African Americans
in the United States Army
in World War II

African Americans in the United States Army in World War II

Bryan D. Booker

McFarland & Company, Inc., Publishers
Jefferson, North Carolina, and London

The present work is a reprint of the illustrated case bound edition of African Americans in the United States Army in World War II, *first published in 2008 by McFarland.*

LIBRARY OF CONGRESS CATALOGUING-IN-PUBLICATION DATA

Booker, Bryan D., 1956–
African Americans in the United States Army
in World War II / Bryan D. Booker.
       p.   cm.
Includes bibliographical references and index.

ISBN 978-0-7864-6904-8
softcover: acid free paper ∞

1. World War, 1939–1945 — Participation, African American.
2. United States. Army — African Americans — Social conditions —
20th century. 3. African Americans — Social conditions — To 1964.
I. Title
D810.N4B66   2012   940.54'03 — dc22   2007040063

BRITISH LIBRARY CATALOGUING DATA ARE AVAILABLE

© 2008 Bryan D. Booker. All rights reserved

*No part of this book may be reproduced or transmitted in any form
or by any means, electronic or mechanical, including photocopying
or recording, or by any information storage and retrieval system,
without permission in writing from the publisher.*

On the cover: 6888th Central Postal Directory Battalion
members in a ceremony on May 27, 1945, honoring
Joan of Arc at the place where she was burned at the stake
(National Archives 111-SC-42644426441)

Manufactured in the United States of America

*McFarland & Company, Inc., Publishers
Box 611, Jefferson, North Carolina 28640
www.mcfarlandpub.com*

To the men and women
who gave the ultimate sacrifice
to preserve the freedoms of this nation

Table of Contents

Preface 1
Introduction — "The Good War" 5

    I. **World War I** 11
   II. **Between the Wars** 32
  III. **The African American Press** 52
  IV. **Combat Service Support Units** 60
       Early Deployments — Pacific Theater 68
       Liberia Task Force 75
       Road Builders 76
       Combat Service Support Deployments 83
       Truck Drivers — The Red Ball Express 85
       Combat Support Units 87
   V. **Women's Army Corps** 96
       6888th Central Postal Directory Battalion 105
       Demobilization 108
  VI. **Artillery** 111
       Antiaircraft Artillery 127
 VII. **Tank Destroyers** 131
VIII. **Separate Infantry Regiments** 145
       24th Infantry Regiment 146
       364th Infantry Regiment 150
       366th and 372nd Infantry Regiments 159
       65th Infantry Regiment (Puerto Rico) 160

IX. Paratroopers ... 162
X. 2nd Cavalry and 93rd Infantry Divisions ... 167
Army Divisions ... 167
2nd Cavalry Division ... 168
93rd Infantry Division ... 172
XI. 92nd Infantry Division ... 192
366th Infantry Regiment ... 210
December Offensive ... 212
Operation Fourth Term ... 223
Reorganization ... 247
Operation Second Wind ... 252
XII. Combat Infantry Replacements ... 274
XIII. Armored Forces ... 285
761st Tank Battalion ... 288
Camp Hood, Texas ... 290
Deployment to War ... 293
Baptism by Fire ... 295
Aftermath ... 323
XIV. Conclusion ... 329

Appendix: The Medal of Honor ... 335
Chapter Notes ... 339
Bibliography ... 353
Index ... 357

Preface

THE HISTORY OF WORLD WAR II HAS BEEN well documented, often focusing on the deeds of the great leaders such as Franklin Roosevelt, Winston Churchill, Josef Stalin, Dwight D. Eisenhower and others. History has gone through many transformations in the past few decades. The past has not changed, only the way Americans interpret history has changed. With those changes have come different interpretations, which have sometimes incited bitter controversies. Before, the role African Americans played in the war was often ignored, or left to the interpretations of those who documented their deeds, often white officers. In 1946, the army in a special study tasked Captain Ulysses Lee, a black officer, to compile a history of the role of African Americans in the war. Using the standard research methods of the time, Captain Lee sorted through the National Archives finding records, official documents, and reports of what occurred during the war. After twenty years, the army finally published *The Employment of Negro Troops* in 1966.

The popularity of American history and the turbulence of today's world have encouraged historians to ask new questions of the past in an effort to better understand its complexity. Minorities were often ignored by mainstream America. Historical narratives once recounted only the experiences of great white men and the unfolding of great public events as they related to white men. The United States has always been a nation of many cultures. To understand its history, we must understand the experiences of many groups who have shaped America's history. Over one million African Americans served in the military during World War Two, yet, very little is known about their struggle, accomplishment, and contribution in helping to reshape a modern world.

While working on my graduate studies at the Fayetteville State University in North Carolina in the late 1990s, I was amazed that Ulysses Lee's study, now over thirty years old, was still the primary document for the role of African Americans in World War II. Working with the Department of Government and History at the university, I began to interview local veterans of that war and got a new perspective on the role these men and women played. Often relegated to combat support units, their participation in the war was just as important as the front line combat soldiers. I began to do research on the segregated units of the war and discovered through files often deep within the National Archives that many of these units had distinguished war records. They were the engineers that helped build the Alaskan Highway and Burma Road, the transportation units that delivered vital supplies and war materials all over the world, and the quartermasters that loaded and unloaded often dangerous material and ammunition on the supply ships. Also located within the National Archives were hundreds of photographs. The military during World War II enlisted photographers to record not only the battlefield carnage, but also the day to day life of the soldiers, sailors, and airmen. The United States Army Center for Military History, the official Department of Defense historical site, has also done extensive research and compiled the history of African Americans and their long and distinguished service in the army. But it was St. Augustine College in Raleigh, North Carolina, and the Division of Social Science under the guidance of division chair, Dr. Joyce Blackwell, that encouraged my research.

The United States emerged from World War II in 1945 vastly different from the country of that tragic Sunday morning of December 7, 1941. A united effort at defeating the Axis powers would bring the country together like no other period in American history. But this unified task did not come without its share of problems, for America in the 1940s was a country that practiced segregation and discrimination based on the color of one's skin, and the military encapsulated society's norms. In 1940 as the country anticipated its entry into this global conflict, there were no African Americans serving the Marine Corps or the Army Air Corp. In the Navy and Coast Guard, African Americans were relegated to duties as mess attendants or cooks. Yet on December 7, 1941 as the Japanese attacked Pearl Harbor, Hawaii, one of these mess attendants, Dorie Miller, became one of America's first heroes, and won the Navy Cross for manning a machine gun and downing several enemy aircraft.

There were in essence two armies, one black, and one white. In 1940, when war in Europe was raging on, America knew that it was only a matter of time before they would be drawn in. The army's general staff devised a plan for the mobilization of America to meet this new threat. They knew that African Americans, as in every previous war, would also have to be included into the general planning scheme. In the Army, the four African American regiments that became a permanent part of the regular army in 1866 as mandated by Congress, the 24th and 25th Infantry, and the 9th and 10th Cavalry Regiments, were still led by a cadre of white officers. These regiments served with distinction during the Indian Wars of the late 1800s, in the Spanish American War in Cuba in 1898, during the Philippine Insurrection that lasted from 1899 to 1902, and as members of the American Expeditionary Force that pursued the Mexican revolutionary Pancho Villa in Mexico in 1916. But during World War I, those African American regiments were relegated to duty along the Mexican border and in the Philippines Islands. America was not willing to send their regular army segregated regiments into war. On the dawn of another great conflict, these soldiers were not being utilized as combat forces, but were made to collect trash at Fort Benning, Georgia, or to maintain the horse stables for the cadets at West Point. But this would change with the advent of war, swelling the ranks of the military with nearly one million African American men and women.

Prior to the United States' entry into World War II, Charles Houston, an attorney and civil rights activist, warned that African Americans would no longer tolerate the indignities and mistreatment that they had endured during the First World War. President Franklin D. Roosevelt remained wary of challenging institutionalized racism in spite of the views of Houston and other African American leaders. The president hoped to include African Americans in the defense effort without offending those powerful southern politicians who believed in the separation of the races. Roosevelt proposed to incorporate African Americans into the armed forces without integration. In working toward that objective, his administration affected a number of changes intended more as symbolic gestures than genuine reform. For example,

William H. Hastie, an African American federal judge and former dean of the Howard University School of Law became an assistant to the Secretary of War for matters involving black soldiers. Colonel Benjamin O. Davis, Sr., was promoted to brigadier general, becoming the first African American to obtain that rank, but would not lead combat forces throughout the duration of the war.

The census of 1940 indicated that African Americans represented 10.3 percent of the total population. Thus, each branch of the army would include in its planning to have 10 percent of their forces comprised of African American soldiers. This, of course, met strong resistance from the general staff. To have African American soldiers operating tanks, firing artillery, staffing hospitals, and flying aircraft was unheard of in these times. But this directive was from the White House and President Roosevelt himself. African American civic leaders had long sought out equal representation throughout the military and in defense contracting factories. America did not want to be perceived as not being a united country in the face of potential enemies.

Each branch in the army had segregated units, but in some sections, mainly the combat arms, that goal of 10 percent was never met. Instead, there would be token representation, and these units were never meant to be sent into combat. The two African American infantry divisions that had fought in the First World War, the 92nd and 93rd, would be reactivated. A cavalry division centered on the 9th and 10th cavalry regiments would also be formed. These divisions would be commanded and staffed with white officers because it was felt that African Americans were not capable of leading men in combat. After an outcry from the black population, African American junior officers would be allowed to serve in these units. There would also be African American paratroopers. But unlike the white paratroopers who would be known for their heroic exploits during the war, the African American paratroopers were denied the opportunity to defend their country in combat.

The overwhelming majority of African American soldiers would go on to serve this country as they had in the previous war, as combat service support troops. They would be the truck drivers, the engineers, the cooks, fuel handlers, and supply personnel. But, this war would be unlike any war previously fought. This was truly a global war, and the role of the support soldier would forever be changed. Armies could not fight unless they were well armed and supplied. Military forces could not deploy troops without fuel for the many vehicles and tanks of the new armored divisions. So, the contributions of these second class citizens gained a new importance throughout the course of the war.

But it is in combat where a soldier proves his worthiness. Eventually a shortage of manpower in 1944 would force the army to utilize these segregated combat forces in every theater of operations. Some would even fight side by side with white soldiers. It was the accomplishment of these chosen few that would eventually lead this nation to integrate its military.

Introduction — "The Good War"

WORLD WAR II HAS OFTEN BEEN REFERRED TO as "The Good War." When war is glamorized as supporting a noble cause, it masks the horrors and destruction that inevitably accompany combat. But this was the war that changed the face of America. The United States in 1940 was far from being united. There was vast separation by race, social status, religion and ethnicity. The country's social order was also separated by geographical locations. The American society in the South, with its strict segregation of race and "Jim Crow" laws, differed from the urbanization of the cities in the northeast. The Second World War was started by the alliance of the Axis Power nations in order to force their ideology and to dominate large regions of the world. The Allies' goal was to rid the world of these same evil factions that chose to make war, and to create a world safe for democracy. The majority of Americans were in support of President Franklin Roosevelt and his efforts to defeat the Axis Powers. For it had been this country that was attacked at Pearl Harbor, Hawaii, without warning on December 7, 1941.

World War II brought this country out of ten years of financial depression. Industry, which had been virtually shut down, was now mobilized to produce the weapons of destruction. It afforded almost everyone the opportunity to work. Women were being employed by industry in large numbers for the first time in history. Most Americans were now making more money than they had in the previous ten years. Yet, for all its new opportunities and the will to fight oppression overseas, most of America existed in a segregated society, with African Americans relegated to second-class citizenship due to the color of their skin. This is the aspect of World War II that most of America has forgotten, and that history has often neglected.

But in spite of being regarded as second-class citizens, and not benefiting from the rights that were guaranteed to most Americans, during times of conflict, African Americans would put these injustices aside and unilaterally support the war effort. Since the beginnings of this nation, African Americans have fought for the freedoms of this country in every major conflict. More than 5,000 African Americans, both free men and slaves, served in integrated military units during the Revolutionary War. In 1778, Rhode Island formed the first regiment comprising both slaves and free men of color, commanded by white officers.[1] But it was during the Civil War where this practice of African Americans organized into segregated regiments, led by white officers, would serve for the Union forces. The Union Army had suffered major setbacks early during the war, with the defeats at Fredericksburg, Maryland, and Vicksburg, Mississippi, in 1862. At that time, the Union Army forbade the recruitment of African Americans, but after enduring heavy casualties, in the summer of that same year, Colonel James Williams organized the First Kansas Colored Regiment. In September, General Benjamin F. Butler formed the Louisiana Native Guards made up of free African American men of that state. In the Union Army's Department of the South, General David Hunter took it upon himself to form a regiment of recently freed slaves called the First South Carolina Regiment. After President Lincoln issued the Emancipation Proclamation on 1 January 1863, freeing the slaves in the Confederate states, Massachusetts raised the first African American regiment in the northern states east of the Mississippi River on 26 January 1863, the 54th Massachusetts Volunteer Infantry. Another African American regiment, the 55th Massachusetts Volunteer Infantry, would soon follow it.

The decision to use African Americans as soldiers in the Union Army was still hotly debated, but the horrors of this grueling war dictated that their utilization was sorely needed. One historian wrote, "This decision to use the Negro as a soldier did not necessarily grow out of any broad humanitarian resolve; it seems to have come more largely out of the dawning realization that, since the Confederates were going to kill a great many more Union soldiers before the war was over, a good many white men would escape death if a considerable percentage of those soldiers were colored."[2] This, the practice of organizing African American regiments led by white officers, would exist for the next 80 years. During the Civil War, there would be 167 African American army regiments of all branches, enlisting 186,097 men.[3] They would suffer 33,380 deaths, and yet many doubted that the African American would be a valuable asset in the military forces. Their contributions and sacrifices would be a major contribution to a Union victory.

After the war ended, it was a Republican-led Congress that would determine the future of the African American soldiers in the Army. On 26 July 1866, Congress mandated that there would be six permanent regiments made up of African Americans, two of cavalry and four of infantry. This would later be reduced to a total of four regiments, with only two infantry regiments. Through this legislation, Congress opened a new chapter in military history, and afforded the erstwhile slave an opportunity to play a major role in the settlement of the western portion of the nation. With no experienced African American officers available, Congress provided that all officers of the new regiments would be white, with the provision that they take a special examination before a board of experienced officers appointed by the Secretary of War. Two years of active field service in the Civil War were required of all these officers.[4] Thus, the formations of the 9th and 10th Cavalry, and the 24th and 25th Infantry Regiments were created. Known as the "Buffalo Soldiers," they would go on to forge a permanent presence in the westward expansion of the United States. Fighting side by side with their white counterparts, they protected the building of the railroads and the influx of new settlers against bandits and warring Native Americans. By stationing all four regiments in the remoteness of the west, it also ensured there would be little resistance against seeing armed African American soldiers.

Henry Ossian Flipper became the first African American to graduate from the military academy at West Point. Born in Thomasville, Georgia, on 21 March 1856, into slavery, he spent his formative years in Georgia. Following the Civil War, he attended the American Missionary Association Schools in his home state. In 1873 Flipper was appointed to the United

States Military Academy, and in 1877, after four years of isolation and being totally ignored by his fellow classmates, he became the first African American to graduate from the institution. He was commissioned a second lieutenant and assigned to the 10th Cavalry Regiment. From 1878 until 1881, Lieutenant Flipper served on frontier duty at various installations throughout the southwest. His duties included scouting, as well as serving as the post engineer surveyor and construction supervisor, post adjutant, acting assistant and post quartermaster, and as the commissary officer. In August 1881, Lieutenant Flipper's commanding officer accused him of embezzling $2,000 while performing duties as the post quartermaster and of conduct unbecoming an officer and a gentleman, for allegedly being in the company of one of the eligible young white ladies of the post. As a result of these charges, he was confined to the Fort Concho, Texas, guardhouse and later court-martialed. He was acquitted of the embezzlement charge but was found guilty, by general court-martial, of conduct unbecoming an officer. On 30 June 1882, he was dismissed from the Army as required by this conviction.[5] This would set the precedence for the treatment of the few African Americans that would achieve officer status in the future.

By the time of the Spanish-American War in 1898, the four African American regiments were some of the best-trained and highly disciplined units in the military. As the United States mobilized for war, these units were among the first to be deployed to Cuba. The 9th and 10th Cavalry, and the 24th Infantry Regiments fought in the famous battle of San Juan and Kettle Hills and the 25th Infantry Regiment fought at El Caney. Future president and commander of the 1st Volunteer Cavalry Regiment (the Rough Riders) during the battle, Lieutenant Colonel Theodore Roosevelt, would forever have praise for the African American regiments that he fought side by side with. A future general that would lead American forces in World War I, Lieutenant John Pershing, was assigned to the 10th Cavalry Regiment as its adjutant during the war. Five troopers of the 10th Cavalry would be awarded the Medal of Honor for bravery in Cuba. Also deployed for the first time were African American state militia and volunteer units. The 9th Volunteer Infantry Regiment, the 8th Illinois, and the 23rd Kansas Militia participated in the hostilities. The four regular army units would be deployed to the Philippine Islands, along with the 48th and 49th Voluntary Infantry Regiments (Colored), where they helped to suppress the native insurrections against American colonial rule and served as occupation forces until 1909.[6]

During the first 15 years of the 20th century, the plight of African American servicemen significantly worsened despite stellar performances in combat. In 1896, the *Plessy v Ferguson* case legalized segregation, and racism became prevalent in this country.[7] The early 1900s found African Americans in the military facing a bleak future, with the very right to serve in the armed forces threatened, and their opportunities limited. Many whites disapproved of arming African Americans. Arming men that were treated as second-class citizens and often abused because of the color of their skin might lead to retaliation.

While the overall number of army regiments and navy ships increased in the period that followed the Spanish-American War as the United States projected itself as a new world power, the number of African Americans in the military decreased. On 2 February 1901, Congress authorized an additional 1,135 new officers for the regular army. Most of them came from the volunteer regiments that were mobilized during the Spanish-American War. These enlisted soldiers received their commissions on the recommendations of their commanders. No African Americans received any of those commissions. In addition to the authorization for additional officers, Congress also directed the formation of five additional infantry regiments and five additional cavalry regiments into the regular army. But unlike the post–Civil War Congress that authorized the formations of the first African American regiments, there would be no addition regiments of color.

There would also be fewer opportunities to serve in the individual state National Guard units. Both the military and the state governments defined the Militia Act of 1903 as limiting federal control of the National Guard.[8] All agreed that the racial composition of the National Guard remained an individual state's prerogative, and as a result, many state units no longer accepted African Americans into their ranks. By the time the United States entered World War I in 1917, the National Guard contained only 5,000 African Americans, which was less than 3 percent of its total strength. The majority of African Americans served in the 8th Illinois Regiment based in Chicago, and the 15th New York Regiment from Harlem. Single African American National Guard companies comprising approximately 100 men each represented the states of Massachusetts, Maryland, Ohio, Tennessee, and the District of Columbia. No African Americans served in the National Guard of any other state.

Complaints about the dearth of black officers and the paucity of African American regular army and reserve units did produce a few minor changes. Benjamin O. Davis, an enlisted man in the 9th Cavalry Regiment, received a regular army commission to second lieutenant on 19 May 1901. Davis, a former first lieutenant with the 8th Illinois Regiment during the Spanish-American War, reverted back to his enlisted rank at the conclusion of the conflict. He became the first African American soldier to rise up from the enlisted ranks to become a regular army officer. Corporal John E. Green of the 24th Infantry Regiment would receive his commission the following June. But these token appointments did little to appease African American activists, who continued to lobby for additional officers and units. They also continued to lobby campaigns to open the artillery branch to African Americans. Both the majority of congressmen and many senior army officers stood by the Civil War–vintage argument that African American soldiers lacked the intelligence to master the technical skills required of artillery crewmen.

During the spring of 1906, the War Department ordered the 1st Battalion, 25th Infantry Regiment, comprising African American soldiers from Fort Niobrara, Nebraska, to transfer to Fort Brown, a post at the mouth of the Rio Grande, just outside the town of Brownsville, Texas. Both the African American enlisted men and the white officers of the 25th Infantry Regiment protested the orders, citing troubles with racist Texans during the regiment's previous assignments to that state. Since the Reconstruction Era, the white population had resented the stationing of African American army regiments in Texas, although the soldiers were located there for the protection of the local community.

The citizens of Brownsville also protested the reassignment of the African American soldiers, and the local United States Commissioner wrote to Secretary of War, William Howard Taft, requesting that he revoke the orders for the 25th Infantry and to instead keep the white 26th Infantry Regiment at Fort Brown. After much debate, the War Department refused to revoke the orders transferring the 1st Battalion to Texas. The battalion arrived at Fort Brown on 28 July 1906, without incident, but the local population remained hostile to the newly arrived African American soldiers. A few minutes after midnight on the morning of 14 August, a group of men numbering between six and twenty gathered across the road from Fort Brown at a narrow passage know as Cowen's Alley. The men began firing shots into buildings and at streetlights and proceeded to shoot up the alley for about ten minutes. The random bullets killed a local bartender, and wounded two others. Several Brownsville citizens alleged that they saw black men among the shooters. In the morning, Major Charles Penrose, the battalion commander, conducted an inspection of the battalion's arms room and found all weapons secured and with no evidence that they had been fired. Local citizens began coming forward, however, with spent military rifle cartridges and clips from Springfield rifles, the kind recently issued to the 25th Regiment. Supposedly, this was the only source of this type of ammunition.

On August 16, President Theodore Roosevelt ordered an immediate investigation and dispatched Major August Blocksom, assistant inspector general of the army's Southwestern Division, to Brownsville to take charge of the proceedings. The President also ordered the 1st Battalion to remain confined at Fort Brown until the conclusion of the investigation. However, renewed protests by the citizens of Brownsville forced the president to change his mind. On 25 August, the soldiers of the battalion were transferred by train to Fort Reno in the Oklahoma Territory. Twelve soldiers who remained in Texas were prisoners at Fort Sam Houston in San Antonio, awaiting trial as members of the raid. A Cameron County, Texas, grand jury, meeting in Brownsville, heard no convincing evidence despite much emotional testimony about the guilt of the dozen men. The court released the twelve soldiers, and they rejoined their battalion in Oklahoma.

Although there was a lack of any evidence that would place guilt on any of the African American soldiers, Major Blocksom still recommended that if the guilty parties did not come forward, "all enlisted men of the three companies present on the night of August 13th be discharged from the service and debarred from reenlistment."[9]

On 4 October 1906, President Roosevelt ordered still another investigation into the Brownsville incident, this time sending Brigadier General Ernest Garlington, the Inspector General of the Army, and a native of South Carolina, to once again conduct interviews and to study the evidence. He reported that every soldier he interviewed denied any knowledge of the affair. General Garlington admitted he could find no proof of collusion on the part of the members of the battalion to withhold information, but that fact did not deter his concurrence with Major Blocksom's recommendations. Garlington concluded: "The secretive nature of the race, where crimes charged to members of their color are made, is well known.... It has been established by careful investigation, beyond reasonable doubt, that the firing into the houses of the citizens of Brownsville ... was done by enlisted men of the 25th Infantry...."[10]

Without any evidence and relying solely on prejudiced beliefs, General Garlington recommended to the president that all the enlisted members of Companies B, C, and D be immediately dismissed from the service. President Roosevelt approved the discharges, but ordered that the announcement be withheld until after the elections, held on 9 November, "for fear of its effect on the colored vote."[11] Between 16 November and 26 November, the army discharged all 167 enlisted African American soldiers of the 1st Battalion, 25th Infantry Regiment, who were present for duty on the night of 13 August at Fort Brown. The discharges were without honor, all back pay and pension benefits were denied, and they were barred from enlisting into any branch of the military service. Of those discharged, more than 15 had earned medals for valor in Cuba or in the Philippines, including three Congressional Medal of Honor awardees.[12]

Chapter I

World War I

With America's entrance into World War I on 6 April 1917, African American soldiers and sailors stood ready to serve overseas. The African American communities were prepared to support the war effort; however, as in previous wars, racism initially thwarted opportunities to contribute. Despite their outstanding duties along the Mexican border the previous year, the four African American regiments did not receive orders that would deploy them to Europe after the declaration of war because many senior military and political leaders still believed that African Americans lacked the intelligence, courage, and dedication to serve in sustained combat roles. Under President Wilson's administration, it was maintained that African Americans would be limited to menial labor positions within the navy, and restricted from combat roles in the army. Although the four African American regiments contained some of the best trained and most experienced soldiers in the United States Army, the War Department assigned them to continue their security duties. The 9th Cavalry was stationed at Stotsenburg Camp at Luzon, in the Philippine Islands, throughout World War I. The 10th Cavalry was stationed at Fort Huachuca, Arizona, and several of its companies spent the war years patrolling the border and suppressing uprisings on the Mexican side. The 24th Infantry Regiment was headquartered at Camp Furlong near Columbus, New Mexico, with its battalions deployed throughout Texas. When the war began, the 25th Infantry Regiment was stationed at Schofield Barracks in Hawaii, but when a native Hawaiian National Guard infantry regiment was activated in the summer of 1918, the 25th Infantry was brought stateside for Mexican border patrol, and thus a white regiment was released for combat duty in France. By such assignments, the African American regular army soldiers were kept out of the limelight that a combat assignment would warrant, while at the same time performing vital, although thankless, security duties for their country.

In July 1917, the 3rd Battalion, 24th Infantry Regiment, received orders to report to Houston, Texas, to guard the construction of Camp Logan, where white National Guard soldiers were to train before transferring overseas. Some African American soldiers resented not being included in the units deploying to the European battlefront. Others were frustrated with the segregated facilities and the racial discrimination that they encountered in Houston. Within a month, pent-up frustrations led to the first racial riot in American history in which more whites died than African Americans. On the morning of 23 August 1917, the Houston police arrested Mrs. Sara Travers, a local African American housewife, for complaining about two patrolmen shooting into her neighborhood while attempting to apprehend two young gamblers. While the policemen and Travers stood waiting, a group of African American civilians gathered to complain about the mistreatment of Travers. Private Alonzo Edwards, of Company L, 3/24th Infantry, joined the group and offered to pay Mrs. Travers' fine if the police would release her. One of the policemen, Lee Sparks, drew his revolver and struck Edwards several times on the head, later explaining, "I wasn't going to wrestle with a big nigger like that. I hit him until he got his heart right." Sparks then took Edwards as well as Travers to the city jail. Early that afternoon, Corporal Charles Baltimore, a senior member of the 3/24th Infantry's provost guard, went to the jail to check on Edwards's welfare. He too was beaten by Sparks and put in jail with Edwards.[1]

Although several of their unit's white officers attempted to stop them, about 100 armed infantrymen marched out of Camp Logan and into the streets of Houston. Several noncommissioned officers joined the formation, including a battered and humiliated Corporal Baltimore, recently released from jail, who sought revenge on the Houston Police Department. Sergeant Vida Henry, the acting first sergeant of Company I, took command of the group. Over the next two hours, the soldiers proceeded to deliberately shoot and kill policemen as well as any civilian bystanders who got in their way. Destroying no property, they remained focused on their targets, the members of the Houston police force. After two hours of searching the Houston streets for their prey, the soldiers broke into small groups and either returned to Camp Logan, or sought refuge with local families. In their wake, they left 15 dead, including four policemen, two white soldiers of the Illinois National Guard, and two civilians assisting the police. The ensuing riot and mob wounded 12 more white Houston citizens, including a policeman who would later die of his wounds. Four African American soldiers died during the violence, including Sergeant Henry, who committed suicide. Some investigations later credited him with planning the entire mutiny, while others claimed that Sergeant Henry participated only out of a sense of responsibility to his men, and then killed himself rather than live with the consequences.[2]

Unlike its actions following the Brownsville incident, the army did not resort to mass punishment. Extensive investigations both by the army and the city of Houston attempted to discover exactly what had happened and who the individual guilty parties were. The investigations cited the arrest and pistol-whipping of Private Edwards and Corporal Baltimore by Officer Sparks, and the subsequent rumors of Baltimore's death, as the flash point for the mutiny, but not a single witness in Houston could identify any of the soldiers who shot the victims. Finally, after granting immunity to several of the participants, comparing roll call rosters, and collecting observations by the battalion's white officers in camp, the army identified individual defendants and assembled its charges against each.

The first court-martial convened at Fort Sam Houston in San Antonio, Texas, on 1 November 1917 to try 63 of the soldiers charged with mutiny and premeditated murder. The trial, the largest military court-martial in United States history, involved 196 witnesses and resulted in 2,100 pages of testimony. Separate individual lawyers did not represent the defendants. On 12 November, the board pronounced 54 of the defendants guilty of all charges. Of those, 13 received the death sentence and 41 were sentenced to life in prison. Four soldiers received lesser sentences and five were proven innocent of all charges and set free. Before dawn on 11 December 1917, army executioners hanged Corporal Baltimore and 12 other solders at Camp Travis, just outside of Fort Sam Houston, Texas. There was no notice to the public or the press. Not until two hours after the executions occurred did the army announce the facts.[3]

Neither the War Department nor the president had reviewed the trial findings. When African American civilian leaders protested the lack of high-level review, the army responded that it had acted properly in enforcing the sentences, "since military law specified that the area commander had final authority in time of war." When the African American leaders and newspapers protested to President Wilson that Texas and the trials were far from the European war, they were able to secure a promise of high-level review of any future death sentences. Provost Marshal General Enoch Crowder drafted General Order No. 7, which stated that in the future no death sentence could be carried out until it was reviewed and upheld by the president of the United States.

W.E.B. Dubois expressed perhaps the most widely felt belief of the African American community about the Houston Mutiny in the January 1918 edition of *The Crisis*:

> They have gone to their death, 13 young, strong men: soldiers who have fought for a country which never was wholly theirs; men born to suffer ridicule, injustice, and, at last, death itself. They broke the law. Against them punishment, if it was legal, we cannot protest...the shameful treatment which these men, and which we, their brothers, receive all our lives, and which our fathers received, and our children await; and above all we raise our clenched hands against the hundreds of thousands of white murderers, rapists, and scoundrels.[4]

Two subsequent trials tested the review system as 16 additional members of the 3/24th Infantry received death sentences and 12 received life terms. After strong lobbying from African American leaders, President Wilson, in an effort to appease both the African American and white communities, changed the sentence of ten of the soldiers to life in prison and authorized the execution of the remaining six on September 16, 1918.[5]

Over the years, continued lobbying by African American organizations, including the National Association for the Advancement of Colored People (NAACP), secured reductions in many of the sentences. However, it was not until 1938 that the final Houston mutineer was released from the United States Army Disciplinary Barracks at Fort Leavenworth, Kansas.

Unlike Brownsville, where the African American soldiers received mass punishment rather than fair trials, the army adjudicated the Houston Mutiny through proper procedures. Certain soldiers of the 3rd Battalion mutinied against their officers and murdered local civilians. While a long history of discrimination and mistreatment may have provided the background about why their actions took place, the fact remained that there was no justification for the soldiers to take the law into their own hands. Whether or not African Americans felt that through violence it would be possible to show white America that it would not be subjugated to unfair and unlawful treatment, the subservient attitude perceived of African Americans had changed.

The 3rd Battalion, reinforced by new recruits, served at several isolated posts in New Mexico before the army finally disbanded it altogether in 1921 due to the War Department's reductions in strength. A congressional mandate at the formation of the African American regiments in 1866 forbade the deactivation of any of those regiments as a whole. The remainder of the 24th Infantry Regiment served similar postings, remaining beyond consideration for favorable assignment for the next two decades before the magnitude of World War II required an entirely new look at the utilization of African American units. It would be one of the first infantry regiments deployed to the Pacific Theater during the Second World War in 1942, and would serve with such distinction as to be the only African American regiment to receive the coveted Combat Infantry Badge in that theater.

Non-white soldiers served in World War I from its very inception in 1914. All the major European powers utilized native soldiers from their colonies in Africa, the Caribbean, and

Asia. The *Literary Digest* reported: "The French Army included 340,000 natives of North Africa, mostly Berbers; at least a quarter of a million black men from the Sudan and Senegal; and 30,000 from the French West Indies. A number of black men held high command in the French army, and at least two were generals."[6] Reports varied as to the efficiency of these soldiers in combat. Early in the war, a white American correspondent wrote, "that such troops could not possibly be of any value in modern European warfare, and that only in desperation could France delude itself into using them."[7] But in their desperate need, the French army continued to utilize African and West Indian soldiers on every front. A Senegalese infantry regiment was one of the highest decorated units in the French Army.

Once the United States entered the conflict, African Americans would be required in the war effort. While the four regular African American army regiments would be denied the opportunity to serve in Europe, thousands of new inductees would be employed in combat. More than a month before the United States declared war in April 1917, the First Separate Battalion (Colored) of the Washington, D.C. National Guard was federalized to guard the White House, the Capitol, and other federal buildings. It was planned that the African American National Guard units would be formed into segregated infantry divisions, but the majority of draftees would be used to perform the manual labor tasks in service support units. For the first time, intelligence testing was used to categorize the new inductees.

For this intense mobilization of military forces, Secretary of War Newton Baker, at the urging of African American leaders, initiated the first Officers Training Camp for African Americans at Camp Des Moines, Iowa, predicated upon certain criteria: (1) that no more than 2 percent of the officers would be African American (although 13 percent of the new inductees into the army were African American); (2) few of these officers would ever be utilized in combat; (3) that if charged with incompetence, these officers would be removed from the army; and (4) that no African American officers will achieve field grade ranks (major or higher).[8] The class began in July 1917 with 1,250 candidates, of which 1,000 had been recruited from the civilian population and with the rest being noncommissioned officers from the four African American regular army regiments. The two infantry regiments detailed 84 men each for this assignment. The 10th Cavalry Regiment sent 57 men and the 9th Cavalry Regiment provided 25 noncommissioned officers.[9] Newly promoted Brigadier General Charles Ballou, whose previous assignment had been as the executive officer of the 24th Infantry Regiment, would command this new training.

On 15 October 1917, 639 commissions were awarded to those who had completed the training, which included 106 captains, 329 first lieutenants, and 204 second lieutenants.[10] Most of the captains would be former noncommissioned officers of the regular army units, who were selected by their white commanders. They were selected to the highest rank based more on their military experience rather than intelligence, education, or potential leadership capabilities. An important element of their experience was the learning of their role in relations to white officers; obviously, they would not have achieved noncommissioned officer status, nor have been recommended for officer training by their white superiors if they had not learned their role well and practiced it consistently.[11] All the graduates were assigned to the 92nd Infantry Division, and there would be no additional classes for African American officer candidates.

The few additional African American officer candidates that followed would be trained at the regular officer training courses. At some of these facilities, they faced extreme hardships as every effort was made to eliminate the candidates from the training. Of the 96 potential African American artillery officers training at Camp Taylor, Kentucky, only 44 graduated, and it was recommended that they all be assigned to battery service, the most hazardous duty for an artillery officer. At Fort Sill, Oklahoma, of the 24 artillery officer candidates, all from regular army regiments, only 6 completed the course. The candidates were housed and fed in segregated facilities on the post. At the aviation school on Fort Sill, the African American soldiers were treated so harshly that three of the four officer candidates requested transfers back to their original units, and the fourth was eliminated two days prior to graduation. But not every facility practiced unfair treatment of African American officer candidates. At Camp Hancock, Georgia, of the 56 officer candidates attending the machine gun course, 43 graduated. These training classes were staffed with veteran British and French officers as instructors, and did not share in the same prejudiced beliefs as many of the American military officers.[12]

But the greatest injustice inflicted on an African American officer during the war was the treatment directed at Colonel Charles Young. Born in Kentucky in 1864, Young had been the third African American to graduate from the military academy at West Point in 1889, and the only one still remaining in the service at the outbreak of the war. He had met discrimination throughout his military career, but was such a dedicated and generally well-regarded officer that he managed to achieve promotions. Young was an accomplished linguist, fluent in Latin, Greek, French, Spanish and German. He served as Professor of Military Science at Wilberforce University, Ohio. From 1894 through 1898 and during the Spanish–American War, he was assigned to the 9th Ohio Volunteer Infantry. In 1903 he was superintendent of parks at Sequoia and General Grant National Parks in California. In 1908, now a major, Young was sent to the Philippines to join his 10th Cavalry Regiment and commanded a squadron of two troops with white officers subordinate to him.[13]

The government also found it advantageous to have an African American field grade officer within its ranks when it came time to send a military attaché to the countries of Haiti or Liberia. Colonel Young served at both locations. While stationed in Liberia, he contracted a severe tropical fever, and was returned to the United States in 1915 with high praise from the Liberian president for his excellent services. When he recovered, he rejoined the 10th Cavalry Regiment and commanded the 2nd Squadron on the Mexican border.

He was most renowned for his leadership during the 1916 Punitive Expedition, which marched into Mexico in pursuit of the revolutionary bandit Pancho Villa, who had murdered American citizens on his raids across the border. On 9 March at Agua Caliente, Mexico, Major Young led the 2nd Cavalry Squadron in a pistol charge against the Villista forces, threatening to envelope the right flank of Mexican General Beltran. General Beltran's 150 Mexican Federalist soldiers were able to escape without any losses thanks to Major Young's aggressive cavalry squadron.

On 12 April, at the Hacienda Santa Cruz de la Villegas, Major Young was the hero of the hour when he led with his squadron to the relief of Major Frank Tompkins, who was severely wounded while his squadron of the 13th United States Cavalry Regiment fought a heavy rear guard action against Mexican federal soldiers. Major Young's reinforcement of Major Tompkins' cavalry troopers at this critical time is credited by many as preventing an all-out war with Mexico.[14] Major Young was one of the few field grade officers serving with General Pershing in the Mexico Campaign that the general had recommended to command militia forces in the federal service.[15]

Major Young's brilliant and aggressive operations in Mexico won him a promotion to lieutenant colonel in the 10th Cavalry Regiment in 1916. A year later he was promoted to full colonel. Colonel Young was sixth on the list of colonels to be promoted to brigadier general, and the current commander of Fort Huachuca, Arizona, in 1917. With the rapid wartime expansion of the military, it was certain that he would be promoted to brigadier general that year, and thus would be eligible for a position such as the Assistant Division Commander of one of the African American infantry divisions. The promotion board approved his promotion, and he was ordered on 23 May 1917 to the military hospital in San Francisco for a physical examination. The doctors diagnosed him with high blood pressure and he was retired from active military service the day before he would have been promoted to general. Colonel Young protested that he was not sick and had his personal physician verify that his blood pressure was normal for a man of his age. In a dramatic effort to prove his fitness for duty, Colonel Young rode on horseback from his home in Chillicothe, Ohio, to Washington, D.C. But his protest gained him nothing, and he became officially retired on 30 July 1917. His loss as a potential commander of African American soldiers during the war stirred anger, protest, and deep disappointment in the African American community, which felt sure that he had been forced from active service.[16]

The papers of Secretary of War Baker give further explanation for the plight of Colonel Charles Young. While Colonel Young was having his physical in San Francisco, Senator John Williams of Mississippi, one of President Wilson's strongest supporters and an outspoken racist, forwarded to the president a complaint from a young white lieutenant assigned to the 10th Cavalry Regiment. President Wilson passed the message on in a letter to Secretary Baker, informing him that the lieutenant wanted to be transferred because he found it "not only distasteful but practically impossible to serve under a colored commander,"[17] and asking Secretary Baker what could be done about it. Although Secretary Baker had small patience with such complaints, he consulted with the Chief of Staff, General Tasker Bliss, and wrote the president that Colonel Young would be in a hospital under observation "for the next two or three weeks to determine whether his physical condition is sufficiently good to justify his return to active service." Secretary Baker added: "There does not seem to be any present likelihood of his early return to the 10th Cavalry so that the situation may not develop to which you refer."[18] Three days later, President Wilson wrote to Senator Williams that Colonel Young "will not in fact have command because he is in ill health and likely when he gets better to be transferred to some other service."[19] Since Colonel Young's medical condition had yet to be diagnosed, it is evident that political decisions within the highest offices of government would determine the fate of the ranking African American officer in the army.

In Colonel Young's retirement, he was assigned duties with the Adjutant General of his home state of Ohio. He raised a regiment of dismounted cavalry, but the War Department, not wanting any additional African American combat forces, decided that the regiment was not needed and had it disbanded before the conclusion of the war. Ironically, after the war had ended, and there was no longer a chance of being promoted to general, Colonel Young was called back to active duty, due to the fact that a military attaché was required for Liberia. There, Colonel Young suffered a recurrence of "blackwater fever" and died on 8 January 1922. At the time he was on a research expedition in Lagos, Nigeria. His body was returned to the United States and interred with honors at Arlington National Cemetery in Washington, D.C.[20]

In World War I the majority of the 404,348 African American soldiers, including 1,353 commissioned officers and 15 Army nurses, were assigned to the Services of Supply Branch performing quartermaster, stevedore, and pioneer infantry duties. Two infantry divisions, the 92nd and 93rd, were activated and eventually sent into combat in France.[21]

The 93rd Infantry Division was designated a provisional division because it never had the opportunity to be brought up to its full authorized strength. It was comprised of four separate infantry regiments, three National Guard and one of draftees, but with none of the supporting units associated with an infantry division such as artillery and engineers. All three National Guard regiments had been ordered to train with the infantry divisions formed within their perspective states, but the white units immediately rejected them.

When the African American guardsmen were federalized for active duty, all the regiments were under strength in personnel. The 15th New York Regiment had 2,053 enlisted men and 54 officers assigned; the 8th Illinois had 1,405 enlisted men and 42 officers; the 1st Separate Battalion of Washington, D.C., had 950 enlisted men and 55 officers, the 9th Separate Battalion of Ohio had 650 enlisted men and 15 officers; and the National Guard separate companies of Tennessee, Massachusetts, Maryland, and Connecticut averaged 150 enlisted men and 2 officers each.[22]

The 15th New York Regiment had been organized in 1916, and commanded by Colonel William Hayward, a prominent white New Yorker. When the regiment was federalized, it would be redesignated the 369th Infantry Regiment. The regiment was ordered to training at Camp Whitmen near Peekskill, New York, in May 1917. There, the regiment was assigned to guard duty at several locations throughout the state and thus were unable to train for combat duties. In the fall of 1917, the regiment, along with the 12th and 71st New York Regiments, was ordered to Camp Wadsworth in Spartanburg, South Carolina, where they were immediately greeted with hostility from the local population. The camp commander, General Charles L. Phillips, praised the men of the 15th New York for their discipline under such harsh conditions, but foreseeing eventual trouble, he urged Colonel Hayward to persuade the War Department to send the regiment immediately to France.[23]

While Colonel Hayward was in Washington, D.C., the drum major of the regimental band, noted composer Nobel Sissle, was in Spartanburg buying a newspaper from a hotel lobby when the manager assaulted him. When the soldiers attempted to retaliate, the bandleader, Lieutenant James Reese Europe, restrained them. Fearing another Houston incident, Secretary Baker sent his Aide on Negro Affairs, Emmett Scott, a former assistant of Booker T. Washington, to investigate the incident.[24] The 15th Regiment departed Spartanburg after only 12 days of training, and sailed for duty in France on 10 December 1917. There, the unit would officially be redesignated as the 369th Infantry Regiment of the 93rd Infantry Division (Provisional).

The 8th Illinois National Guard was mobilized for duty in March 1917. Commanded by Colonel Franklin A. Dennison, this guard regiment had the distinction of being the only unit fully staffed with all African American officers. Colonel Dennison was originally from Texas, but moved to Chicago to practice law. After serving as assistant city prosecuting attorney, he became assistant corporation counsel for the city. The regiment was ordered in October 1917 to Camp Logan, Texas, the scene of the Houston Mutiny, to train with the other regiments of the Illinois National Guard. Trouble immediately started for the 8th Illinois upon their arrival at Camp Logan. Soldiers were put in the guardhouse for fighting with the citizens of Houston. A policeman shot a soldier for allegedly interfering with an arrest. Men of the regiment were barred from public transportation for refusing to obey Jim Crow laws. As tensions in Houston grew, the General Staff of the Army was trying to decide how to employ the regiment. White infantry divisions rejected this regiment. Redesignated the 370th Infantry Regiment of the 93rd Infantry Division (Provisional) in March 1918, the unit departed Camp Logan and sailed to France from Newport News, Virginia on 6 April.[25] Together with the 369th Infantry, these two regiments formed the 185th Infantry Brigade under the command of Brigadier General Albert H. Blanding.

The War Department decided to group all the separate African American National Guard battalions and companies into a single regiment. Secretary Baker decreed that all African American officers that had been mobilized with their units would be retained in spite of harsh criticism of their leadership capabilities. Approximately 250 draftees from Michigan, Illinois, and Ohio were transferred to this newly formed 372nd Infantry Regiment as replacements and to bring the unit up to strength. Two white officers, Colonel Glendie B. Young and Lieutenant Colonel Albert W. Cole, were selected as the commander and executive officer of this new regiment. Surplus white National Guard officers filled the vacant officer positions. Originally, each of the three infantry battalions was commanded by an African American officer, but the 1st Battalion's commander, Major James E. Walker, was replaced due to alleged illness, although the reason was more likely the army's abhorrence of African American field grade officers. This trend would continue to plague African American officers that achieved this status. White officers within and outside of the regiment worked toward discrediting African American officers' leadership abilities. The regiment sailed for France on 30 March 1918.

With no other African American guardsmen available, the fourth regiment would be made up entirely of draftees and white officers. Designated the 371st Infantry Regiment, this unit was staffed with southern draftees from the Carolinas, Georgia, Florida, and Alabama. Colonel Perry L. Miles and Lieutenant Colonel Robert M. Brambila, both from the regular army, led the regiment. According to Emmett Scott, the regiment was slow in forming because the African American draft in the South was delayed until the cotton crop had been harvested. In October, 3,380 men of the 371st Infantry Regiment were assigned to Camp Jackson, South Carolina, for training.[26] Many of the officers were also from the South, inexperienced, and not happy about being assigned to lead African American soldiers.

Together with the 372nd Infantry Regiment, these two units formed the 186th Infantry Brigade, commanded by Brigadier General John H. Harries. The headquarters staff of the 93rd Infantry Division (Provisional) sailed for France on 18 February 1918.

The War Department then had the problem of what to do with the large number of African American draftees that would form the 92nd Infantry Division. Originally, 40,000 men were considered for the division, of which the best 26,000 would be retained. In order to not have any large concentration of African American soldiers based at a single location, the War Department decided to train elements of the division at various military installations. To avoid the racial problems encountered in the South, it was also decided that all the training would take place at northern military facilities. By the end of October 1917, the units were training at the following military posts: Camp Grant, Illinois, the 365th Infantry Regiment, the 350th Machine Gun Battalion, and headquarters of the 183rd Infantry Brigade; at Camp Upton, New York, the 367th Infantry Regiment, the 351st Machine Gun Battalion, and headquarters of the 184th Infantry Brigade; at Camp Dix, New Jersey, the 349th and 350th Field Artillery Regiments, the 317th Trench Mortar Battery, and headquarters of the 167th Field Artillery Brigade; at Camp Meade, Maryland, the 368th Infantry Regiment and the 351st Field Artillery Regiment; at Camp Sherman, Ohio, the 317th Engineers and the 325th Signal Battalion; and at Camp Funston, Kansas, the 349th Machine Gun Battalion, Headquarters' Troop, Divisional Headquarters, and the divisional logistics trains. The 92nd Infantry Division was the only American division to be trained in this manner.[27] General Ballou, the commander of the Camp Des Moines Officer Training Course, was given command of the division.

The African American officers of the division were all Camp Des Moines graduates, none higher than the rank of captain. Excess white officers within the National Guard were assigned to the 92nd Infantry Division, not for their leadership abilities, but due to the fact that they were available, and that some of the southern officers had "experience with colored men."[28] All of the field grade and staff officers were white with special care taken to ensure, within a given unit, that no African American officer outranked any white officer.[29]

During World War I, the infantry regiments were formed with soldiers who were from a specific region of the United States. The 365th Infantry Regiment was filled with new inductees mainly from Texas and Oklahoma, and was commanded by Colonel Vernon A. Caldwell. The 366th Infantry Regiment, commanded by Colonel Ralph B. Parrott, had soldiers reporting mostly from the mining districts of Alabama. These two regiments formed the 183rd Infantry Brigade under the command of Brigadier General Malvern Hill Barnum, who had previous leadership assignments with the 9th and 10th Cavalry Regiments.[30]

The 367th Infantry Regiment was formed with draftees mostly from New York, and was led by Colonel James A. Moss, a southerner with experience commanding African American soldiers in the regular army regiments. He nicknamed his regiment the Buffaloes, a name given to African American soldiers of the west by the Native Americans. This symbol was later adopted by the entire 92nd Infantry Division. In this regiment were 108 officers, of which only 8 were white. The 368th Infantry Regiment was composed of draftees and volunteers from Maryland, Tennessee, and Pennsylvania, and was commanded by Colonel William P. Jackson. There were 97 African American officers assigned from Camp Des Moines. Together, these two regiments formed the 184th Infantry Brigade.[31]

Also assigned to the division were three field artillery regiments, the 349th, the 350th, and the 351st. The African American officers and enlisted men never received any specialized training in artillery tactics or procedures. It was not until the division was preparing to deploy to combat in France that the artillerymen were finally provided with training.

After the war, Lieutenant William N. Colson, an African American officer with the 92nd Infantry Division, charged that the army had deliberately misassigned men to various parts to the division so that it would fail; he claimed that the South Carolina illiterates formed the nucleus of the 351st Machine Gun Battalion, while men well qualified for such technical work were put into labor regiments.[32] It was also alleged that the 350th Machine Gun Battalion received inadequate training with obsolete weapons by unqualified white instructors. In the 317th Engineer Battalion, the men only received rudimentary instructions in basic engineering because the African American officers assigned to the battalion lacked the qualifications to be engineers. Consequently, white officers replaced all the African American captains after only seven months, and the lieutenants were replaced after the unit's arrival in France. The only exceptions were the battalion chaplain, the officers of the medical detachment, and two line officers. The 325th Signal Battalion performed extremely well as all of its officers were high school and college graduates. Some of the officers were afforded the opportunity to receive specialized radio training at a civilian technical school, which was endorsed by Secretary of War Baker, despite objections that it was useless to provide African Americans with such technical instructions. Two African American service companies, the 332nd Butchery and the 316th Laundry, were formed on 4 June 1918, just prior to the division's departure for overseas duty.[33]

But the majority of African American soldiers would be assigned to stevedore regiments, labor battalions, development battalions, or pioneer infantry units. Before the war's end, at least ⅓ of all the labor forces in the military were African American. The General Staff felt certain that, because most African American inductees had been manual labor workers as civilians, this was the work proper to them, and they should continue to do it for the army.

Colonel E.D. Anderson added his opinion that the "poorer class of backwoods Negro has not the mental stamina and moral sturdiness to put him in the line against opposing German troops who consist of men of high average education and thoroughly trained."[34]

With the induction of 83,400 African American soldiers in September 1917, General Tasker Bliss authorized the formation of four stevedore regiments consisting of 2,400 men, supervised by noncommissioned officers of the 24th Infantry and 10th Cavalry Regiments, and staffed with white officers. At Camp A.P. Hill, Virginia, the four regiments were hastily formed in order that they could be immediately shipped overseas in preparation for the large influx of American soldiers and equipment.[35] Also in September 1917, 12 African American labor companies were formed as a result of urgent requests from General Pershing for warehouse workers and men to load and unload trucks. The War Department still recommended that, as many of the soldiers in these units were to be volunteers with noncommissioned officers from the African American regular army regiments. Realizing that these 250-man companies were insufficient for this task, the War Department authorized that African American inductees would be assigned to labor battalions made up of 3,500 men. They would be assigned the duties of working on the docks, maintaining the cleanliness of the military camps, digging ditches, providing wood and coal for fuel, caring for livestock, and disposing of garbage. In some cases, they were trained for more technical duties as truck drivers and mechanics.[36]

The pioneer infantry battalions were originally formed in the summer of 1918, in order to keep front line units supplied. In a typical unit, white officers would have a nucleus of African American noncommissioned officers from the regular army regiments, assisted by such specialists as mechanics, blacksmiths, horse grooms, and carpenters who had received technical training at vocational schools. The rest of the men would be draftees that were classified higher than those assigned to the labor battalions. The pioneer infantry battalions were given some training on marksmanship, gas defense, tactical defense and open-position warfare. This training was not provided to the labor battalions. Some pioneer infantry battalions were also instructed in engineering technical matters such as bridge and railroad construction, laying barbed-wire entanglements, demolition, and digging fortified trenches.[37]

The first American troop convoys sailed for France in June 1917. They did not carry any African American soldiers, but they did transport up to 500 African American stevedores under contract to the military. Although not soldiers, they still wore uniforms, some surplus Union Blues from the Civil War, which a quartermaster officer had located. They were sent to speed the unloading of American ships on arrival in France. These men, like the thousands of African American soldiers that would follow them, drew the worst berthing aboard ship and were provided no dining facilities. Many ate and slept on deck in all weather, rather than in the hot airless lower holds assigned to them. The few African American officers who accompanied them were provided segregated facilities. While the combat soldiers of the white divisions were sent inland for training, the stevedores remained on the docks unloading ships.[38]

The 369th Infantry Regiment was the first African American combat unit to arrive in France in December 1917. The soldiers were immediately put to work along with the labor battalions laying railroad tracks from the docks to the forward supply depots. During the first two months of 1918, the General Staff of the Army debated the best utilization of the African American infantry regiments. General Pershing cabled to Washington, D.C., that he intended to use the regiments as labor forces for a time, after which they would be utilized as pioneer infantry.[39]

It had never been decided to actually use any of the African American infantry regiments in combat. The War Department had no plans to train additional African American infantry soldiers to be used as replacements for the combat casualties. The opportunity to fight, and even die for their country on an equal basis with white Americans was to be denied in this global conflict which had come to be known as the Great War. For if African Americans were to shed their blood on the same basis as white Americans, then just maybe they would eventually be accepted on equal terms within white America.

Initially, the French government wanted the infantry divisions of the American Army to fall within the command and control of the French Army. After nearly four year of intense combat against the German Army, the French Army had been decimated, and by 1918, were desperate for any type of relief. After nearly four years of war on the French countryside, the United States' entry into the war offered France some relief from the strain on the demand for personnel. All of the French colonial territories had by 1918 contributed men to the war effort. But General Pershing insisted that the American forces fall within the command of the United States Army on an equal basis with Great Britain and France. Still desperate for additional manpower, the French government pleaded with the United States for American forces to augment their army. General Pershing, wanting to maintain the command of the American Army under a single commander, and faced with the dilemma of supporting his allies, now had four separate infantry regiments and could not determine how best to use them. This proved to be an answer to his French allies. The four separate infantry regiments of the 93rd Infantry Divisions could be attached to the French Army. Later, General Pershing wrote in his war memoirs that the regiments were only lent to the French temporarily, "with the provision that they were to be returned for the formation of the 93rd Division when called for. Unfortunately, they soon became identified with the French and there was no opportunity to assemble them as an American division."[40]

There would be some logistical problems associated with integrating the American infantry regiments into the French Army. The American M1903 Springfield rifles were much more accurate than the ancient French Lebel rifles with their three-shot magazines, which had been employed in the Franco–German War of 1870. Superior French artillery augmented the deficiencies of the basic French rifle. It was decided to equip the American regiments with French armament, helmets, rations, and equipment. Since the American regiments received very little combat training prior to their deployment to France, they easily gave up their American shovels and adapted to the French weapons.

Just prior to the African American infantry regiments' being attached to the French Army, there was concern by the American Expeditionary Force Headquarters on how the French would treat the African American soldiers. They feared that if the French treated the African Americans as equals, it would have an adverse affect on the men when they returned to the United States after the conclusion of the war. Men accustomed to being treated as second-class citizens would now demand equal rights. Colonel Linard, of the American forces headquarters, stated the concern in a document called "Secret Information Concerning Black American Troops," explaining to the French how African American soldiers should be treated and why.[41] Colonel Linard explained "that the French people must understand the position of Negroes in America, whether or not they agreed with it. Approximately 15 million Negroes in the United States presented a threat of race mongrelization unless coloreds and whites were kept strictly separated. Since the danger did not exist in France, the French people were accustomed to being friendly and tolerant toward Negroes; but such behavior deeply offended Americans as an attack on their national beliefs and aroused the fear that it might give American Negroes intolerable pretensions to equality...."[42]

The 369th Infantry Regiment was the first to be incorporated into the French Army after they left their camp at St. Nazaire on 13 March 1918, and moved forward to Givry-en–Argonne to become attached to the French 16th Division, commanded by General Gouraud. In April, the 369th Infantry Regiment was given the responsibility for the defense of a sector that covered 4.5 kilometers of the front lines. The area covered approximated 20 percent of the sector then defended by American forces at the front lines.

By late May, the Germans were curious about these American forces in French uniforms and set out to capture some of the soldiers. Sergeant Henry Johnson and Private Needham Roberts were manning a forward observation post when a German patrol attempted to capture them. In the ensuing battle, both soldiers were wounded in the initial moments, but with grenades, Lebel rifles, and Bolo knives, they beat off the Germans, inflicting serious casualties. Private Roberts was seriously wounded early in the conflict, and most of the fighting fell to Sergeant Johnson. Captured German documents later revealed that their forces had suffered four killed and 32 wounded in this futile attempt to capture the African American soldiers.[43] For their heroic actions that day, Sergeant Johnson and Private Roberts would be the first American soldiers to be awarded the croix de guerre, France's highest medal for valor. Yet the United States Army refused to recognize the heroic deeds of these African American soldiers. On 13 February 2003, the United States Army posthumously awarded the Distinguished Service Cross, this nation's second highest award, to Sergeant Henry Johnson's 86 year old surviving son, Herman Johnson, a member of the Tuskegee Airmen during World War II, at the Pentagon's Hall of Heroes.[44]

The 369th Infantry Regiment continued to fight heroically for the French Army's 16th Division during the battles of the Argonne Forest, Chateau–Thierry, and Belleau Wood, all major conflicts. With no replacements available, by October 1918, the first battalion of the regiment was reduced to three officers and 100 enlisted men; the second battalion to ten officers and 300 men; and the third battalion to seven officers and 137 men. Casualties included 125 killed in action with 36 others who would later die of their wounds; and 636 wounded seriously enough to require hospitalization. On 26 November, the 369th Infantry Regiment became the first American unit to reach the Rhine River. According to Colonel Hayward, the regiment had been in combat 191 days, longer than any other unit in the American Expeditionary Force, after the shortest combat training of any regiment.[45]

For its valor, the entire regiment was awarded the croix de guerre (the equivalent of today's Distinguished Unit Citation) for securing the town of Sechault. The individual croix de guerre had been awarded to 170 officers and enlisted men of the regiment. Secretary of War Baker was reported to have called the 369th Infantry the all-around most serviceable regiment sent to France. By the time all the awards were presented, all of the original African American officers, with the exception of bandmaster Lieutenant Europe, had been transferred. Captain Fillmore, who had won praise for his valor at the battle of Butte de Mesnil, and Lieutenants Lacy and Reid were transferred to the 370th Infantry Regiment; and Captain Marshall was sent to the 365th Infantry Regiment of the 92nd Infantry Division.[46]

The 370th Infantry Regiment arrived in France in April 1918, and almost immediately began to lose their African American officers. Captain George Marvin, an American liaison officer with the French Army, submitted a biased and for the most part untrue report of the all-black regiment, which criticized the leadership capabilities of the officers in the unit. Captain Marvin's report stated "the Negro officers could not speak French and were bewildered by their assignment; the men disliked the French equipment and threw most of it away; and that the logistics system had failed because the Negro officers did not know which French supplies were available to them or how to transport them from the depot to their location." He stated in his report dated 14 June 1918: "From all the above it is clearly evident that this regiment is unavailable for service at the front now and, in my opinion, will not be fit for two months to come, if ever. It was plainly evident that there had been a serious loss of morale throughout the entire command."[47] Colonel Dennison was relieved of command due to alleged ill health on 12 July, and ordered to report to the American Expeditionary Force Headquarters for duty. He was replaced with Colonel T.A. Roberts, who became the first white officer in the regiment's 24-year history. Shortly after the change of command, one African American major and three captains were also relieved.[48]

The 370th Infantry Regiment's first action was in the Argonne Forest in July. On 16 July, Lieutenant Harvey Taylor sustained six wounds during a raid, thus winning the regiment's first Croix-de-Guerre. The following month, the regiment captured over 1,900 German prisoners, four cannons, 45 trench mortars, and 200 machine guns in assaults against the enemy. The 370th Infantry Regiment was attached to the 10th, 34th, 36th, 59th, and the 73rd French Divisions throughout the war. Sergeant Matthew Jenkins was awarded both the croix de guerre and the American Distinguished Service Cross for capturing a fortified German tunnel with his squad of Company F, 2/370th Infantry and holding it against enemy counterattacks for over 36 hours.[49]

By the end of the war, 71 individuals of the regiment were awarded the croix de guerre, and another 20 received America's Distinguished Service Cross for valor. The croix de guerre with Palm was awarded to the entire Company C, 1/370th Infantry for valor. Lieutenant Colonel Otis Duncan, commander of the 2/370th Infantry, remained the sole African American battalion commander in the regiment. Yet this regiment, which was reported unfit for combat upon their arrival in France, served throughout the conflict with distinction.

The 372nd Infantry Regiment, the third of the National Guard units, received a new commander upon its arrival in France. Colonel Hershel Tupes immediately requested the transfer of all the African American officers, to be replaced with white officers. He arranged a board consisting of white officers from the 371st and 372nd Infantry Regiments to evaluate the capabilities of the African American officers before they were even tested in the rigors of battle. Twenty out of the first twenty-one officers that appeared before the board were recommended for removal. Colonel Tupes' request for replacement of all of his African American officers was not on the grounds of inefficiency, but rather due to racial distinctions, which to him presented a formidable barrier to comradeship among the officers. Tensions rose to a dangerous degree, and all the white officers were ordered to wear sidearms at all times.[50]

The regiment was ordered to the front lines in September, where they relieved the 371st Infantry Regiment at Trieres Farm, which they were ordered to fortify and hold. Next the regiment was ordered to clear pockets of enemy resistance in the town of Monthois. It was during these actions that the first and second battalions suffered so many casualties that the survivors had to be consolidated into a single battalion. A young white lieutenant stated that the casualties were so high because the soldiers refused to surrender or retreat. The veteran French 157th Division, whom the regiment was attached to at the time, commended the soldiers for their many acts of heroism. Corporal Clarence Van Allen, originally a member of the Massachusetts National Guard Company, singlehandedly destroyed a German machine gun emplacement and captured a trench mortar battery and its crew. These exploits earned him the croix de guerre with Palm, the Medaille Militaire, and the Distinguished Service Cross. In all, the French Army awarded 52 individual croix de guerre and four Medailles Militaires to the soldiers of the 372nd Infantry Regiment.[51] In spite of the discrimination and the unjustified removal of the African American officers of the regiment, the French Army awarded the entire unit the croix de guerre with Palm, the highest unit decoration conferred by France, with a citation praising "a superb spirit and an admirable scorn of danger."[52]

The southern draftees of the 371st Infantry Regiment were immediately sent to the front lines upon their arrival in France in April 1918. The regiment was also attached to the French 157th Division. The division, famous for their heroic defense of Verdun in 1915, wore a red hand shoulder patch, and called itself the Red Hand Division. The 371st Infantry adopted this shoulder patch and called themselves the Red Hand Regiment.

On 28 September 1918, Company C, 1/371st Infantry was assigned the task to lead an assault on Hill 188 in the Champagne Marne sector. As the company attacked the enemy positions, the Germans ceased fire and began climbing atop the parapets of their trenches, waving their weapons in the air as if to signal an intent to surrender. When the American soldiers were within 300 feet of the trench line, the Germans leaped back behind cover and opened fire. Within minutes, over 50 percent of Company C were casualties. Corporal Freddie Stowers, a 21 year old from Sandy Spring, South Carolina, took charge and beckoned his soldiers to follow him in the attack. Under devastating fire, Corporal Stowers crawled forward, leading his squad toward enemy machine gun emplacements which were killing and wounding the men all around him. After fierce hand-to-hand combat, the machine gun positions were silenced, and the German soldiers killed. While leading his men to assault a second trench line, Corporal Stowers was mortally wounded, but continued to press the attack, urging his men forward until he succumbed to his wounds. Corporal Stowers' leadership inspired his men, and the company continued the attack against incredible odds, finally capturing Hill 188 while inflicting heavy German casualties. For his bravery that day, his company commander recommended Corporal Stowers for the Congressional Medal of Honor. But the award presentation would languish for over 70 years. On 24 April 1991, President George H. W. Bush presented the award to his two surviving sisters, Georgia Palmer of Richmond, California, and Mary Bowens of Greenville, South Carolina. Also in attendance was his nephew, Staff Sergeant Douglas Warren of the 101st Airborne Division, who was flown in from combat duties in the Persian Gulf War. Corporal Freddie Stowers would be the only African American soldier awarded this nation's highest honor for valor in World War I.[53]

By the time the hostilities had ended in November, the 371st Infantry Regiment had also been awarded the Croix-de-Guerre with Palm. In addition, 60 officers and 124 enlisted men received either the American Distinguished Service Cross or the croix de guerre, more than any other regiment of the 93rd Infantry Division.

As a whole, the four regiments of the 93rd Infantry Division suffered a total of 584 men killed in action and 2,582 wounded. That represents 32 percent of the division, yet those regiments fought with great valor, never receiving any replacement soldiers. They were welcomed and treated with the utmost respect by the French Army divisions to which they were assigned.[54]

The 92nd Infantry Division, commanded by Major General Charles C. Ballou, had the misfortune to be assigned to the American 2nd Army, commanded by General Robert Bullard, upon their arrival in France in June 1918. General Bullard had no desire to have an African American infantry division serving within his army and expressed in his diary: "Poor Negroes! They are hopelessly inferior. As fighting troops, Negroes were simply failures." He declared: "If you need combat soldiers, and especially if you need them in a hurry, don't put your time upon Negroes. The task of making soldiers of them and fighting with them, if there are any white people near, will be swamped in the race question. If racial uplift or racial equality is your purpose, that is another matter." In referring to General Ballou, he said: "I'm inclined to think he will have to be 'S.O.S.ed,' and I'll have to get this done.... all this constructive equality I regarded as an injustice: it is not real."[55] S.O.S. pertained to the Service of Supply branch to which most African American soldiers were assigned to perform the manual labor duties. General Bullard also strongly believed that African American officers were inferior to white officers solely by virtue of their color.

Many of the white officers of the 92nd Infantry Division felt the same as General Bullard about African American soldiers. General Ballou stated: "It was my misfortune to be handicapped by many white officers who were rabidly hostile to the idea of a colored officer, and who continually conveyed misinformation to the staffs of the superior units, and generally created much trouble and discontent. Such men will never give the Negro the square deal that is his due."[56] General Ballou's own chief of staff, Colonel Allen J. Greer, was a man who, either due to bigotry or thorough racial hatred, circulated derogatory and untrue stories about African American soldiers, and especially the officers in the division, to his higher headquarters without ever consulting General Ballou.

In addition to the low opinion that higher headquarters held in regard to the 92nd Infantry Division, the division had additional obstacles to overcome. When the division arrived in France, the African American officers were segregated from the white officers in billeting and dining facilities. General Pershing had requested that the British Army train the division prior to its being deployed into combat, but the British did not want to have anything to do with these African American soldiers. The French, who were more tolerant of racial differences, instructed the 92nd Infantry Division in combat tactics. The division was also hampered in other ways that did not affect the white infantry divisions deployed to France. General Ballou had not been afforded the opportunity to come to France prior to the division's arrival in order to observe actual battle tactics like his fellow commanders of the white infantry divisions. The 92nd Infantry Division had not received any training as a consolidated unit in a single location like the other infantry divisions. Their units were dispersed at several military installations. Being restricted to military posts located only in northern states, the division was unable to receive adequate training when adverse winter weather conditions curtailed the division's training schedule.

Many of the division's African American officers had not been afforded the opportunity to complete their specialized training prior to deploying to France. Most of the artillery and engineer captains were replaced upon their arrival to the country. The 317th Engineers were immediately tasked with building docks and barracks when they arrived in country. The artillery regiment had a shortage of trucks and horses to transport their artillery pieces to the front lines.

But the major concern of white officers while the 92nd Infantry Division was involved with training was the interaction of African American soldiers with French women. One white officer instructed his soldiers that French women were to be treated the same as they would American white women, which meant that all contact was prohibited. The French were informed that African Americans were inferior to whites and that in the United States they were therefore not permitted to ride in the same railway cars with whites or to live in white neighborhoods.[57] Soldiers of the division were restricted to a curfew and could not be more than one mile away from their training post.

White officers also saw to it that African American officers had no conceptions about such subversive ideas as equality. Captain M. Virgil Boutte, a graduate of Fisk and Illinois Universities, because of his fluency in French, had been assigned as an interpreter for the division. The white officers of the division had him returned to his original unit, the 350th Machine Gun Battalion, because they could not tolerate his interaction with the French people in his duties as the billeting officer. He was immediately brought before an efficiency board where he was cleared of all the charges. His battalion commander was shown to have acted entirely from prejudice and was relieved of his command.[58]

The Army War College also saw to it that officers were not to be treated on an equal basis. On a new table of organization for the 92nd Infantry Division, it was determined that there would be 373 white officers and 684 African American officers assigned to the division. Specifically reserved for white officers were: divisional headquarters staff, aides to brigade commanders, captains in the field artillery and engineer battalions, all adjutants, logistics officers, and the commanders of headquarters companies. There was no opportunity for an African American officer to advance higher than the rank of captain in the divisions, and many of those captain positions were reserved for white officers. The War College plan concluded: "The War College Division strongly recommends that no reduction from this table be made in the number of white officers assigned to this division, as this is considered the minimum with which any degree of efficiency can be reached. Colored officers who are incompetent will not be retained, nor will their own estimate of their fitness be accepted." The policy contained no statement in reference to incompetent white officers, although General Ballou complained that he had many, stating: "The division is a dumping ground for incompetent white officers as well as colored."[59] Of the 144 captain positions in the 92nd Infantry Division, only 74 were authorized to be filled by African American officers.[60] African Americans, while being allowed to become officers, would be relegated to the most junior ranks, with no opportunity of being promoted. The division, which had started the war with 82 percent of its officers being African American, ended the war with only 58 percent of the officers being black.[61]

By late August 1918, the 92nd Infantry Division was finally moved to the front lines in the St. Die sector, not far from the German border. While assigned to this sector, the division's primary duties were patrolling and casualties occurred daily. On the night of 4 September, Lieutenant Aaron Fisher earned a Distinguished Service Cross when his squad of seven riflemen from Company E, 2/366th Infantry, repulsed a numerically superior enemy attack.

When the 92nd Infantry Division was deployed to the front lines, German propaganda leaflets were dropped on their sector.

> Hello, boys. What are you doing over here? Fighting the Germans? Why? Have they ever done you any harm? Of course some white folks and the lying English–American papers told you that the Germans ought to be wiped out for the sake of humanity and democracy. What is democracy? Personal freedom; all citizens enjoying the same rights socially and before the law. Do you enjoy the same rights as the white people do in America, the land of freedom and democracy, or are you not rather treated over there as second class citizens?
>
> Can you get into a restaurant where white people dine? Can you get a seat or berth in a railroad car, or can you even ride in the south in the same streetcar with the white people?
>
> And how about the law? Is lynching and the most horrible crimes connected therewith, a lawful proceeding in a democratic country? Now all this is entirely different in Germany, where they do like colored people; where they treat them as gentlemen and as white men, and quite a number of colored people have fine positions in business in Berlin and other German cities. Why, then, fight the Germans only for the benefit of the Wall Street robbers, and to protect the millions that they have loaned to the English, French, and Italians?
>
> You have been made the tool of the egoistic and rapacious rich in America, and there is nothing in the whole game for you but broken bones, horrible wounds, spoiled health, or death. No satisfaction whatever will you get out of this unjust war. You have never seen Germany, so you

are fools if you allow people to make you hate us. Come over and see for yourself. Let those do the fighting who make the profit out of this war. Don't allow them to use you as cannon fodder.

To carry a gun in this service is not an honor, but a shame. Throw it away and come over to the German lines. You will find friends who will help you.[62]

Although there was much truth in these propaganda leaflets, they produced very few American desertions. Soldiers on the front lines fought for their fellow soldiers and not for their country, especially when that country felt as though they were not worthy of fighting for it. A camaraderie develops when the soldiers of a unit are together from its inception through combat. There is a bond between the officers that lead and the enlisted soldiers that follow, but with the racism and discrimination in the 92nd Infantry Division, this bond rarely happened.

In mid–September, the 92nd Infantry Division was quickly moved to the Meuse–Argonne sector for the offensive attacks. The division was kept in reserve, but a gap existed in the front lines between the American 77th Infantry Division and the 4th French Army. The 368th Infantry Regiment was ordered to deploy at night to fill this breach in the lines on 25 September. When the attack began the next morning the regiment lacked it own organic artillery support, which had been attached to another infantry division, and the proper tools for clearing the wire obstacles along the path of their frontal attack. In the confusion of battle and a due to a lack of communications to the units on their flanks and with their regimental headquarters, the three infantry battalions were ordered to fall back.[63] On the second day of the battle, the 368th Infantry Regiment encountered the same obstacles, but managed to capture one of their objectives, the town of Binarville. On 28th September, the regiment continued the attack, but intense German artillery fire, bypassed machine gun emplacements, and enemy sniper fire forced the regiment to retreat again. One battalion commander ordered a withdrawal without specifying the new line of defense. Other soldiers, not receiving orders from higher command, maintained their present positions throughout the night.[64]

The 368th Infantry Regiment was finally relieved after five days of fighting on 30 September. Its casualties in the Meuse-Argonne offense were 42 men killed in action and 16 who would later die of their wounds; and over 200 wounded. By now, rumors had been spread by white officers, not only of the failure of the regiment in combat, but the failure of the entire 92nd Infantry Division. Instead of another regiment of the division replacing the 368th Infantry, the entire 92nd Infantry Division was ordered out of the Argonne sector on 5 October. Naturally blame for the confusion in battle was placed entirely on the alleged incompetent leadership of the African American junior officers. In comparison to the white infantry divisions assigned to the front lines of the attack, the 368th Infantry Regiment fared no worse. One historian in describing the battles of the Argonne Offense stated: "Under the galling fire from the Germans, reinforced in their line of resistance, the forward units of these three divisions had retreated. Some sort of battle line was formed, but the morale of these troops was too badly shattered to permit reorganization on the field."[65] Those three infantry divisions had to be replaced, but nothing was ever mentioned about white soldiers not being able to withstand the stress of modern warfare and that white officers were unsuited for combat leadership.

Colonel Greer, the chief of staff for the 92nd Infantry Division, was reported as saying: "They failed in all their missions, laid down and sneaked to the rear, until they were withdrawn."[66] Colonel Fred Brown, the commander of the 368th Infantry Regiment, made a long, if not objective investigation of the charges of cowardice and incompetence and reported the results in a paper entitled "Inefficiency of Negro Officers." Colonel Brown concluded that all the derogatory rumors and unproven reports were true. "Two battalions disintegrated without reason," he reported, "and failed to advance when ordered to do so. They fled back to the regimental command post. I personally stopped the entire mob and put them in the trenches near my C.P. [Command Post]. No colored officer or noncommissioned officer exercised any command at the time and could not be distinguished from the enlisted men. I wish to go on record as expressing my opinion that colored officers as a class are unfit to command troops in present day warfare."[67] This tribute to Colonel Brown's bravery appears nowhere but in his report. Similarly unique is his further statement that said he "went forward with headquarters' personnel [white soldiers], out-distancing the advance of any combat companies and taking prisoners and machine guns."[68] Also proven to be untrue.

At a time when all aspects of military operations were being documented, it was not unusual for white officers to fabricate their actions in combat, especially when they were assigned to an African American unit. Racial prejudices ensured that the stereotypes of the African American soldier as a coward and incapable of succeeding in combat unless a white man led them, would keep these fabricated reports circulating throughout two world wars. No one ever thought to question the African American soldiers as to the validity of these reports. It would be years before that concept ever came to light, tucked away in the National Archives and unit histories. Occasionally, a white officer would actually state the truth, but it often meant an abrupt end to his military career.

In the investigation that followed the battle, the white battalion commanders would make several statements against the African American officers under their command. This was mainly in an effort to relieve these battalion commanders of any blame for failure. The African American officers made an easy target upon whom to place blame due to prejudice and since many of the white officers of the division did not want to be placed on an equal level with them. Major J.N. Merrell, commander of the 1/368th Infantry, stated, "not a single officer of the battalion has shown any anxiety to get to close quarters with the Germans." Major B.F. Norris, commander of the 3/368th Infantry, also described his men as cowards. But an African American officer of the battalion testified that Major Norris hid in a ditch during the attack, a fact to which Major Norris admitted in later testimony. One officer testified that that Major Norris deserted his men under fire and returned to his command post. Another officer testifying in his defense at his own court-martial stated that none of his messages to the battalion commander requesting guidance during the battle had ever been answered.[69]

In time, a number of the African American officers of the 368th Infantry Regiment were tried by court-martial. Five were found guilty of cowardice and sentenced to death, but were later exonerated by a War Department investigation, led by Secretary Baker, which attributed the failure of the regiment to a lack of experience and equipment and added, "there is strong evidence that withdrawal orders were carried to the front by runners," just as claimed by the African American officers.[70] Colonel Brown and his battalion commanders were found to have ordered the battalions of the regiment to retreat. In order to shift the blame of their inadequate leadership and incompetence in combat, African American officers took the brunt of the blame for these failures.

Major Max Elser, who commanded the 2/368th Infantry, which was the leading battalion during the initial attack, would testify that he relocated his command post without informing any of his company commanders, and never knew what happened to his men once they moved forward.[71] Colonel Brown noted in his After Action Report on the battle that Major Elser had withdrawn his battalion without orders and had been missing from his command post over four hours on the night of 26 September. On 28 September, Colonel Brown was forced to relieve Major Elser due to what he termed "physical exhaustion."[72] When the African American officers were finally questioned about the battle, one officer stated that "Major Elser became hysterical, that he placed his hands to his face and cried out to his personal runners to take him out of there, that he could not stand it. As a result, he was in a hospital for a period of three weeks and would have been court-martialed but for the intercession of his influential friends...." An African American doctor reported that Major Elser was treated at the 365th Infantry Regiment's field hospital for psychoneurosis, and that the white commander of the hospital sent him elsewhere for further treatment.[73] The actions of Major Elser would never be considered a factor in the failure of the 368th Infantry Regiment during the battle in the Meuse-Argonne sector.

The 92nd Infantry Division would be relegated to patrolling and labor duties for the remainder of the war, and the African American officers who led these soldiers were highly criticized from white superior officers within the division. The irony is that 21 soldiers of the division were awarded the Distinguished Service Cross, a greater number than the 6th, 35th, 81st or the 88th Infantry Divisions, which had been assigned duties in the same sector. The 92nd Infantry Division suffered over 1,700 casualties, but due to the false statements made by white officers of the American Expeditionary Force, the division would forever be considered a failure for their performance in World War I.

Both the 92nd and 93rd Infantry Divisions would perform occupation duties in Germany at the close of the war. It remains to be answered, if the 92nd Infantry Division had been attached to the French Army, would their combat record have been as stellar as the 93rd Infantry Division? Obviously, racism, hatred, and discrimination were to the detriment of the soldiers who served under the American army. Both of these divisions were ordered from occupation duty in Germany to return to France for possible debarkation back to the United States. Both divisions were restricted to their camps to minimize contact with the French population. The African American laborers of the Service of Supply Branch and the Pioneer Infantry Battalions had the arduous task of returning the battlefields of France back to normalcy so the French farmers could plant their crops in the spring of 1919. Old battlefields had to be cleared of mines and wire entanglements. Demolition teams were sent in to detonate unexploded ordnance. Trenches had to be filled in. The docks had to be maintained so that equipment and men could be shipped back to the United States.[74] Over 6,000 pioneer infantrymen of the 813th, 815th, and 816th Regiments were sent to Romagne and detailed to the Graves Registration branch to collect all the bodies within a 50-kilometer radius. Many of the bodies found were in advanced stages of decomposition. At least 23,000 bodies were located and reburied.[75]

On 31 January 1919, secret instructions were issued from the American Expeditionary Force Headquarters to all American counterespionage and intelligence officers, warning them to watch for evidence that a secret radical organization existed among African American officers: "Among the alleged avowed purposes of the organization, is protection of Negro interests, collective combating of any white effort, especially in the south, to reestablish white ascendancy, the securing of equal intellectual and economic opportunity for Negroes and the maintenance of the social equality between the races as established in France."[76] When W.E.B. Dubois was scheduled to visit the 92nd Infantry Division in January 1919, Major F.P. Schoonmaker, the division G-2, issued special instructions to all intelligence officers.

1. A man by name of Dubois, with a visitor's pass, reported on his way to visit this Division. His presence at stations of any unit will be immediately reported in secret enclosures to

the Assistant Chief of Staff, G-2 [Major Schoonmaker], of these headquarters. Likewise prompt reports will be made to G-2 of all his moves and actions while at stations of any unit.

2. The fact of this inquiry as to Dubois and his moves will not be disclosed to any person outside the Intelligence Service.[77]

Amid the suspicion surrounding subversive activities of African American officers, there were also allegations that African American soldiers had been executed in France for minor offenses without trial. Senator Tom Watson of Georgia presented to a Senate investigating committee the names of 62 men, many of them African American, who had been executed without trial by order of military officials.[78] The military denied all charges, with the advocate general insisting that if these illegal executions had occurred, there would have been some record of them. When Senator Watson produced a photograph of a hanging at the town of Gievres, the advocate general had to admit that it occurred. There was also convincing testimony that other hangings had taken place, even if they were not recorded. In the Graves Registration Service, staffed by white personnel, Captain Charles Wynne and Richard Sullivan testified that among the dead who had been reburied were men who bore the marks of a hanging.[79] But in the end, nothing was ever done about the illegal execution allegations. The Senate concluded that the charges were without foundation.

The African American infantry divisions were finally shipped back to the United States in early 1919, but little attention was paid to their triumphant return, in contrast to the receptions received by the white combat divisions. The 369th Infantry Regiment returned to New York on 12 February 1919. They were the first New York soldiers to return from the war, and the city gave them a parade up Fifth Avenue a few days later. After the parade, city officials entertained the soldiers with a dinner at the armory of the 71st New York Infantry Regiment. It would be the first and last time that the entire regiment would be assembled under one roof. The 367th Infantry Regiment returned to New York one month later and also paraded through the city. In the South, things were vastly different. In St. Joseph, Missouri, African American soldiers refused to take part in the victory parade because they were forced to march at the very end. There were reports that African American soldiers were stopped at Southern railroad stations, beaten and stripped of their uniforms.[80] The NAACP reported such incidents occurring in Texas, Mississippi, Alabama, South Carolina, Kentucky, and Wyoming. The white assailants included a local banker, a deputy sheriff, and a town marshal.[81]

African American soldiers who wished to remain in the army also faced obstacles. With demobilization, the only remaining African American units were those original four cavalry and infantry regiments. Once those regiments reached full strength, no additional enlistments were allowed. African American officers wishing to remain on active duty faced an even larger hurdle to overcome. They had to go before a retention board of white officers to determine whether they could keep their commissions. Prejudices and stereotypes formulated the opinions of the board members. One board stated the following on refusing to allow an officer to retain his commission: "The Board recommends that he be not examined. Reason: unqualified by reason of the qualities inherent in the Negro race; an opinion of the Board, based on the testimony of five white officers serving with the 368th Infantry. Negroes are deficient in moral fiber, rendering them unfit as officers and leaders of men."[82] In this particular case, the War Department overruled the examining board, but such actions did not speak for the entire army.

Colonel Greer, again writing to Senator McKellar of Tennessee on the matter of retaining African American officers, stated: "Now that a reorganization of the army is in prospect, and as all officers of the temporary forces have been asked if they desire to remain in the regular army, I think I ought to bring a matter to your attention that is of vital importance not only from a military point of view but from that which all Southerners have. I refer to the question of Negro officers and Negro troops. The 92nd Division had failed in all its missions because the officers and men were cowards."[83]

In a more typical case, Colonel I.C. Jenks stated: "If the time has come for Negroes and dagoes to be officers in the regular army, it is time for the white man to step out." Colonel Jenks refused to endorse the retention of Major Milton Dean, an African American officer with 22 years of military experience, saying: "Major Dean is a very efficient officer, but for reasons which I care not to state, but which are well known, I cannot recommend him."[84]

Those few African American officers that were retained were of the junior grades of lieutenants and captains and were restricted to duty in those four African American regular army regiments. Although there were exceptional artillery and engineer officers, none were retained. Colonel Hayward resigned his commission with the 369th Infantry Regiment shortly upon his return to the United States. "Colored officers had proved their merit," he felt; "therefore, some capable Negro should be selected to take over the regiment."[85]

African American women also suffered discrimination in their efforts to support the war effort. When the United States declared war on Germany, Ada Thoms, cofounder of the National Association of Colored Graduate Nurses, encouraged African American nurses to join the American Red Cross. The Red Cross registered interested African American nurses, but then rejected their applications on the grounds that the army would not accept them for duty. It was not until after the conclusion of the war, in December 1918, that the army finally accepted African American nurses. In an openly declared experiment, the Army accepted 18 African American nurses and assigned them to hospitals at Camp Sherman, Ohio, and Camp Grant, Illinois, due to the influenza epidemic that killed an estimated half million Americans, including many military personnel. Although living in segregated facilities, the nurses attended to both white and African American patients.[86]

The only other opportunity during World War I for African American women to directly assist those in military uniform was with the Young Men's Christian Association (YMCA). The War Department had authorized the YMCA to operate service centers to provide recreation, refreshment, and a comfortable location to write letters, read, or just relax. At the beginning of America's involvement in the war, the YMCA promised to provide equal services to both white and African American service members, but those facilities were strictly segregated. More than 200 African American women served as hostesses in YMCA centers throughout the United States. Fifteen centers, operated by 68 male and 19 female volunteers, also supported African American soldiers in France. In addition to the usual comforts provided by the YMCA, those which served the African American soldiers also offered classes that taught thousands of previously illiterate soldiers how to read and write.

Chapter II

Between the Wars

As a result of its participation in World War I, the United States gained international prominence and influence, and with its newfound position as a world leader, America had changed. During the war, Europeans were banned from immigrating into the United States. With factories in the north increasing their output of war materials, and four million men being removed from the labor force to serve in uniform, there was a void in manpower to support these industrial requirements. Between 1916 and 1918, an estimated one million African Americans were recruited from the South to fill this void. Along with improved employment opportunities, African Americans, though still experiencing segregation in these northern cities, were afforded better individual rights than they had in the South. Once the war concluded, white Americans, wishing to revert to prewar employment practices that would allow returning soldiers to regain their previous employment positions, expected African Americans to accept their previous subservient, less than equal status.

To meet the peril of retuning African American veterans who might have been infected with foreign ideas of liberty, equality, and fraternity, the Ku Klux Klan, which had been revived in 1915, now became very visible. White America, especially in the South, was outraged by the fair treatment extended to African American soldiers by the French and other European powers, which regarded them as equals as opposed to the subhuman treatment they received in their own country. The postwar years became a period of racial tension and fear, for the United States was evolving into a new world order, but many white Americans were not willing to accept this new change in status.

In 1919, the level of violence increased as 83 people were lynched by hostile mobs. Of that total, 77 were African Americans, with at least ten being returning veterans. Most were killed for the usual false allegations of raping a white woman or just "not knowing their place." In Sylvester, Georgia, Daniel Mack allegedly told a white man that he had fought in France and did not intend to take mistreatment from white people. He was sentenced to jail for 30 days, but was removed from his cell by an angry mob and beaten to death, still in his uniform. In Pine Bluff, Arkansas, a returning African American veteran refused to move off the sidewalk when ordered to do so by a white woman. He replied that it was a free country and would not move. A mob took him forcefully from town, lashed him to a tree with tire chains, and shot him 50 times.[1] As one historian would put it: "To the reactionary, the uniform on a Negro man was like a red flag thrown in the face of a bull."[2]

The summer of 1919 has been referred to as the "Red Summer" due to the quantity of blood spilled in race riots throughout the country. At least 38 clashes, which could be classified as race riots, occurred that year, mainly during the summer. Whites believed that African Americans created the tensions that led to this extraordinary violence by returning from the war armed and defiant, and whites supposedly organized only in self-defense. Yet the worst rioting occurred in the African American neighborhoods of Washington, D.C., Chicago; Omaha, Nebraska; New York City; Norfolk, Virginia; Knoxville, Tennessee; and Longview, Texas, with marauding white mobs attacking innocent blacks. This epidemic of violence even broke out in Bisbee, Arizona, with the local townspeople and police harassing the soldiers of the 10th Cavalry Regiment, which had been a mainstay in the community for decades.

Although the underlying causes of the violence were profoundly economic, social, and psychological, it was the return of the African American soldier with his perceived "foreign ideology" from Europe that seemed to trigger violence throughout the country. Yet, it was the reasoning of defending their country and bringing forth democracy to the world that instilled newfound pride in African Americans. Most newspapers criticized the African Americans as causing the violence, but when police refused to do anything to stop the mobs or to protect the people who were suffering from their abuse, African Americans took it upon themselves to provide their own defense. However, once whites realized that African Americans, no longer docile but resisting oppression, were willing to arm themselves and fight back, the riots waned, giving way to the smaller-scale atrocities and terror tactics, such as the lynching and burnings. The strict enforcement of Jim Crow laws symbolized a last-ditch effort to keep African Americans in their unequal status.

The military made no effort to end discrimination in the postwar army. African Americans found themselves no more welcomed as soldiers than they were in the towns and cities of white America. White army officers harbored racist agendas based on the belief that African American subordinates had adversely influenced their careers during the war. These officers devalued the combat abilities of African Americans and advanced the stereotype of the race's inferiority.

The army's general staff, in determining what the future role of African American soldiers in combat would entail, conducted studies and testimonies. Most of the testimony came from regimental and higher commanders of units of the 92nd Infantry Division, the only full-strength African American combat division with the American Expeditionary Forces. This testimony was almost uniformly condemnatory of the performance of African American infantry soldiers, and particularly with an emphasis on the leadership performances of African American officers. Infantry commanders were especially convinced that the training and performance of their soldiers had been a failure. Never was it mentioned that the 92nd Infantry Division was never able to train at a single location like the white infantry divisions, due to the fear of not wanting to place such a large number of armed African American soldiers at one place. Commanders of supporting units, such as engineers and field artillery, reported relatively greater success, but they too felt that combat duties, especially those under the command of African American officers, should not be assigned. Commanders of the regiments of the 93rd Infantry Division, whose experiences were with combat soldiers organized in separate infantry regiments attached to French divisions, made similar comments on the inadvisability of employing African Americans as combat soldiers, especially under the leadership of African American officers, although their reports showed that their own organizations were relatively more successful than those of the 92nd Infantry Division. No formal comments were sought from the officers of the four regular army African American regiments, for these units had not been sent to France. The testimony was therefore confined to units of volunteers, draftees, and National Guardsmen.[3]

The commanding officer of the ill-fated 368th Infantry Regiment, 92nd Infantry Division, for example, felt that "Negro soldiers were absolutely dependent upon the leadership of white officers," never mentioning that some of his own white battalion commanders broke down the first time they were exposed to combat. Since, he said, "combat units may expect heavy officer casualties I consider the Negro should not be used as a combat soldier." The commanders of the 371st and 372nd Infantry Regiments of the 93rd Infantry Division agreed, saying that "in a future war, Negroes should be used principally in labor organizations." The 372nd Infantry Regiment's commander added "that if they had to be used in combat organizations, then combatant officers should be all white, also the non-commissioned officers." Yet, the commander of the 369th Infantry Regiment, Colonel Hayward, whose unit had been in combat longer than any other American infantry regiment during the war, and had dispelled the myth that African Americans were incapable of being effective combat soldiers and leaders, was not solicited to provide any testimony during these procedures.

The commander of the 365th Infantry Regiment, 92nd Infantry Division, along with others, added a further provision, "a period of training at least twice as long as is necessary in the training of white troops otherwise they should be used as pioneer or labor troops." Frequently, comments included a statement such as that of the commander of the 367th Infantry Regiment of the 92nd Infantry Division: "As fighting troops, the Negro must be rated as second class material, this due primarily to his inferior intelligence and lack of mental and moral qualities." Others, like the commanding general of the 92nd Infantry Division, Major General Ballou, reduced to the rank of colonel in the peacetime army, blaming his division for his military failures, recommended that "no Negro units larger than a regiment be formed in the future."[4]

The conviction that the army, instead of limiting the use of African American combat soldiers, should rather attempt to increase their efficiency was strongly expressed in some of the reports. To heighten their self-identification as a vital part of the army team, some officers recommended that smaller African American units be attached to or integrated into larger white units. One commander wrote: "Personally I think it is a waste of time to consider whether we shall have colored troops and colored officers. It is quite possible that in the future as in the past, circumstances will arise to compel us to have both. I think our past policy of massing them by themselves has not been wise. I believe under conditions as they are, this policy should be modified by doing away with the colored regiments and putting a colored unit in every regiment, said unit not to be smaller than a company and not larger than a battalion. I believe in having colored officers for these colored units to the extent that suitable colored personnel is available under the conditions for qualifying for the position of an Army officer."[5]

After World War I, the United States took an isolationist stance on international affairs. Although the National Defense Act of 1920 reduced the regular army forces to 30,000 soldiers, the four African American regular army regiments were left untouched. Throughout the 1920s and 1930s, the regiments were maintained at full strength, though they rarely trained for combat duties or operated as complete units. Instead, the African American infantrymen and cavalrymen were detailed to installation maintenance and labor support positions, which often required keeping the post cleaned. The 10th Cavalry Regiment, stationed at West Point for most of the 1930s, acted as orderlies and servants for the academy's staff and cadets. At Fort Benning, Georgia, the 24th Infantry Regiment rarely practiced marksmanship or any other infantry tactics. Instead, they performed duties as truck drivers, cooks, garbage collectors and stable hands for the installation's white units.

Congress authorized an expansion of the Army Air Corps in 1926. This expansion was to take place in five yearly increments. To maintain a balance in the strength of the army, the men for the Air Corps units were to come from allotments allocated to units from the other branches. African American ground units were not required to contribute to the first four increments, but in the fifth, or during the 1931 increment, they took their share of the reductions all at once, although there had not been any African American positions allocated in the Army Air Corps.[6] The African American regular army regiments once more found themselves over-strength both in numbers and in enlisted ratings. During 1931, the War Department had to order a temporary cessation of enlistments, re-enlistments, and promotions for African American soldiers. Only transfers could absorb the excess men, and the cessation of enlistments and promotions, planned to last not more than six to twelve months, persisted until 1934 in an acute form.[7]

Although the original War Department letter of instructions plainly indicated that the orders suspending recruiting for Negro units were "*Not for Press Release*," it was difficult to keep the news quiet. Before the month was out, the NAACP had received copies of the orders from "two sources" and had written President Herbert C. Hoover to inquire about their authenticity. "If we interpret these facts correctly," the NAACP said, "it appears ... that it is the intention of the War Department to abolish the so-called colored regiments."[8]

It was still perceived by the public that the War Department was attempting to abolish the four African American regiments. As the dissatisfaction of the African American population continued, Robert R. Moton, the successor to Booker T. Washington at Tuskegee Institute, made impassioned pleas to President Hoover for the preservation of the units, pointing out that, from his own observations at nearby Fort Benning, "The fate of the 24th Infantry had been a slow withering away." Moton wrote: "The original declaration was that these Negro troops from the 24th Infantry were transferred to Fort Benning as a special training unit. Whatever the original intention, this program has been entirely abandoned. Negro troops at Fort Benning are without arms or equipment of any sort that could be used in training for combat service. They are called out twice a week for what are virtually the rudiments of drill, the only elements of training which they get." Continuing, Moton urged the President: "I would respectfully ask you to consider the long and honorable career of Negro troops in the service of the United States. It is the universal testimony that they are excellent soldiers and possessed with eager willingness in the performance of their duties under all conditions of service. It is more than unfortunate, it is an injustice, that regiments that have distinguished themselves in the way the 10th Cavalry and the 25th Infantry have done, should be reduced from combat service to be menials to white regiments, without chance for training or promotion and be excluded from other branches of the service. It is merely a pretense that Negroes are accorded the same treatment in the United States army as are given to white troops. It has never been the case and is not so now. This applies both to the rank and file, as witness the presence of the highest ranking Negro officer in the United States army (Colonel Benjamin O. Davis Sr.) at Tuskegee Institute at the present time, who, by reason of his color is denied service according to his rank and with his own regiment."[9]

Even after the resumption of enlistments in 1934, the tight vacancy situation within the African American regiments allowed for little recruiting. Because enlistments could be accepted for vacancies only, an African American candidate who wished to join the Regular Army could not present himself at a typical recruiting station, make an application, be examined, and then be accepted or rejected. During the earlier years of the depression, the same situation with regard to an excess of applicants over vacancies existed for white units. White recruiting, however, never came to a complete halt, and in the middle and late 1930s, recruiting stations were nearly always able to accept well-qualified white applicants. But an African American seeking to join the army had to find out which installation had elements of an African American regiment stationed there, discover where vacancies existed, apply to the commanding officer of the post or unit where service was desired, and present himself at the post at his own expense once enlistment was authorized. The army explained that it had no funds for transporting recruits over the great distances outside their own regional corps areas, which many African Americans had to travel to reach installations where the vacancies existed.[10]

The restrictions on the size, number, and types of authorized African American units, added to the high proportion of re-enlistments and the consequent inability to enlist many new recruits, made it difficult for the African American regiments to prepare themselves for the job of providing a nucleus of young, well-trained African American soldiers who might be valuable in an expanded wartime army. During the depression, the African American regiments consisted of career soldiers who did not leave the service until forced into retirement. Not only did this keep recruitment low, but it also kept promotions at even a lower rate. Because all elements of the regiments were seldom assembled and stationed at the same military installation, and because so many of the companies and detachments were used for "housekeeping" duties and menial labor tasks, training beyond the level of the disciplined life of the garrison soldier was difficult. The combat efficiency of the African American regiments plummeted. The regiments, or those portions when available, did participate in occasional field training exercises with other white units of the army, but for the most part they had little save ceremonial and rudimentary training duties to perform. The African American press and public, in their long campaign for increased enlistment opportunities, did not overlook the ready opportunity to cite the disadvantages of a situation in which recruiting posters and stations were in evidence in the business sections of most cities, while potential African American trainees lacked vacancies in which they could be placed. The young African American male, who successfully found his way into the regular army as an enlisted man during the depression years, was looked upon as an extremely fortunate individual.

Opportunities for African American officers where also very limited. By the time the military had been reduced to its postwar strength, less than six African American officers remained on active duty in the regular army. Many of the African American officers that had served during World War I were rejected when they applied to remain in the regular army. Some took reductions to the enlisted ranks in order to remain in the service and receive a retirement pension. The primary source of regular army commissioning remained at the United States Military Academy at West Point, New York. After Charles Young had graduated in 1889, not another African American was appointed until 1929 when Alonzo Parham from Illinois entered the academy. He left after one year. In 1932, the son of an army officer, Benjamin O. Davis Jr., was accepted to West Point, and graduated in 1936, becoming only the fourth African American to graduate from that institution. But by 1940, the total number of African American officers in the regular army stood at five, of which three were chaplains, and the senior and junior Davises.

The War Department left the policy of the racial composition and recruiting methods of the National Guard entirely up to the individual states. All 30 of the National Guard's white infantry regiments were formed into its 16 authorized infantry divisions. During the period between the World Wars, several large northern cities had National Guard units allocated for the enlistment of African American soldiers, most of which were the same units that had existed prior to World War I. Only one of these, the 369th Infantry Regiment (New York), was maintained with all of its battalions fully staffed. The 8th Illinois Infantry was maintained minus one of its infantry battalions. The 372nd Infantry Regiment, with two battalions and one company of a third, was divided among Massachusetts, Ohio, and the District of Columbia, with a New Jersey infantry company added just prior to mobilization in 1940. Maryland had a separate infantry company, which became the Service Company of the 372nd Infantry Regiment in 1940. The regiment's headquarters, band, and medical detachment were not authorized. Agreements made between the states' National Guard Bureaus within the regiment were necessary before a commanding officer or any other field officers could be appointed. Separated as it was, among three states and D.C. in four different corps areas, supervision of this unique regiment for peacetime training as a unit was practically impossible.

Senior infantry units of the Reserve Officers' Training Corps (ROTC) were established at Howard University in Washington, D.C., and at Wilberforce University in Ohio. Although African American students at other northern universities were permitted to take ROTC training in integrated units provided that they met the prerequisite qualifications, African Americans students in ROTC units outside of Howard and Wilberforce Universities were extremely rare. Charges were alleged during the peacetime years that at certain colleges, the primary qualification was that the candidate had to be white. Despite investigations, such charges were difficult to prove, for the decisions on academic qualifications for the ROTC program were not centralized and rested within the school's authorities.[11] African American reserve officers, numbering 353 eligible reservists in 1940, were assigned to regiments of the Organized Reserves and were given summer camp training when they requested it. The only African American reserve regiment, which was almost fully staffed, was the 428th Infantry from Washington, D.C.[12]

The 1937 War Department Plan for the utilization of military forces in any future war included a provision to enlist a proportionate number of African American soldiers in regard to the total population. This came to approximately 10 percent of the total army that would be composed of African American soldiers, fielded in segregated units.

The approved features of the 1937 War Department G-1 plan, as published in the Mobilization Regulations as they made their successive appearances, included the following provisions:

1. Negro manpower was to be indicated in mobilization plans, "when applicable," at a percentage of the total mobilized strength approximately equal to the ratio between the Negro manpower of military age and the total manpower of military age.

2. Each corps area was to furnish manpower approximately in the ratio of the total manpower mobilized, period-by-period, which the area's male population of military age bore to the total population of military age. "In the application of this provision whites and Negroes will be computed separately." Each corps area would therefore provide Negroes in a ratio equal to the ratio of its Negro manpower of military age to the total Negro manpower of military age.

3. "Unless conditions require modification in the interests of national defense, the ratio of Negroes mobilized in the arms as compared with those mobilized in the services will be the same as for white troops."

4. "Where desirable for training or other purposes, the War Department will provide for the early mobilization of Negro units at war strength."

5. Negroes, except when assigned to pools, were to be placed in Negro organizations. All warrant officers and enlisted men of Negro organizations were to be Negroes. "Negro personnel requirements for units are provided for and established by the Negro units scheduled for mobilization by the War Department." Warrant officers and enlisted personnel of another arm or service attached to Negro units were, except as otherwise prescribed by the War Department, to be Negroes.

6. Reserve officers for Negro units of the Organized Reserves, officers for Negro organizations in installations, and chaplains for Negro Regular Army units would be Negro. For National Guard units, Negro officers were to be restricted to those positions in Negro units authorized for Negro officers. Whether such authorized positions were to be filled by Negro officers would depend upon the availability of qualified personnel.

7. The number of Negro officer candidates would not exceed the number required to provide officers for organizations authorized to have Negro officers, account being taken of the necessary loss replacements and of the number of Negro officers already available on initiation of mobilization. "The actual number procured, trained, and commissioned will depend, as for all other eligible, upon the number who qualify under the prescribed standards. The prescribed standards will be rigidly applied on the basis of individual merit, without exception as to such factors as race, religion, financial status, or social position."

8. Negroes were to be assigned to service command and War Department overhead installations in a percentage "not less than" the percentage of Negroes in the total male population of military age within the corps area in which these installations were located. In overhead installations controlled by the chiefs of arms and services, Negroes were to be employed in a percentage "at least equal to the percentage of Negroes in the total male population of military age." Rare exceptions might be made by the War Department on the basis of the merits of each case.

9. So far as practicable, Negroes assigned to zone of interior installations such as reception centers, replacement centers, and unit training centers for processing, training, or permanent duty during mobilization, were to be assigned to installations in the general areas where they were procured.[13]

A letter supplementing the issuance of the new Mobilization Regulations, the percentage ratio of African Americans to whites for the United States at large and for the installations under the control of chiefs of arms and services was fixed at approximately 10 percent. The army established their corps by geographical locations. For the several corps areas and installations of the War Department not under the control of the chiefs of arms and services located therein, based on the 1930 United States Census, the percentages of African American soldiers that were to be recruited during mobilization were fixed as follows: First Corps Area, 1.26 percent; Second Corps Area, 4.26 percent; Third Corps Area, 11.25 percent; Fourth Corps Area, 33.37 percent; Fifth Corps Area, 6.45 percent; Sixth Corps Area, 4.25 percent; Seventh Corps Area, 5.58 percent; Eighth Corps Area, 10.52 percent; Ninth Corps Area, 1.03 percent.[14] These percentages were approximately the ratios of African American military age males to white manpower in each corps area. They provided a forecast of the distribution of African American enlisted men by geographical area.

The 1937 plan provided that African Americans would be organized into the following types of units:

Infantry regiments, General Headquarters Reserve
Cavalry regiments, General Headquarters Reserve
Artillery regiments, heavy, long-range calibers, General Headquarters Reserve
Harbor defense forces, coast artillery
Corps and army ammunition supply trains
Engineer general service regiments, separate engineer battalions, and dump truck companies
Quartermaster service, remount, and truck regiments; service and port battalions; railhead and salvage companies; and pack trains
Ordnance companies (ammunition handlers)
Corps area service command units
War Department overhead

From the listing of African American units in the Protective Mobilization Plan (PMP) of 1940, as shown in Table 1, it is obvious that, even within the limits of planning, in which inactive units could be shifted as necessary, the published mobilization planning policy as it affected African American soldiers was not being adhered to. The 1937 policy required that African American manpower be maintained at a ratio approximately in proportion to the total manpower available, that is, from 9 to 10 percent. The units provided in the 1940 Protective Mobilization Plan contained 5.81 percent African American soldiers in the total of enlisted strength. The policy required further that the ratio of African American combat forces to combat service support forces be the same as that of white soldiers. Of the 5.81 percent African American personnel in the Protective Mobilization Plan, by far the largest proportions were assigned to the infantry, the engineers, and the quartermaster branches. Other branches of the army, such as the medical and signal corps, had no African American units or disproportionately small numbers of units and personnel. None of the revisions of the Protective Mobilization Plan since 1938 had complied with the provision on the ratio of combat-to-combat service support soldiers. In those branches which contained both the combat and non-combat types of units, African American soldiers were placed principally in the non-combat units, such as engineer separate battalions, where they would be tasked with performing most of the manual labor. Aside from the active regiments of infantry and cavalry already in the regular army and the National Guard, the number of combat units in the Protective Mobilization Plan was limited to one field artillery and one coast artillery regiment.[15]

Table 1— Negro Units in Protective Mobilization Plan 1940
(Continental United States)

Unit	Corps Area	Status	Enlisted War Strength
Total			44,737
24th Infantry Regiment	IV	RA-PA	2,660
25th Infantry Regiment	VIII	RA-PA	2,660
369th Infantry Regiment	II	NG-A	2,660
8th Illinois Infantry Regiment (less 1 Battalion)	VI	NG-A	1,910
372d Infantry Regiment			
2d Infantry Battalion	V	NG-A	750
3d Infantry Battalion	I	NG-A	750
Rifle Co A	III	NG-A	188

(Table 1—Negro Units in Protective Mobilization Plan 1940
[Continental United States]—*continued*)

Unit	Corps Area	Status	Enlisted War Strength
1st Separate Infantry Rifle Company	III	NG-A	188
9th Cavalry Regiment	VII	RA-PA	1,272
10th Cavalry Regiment		RA-PA	1,244
94th Field Arty Regiment (8-in. How)	IV	RA-I	1,968
44th Coast Arty Regiment (155-mm. Gun TD)	III	RA-I	1,865
41st Engineer Regiment (Gen Service)	IV	RA-I	1,176
59th Engineer Battalion (Separate)	IV	RA-I	1,079
66th Engineer Battalion (Separate)	IV	RA-I	1,079
65th Engineer Battalion (Separate)	V	RA-I	1,079
99th Engineer Battalion (Separate)	IV	RA-I	1,079
62d Engineer Battalion (Separate)	III	RA-I	1,079
63d Engineer Battalion (Separate)	IV	RA-I	1,079
67th Engineer Battalion (Separate)	IV	RA-I	1,079
69th Engineer Battalion (Separate)	V	RA-I	1,079
70th Engineer Battalion (Separate)	VI	RA-I	1,079
98th Engineer Battalion (Separate)	VI	RA-I	1,079
16th Engineer Company (Dump Truck)	II	RA-I	150
17th Engineer Company (Dump Truck)	V	RA-I	150
21st Engineer Company (Dump Truck)	VII	RA-I	150
47th Quartermaster Regiment (Truck)	VIII and IX	RA-PA	1,300
48th Quartermaster Regiment (Truck)	IV and V	RA-PA	1,300
354th Quartermaster Regiment (Service)	IV	RA-I	2,518
255th Quartermaster Regiment (Service)	IV	RA-I	2,518
201st Quartermaster Regiment (Gas Supply)	II	RA-I	388
202d Quartermaster Regiment (Gas Supply)	VI	RA-I	388
203d Quartermaster Regiment (Gas Supply)	V	RA-I	388
204th Quartermaster Regiment (Gas Supply)	V	RA-I	388
205th Quartermaster Regiment (Gas Supply)	IV	RA-I	388
206th Quartermaster Regiment (Gas Supply)	IV	RA-I	388
207th Quartermaster Regiment (Gas Supply)	VII	RA-I	388
208th Quartermaster Regiment (Gas Supply)	VII	RA-I	388
209th Quartermaster Regiment (Gas Supply)	III	RA-I	388
210th Quartermaster Regiment (Gas Supply)	III	RA-I	388
211th Quartermaster Regiment (Gas Supply)	VI	RA-I	388
212th Quartermaster Regiment (Gas Supply)	VI	RA-I	388
391st Quartermaster Battalion (Port)	II	RA-I	807
394th Quartermaster Battalion (Port)	IX	RA-I	807
86th Quartermaster Company (Railhead)	II	RA-I	100
88th Quartermaster Company (Railhead)	IV	RA-I	100
92d Quartermaster Company (Railhead)	VII	RA-I	100

On 14 September 1940, Congress passed the Burke-Wadsworth Bill, which authorized the first peacetime draft in American history. Two days later, President Roosevelt signed it into law as the Selective Service and Training Act of 1940. The main provision of the act called for the registration of all men between the ages of 21 and 35, and the induction of 800,000

draftees. As a concession to African American community leaders, Section 4(a) stated: "There shall be no discrimination against any person on account of race or color." Yet the War Department initially objected to the addition of this provision, stating: "it would disrupt completely plans for the organization of an effective military force."[16]

But the real threat of this provision as perceived by the War Department was that it would curtail the status of segregated units within the army. The General Staff of the Army was still highly opposed to any form of integrated military forces. After getting the General Staff divisions' views, Secretary Woodring summarized the department's objections to the provision, linking them to the potential Japanese threat and to the possibility that passage might endanger the maintenance of segregated units: "It is impossible to forecast definitely what its effect might be. Its retention in the bill might result in the enlistment of Negroes or Japanese in numbers out of all proportion to the colored population of the country. Such a result would demoralize and weaken the effectiveness of military units by mixing colored and white soldiers in closely related units, or even in the same units. It might also have a dangerously adverse effect upon discipline should it be necessary to have colored and white troops in the same units or closely related units. I have no objection whatever to Negro troops but must not be required to take them in such numbers as to prevent the proper organization of the army. I strongly urge the conferees to strike this provision from the bill."[17]

The joint conferees of the House and Senate substituted a provision which read, as passed: "Provided, That no Negro, because of race, shall be excluded from enlistment in the Army for service with colored military units now organized or to be organized for such service."[18] This substitution left the manner of the enlistment and utilization of African American soldiers exactly where it had been before.

But the net effect of the original proposal was to increase the allotment of African American combat units in the army for the first time in twenty years and to provide the types of units to which African American soldiers had not previously been assigned. For although the provision, as originally worded, was stricken from the bill, the War Department could not be certain that it would not reappear and become a part of final legislation. In an effort to "forestall the reinclusion of this provision," the Chief of Staff authorized Major Wilton B. Persons, Office of the Secretary of War, to inform "appropriate conferees" that the War Department was making definite plans to organize "a considerable number of additional Negro units of the ground forces under the provisions of a second bill, authorizing an increase of the Regular Army by another 95,000 men." Major Persons reported that the matter was "handled with satisfactory results."[19]

The new African American units added under this compromise were: one 155-mm field artillery regiment; two coast artillery antiaircraft artillery regiments; one general service engineer regiment; twelve quartermaster truck companies; and one chemical decontamination company. Each of these units, except the second coast artillery regiment and the chemical company, was within the allocated allotment contained in the current Protective Mobilization Plan, although not all of those activated were units designated specifically in the Protective Mobilization Plan as being allocated for African Americans. The total strength of the new African American units was to be 4,595 men, or 8.4 percent of the projected 55,000-man increase authorized for army ground forces. The African American strength of the army was to be more than doubled with the addition of these new units.

The provisions of the Selective Service Act did little to appease the concerns of the African American community about military segregations. On 27 September 1940, Walter White of the NAACP; A. Phillip Randolph of the Association of Sleeping Car Porters; and T. Arnold Hill of the National Youth Administration, met with Secretary of the Navy Frank

Knox and Assistant Secretary of War Robert Patterson to present their ideas on eliminating discrimination within the military services. The seven-point program presented by the African American leaders centered on the integration of officers and enlisted men throughout the armed forces. The portion of the program applying to the military forces read:

The following are important phases of the integration of the Negro into military aspects of the national defense program.

1. The use of presently available Negro reserve officers in training recruits and other forms of active service. At the same time, a policy of training additional Negro officers in all branches of the services should be announced. Present facilities and those to be provided in the future should be made available for such training.

2. Immediate designation of centers where Negroes may be trained for work in all branches of the aviation corps. It is not enough to train pilots alone, but in addition navigators, bombers, gunners, radiomen, and mechanics must be trained in order to facilitate full Negro participation in the air service.

3. Existing units of the army and units to be established should be required to accept and select officers and enlisted personnel without regard to race.

4. Specialized personnel such as Negro physicians, dentists, pharmacists and officers of chemical warfare, camouflage service and the like should be integrated into the services.

5. The appointment of Negroes as responsible members in the various national and local agencies engaged in the administration of the Selective Service Training Act of 1940.

6. The development of effective techniques for insuring the extension of the policy of integration in the Navy other than the menial services to which Negroes are now restricted.

7. The adoption of policies and the development of techniques to assure the participation of trained Negro women as Army and Navy nurses as well as in the Red Cross.[20]

The demands were not well received. When newly appointed Secretary of War Henry L. Stimson was briefed on the meeting, he noted in his diary that he did not support the seven points: "I saw the same thing happen 23 years ago when Woodrow Wilson yielded to the same sort of demands and appointed colored officers to several of the Divisions that went over to France, and the poor fellows made perfect fools of themselves and one at least of the Divisions behaved very badly. The others were turned into labor battalions."[21] These opinions were based on the negative testimony provided by those officers who wished to further their military careers by not going against what was considered command policy on the effectiveness of African American officers in World War I.

As a result of the 27 September conference, on 8 October 1940, Assistant Secretary Patterson submitted to President Roosevelt a full statement of policy, already approved informally by the Secretary of War and the Chief of Staff. The President penciled his "O.K." and initials on this memorandum, thereby giving his approval to a policy which remained in effect throughout the war. On the morning of 9 October the White House released a statement to the press.[22] This first comprehensive statement on the subject read:

"It is the policy of the War Department that the services of Negroes will be utilized on a fair and equitable basis. In line with this policy provision will be made as follows:

1. The strength of the Negro personnel of the Army of the United States will be maintained on the general basis of the proportion of the Negro population of the country.

2. Negro organizations will be established in each major branch of the service, combatant as well as noncombatant.

3. Negro reserve officers eligible for active duty will be assigned to Negro units officered by colored personnel.

4. When officer candidate schools are established, opportunity will be given to Negroes to qualify for reserve commissions.

5. Negroes are being given aviation training as pilots, mechanics and technical specialists. This training will be accelerated.

6. At arsenals and army posts Negro civilians are accorded equal opportunity for employment at work for which they are qualified by ability, education, and experience.

7. The policy of the War Department is not to intermingle colored and white enlisted personnel in the same regimental organizations. This policy has been proven satisfactory over a long period of years, and to make changes now would produce situations destructive to morale and detrimental to the preparation for national defense. For similar reasons the department does not contemplate assigning colored reserve officers other than those of the Medical Corps and chaplains to existing Negro combat units of the Regular Army. These regular units are going concerns, accustomed through many years to the present system. Their morale is splendid, their rate of reenlistment is exceptionally high, and their field training is well advanced. It is the opinion of the War Department that no experiments should be tried with the organizational setup of these units at this critical time.[23]

The White House, in releasing this policy statement, implied that it was the result of the 27 September conference with the African American leaders. The measure of the protests which went up from African Americans was the measure of the distance between the White House announcement and their proposed program. The men who had attended the White House conference were especially annoyed by the implication that they had endorsed the announced policy, which supports total segregation in the military forces. Press Secretary to the President, Stephen Early, implied that White, Randolph, and Hill had conferred with the President, when in actuality they had just met with representatives of the War and Navy Departments. They were specifically disturbed about points five and seven.[24] The announcement embodied the main points of a policy adopted (although not publicized) by the War Department in 1937, in its planning for mobilization; and the final paragraph repeated, in almost identical phrases, the statements made in the many Adjutant General letters which had gone out to individuals all over the country. Nevertheless, this statement, which contained the basic army policy that would be enforced throughout much of the war, was afterward referred to within the War Department as the "Presidential Directive on the use of Negro Troops" and as a Presidential sanction for policies derived therefrom.

"Of all the shabby dealings of America with a tenth of her citizens," *The Crisis* commented in its issue following the announcement, "none is more shameful or more indefensible than the refusal to give Negroes a fair chance in the armed forces." The editorial continued: "The citizens' army that is to be trained under the Selective Service Act will find shortly that the Army and the Navy are being run very much like country clubs. Americans discovered that in 1917, but there was a war to be fought at once then and there was not much they could do about it. Now it should be different and the peacetime army and its civilian relatives, given a space to think and act before actual warfare interferes, may force some changes."[25]

African American political power was beginning to match the influence of the wartime requirements for African American support. As a measure to further control the damage, President Roosevelt communicated with African American leaders to reassure them that he supported the admission of African Americans into all military specialties, and promised that they would have equal chances to gain commissions as officers, leading to appropriate command opportunities. To enhance this even more, on 25 October 1940, a little more than one week before the presidential elections, Colonel Benjamin O. Davis Sr. was nominated for promotion to the rank of brigadier general, becoming the first African American flag officer in the United States military.[26] It had been rumored that, like Colonel Charles Young in World War I, Colonel Davis would be ceremoniously retired to prevent the opportunity of his ever being in charge of white officers. Colonel Davis, born in 1877 in Washington, D.C., by this time had served in the army since the Spanish-American War as a first lieutenant in the 8th Volunteer Infantry Regiment. He enlisted in the 9th Cavalry Regiment in 1899, and was commissioned as a second lieutenant in the regular army on 19 May 1901. By 1930, he had been promoted to colonel, filling the requirement for a senior African American officer to serve at posts like the American Consulate in Liberia, and as an instructor for the National Guard and the ROTC program at Wilberforce University. He was presently serving as the commander of the 369th Infantry Regiment.

The White House also ensured that General Lewis B. Hershey, the national director of the Selective Service System, announced prior to the election the appointment of an African American officer, Major Campbell C. Johnson, to his staff to advise and assist in questions pertaining to the drafting of African American inductees.

On 1 November, President Roosevelt announced that Judge William H. Hastie, Dean of the Howard University Law School, had been appointed as an assistant secretary in the War Department to advise on African American military affairs. Judge Hastie had been the assistant solicitor for the Department of the Interior from 1933 to 1937; the first African American judge appointed to the federal bench by serving as the Federal District Judge for the United States Virgin Islands, 1937–1939; chairman of the National Legal Committee of the NAACP, and a prominent spokesperson in civic activities in Washington, D.C.[27]

Technically, Judge Hastie was slotted in the War Department as Head Attorney under Executive Order 8044. Judge Hastie undertook his duties on 1 November 1940. In his letter of appointment, Secretary Stimson described these duties to be "to assist in the formulation, development and administration of policies looking to the fair and effective utilization of Negroes in all branches of the military service." The secretary's letter continued: "I hope that you will be able to assist us in the development of and improvements in the War Department's plans for the organization of Negro units in each major branch of the service, and for the utilization of Negro reserve officers, candidates for commissions, and aviation cadets. I also hope that you will be of assistance to us in connection with policies involving the employment of Negroes on civilian status at army establishments and by army contractors. It will be part of your duties to investigate complaints concerning the treatment of Negroes in the military service or in civilian employment in the War Department. In this connection, I hope it will be possible for you to spend time visiting camps, posts and stations for the purpose of observing and reporting to me upon matters of Negro participation in the national defense. It is my expectation that you will cooperate with the Negro representatives on the Selective Service Committee and in the Labor Section of the Advisory Commission to the Council of National Defense, where appropriate. Such recommendations as you may from time to time wish to make should be submitted to me through the Assistant Secretary of War. You may be assured that the officers and establishments of the War Department will cooperate with you in carrying out the tasks which I have outlined. Instructions are being issued that you be consulted on matters affecting Negroes in the army, and that all information necessary to the effective execution of your duties be made available to you."[28]

In an interview conducted in 1972, Judge Hastie recalls why he accepted this position: "This was at a time when there was tremendous bitterness and vocal expression of dissatisfaction in the black community as to the result of the exclusion of blacks both from rapidly developing defense industrial mobilization, and from the rapidly expanding Army. Secretary Stimson wanted to bring someone onto his staff with a general responsibility to assist in and recommend and criticize action or non-action by the War Department in this field. So with some reluctance I agreed to take that rather general responsibility. I was reluctant not because of any lack of interest or because it was not an important area, but I was rather skeptical as to what a person with no authority of his own whom I was sure the military did not want serving in the Secretary's office. But I did agree to come in and worked for about two years with Secretary Stimson, and more directly with Under Secretary [Robert] Patterson, who was my immediate and day-to-day contact, though from time to time there were occasions, of course, when I was dealing directly with Secretary Stimson.... Mr. Stimson was concerned but he, in my judgment, had no feel for, no real perception of the problems of race in America, or their impact, or the relation of the military to them. He was a most honest and dedicated man, a patriot in the best and the highest sense of the word, but he was a man whose whole life in his practice of law, in his social contacts, his whole background, had isolated him from the areas, the problems, of which I was basically concerned."[29]

The Selective Service Act had ordered that inductees be selected and trained without discrimination and, the War Department reiterated, it did not itself discriminate against any of its soldiers. Here was one of the major points of disagreement, for, as shown in the congressional debates on the inclusion of nondiscriminatory clauses in the Selective Service Act, the distinction between discrimination and segregation in normal usage was not always clear. The meaning of these terms then and later depended in large measure upon the view of the user. Segregation, implying only separation, was often considered nondiscriminatory by those who believed that equal, but separate facilities and opportunities could be afforded to both races. To others, including most African Americans, this concept of enforced racial segregation was in itself discriminatory. The fact of separation not only prevented freedom of movement and action on the part of the segregated minority, and was therefore considered an abridgment of basic personal liberties, but also produced inequalities of facilities and opportunities for the minority. The minority, being numerically smaller, had no means of enforcing guarantees of the so-called equal facilities and opportunities. Moreover, the argument ran, the very act of formal segregation implied inescapable differences among people of different races, which made common action impossible and which, by denying the common aims and similar objectives of the population was, per se, discriminatory. On the other hand, the federal courts, throughout the early years of World War II, held that segregation, as such, was not discriminatory where equal facilities were provided. Field commanders therefore saw nothing anomalous in announcing that their racial policy was "segregation without discrimination," or that "no discrimination could exist in a command or camp, which had Negro enlisted men only."[30]

In the months following President Roosevelt's reelection, African American leaders recognized that other than the token appointments, the administration was not honoring its promises of opening more military job specialties to greater numbers of African American volunteers and draftees. Fewer than one percent of the appointees to the various staffs of local draft boards were African Americans. By November 1941, African Americans made up only 5.9 percent of the army's total strength rather than 10 percent as prescribed by the legislation.[31] The War Department, in having to provide segregated facilities at army installations for this influx of African American draftees, was not prepared for this mobilization. The result was that for several months, African American inductees were assigned to units neither by occupational specialties, by educational background, by tested aptitudes, nor by any other classification method. They were assigned according to the numbers of men received and to the availability of space in units. A unit which required 250 men in order to reach its authorized strength would not receive them if its installation had no additional housing for African American soldiers, while a unit which needed no additional men but whose post had available housing might be overwhelmed with successive increments of men.

Again, housing for African American soldiers had to be located so as to carry out the principle of separation of the units based on race. This required an extension of segregation into the allotment of housing. The main portion of a military installation, often constructed in a huge arc with parade grounds and headquarters near the center and hospital wards and warehouses at either end, was often allotted to division-sized units assigned to that installation. Away from the main portion of installation buildings, a regimental or smaller size area was constructed for African American soldiers. All African American units assigned to the installation had to be fitted into this or similar blocks of housing. Initially these areas at installations like Fort Dix, New Jersey, and Fort Devens, Massachusetts, were at a considerable distance from the main post facilities. Later construction filled in the intervening vacant spaces, usually with warehouses, stockades, and motor pools rather than with barracks. This afforded a large area void of barracks to avoid any possible confrontation between the races. Usually the African American section remained distinct and separate, though in some of the newer installations, such as Camp Breckinridge, Kentucky, and Camp Ellis, Illinois, they were separated from identical white quarters only by a parade ground or a firebreak. The "Negro Area" came to be known as such; often it was so shown on installation diagrams and blueprints. It was, essentially, a separate segregated camp adjoining the major portion of the post. On some military installations, the newer constructed barracks were allocated for white soldiers, while the older buildings, usually in need of repair, were designated for the African American soldiers. The segregated area designated for African American soldiers was provided with its own, although usually inadequate post exchange (PX), its own recreation hall, and, later, movie theaters, chapel, and, if the area were large enough, its own service club and guesthouse. In November 1941 General Marshall directed his staff to resurvey the allocation of African American units, "with the idea of planning a proper proportion of Negro personnel at locations adjacent to communities with a large colored population."[32]

In addition to the availability of housing at military installations designated for the receipt of African American soldiers, the physical location of posts to which these soldiers were to be sent was itself a determining factor in procurement and assignment. Finding suitable military installations for the training of large numbers of African American soldiers was to vex the War Department throughout the war. The answer was not simply one of locating suitable segregated barracks space and training facilities within areas under army jurisdiction. Purely military considerations played but a small part in determining the location of African American soldiers in the early period of this mobilization. The main considerations were: availability of separate segregated housing and facilities on the installation concerned; proportions of white and African American soldiers at the post; proximity to civilian centers of African American population with good recreational facilities that could absorb sizable numbers of soldiers on pass; and the attitude of the nearby civilian community to the acceptance and presence of African American soldiers. The riots in Houston, Texas, in 1917 had not yet been entirely forgotten by the War Department.

Many communities objected to the presence of any African American soldiers being stationed close to their neighborhoods. Others objected to the presence of certain categories: military policemen, combat soldiers, officers, and soldiers from the north. After many years of harsh treatment of African Americans in their community, fears of armed African American soldiers, or the presence of soldiers from the north, not accustomed to their "Jim Crow" laws, would cause turmoil in their cities, and upset the status quo of their lives.

Many communities could not be convinced that the exigencies of the situation demanded the stationing of African American soldiers close to their towns and cities. Concerned civic leaders often made their views known through their congressmen. An early and typical protest came from Congressman Patrick H. Drewry of Virginia on behalf of the citizens of Petersburg. In September 1940, before the opening of Camp Lee and before the large mobilization of African American soldiers, Congressman Drewry visited General Marshall and the Chief of the War Plans Division to request that, "in view of racial difficulties in Petersburg during World War I, no Negro troops other than a small number of labor troops be stationed at Camp Lee."[33] One of the first forms of corrective action to the fear of potential race riots was formulated in connection with this request. As a supplement to plans already made to establish a quartermaster and medical replacement center at Camp Lee with a peak load of 19,000 newly inducted soldiers, 3500 of whom would be African Americans, the Chief of Staff G-3 proposed that a rifle company of the 12th Infantry Regiment be made available if necessary to help prevent race riots. The Chief of Staff approved the G-3 proposal and African American soldiers were assigned to Camp Lee. The 12th Infantry Regiment's rifle company was never required.[34] Segregated facilities, local "Jim Crow" laws, racial hatred and fear, would continue to plague the War Department throughout the war until large numbers of African American soldiers were deployed overseas.

Unhappy with the lack of progress following the pre-election appeasement appointments, including the foot-dragging in drafting African Americans into the army, A. Philip Randolph, in January 1941, called for a march on Washington, D.C., the following July to protest the exclusion of African Americans from working within the defense industries and their humiliation in the armed forces. As the leader of the Brotherhood of Sleeping Car Porters, Randolph's primary interests were equal job opportunities for African Americans in the rapidly expanding war industries, but his ideas about integration also extended to the military. In its annual meeting, the NAACP endorsed Randolph's movement and promised to join the demonstration. Randolph's threat of 50,000 to 100,000 angry African American protesters and their supporters marching on Washington worried government officials that the protest might appear to Tokyo and Berlin as a weakness in American resolve and unity to defend itself in war.

Eleanor Roosevelt met with Randolph in an attempt to get him to cancel the march, and finally the president himself met with the labor leader to seek a resolution. President Roosevelt agreed to make some concessions, although some African American groups encouraged Randolph not to settle for anything less than total integration of the workplace and the military. On 25 June 1941, President Roosevelt signed Executive Order 8802, the Fair Employment Practices order, which banned discrimination in the defense industries and the government. The order stated "it is the policy of the United States to encourage full participation in the national defense program by all citizens of the United States, regardless of race, creed, color, or national origin, in the firm belief that the democratic way of life within the Nation can be defended successfully only with the help and support of all groups within its borders...."[35]

While African American organizations and leaders still protested segregated facilities, they had at least secured equality of the workplace, if only on paper. Now they concentrated their efforts on eliminating segregation in the armed forces. Judge Hastie lobbied from his position in the War Department for total integration in the army. Judge Hastie comments on some of his accomplishments before he resigned from the position in 1942: "We were able to get a substantial amount of unsegregated training in places like officers' candidate schools; we were able to get significant numbers of black soldiers admitted to officers' candidate schools, and earning their commissions, who theretofore would have found their application for one reason or another, pigeonholed or rejected. We were able to get in many commands affirmative encouragement of blacks to apply for officer training, when theretofore the attitude would have been either to prevent or effectively discourage them from training. We were able to get a great many improvements in the conditions which blacks experienced on military bases, and some in the civilian communities around the bases. Weather conditions and the availability of land meant that a disproportionately large number of the training centers were in the deep South, and this created, of course, a great number of very serious racial problems; and I think we were able to ameliorate conditions, though they remained really very bad throughout the war. The black medical officers were just nonexistent in 1940, and there was a great deal of resistance to taking black medics into the Army as doctors, and very strong resistance to taking them into Army hospitals for the practice of their specialty in the military hospitals. So I think there were numbers of worthwhile things accomplished, but the basic resistance of field commanders and of many persons in the general staff in the War Department, never let down. The episode which caused my resignation was just one of the most glaring examples of movement directly counter to the direction in which I was trying to get the Army to move. I know Secretary Patterson was entirely sympathetic with what I was trying to do. Like all civilian heads of defense establishment, to some extent he himself was a prisoner of the military. And I must say that I also think that General Marshall was quite sympathetic to the things that I wanted to accomplish."[36]

In September 1941, Judge Hastie submitted a survey with recommendations for improving the plight of African American soldiers in the army. In his specific recommendations for the organization of African American soldiers, Judge Hastie proposed four points "in order that the progressive integration of Negro soldiers into the Army shall proceed in such manner as to achieve the greatest possible Military advantage." These recommendations were:

1. New organizations must be provided as speedily as possible to accommodate the anticipated excess of Negro selectees.
2. Negro combat regiments should be made components of higher units; isolated single companies and detachments should be eliminated.
3. Isolated small units which are the only Negro troops at their stations should be transferred to other stations (in order to obviate the need of providing expensive separate recreational facilities for them).
4. At some place in the armed services a beginning should be made in the employment of soldiers without racial separation.

It was not until December 1941 that anyone from the War Department responded to Judge Hastie's memorandum. No one quarreled seriously with the first three recommendations of Judge Hastie. The G-1 and G-3 for the Chief of Staff responded: "New Negro units, as described above, were activated as rapidly as possible. The possible organization of all–Negro divisions," although Hastie had not urged it, "was expected to answer the question of making smaller combat units parts of larger units. The organization of the 2nd Cavalry Division," although Judge Hastie was not informed of this, "was considered proof that the Department is not opposed in principle to the inclusion of Negro regiments in higher units. The General Headquarters' separate tank battalion, the 78th, later the 758th Tank Battalion, and the 99th Pursuit Squadron were cited as evidence of willingness to activate units of the 'new type' organizations. More would be activated as qualified men became available, but comparatively low Army General Classification Test scores seemed to indicate that such an event was unlikely."[37]

In the formal memorandum of the Chief of Staff to the Secretary of War on the subject, dated 1 December 1941, General Marshall wrote:

> A solution of many of the issues presented by Judge Hastie in his memorandum to you on 'The Integration of the Negro Soldier into the Army,' dated September 22, would be tantamount to solving a social problem which has perplexed the American people throughout the history of this nation. The Army cannot accomplish such a solution, and should not be charged with the undertaking. The settlement of vexing racial problems cannot be permitted to complicate the tremendous task of the War Department and thereby jeopardize discipline and morale. The problems presented with reference to utilizing Negro personnel in the Army should be faced squarely. In doing so, the following facts must be recognized; first, that the War Department cannot ignore the social relationships between Negroes and whites which has been established by the American people through custom and habit; second, that either through lack of educational opportunities or other causes, the level of intelligence and occupational skill of the Negro population is considerably below that of the white; third, that the Army will attain its maximum strength only if its personnel is properly placed in accordance with the capabilities of individuals; and fourth, that experiments within the Army in the solution of social problems are fraught with danger to6 efficiency, discipline, and morale.[38]

To all practical intents and purposes, Judge Hastie and the army's high command had reached an impasse on this particular question before the formal entry of the United States into war. The bombing of Pearl Harbor, Hawaii, on 7 December 1941, and the declaration of war by the United States the following day, provided the army with a ready excuse to continue to ignore the racial problems within its ranks.

Once the fighting actually began, neither white political leaders nor military commanders were interested in sociological experiments of equality for African Americans in the military. Despite continued discrimination, African Americans came forward, as in all previous wars, to share in their country's defense and to willingly risk their lives for the freedoms which they did not share. However, during this global conflict, African Americans preparing to fight in World War II had fewer illusions that their service and sacrifice would yield civil rights and equality. They were willing to fight, but they had learned that any true advances in their social standing would come not from their military service, but from racial unity and political influence. The desire of politicians to win the African American vote in the election system of the United States would prove to be a greater ally to equality than the service of hundreds of thousands of African American men and women in uniform.

With America's entry into World War II, the Navy and Coast Guard relegated African Americans to being only mess attendants and cooks. No African American had ever graduated from the Naval Academy at Annapolis. But when the Japanese attacked, a mess attendant on the battleship *West Virginia* would display untold heroism. When the attack began, the captain of the *West Virginia* was gravely wounded. Dorie Miller, a young mess attendant, moved his captain to safety. Then he manned a .50-caliber machine gun, a weapon with which he had received no training, and was credited with downing two Japanese aircraft, and

Military Policeman, MP Detachment, Fort Benning, Georgia, 13 April 1942. (National Archives)

damaging three others. For his actions that day, Miller would be awarded the Navy Cross, the second highest medal for valor, and returned to his mess attendant duties. He would be killed the following year when the aircraft carrier *Lipscomb Bay* was sunk in the South Pacific.

By the time the war had come to an end in 1945, the Navy and Coast Guard were allowing African Americans to train in all military skills. One of the first African American journalists in the Coast Guard was author Alex Haley. He joined the Coast Guard in 1939 as a mess attendant and retired in 1959. He would then go on to write *The Autobiography of Malcolm X* and *Roots*. For the first time, the Navy allowed African Americans to become commissioned officers, with the first receiving their rank of ensign in 1944. Also in 1944, a navy warship, the destroyer escort USS *Mason*, would have an all African American enlisted crew, and would serve in the Atlantic escorting convoys to and from Europe.

The Marine Corps, the smallest of the military branches, never allowed African Americans to enlist. In 1942, African Americans were allowed to enlist in the Marines and were trained at a small segregated facility next to Camp LeJeune, North Carolina, called Montford Point. Over 12,000 African American marines would serve overseas in combat zones in the Pacific throughout the duration of the war. After the war ended the Marine Corps would be the first branch to integrate their forces.

In 1941, the Air Corps, then a separate branch of the Army, allowed the first African Americans to train as pilots. This was contrary to what the general officers wanted because they believed that African Americans did not possess the mental and physical attributes for the strenuous duties of a pilot. This experiment with African American pilots, which many deemed would be a failure, is now famously known as the Tuskegee Airmen, named after the place where the first pilots trained. In command of this first unit, the 99th Pursuit Squadron, and later the 332nd Fighter Group, was Colonel Benjamin O. Davis Jr., son of the first African American general. When he graduated from West Point in 1936, he requested to be assigned to the Air Corps but was denied due to the fact that the Air Corps barred blacks from joining. Instead, he was assigned to the infantry. On January 9, 1941, the War Department approved plans to have an African American pursuit squadron assigned to the Air Corps. Pilot preflight and primary training was awarded to Tuskegee Institute, and basic and advanced training would be given at a new Air Corps field to be built seven miles northwest of the town of Tuskegee. The training of 460 African American enlisted personnel would take place at the Air Corps Technical School, Chanute Field, Rantoul, Illinois. These were the mechanics, electricians, armorers, fuel handlers, air traffic controllers, and other administrative support personnel for the squadron. The pilots and enlisted support personnel faced more stringent requirements than their white counterparts. This was done in part to show that African Americans were not capable of being airmen, when in fact it produced a unit far superior, keeping only the best of the best. Once allowed to deploy to a combat zone, the 99th Pursuit Squadron first went to North Africa. The 332nd Fighter Group joined them in Italy where they had the mission of flying bomber escort. In spite of discrimination and prejudices, the 332nd amassed an outstanding flying record, receiving the Distinguished Unit Citation, the highest award for valor going to an entire unit.

Chapter III

The African American Press

OFTEN EXCLUDED BY THE WHITE NEWSPAPER CORPS, the black press assumed the role of being the voice of African Americans throughout the first half of the 20th century. While most urban areas with large African American populations had their own local black newspapers, it was newspapers like the *Atlanta Daily-World,* the Baltimore, Philadelphia, Richmond, and Washington, D.C. *Afro-American,* the *Chicago Defender,* the *Pittsburgh Courier,* the *Indianapolis Freeman,* the *New York Amsterdam News,* and even the periodical *The Crisis* of the NAACP, that would play pivotal roles in expressing the opinions and reporting the news of the African American soldiers' experiences in World War II. These newspapers would report on both the battle overseas against the Axis powers, and the battle against racism on the home front.

In 1938, the *Pittsburgh Courier,* then the largest and one of the most influential African American newspapers of national circulation, opened a campaign for the extension of opportunities for African Americans in the military services. The paper published an open letter to President Roosevelt, organized a Committee for Negro Participation in the National Defense, and encouraged its readers to send letters, telegrams, and delegations to congressmen and other national political leaders asking for an opinion on the wisdom of forming an all African American infantry division in the peacetime army. Many of these letters, especially those to congressmen, were forwarded to the War Department for information. As the campaign spread to other African American newspapers and to local organizations, similar letters arrived from other sources.[1] This campaign was well organized and well publicized. Quantities of correspondence poured into the War Department. When the War Department was noncommittal, the African American press, having obtained no positive information, became even more cynical and critical.

With the United States military buildup beginning with the draft in 1940, the newspapers campaigned for the army to recruit its full quota of African Americans. Of the 585,000 soldiers presently in the army in 1940, only 9,000 were African Americans, of which only five were regular army officers. The army's rebuttal was that African Americans could only be recruited for the four regular army regiments, and those units were already at full capacity. As early as 1938, the *Pittsburgh Courier* had advocated full participation of African Americans into every branch of the armed forces. Although it disapproved of racial segregation in the army, the *Courier* was nonetheless willing to accept those terms if the army enlisted African Americans in proportion to their total representation of the entire population, which was approximately ten percent. Their segregation in African American units was preferable to complete exclusion from the military. As a result of the collective lobbying by the African American press, the Burke-Wadsworth Draft Bill of 1940 included a mandatory ten percent African American quota of inductees. All branches of the army were to include African American officers and enlisted men in that same proportion, although it would be restricted only to segregated units.[2] But the reality was, just as was the case in World War I, that the majority of African Americans in the army would be relegated to combat service support units, performing many of the thankless manual labor tasks.

The *Chicago Defender* represented the sole opposition to the draft, noting that "conscription would not ensure full Negro participation in the armed forces but would silence Negro opposition to domestic and military racial abuses."[3] Even the *Baltimore Afro-American*, a strong supporter of the draft to achieve both preparedness and racial justice, changed its view and endorsed Republican Wendell Willkie, who advocated total desegregation of the armed forces, over Franklin Roosevelt in the 1940 presidential election. Once the goal of increased African American participation in the armed forces had been achieved, the press could now focus on a complete end to racial segregation in the military.

With America's entry into World War II on 7 December 1941, the black press proclaimed that African Americans had as much at stake in the nation as anyone else, and would do their share to defend it. However, African Americans could not defend the country with a "dust brush, a mop, and white apron ... armed only with a whiskbroom and a wide grin." The *Baltimore Afro-American* pleaded for an end to racial segregation in and exclusion from the armed forces and defense industries.[4] The black press strongly believed that African Americans had to participate fully in all aspects of the war effort if they were to successfully claim the right to full equality in American society. But this was the same stance taken by W.E.B. Dubois in World War I in a belief that racial discrimination and segregation would end upon the conclusion of the war. That was an illusion not to be fulfilled, as racism in America prevailed. The black press would have an arduous task of persuading African Americans to support this war effort.

Through the newspapers' "Double V" campaign, the black press would persuade the African American community that World War II would be an effort to end racism and tyranny in the United States as well as abroad. The newspapers would provide extensive coverage of the exploits of African American servicemen and any racial abuses that occurred. The newspapers reported on the injustices that the African American soldiers encountered, especially when stationed at military installations in the southern states. Often denied the opportunity to have reporters at all these locations, the newspapers relied on personal correspondence from the soldiers themselves, explaining in detail the racial abuses and discrimination that they encountered as explained in these letters to the *Pittsburgh Courier* and the *Afro-American*.

> Company E, 25th Infantry
> Camp Bowie, Texas
> April 13, 1941

Pittsburgh Courier Publishing Company
Dear Sirs:

I'm a soldier of the U. S. Army and a constant reader of the Pittsburgh *Courier*. I've noticed that you've helped soldiers in the various Jim Crow problems.

We, as colored soldiers of the U. S. Army of the 25th Infantry, Fort Huachuca, Arizona, are now on maneuvers through Texas, and we have a problem that we wish you'd help us solve.

Fort Huachuca is an exclusive colored camp with about 5,000 enlisted men. The 2nd Battalion left Arizona on the 7th of May "to start the maneuver" and arrived at Camp Bowie, Texas on May 11th to stay here for about a month.

The Army post here have approximately 22,000 white soldiers, and from these "white" soldiers we're jeered by them both day and night, calling us various unpleasing names as *Niggers, Snow Ball,* and the *Black African Army.* Also, they don't allow us to ride the post buses. We either have to hire a special cab, or ride in the extreme rear of the buses. If we ride the buses, we're talked about like dogs and pushed and shoved around in the same manner. When we try to defend ourselves, we're outnumbered ten to one. This went on for a few days "until we got tired of it." We thought we'd take this matter up with our officers, "as you understand our officers are all white." There were various questions asked by different soldiers to the senior officer of the 2nd Battalion (the Colonel). They were, if a white soldier calls you nigger, curse or call you various names what to do? His answer was, to not to look at them, pay them no attention, just completely ignore them, if necessary walk a little faster. In other words he meant for us to run and let them call us anything, and us not say nothing to them. Another question was, if a white soldier hits, kicks or pushes on you, what to do? His answer was "to say" "Gwan white man don't bother me now. I'm a soldier just like you and you ain't suppose to bother me. Ain't no use for you to bother us colored soldiers, we ain't going to bother you." He also says if the white soldier continue to hit you, get on out of his way, and not "what ever we did," hit them back.

Also since we've been here, our guards were put around the areas in which we live, they were all given guns but not any ammunition of course. All the white soldiers have ammunition. They also decided to put on colored military police in the colored section of town to keep down disturbance between one another, but they have no guns or ammunition, nothing but the M.P. badge, not even a club. That's in order that we don't fool with the white soldiers. The white soldier M.P.s have pistols, clubs and ammunition. They are allowed to arrest colored soldiers, but we're not allowed to touch the white soldiers.

This is our problem. I wish that you could help us in some respect, and if possible please publish this letter so that the rest of the country would know how they're treating colored soldiers in the U.S. Army.

Anything that you can do to help us will be very, very much appreciated.

> Co. E, 25th Inf.
> Camp Bowie, Texas
> Signed,
> All the soldiers of the 2nd Battalion

Not only did the newspapers rely on the soldiers to provide information about injustices, but the soldiers sought out the African American press to present these issues to the masses. By presenting this information to the public, the papers forced political leaders to bring about change. When African American infantry soldiers stationed in Arizona in February 1943 reported to the press that they were about to be utilized to harvest the cotton crop, instead of preparing for combat, the War Department was forced to rescind those orders.[5] The black press reported on the racial riots at Camp Stewart, Georgia; Camp Van Dorn, Mississippi; and Fort Bragg, North Carolina, which occurred during the turbulent months of 1943, as large numbers of African Americans were inducted into the military, and mainly being utilized in menial labor tasks. When the commanding officer of Camp Stewart, Georgia, issued a directive ordering African American soldiers to accept unfair discriminatory policies dictated by the "Jim Crow" laws of that state, and to be polite and respectful to white people, the *Baltimore Afro-American* called the incident "another disgraceful chapter in army history and declared racial segregation in the army unconstitutional."[6]

The nationwide impact of the black press' war coverage aroused the government's concern over its effects on the African American community's morale. But stifling the newspapers would not have lifted the low regard many African Americans had for the armed forces. Ending racial segregation and oppression may have accomplished this. By emphasizing racism in the military during the midst of World War II, the African American news service was not merely performing its journalistic duty, but also bringing attention to problems that were far more dangerous to the war effort.

The federal government began scrutinizing the African American press and its criticism of American racial disorder during World War II. On the question of the relationship of the press to morale, the army's Bureau of Public Relations, which was centrally concerned with public and press reactions, was especially disturbed not only by the army's relations with the African American press but also by recurring suggestions from the military intelligence corps and from field commanders that portions of the press be censored or otherwise controlled.[7] In the summer of 1942, when such suggestions had been frequently made as a result of the African American press coverage of the racial disturbances of that year, the bureau replied that "it was attempting to help, rather than hinder, the Negro press in obtaining and printing accounts of Negroes in the army. The policy of this Bureau," it told the Operations Division of the War Department, "has been to work for a higher degree of factual accuracy in published reports of the activities of Negro troops, to emphasize the many favorable aspects of Army practices and policy in racial matters, and to encourage the reconsideration of articles or editorials of a critical or controversial nature."[8]

In an effort to improve communications between the press and the military, the Bureau of Public Relations gradually became a center for the regular visits of African American news correspondents, and it in turn sent its representatives for visits to the African American publishers and to their annual conferences. A weekly illustrated material service especially planned for African American newspapers and the encouragement of sending public relations officers in the field and military installations to stimulate the reporting of news of African American activities brought an increase of information on black soldiers in all the news agency services. A Special Interest Section created to serve the requirements of the African American press was organized within the bureau during the summer of 1942 and staffed by African American commissioned officers beginning in 1943. Visits to maneuver training areas were arranged for African American correspondents so that the progression and seriousness of the training of African American soldiers could be observed and documented firsthand.[9] But this effort to change the focus of the African American press away from the army's policy of racial discrimination would not deter reporters from attempting to convey the full story to not only the African American community, but to the entire American public.

Despite these efforts, the reporting of events in a manner critical of the army continued. In the opinions of white field commanders, such articles were damaging to the morale of soldiers. In addition to making suggestions that all or particular Negro papers be placed under surveillance for possible subversive activities, a number of military installations and army bases from time to time banned one or another paper from the post exchanges or libraries.

A few military installations even went so far as the Antiaircraft Artillery Training Center at Fort Bliss, Texas. There, after the racial disturbances in 1943, African American newspapers, which in the opinion of the commanding general of the base contained material of "such an agitational nature as to be prejudicial to military discipline within the training center," were banned from the post entirely. All mail received at the Fort Bliss post office for the African American battalions was first delivered to the installation's postal officer, who extracted the "objectionable newspapers." The remaining mail was then delivered, with the training center's commander directing the final disposition of newspapers. The legality of this procedure was endorsed by the Eighth Service Command's Director of Military Intelligence, and by the Censorship Officer, El Paso Branch, Office of Postal Censorship, but the Antiaircraft Artillery Branch, when informed of the practice, sought advice from the War Department.[10]

Army Ground Forces, upon receipt of the Antiaircraft Artillery Branch's report, telephoned the commanding general of the branch to have the commanding general of the Fort Bliss Training Center discontinue his practices of non–delivery of certain items of mail immediately. As an emergency measure, the Army Ground Forces Intelligence Section thought a commander might properly stop a particular paper or an issue, but to do so permanently "would only serve to supply ammunition for agitation to colored papers."[11] Yet local commanders still kept African American newspapers out of the hands of the soldiers.

Inquiries of the various service commands revealed no formal bans of African American publications, for actions of this type had not been taken through regular military channels. But in some cases, the military installation's intelligence officers, without an order from the post commander, had proceeded to ban the release of all African American newspapers. In at least one case, a unit's intelligence officer took it upon himself to keep those publications from the African American soldiers after receiving from his chain of command the information that, although they had no War Department approved or disapproved list of newspapers, on certain military installations, specific African American newspapers, which were named, had been banned. The Army Bureau of Public Relations felt that if it had not pursued its investigations below the level of installation commanders, it "might have been placed in the position of stating that there was no truth in the report...." The Bureau of Public Relations took the position endorsed by Army Ground Forces, that so long as the newspapers and magazines enjoyed postal office privileges, local commanders should not ban them from installations without the War Department's approval. The Bureau was certain that, through its liaison officers, it would be able to remedy public relations situations considered damaging to morale. The bureau's position was approved by the War Department and commanders were informed.

Yet the African American press' intense coverage of racial discrimination and abuses in the armed forces still worried government agencies such as the Office of War Information, the Federal Bureau of Investigation, and the Justice Department. They believed reporting on these issues would diminish the African American community's support of the war effort. Their concerns reached the White House, and President Roosevelt spoke with Walter White of the NAACP to use his influence to help diminish these detrimental reports. Mr. White met with the publishers of many of the papers to convey the president's concerns, and to warn against criticism of wartime racism in the military and on the home front. There was even speculation that some of the newspapers would be charged with sedition should they continue this type of reporting. But United States Attorney General, Francis Biddle, was a strong supporter of the First Amendment and freedom of speech. The Federal Bureau of Investigation and the United States Postal Service did subject the African American newspapers to intense surveillance. The FBI could uncover no incidents of sedition, although its director, J. Edgar Hoover, would have shut down the papers without any evidence.[12]

The government was not the only entity that considered the African American press corps subversive. Many prominent civilians felt that the news articles and editorials would circumvent any progress African Americans had made toward equal rights and desegregation. Southern white liberals such as Mark Ethridge and Virginius Dabney, the editor of the *Richmond Times-Dispatch*, believed that the militancy expressed by African American publications would "undo their efforts, along with those of 'responsible Negroes,' to effect a gradual amelioration of Southern racial policies." In their opinion, "the radicalism expressed by colored newspapers would encourage white racist extremists to resort to lynchings, race riots, and other horrors to preserve the South's racial order." By the end of 1942, this criticism had reached the pages of the *Atlantic Monthly* and the *Saturday Review of Literature*.[13] In the January 1943 issue of the *Atlantic Monthly*, Dabney harshly criticized the African American press for "demanding an overnight revolution in race relations." He is quoted as saying, "The radical element in the Negro press both North and South, were stirring up interracial hate.... [It has] encouraged Negroes to more militant protest, thereby disturbing the delicate balance of Southern race relations."[14]

But the government's intimidation, surveillance, and white press criticism did not deter the African American press from its coverage and criticism of racism in the armed forces. The press was highly critical of the army's failure to use African American combat forces in the war. As a result of this constant criticism and pressure from both the press and African American civic leaders, the army reluctantly sent the 93rd Infantry Division to the Pacific Theater in January 1944. While the 24th Infantry Regiment, one of the oldest African American regiments in the military, had been in the Pacific Theater since April 1942, they had been relegated to non–combat, manual labor, support service duties. But with the African American press working in conjunction with the army's own Bureau of Public Relations, the War Department began putting pressure on the commanding generals to utilize these forces in combat. So totally unprepared was the War Department to actually utilize any African Americans in combat, that no form of training personnel to be utilized as infantry or armored replacements for the African American ground combat casualties was ever incorporated during World War II. This would have detrimental effects on the combat efficiency and morale of the armored and infantry units deployed in the combat theaters.

Through the assistance of the Bureau of Public Relations, the press also emphasized the accomplishments of the African American soldier. In 1943, the Bureau of Public Relations and the Civilian Aide on Negro Affairs in the War Department encouraged thirteen African American newspapers to organize a pool of war correspondents so that better coverage might be available to all from among the limited number of war correspondents available. By the end of the war, every major theater was being covered by at least one African American war correspondent. In 1944, the bureau established a special European clearing office dedicated to the news of African American soldiers.[15] This agency followed soldiers in the European and Mediterranean Theaters of Operations, and provided war correspondents from African American newspapers with news of their exploits. Downplayed was the large number of African American soldiers that were assigned to combat service support units, while the exploits and failures of the few combat units received the majority of the press coverage. Even overseas, the soldiers continued to use the African American newspapers as a method to voice their concerns.

                                          Company B, 1st Battalion, 5182 Maintenance (Truck)
                                          APO NY 467

The Afro-American Newspapers   December 10, 1944
Dear Editor:

We are writing you enlisting your aid concerning segregation of Negro troops in India, and we would like you to take an appeal to the NAACP.

First off, on the ship, a lecture was given by Dr. Paul D. Lindbergh, and he asked the Negro

Associated Negro Press War Correspondent and men of a Signal Construction Battalion somewhere in France, 13 July 1944. (National Archives Photo)

troops not to mention racial prejudice in the states. And right on the ship we weren't allowed to drink from the cool water fountains.

Then, the first thing we encountered in India is segregation. American, British, Indian, Chinese, and Negro troops, all attend the same show and the Negroes are piled in a huddle right in the rear.

These boys are getting plenty fed up of being troddled [sic] on when they are giving their lives for America. And when a complaint is taken to an officer, the only answer we receive is, "I'll see about it tomorrow."

And we would greatly appreciate you giving this letter to the NAACP and let them see if they can do anything concerning it. We would also like for this to get into some Negro paper.

Yours with thanks,
Negro Troops in India.[16]

By late 1944, both the 92nd and 93rd Infantry Divisions had been deployed to combat theaters, and their exploits were closely followed by African American war correspondents. Some of the restrictions imposed by the military had been lifted by this time. Large numbers of African American soldiers had been deployed overseas to support the war effort. The Women's Army Corps had established African American units with many of the female soldiers performing critical duties at stateside military installations.

These small, though welcomed improvements in the lot of African American military personnel were due in no small part to the constant agitation by African American organizations, especially as they expressed themselves through the various news organizations. African American newspapers' unrelenting scrutiny of the military's treatment of African American soldiers was instrumental in lowering racial barriers somewhat. In that sense, the African American press' "Double V" strategy was a qualified success.

Chapter IV

Combat Service Support Units

During World War I, the vast majority of African Americans that served in the military were relegated to perform duties in combat service support units. These units performed the manual labor and logistical tasks that were required to ensure the combat forces succeeded on the battlefield. The military commanders, just prior to World War II, decided that in the segregated army of the 1940s, African American soldiers, often criticized as not being capable to withstand the rigors of front-line combat, would be best utilized in combat service support units. But World War II would not be fought like previous wars. Warfare would not be confined to static battlefields. Battles would be fought from island to island in the Pacific Ocean, across the vast mountain ranges of Central Asia through China, from North Africa to the Mediterranean, and across the English Channel through France to Germany. Engineers would be required to build roads, airfields, bridges, and hospitals, where there had before been only empty desert, tropical jungles, or the frigid cold of Alaska. They were tasked to install pipelines to furnish water and fuel to the military forces in every theater of battle. Trucks were required to transport supplies and soldiers to the front lines over these newly constructed roads. Petroleum specialists would be required to keep aircraft, ships, and vehicles fueled. Maintenance personnel would be required to keep the vehicles operational. Dock personnel and stevedores were needed to load and unload the tons of supplies required to keep a mobile military force moving. Cooks were required to keep soldiers fed. Ambulances were needed to transport the wounded from the battlefield. These vital tasks fell to the African American soldiers. Hardly could the commanders foresee the importance of the service these soldiers would contribute to the total victory of the war. As the war progressed, the requirement for combat service support personnel increased drastically. For every one infantryman on the front lines, it would take ten soldiers to support him. African American combat units such as the 2nd Cavalry Division and several armored, artillery, and tank destroyer battalions were disbanded and the soldiers transferred to combat service support units. While the performance of combat forces often overshadowed the contributions of these combat service support units, total victory could not have been achieved without them.

The demand for combat service support units became an ever-increasing one in the expanding army. The provision of combat service support units for African Americans, especially in the Corps of Engineers and the Quartermaster Corps, was originally accompanied with little debate, for it was generally agreed that African American soldiers could be best utilized to their advantage in such units. By April 1942, 42 percent of all engineer and 34 percent of all quartermaster units were made up of African Americans, while only four percent of the total combat units were African American.

Only one African American engineer service regiment was provided for in the 1940 Protective Mobilization Plan for the army. From the formation of the 41st Engineer General Service Regiment in August 1940 through the end of 1942, twenty-seven engineer general service regiments were activated. An equal number was to be added in the remaining years of the war. One engineer aviation regiment and 13 separate engineer battalions were activated by the end of 1942, with a larger number activated in the succeeding years of the war. Separate engineer battalions, engineer water supply battalions/companies, dump truck companies, and aviation engineer companies accounted for the majority of the remaining engineer units activated with African Americans during the period of 1940 through 1942.

The 41st Engineer General Service Regiment, one of the first new engineer units to be activated during the mobilization, discovered that by December 1940, most of its newly inducted soldiers did not possess the qualifications or the background experience required for an engineer general service regiment.[1] Engineer General Service Regiments were required to be able to perform the various types of engineering tasks conducted while supporting military operations, including the construction of roads and bridges, and the operations of utilities. These segregated African American engineer regiments were often confused with the unskilled labor units that the army utilized prior to World War II. These units were called Engineer Separate Battalions, but as the complexity of the conflict increased, so too would the role of these units change. It was not widely realized that general service engineer regiments required a high percentage of skilled technical labor and a relatively high average of ability to learn and adapt on the part of the individual soldier. The Chief of Engineers recommended that reception centers assign soldiers of average or high classification to these units. The War Department in denying this request stated that it was "impossible, at the time, to assign Negroes on any other than a numerical basis." It suggested that "whenever new Negro engineer units with lower requirements, such as separate battalions, become available, the 41st Engineers could transfer its unsuitable men to these units."[2] But while the soldiers assigned to these units did not always meet prerequisite aptitude or technical standards, they quickly adapted and became extremely proficient in their jobs, exceeding all expectations.

Available segregated housing for African American soldiers was not adequate in early 1941 when most new draftees were being inducted into the army. Soldiers were assigned wherever billeting space was available, regardless of military qualifications. The 41st Engineers spent their first winter living in tents at Fort Bragg, North Carolina. But these obstacles would not deter the success these units would accomplish on the battlefield.

The housing shortage of segregated facilities on many bases in 1941 postponed the activation and training of many African American units in order to carry out the principle of separation by units and race. Usually, the African American section of a military installation remained distinct and separate, essentially becoming a separate camp within the installation. Many post commanders considered total separation of the races, especially with such a large number of soldiers, as the only method of preventing racial conflicts. The 41st Engineer General Service Regiment, being stationed at Fort Bragg, North Carolina, could not expect housing accommodations for its full complement of 1,176 men until 15 January 1941. In October 1940, the unit requested 800 additional men as soon as possible since by 15 February 1941, it was scheduled to provide 562 cadres for newly activated African American engineer regiments. The unit was told that housing difficulties precluded expansion beyond a total of 835 men. By December 1940, the 41st Engineer Regiment only had 697 soldiers with 425 new draftees expected from the 4th Corps Area (all the southeastern states excluding Virginia and Kentucky) in January. During the mobilization plan of 1940, new draftees were inducted and trained in the same geographical region of the country from which they came.

Quartermaster truck and service units were always in high demand. Later, as more soldiers were shipped to overseas theaters, requests for these types of units were generally greater than the number and the shipping space available for them. The many types of quartermaster units activated between 1940 through 1942 for the utilization of African American soldiers included truck, service, car, railhead, bakery, salvage repair, salvage collecting, laundry, fumigation and bath, fuel supply, sterilization, and pack units, ranging in size from small detachments through entire regiments. Before the conclusion of the war, there were more than 1,600 quartermaster companies with headquarters; bakery, laundry, and driver detachments; separate platoons and provisional units of various sizes and types. During that same period, the Quartermaster Corps, before the establishment of a separate Transportation Corps, organized separate African American port battalions and companies. Subsequently, the Transportation Corps itself organized a considerable number of port and amphibian truck companies for use throughout the United States and in theaters overseas.

Chemical detachment lays down a smoke screen for the 3rd Army crossing of the Moselle River, France, November 1944. (National Archives)

In the rapid expansion of its African American units, the Quartermaster Corps could not avoid the personnel problems common to the other branches of the army. As early as August 1941, the personnel requirements of African American quartermaster units began to exceed the current supply of available trainees graduating from the quartermaster replacement training centers. To fill high priority quartermaster units scheduled for activation during the autumn of 1941, some units were staffed with African American soldiers from existing engineer, artillery, infantry, and cavalry replacement training centers. Each of these centers had a surplus of African American trainees who, classified as over–strength personnel, lacking units for assignment, would otherwise present housing and assignment difficulties for their branches. Filling high priority quartermaster units with these surplus soldiers helped resolve the problem of placement for these men.[3]

A third branch, the Chemical Warfare Service Branch, continued to provide units for more than its proportionate share of African American soldiers from the activation of the 1st Chemical Decontamination Company onward. Soldiers were placed in smoke generator companies, aviation chemical maintenance companies, aviation chemical depot companies, and airdrome chemical platoons. One chemical service, one chemical motorized, and one chemical processing company were activated in 1942. But the majority of the new chemical units were the smoke generator companies, many of them added to the troop basis schedule during 1942 to fill expected needs of camouflaging amphibious operations being planned for that year. A number of these units were to be activated, trained, and initially utilized by the defense commands.[4]

The Medical Corps, reluctant to have African American soldiers within its ranks, experienced considerable difficulty in providing units for its share of African American inductees. The whole question of medical units, as distinct from the medical detachments that were attached to units of other branches and services, was inextricably interwoven with the utilization of African American physicians, dentists, and nurses, which in turn was part of the larger question of the utilization of African American officers in general. Initially, African American draftees designated for the Medical Corps could be trained as medical corpsmen and technicians and assigned to the medical detachments of the newly activated African American regiments and battalions.

In the late summer and fall of 1940, the Medical Corps initiated plans for the utilization of African American soldiers. These plans included provisions for both officers and enlisted men. The major feature affecting the provision of units for African American soldiers was the proposal for a separate African American unit, which would become the medical sanitary company of World War II. Originally called "Medical Company, Separate (Colored)," by the Surgeon General's Office, these units were organized in conformance with the policy that no organizations were to be designated by race and that no special tables of organization were to be made for African American soldiers which did not apply to white soldiers as well.[5]

The medical sanitary companies were originally intended to provide hospital ward and professional services for hospitals having 100 or more African American patients, cared for in separate, segregated wards. After it was determined that such services would be administratively uneconomical, the units were thought of as hospital service units, containing men who could replace the approximately 180 white enlisted men normally used for menial labor tasks such as drivers, cooks, cooks' assistants, orderlies, and basic labor service in a general hospital. It was planned that they would be housed, fed, and administered in segregated facilities, under the command of African American officers. When African American doctors and nurses

Captain Della H. Raney, Army Nurse Corps, who now heads the nursing staff at the station hospital at Camp Beale, CA, had the distinction of being the first African American nurse to report to duty in World War II, on 11 April 1945. (National Archive 208-PU-161K-1)

were assigned to a hospital, these companies could provide the segregated facilities to support them administratively.

As the units actually developed, the medical sanitary companies became primarily manual labor organizations, utilized in addition to the general hospital personnel. They became general service units, which might be utilized for any duty considered appropriate by the commander of the unit or installation to which they were assigned. No medical training was ever provided for these men, and the African American soldiers were usually assigned duties that were in a menial manual labor capacity. Only two medical sanitary companies were activated in 1941. These two companies were activated "because of pressure on the Adjutant General to put colored medical personnel on duty," and not, as was the case in certain other units, for the purpose of absorbing the increasing number of African American draftees.[6] An additional 54 of these medical sanitary companies were activated during 1942. An even larger number of medical sanitary company activations were scheduled for 1943, but not all of the units were activated. Thirty medical sanitary companies were actually activated in 1943 and only one in 1944. Many of the 1943 companies were later disbanded in the fall of that year when more vitally needed combat service support units were required for the different overseas theaters.[7] Also, complaints reached the American public of the menial jobs that these African American soldiers were being tasked to perform in the medical department via the African American press corps. Aside from the two segregated station hospitals located at Tuskegee, Alabama, and at Fort Huachuca, Arizona, four field hospitals, and numerous veterinary, ambulance, and administrative companies were activated. Unfortunately, the medical sanitary companies still remained the major medical units provided for the utilization of African American soldiers in the Medical Corps.

IV. Combat Service Support Units

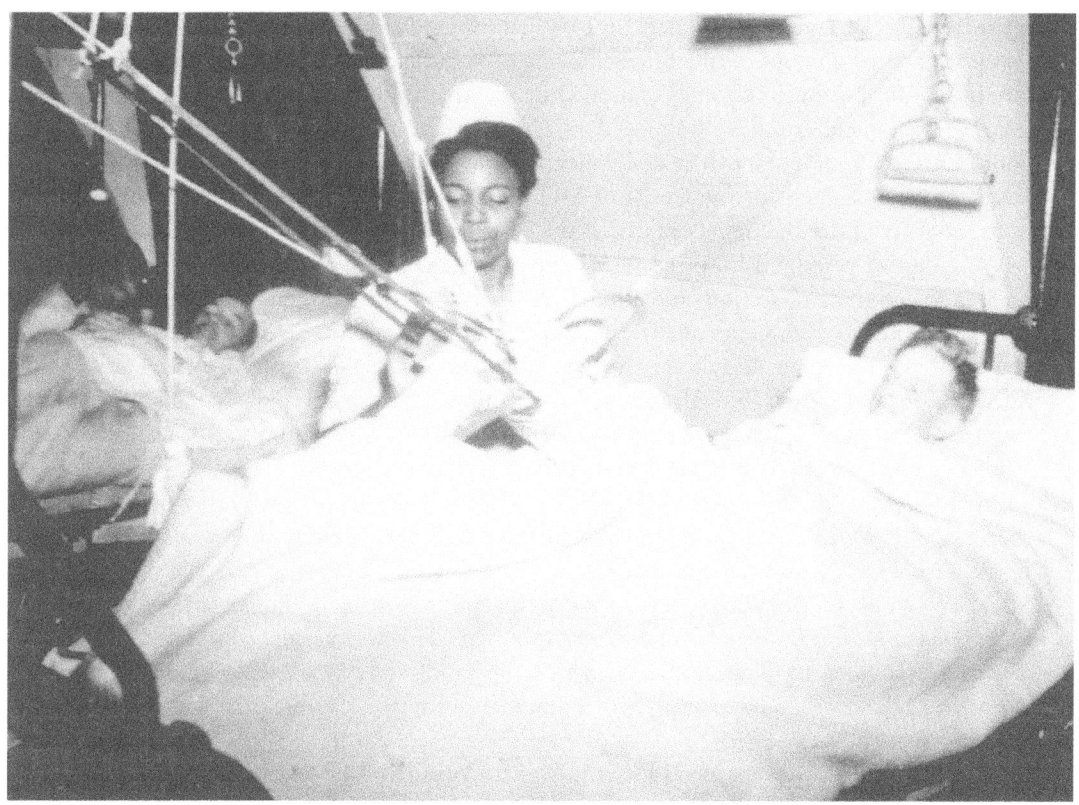

Lieutenant Florie E. Gant tends a patient at a prisoner-of-war hospital somewhere in England, 7 October 1944. (National Archives 112-SGA-Nurses-44-1676)

In January 1941, the army opened its nurse corps to African Americans but established a ceiling of only 56 personnel. On 25 June 1941, President Roosevelt's Executive Order 8802 created the Fair Employment Practices Commission, which led the way in eradicating racial discrimination in the defense program. In June 1943, Frances Payne Bolton, congresswoman from Ohio, introduced an amendment to the Nurse Training Bill to bar racial bias. Soon 2,000 African American women were enrolled in the Cadet Nurse Corps. The quota for African American Army nurses was eliminated in July 1944. One group of 15 nurses deployed to the Southwest Pacific Area in the summer of 1943 with the segregated 268th Station Hospital. In June 1944 a unit of 63 nurses deployed with the 168th Station Hospital to England to care for German prisoners of war. More than 500 African American Army nurses served at stateside hospitals and overseas during the war.[8]

African American military police units were not planned for activation until experiments with African American military police detachments showed that their utilization in areas populated with large African American soldier concentrations paid dividends in better order, better relations between soldiers and the military police, and better relations with civilians in those communities which had learned to look upon African American military police as something less than a threat to local customs. But conflict did occur between African American soldiers and their military police counterparts. Also, some southern army installations did not allow African American military police to carry the standard .45-caliber sidearm while on patrol in the local communities. Fear of attacks on armed African American servicemen by the local residents and white soldiers, in part, contributed to this policy. Prior to World War II, most of these units were small detachments of men detailed to perform temporary military police duties from the locally stationed units. Among them, there was little uniformity in procedure, organization, or training. Some installations utilized African American military police on special temporary duty assignments, while others used them on a full-time basis. Until the establishment of the Corps of Military Police on 26 September 1941, these units were generally under the direct control of the installation and service commanders.

The directive establishing the new Corps of Military Police required commanders to report the designation, station, and strength by race of existing military police units.[9] There were 22 of these detachments of African American military police on 30 June 1942, ranging in size from a two-man detachment at Fort Sam Houston, Texas, to 65 men at Camp San Luis Obispo, California. Ten African American military police battalions (zone of the interior) and three companies were activated in August 1942. Two additional battalions were scheduled for activation, but the War Department decided not to activate any additional African American military police battalions, and converted them to white battalions. Both the 92nd and 93rd Infantry Divisions included an African American military police platoon in their table of organization and equipment.

The Ordnance Branch provided that only ammunition handling companies be designated for the utilization of African American soldiers. This was usually considered very hazardous duty, due to the dangers associated with the handling of explosives. Aviation ordnance depot and aviation ordnance supply and maintenance companies were provided in the Army Air Forces.

In the mobilization plan of 1940, the Signal Corps believed that "it would be difficult to obtain qualified personnel who could be properly trained for duty and function efficiently in units such as Signal Battalions, Signal Companies, Signal Troops and Signal Service Companies." The Signal Corps was willing to consider an exception in the event that "a Negro Division is ever organized." Even then, it felt, "it would be difficult to obtain properly qualified men such as radio electricians, telephone technicians, and radio operators."[10]

Prejudice and racism of the senior white officers of the Signal Corps led to this conclusion. Thus, the Signal Corps restricted African American communicators to signal construction companies. These companies provided the manpower for most of the labor-intensive tasks associated with providing viable communications in a theater of combat. Their duties normally included erecting telephone poles and digging ditches used for underground wiring conduits. One signal construction company was activated in May 1941, and saw early duty in the Panama Canal Zone, as newly constructed defense facilities required communications operating centers. Except for three separate signal construction companies and three signal construction battalions, all other signal units activated in 1942 were Army Air Force assets. Later, each of the African American infantry divisions had a signal company assigned that was responsible for providing all of the division's communications support. Other separate African American combat regiments and battalions had trained signal personnel assigned, but the Signal Corps remained well below its proportionate percentage of African American soldiers throughout the war.[11]

A number of miscellaneous units were activated for the utilization of African American soldiers from 1940 through 1942. Among these were bands, replacement companies, postal units, service command companies, and a special service unit. Various provisional units, training units, school detachments, and special supply detachments were activated also, solely for the placement of African American soldiers. Several medium automotive maintenance companies in the Army Ground Forces were activated with African American enlisted men. This would ensure the total segregation of transportation units that required vehicle maintenance companies to support them.

With the military expansion, requests increased for truck regiments and special service companies to be used at service schools and school detachments to replace civilians, performing such duties as janitors and table waiters for the instructors' and student officers' living quarters and dining facilities. A number of African American soldiers were assigned to these units, which provided none of the combat or combat support skills required for the successful operations of the army. The Field Artillery School at Fort Sill, Oklahoma, explained its requirement for additional African American enlisted men in its school detachment. "Until recently, civilian colored kitchen police and table waiters were available in sufficient numbers to maintain officer and instructor messes without difficulty. Lately, we have not been able to employ the required number, since a large percentage of this labor has been drafted. Other eligible men who would be desirable in the messes are now employed elsewhere at more attractive wages and better working hours. The problem of securing adequate kitchen police and table waiters is becoming more acute."[12]

But African American soldiers did not desire to be permanent kitchen police and waiters for the army. Many equated this type of duty with slavery, and could not see how it contributed to the war effort. Disgruntled African American soldiers used the African American press corps as a forum to inform the American public how they were being treated.

Richmond Afro-American
503 N. 3rd Street
Richmond, Virginia

328th Aviation Squadron
Pampa Army Air Field
Pampa, Texas
November 22, 1943

Dear Sirs:

I am writing this letter to acquaint you with the horrible and Un-American treatment of Negro personnel of this field and beseeching you to please come to our rescue. Every Negro man on this post is absolutely fed up and disappointed with the bad treatment and discrimination, segregation and injustice imposed upon us. You must please understand that we do not resent serving our country (we are proud to serve), but we would like and want very much to serve it in a more important capacity than we are at this time. We can and would fight if trained to do so, but as yet we hardly know what a gun, or tank, combat planes, a hand grenade, machine gun look like. We haven't had any drilling to speak of that could be classed as drilling. We had three weeks of basic training. It takes that long to learn to do the manual of arms (arms are something we haven't even seen except a 45 on the M.P.'s side, ready to blow your brains out if you resent being treated like a dog or being called a nigger or a black son of a bitch), much less call it Basic Training.... We are a group of permanent K.P.'s. We are allowed no other advancement whatsoever. It is true that K.P. pusher (Head K.P.) are made Corporal and Sergeant, but the K.P.'s themselves are a miserable group that will be worked like slaves without any ratings to speak of. We are confined to this job not because we are not fit for anything else but because we are dark. We are referred to on this post as "that Nigger squadron at the end of the field."

So gentlemen if you will please see fit to help us in some way we the whole squadron and the 908th Quartermaster Company (Negro) will greatly appreciate it and will cooperate 100% if investigated.

Copies of this letter are being sent to Colonel B.O. Davis, the NAACP and the War Department at Washington D.C.

Thanking You Very Much
328th Aviation Squadron and
908th Quartermaster Company[13]

The Parachute School at Fort Benning, Georgia, requested an African American service company to relieve its own students of such duties as kitchen police, guarding installations, cooks, and cleaning training areas, hangars and administrative buildings.[14] Ironically, some members of this service company would become members of the initial African American airborne test platoon for the 555th Parachute Infantry Battalion. The service company's first sergeant, Walter Morris, became the first enlisted man recruited into this elite airborne battalion.

Table 2 — Racial Distribution by Types of Service (Enlisted Only)
31 December 1942

TYPE OF SERVICE	White	African American	Percentage of African American	Percentage of All Servicemen	
				White	African Americans
Army Totals	4,531,117	467,883	10.3	100	100
Combat Units	1,814,094	92,772	4.8	40	19.7
Service Units	616,851	161,707	20.7	13.6	34.5
Army Air Force	1,190,363	109,637	8.4	26.4	23.5
Replacement Depots/ Hospitals	363,820	65,880	15.3	8	14.1
Replacement Training Centers	238,500	27,500	10.3	5.3	5.9
Officer Candidate School	72,200	800	1.1	1.5	0.2
Unassigned	235,289	9,587	3.9	5.2	2.1

Source: Extended from Tab B, Memorandum, G3 for Commanding General Army Ground Forces and Supply of Service, 25 Jan 43, File WDGCT 320.2 Gen (1–25–43) National Archives.

EARLY DEPLOYMENTS — PACIFIC THEATER

The greatest in demand and most consistently utilized were the African American engineer and quartermaster units. These were among the first to be notified and deployed to overseas theaters. Often, they preceded the combat units' deployment in order to prepare staging areas and constructing airfields for aviation support. By early 1942, these units were being deployed to the South Pacific, Iran, and India. In Task Force 6814, the first large task force to be deployed to the Pacific Theater after the attack on Pearl Harbor, were the 810th and 811th Engineer Aviation Battalions. The 811th Engineers were a newly activated unit, with its men reporting to Langley Field, Virginia, on 7 December 1941. The unit was a little more than a month old when the task force departed on 23 January 1942, bound for Australia. The 810th Engineers were activated on 26 June 1941 at MacDill Airfield, Florida, with a cadre of enlisted men from the 41st Engineer Regiment and four officers. The unit had spent the first six months of activation prior to deployment, learning to operate its heavy equipment by building roads, bridges, and fortifications, and by performing general construction work at its home station and at other new and expanding posts in the region. The individual companies of the 810th Engineers were activated separately and trained and worked at different levels and locations.

Given a one-week warning order, the 810th Engineer Aviation Battalion assembled at the New York Port of Embarkation. Seventy railway cars transported the battalion's heavy equipment to the west coast for shipping to the Pacific Theater. After two days of loading additional equipment on ships, the battalion boarded the United States Army Transport Ship *J.W. McAndrew*, which in a convoy of the other six ships of Task Force 6814 departed New York for Australia on 23 January 1942. On shipboard, the 810th Engineers were joined by the 811th Engineer Aviation Battalion, which had only spent one month becoming familiar with their new equipment. The convoy arrived at Melbourne on 26 February. Both battalions remained occupied with their duties of unloading ships and reloading them with badly needed ordnance supplies that were to be positioned closer to the combat zones. On 7 March the two battalions departed for New Caledonia, Noumea, on the United States Army Transport *Erickson*.

In Noumea, the units, both of which were later attached to the Americal Division, went to work before unloading. Companies A, B, and C of the 810th Engineer Aviation Battalion moved ashore to assist in unloading ships of the task force already tied up in the Noumea harbor. The Headquarters Company remained aboard the *Erickson* to assist unloading a French ship, the *Polynesian*, which was tied up alongside. The 811th Engineers unloaded their equipment and proceeded 30 miles up the coast to Bouloupan to repair roads.

As the 810th Engineer Aviation Battalion's heavy equipment arrived, the battalion deployed to the Nepoui Peninsula, 245 kilometers away. After several weeks of transporting equipment over roads and bridges never intended to be utilized for heavy vehicles of that size, the 810th Engineers took over the construction of the Plaine Des Gaiacs Airport from a civilian construction company. It was to be converted to a bomber base before the invasions of the southern Solomon Islands. While the majority of the battalion worked on the construction of the airfield, separate engineer platoons constructed fighter airstrips and docks. One platoon of Company C repaired an old French airfield at Koumac to be used for emergency landings. Originally, the platoon was ordered to merely level and lengthen the airstrip, but after the first week of construction, the commander of Task Force 6814, Major General Alexander Patch, ordered that it be converted into an all-weather runway. During the next week, Company C was informed that the runway was to be long enough to support the B-17 Flying Fortress bomber, with at least 12 available aircraft parking areas. The job, to be completed by the end of July, required the efforts of the entire company, a platoon from the 811th Engineers, and 12 drivers and trucks from the 57th Combat Engineer Battalion of the American Division. Working in shifts 24 hours a day, 7 days a week, they completed the task on time. On 1 August 1942, a squadron of B-17 Flying Fortresses landed at Koumac. The next morning, the bombers took off to bomb enemy targets in the Solomon Islands. Units at the Plaine des Gaiacs Airport, with the assistance of native Javanese labor gangs hired to dig drainage ditches, worked around the clock until the airport became operational. B-17s, bombing enemy targets on Guadalcanal, were using the airfield before the construction was completed.

The heavy equipment of the 811th Engineers trickled in for months. The battalion began to work on airfield projects in April 1942, widening access highways into landing strips, building equipment dispersal areas, and constructing aircraft and bomb shelters at Tontauta, learning the techniques of the job as it worked. The Headquarters Company transported crated fighter aircraft from the docks to assembly points 35 miles inland. Two platoons constructed a fighter airstrip at the Bourake Peninsula in a valley bounded on three sides by hills and by the sea on the fourth side. Meant only to be used as a temporary emergency landing strip, it remained in full operation for over a year.

These tasks were typical of the jobs performed by aviation engineer battalions. Platoons and companies often operated independently of the battalion on separate remote projects. On 7 September 1942, Company B of the 810th Engineers proceeded to Espiritu Santo in the New Hebrides Islands, where it constructed a bomber airbase in the mists of a teakwood forest. The unit did not rejoin the rest of the battalion until after its arrival on Guadalcanal on 2 May 1943. In the meantime, the battalion acquired its first African American officers from the Engineers Officers Candidate School. The remaining companies of the battalion in the intervening months constructed roads, built radar stations, and worked at ration supply depots. Assembling the battalion on Guadalcanal on 15 June, the 810th Engineers built installations, aircraft taxiways, and hardstands for the 13th Air Force.[15]

Guadalcanal's Carney Field (Bomber One), the only airfield on the island from which heavy bomber aircraft could operate efficiently, was deteriorating due to the heavy rains of the monsoon season. The 810th Engineers had been tasked to repair it, and had the field restored to operational condition in only four days. The battalion performed reconstruction jobs on other airfields, built new hangars, and assisted with construction jobs for the Navy. In conjunction with Navy and Marine Corps construction battalions, it built Kili Field. After the airfield became operational, Company B maintained its upkeep. By this time, the unit had been deployed overseas for over two years. The 810th Engineers had no unit holiday until 26 June 1944, when it celebrated its third anniversary. Despite its early arrival in the theater and the fact the unit remained overseas for the duration of the war, the battalion was never permitted to take time off to go on furlough at a rest camp or to train its replacement personnel.[16]

Upon completion of its tour on Guadalcanal, in July 1944, the 810th Engineer Aviation Battalion was assigned to the Southwest Pacific Area's Services of Supply (USASOS) and deployed to the island of Biak, where it constructed a hospital for the 41st Field Hospital. Assigned to the 6th Army in November 1944, the 810th Engineers were assigned to the Luzon invasion forces, leaving Biak on 4 January 1945 and arriving at Lingayen Gulf in the Philippines on 13 January. The battalion's companies were attached to the 1178th and 1180th Engineer Construction Groups, a typical operational arrangement for smaller engineer units in the last years of the war. The battalion went ashore at Yellow Beach and White Beach 2 (San Fabian). After the landings, the battalions filled and laid corrugated steel mats on hardstands, constructed unloading aprons, maintained roads, constructed and maintained water supply points, built fuel tank foundations and fire trenches, painted and erected road signs, built tent hardstands, constructed a 1,000 bed hospital of prefabricated building material at San Fabian, rebuilt and constructed bridges, maintained pontoon bridges, and made topographic surveys of proposed signal and quartermaster areas. It was not until December 1945 that the battalion sent all of its original soldiers home on leave. By then the war had been over for four months.

The 811th Engineers remained on New Caledonia until the spring of 1944. In its tenure there, it worked with the Navy's construction battalions (Seabees) on many construction projects, often competing to see who would complete their assigned task first. After having undertaken almost every conceivable job associated with airport construction, the battalion deployed to Guadalcanal in March 1944. It found mainly minor odd jobs waiting to be completed there. The 811th Engineers, like many other African American units, was to discover that assignment to a new headquarters often meant demonstrating all over again that it was capable of doing even the average job well. Units sometimes noted that inspecting and supervisory personnel were skeptical of their capabilities, especially if they had both African American and white officers assigned, but they were often unaware that the battalion already had a distinguished record while deployed in the combat theater.[17]

In September 1944, the 811th Engineers departed Guadalcanal for Honolulu. There, it performed various construction and repair jobs at Hickham and Bellows Airfields, and throughout Oahu until 10 December 1944, when it was alerted to prepare for deployment to a forward area. After a period of amphibious combat training at the Jungle Training Center, the battalion departed on 28 March 1945 for Iwo Jima.[18] On Iwo Jima, while constructing airstrips and quarters for the bomber groups, its platoons continued to encounter pockets of enemy resistance as their bulldozers were utilized to cut into caves. The hiding Japanese were promptly captured by the 811th Engineers and their accompanying infantry squads.

The 810th and 811th Engineer Aviation Battalions were among the first deployed African American units with the longest overseas service tours. Equally as long, and very similar in some respects to their overall achievements, were those of the 96th and 91st Engineer General Service Regiments, which arrived in Brisbane, Australia, on 6 April 1942, organized as separate engineer battalions. The battalions left the next night on the same ships for Townsville, Australia. There, the 96th Engineers began clearing an area by hand for a 7,000-foot runway, as their heavy equipment had yet to arrive. Two companies remained at this location until June, constructing three 7,000-foot dirt runways. The remainder of the battalion deployed to Port Moresby, New Guinea, where a small Australian garrison had been under siege by Japanese air attacks since 3 February 1942.[19]

Port Moresby, on the Gulf of Papua near the southeastern tip of the island of New Guinea, had inadequate facilities for either its own defense or for the receipt of additional supplies and equipment from Australia, over 700 miles away. Its port facilities were inadequate; its two existing airfields were too small, poorly built, and subjected to continuous bombings, so that they were at first only utilized as a refueling point for aircraft flying from Australia to attack enemy targets. Construction of new airfields, improving the port facilities, and repairing existing airfields were required before Port Moresby could either be defended or used as a base of forward operations.

The 96th Engineers were deployed to Port Moresby to improve existing prewar airfields. On 20 April 1942, an advance party of two officers and 40 enlisted men departed Australia by C-47 aircraft to survey the area and prepare for the arrival of the remainder of the battalion. The rest of the battalion, minus two companies, arrived at Port Moresby on 28 April, having the distinction of becoming the first American soldiers on New Guinea. That night, Port Moresby suffered an enemy air raid. The Japanese concentrated on the airdrome at Seven-Mile, where Company B was located. They became the first African American unit to come under enemy fire during the war. The next day, they assisted with the installation of .50-caliber machine guns and 37-mm cannons into 26 newly arrived P-39 Airacobras fighter aircraft.

Engineering equipment arrived from Townsville on 5 May 1942. Although not trained as an aviation engineer battalion like the 810th or 811th Engineers, and lacking the heavy equipment that those aviation engineer battalions were authorized, the companies began to improve facilities at those airfields. On 8 May, the battalion was incorporated into the defense of Port

Moresby, and alerted against the possibility of a Japanese invasion. The battalion continued to be harassed by enemy air attacks, often resulting in the destruction of their equipment, which was already in short supply. At the end of June, the engineers remaining in Australia rejoined the battalion, bringing with them badly needed construction equipment. In July, the battalion was relieved of its airfield construction duties by the 808th Aviation Engineer Battalion, a newly arrived white unit.[20] The 96th Engineers could now assume a role more in line with the duties required of a general engineer battalion. Gradually, the battalion took on the construction of barracks, dining facilities, and roads. When Australian combat forces halted the Japanese offensive on Port Moresby on 14 September 1942, the enemy was only 30 miles away. On 25 September, when the Japanese retreated toward Kokoda, north of the Owen Stanley Mountains, a 37-mm antitank gun and crew from the 96th Engineers departed to assist driving the enemy back. In December 1942, Port Moresby had obtained M-4 Sherman tanks, badly needed by the Allied forces fighting at Buna, but had no personnel available to unload the tanks under heavy enemy fire, and then defend the cargo until it could be turned over to the consignee Australian and New Zealand soldiers. Volunteers were sought from the 96th Engineers. On 8 December, a force of 15 enlisted men and one officer landed the tanks on the beach without mishap, but constant enemy fire killed one and wounded another of the soldiers of the 96th Engineers.[21]

In spite of frequent air attacks on Port Moresby, the 96th Engineers continued to perform various construction jobs. The construction of the Tatana causeway and docks, for which General MacArthur personally commended the unit, more than doubled the capacity of the port. In addition to the construction and maintenance of airfields and docks, the unit was engaged in miscellaneous projects: five months of manual labor duties at the engineer depot; loading, shipping, and laying pierced steel landing mats for emergency airstrips; repairing and extending runways at Kokoda during the Japanese retreat; and constructing a 500-bed hospital for the air force. After an inspection and review on the anniversary of its arrival in New Guinea, Brigadier General Hanford McNider, then of the Combined Operational Service Command, declared to the 96th Engineer's soldiers: "Fellow soldiers, a year ago today, when you stepped ashore as the first American troop unit in New Guinea, you were making history. You've been making it ever since. You've had a part in the building and upkeep of all our airfields; and thus you've help make possible the destruction of the convoy in the Bismarck Sea, the flying of the infantry over the mountains, a hundred enemy actions. You've contributed your share to every crack we've taken at the Japs. You've carried out important works projects, even unloaded ships so we could eat and fight. You've built roads and the mains, which give us power and light. You're one of the workingest outfits in this man's Army. All of us here are proud of you. All America will be proud of you when your record gets into the histories. Some of you have been to war with the tanks. You all know about bombs from hanging them on planes and having them hung on you. You've been good soldiers and you're going to be good soldiers. The harder we work and the better we do our jobs, the quicker you and I are going to get back where we belong, to the United States of America, which is all wrapped up in that flag which you are saluting today."[22]

The 96th Engineers had performed an outstanding job under the most adverse conditions. It was a general service regiment, not an aviation engineer battalion; as such its equipment allocation never called for the heavy earth-moving equipment assigned to the aviation engineer battalions. But with its inadequate equipment, it had completed all assigned tasks, working ahead of the airplanes and ground forces, which would later carry the war against the Japanese from the airfields and docks constructed by the 96th Engineers. The unit would experience this later in the war, but Port Moresby and the former outposts at Milne Bay, where some of its soldiers were now located, were rapidly becoming rear areas of operation.

The 91st Engineers, which had been left in Australia, had been performing various construction jobs throughout that country. The 91st Engineers was another one of the units activated with cadre from the 41st Engineers, during the period when the 41st Engineers had abandoned its engineering duties to concentrate on cadre training. The majority of the cadres were old infantry soldiers of the 24th and 25th Infantry Regiments, none of which had any engineering training.[23] It was also one of the units whose 13-week basic training cycle was frequently interrupted to perform labor duties at Camp Shelby, Mississippi. The unit departed Camp Shelby on 28 July 1941 for field maneuvers, and never returned to any training camp or permanent barracks prior to their departure for overseas.

On 8 September 1942, the 91st Engineers departed Australia for Port Moresby, minus a provisional battalion, which had been left at the Cape York Peninsula to repair an airfield for use by B-17 bombers. The battalion remained at Cape York until December, when it rejoined the rest of the regiment. The 91st Engineers, now reorganized as a general service regiment, was authorized improved equipment in order to complete its mission. But those early days on New Guinea, the 91st Engineers was forced to improvise in order to finish vital construction projects, as this new equipment had yet to arrive in theater. The 91st Engineers continued to perform construction duties in the Port Moresby area until mid–1944, after all other engineers and most of the air units had redeployed to forward areas. Road construction and maintenance, operation of gravel pits, excavation of sites for oil storage tanks, expansion of the Tatana dock area, and construction of utility systems were among the tasks it performed during its tenure there.

In additional to the engineers, segregated units also deploying early in the war to Australia and New Guinea included the 394th Quartermaster Battalion (Port), later redesignated a Transportation Corps Port Battalion. This, the oldest of the port battalions, departed the United States and arrived in Australia prior to engineering regiments due to departing from the west coast. The unit was activated with three companies on 27 June 1941 at Oakland, California. A fourth company was activated on 20 January 1942. After its arrival at Brisbane, Australia, on 9 March 1942, the companies of the battalion pursued the semi-independent course typical of port battalions. Company D (611th Port Company)[24] remained in the Brisbane area for a month, moving then to Charters Towers, where it remained for a month and a half before embarking on 15 June for Port Moresby. Company C (610th Port Company) moved from Brisbane to Cloncurry, then to Mount Isa, where it stayed until it left for Port Moresby on 26 November 1942. The headquarters element and the two remaining companies stayed in Brisbane, then deployed to Birdum in the Northern Territory. There, Company A (608th Port Company) worked for two months, deploying forward for Milne Bay on 23 July 1942. This company was located at Milne Bay until April 1943, when it joined the other units of the battalion at Port Moresby. It deployed to Finschhafen in December of that year. The battalion Headquarters Company and Company C arrived at Port Moresby in November 1942. The bulk of the battalion's work at Port Moresby was conducted on the Tatana docks, unloading and forwarding cargo that was vital to the war effort on New Guinea.[25]

In April 1944, when a second port company departed Port Moresby for Finschhafen, the battalion requested support from personnel of the 91st Engineers and the 55th Ordnance Ammunition Company for aid in handling cargo. A commendation from the 394th Port Battalion, stressing the excellent spirit and fine discipline of the 91st Engineer's men, enabled the battalion to move a record amount of cargo in a very short time.

Amphibious Truck Company, Iwo Jima. From left to right, back row, they are T/5 L.C. Carter, Jr., Private John Bonner, Jr., Staff Sergeant Charles R. Johnson. Standing, from left to right, are T/5 A.B. Randle, T/5 Homer H. Gaines, and Private Willie Tellie, 11 March 1945. (National Archives)

Meanwhile, the 96th Engineers worked on general construction and airfield projects throughout New Guinea. The full regiment, after over a year of working on separate projects, was assembled at Oro Bay in June 1944 for training, reequipping, and preparation for a new assignment. The regiment departed Oro Bay to join a convoy for Maffin Bay on 21 July, leaving one company and a detachment to follow later. After a brief layover at Maffin Bay, the regiment's Company C deployed to Wakde Island, charged with carrying out engineer, construction, and maintenance jobs. The remainder of the regiment proceeded to Cape Opmarai on 9 August 1944. After unloading their equipment, the 96th Engineers began work constructing buildings, roads, gasoline bulk storage tanks, and supply depots. The regiment remained in the Cape Opmarai area until April 1945. Toward the end of their stay, as this base also declined in population, and as the taxiways of the airfield emptied of aircraft, the pockets of bypassed Japanese resistance began harassing raids on the remaining soldiers at the base. Companies A and B of the 96th Engineers took over the defense at the Table River, while soldiers of the 167th Infantry Regiment, 31st Infantry Division, to which the engineer regiment was then attached, patrolled in search of the elusive enemy. All companies of the 96th Engineers deployed security and reconnaissance patrols in addition to their engineering duties.

The unit remained at Cape Opmarai until the base was closed out. The unit destroyed the runways and taxiways by cutting dozer ditches across them. It dismantled and crated fuel storage tanks and prepared all bridges for demolition. The unit was now critically short of enlisted personnel due to rotations and attrition. The replacement system of African American soldiers failed to provide trained soldiers where they were needed the most. In April 1945, the enlisted strength of the 96th Engineers had decreased to 675 men before they received 250 replacements that had come from the 1315th Engineer Construction Battalion, disbanded for the purpose of providing replacements for older African American engineer regiments. The last major project of the war for the 96th Engineers was to maintain roads and bridges along the supply route of the 31st Infantry Division in the Mindanao offensive campaign of the Philippine Islands.

On 8 March 1943, the 2nd Battalion, 29th Quartermaster Regiment was en route to New Guinea on a transport ship, when Japanese bombers attacked their convoy. When the ship was ordered abandoned, Private George Watson, instead of seeking to save himself, remained in the water assisting several soldiers who could not swim to reach the safety of the life raft. This heroic action, which subsequently cost him his life, resulted in the saving of several of his comrades. Weakened by his exertions, he was dragged down by the suction of the sinking ship and was drowned. Private Watson's body was later recovered, and he was buried at sea. For his heroic actions, he was posthumously awarded the Distinguished Service Cross, the nation's second highest award for valor, and the first African American soldier to do so during the war.[26]

LIBERIA TASK FORCE

In early 1942, Liberia granted the United States unrestricted access to construct, control, operate, and defend such commercial and military airfields as might be deemed necessary by mutual agreement, and the army was given the task of defending Liberian airfields.[27] The task force for Liberia consisted mainly of segregated African American units. Freed American slaves that were granted the right to return to Africa had formed this country during the early 1800s. The officers and enlisted men of the task force's headquarters, signal, and quartermaster detachments, the commander and four staff officers of the 25th Station Hospital, and personnel of the ferry command and supporting Army Air Corps units were white. An advance construction force, set up to prepare installations and provide defense pending the arrival of the full task force, comprised the 41st Engineer General Service Regiment (less the 2nd battalion), Company A, 812th Engineer Aviation Battalion (later redesignated the 899th Engineer Aviation Company), the 802nd Coastal Artillery Battery, and an advance detachment 25th Station Hospital, one of the four African American field hospitals.[28] These units arrived in June 1942. A detachment with African American cadre, assigned to train the Liberian Frontier (Guard) Force, went on to the capital city of Monrovia. Originally the 1/367th Infantry Battalion was scheduled to deploy at the same time, but shipping difficulties caused their deferment. The 41st Engineers received additional armament for their defensive mission, making the regiment comparable to a unit of combat engineers. The 99th Pursuit Squadron of the Tuskegee Airmen and its supporting service units were to join the Liberia Force at a later date, but were deferred to the Mediterranean Theater after the danger of enemy attacks on Liberia diminished. Although the strategic importance of Liberia no longer existed, the remaining ground forces proceeded to this country due to a prior agreement with the United States government. There were no provisions to include air units. After being on alert for nearly a year, the 1/367th Infantry, now a separate battalion, proceeded and arrived on 10 March 1943 at Marshall, Liberia.[29]

Aside from the construction of Roberts Airfield and its adjoining access roads, soldiers

Company of African American Women's Army Auxiliary Corps being reviewed by the Honorable Lester A. Walton, United States Minister to Liberia, recently on a visit to an American camp near Monrovia, Liberia, 1943. (National Archives 208-NP-6KKK-5)

in Liberia Task Force encountered no particular problems. The Liberia garrison dwindled gradually as the requirement for defense and for specific units decreased. Male nurses replaced the female nurses of the 25th Station Hospital late in 1943. After ten months, the 367th Infantry Battalion transferred to Oran, arriving in February 1944. The battalion would then perform airfield security duties throughout North Africa and Italy for the duration of the war. The 41st Engineers deployed to Corsica, and later on to France and Germany in the European Theater of Operations, where engineers were urgently needed. The 802nd Coastal Artillery Battery was disbanded in Liberia, and its soldiers transferred to combat service support units.[30] Instructors for the Liberia Guard Force, the hospital and air service soldiers remained, for Roberts Airfield continued to be a valuable asset for transatlantic service to the air transport and ferry commands until the end of the war.

ROAD BUILDERS

The first engineer and port battalions sent out to the Pacific Theater were followed within a few weeks by engineer units that were deployed to Alaska and Canada for construction of the Alaska (Alcan) Highway from Dawson Creek to Fairbanks. Three of the seven engineer regiments constructing this road through the northwestern wilderness were African American units. All originally designated as separate engineer battalions, they were utilized to perform many of the manual labor tasks assigned to this project. Later, the battalions were expanded in personnel and authorized equipment to engineer general service regiments. The 3,695 African American engineers accounted for more than a third of the 10,607 soldiers employed on the construction of the highway.[31] The commanding officer of the project did not want the African American engineers assigned for fear that they would intermingle with the native Alaskan population, but the War Department superseded his decision.

The 93rd Engineer General Service Regiment, arriving in April 1942, constructed the portion of the highway from Tagish north to the McClintock River and east and southeast toward Teslin; the 97th Engineer General Service Regiment, arriving at the same time, constructed the section from Slana north toward the Tanana River, and then south to the Alaska-Canada border. The 95th Engineer General Service Regiment, the last of the units to arrive, begin to follow the white 341st Engineers in June, improving the road cut by that regiment from Fort St. John to Fort Nelson. Having completed the pioneer road on 25 October 1942, the regiments remained there to improve and maintain the road or to perform other construction duties in Alaska and the Aleutian Islands. Units of the 97th Engineers, in addition to maintaining roads, operated terminals for trucks on the "Fairbanks Freight Route," the truck supply road over the highway. All three units later deployed to other theaters of operation, the 93rd and the 97th Engineers to the Pacific Theater, and the 95th Engineers to the European Theater of Operations.

Halfway around the world, in the China-Burma-India Theater, 60 percent of the 15,000 American soldiers assigned to the construction of the main supply route for that region, the Ledo Road, were African Americans. After the early successful Japanese campaign in the Pacific Theater, and their capture of the Burma Road, a new route had to be developed to supply the Chinese Army. This road, which ran 271 miles from Ledo, Assam, India, to the connecting Burma Road to Kunming, China, was vital for connecting supply bases in India to allied forces fighting in China. Until this road was completed, supplies had to be delivered via airlift. The first two army units to be assigned to this task of constructing the new road were the 45th Engineer General Service Regiment and the 83rd Engineer Aviation Battalion, both segregated African American units that had previously constructed airfields in Assam and elsewhere in India as the first American engineer units in the theater. Already performing construction on the road were one bridging and several pioneer engineering units of the British Army, and 8,000 local laborers.[32]

The 45th and 83rd Engineers began construction on 15 December 1942. The 45th Engineers' commander, Colonel John Arrowsmith, was assigned to the project as the original commanding officer of Base Section Three (later designated Advanced Section Three and then Advance Section), headquarters for road operations at Ledo.

The road, with its first section extending from Ledo through the Patkai Mountains to Shingbwiyang, 103 miles distant, traversed through previously unsurveyed territory. It followed roughly the steep narrow trail over which thousands of refugees had fled into India during the Allied retreat from Burma. Rising as high as 4,500 feet in elevation, the road ran through five mountain ranges of the Patkais. For each mile between Ledo and Shingbwiyang, 100,000 cubic feet of earth had to be removed. Steep grades, curves, and sheer drops as much as 200 feet, all surrounded by tropical rain forest and jungle, characterized this first section of road.

When the construction commenced, equipment used on the road was almost entirely the organizational equipment of the 45th Engineer Regiment and the 83rd Engineer Aviation Battalion, supplemented by road rollers, graders, rock crushers, air compressors, and small tools available from the China Defense Supply stocks. By 1 January 1943, the 83rd Engineers, continuing where the British forces left off, had cut five new miles of the road through the harsh terrain. During February, the work continued with the 83rd Engineers coming into Japanese-held Burma at mile marker 43.3.[33] Work proceeded slowly during the months thereafter as difficulties with equipment, shortages of trained engineer soldiers, and the monsoon rains plagued the efforts of the engineers. Landslides, washed-out bridges, and swollen streams hampered progress. By the beginning of the heavy rains, the road head had advanced so far as to be beyond practical resupply distances. Soldiers began to widen the existing portion of the road and slope the banks beyond mile 34, with Indian tea plantation contract laborers doing most of the rigorous manual labor.

Construction of the road followed the advancing combat forces as closely as possible. On 1 April 1943, the 45th Engineers organized to meet a possible Japanese attack. Enemy patrols had been sighted south of the road, not far from Ledo, and there were reports that others were operating to the north of the road. The 45th Engineers sent patrols out in both directions, but the threat diminished within a few days.[34]

During the monsoon seasons, soldiers working on the road strove to maintain what they had already constructed. The 10th Chinese Engineers, who arrived in March 1943, worked on drainage and built revetments. In the months that followed, new American units, including the 330th Engineer General Service Regiment and the 849th and 1883rd Engineer Aviation Battalions, the latter two African American units, arrived in theater. The 330th Engineers assumed the duties of clearing ground for the lead portion of the road beginning in August 1943, while the other organizations widened, improved, and bridged the road, and built adjacent airstrips and connecting combat roads. Engineer units on the road were joined by other units necessary for road operations: Three light pontoon bridge companies, including two African American units of this type, were deployed to bridge the swift mountain rivers and to operate ferries. The 45th Quartermaster Regiment was a unit whose trucks delivered surfacing materials and, later, supplied and provided transportation for newly arrived engineering units. Just prior to the end of the year, on 27 December 1943, the lead bulldozers reached Shingbwiyan, three days ahead of schedule. The most difficult part of the road was completed, but the job of widening, clearing and preventing slides, bridging, and managing the operations of the road, as well as completing it through the lower lands was yet to be accomplished. Much of the remaining planned portions of road construction, including routes to Myitkina and Bhamo, were still in the hands of the enemy forces.

The pontoon bridge companies, arriving in late 1943, deployed forward in January and February 1944 beyond Shingbwiyang to operate ferries and to build pontoon bridges. The 76th Engineer Light Pontoon Company, in February, deployed up the Ningham Combat Trail to the Tarung River, building a standard pneumatic float twelve-ton bridge, 470 feet long, the first in Burma and the first built in the construction of the road.[35] The bridge was not built under enemy fire, but the company's temporary encampment received harassing sniper and mortar fire. The 76th Engineers constructed a 540-foot pontoon pier on the Tarung River for use by the 209th Combat Engineer Battalion, a white unit constructing a fixed bridge across the river. One of the 76th Engineer's platoons widened and improved the Ningham Combat Trail in order to transport the larger pontoon bridging equipment forward to construct an 80-foot bridge farther up river. Since the unit had to maintain the combat trail to supply itself and its bridges, it sent a detachment back to Ledo to requisition dump trucks for use in this mission, but that detachment, on the return trip during monsoon season, was diverted at mile 55 to deliver gravel for washed-out sections of the road. The 76th Engineers found itself trying to maintain the Combat Trail during the monsoon without equipment. It had to replace a washed-out bridge when the Tarung River rose eleven feet in one day on 1 May 1944. Its ferries over the Tanai River could not be operated in June due to the swiftness of the rising river. The unit, stranded for six days, was moved across the river by assault boats. With the assistance of the 71st Pontoon Company, it built a 775-foot bridge over the Tawang River in eleven hours under the difficult conditions of the July floods. When not operating as bridging units, the pontoon companies, moving at times by cargo aircraft to the sites where they were most needed, helped to maintain roads and operate waterworks, or performed additional duties as construction soldiers.[36]

Other engineering units utilized the completed section of the road to construct B-29 Superfortress bomber airbases in India in early 1944. These bases would be used to bomb Japanese targets in China and in the Pacific Theater. The 382nd Engineer Construction Battalion arrived at Kharagpur in late January with the mission of building a limited operational airfield by 15 March 1944. The battalion left its organizational equipment on the road for continued use by other engineer units operating there. It was therefore dependent upon the China-Burma-India Theater Engineer District's equipment. The 382nd Engineers, not being an engineer aviation battalion, had very few qualified equipment operators for airfield construction at the commencement of this task. Through diligent hard work, the engineers met the target date, and remained for another 90 days to improve the airfield, bringing it up to fully operational status by 30 June.[37] The 1888th Engineer Aviation Battalion took over the construction of Piardoba Airfield in February 1944 from another battalion, inheriting a difficult schedule, which it met successfully. Neither enlisted men nor officers in this battalion possessed the full knowledge of airfield construction methods, but showed a "great willingness" to learn and adapt which resulted in completion of their task on schedule.

From the beginning, the Ledo Road was a combat support road as well as a potential main supply route into China. Along with the engineers, the Advance Section, performing administration duties for the command and control of construction in the region, acquired replacement soldiers to support the combat forces as well as to support soldiers constructing the highway, the airfields, and the fuel and water pipelines that ran adjacent to it. The 60th Ordnance Company maintained supply depots to stock forward ammunition points located along the road and along combat trails branching out from the road. African American laundry detachments at Ledo and Myitkyna, and a semi-mobile salvage repair company, were utilized in Advance Section Three. Truck convoys began operations as soon as enough of the road was open to enable the drivers to proceed. The 45th Quartermaster Regiment arrived in November 1943 to operate convoys between Ledo and Shingbwiyang and remained throughout the period of road operations.

In the early months of convoy operations, trucks transported supplies to support the engineers and combat forces, with little organized convoy operational control. Operating in the mud of the still developing road, trucks and other wheeled vehicles could only follow the combat forces and engineers as far as the road would take them. In the Burma campaign, Chinese, American, and Indian combat forces were often deployed deep within the jungles, and high in the Naga Hills, far removed from the nearest roads. Neither native porters nor pack mules could reach them throughout the monsoon season.

The only American infantry force in the theater was the 5307th Composite Unit (Provisional). Code Name: "GALAHAD," later it became popularly known as "Merrill's Marauders" named after its leader, Brigadier General Frank Merrill. This regiment-sized unit was formed into six combat teams (400 men per team), color-coded Red, White, Blue, Green, Orange and Khaki. Two teams were assigned to a battalion, with the remainder of its personnel formed into the Headquarters, and the Air Transport Commands Detachments.

To provide logistical support for these combat forces, the theater resorted to airdropping their required supplies. Experimental airdrops in March 1943 proved the most feasible method of supply delivery, despite the absence of trained parachute riggers, proper aircraft, or containers sturdy enough to withstand the impact of the airdrop. For the first airdrops, enlisted men of laundry and ordnance units packed and dropped supplies, utilizing basket containers and parachutes from a fighter aircraft control group and airplanes from the Ferry Command stationed at Chabua. By the end of the month, a regular airdropping organization had been improvised. Personnel of the 3841st Quartermaster Truck Company at Sookerating Air Base were used for warehousing, packing, and airdropping operations. African American personnel of the 3304th Quartermaster Truck Company, divided into seven detachments of one officer and nine enlisted men, were used to receive and process airdropped supplies at forward resupply stations.[38]

As the airdropping missions increased in scope, the 518th Quartermaster Battalion (Mobile), an African American battalion just arriving into the theater, was assigned the mission of procuring, warehousing, packing, and loading all subsistence and other vital supplies for air delivery. Its headquarters and two companies worked out of Dinjan. The other two companies deployed to Sookerating Air Base. The 3841st Quartermaster Company, now supplemented by additional volunteers, was attached to this battalion for duty. Its personnel, divided between the two air bases, continued as the "kickers," personnel who rode the airplanes of the 2nd Troop Carrier Squadron. Their duties were pushing packaged supplies from the open doors of the C-47 cargo airplanes in flight over the designated targets area. Two detachments of one officer and four enlisted men of the 518th Quartermasters deployed to forward areas to assist the 3304th Truck Company in its receiving and issuing supply duties. These African American detachments sent back periodic After Action Reports on the effectiveness of the airdrops and provided valuable information in the development of improved airdropping techniques and standard operating procedures.

In November 1943, when Chinese soldiers launched an offensive drive into the Hukawng Valley, supplies were directly airdropped to the receiving combat soldiers, and the 3304th Truck Company was relieved of its resupply duties and returned to its original transportation support mission.[39] Nineteen Chinese and two Indian infantry divisions, as well as the American 5307th Composite Unit, received their supplies solely through this method. The 518th Quartermasters continued its air resupply duties until the end of December 1944, when it was relieved to begin convoy duties on the now nearly completed Ledo Road. Sufficient specialized provisional airdropping units had by now been organized and were being deployed to the combat theaters.

During the period of its airdropping duties, the 518th Quartermasters, with less than ten days of instruction and orientation in its new assignment, experimented with, packed, and dropped a number of unusual items, including the first 75-mm pack howitzer airdropped in Burma, oil and gasoline in 55-gallon drums lashed with rope around sacks of rice husks used to absorb the impact, ammunition carts cut into sections so that they could get through the aircraft doors, delicate medical supplies and instruments, bulky operating tables and generators, blood plasma, and even live ducks and fresh eggs for special holidays. The 518th Quartermasters operated virtually a specialized sub-depot, shifting its personnel about so that they all were trained in every phase of air delivery methodology. The 518th Quartermasters also instructed the personnel of other organizations for airdropping duties. The battalion was proud that it used only its own organic personnel, other than native personnel for manual labor and less technical work, and that it never allowed the aircraft of the air cargo squadrons to remain idle while waiting for packaged supplies.

When the monsoon was over in October 1944, completion of the Ledo Road was in sight. By this point in the war, sufficient American forces had been trained and mobilized to allow additional engineer soldiers to deploy to the theater to reinforce the road builders. Among them were more African American units, including the 1327th Engineer General Service Regiment, flown in directly from the United States. Also, the 352nd Engineer General Service Regiment, which, since January 1943, had been building and maintaining highways, railroads, and airfields throughout Iran for the Russian lend-lease supply route.[40] Every available truck and driver was being assigned to convoy service in order to deliver urgently needed supplies. In December 1944, 36 of the 59 quartermaster truck companies assigned to the China-Burma-India Theater were African American. The call also went out for volunteer truck drivers to supplement the drivers on the route into China.

By early January 1945, the first convoy was readying at Ledo to move over the road to Kunming, China. It began to move before the road was completed and cleared of the still-fighting Japanese soldiers. At first, it was thought that a critical situation might arise over the use of African American drivers in China, but the Chinese government, which had opposed the use of African Americans in its territory, permitted the drivers to go as far as Kunming. China authorities requested that unless the tactical situation demanded it, African American units not be used east of Kunming. Fueled by the prejudice and racism spread by white Americans, the Chinese government did not want to expose their people to the "inferior" African American soldiers. The western Chinese had never seen African American soldiers, Generalissimo Chiang explained, and he felt it better not to send them there unless absolutely required.[41] The first convoy consisted of 50 African American and 50 Chinese drivers. These Chinese drivers were specially trained for the convoy and were prepared to assume the drivers' duties upon the convoy's entering Kunming. Also on the first convoy were eight white American enlisted men: one truck master, four section leaders, one mechanic, one medical corpsman, and one ambulance driver. The number of African Americans remaining after the Chinese ruling was reduced to ten, with two African American war correspondents included.[42] The China restriction did not interfere with future convoys on what was now renamed the Stilwell Road.

For operations on the Stilwell Road, officially commencing 1 February 1945, 58 truck companies assigned to three groups and eleven battalion headquarters were in use when the Motor Transport Service was formally organized on 25 February. Of the 58 truck companies, 52 were African American; the three groups and nine of the battalion headquarters were also staffed with African American junior officers and enlisted men. In addition to the African American truck companies were one service and one railhead company being utilized as truck companies. Remaining on the road for maintenance and continuing construction at this time were four engineer general service regiments, three of them African American; seven engineer aviation battalions, four of them African American; two dump truck companies, both African American; and two light pontoon bridging companies, one of which was African American. The first engineer unit to deploy into China to work on the Stilwell Road was the 858th Engineer Aviation Battalion, which arrived in May 1945 to maintain the road from the Salween River to Kunming, China. This unit, the only African American battalion sent into China, remained there until the war ended as one of two engineering battalions then working on the China portion of the Stilwell Road. Its companies, with the white 71st Light Pontoon Company attached for maintenance between the Salween River and the China border, eventually constructed roads to a point nearly 500 miles east of Kunming.[43]

In addition to the medical dispensaries of the engineering units located along the convoy route, the 335th Station Hospital, one of the four African American field hospitals organized for overseas duty, was located at the 80-mile mark, at Tagap, Burma. From excess personnel of this unit the 383rd Station Hospital was activated as of 6 December 1944.[44] Both units operated at Tagap, with the 383rd Station Hospital attached to the 335th for command and control. With the high concentration of African American soldiers in this theater, these two hospitals were the only ones along the road operating "strictly in the manner for which they were designed," to provide segregated medical care strictly for African American soldiers.[45]

Other units previously working on the Stilwell Road relocated to airfields, to the sub-base at Myitkina, and to supply depots at Ledo, whose work level increased to meet rising demands for additional equipment. The quartermaster section at Ledo acquired the 547th Quartermaster Depot Company, one of two African American units of this type, "and an exceptionally good one," in late 1944.[46] This unit specialized in managing and operating supply depots, and was the only company of this type in the theater. After the command lost this company to duties in China in May 1945, it utilized the 43rd Veterinary Company, converted to a composite supply platoon, and the 2nd Veterinary Company on temporary duty.[47] Both of these were African American units.

In their work on the Stilwell Road and on supporting and operating missions in the Advance Section of the China-Burma-India Theater, African American units were fully utilized, mainly in the duties for which they were trained. This theater had a low priority on personnel and supplies and it was the one theater where, for most of its existence, a logistics

Army trucks wind along the side of the mountain over the Ledo supply road now open from India into Burma, 1944. (National Archives)

and engineering mission was the primary focus. The construction of the Stilwell Road took precedence over combat operations. The vast majority of personnel in this theater were designated to provide a route for the transportation of supplies from India to China.

COMBAT SERVICE SUPPORT DEPLOYMENTS

It was in the ports, base sections, and depots that the great majority of African American service units were utilized overseas. Aside from the theaters previously mentioned, in the Persian Gulf, in accordance to its operations order, in the initial landing of American soldiers, there was a requirement for an African American quartermaster unit, the 2nd Platoon, 350th Quartermaster Company. In its second priority requirement were two African American port battalions, the 480th and 481st Port Battalions, and the 49th Truck Regiment. In its third requirement were the 352nd and 357th Engineer General Service Regiments, and the 435th and 436th Dump Truck Companies. As the worldwide deployment of the United States Army increased after mid–1944, and as the greater number of African Americans inducted into the army in 1942 and 1943 became available in units completing their training in either their original or converted forms, the proportions of African American soldiers deployed overseas increased rapidly. The requirements for combat service support elements also increased as American forces were deployed in greater numbers to the various theaters of combat. In March 1944, there were still 357,802 African American soldiers stationed in the United States as compared to 314,075 deployed overseas. By December 1944, the number overseas rose to 477,421, with only 214,000 remaining in the United States. By April 1945, there were 511,493 African Americans deployed in overseas theaters and 188,811 in the continental United States. This was the peak overseas figure of the war.[48] Of the 477,421 African American soldiers deployed overseas to every combat theater in December 1944, 169,678 were quartermaster soldiers, 111,012 were engineers, and 64,458 were transportation soldiers.[49] Of all the African American soldiers deployed overseas in December 1944, less than 4% were in the combat arms branches.

With so large a portion of the African American force overseas in the services and with the majority of the combat service support soldiers in rear echelon areas, a number of problems were faced by both the soldiers and by the theater commands. To many white soldiers and commanders, especially in the European Theater of Operations, the sole African American soldiers seen were those in the rear echelon areas, far removed from the rigors of front-line duty. Rear echelon soldiers are often despised by front-line soldiers, no matter what the color of the skin happens to be. This, coupled with the rumors of the lack of combat efficiency in the two African American infantry divisions, left an impression that African American soldiers were unfit for being utilized in battle, whereas it was a policy set forth by the military commanders that kept the majority of African American soldiers in these "rear echelon" positions.[50] In the towns and villages of the war-crowded British Isles, in North Africa, and in Italy, the problem of African American/civilian and African American/white soldier relationships sometimes became acute, although African American and civilians often got along much better than they were expected to and sometimes better than many white American soldiers thought they should.

With the arrival of increasingly large numbers of African American combat service support

General Eisenhower talks with an ammunition handler at Cherbourg, France, during a routine inspection, November 1944. (National Archives)

soldiers in the British Isles in 1942, the European Theater developed a well-defined policy intended to decrease friction between African American and white soldiers, and between American soldiers in general and the British population. This policy extended to the European continent after the D-Day invasion. The European Theater would have the largest concentration of African American soldiers deployed overseas of any theater. In the European Theater, there were 154,000 African American soldiers assigned in August 1944, as compared with 81,870 in the Mediterranean Theater, the next largest concentration at the time.[51] The concern for racial harmony was so great that in July 1942, General Eisenhower's headquarters issued a statement of policy:

1. The presence of Negro troops in this Theater will present a variety of problems that can only be solved by constant and close supervision of Commanding Officers. It is the desire of this Headquarters that discrimination against the Negro troops be sedulously avoided. So far as London and other cities and leave areas where both Negro and White soldiers will come on pass and furlough, it would be a practical impossibility to arrange for segregation so far as welfare and recreation facilities are concerned. The Red Cross has been notified that Negro soldiers will be accorded the same leaves and furlough privileges as other soldiers and consequently they can expect them to come into their clubs. The Red Cross has been informed that wherever it is not possible to provide separate accommodations, the Negro soldiers will be given the same accommodations in the clubs on the same basis as White soldiers.

2. A more difficult problem will exist in the vicinity of camps where both White and Negro soldiers are stationed, particularly with reference to dances and other social activities. This Headquarter will not attempt to issue any detailed instructions. Local Commanding Officers will be expected to use their own best judgment in avoiding discrimination due to race, but at the same time, minimizing causes of friction between White and Colored Troops. Rotation of pass privileges and similar methods suggest themselves for use, always with the guiding principle that any restriction imposed by Commanding Officers applies with equal force to both races.[52]

3. Carrying out this directive fell primarily to Major General John Lee, whose Services of Supply Command contained most of the African American soldiers in Great Britain. To his base section commanders and unit commanding officers he transmitted the directive, declaring that it "sets forth clearly and unmistakably, the basic principles which must guide every commanding officer in the exercise of his responsibilities of command. These fundamental principles, enunciated by the Theater Commander, are founded on fairness, justice, and common sense; they permit of no deviation or compromise."[53] Command attention addressing the problem of racial friction in the British Isles did not eliminate it entirely, but by May 1944, with over 1,500,000 American soldiers stationed there in preparation for the invasion of France, reports of racial incidents did not increase. Official concern that no untoward racial disturbance interfere with mounting an invasion from Great Britain led to certain administrative practices in the utilization of African American soldiers. Keeping the races separated as much as possible became the emphasis of the commanding officers. Port battalions and companies were separated by race and geographical location. For example, in the port city of Southampton, 25 of the 27 port companies were African American. In addition, eight truck companies, two truck battalions, three quartermaster service companies, a quartermaster fuel supply company, a quartermaster fumigation company, an engineer general service regiment, and the medical sanitation companies for handling and unloading wounded men, were composed of African American soldiers.

TRUCK DRIVERS — THE RED BALL EXPRESS

During the rapid advance of the Allied armies in Europe after the breakthrough at Avranches, France, in August 1944, the movement of large tonnages of supplies to the 1st, 3rd and 9th U.S. Armies, and later the 7th Army became imperative. The French railway system had been almost totally destroyed by retreating German armies and attack aircraft of the United States 9th Air Force. To meet the logistical requirements, the Transportation Corps devised the Red Ball Plan on 21 August 1944, and implemented it four days later. This plan called for two one-way reserved highway routes marked "Red Ball Trucks Only." The original route, from St. Lo to Paris and return, was later extended to Sommesous, Reims, and Hirson. Red Ball convoys operated from 25 August until 13 November 1944. The truck drivers carried 412,193 tons of supplies to the armies, covering a total of 121,873,929 tonnage miles during this period. On the average day, 899 vehicles deployed forward, traveling 1,504,616 ton-miles. The average time for the trip to Paris and return to St. Lo was 53.4 hours; the maximum number of truck units operating on the route was 140, supplemented at the height of operations by trucks manned by personnel of combat units and other combat support services. The majority of the units and enlisted personnel participating in the operation were African Americans. Seventy-three percent of the truck companies in the Motor Transport Service in the European Theater were manned by African American soldiers.[54]

Supplementing the Red Ball Express and replacing it after its operations closed down were several others through highways modeled on its original concept. The White Ball Route transported supplies from Le Havre and Rouen to the forward support areas at Beauvais and Reims for the northern French and Belgian campaigns. Supplies shipped to rail transfer points at Paris, the White Ball began operating with six companies on 25 September, clearing the ports of Le Havre and Rouen as its first mission. The B-B (Bayeaux-Brussels) Red Lion Route transported 500 tons of British petroleum and other supplies daily from Bayeaux to the British 21st Army Group Roadhead 1 at Brussels for approximately thirty days, beginning 16 September 1944. Four of the nine truck companies on this route were African American. The ABC (Antwerp-Brussels-Charleroi) Route began to operate on 30 November. The Green Diamond Route, operating from 10 October through 1 November, ran between the ports and beaches of Normandy and Dol at the northern base of the Brest peninsula, passing through Avranches and Granville en route. Two truck battalions, one of which was African American, provided command and control for 19 truck companies on this route at its peak of operations. Two POL (petroleum, oil, and lubricants) battalions, the 467th and the 519th, the latter an African American unit, operated the POL routes of the Motor Transport Service. Operations for these units commenced on D-Day plus eight, deploying forward as pipelines were laid, loading from pipe taps and storage tanks along the line, and transporting POL to forward fuel depots for the rapidly advancing armies.[55] In the Advance Section of the Communications Zone, fuel supply companies like the 3877th Quartermaster Company (POL), a corps level asset, supported divisional soldiers. The 3917th Quartermaster Company (POL) supplied 3rd Army units from August 1944 through the end of the war. These units managed and operated the forward fuel depots, transporting fuel to divisional units, especially the armored divisions and separate tank battalions, which could consume up to 165,000 gallons of fuel per day.[56]

The role of the combat service support soldiers at the ports, the bases, and on the road, was usually that for which they were originally organized. Occasionally, an engineer general service regiment or a chemical company would be employed on guard, prisoner of war escort, or transportation duties in order to meet the war's rapidly changing requirements. The 1323rd and the 388th Engineer General Service Regiments, while stationed in Great Britain, formed seven truck companies, each with its own internal command structure. The 84th Chemical Smoke Generator Company, before deploying forward to provide smoke screens for 3rd Army's Moselle River Crossing at Arnaville, France, operated as a truck company, transporting supplies forward via the Red Ball Express Route.

In the North Africa and Mediterranean campaigns, earlier in the war, the 22nd Quartermaster Truck Group, as the 22nd Quartermaster Truck Regiment, landed at Casablanca on 18 November 1942 in the D-Day plus five convoy of the Western Task Force. They operated convoys for both American and French forces, and trained 3,500 French enlisted men in the operation and maintenance of the lend-lease American vehicles. At Naples, beginning in October 1943, the 22nd Quartermasters operated a civilian truck pool and in April 1944, it began training Italian truck companies. As the 22nd Quartermaster Group, it had both African American and white battalions under its operational control. The group consisted of 15 separate African American truck battalions, four white truck battalions, two British truck battalions, seven Italian battalions, and two African American service companies. While the group headquarters staff and the separate battalions headquarters staff were all white, the

These drivers of the 666th Quartermaster Truck Company, attached to the 82nd Airborne Division, who totaled up 20,000 miles each without an accident, since arriving in the European Theater of Operations. Left to right: T/5 Sherman Hughes, T/5 Hudson Murphy, PFC Zacariah Gibbs, May 1945. (National Archives 208-AA-32P-3)

enlisted men and some of the junior officers were African Americans. Its units performed efficiently with its two original battalions, the 37th and the 110th, plus the 125th Truck Battalion, all African American units, were the first truck battalions in the theater to be awarded the Meritorious Service Plaque. The group allowed no segregation among its officers, and used a single standard for promotions. It departed from general army policy by promoting African American officers to positions where they would have subordinate white officers. This policy was more of an exception to the rule as African American officers commanded only two of its companies.[57]

COMBAT SUPPORT UNITS

Most African American combat service support units remained part of the rear echelon, assigned to the Communications Zone for command and control. The difference between combat service support and combat support is that soldiers assigned to combat support missions have direct interaction with the infantry or armored forces that they're supporting. Often these units are attached to a division or regiment for a specific mission, and in some cases, for the duration of the war. Many African American combat support units were assigned as elements of landing assault forces or attached to divisions or other combat units engaged in front-line battle.

African American units in the Pacific Theater landing forces usually consisted of quartermasters, port personnel, or combat engineers attached to infantry divisions, engineer special brigades, construction groups, or boat and shore battalions. These forces, acting first as combat support forces, reverted to a garrison force once the island was declared secure. For the invasion of Angaur in the Palaus Islands on 17 September 1944, the assault echelon contained an African American engineer aviation battalion and a port company among other service units required for immediate use on the beaches. One port company and a platoon of a quartermaster service company were attached to the 81st Infantry Division for its landings. The first echelon also included a quartermaster service company, an engineer service company, and a laundry truck company. A DUKW (an acronym based on D-model year 1942, U-amphibian, K-all wheel drive, W-dual rear axles) company was assigned to transport the assault forces. This unique unit's primary function was to ferry ammunition, supplies, and equipment from supply ships in transport areas offshore to supply depots and combat forces at the beachhead. Commonly referred to as "duck," the DUKW, which operated on land or sea, was shaped like a boat. It had a hollow airtight body for buoyancy and used a single propeller for forward momentum. It was designed according to army specifications and was based on the frame and chassis of the standard army 2.5-ton truck. The vehicle had a capacity of transporting 25 soldiers and their equipment, a 105-mm howitzer, or 5,000 pounds of general cargo. At sea the vehicle could maintain a speed of 5 knots, and on land it could attain a speed of 50 miles per hour. The United States produced 20,000 DUKWs during World War II.

When the assault forces departed Humboldt Bay, New Guinea, on 13 October 1944 to participate in the Leyte invasion on 20 October, the 609th Port Company had one platoon attached to each of the three infantry battalions of the 34th Infantry Regiment. Each platoon was assigned to a separate ship with the battalion to which it was attached. While the ships were under fire, the three platoons of the 609th Port Company assisted in unloading soldiers and equipment. Two of the platoons proceeded to shore, establishing supply points where the infantry had just advanced 200 yards inland beyond the beaches. The third platoon transferred to a Navy supply ship and discharged cargo until nightfall. Throughout the night, the port platoon received intense small arms and automatic weapons fire, suffering their first casualties.

The next morning, the two platoons on shore returned to the ships to complete their cargo unloading tasks. For the next three days, while enemy aircraft attacked the harbor, the entire company, minus the headquarters staff, remained, unloading the liberty ships of the convoy. A burning Japanese bomber, hit by American antiaircraft fire, went into a dive and struck a vessel where the 609th's soldiers were unloading supplies in the ship's hold, causing additional casualties. Two days later, a typhoon injured two other soldiers operating a resupply point on the beach. While men of the company were salvaging cargo in another ship that was damaged by enemy bombs, another explosion killed three men, while two others were severely burned. The 609th Port Company remained on the beaches throughout December, unloading, sorting, and transporting supplies throughout continuous air attacks. On 10 December, another explosion of unknown cause killed and wounded several other soldiers. These were the inherent dangers of handling hazardous cargo such as fuel and ammunition in a combat zone. Despite the air attacks, which caused additional casualties, the unit averaged 300 tons of supplies transported during an eight-hour period.[58]

During the Iwo Jima assault landings, commencing on 19 February 1945, there were several African American combat support units that were assigned to the Garrison Force. While this was primarily a Marine Corps combat operation, some of the combat support duties were performed by African American army units. They included a quartermaster company, two quartermaster service companies, a salvage repair company, a truck company, an amphibian truck (DUKW) company, two aviation support squadrons, one aviation engineer battalion, and a medical sanitary company. The 442nd and 592nd Port Companies and the 471st, 473rd and 476th Amphibian Truck Companies were assigned to the Garrison Force, but attached to the V Amphibious Corps (Marines) for the assault. One port company remained attached to the V Amphibious Corps, while the others were directly attached to the 5th Marine Division. One DUKW company was attached to the 13th Marine Regiment, a second DUKW company remained with the V Amphibious Corps, and the third was attached to the 4th Marine Division with the primary task of transporting ammunition and cargo ashore for the 14th Marine Regiment, and evacuating the wounded marines from the beaches to the hospital ships.[59]

The 592nd Port Company, divided into three sections, landed in the fourth assault wave and began unloading small supply boats as they arrived on the beach. Three of its crane operators were attached to the 5th Pioneer Battalion, where they operated eight-ton cranes on the beach. The Marine Corps, for their outstanding work in the Iwo Jima landings, gave the DUKW companies commendations for transporting ammunition and supplies between ship and shore, and then returning with the wounded from the beaches.

Occasionally, special purpose units were employed in the amphibious assault landings. At Salerno, in the first Mediterranean assault landing to use smoke screens extensively, navy and army chemical units laid smoke screens over an area 20 miles long in order to screen landing craft from enemy fire. In the D-Day assault on 9 September 1943, a detachment of the 24th Chemical Decontamination Company, equipped with M1 smoke pods, and navy personnel with smoke generators mounted in boats, screened the Paestum beaches where the ships were being unloaded. During the following days, the personnel of the 24th were trained on and operated 36 naval mechanical smoke generators ashore. The men laid a smoke haze daily at twilight to conceal anchorage and the unloading areas from enemy aircraft attacks, and screened the beaches during air attack alerts. Smoke generated usually covered an area of a 20 to 30 square mile radius. An enemy bomb did not hit a single allied ship that was hidden by the smoke screen.[60] The 24th Chemical Decontamination Company, along with other chemical companies, deployed to Naples, Italy, to maintain the smoke screens for the advancing forces at that location. For the Anzio landings on 22 January 1944, the 24th Chemical Decontamination Company was attached to VI Corps to provide a smoke concealment as needed. Equipped with eight large Navy smoke generators and a quantity of smoke pods, they went ashore, laying the first screen on 24 January. Additional Navy generators were brought ashore later. A British smoke unit took over the operation of smoke pods on 8 February, allowing the 24th Chemical Decontamination Company to operate the 36 mechanical smoke generators. These two units ran the antiaircraft smoke screen until 24 February, when the 179th Smoke Generator Company arrived and extended the smoke line to Nettuno, Italy. At Anzio the smoke operators shared the rigors of front-line infantrymen, living in their foxholes. For its performance at Anzio, the 24th Chemical Decontamination Company received one of the first four 5th Army plaques, and the first awarded to a chemical unit. The company later performed the duties of managing and operating chemical depots.

The first platoon of the 387th Engineer Battalion (Separate) landed in the initial assault wave at Anzio, going ashore from a Landing Craft Tank (LCT) at 0400 on 22 January 1944 with the advance party two miles south of Nettuno. The remainder of Companies B and D, after sitting through two air attacks on a Landing Ship Tank (LST) offshore, landed in the afternoon. Separate engineer battalions were organized to perform only basic engineering tasks and did not receive any type of specialized training with heavy equipment. The 387th Engineers prepared defensive fighting positions, erected shelter tents, and began unloading supplies. The rest of the battalion, though arriving later on D-Day, had to wait, as corps element soldiers, until the next morning to land. Utilizing hand tools, they worked on improving roads, cleared mine fields to enable medical personnel to evacuate the wounded, unloaded supplies from ships into the DUKW's, and handled supplies on the beaches through the many weeks of day and night air and artillery attacks. For seven days, the 500 men of the battalion averaged 1,940 tons of supplies unloaded per day, all completed manually.

Gradually the companies of the 387th Engineers were released from port duties. They moved to construction operations of the engineer depot, maintenance of the runway at the Nettuno Airport, and the operation of quarries. At times, they were attached to white combat engineer and aviation engineering units. This battalion, described by the Associated Press in a dispatch of 29 February 1944 as having been under "more fire than any other Negro unit in the 5th Army," remained at the Anzio-Nettuno beachhead for five months. It lost four officers and eleven enlisted men killed, three officers and 58 enlisted men wounded, and

T/5 Dexter Clayton and M/Sgt. Nelson T. Ewing are tying wire to a pole in France, 25 July 1944. (National Archives 111-SC-191834-S)

received three Silver Star medals for gallantry during this period.⁶¹ During the attack on Rome, it maintained the Nettuno-La Ferriere and, later, the Anzio roads. It operated asphalt mixing plants, salvaged steel, repaired anti-submarine cables, operated trash and rubbish dumps, unloaded Bailey bridges, and furnished bulldozers, air compressors, and motorized graders for various jobs, all in heavily mined areas.

While attached to the African American 92nd Engineer General Service Regiment for operations on 9 June 1944, one of its companies removed its first Bailey portable bridge. The 387th Engineers returned to Anzio at the end of June. There it relieved the 540th Combat Engineer Battalion, a unit with which it had worked during the initial beachhead operations. Now, the unit built and removed Bailey bridges. Designed by British engineer Sir Robert Bailey, these portable bridges were utilized in every theater of the war. Two of the battalion's companies converted to bridge companies in support of the American IV Corps and the French Expeditionary Corps. The companies had to learn quickly the nomenclature and the loading method for all Bailey and treadway bridge parts, train 30 new drivers for 2.5-ton trucks that transported the bridging equipment, and instruct eight new drivers for the six-ton Brockway Bridge construction trucks (vehicles that mounted huge hydraulic cranes for lifting and placing bridge parts). They required additional mechanics to maintain this equipment, which was already in unsatisfactory condition when they received it. These companies delivered bridges to combat engineers, a task on which one officer and two enlisted men lost their lives. Another company took over the operations of the 5th Army Bridge Depot on 5 July 1944, learning all new terms, operating new types of river crossing equipment, and learning to repair pneumatic floats, assault boats, and floating Bailey bridges. When two other bridge depots opened, the company also operated these, training two Italian engineer companies to perform the bulk of the manual labor. These depots deployed forward by leapfrogging, following the combat units of the 5th Army.

Vernon C. Stephens, while stationed in Italy, was attached to a glider detachment of the 517th Airborne Infantry Regiment. He was one of three African American engineers attached to that unit. He had joined the North Carolina National Guard segregated engineer detachment as a teenager in 1936. By the beginning of World War II, he had switched over to the regular army, and was assigned as an engineer at Pearl Harbor. Surviving the Japanese attack, he was soon deployed to Liverpool, England, then to North Africa, Sardinia, Sicily, and finally on to Italy. Stephens had volunteered to attend every course being offered and later received parachute training with the 555th Airborne Infantry Company. As he was being loaded into the glider for an airborne assault, the sergeant told him, "Now, you're not supposed to be on here with these white people. If they kill you, don't say nothing." Stephens recalls replying, "They won't bother me, I hope. I got on there with 'em; they didn't bother me. They spoke to me just as nice."⁶² He was one of the few African American soldiers that would participate in an airborne assault during World War II.

For the larger landings at Normandy, France, on 6 June 1944, very few African American soldiers were utilized in the initial assault. The 1st United States Army's assault force on D-Day at Omaha Beach contained fewer than 500 African American soldiers out of a total of 29,714 troops that participated in the initial attack. These were the soldiers of one section of the 3275th Quartermaster Service Company and the 320th Antiaircraft Balloon Battalion (Vertical Low Altitude) minus one battery. One soldier in the 320th who distinguished himself above many others that day was Corporal Waverly B. Woodson, Jr. Serving as a medical corpsman within the battalion, Corporal Woodson rode an LST onto Omaha Beach in the third wave and suffered shrapnel wounds when the vessel struck a mine as it approached the

A platoon of combat engineers surrounds a farmhouse in a town in France, as they prepare to eliminate a German sniper holding up an advance. Omaha Beachhead, near Vierville-sur-Mer, France, 10 June 1944. (National Archives 111-SC-190120)

landing site. Disembarking while under continuous mortar and machine gun fire, Woodson assisted in establishing an aid station on the beach and remained on continuous duty in treating casualties for the next 18 hours. He then assisted in retrieving and reviving three soldiers who had nearly drowned while leaving a landing craft which had slipped its anchor and drifted into deep water. Corporal Woodson was then hospitalized for treatment of the wounds he had received the previous day. For his valor that day, Corporal Woodson would be awarded the Bronze Star Medal.[63]

In the force of 31,912 troops landing on Utah Beach, 1,200 African American soldiers were deployed with the initial assault force. These were soldiers of the remaining battery of the 320th Antiaircraft Balloon Battalion, the 582nd Engineer Dump Truck Company, the 385th Quartermaster Truck Company, and the 490th Port Battalion with its 226th, 227th, 228th, and 229th Port Companies. In the follow-up forces arriving later on D-Day after the beaches had been secured, and on the ensuing days when more of the needed combat support units had come ashore, including quartermaster truck companies that were attached directly to the infantry and armored divisions for transporting soldiers and equipment, the 100th Ordnance Ammunition Battalion arrived. It was to supply ammunition for 1st Army's drive across Europe, amphibian truck companies to work across the beaches and later at heavily damaged ports like Cherbourg and Le Havre, and the medical sanitary companies for the evacuation of the wounded back to England. Though they were neither trained nor equipped for this mission, truck and transportation companies attached to combat divisions had frequent contacts with the enemy and often joined in the fighting. Some of these units were attached so long to the same divisions that they were treated as its organic units. The commander of the 22nd Infantry Regiment, 4th Infantry Division, motorized by the attachment of two African American truck companies, described their actions as part of a special task force attacking German positions south of St. Lo, France, when, shortly after daylight, the regiment encountered the enemy:

> As daylight neared, confusion mounted. Our columns clogged in endless traffic jams, bogged down in bomb craters, crawled through detours over broken fields, struggled across improvised stream crossings. All around us, the night erupted with flaming towns, German artillery and bombs added to the confusion. Every once in a while a huge German tank would pound out of the darkness and cut into our column, thinking it his. Running fights ebbed and flowed about us. As daylight broke, we were literally cheek by jowl with the Germans — in the same villages, in the same fields, in the same hedgerows, in the same farm yards. A hundred sporadic fights broke out to the front, to the flanks, to the rear, within the columns, everywhere. It was early that morning that I first became aware of the fact that our Negro truck drivers were leaving their trucks and whooping it up after German soldiers all over the landscape. This, I might add, is not hearsay. I personally saw it over and over again in the early hours of that wild morning. But in addition to my own personal observation, many reports reached me throughout the day of the voluntary participation of these troops in battle and their gallant conduct.[64]

The 3398th Quartermaster Truck Company, attached to the 6th Armored Division moving into Brittany, put out its defenses and joined an armed reconnaissance with other units in division supply trains when it was reported that over 200 enemy soldiers were headed for the area where this truck company was located. Late in the afternoon, eight German attack fighter aircraft strafed and bombed the truck convoy. Two officers and enlisted men of the company captured a German pilot that had parachuted from one of three planes shot down by truck-mounted .50-caliber machine guns. Enemy planes attacked the company's convoys thereafter, and shrapnel and shellfire struck trucks.[65] The 57th Ordnance Ammunition Company, during the pursuit across France, found itself engaging 65 of the enemy soldiers at Peronne when no other American units were in the area. It killed 50 and captured the other 15. Members of the unit were awarded two French croix de guerre, one Silver Star, and one Bronze Star for their valor in combat.[66]

Another transportation unit, the 666th Truck Battalion, while supporting the 82nd and 101st Airborne Divisions during Operation Market Garden in Holland, had trucks destroyed and drivers killed and wounded during the enemy bombings of "Hell Highway," the route between Eindhoven and Nijmegen. While transporting soldiers of the 82nd Airborne Division after the Battle of the Bulge in February 1945, it had several trucks shelled near Schmitt, Germany, with the losses of both airborne infantrymen and drivers. Enemy shells and bombs were not the unit's only concern. It considered its greatest difficulties to be shell fragments, glass, bullets, and cartridge cases exposed in the roadways when warmer weather cleared the roads of snow and ice. In one 24-hour period, the company had over 100 tire punctures on its 40 vehicles. The 666th transported forward 2,800 tons of supplies and 17,350 soldiers for 188,587 vehicle miles over icy and snowbound roads between 1 January and 31 March 1945. For its "outstanding accomplishments" it received a formal commendation from the commander of III Corps.[67]

Medical ambulance companies were often as close to the enemy and as closely associated with forward combat units as the truck companies. The 588th Medical Ambulance Company, attached to the 66th Medical Group, worked in such close support of the 7th Armored

This combat engineer crew is demonstrating clearing mines around telephone poles in France. Left to right: M/Sgt. Bennie Burns, Sgt. Vincent McNeill, Sgt. Frank Mack, Pfc. Riggles McCutcheon, T/Sgt. John A. Barbee, and Sgt. Thomas G. Alexander, 13 July 1944. (National Archives 111-SC-191360-S)

Division as it spearheaded the XX Corps' drive across France that its ambulances were an integral part of the division so far as rations, gasoline, convoys, communications, priorities in bridge crossings, and bivouac sites were concerned. Armored divisions and their medical companies moved so fast that the distance of the ambulance's trip to transport wounded soldiers from battalion aid stations to the combat support hospitals in the rear was usually twice that of ambulances attached to the infantry divisions.

Early in the Battle of the Bulge, on 20 December 1944, the enemy attacked the 7th Armored Division's supply convoys near Samree, Belgium. The division's quartermaster, with soldiers of its own unit, attached African American soldiers of the 3967th Troop Transport Company, and a platoon of antiaircraft guns from Battery D, 203rd Antiaircraft Artillery Automatics Weapons Battalion, threw up a defense and held off the enemy attack for over four hours while awaiting reinforcements from the 3rd Armored Division that was located to their north. Medium tanks dispatched to relieve the embattled soldiers never arrived. The antiaircraft gunners lost their weapons to enemy fire, but not before they destroyed two enemy tanks and had depleted all of their ammunition. With their ammunition exhausted, the quartermaster and antiaircraft soldiers were forced to retreat. After the Battle of the Bulge, the 7th Armored Division equipped and trained each of its support units, including the 3967th Troop Transport Company, with a 57-mm antitank gun for defense. Both white and African American combat support soldiers found themselves fighting as infantrymen during the battle to halt the enemy advance.[68]

With the cessation of hostilities, the requirements for combat service support units became even more prevalent, while the role of the combat forces diminished. The rebuilding of war-ravaged countries required the extensive use of engineer, transportation and quartermaster units. In Europe, they assisted in the clearing of minefields, providing supplies that were essential to restoring countries back to normalcy, and reestablishing the transportation and communications systems. In the Pacific Theater, the combat service support soldiers had the arduous task of closing out installations on islands that were no longer being utilized. This often included dismantling airfields, evacuating supplies, and disinterring bodies from American cemeteries. Many African American soldiers volunteered to remain overseas as opposed to returning to a segregated United States.

While gaining very little recognition, the Combat Service Support Units of World War II performed an invaluable service without which total victory could never have been achieved. But this war would change the face of America. The prejudices against and stereotypes of the African American soldier had changed after nearly four years of fighting in every theater of the war. African American combat service support soldiers would put their lives on the line to accomplish their mission. Often exposed on the front lines, they carried out their tasks supporting their fellow soldiers regardless of race. They worked side-by-side with white combat service support units in order to accomplish the mission.

Chapter V

Women's Army Corps

OVER 150,000 AMERICAN WOMEN SERVED IN THE Women's Army Corps (WAC) during World War II. Members of the Women's Army Corps were the first women other than nurses to serve within the ranks of the United States Army. Both the army and the American public initially had difficulty accepting the concept of women in uniform. However, political and military leaders, faced with fighting a global conflict and supplying men and materiel for that war while continuing to manufacture and transport lend-lease equipment to the Allies, soon realized that women could provide the additional resources so desperately needed within the military and industrial sectors.

Early in 1941 Congresswoman Edith Nourse Rogers of Massachusetts met with General George C. Marshall, the Army's Chief of Staff, and informed him that she intended to introduce a bill to establish an Army Women's Corps, separate and distinct from the existing Army Nurse Corps. Congresswoman Rogers remembered the female civilians who had served overseas with the United States Army under contract and as volunteers during World War I, working as communications specialists and dietitians. Because these women had served the army as contractors without the benefit of official status, they had to obtain their own food and quarters, and they received no legal protection or medical care. Upon their return to the United States, they were not entitled to the disability benefits or pensions which were available to United States military veterans. Congresswoman Rogers was determined that if women were to serve again with the army in a wartime theater they would receive the same legal protection and benefits as their male counterparts.[1]

The Women's Army Auxiliary Corps (WAAC) was established to work with the army, "for the purpose of making available to the national defense the knowledge, skill, and special training of the women of the nation." The army would provide up to 150,000 "auxiliaries" with food, uniforms, living quarters, pay, and medical care. Women officers would not be allowed to command men. The Director of the Women's Army Auxiliary Corps was originally assigned the rank of major. Women's Army Auxiliary Corps first, second, and third officers served as the equivalents of captains and lieutenants in the regular army, but received less pay than their male counterparts of similar rank. For example, although the duties of a Women's Army Auxiliary Corps first officer were comparable to those of a male captain, she received pay equivalent to that of a male first lieutenant. Enlisted women, referred to as "aux-

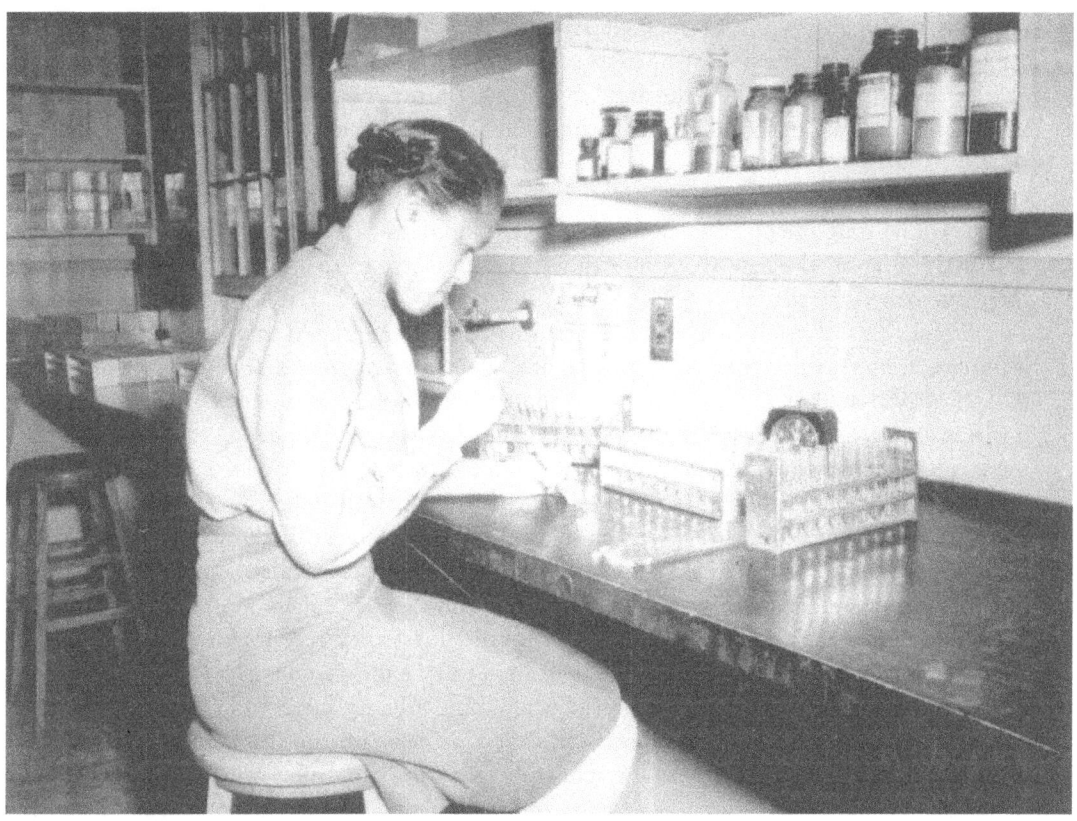

Private First Class Johnnie Mae Welton, laboratory technician trainee, conducts an experiment in the serology laboratory of the Fort Jackson Station Hospital, Fort Jackson, SC, 20 March 1944. (National Archives, 111-SC-34153)

iliaries," were ranked in descending order from chief leader, a position comparable to master sergeant in the regular army, through junior leader, comparable to corporal, and down to auxiliary, comparable to private.[2]

Congresswoman Rogers introduced her bill in Congress in May 1941, but it failed to receive serious consideration until after the Japanese attack on Pearl Harbor in December. General Marshall's active support and congressional testimony helped get the Rogers Bill through Congress. General Marshall believed that the two-front war in which the United States was engaged would cause an eventual manpower shortage. The army could ill afford to spend the time and money necessary to train men in essential service skills such as typing and switchboard operations when highly trained women were already available who could perform these tasks. General Marshall and others felt that women were inherently suited to certain critical communications jobs which, while repetitious, demanded high levels of manual dexterity. They believed that men tended to become impatient with such tasks and might make careless mistakes, which could be costly during war. After a long and acrimonious debate, which filled ninety-eight columns in the *Congressional Record,* the bill finally passed the House by a vote of 249 to 86. The Senate approved the bill 38 to 27 on 14 May 1942. When President Franklin D. Roosevelt signed the bill into law the next day, he set a recruitment goal of 25,000 for the first year. Women's Army Auxiliary Corps recruiting topped that goal by November, at which point Secretary of War Henry L. Stimson authorized enrollment be set at 150,000, the original ceiling set by Congress.

On 16 May 1942, Mrs. Oveta Culp Hobby, the wife of a former governor of Texas, took the oath of office as Director, Women's Army Auxiliary Corps, and would be assigned to the Services of Supply Division of the army. By 27 May, army recruiting stations were supplied with blank applications for officer candidates. The initial group of candidates would be highly selective. There would be no directly appointed officers, as had been the case with their male counterparts. All applicants would have to go through Officer's Candidate School. Male officers would train the first class of female officer candidates. The first class began on 20 July, and on 29 August, 436 new Women's Army Auxiliary Corps third officers (equivalent of second lieutenants) graduated.

From its conception in 1942, African American women were an integral part of the Women's Army Auxiliary Corps. When the first Women's Army Auxiliary Corps officer candidates arrived at Fort Des Moines, Iowa, there were 400 positions allocated, of which 40 positions were dedicated solely for African American women. Dubbed "ten-percenters," recruitment of African American women was limited to ten percent of the Women's Army Auxiliary Corps population, matching the approximate African American proportion of the national population. Later, the Women's Army Corps, like that of the regular army, was directed to accept 10.6 percent of its strength in African American recruits. The Women's Army Corps was totally dependant on voluntary service, and this percentage would never be met.

Columbia, South Carolina, native Charity Adams-Earley remembers a nation where even those who were willing to sacrifice their lives to save their country had to endure prejudice. It came as no surprise that when she entered the military she lived in segregated quarters with other African American women and served in a separate unit. Born in 1918, the oldest of four children of a minister and a teacher, she grew up in a family where reading was as natural as breathing. Her father was a scholar who was fluent in Greek and Hebrew. Her mother ensured the children used the English language correctly, even marking with a red pen the letters that Charity wrote to her from college. As valedictorian of Booker T. Washington High School, she selected to attend Wilberforce College, located in Ohio. After graduation, Adams returned to Columbia and taught for four years. In the summers she attended graduate school at Ohio State University. She had discovered a love for vocational psychology and hoped to earn a master's degree. In June of 1942 she received a letter, which was an invitation to join the Women's Army Auxiliary Corps. The letter focused on the career and leadership opportunities available. Miss Adams submitted the application and promptly forgot all about it. On her return trip to Ohio for graduate school her aunt met her at the railroad station in Knoxville with a telegram message to call home. The army was interested in her services. After completing the arduous process of health examinations and interviews, in July of 1942, Charity Adams was sworn into the Women's Army Auxiliary Corps as an officer candidate.[3]

Joining the other women who would be part of this first officer candidate class for the Women's Army Auxiliary Corps, Miss Adams found herself stationed at Fort Des Moines, Iowa. The 25 women, both African American and white, with whom she had traveled to Iowa had become close, but the army did not allow that closeness to last. Having traveled together, the women now found themselves segregated by race. Later, the African American women were visited by their commanding officer, who apologized for the army's segregation policy. All of the women, regardless of race, had similar quarters, and all had to adjust to the lack of privacy.

Within a few days, other women begin to arrive. Adams became part of the Third Platoon, the first 39 African American women, who had joined the military for a variety of reasons: to go to work, to change their lives, or to help to bring about a quick end to the war.

Some other women's service organizations had no intention of offering any opportunities to African American women at all. Later in life, Charity Adams-Earley comments, "Despite their differences, all these women had much in common. No real class differences existed among African Americans in that day, despite differences in income and education. All had lived in a world of daily discrimination." The Third Platoon bonded as they trained, supporting and bickering with each other much like members of a family, Adams-Earley recounts in her autobiography. "The women learned to drill, to read maps, to prepare for inspections, and in time, they became soldiers." In August of 1942, Charity Edna Adams became the first African American to be commissioned an officer in the Women's Army Auxiliary Corps. Alphabetically, she should have been the first woman of either race sworn in, but for this graduation, the army broke with tradition and each class was sworn in by platoon.[4]

Most African American organizations alleged that the policy of segregation in the military would deter the best-qualified African American women from enlistment. This possibility was recognized and provided for in the original War Department policy concerning African American in the Women's Army Auxiliary Corps, which stated: "There is a definite reluctance on the part of the best qualified colored women to volunteer in the Women's Army Auxiliary Corps. This is brought about by an impression on their part that they will not be well received or treated on posts where they may be stationed. This could be overcome by an intensive recruiting campaign with the idea in view of interesting the desired class of colored women in this project and arriving at a thorough understanding of their rights and privileges while in the service…. An eminently qualified person, preferably a Negro recruiter, will be sent out to colored colleges in order to secure the proper class of applicants."[5]

Definite instructions requiring the acceptance of African American applicants were sent out to recruiting stations. Noncompliance was discovered, but reported in only five cities and was corrected via telegraph in the Women's Army Auxiliary Corps' first week of recruiting. The cities were Pittsburgh, Pennsylvania; Winston-Salem, North Carolina; Columbia, South Carolina; Dallas, Texas; and St. Paul, Minnesota.[6] The work of investigating recruitment complaints was assigned to one of the first African American officer candidates to graduate, Third Officer Harriet West, of the Director of the Women's Army Auxiliary Corps staff, and a former assistant to Dr. Mary McCloud Bethune.[7] Although African American Women's Army Auxiliary Corps recruiting officers were sent to assist with the recruiting effort as soon as the first officer class graduated, African American recruits from the first months failed to meet expectations in either quantity or quality.

The Recruiting Command indicated that there were sufficient applications, but in some localities, as many as 85 percent allegedly failed the various aptitude and physical tests. The women were hampered by the same inequalities that African American males encountered. In a society where African Americans were regarded as second-class citizens, they often lacked the educational or technical skills required when evaluated against white Americans. Prejudices and discrimination in American society during the years of the Second World War played a major factor. Many men and women felt that it was not acceptable for females to serve in the military forces. Also, recruiting duty, which was delegated solely to white males, did not actively seek to recruit qualified African American females. Their primary focus at that early stage of the war was to recruit males for the vacancies of a rapidly expanding military force. The Second Service Command reported that, in the span of several months, it had only been able to secure one qualified African American typist and one clerk against its quota. Yet vocational and technical schools, especially in the larger northern cities, actively taught these skills to African American women.

Women auxiliaries Ruth Wade (left) and Lucille Mayo demonstrate their ability to service trucks at Fort Huachuca, Arizona, 8 December 1942. (National Archives 111-SC-16246)

Director Hobby had already done much to dispel the fear that African American women in the Women's Army Auxiliary Corps were neither wanted nor needed. Her first public address after her appointment as the director was at Howard University before members of a college sorority on 6 July 1942. She spoke of the high qualifications of the applicants for the first officers' class, explained that the first two African American Women's Army Auxiliary Corps companies, both commanded by African American female officers, would be stationed at Fort Huachuca in November, and announced that "she was certain that Negro women would serve faithfully and loyally in all parts of the Women's Army Auxiliary Corps."[8]

The assignment of African American Women's Army Auxiliary Corps personnel to military installations and stations was conditioned by the same considerations that governed the location of male units: "the presence of a military or civilian Negro population and the willingness of installations and station commanders to receive them." To clarify further the position of African American women within the corps, Military Personnel, Services of Supply, suggested that the policy of the director of the Women's Army Auxiliary Corps be specifically confirmed by instructing: (1) that there be no discrimination in the types of duties to which Negro women might be assigned; (2) that no lowering of standards to meet racial ratios be prescribed and that, therefore, intensive recruiting among Negro women be inaugurated; (3) that colored units be provided on the basis of 10.6 percent of the overall strength of the Women's Army Auxiliary Corps and that this percentage be maintained in each type of unit within the Women's Army Auxiliary Corps, thereby paralleling the policy for men in the army; and (4) that an eminently qualified person, preferably a Negro Women's Army Auxiliary Corps recruiting officer, be sent out to colleges "in order to secure the proper class of applicants for colored units of the Women's Army Auxiliary Corps."9 Each of these policies was adopted.

Third Officer Adams was soon assigned to the Third Company, Third Training Regiment, which had two white and one African American platoons. The army assigned all of the African American enlisted women recruits at Fort Des Moines and placed them all in two segregated companies. Soon the newly appointed officers were training all of the enlisted personnel, and in December the first group of Women's Army Auxiliary Corps trainees was transferred out to various army installations. Because African American recruits were few in number, Third Officer Adams and the other African American officers trained them in a wide variety of procedures, which normally would have been handled by specialist companies.

The Adjutant General had come to the conclusion that of the total of 628 military occupation skills listed in the army, 406 were suitable of being performed by women. A job was considered unsuitable if it required combat, considerable amounts of physical strength, or a working environment that was improper for women. All supervisory jobs were also deemed unsuitable for women. Using this list, the Adjutant General determined that in 1943, there would be 3,972,498 men in job positions that could be performed by women. That was over half of the army's strength to date. In the early months of 1943, it was determined to expand the Women's Army Auxiliary Corps in order to meet the expanding needs of the military.

With additional African American women entering the army, reports of their alleged unsatisfactory performance began to be reported to the highest levels. As was the case with the male soldiers, low Army General Classification Test scores were keeping many of the African American recruits from attending some of the more technical training. As was often done during the war, comparisons between white and African American test scores were used as a determining factor for the quality of the soldier. In a May 1943 sample, 66 percent of African American female recruits scored in the lowest two categories of the Army General Classification Test as compared to 15 percent of white female recruits; only 6 percent of African American female recruits scored in the upper two categories, as opposed to 43 percent of white female recruits.[10] In a further effort to discredit the abilities of African Americans, the Women's Army Auxiliary Corps Control Division commented that the problem was one of the Corps' most serious, and would become worse when the women reached the field. This was not to be the case, because in spite of lower test scores, local commanders gave high praise to the job performances of African American Women's Army Auxiliary Corps personnel.

Congress opened hearings in March 1943 on the conversion of the Women's Army Auxiliary Corps into the regular army. Army leaders asked for the authority to convert the Women's Army Auxiliary Corps into the Women's Army Corps, which would be a regular branch of the army rather than merely a supplementary auxiliary serving within it. The Women's Army Auxiliary Corps program had been an unqualified success, and the army received more requests for Women's Army Auxiliary Corps personnel than it could provide. Although Women's Army Auxiliary Corps personnel were desperately needed overseas, the army could not offer them the protection if captured or benefits if injured which the regular army soldiers received. The plans for an eventual second Allied front in Europe required a substantially larger military force, with many more positions that women could fill. Establishment of a Women's Army Corps with pay, privileges, and protection equal to that accorded to men was seen as a partial solution to the military's problem. On 3 July 1943, after a delay caused by congressional hearings, the Women's Army Corps bill was signed into law. All Women's Army Auxiliary Corps personnel were afforded the opportunity of joining the regular army as a member of the Women's Army Corps or returning to civilian life. Although the majority decided to enlist, 25 percent opted to leave the service at the time of conversion.[11]

With the conversion of the Women's Army Auxiliary Corps to the Women's Army Corps, former Women's Army Auxiliary Corps first, second, and third officers became captains and first and second lieutenants, respectively. Director Hobby was officially promoted to the rank of colonel; Women's Army Corps service commanders and theater staff directors were promoted to lieutenant colonels. Company commanders became captains or majors depending upon the size of their command and their time in service. Enlisted women were ranked as master sergeant through corporal and private, the same as their male counterparts.

In April of 1943, the Secretary of War's civilian aide on Negro affairs, Truman Gibson, sent the War Department a complaint that the "failure to give Negro women radio and other specialist training represented manipulation of test scores rather than the women's inaptitude." The training authorities formally denied this. In May, representatives of the NAACP called on upon Colonel McCoskrie at Fort Des Moines with the same and other complaints, and were again informed that women's alleged qualifications for radio and other training was not reflected upon their test scores. In September 1943, Truman Gibson again complained that "Negroes were being sent only to cooks' and bakers' school instead of to higher technical schools, and that white women were being assigned to field jobs, while Negro women were not." Colonel Hobbs in turn replied, "Negroes could and did go to every specialist school upon the same basis as other women, and in fact had received more educational attention than white women in an effort to make up their deficiencies and permit their assignment to military jobs."[12]

Most branches of the service were initially reluctant to accept any African Americans that scored in the lower Army General Classification Test categories for technical training. The Surgeon General's Office in 1943 and 1944, which was also reluctant to accept African American male soldiers into the Medical Corps, refused to accept African American Women's Army Corps personnel even as ward orderlies, stating, "No suitable assignments exist for such personnel upon completion of training and further accumulation of surplus colored Women's Army Corps enlisted women thus trained would constitute an increasing embarrassment to the service."[13] The Medical Corps utilized the majority of African American male soldiers in medical sanitary companies, which performed manual labor tasks. In order to appease opposition, a limited select few of the enlisted African American female recruits who met or exceeded the intelligence qualifications were successfully given training in such specialist fields as medical, surgical, laboratory, X-ray, and dental technicians. Army posts and air force installations where large numbers of African American soldiers were stationed, expressed a consistent eagerness to obtain African American Women's Army Corps clerical companies, which contained stenographers, typists and other office workers.

Once the African American Women's Army Corps companies completed training and began arriving at the various army installations, favorable reports came in on their stellar job performances in a number of varieties of administrative and technical skills. At Fort Jackson, South Carolina, a sergeant was the medical stenographer to the chief of general surgery. At Fort Bragg, North Carolina, a Technician 5th Class performed duties as the primary instructor at the recreational therapy section. At Fort McClellan, Alabama, 15 Women's Army Corps clerks operated the post locator section of the installation post office, forwarding mail and maintaining locator files on all the soldiers that processed through that base for training prior to overseas deployment. At the post hospital at Fort Riley, Kansas, home of the 2nd Cavalry Division, members served not only as ward orderlies, but also in the more technical positions as physical therapy aids, laboratory technicians, X-ray technicians, and dental technicians. At Fort Sheridan, Illinois, the women operated and maintained the graphotype machines, which were used for processing soldiers' military records. At Camp Knight, California, 105 Women's Army Corps personnel performed the clerical duties in the overseas logistical and supply division.

There was better utilization of African American Women's Army Corps personnel at the Army Air Force installations. An entire clerical unit received highly favorable reviews for their job performances at Walla Walla Air Base, Washington. At Sioux City Army Air Base, the Women's Army Corps were assigned duties in the technical inspector's office. At Douglas Army Airfield, the women were assigned to duties including aircraft maintenance, flight line integrity, hospital laboratory work, and one also served as the photographer for the installation public relations office. In the Air Service Command Headquarters at Fresno, California, two women soldiers performed duties in the war room as map editors.

Other duties noted at different stations were those of teletype operators, radio operators, motion picture projectionists, parachute riggers, drivers, cooks, chaplains' assistants, and librarians. The commanding officer at Fort Huachuca wrote, "These young women are showing marked ability in taking over essential jobs.... The performance of the WACs has been very satisfactory in every respect." The commanding officer of Douglas Army Airfield stated, "I've found them cooperative at all times, and their enthusiasm, industry, attention to duty, and conduct make them a real asset to this post." Colonel Bandel reported later, "In several cases, their efficiency and spirit were highly praised by airbase commanders."[14]

African American Women's Army Corps officers served not only as company officers and instructors, but in operational positions, a number also having graduated from the Army's Quartermaster Officer's Course at Camp Lee, Virginia. Using the higher enrollment standards and with newly appointed Women's Army Corps officers assisting with recruitment, recruiters experienced increased success in obtaining qualified women for the army. Another racial comparison of skills, conducted in 1944, showed that 25 percent of African American recruits enlisted with clerical and professional skills as opposed to 50 percent of white recruits. In addition, 30 percent of African American recruits, as compared to 34 percent of white recruits, had experience in skilled or unskilled vocational trades.[15]

In employing higher skill and aptitude standards, recruiters were never able to reach the desired goal of 10 percent of the Women's Army Corps strength being African American. The peak strength of African American Women's Army Corps soldiers was reached early in 1945 and totaled 6,520 personnel, or only approximately 6 percent of the Corps. These women were assigned to twenty duty stations in the Army Service Forces, and ten duty stations in the Army Air Forces. The Army Ground Forces did not utilize any Women's Army Corps, since most of their soldiers trained on installations where the Army Service Forces performed the administrative duties.

Over the next two years Lieutenant Adams remained on duty at Fort Des Moines, Iowa. In mid–1943 Lieutenant Adams received a new assignment, as a training supervisor at the Fort Des Moines Headquarters. She spent much of her time observing the classes of trainees of both races and interacted well with the other supervisors, who were all white officers. In June she received the first of many assignments away from Fort Des Moines, to Washington, D.C. Soon, she was on an inspection tour to Massachusetts, New Jersey and North Carolina to observe the performance of African American Women's Army Corps that had been transferred to permanent duty stations, and would report her findings to higher headquarters. In early 1944, Lieutenant Adams, now officially a part of the army's new Women's Army Corps,

Women's Army Corps Officer Candidate Class Number 50 graduates, 20 May 1944, Third Women's Army Corps Training Center, Fort Oglethorpe. (National Archives)

was given the assignment of Training Center (TC) Control Officer back at Fort Des Moines. As the majority of the male officers departed for other wartime assignments, Lieutenant Adams acquired more of the responsibilities associated with the normal duty performance of an army officer. She was managing nine new duty assignments in addition to her other daily responsibilities. As a summary court-martial officer, she handled trials for women charged with minor offenses. As surveying officer, she had to locate lost property and determine responsibility for the lost items. For much of this time, she was the only African American officer assigned to the Training Center Headquarters.

Adams, now promoted to major, traveled frequently and often served as convoy officer when soldiers were transferred to other military installations. During these trips, she encountered discrimination and prejudice in spite of the fact that she was a military officer in uniform on official business. On one train trip, a white woman tried to have her removed from the car, claiming that since she was African American, she must be an impostor in an officer's uniform. Another time, while Adams was sitting with her parents in the "colored" waiting room in the Atlanta train station, military police asked to see her identification. When Major Adams asked why she was being questioned, the military policemen stated that someone had questioned her status. By 1944, federal regulations had started forbidding discrimination on interstate travel, and African American attitudes about such unfair treatment were beginning to change.

6888TH CENTRAL POSTAL DIRECTORY BATTALION

By early 1945, as army units advanced quickly across Western Europe into Germany, a gigantic backlog had developed with regards to the delivery of mail to servicemen. A shortage of manpower had allowed mail to accumulate in British warehouses for months and delayed its delivery to the frontline soldiers. Further delays in the delivery of mail had the potential of dampening soldiers' morale as American armies thrust into the German homeland, where they expected to meet stiff enemy resistance.

To alleviate the backlog of undelivered mail, and after an outcry from the African American community and press corps to deploy African American women to a combat theater, military leaders activated the 6888th Central Postal Directory Battalion under the command of Major Charity Adams. Women's Army Corps personnel from both Army Air Forces and the Service of Supply Forces were afforded the opportunity to volunteer for service in this battalion in order to give all women the opportunity to serve in an overseas theater of operations. But sufficient volunteers with the proper military occupational skill of postal clerks to fill all of the job vacancies in the newly activated battalion could not be found. Many of the trained postal clerks were already working in vital positions, and installation commanders were reluctant to release them for overseas duty. There were sufficient volunteer personnel to fill the available support positions within the battalion. Since this was a newly organized battalion with an urgent requirement to deploy overseas, many of the volunteers selected would have to receive on-the-job training as postal clerks.

The battalion was the only unit of that size composed of African Americans in the Women's Army Corps to serve overseas in a combat theater. With an authorized strength of 855 African American women — 824 enlisted women and 31 officers — the 6888th Central Postal Directory Battalion was composed of African American women from a variety of military occupation skills who previously had been assigned throughout the United States. While the majority of the African American women of the 6888th Postal Battalion were trained as postal clerks, others held service and support military occupation skills and operated the 6888th's own dining facilities, motor pools, administration facilities, and supply rooms, making the battalion almost entirely self-sufficient.[16]

In December of 1944, the army issued Major Adams orders for deployment of the battalion to an overseas assignment. The staff officers of the 6888th Central Postal Directory Battalion would deploy to England as an advanced party to prepare for the arrival of the remainder of the battalion. When the Women's Army Corps personnel of the 6888th central Postal Directory Battalion arrived at Birmingham, England, in January 1945, floor-to-ceiling stacks of undelivered mail and packages, and the trainloads of mail that continued to arrive, overwhelmed them. The magnitude of the task and limited workspace area necessitated working around the clock in eight-hour shifts, seven days a week. Poor working conditions added to the stress of their monumental task. Eyestrain was common because of the poor lighting from windows painted black for war-related light discipline at nights. The inadequate heat forced women to work in their winter military clothing and field jackets. Ventilation was especially poor. Wartime security required that all outgoing letters being sent back to the United States from the combat zones had to be read and censored, a task usually assigned to the company grade officers. As the assignment to Birmingham, England, was only to be temporary, Major Adams had trouble acquiring the proper equipment required for their postal facility. Within four months, through their vigilance and hard work, the 6888th Postal Bat-

Somewhere in England, Major Charity E. Adams (right front) and Capt. Abbie N. Campbell inspect the first contingent of African American members of the Women's Army Corps assigned to overseas service. (National Archives)

talion had reduced the backlog of mail in England at the cessation of hostilities in Europe in May 1945.

In spite of their performance in accomplishing these monumental tasks, white mail inspectors were highly critical of this unit, as were most inspectors of any African American unit in the theater. Before the unit's arrival, the central directory operated with enlisted men and civilians and reported itself swamped by mail, and with an undelivered backlog of over three million pieces. It also faced the necessity of an impending deployment to France, where English-speaking civilians would be more difficult to find. Army mail inspectors reported that within the 6888th Postal Battalion, "production appeared to be low," and that "the girls relax on their jobs while mail accumulates."[17] But these reports sent to higher headquarters were highly prejudicial and without merit. The battalion's success in accomplishing the mission well ahead of schedule would often contradict the reports being submitted by these inspectors.

Late in April of 1945, Major Adams and an advanced party from the 6888th Postal Battalion deployed to France, traveling between the cities of Paris and Rouen, making preparation for the movement of the remainder of the battalion to Rouen. Transferred to Rouen in May 1945, the 6888th Central Postal Directory Battalion faced similar difficult tasks. As was the case in England, the majority of the mail in France had been held up for months, some items for as long

Members of the 6888th Central Postal Directory Battalion take part in a parade ceremony in honor of Jeanne d'Arc at the marketplace where she was burned at the stake. (National Archives 111-SC-426441)

as a year. As units quickly advanced across Western Europe, the mail often could not catch up with the soldiers. Directed to eliminate the mail backlog in France in six months, members of the battalion, aware of the importance of mail for front-line soldiers, were determined to accomplish the task in three months. Despite living and working in less than ideal conditions at Rouen, members of the 6888th Postal Battalion developed strong group ties and a high sense of esprit de corps that enabled the battalion to operate more efficiently. Often, mail had to be redirected as units were deploying back to the United States in anticipation of an offensive against Japan. Selfless individual dedication, teamwork, and methodical attention to detail by members of the 6888th reduced the backlog of mail France at the conclusion of the war in Europe.

For the vast majority of American soldiers in Europe in 1945, the African American women of the 6888th Postal Battalion were anonymous, as were the names on the millions of pieces of mail that members of the battalion processed. The 6888th Postal Battalion took great satisfaction in their accomplishments, recognizing that their work improved the quality of life for the millions of soldiers in Europe. For each member of the 6888th Postal Battalion, enlistment in the army also fulfilled some individual needs as well. For women, and for African American women in particular, World War II offered unprecedented opportunities to serve their country. The deployment of racial minorities and women in the army during World War II represented milestones that led in subsequent years to racial and gender integration in the army and all the armed services.

Charity Adams Earley, commander of the 6888th Central Postal Directory Battalion in World War II, summarized the history of women in the military when she wrote in 1989: "The future of women in the military seems assured.... What may be lost in time is the story of how it happened. The barriers of sex and race were, and sometimes still are, very difficult to overcome, the second even more than the first. During World War II women in the service were often subject to ridicule and disrespect even as they performed satisfactorily.... Each year the number of people who shared the stress of these accomplishments lessens. In another generation young African American women who join the military will have scant record of their predecessors who fought on the two fronts of discrimination — segregation and reluctant acceptance by males."[18]

With the end of the war in Europe, some of the women began to return to the United States, and in late 1945, the 6888th Postal Battalion was transferred to Paris. Finally, with a much smaller unit in place, the army ordered Major Adams to the United States for an assignment at Women's Army Corps Headquarters at the Pentagon. Major Adams left the Army in March of 1946, having been promoted to the rank of lieutenant colonel after only four years of service. She was the highest-ranking African American female officer to serve in the army at that time.

DEMOBILIZATION

At the conclusion of the war in the Pacific on 2 September 1945, the Women's Army Corps boasted a membership of 90,779. In point of fact, the Reserve Policy Committee of the War Department had recommended, in May 1945, that women be given reserve status in the postwar army; army leaders had commended Women's Army Corps performance in the field; and, later that fall, Lieutenant General Ira C. Eaker, who had commanded the 8th and 9th Air Forces in Europe before becoming deputy commander of the Army Air Forces, would recommend that the Women's Army Corps "be retained as part of the postwar military plans." General Eaker based his recommendation on the Women's Army Corps' performance during the war. Other male Army leaders also praised Women's Army Corps performance. General Eisenhower wrote, "During the time I have had WACs under my command, they have met every test and task assigned to them.... Their contributions in efficiency, skill, spirit, and determination are immeasurable." General MacArthur, in complimenting their effectiveness and efficiency to Colonel Westray Battle Boyce, who succeeded Colonel Hobby as the director of the Women's Army Corps, called the Women's Army Corps "my best soldiers" because they worked harder than the men, seldom complained, and were well-disciplined troops.[19]

Their commanders praised their performance of duty, deportment, and appearance in uniform. One woman was awarded the Distinguished Service Medal; 62, the Legion of Merit; 565, the Bronze Star Medal; 3, the Air Medal; 10, the Soldier's Medal for heroic actions (not involving combat); and 16, the Purple Heart for being wounded in combat.[20]

On 5 February 1946, the newly appointed Chief of Staff of the Armed Forces, General Eisenhower, charged the G-1 with the responsibility of preparing the plans and drafting the legislation to establish a permanent Women's Army Corps within the regular army with concurrent Reserve Corps status. Both he and General Marshall had recognized the role women had established in the army during World War II. The postwar introduction of women into the regular army stemmed from that recognition. The idea was not to provide equal opportunity for women or to set a precedent for society; it was to relieve as many men as possible from administrative jobs so that they would be available for combat.[21]

World War II had proved that women could play an important role in the defense of this nation. African American women continued to serve in the Women's Army Corps in the postwar years, when the military was eventually integrated as a result of President Truman's executive order in 1948. Some felt that the opportunities of an integrated army were preferable to a segregated society that still prevailed in the majority of this country. African American women would remain a viable part of the Women's Army Corps with ever-increasing numbers until the corps was abolished in 1978, and women were fully integrated into all branches of the Army with the exception of the combat arms.

Table 3 — African American Women in the Services, 1945 and 1947

Service	1945		1947	
	Officer	Enlisted	Officer	Enlisted
Women's Army Corps	111	8,892	7	307
WAVES (Navy)	2	58	0	6
Women Marines	0	0	0	0

Source: Congressional Record, 23 Feb 48, p. 5604.

Table 4 — Strength of African American Members of the Women's Army Corps, 1945–1978

End of Fiscal Year	Total	Officers	Warrant Officers	Enlisted
1945	3,849	117	0	3,732
1946	673	15	0	658
1947	319	9	0	310
1948	125	4	0	121
1949	352	12	0	340
1950	648	18	1	629
1951	1,046	30	1	1,015
1952	1,332	40	1	1,291
1953	1,169	38	0	1,131
1954	869	31	0	838
1955	983	29	0	954
1956	1,061	32	0	1,029
1957	965	28	0	937
1958	933	24	0	909
1959	1,042	27	0	1,015
1960	1,183	28	0	1,155
1972	2,453	52	5	2,396
1973	3,188	56	4	3,184
1974	5,519	63	6	5,450
1975	8,122	85	6	8,031
1976	9,785	98	6	9,681

Table 43 — Strength of African American Members
of the Women's Army Corps, 1945–1978

End of Fiscal Year	Total	Officers	Warrant Officers	Enlisted
1977	11,537	236	8	11,293
1978	14,688	264	12	14,412

No statistics maintained on African American Army personnel from 1961–1971. Source: *Strength of the Army Reports* (STM-30), 1945–1959 and (DCSPER 46), 1960–1978; Report, ODCSPER, Ten Year Review of Equal Opportunity in the Army, 10 Dec 1974, Tables 9, 17; Third Annual Assessment of Army Equal Opportunity Programs, Mar 1979.

Chapter VI

Artillery

IN WORLD WAR I THE ARTILLERY BRANCH OF THE United States Army had fought in Europe equipped entirely with French or British weapons. There were many reasons for this: the need to standardize Allied artillery, lack of shipping space, and lack of industrial capacity to develop and produce new artillery guns. However, another factor was that many ordnance specialists in England and France felt that the indigenous American gun designs were not up to European standards after four years of war. As a result, in 1921 the United States Army Chief of Staff, General Charles P. Sommerall, noted as one of the most brilliant artillerymen in United States Army history, established the Westervelt Board to examine the army's ordnance requirements for the future. The board's report was impartial and farsighted, and it had dramatic consequences for the United States Army artillery in World War II. The board recommended that the standard divisional artillery piece be increased in caliber from 75-mm to 105-mm howitzer, while the general support weapon for the infantry division was to be standardized as the 155-mm howitzer. The 4.7-inch corps general support gun, a British design, was to be discarded in favor of the 155-mm gun, which was of French design.[1] In addition, the board recommended that heavier artillery pieces of the most modern type be designed, and that all artillery be suitable for rapid motorized road movement. Finally, improvements in fire control methodology and communications were recommended, based upon concepts that had been pioneered by General Sommerall as an artillery brigade commander in France.[2]

Divisional artillery pieces included the M1 105-mm howitzer and the M1 155-mm howitzer. Both were excellent weapons, with good range and, particularly in the case of the 155-mm, excellent accuracy. Other new weapons were the M1 75-mm pack howitzer and the M3 105-mm howitzer. Both were lightweight and could be easily broken down into manageable loads suitable for transportation by pack animal (horse, mule, or man as available) or by air, and although relatively short-ranged, were ideal for the airborne forces. The M3 also saw service after 1943 in the Cannon Company of the standard infantry regiment. A self-propelled version of the M1 105-mm, the M7 Priest Armored Vehicles, also equipped the field artillery battalions of the armored divisions, and were incorporated as platoons in the separate tank battalions.

Non-divisional or corps artillery units included battalions equipped with these same weapons, as well as other, heavier pieces. A companion of the 155-mm howitzer was the 4.5-

inch gun (an indigenous 120-mm gun was one of the few failures of the inter-war design projects). The tube of this gun was of British design, while the carriage was that of the 155-mm howitzer (carriage commonality between companion guns and howitzers was one of the hallmarks of United States artillery designs). Unfortunately, the 4.5-inch gun was not well liked by American artillerymen. The shell, also of British design, was composed of low-grade steel, thick-walled and with a small bursting charge compared to the shell weight. Its range was insufficient to compensate for the relative ineffectiveness of its round and it was withdrawn from service soon after the end of the war.

A much better weapon was the M1 155-mm gun, known as a "Long Tom," an appellation with a long and glorious tradition in the United States artillery. It combined long range, accuracy, and striking power with a well-designed mobile carriage.

A different 155-mm gun was the M12 Self Propelled. Developed in 1942, it was an interesting amalgam of the old and the new, utilizing the tube of the French-designed GPF (Grand Puissance, Failloux), itself developed in World War II, and the chassis of the obsolescent M3 Grant tank. It was an experiment by the Ordnance Department that had been turned down by the Army Ground Force in October 1943 on the basis that there was no requirement for it. However, in early 1944 urgent requests from United States Army forces in England for a heavy self-propelled gun resulted in 74 of these vehicles being rebuilt. They eventually equipped seven field artillery battalions in the European Theater of Operations and proved invaluable while supporting the armored divisions in the mechanized advances across France and Germany. An improved model, the M40, based upon the M1 gun and the chassis of the M4 Sherman tank, was produced in 1944 and deployed in limited numbers to the European Theater of Operations toward the end of the war in March 1945.

Heavier supporting artillery pieces were the M1 8-inch howitzer, an excellent and very accurate weapon; the M1 8-inch gun, which was developed as an answer to the superb German 17-cm gun, had greater range and a more lethal shell than the German weapon, but suffered from poor accuracy and excessive barrel wear; and the 240-mm howitzer, a good, if very heavy, weapon.

Nearly all artillery battalions were organized with three firing batteries (companies) for a total of twelve artillery pieces. The exceptions were the eighteen-tube armored self-propelled field artillery battalions, the six-tube 8-inch gun battalions, and 240-mm howitzer battalions. A major advantage for the American artillery was that it was fully motorized and highly mobile. All 105-mm and 155-mm howitzer battalions in the European Theater of Operations were truck-drawn, although a Table of Equipment (TE) for a tractor-drawn 155-mm battalion existed. The 155-mm gun artillery battalions were almost all tractor-drawn, although a few evidently were also truck-drawn. The 4.5-inch gun, the 8-inch gun, the 8-inch howitzer, and 240-mm howitzer battalions were all tractor-drawn, although, again, a TE for truck-drawn battalions existed. The standard prime mover was a two-and-one-half ton truck for the 105-mm and a five-ton truck for the 155-mm howitzers. Tractors, including the M4 thirteen-ton prime movers, were utilized for the 90-mm antiaircraft gun, the 4.5-inch gun, and the 155-mm howitzer. The M5 eighteen-ton, high-speed, full-tracked, heavy prime mover was utilized for the 155-mm gun, the 8-inch howitzer, the 8-inch gun, and the 240-mm howitzer. Redundant M3 medium tank chassis, without armament, and the M31 and M32 armored recovery vehicles were also utilized as prime movers for the heavier artillery pieces.

Corps artillery battalions were normally subordinated to field artillery groups. The groups were formed in 1943 from the headquarters battery of the deactivated field artillery regiments. The field artillery group consisted of a headquarters and headquarters battery, with a command element, a fire-direction center element, and a service battery, and was normally under the command and control of the corps artillery commander. A group was usually assigned from two to six artillery battalions, although one or more of the battalions might be attached for direct support of an individual division. Usually, the groups were assigned howitzer and gun battalions of companion caliber, which meant the 155-mm howitzers were grouped with 4.5-inch guns, the 8-inch howitzers with 155-mm guns, and the 8-inch guns with 240-mm howitzers. The normal ratio was one gun battalion for every two howitzer battalions, although this was not always firmly adhered to in times of war.

Field artillery brigades were also created, originally to command the separate field artillery regiments, and later to command the field artillery groups. However, the brigade eventually was seen as a redundant and unnecessary additional layer of command structure. Most of the brigades were inactivated or were redesignated as headquarters and headquarters batteries and assigned to different corps and divisions. A few artillery brigades were retained and served as such: the 13th Brigade in the Mediterranean Theater of Operations and the 32nd, 33rd, 34th, and 61st Brigades in the European Theater of Operations. In the First Army of the European Theater of Operations, two field artillery groups were attached to the 32nd Field Artillery Brigade. This artillery brigade controlled all the larger 8-inch gun and 240-mm howitzer battalions of that army, making it, in effect, a heavy artillery brigade. The 3rd, 7th, and 9th Armies followed a similar, but less centralized system for control of their heavy artillery battalions. The United States Army Artillery Corps was equipped with armament that was at least as well designed as, if not better than, any other in the world. The artillery corps further benefited from improved communications equipment and a fire control system that was equaled only by that of the Royal British Artillery. Individual forward artillery observers and teams operated close to the front lines and had access, via powerful radios and extensive telephone landlines, to a formidable array of weapons. The highly redundant signal system meant that, even when all other contact with front-line units and their headquarters was lost, the artillery communications net usually remained open.

On 31 December 1944 the artillery branch of the army reached its maximum strength. On that date there were a total of 346 artillery battalions active: 137 heavy, 116 medium and 93 light. On 31 March 1945 there were 137 heavy, 113 medium and 76 light battalions active, of which 307 artillery battalions were deployed or were about to deploy to active theaters of war.[3]

As of 8 May 1945 there were a total of 238 separate field artillery battalions in the European Theater of Operations. Of this number, only nine of those battalions consisted of African American soldiers, far less than the 10 percent that was planned by the Army General Staff in 1940.

In the artillery branch, the expansion of the number of segregated African American units proceeded in an orderly fashion, in accordance with theories developed during peacetime by the Army General Staff. On the basis of World War I after action reports, it was believed that African Americans could be utilized efficiently in the supporting corps artillery units, especially in the heavier caliber types where direct contact with the enemy would be least likely. In this way, there would be no need to train replacement artillerymen after the original battalions had been activated. Two antiaircraft artillery regiments and one field artillery regiment were provided for in the August 1940 military expansion. These were the 76th and 77th Coast Artillery (Antiaircraft) and the 349th Field Artillery Battalions. Two African American National Guard infantry regiments that had served with distinction during World War I with the 93rd Infantry Division were also converted into artillery regiments when they were federalized in early 1941, much to the dismay of the African American public. The 369th Infantry Regiment (Harlem Hell Fighters) from New York was converted to the 369th Coast Artillery (Antiaircraft) Regiment on 13 January 1941. The 8th Illinois Infantry Regiment was converted to the 184th Field Artillery Regiment on 10 February 1941. One additional coast artillery battalion, two more antiaircraft artillery battalions, three field artillery regiments, and a field artillery brigade headquarters were activated in later 1941. They were the 54th Coast Artillery Battalion, the 99th and 100th Coast Artillery (Antiaircraft) Battalions, the 350th, 351st, and 353rd Field Artillery Regiments, and the 46th Field Artillery Brigade. By the end of 1942 eight additional segregated African American antiaircraft artillery regiments, four barrage balloon battalions, six separate antiaircraft artillery battalions, and two separate searchlight batteries had been activated. At the same time, in addition to the one field artillery brigade headquarters and the division artillery for the 92nd and 93rd Infantry, and the 2nd Cavalry Divisions, a total of seven field artillery regiments, with fourteen artillery battalions consisting of two 75-mm howitzer, two 155-mm, gun, eight 155-mm howitzer, and two 8-inch howitzer, had been activated.

In August 1943, the army decided to convert many of the African American ground combat forces into combat service support units with the dual purpose of filling a shortage of manpower and of releasing white soldiers serving in these support units for duty in combat divisions. Of these units, 23 field artillery and antiaircraft artillery battalions were deactivated. A total of 14,288 African American enlisted men from disbanded artillery and tank destroyer battalions were transferred to the quartermaster, transportation, and engineer branches to perform much of the combat support duties.[4]

All of the nine African American separate field artillery battalions that remained in the United States after the conversions were deployed to the European Theater of Operations. The two African American infantry divisions had their own organic artillery battalions and cannon companies that utilized the 105-mm and

155-mm howitzers. All of the nine separate artillery battalions were heavy caliber units that would be used as corps artillery for general support or for reinforcing the artillery fires of one or more divisions. Each battalion was composed of three firing batteries for a total of 12 heavy guns, a headquarters battery, and a maintenance support company. Artillery has been known to be the most devastating weapon by inflicting the largest number of enemy casualties on the battlefield.

Shortly after D-Day and the invasion of Nazi-occupied Europe, the 333rd Field Artillery Group, with its headquarters and headquarters battery, landed in France on 29 June 1944 with the VIII Corps Artillery. The 333rd Field Artillery Group was a segregated unit. Its commanding officer and all of the senior staff officers were white. The junior officers, the captains and lieutenants at the battery level, and all of the enlisted men were African Americans. The same would hold true for all of the African American artillery battalions that were assigned to the theater. The United States Army still followed the guidelines that hindered the segregated units during World War I. While African Americans could become officers, rarely would they achieve the field grade status of major or above, and never would they be put in a position where they outranked a white officer. In addition to that, highly qualified African American officers were often passed over for promotion, while less qualified white officers quickly rose through the ranks. This would be a problem that would continue to hurt morale, especially in the few units that were assigned a combat role in the war.

The VIII Corps Artillery utilized the battalions of the 333rd Field Artillery Group as the tactical need required heavy artillery support. The 333rd Artillery Group's African American artillery battalions were often assigned to other artillery groups, as white artillery battalions also served under the command and control of the 333rd Field Artillery Group. During the siege of Brest, France, VIII Corps Artillery, which had three African American battalions and the 333rd Field Artillery Group among its 15 corps artillery battalions and several group headquarters initially available to it, distributed its artillery forces into two reinforcing groups, two mixed-caliber general support groups, one reinforcing battalion, and one attached group. The battalions were assigned to groups and attached to infantry and armored divisions as the mission required. During the siege, for example, the 333rd Field Artillery Group had control of one African American battalion, the 333rd Field Artillery Battalion (155-mm howitzer), and two white battalions. The African American 969th Field Artillery Battalion (155-mm howitzer), formerly attached to the 333rd Artillery Group, was at first given the task of reinforcing the artillery fires of the 2nd Infantry Division, and later placed under the control of the 402nd Field Artillery Group, through which it supported the 8th Infantry Division in its attack on the Crozon Peninsula. A third African American battalion, the 578th Field Artillery Battalion (8-inch howitzer), was attached to the 202nd Field Artillery Group, one of the two general support groups responsible for counterbattery fire.[5]

The 969th Field Artillery Battalion arrived on Utah Beach on 9 July 1944 under the command of Lieutenant Colonel Hubert D. Barnes. Its first mission was to reinforce the artillery fire of the 8th Infantry Division through the control of the 333rd Field Artillery Group. On 10 July, the battalion took its first positions at Lattage du Pont in the vicinity of Le Haye du Puits. At 2205, Battery A fired the unit's first rounds in combat. The battalion commander was slightly wounded that night by enemy counterbattery fire, and the battalion continued to support the 8th Infantry Division for the next four days under the command of the executive officer, Major Einar Erickson. After 14 July, the battalion was attached to the 8th Infantry Division for command and control. The 969th Artillery Battalion also fired special missions for the 90th Infantry Division. On 26 July, Battery A was attached to the 4th Armored Division. By 1 August, the rest of the battalion was also attached to the 4th Armored Division, where it occupied positions near Rennes, France. The battalion was given credit for 79 enemy prisoners captured while it maintained firing positions there. In late August, the 969th Artillery Battalion began its participation in the siege of Brest, France, continuing until hostilities in the area ceased on 19 September. In October, the battalion, now back in support of the 8th Infantry Division, deployed from Brest to the Bastogne, Belgium, sector, where, attached to the 174th Field Artillery Group, it remained until December.[6]

In the Bastogne-Houffalize sector of Belgium, the three VIII Corps African American field artillery units were assigned to support the infantry and armored divisions in that region: the 333rd Field Artillery Group at Atzerath initially supporting the 2nd and later the 106th Infantry Divisions; the 333rd Field Artillery Battalion, headquartered at the town of Schonberg, was attached to the 333rd Artillery Group; and the 578th Field Artillery Battalion of the 402nd Artillery Group was stationed around the town of Burg Reuland. The 333rd Artillery Group arrived at Houffalize, Belgium, on 5 October, with the 333rd Field Artillery Battalion and the white 771st Field Artillery Battalion attached. The group's mission throughout December continued to be the general support of VIII Corps, reinforcing the fire of the 106th Infantry Division with the 333rd Field Artillery Battalion's 155-mm howitzers augmenting the division's 590th Field Artillery Battalion.

The Bastogne-Houffalize area was considered the quiet sector of the front lines. Newly arrived infantry and armored divisions and battle-weary units requiring rest and refit were stationed in this sector. In the a333rd Artillery Group, firing was averaging only 150 rounds per day. At Burg Reuland, the 578th Field Artillery Battalion, like the other artillery units in the sector, was constantly improving its billets and firing positions. After three months in this quiet sector, most units had become complacent and all personnel were billeted in either houses, wooden cabins, or winterized tents. Due to a worldwide shortage of artillery shells, ammunition expenditure for a four-day period was limited to a total of only 250 rounds. Enemy activity consisted of occasional shelling of forward observation posts, harassing fire on the battalion command post, and an occasional V-1 rocket attack. Though the weather was damp with freezing rain and snow, and the roads nearly impassable, the battalion found the days at Burg Reuland similar to garrison life in the United States. Soldiers were able to attend USO shows and movies, and officers and enlisted men were scheduled for trips to Paris over the Christmas holidays.

When the Germans launched their attack on this quiet sector against the VIII Corps units on 16 December, the forward artillery observation posts of the 333rd Field Artillery Battalion at Bleialf, Belgium, taken totally by surprise, were overrun by 1100 that morning. The soldiers withdrew to the command post of the 590th Field Artillery Battalion, where the 333rd's liaison officer was located. These were the first positions of the 333rd Field Artillery Battalion to be lost to combat.[7] To the north, at its St. Vith command post, the 402nd Artillery Group was sending warning orders for a retrograde (retreating) movement to all of its artillery battalions. The 578th Field Artillery Battalion's forward artillery observation post at Heckhuscheid, Belgium, a town held by a battalion of the 424th Infantry Regiment of the 106th Infantry Division, was subjected to heavy artillery fire and attacked by enemy forces. The artillery battalion commander, Lieutenant Colonel Thomas Buckley, the forward artillery observer and his radio operators held off the Germany infantry with their carbines and M1 rifles. Being attacked by a numerically superior force of German infantry and tanks, the observation team withdrew to another of the battalion's observation posts, taking 12 German prisoners with them. During the first day of the Ardennes campaign the 578th Field Artillery Battalion had 23 fire missions, expending 774 artillery rounds in support of infantry and armored units engaged in combat.

The seriousness of the German attack was apparent the following day as the battalions of the 333rd Artillery Group began to retreat to prepared alternate positions on the night of 16 December. Each artillery battalion was ordered to leave one battery forward at the request of Major General Alan W. Jones, the Commanding General of the 106th Infantry Division, who assured VIII Corps Artillery that his positions would be held. The untested 106th Infantry Division landed in France on 6 Dec 1944 and replaced the veteran 2nd Infantry Division in the Schnee Eifel sector of Belgium on 11 Dec 1944. When the German Ardennes Counteroffensive, better known as the "Battle of the Bulge," struck the division on 16 Dec 1944, the 424th Infantry Regiment was headquartered at the town of Winterspelt, and the 422nd and 423rd Infantry Regiments were in the Schnee Eifel salient. Both the 422nd and 423rd Infantry Regiments, along with the division headquarters and all supporting units, surrendered on 19 Dec 1944 after being encircled at their defensive positions near the town of Schonberg the previous day.[8] This was the only time in World War II that the majority of an American infantry division would surrender to enemy forces. Many of the artillerymen of the 333rd Artillery Group and its attached battalions became prisoners of war when the 106th Infantry Division surrendered. The African American prisoners that were displayed on German propaganda newsreels during the Battle of the Bulge were many of the artillerymen captured with the 106th Infantry Division. After the war, 87 soldiers, including 3 officers of Battery C, 333rd Field Artillery Battalion were repatriated from German Prisoner of War and work camps.⁹ Ironically, the Germans treated these African American soldiers the same as any other prisoners of war. But the bodies of 11 soldiers of this battery were found near the hamlet of Wereth, Belgium, murdered by German SS troops after they surrendered.¹⁰

As the infantry and cavalry reconnaissance units began retreating under the German onslaught and the confusion of the battle, the heavy artillery units, with their slower-moving vehicles, lost several howitzers and artillery guns to enemy action and adverse weather, which left many of the roads impassable. The surviving members of the 333rd Field Artillery Battalion at the end of the day possessed only five of their twelve 155-mm howitzers. On 18 December, the 969th Artillery Battalion, retreating toward the town of Vecmont, was attached to the 333rd Artillery Group by verbal orders of the Commanding General, VIII Corps Artillery.

The 578th Artillery Battalion, along with the white 559th Field Artillery Battalion, lost communications with the 402nd Artillery Group headquarters and temporarily organized under the command of the 578th Artillery Battalion as they planned to retreat to Cherain. The two battalions conducted reconnaissance and with the fire support of three 105-mm howitzers, occupied their positions without opposition. Once they were able to contact VIII Corps Artillery, they were ordered further to the rear, so as not to be isolated from the main retreating forces. Using tractors to transport the heavy artillery guns, the 559th Artillery Battalion suffered casualties on the highway from Houffalize, which was now in enemy hands. The 578th Artillery Battalion encountered tank fire, but suffered no casualties nor lost any equipment. "The steadiness and determination of all concerned in this trying movement when a heavy artillery battalion was fighting a rear guard action is worthy of higher praise," declared the commander of the 578th Artillery Battalion.¹¹

On that same day, 19 December, the 333rd Artillery Group was released by VIII Corps Artillery for attachment to the rapidly deployed 101st Airborne Division, and ordered to proceed to the vicinity of Bastogne. The 101st Airborne Division had been at a rear area in France, being refitted after months of battle in Holland. Many of its soldiers arrived in Bastogne without ammunition or winter clothing. Bastogne was a major highway junction and of strategic importance to the advancing Germans. The 333rd Artillery Group, receiving its verbal orders at 1300, undertook a reconnaissance, and began to displace at 1430. By 1730, the 333rd Artillery Group, with its three battalions, arrived at their new positions. The command post established its position at Mande-St. Etienne, with the 771st Artillery Battalion stationed around the town of Flamierge, the 969th Artillery dispersed in the Flamizoulle area, and the remainder of the 333rd Artillery Battalion that had not been captured or killed, set up their firing positions in the vicinity of Rennamount. All these sites where to the north and west of Bastogne. During the night, the Germans cut the Bastogne-Marche highway. Reports and rumors continued to circulate indicating that the enemy was infiltrating American positions from all sides. When small arms fire was received in vicinity of the 771st and the 969th Field Artillery Battalions, the 333rd Artillery Group commander ordered all his units to retreat toward the town of St. Hubert, west of Bastogne. Considerable confusion resulted from this uncoordinated displacement. In the panic that ensued, the 771st Field Artillery Battalion was forced to abandon its large guns as their tractors had become mired in the snow and mud. The 333rd Field Artillery Battalion, receiving counterbattery and small arms fire, was forced to abandon three of its remaining five howitzers.

The 101st Division Artillery, not being able to communicate with the 333rd Artillery Group headquarters throughout 20 December, eventually learned from the group's executive officer that the commander had ordered all his battalions to displace without coordinating first with the 101st Division Artillery. When the units had proceeded five miles to the southwest along the Bastogne-Neufchateau highway, the columns were finally contacted and ordered to halt. An hour later, they were ordered to return to their old positions. Once they arrived, they discovered that Lieutenant Colonel Barnes, the commander of the 969th Field Artillery Battalion, had been placed in command of the entire 333rd Artillery Group. Brigadier General Anthony McAuliffe, temporary commander of the 101st Airborne Division and its artillery officer, as the division commander, Major General Maxwell Taylor, was at a conference in Washington, D.C., relieved the commander of the 333rd Artillery Group.[12]

By 1600 and repositioned at their original positions, the 333rd Artillery Battalion found two of its gun crews attempting to get the abandoned howitzers out of the mud with borrowed tractors. The battalion reclaimed all its remaining weapons, which were still usable. An armored unit had already retrieved one of the 771st Artillery Battalion's tractors and guns. Their other three tractors and guns remained mired in the mud. Thirty minutes later, the 101st Division Artillery ordered the 333rd Artillery Group to move again, first to Morhet and then to the area around the towns of Chenogne, Sibret, and Villeroux, three miles southwest of Bastogne. There, elements of the 28th Infantry Division would provide security for the heavy artillery battalions. Displacement began immediately, and the 771st Artillery Battalion, unable to remove its mired guns, destroyed them in place. The 771st Artillery Battalion then occupied positions at Sibret, the southwesternmost of the towns and the location for the headquarters of the 28th Infantry Division. The 969th Artillery Battalion set up their howitzers in the vicinity of Villeroux; and the 333rd Artillery Battalion positioned its remaining five 155-mm howitzers near Chenogne, where the 333rd Artillery Group located its headquarters. The battalions fired harassing missions on enemy targets throughout the night. The unit's rear echelon and logistical support personnel remained at the towns of St. Hubert and Molinfaing.

On the morning of 21 December, with the enemy tightening their lines around Bastogne, the Germans approached the town of Sibret from the south and west. At 0800, enemy tanks and mortars began to fire into the town. The 28th Infantry Division commander, Major General Norman D. Cota, ordered all personnel into the streets to defend the town. The 771st Artillery Battalion relocated some of its remaining 4.5-inch guns to the northwest of town in search of improved firing positions with no minimum elevation so that heavy artillery fire could be placed on enemy targets as close as 1,500 yards away. Heavy German artillery fire began to fall in the town and on the 771st Artillery Battalion's gun positions. As the vehicles of the 28th Infantry Division started to retreat northwest through the town toward the rear, the 771st Artillery Battalion commander ordered his headquarters battery to follow in order to maintain contact. The battalion's S-3 operations officer, at Chenogne for a 333rd Artillery Group conference, received orders to have the 771st Artillery Battalion remain in its present position, firing in support of the 101st Airborne Division. The operations officer, on his way back to Sibret, met one battery on its way out of town and ordered it and another battery to establish new firing positions to the northwest of Sibret. Under intense enemy fire, the remaining batteries were finally forced to retreat toward Chenogne. When the 28th Infantry Division was finally forced to evacuate Sibret around 1000, all remaining firing batteries of the 771st Field Artillery Battalion had displaced to positions near Chenogne.

Elements of the 28th Infantry Division, including one of the division's organic field artillery battalions, and the 58th Armored Field Artillery Battalion, passed through the firing positions of the 771st and 333rd Artillery Battalions as they retreated. When German infantry and tanks approached one of the 771st Artillery's gun positions, the defending American infantry broke and retreated northward, leaving the cannoneers exposed and unprotected. Direct tank fire destroyed one gun, its prime mover tractor, and an armored command car of one of the 771st Artillery Battalion. Another tractor displacing a gun to a new position was also destroyed. As enemy Panzer tanks appeared over the ridge that was previously selected for minimum elevation fire, all the remaining elements of the battalion began to hastily retreat from their positions without orders from their commanders, abandoning all equipment. The battalion S-2/intelligence and S-3/operations officers gathered the remaining members of the 771st Artillery Battalion together, and on orders from VIII Corps Artillery, retreated all the way to Matton, France, well to the rear of the battle, where scattered surviving elements of the battalion straggled in over the next few days. All guns except two were either destroyed or abandoned en route to Matton. The battalion commander, 5 staff officers, and 14 enlisted men joined elements of the 333rd Artillery Group headquarters.[13]

In the meantime, the two African American battalions of the group remained in position, with the 333rd Artillery Battalion in the Chenogne area, and the 969th Artillery Battalion at Villeroux. The 333rd Artillery Group headquarters deployed back toward Bastogne as the enemy approached Chenogne, issuing movement orders to the 333rd Field Artillery Battalion. Before the 333rd Artillery Battalion could displace, incoming enemy tank fire destroyed a prime mover tractor and two of the remaining howitzers, killing many of the soldiers. An additional tractor had to be abandoned as the remnants of the battalion relocated to new positions closer to the protection of Bastogne. Throughout the afternoon of 21 December, the 333rd Artillery Group maintained a temporary command post at Senonchamps with the 420th Armored Field Artillery Battalion of Combat Command B, 10th Armored Division. The group reinforced the fire of this battalion. As the enemy forces approached Villeroux, they subjected the 969th Artillery Battalion to incoming artillery and tank fire, which subsequently killed the motor officer and wounded several enlisted men. The 969th Artillery Battalion, on orders from the 101st Division Artillery, retreated to the northwest to a position one half mile west of Bastogne. There, as the 101st Airborne Division formed its perimeter defensive line around the outskirts of the town, the three remaining serviceable 155-mm howitzers of the 333rd Artillery Battalion were incorporated with those of the 969th Artillery Battalion. The two battalions, with the 969th operating the recovered 4.5-inch guns abandoned by the 771st Artillery Battalion and other retreating artillery units, operated as one unit throughout the siege of Bastogne, reinforcing the fire of the 420th Armored Field Artillery Battalion in their support of the 10th Armored Division, as well as giving general fire support to the 101st Division Artillery. The 333rd Artillery Group had only 450 rounds of high explosive shells available. Fire missions were still conducted, but not on the intensive scale that was normally provided. All the primary roads into Bastogne were now cut off and held by the enemy. There would be little possibility of resupply.

On 23 December, the third day after Bastogne had been isolated, C-47 cargo aircraft delivered the first aerial resupply for the besieged area, but no 155-mm howitzer ammunition was included. Along with the other units, the 333rd Artillery Group and its subordinate battalions received enemy aerial bombardment on Christmas Eve. They lost two battery commanders and three enlisted men killed.[14] Allied infantry lines were now within 500 yards of the artillery positions. On 26 December, as the 969th Artillery Battalion continued to fire its dwindling supply of ammunition, C-47 cargo aircraft airdropped the first 155-mm howitzer ammunition during the siege. It was also learned that General Patton's 3rd Army, with the 4th Armored Division in the lead, was at Assenois, two miles away, attempting to break through to the besieged forces.

On 27 December, 50 gliders landed with supplies, including additional 155-mm howitzer ammunition. The 333rd Artillery Group headquarters and headquarters battery, the surviving members of the 333rd Artillery Battalion, and the small detachment of men from the 771st Artillery Battalion were ordered by VIII Corps Artillery to displace on 28 December over the now-opened road to Matton, France. There, most of the VIII Corps Artillery units that had escaped encirclement or capture were assembling. The rear echelon of the 333rd Artillery Battalion was maintaining roadblocks and a mobile reserve force for security purposes there. They had attempted vainly to resupply the main elements of their battalion in Bastogne. On 26 December, a convoy led by the 333rd Artillery Group's supply officer, Major Oscar Lewis, delivered fuel, ammunition, and rations to their unit.

The 333rd Field Artillery Battalion, which sustained heavier losses during the Battle of the Bulge than any other VIII Corps Artillery unit, lost a total of 6 officers and 222 enlisted men either killed or captured. They also lost nine 155-mm howitzers, 34 trucks and 12 weapons carriers. The other 11 artillery battalions of the corps combined lost a total of 346 enlisted men. Since the army was not training any more African American soldiers at the artillery school as artillerymen to replace battlefield losses, there was little chance of reconstituting the 333rd Artillery Battalion. The Army Ground Forces Command had not anticipated any of the African American artillery battalions ever being used directly in combat, let alone being exposed to the horrific conditions in the Battle of the Bulge. The 333rd Artillery Group, which now had the 771st, 333rd, 58th Armored, and 740th Field Artillery Battalions attached to it, reorganized and reequipped all of the battalions except the 333rd. The 771st Artillery Battalion, having abandoned or destroyed all of its 4.5-inch guns, was reequipped with 155-mm howitzers. The 333rd Artillery Battalion sent the majority of its surviving 286 men to the 578th and 969th Artillery Battalions, and to the 333rd Artillery Group's headquarters battery as replacements. All of those units were still engaged in battle and had sustained large numbers of casualties. The 333rd Artillery Battalion, originally scheduled to be disbanded, remained active as a skeleton unit, performing guard and ordnance duties, while training new volunteer replacements from African American combat service support units. The decision to keep the battalion active was due to its outstanding performance during the siege of Bastogne. The battalion remained and continued to fight, while other units retreated toward safety. It was not until the end of April 1945 that the battalion had received and trained sufficient replacements to return to combat duties. By then, the war in Europe was coming to an end.

The 969th Field Artillery Battalion's commander, Lieutenant Colonel Barnes, returned to his unit upon the departure of the 333rd Artillery Group from Bastogne. The 969th Field Artillery Battalion continued to support the 101st Airborne Division until 12 January when it was relieved and reattached to the 333rd Field Artillery Group. The 333rd Artillery Group returned to its old command post at Bastogne with the mission of supporting the 11th Armored Division, then advancing north to Houffalize. As General Patton and his 3rd Army had the Germans in full retreat in the area south of Bastogne, Major General Maxwell Taylor, commander of the 101st Airborne Division, wrote to the commander of the 969th Field Artillery Battalion: "The Officers and Men of the 101st Airborne Division wish to express to your command their appreciation of the gallant support rendered by the 969th Field Artillery Battalion in the recent defense of Bastogne, Belgium. The success of this defense is attributable to the shoulder-to-shoulder cooperation of all involved. This division is proud to have shared the battlefield with your command. A recommendation for a unit citation of 969th Field Artillery Battalion is being forwarded by this Headquarters."[15]

Major General Troy Middleton, commanding general of VIII Corps, forwarding his commendation to the battalion on 11 January 1945, observed: "Your contribution to the great success of our arms at Bastogne will take its place among the epic achievements of our Army."[16] The 969th Field Artillery Battalion and its attached soldiers, along with other units of the 101st Airborne Division, received its Distinguished Unit Citation through 3rd Army on 7 February 1945, in authority granted by the War Department on 21 January. This would be the first time a Distinguished Unit Citation would be presented to an entire division and its attached supporting units. It would also be the first time that a Distinguished Unit Citation would be awarded to an African American combat battalion in World War II.[17]

The 578th Field Artillery Battalion, moving south and west from Burg Reuland with the 559th Artillery Battalion, reached Mierchamps, west of Bastogne, on 20 December. There, the 402nd Artillery Group resumed control of the battalions. The 578th Artillery Battalion moved into several positions where it expected to be able to fire, but orders kept them retreating further to the rear. Along the way, the 578th Artillery Battalion took control of a number of stragglers and miscellaneous artillery units. A battery of the 740th Field Artillery's 8-inch howitzers, a platoon of antiaircraft artillery soldiers, 50 enlisted soldiers from the 740th Field Artillery acting as infantry, and a battery of 105-mm howitzers were just some of the units that were attached to the 578th Artillery Battalion. On 21 December, the battalion reached the Foret du Luchy where, operating directly under VIII Corps Artillery control, it was instructed to occupy positions near the town of Flohimont so that it could fire to cover any possible withdrawal from Bastogne, which the 101st Airborne Division might be directed to make. The 578th Artillery Battalion was convinced that now its retreat movement would cease and the battalion could make a stand. In spite of the battalion's expectations, a new order came from VIII Corps Artillery at 1135 directing further movement to the rear.[18] The VIII Corps Artillery, in its Matton location, was planning to move its 402nd Artillery Group toward Arlon, 20 miles south of Bastogne, for attachment to III Corps Artillery, which was now heading north with the 3rd Army in the relief of Bastogne. The VIII Corps Artillery considered the current battlefront too mobile to properly utilize the heavy artillery battalions. The 578th Artillery Battalion was among five battalions offered on loan to III Corps Artillery under the command and control of the 402nd Artillery Group on 22 December.

The III Corps Artillery directed the 578th Artillery Battalion to establish firing positions at Nagem. By midday of 23 December, all batteries were in firing positions. From Nagem, the 578th Artillery Battalion fired in general support of III Corps until 26 December when the unit advanced forward. On 29 December, the battalion was attached to the 193rd Field Artillery Group, and later that day, ordered to operate directly under III Corps Artillery, with batteries deploying forward to Neunhausen. On 31 December, the 578th Artillery Battalion was attached to the 203rd Field Artillery Group. Despite its long road marches since 16 December, the battalion had expended 3,455 rounds of 8-inch howitzer ammunition, firing on all but four days for an average of 288 rounds per day. Inspections of captured targets and target areas enabled the battalion to evaluate the effectiveness of a large portion of its fire missions. Fifty-two rounds fired on enemy traffic in and around the town of Boulaide on Christmas Day without adjustment were observed to be 100 percent effective. On 27 December, forward artillery observers noted two tanks immobilized, many vehicles destroyed, and several hits on houses occupied by enemy forces. When the freezing weather hampered the movement to new locations, the battalion borrowed tanks to tow the prime movers and howitzers up slippery hills.

The 578th continued in general support of III Corps, firing from positions near the town of Neunhausen until 16 January 1945. On 4 January, while still in Neunhausen, the battal-

Field artillery 155-mm cannon crew in the Periers Sector, France, 1944. (National Archives)

ion received a fire mission to destroy the enemy-held village of Berle. By the afternoon of the next day, every structure in the village was severely damaged or destroyed with the exception of one, which was marked with a very large red cross. Throughout the mission, the 578th Forward Observation Post No. 1, from which the accurate fire mission was directed, was continuously under mortar and Nebelwerfer (rocket) fire. The battalion commander, Colonel Buckley, departed the unit on 8 January to assume command of the rehabilitated 333rd Artillery Group, now returning from Matton to resume its role in the Ardennes campaign. The 578th Artillery Battalion was attached to the 333rd Artillery Group on 26 January.

After the Ardennes campaign, the 578th Artillery Battalion continued across Europe in general support of VIII Corps. It would be attached to the 333rd, 402nd, 174th, and 220th Field Artillery Groups. In February, two of its batteries were called on by the 4th Infantry Division to assist in repulsing an enemy counterattack with its heavy guns. On 30 March, the battalion crossed the Rhine River, closing in on an area near Limbach, Germany, where it was ordered to clear designated wooded areas. On the morning of 31 March, elements of each battery were formed into infantry platoons, armed with rifles, carbines, bazookas, and vehicular-mounted .50-caliber machine guns to suppress bypassed pockets of enemy resistance. Batteries B and C cleared their assigned objective areas, but Battery A ran into heavy enemy machine gun fire. Members of the headquarters battery reinforced them, and the advance was resumed. This ad hoc infantry unit captured 61 enemy prisoners, including three officers. Rapid advancement of the infantry and armored divisions in this final thrust of the

Allied armies forced the heavy artillery battalions to deploy more frequently, and allowed few opportunities for fire missions. Its patrols cleared wooded areas of bypassed enemy forces immediately after the occupation of a new area. During April, the battalion raced across Germany to the Czech border, firing missions at enemy-held towns and critical road junctions. German resistance was coming to an end, and Germans civilians were rushing to the American and British sectors to avoid the advancing Russian armies. On 26 April, the battalion was ordered to take up occupation duties in Kassell, Germany. Its howitzers were turned into ordnance and weatherproofed with Cosmoline (waterproofed) to be put in storage as the war in Europe was coming to an end.[19]

After the 11th Armored Division linked with friendly forces in Houffalize on 16 January, the 969th Field Artillery Battalion, with over 100 of the 333rd Field Artillery Battalion's personnel being used as replacements, prepared to join the 7th Army in the Vosges sector. Already in Vosges, attached to the 3rd Infantry Division, was another African American artillery unit. The 999th Field Artillery Battalion, an 8-inch howitzer unit, and sister battalion of the 578th Artillery Battalion and the 777th Field Artillery Battalion (4.5-inch gun), had a considerably different employment career from those of the artillery battalions fighting in the Ardennes Forest.

The 999th Artillery Battalion arrived in Normandy on 17 July 1944, after a brief stay in England. With the commitment of the 3rd Army and the XV Corps after the capture of St. Lo, the 999th Field Artillery Battalion was attached on 4 August to XV Corps in pursuit of the retreating German army. In nine days, the battalion traveled 180 miles in the face of stiff enemy resistance, occupying 17 firing positions. From positions around the towns of Flacourt and at Mantes Gassicourt, the battalion fired over 2,000 rounds of ammunition and helped to establish a bridgehead over the Seine River that sealed off the last escape route of the German 7th Army. During this rapid advance, the battalion was attached to the 144th Field Artillery Group, which was supporting the 79th and 90th Infantry Divisions, and the 2nd French Armored Division. The 999th Artillery Battalion was briefly attached to the American 1st Army, when it was establishing a bridgehead at Mantes Gassicourt. The battalion was then attached to the XX Corps and under the command and control of the 333rd Field Artillery Brigade. The XX Corps, having swept east across France, was about to assault the city of Metz when the 999th Artillery Battalion reached the town of Chambley and began to fire in support of the 5th Infantry Division. On 10 September, the battalion rejoined XV Corps and the 40th Artillery Group supporting the 79th Infantry Division and the 2nd French Armored Division as they pushed the Germans across the Moselle and Muerthe Rivers. Along with XV Corps, the 999th Field Artillery Battalion passed to the control of the 7th Army in late October. It participated in the Corps' assault on the towns of Sarrebourg, Saverne, and Strasbourg. It fired in support of the 79th and 45th Infantry Divisions in their advance on the town of Hagenau. On 5 December, the battalion deployed with XV Corps from the Alsace sector back across the Vosges Mountains into Lorraine to support the 100th and 44th Infantry Divisions in their attack on the Maginot Line positions near the town of Bitche. On 21 December, the battalion was relieved from XV Corps and the 194th Artillery Group and attached to the 17th Artillery Group, then supporting the 36th Infantry Division in their attack of the Colmar Pocket area. After a 60-mile night road march, the battalion occupied its new firing positions, changing them slightly when the 3rd Infantry Division replaced the 36th Infantry Division. On 1 January 1945, the battalion was relieved from the 17th Field Artillery Group and attached to the 3rd Infantry Division Artillery, moving on 6 January to the village of Asubure, high in the Vosges Mountains, where it remained until 20 January.

With the elimination of the Colmar Pocket beginning on 23 January 1945, both the 999th and the 969th Field Artillery Battalions were attached to French units. The 999th Field Artillery Battalion was relieved from the 3rd Infantry Division and attached to the ALCA 2, a French artillery group. On 20–21 January, the 999th Field Artillery Battalion established offensive positions for the commencement of artillery preparation fires.

The 969th Field Artillery Battalion, arriving at Selestat on 21 January 1945 after its attachment to the 101st Airborne Division, was attached to the 1st French Division (Division Mobile Infantry), forming a groupment with the division's 4th battalion. With the assistance of this heavy artillery preparation, the attack, which commenced on 23 January, made good progress. The 969th Field Artillery Battalion alone fired 912 155-mm howitzer rounds on the first day of the battle. On 28 January, the 999th Field Artillery Battalion was attached to the 40th Artillery Group in the newly activated XXI Corps. The 969th Field Artillery Battalion on January 25th was attached to the 5th French Armored Division upon its commitment to battle, and later to the American 75th Infantry Division and the French 2nd Armored Division. Both battalions continued in support of the French and American combat divisions engaged in encircling and clearing the Colmar Pocket of enemy forces, a task that was completed by 8 February. Both battalions received commendations from the French and American divisions which they supported, and both were among the units given the right to incorporate the arms of the city of Colmar into their insignia. When heavy artillery was no longer required in the Colmar area, both units were deployed north to XV Corps in the Sarreguemines area where the 999th Field Artillery Battalion was attached to the 144th Artillery

Two French soldiers fill the hands of American soldiers with candy, in Rouffach, France, after the closing of the Colmar Pocket, 5 February 1945. (National Archives, 111-SC-190120)

Group and the 969th Field Artillery Battalion to the 30th Artillery Group. Already attached to the 30th Artillery Group was the newly arrived African American 155-mm howitzer battalion, the 686th Field Artillery, which arrived in France on 1 February 1945 and began its general fire support missions on 10 February. The three artillery battalions fired in general support of XXI Corps' infantry and armored divisions in their attacks along the Saar River and in the advance to and across the Rhine River.[20]

Keeping up with the fast-moving infantry and armored units so that they would be in positions within range of the targets when and if needed became a problem for the heavier caliber artillery units as the spring offensive of the Allied armies across Germany picked up speed. The armored artillery battalions with their self-propelled howitzers were better suited for this fast-paced battle. The 999th Field Artillery Battalion was relieved in April when it received a special mission that took it back to the Atlantic coast of France. The battalion, attached to the 13th Field Artillery Brigade, under the operational control of the French Army of the Atlantic, moved by road and rail from Sarreguemines back across France to the coast. There, the French were attacking German fortifications, which had been blocking the entrance to the harbor of Bordeaux since the June Allied landings. With the other American battalions of the 13th Artillery Brigade, the 999th turned its heavy 8-inch guns on the German-held Ile d'Oleron at the entrance to the harbor and on Pointe de Grave across the Gironde River. The Pointe de Grave pocket was cleared of enemy forces in two days. For ten days, heavy artillery fired on Ile d'Oleron. When the French forces made their amphibious landing on the morning of 30 April, the artillery fire had been so devastating and accurate that German resistance was nonexistent. The enemy surrendered by midafternoon. With the rest of the battalions of the 13th Field Artillery Brigade, the 999th on 6 May started back to rejoin 7th Army. When they arrived in Germany on 11 May 1945, the war in Europe was over, and only occupational duties awaited them.

The rapid advance across Germany in those last few months of the war, and the resulting lack of targets, kept the howitzers of the 969th Artillery Battalion, still in XXI Corps, but then attached to the 4th Infantry Division, silent after 28 April 1945, when the battalion fired its last shots of the war. During its ten months in combat, the 969th Field Artillery Battalion had fought with all four of the American armies in the European Theater of Operations, and with the French Army in the Colmar Pocket. It had fired a total of 42,289 rounds from its howitzers in support of American and French divisions.[21] On 3 May, the 969th Field Artillery Battalion found itself once again attached to the 101st Airborne Division. Though its howitzers were not firing, the battalion's 5-ton trucks were kept busy transporting American infantry and German prisoners. The battalion also assisted in the processing of thousands of German prisoners pouring into the 101st Airborne Division's prisoner of war stockades.

In the winter of 1944–1945, additional African American artillery groups and battalions arrived in England for transshipment to France. Some of those, like the 350th Field Artillery Battalion, had been stripped, refilled, and retrained during the manpower crisis of 1943–1944. The 350th Artillery Battalion, retrained between April and October 1944, arrived in Scotland in December 1944, and deployed to France on 22 February 1945. It was originally attached to the 351st Field Artillery Group, one of the three African American group headquarters and headquarters batteries arriving in Europe during the late winter months. These units were added to the Allied armies' artillery strength for the final attack against Germany. Theirs was generally a combat utilization of brief intensity. The 350th Field Artillery Battalion established its firing position to support both the 63rd and 70th Infantry Divisions in their attacks toward Saarbrucken. By 22 March, the battalion went into bivouac east of Bitche, France,

Easter morning, T/5 William E. Thomas and PFC Joseph Jackson prepare specially decorated eggs on Hitler's lawn, Germany, 10 March 1945. (National Archives 111-SC-202330)

remaining until 5 April, when it moved to Heidelberg, Germany. There, it was attached to the 421st Field Artillery Group in the 44th Antiaircraft Artillery Brigade, with the mission of guarding installations. It would perform these duties until the end of the war. During the month of April, its batteries' soldiers guarded 35 posts, including a prisoner of war hospital, an airfield, a radio repeater station, and various ammunition and fuel depots.

The 686th Field Artillery Battalion with its 155-mm howitzers arrived in Le Harve, France, in January 1945. The battalion would also support the Allied offensive into Germany. The 686th Field Artillery Battalion, similarly, after firing in support of the 4th Infantry Division, which it was detached from on 1 April, went to the 44th Antiaircraft Artillery Brigade on 27 April for duty with its 68th Artillery Group of 7th Army Security Command. As a security force, the unit was charged with maintaining order and safeguarding American soldiers and installations in an area 12 miles wide and 30 miles long adjacent to the Danube River.

Of the remaining African American field artillery units utilized in the European Theater, the 777th Field Artillery Battalion and the 452nd Antiaircraft Artillery Battalion had a more active role on the battlefield. The 777th Field Artillery Battalion, a 4.5-inch gun unit, was one of the African American artillery battalions activated in mid–1943, with cadre personnel from the 969th and 333rd Field Artillery Battalions. It was one of the units whose entire training and most of whose operational service was spent in the attachment of white group artillery headquarters. After a training period of less than a year, it departed Camp Beale, California, on 1 August 1944 for England. It arrived at Utah Beach on 16 September. It was one of the units that arrived just at the time when transportation for men and supplies was in critical demand. Two officers and 76 enlisted men of the battalion took 36 vehicles to form a portion of a truck convoy, which transported men and urgently needed supplies from the beaches to the front lines as part of the Red Ball Express, covering 3,100 miles between 25 September and 6 October. The remainder of the battalion remained in Brioquebosc, France, until 25 October 1944, when it deployed to Tongres, Belgium. There, it joined the XIX Corps as a general support-firing unit attached to the 202nd Field Artillery Group then supporting the 30th Infantry Division. It participated in the Kohlschied penetration (31 October 1944 until 20 November 1944), and in the Julich sector, occupying positions at Richterich and Ubach, Germany. From 24 November, it was in support of XIII Corps at Ubach and at Geilenkirchen. When the 349th Field Artillery Group, an African American unit, became operational at Hontem, Germany, on 1 February 1945, the 777th Field Artillery Battalion was attached to it. The 754th and 548th Field Artillery Battalions joined them, both equipped with 155-mm howitzers.

From the beginning of February, the 777th Field Artillery Battalion supported the British 12th Corps through the command of the 349th Artillery Group. On 6 February, the 349th Artillery Group and its attached battalions supported the XVI Corps for the remainder of the campaign in Germany. In March, the 777th Field Artillery Battalion saw its greatest fire support activity. From positions at Heidhausen, east of the Roer River, the battalion fired 1,337 rounds on the night of 3–4 March. At Weiers, on 4 March, the battalion, in the presence of the corps and corps artillery commanders, fired the XVI Corps' first artillery rounds across the Rhine River into Mehrum, Germany. From the town of Altfeld, between 5 and 10 March, the battalion sank barges, destroyed vehicles, including prime movers for towing artillery pieces, and fired on troop assembly points in the pocket south of Wesel and west of the Rhine River. It fired preparations and supporting fires for Operation Flash Point, XVI Corps' crossing of the Rhine River. On 25 March, the 777th Field Artillery Battalion and 349th Artillery Group crossed the Rhine River, the first of the African American combat units to do so.[22]

ANTIAIRCRAFT ARTILLERY

At the beginning of World War II the antiaircraft artillery force was a small branch of the Coast Artillery

Corps. The units were formed into three types of battalions: an artillery gun battalion, an automatic weapons battalion, and a searchlight battalion, which were either assigned to a regiment, or existed as a separate antiaircraft battalion. They were equipped with a unique array of obsolescent 3-inch artillery guns and single barrel, heavy water-cooled .50-caliber Browning machine guns. The German Blitzkrieg assaults throughout Europe in 1939 and 1940 forced a widespread reevaluation of the army's antiaircraft artillery (AAA) capability. Commencing in 1940–1941, there was a vast expansion of the antiaircraft artillery branch in order to meet the threat of this new type of warfare. On 30 September 1942, it was proposed that 811 antiaircraft artillery battalions be organized, with a total strength of 619,000 men. Finally, in 1943, the antiaircraft artillery became a separate branch of the military.

However, this massive buildup of antiaircraft artillery units became largely redundant when the United States Army Air Corps and the British Royal Air Forces took domination of the skies from the German Luftwaffe in late 1943 and early 1944. Many antiaircraft artillery battalions were disbanded to provide badly needed replacements for infantry divisions in 1944. Some of the battalions were converted to standard field artillery. Most of the African American antiaircraft artillery battalions were disbanded, with their personnel either being transferred to combat service support units, or to the armored and artillery battalions in the theater. A total of 258 antiaircraft battalions were inactivated or disbanded between 1 January 1944 and 8 May 1945. Nevertheless, antiaircraft artillery remained a strong component of the army and achieved something of a resurgence in late 1944 in Belgium, defending the port city of Antwerp from the threat of the German V-1 "Buzz Bomb." On 31 December 1944, there were still a total of 347 antiaircraft artillery battalions with approximately 257,000 men assigned.[23]

In 1943 the antiaircraft artillery regiments were divided into separate battalions, with the regimental headquarter and headquarters companies becoming new Antiaircraft Artillery Group Headquarters. The antiaircraft artillery battalions were organized as either artillery gun, which were equipped with the M1 90-mm antiaircraft gun, or as automatic weapons battalions, which were equipped initially with a United States designed M1 37-mm gun, but later were almost totally reequipped with the famous M1 40-mm Swedish Bofors-designed gun, and with either the M51 or M55 quad-mount .50 caliber Browning air-cooled machine guns. Later in the war, many of the gun antiaircraft battalions were used as standard field artillery battalions, utilizing their powerful 90-mm guns in support of infantry and armored divisions.

Of the African American antiaircraft artillery battalions that were not disbanded, the 452nd Antiaircraft Artillery Automatic Weapons Battalion was the one that saw the most combat duty in the European Theater of Operations. The XII Corps, to which this battalion was attached in combat, considered it to be among the best units of its type. The 452nd was one of those antiaircraft battalions whose batteries were deployed to England in 1943 and early 1944 to protect military installations. After landing in Normandy on 23 June 1944, the battalion spent most of its deployment protecting field artillery battalions from enemy aerial attacks. In August, it protected vital targets such as fuel and ammunition supply depots, river crossings, and road junctions, and sent many of its platoons to protect the XII Corps' field artillery battalions. It made its first claims of downed enemy aircraft on 23 August 1944 when, out of 15 German aircraft attacking the 191st Field Artillery Battalion's gun positions at the Seine River crossing, the 452nd Antiaircraft Artillery Battalion was given credit for two aircraft shot down, two damaged aircraft, and two probable damaged enemy aircraft.[24]

Unlike many other antiaircraft battalions, the 452nd Antiaircraft Artillery remained active throughout its overseas deployment. When protecting field artillery battalions, the 452nd Antiaircraft Artillery's batteries and platoons, as was the standard operating procedure for corps antiaircraft artillery battalions, would be attached to several units simultaneously, responsible for defending them against enemy aircraft attacks. At one point in October 1944, its personnel were detached, providing air defense for eight separate field artillery battalions located throughout France, Belgium, and Holland. No unit or installation defended by the 452nd Antiaircraft Artillery Battalion suffered any major material damage or personnel killed by enemy aircraft. When German counterbattery artillery fire caused casualties in the field artillery batteries, it would be the men of the 452nd Antiaircraft Artillery Battalion which would come to their aid in order to keep the remaining members of the gun crews actively firing. On one such occasion, on 27 September 1944, a platoon sergeant and a medical corpsman of the 452nd Antiaircraft Artillery Battalion came to the aid of several wounded members of the field artillery battalion. When enemy shelling increased in intensity, forcing the antiaircraft platoon and personnel of the artillery battalion to withdraw, the two men remained

Members of Battery A, 452nd Antiaircraft Artillery Battalion, stand by and check their equipment while the convoy takes a break, France, 9 November 1944. (National Archives 111-SC-196212-S)

to assist in the evacuation of all the wounded soldiers. For their heroic action under fire, the Silver Star medal was awarded to Staff Sergeant William Campbell and Technician 5th Class Zeno Ellis. On another occasion, on 4 December 1944, three privates from a 452nd Antiaircraft Artillery platoon protecting a field artillery battalion which had come under heavy enemy counterbattery fire, exposed themselves to incoming artillery shells in order to rescue five injured members of a gun crew. For their bravery, Privates First Class Edward Swindell and Willie Jackson, and Private Samuel Johnson, were also awarded the Silver Star medal.[25]

In March 1945, as XII Corps and 3rd Army drove east to the Rhine River, enemy air activity increased sharply in an all-out effort to stem the Allied advance. The 452nd Antiaircraft Artillery Battalion experienced more combat activity during this period than any other time since entering the theater. It had 133 combat engagements during the month, claiming 42 enemy aircraft destroyed, with 23 probable destroyed. On 17 March, as the two combat commands of the 4th Armored Division were attacked throughout the day by Luftwaffe FW-190 and ME-109 aircraft, the 452nd Antiaircraft Artillery Battalion recorded four additional destroyed aircraft at the Nahe River bridgehead. The Nahe River bridgehead, established at Bad Krueznach on 18 March, was under constant attack for 48 hours. The elements of the 452nd Antiaircraft Artillery Battalion accounted for an additional six German aircraft destroyed. On 20 March, the German Luftwaffe sent 248 aircraft to attack the bridgehead. By now, there were nine antiaircraft battalions defending this sector. Of the 36 aircraft destroyed by antiaircraft battalions, the 452nd Antiaircraft Artillery Battalion was credited with 12 kills. When the 5th Infantry Division reached the Rhine River at Oppenheim on 22 March, and engineers were erecting a pontoon bridge, the 452nd Antiaircraft Artillery Battalion was among the units tasked with providing air defense artillery. That afternoon, 58 German aircraft attacked their positions. Of the 19 enemy aircraft destroyed by antiaircraft batteries, the 452nd was credited with an additional ten enemy aircraft destroyed. The 452nd Antiaircraft Artillery did not suffer any casualties from air activity until April 1945, when in an engagement with 20 Luftwaffe fighters, the unit had four soldiers wounded. By the war's end, with its platoons scattered throughout Germany, Austria, and Czechoslovakia, the 452nd Antiaircraft Artillery Battalion could claim 67 confirmed destroyed aircraft and another 19 probable destroyed.[26]

Chapter VII

Tank Destroyers

THE TANK DESTROYER BATTALIONS WERE CREATED as a mobile antitank reserve force in 1941. On 27 November 1941, the War Department activated the Tank Destroyer Force to carry out the mission to seek, strike, and destroy enemy tanks in defensive and offensive missions. The main battle tank for the army, the M4 Sherman, was inferior to the German's main battle tank, the Panzer. The tank destroyer, a combination of armor and artillery, had the original concept for tank destroyer battalions to be concentrated in brigades and groups for employment en masse against an armored threat like the German Blitzkrieg. In practice, the realities of combat and the erosion of the large, swift-moving German Panzer force meant that the tank destroyer battalions were usually attached individually to an infantry or armored division.

Initial War Department mobilization plans called for the activation of 220 tank destroyer battalions, a figure that was never achieved. By the end of 1943, 106 tank destroyer battalions were in existence, of which 56 served in the combat theaters of North Africa or the Mediterranean, and six battalions operated throughout the Pacific. Eleven of the remaining stateside battalions were converted to armored field artillery, amphibious tractor, chemical mortar, or tank battalions. Thirty-six battalions were disbanded, with their personnel being assigned to the replacement pool. With most of the African American tank destroyer battalions being disbanded, this usually resulted in the men being transferred to combat service support units, which were more urgently required in the combat theaters.

The first tank destroyer battalions organized were fully self-propelled. However, combat experience in North Africa appeared to show that towed guns would be more desirable in the open terrain. As a result, about one-half of the battalions were converted to towed gun units in 1943. Unfortunately, further combat experience on different terrain in Italy proved that towed guns were simply too immobile, making them highly vulnerable to a mechanized armor attack. As a result, in 1944 many of the towed battalions were converted back to self-propelled. On 1 January 1945, a total of 73 tank destroyer battalions were on the active rolls.[1]

Organized similarly to the tank battalions, the tank destroyer battalions were all structured to operate as self-sustained units with three line or combat companies. Each company was equipped with twelve guns, either towed or self-propelled, for a total of thirty-six in the battalion. A reconnaissance platoon was assigned to each line company. Each platoon in the company was led by a lieutenant and consisted of four gun crews that were commanded by a noncommissioned officer. The crew on a self-propelled tank destroyer consisted of five soldiers. In the towed tank destroyer battalion, each gun had a crew of ten personnel. The towed M6, 3-inch Antitank Gun, with the prime mover M3A1 armored half-track vehicle, was a high-velocity antitank gun mounted on a split-trailed carriage (modified from the 105-mm howitzer), with a sloped armor shield. Weighing in at 5,850 pounds, the 3-inch gun required careful coordination and teamwork to operate and maneuver. Its gun crew consisted of a gun commander (a noncommissioned officer), a gunner, a driver, and seven cannoneers. Twenty-seven towed tank destroyer battalions were deployed in the European and Mediterranean Theaters of Operation. All but four of these battalions were later converted to self-propelled tank destroyer battalions by the March/April 1945 timeframe. Two of the four remaining towed antitank gun battalions were composed of African American soldiers.

The tank destroyer battalion also had a service company that was responsible for the administration, logistical support, and the maintenance of the battalion's vehicles. The headquarters company contained an 81-mm mortar platoon and a reconnaissance platoon. The tank destroyer battalion, in addition to attacking enemy armored forces, had a secondary mission to provide highly mobile direct and indirect artillery fire in support of infantry maneuvers. Normally, when a tank destroyer battalion was attached to an infantry division, each of the line companies would support one of the three infantry regiments. The earlier tank destroyer battalions also had antiaircraft and engineer platoons, which were later discarded.[2]

The African American tank destroyer battalions would only have a token representation. When antitank battalions were redesignated tank destroyer battalions in December 1941, thus creating what was in all major respects a new combat arms branch, two African American battalions for the new service were activated with cadres from two of the older field artillery regiments. These were the 846th Tank Destroyer Battalion, activated with personnel from the 349th Field Artillery Battalion on 15 December, and the 795th Tank Destroyer Battalion, activated the following day with men from the 184th Field Artillery Regiment. In 1942, five additional segregated African American tank destroyer battalions were activated, with six more scheduled for 1943. Of these latter six, only four were activated. Out of eleven African American tank destroyer battalions that were activated during World War II, only three would ever be deployed in combat, with the others being disbanded and the enlisted men transferred to combat service support companies.[3]

The tank destroyer battalions first employed two stopgap ad hoc weapons: the M3 half-track, which mounted an older version of the 75-mm howitzer, and the M6 tank destroyer, a Dodge ¾-ton weapons carrier vehicle armed with a 37-mm antitank gun crudely mounted in the truck bed. Later, during the campaign in North Africa in 1943, the tank destroyer battalions began to receive the first standardized tank destroyer vehicle, with the introduction of the M10. The M10 was based on a variant of the M4 Sherman medium tank chassis, which was easily mass-produced, was lightly armored with an exposed opened turret, and had poor cross-country mobility and speed. However, its 3-inch main gun, a development of a prewar antiaircraft gun, was quite powerful for the time, and was capable of destroying any enemy armored vehicle, provided it was able to fire the first round. By early 1944 the first specifically designed tank destroyer appeared, the M18, and began to slowly replace the M10. The M18 was even more lightly armored than the M10, but had very good cross-country mobility and impressive speed. Noted for being the fastest armored track vehicle in the army inventory, it could reach a speed of 60 miles per hour. Furthermore, the gun was an improved version of the 3-inch caliber, known later as the 76-mm high-velocity gun, with a more powerful cartridge case and muzzle-break, giving it greater accuracy and striking power. Finally, also in late 1944, the M36 was deployed. The M36 utilized the same chassis as the M10, but mounted the powerful 90-mm gun (also originally an antiaircraft weapon). The M36 was the most powerful antitank weapon in the United States Army arsenal. With the newly developed high-velocity armor-piercing rounds (HVAP, also known as APCR for Armor Piercing Composite Rigid), the 90-mm was easily capable of defeating all German armor forces, if it could score the first hit while engaged in combat.

The 614th Tank Destroyer Battalion (Towed) was an African American unit that had been activated on 25 July 1942 at Camp Carson, Colorado, and later transferred to Camp Kilmer, New Jersey. The battalion arrived on Utah Beach on 8 October 1944 and was initially committed to combat in the European Theater of Operations on 28 November, when it was assigned to relieve the 705th Tank Destroyer Battalion (Self-Propelled), then supporting the 3rd Cavalry Group (Mechanized) in the 7th Army. The 614th Tank Destroyer Battalion was equipped with the 3-inch gun that was towed by armored half-track vehicles. In the 3rd Cavalry Group, one line company of the 614th Tank Destroyer Battalion was attached to each of the group's three squadrons with the remainder of the battalion kept in strategic reserve. The 614th's commander, Lieutenant Colonel Frank Pritchard, and four of his staff officers were white. The rest of the battalion's officers and enlisted men were African Americans. At this time, the 3rd Cavalry Group was protecting the north flank of XX Corps from the Moselle River to the vicinity of the Ober Tunsdor in Germany, where it maintained contact with the 90th Cavalry Reconnaissance Squadron of the 10th Armored Division, then operating in a zone between the Moselle and Saar Rivers. Before it were the "dragons' teeth," antitank ditches, and pillbox defensive positions of the Siegfried Line. On 1 December 1944, its first day on the front lines, Company A, 614th Tank Destroyer Battalion, scored three direct hits on enemy held pillboxes north of the town of Borg. The Germans raised a white flag, but when an armored cavalry patrol approached, the enemy opened fire. The tank destroyers then resumed firing and the enemy retreated out of their pillboxes. The company, in its first day of combat, also accounted for one German 88-mm antitank gun destroyed through highly accurate indirect artillery fire.

Late that evening, the 614th Tank Destroyer Battalion was relieved from the 3rd Cavalry Group for movement to Luneville, France, where on 7th Army Headquarters orders it was attached to VI Corps. On 5 December the battalion was attached to the 103rd Infantry Division, then headquartered at Kuttolsheim, France.[4] There, Company A was attached to Task Force Forest, composed of the 103rd Reconnaissance Troop, a company of the 756th Tank Battalion, and a company of the 409th Infantry Regiment. Company C was attached to the 411th Infantry Regiment.[5]

The 103rd Infantry Division was relieving the veteran 45th and 79th Infantry Divisions in a sector on the west bank of the flooded Zintzel du Nord River. Beginning on 8 December, as the 103rd Infantry Division deployed into the front defensive lines, the companies of the 614th Tank Destroyer Battalion commenced firing, with Company C destroying an enemy observation post located in a church steeple, taking out a machine gun emplacement, and delivering harassing direct artillery fire on enemy soldiers. The 103rd Infantry Division's attack began before dawn on 9 December, with a crossing of the Zintzel du Nord River to seize the towns of Uttenhofen and Mertzwiller on the opposite bank. The attack progressed through Griesbach and Fortsheim. In both towns, being utilized as short-range, direct artillery support, the 614th Tank Destroyer Battalion's guns eliminated enemy forward artillery observation posts and sniper positions that were located in church steeples. When the attack reached the Maginot Line, German defensive positions grew stronger. In the rugged hills and forest surrounding the Lembach-Climbach area, the 411th Infantry Regiment met strong enemy resistance.

The regiment organized a task force under the command of its executive officer to dislodge the Germans from Climbach, a town in an open valley with high, well-defended ridges guarding its approaches. The task force contained a platoon of combat engineers, a platoon of M4 Sherman tanks, Company B of the 1/411th Infantry, and a platoon from Company C, 614th Tank Destroyer Battalion. The task force had the mission of advancing to the town of Climbach and holding it, thus cutting the lines of enemy communication to Lembach. The third platoon from Company C of the 614th Tank Destroyer Battalion would act as a diversionary force in order to draw enemy artillery fire so that the infantry and tanks could attack the town on the flanks. Private First Class Gordon Roget of Company B, 1/411th Infantry, who would later receive a battlefield commission, recalls: "We were in the woods outside of Climbach on the night of December 13th preparing for the coordinated attack the next morning. We would be backed up by the 614th Tank Destroyer Battalion, so we felt that this must be a very important assignment. There was a massive artillery barrage during the night by our rear support guns."[6]

The task force departed Prueschdorf at 1020 on the foggy, cold morning of 14 December. Visibility was less than 300 yards. The task force, with First Lieutenant Charles L. Thomas, the commander of Company C, 614th Tank Destroyer Battalion, leading the column in the his M20 armored scout car, followed by the halftrack vehicles towing the M6 antitank guns, proceeded through enemy territory. The enemy had the approach coordinates to Climbach pre-sited to deliver devastating fire. When the task force got within range, heavy enemy small arms, M42 machine gun, mortar, and artillery fire fell along the approach route. Once within 1000 yards of Climbach, Lieutenant Thomas' scout car took a direct hit from an enemy mortar shell but proceeded forward. His vehicle was eventually demobilized after striking a land mine. Lieutenant Thomas, though wounded, dismounted from his wrecked scout car and assisted his crew, including another wounded soldier. He then scrambled on top of the vehicle, secured the .50-caliber machine gun, and placed a steady stream of fire on the advancing enemy infantry. In the ensuing firefight, Lieutenant Thomas was wounded again in the chest, arms, and leg, but refused medical evacuation.

Infantry and tanks deployed on both sides of the road. The task force commander ordered the tank destroyer platoon to proceed up the road and establish defensive positions to lay down a base of fire. There, they could place direct artillery fire on the enemy forces in and around Climbach, while the rest of the task force advanced on the flanks of the German positions. Lieutenant Thomas's swift action in firing his heavy machine gun kept the enemy occupied long enough for his gun crews to dismount their half-tracks and to put their antitank gun systems into operation. Leaving the protective cover of his wrecked scout car, Lieutenant Thomas ordered, and then personally directed the dispersion and placement of two of the four tank destroyer crews. These tank destroyers, while totally exposed in the open fields, were soon returning fire on the now alerted enemy, who were directing the fire of all their ridgetop weapons upon the task force. Lieutenant Thomas, in spite of his multiple wounds, continued to direct and encourage his men. Only when he was certain that his men were effectively returning fire and that his platoon leader was in control of the situation, did Lieutenant Thomas allow himself to be evacuated from the battlefield to the battalion aid station.[7]

On their exposed hillside, the ten-man tank destroyer crews went into action, loading, aiming, and firing their towed antitank guns, while laying down suppressive fire with the half-track mounted .50-caliber machine guns. Within minutes, the gun crews, exposed in the open fields, began to take heavy casualties. One tank destroyer crew, although exposed in the open, had better luck than the other crews. Their half-tracked vehicle bogged down in the open muddy fields, but in a slight draw. Unable to proceed to their assigned position, they put their antitank gun into action from this defilade. The Germans poured small arms and tank fire into the position without being able to inflect any serious damage. The gun crews, some reduced to as few as two men, continued to accurately fire from their exposed positions on the Germans, causing severe damage for four hours. The M4 Sherman tanks of the task force also became mired in the muddy fields, and were abandoned when they came under fire from German 88-mm antitank guns. Three infantrymen from the 411th Infantry Regiment, armed with Browning Automatic Rifles (BAR), volunteered to go forward and provide flank security to the exposed gun crews.

When the cannoneers ran out of ammunition for their 3-inch antitank guns, the surviving crewmen continued to return fire with their .50-caliber machine guns, M1 rifles, and carbines, keeping the enemy from mounting a counterattack. Technician 5 Robert W. Harris, knowing that the last gun was running out of ammunition, drove his half-track to the forward supply depot under a barrage of small arms, mortar and artillery fire. After his vehicle was fully loaded with ammunition for the antitank guns, M1 rifles, and the .50-caliber heavy machine guns, he proceeded back up the Climbach hill. About halfway up, the task force commander, who had already withdrawn the rest of the task force to a protective area, stopped him. The task force commander told Harris that the enemy fire was too intense to proceed. Disregarding the warning, and refusing to leave his fellow soldiers stranded without ammunition, Technician 5 Harris drove to within 25 yards of his gun position so as not to become bogged in the muddy field. He unloaded the vehicle, uncrated the ammunition, and began to carry it forward. The surviving men of the platoon made trip after trip, under heavy enemy fire, to carry the 54-pound ammunition boxes to the one gun that was still functioning. Infantrymen of the 411th Infantry Regiment, inspired by the brave feats of the African American gun crews, infiltrated and attacked from the flanks while the enemy concentrated their fire on the remaining antitank gun. The tank destroyer crew continued to engage the enemy until darkness. By then, enemy fire had been reduced to pockets of small arms fire in Climbach, which was cleared out by the advancing infantry.

Colonel Donovan Yeuell, the commander of the 411th Regimental Combat Team, quickly moved his advance command post to a house on the side of a mountain looking straight up the valley toward Climbach, where he could see the battle unfold, and issued prompt commands when the situation demanded it. He would note in his after action reports of the battle: "The men of the 614th Tank Destroyer Battalion made it possible for the rest of the attacking force to be successful in defeating the enemy and capturing the strongly defended town of Climbach."[8]

After the battle, the 103rd Infantry Division reported: "This outstanding performance of mass heroism on the part of the officers and men of Company C, 614th Tank Destroyer Battalion, precluded a near catastrophic reverse for the task force." Their action before Climbach, in which the platoon had more than 50 percent casualties, lost three antitank guns, two half-track vehicles, and an armored scout car destroyed, enabled the task force to capture the town and forced the enemy to retreat to the Siegfried Line. Two enemy infantry/tank counterattacks against the town during the night were repulsed with the assisted firepower of the surviving tank destroyer crewmen. For their heroic action and self-sacrifice at Climbach, France, the Third Platoon, Company C, 614th Tank Destroyer Battalion, was awarded the

Presidential Distinguished Unit Citation. This was a first for any unit assigned or attached to the 103rd Infantry Division, and the first African American unit to do so in the war. In addition to the Distinguished Unit Citation, Lieutenant Thomas received the Distinguished Service Cross, the nation's second highest award, for his valor under fire. The members of this valiant platoon were also awarded four Silver Star medals, two of them posthumously, and nine Bronze Star medals for individual acts of heroism.[9] When Major General Charles C. Haffner, Jr., commanding the 103rd Infantry Division, personally pinned their decorations on two officers and nine enlisted men at a ceremony on 28 December, the unit declared it "a great morale factor in our troops."[10]

The resolve of the enemy was broken and on 15 December, the men of the 103rd Infantry Division were the first soldiers in the 6th Army Group to enter Germany across a very small stream near the Lauter River.

In March 1945, Lieutenant Thomas, still recovering from his wounds, was sent home to Detroit, Michigan. He was hailed as a conquering hero by the African American press. Still, he remained humble: "I know I hung on to one thought, deploy the guns and start firing or we're dead.... I was sent out to locate and draw enemy fire, but I didn't mean to draw that much."[11]

Throughout the winter of 1944–1945, the 614th Tank Destroyer Battalion remained attached to the 103rd Infantry Division. It participated in the division's holding operations and limited offensives on the left flank of the 7th Army's defensive line and along the Moder River line. It fired star illumination shells for night patrols, and indirect fire missions in attachment to the 928th Field Artillery Battalion, thereby relieving a critical shortage of howitzer ammunition in the theater. Its men of the reconnaissance platoons engaged in raids and patrols with elements of the 103rd Infantry Division.[12] On 1 January 1945, an enemy patrol attacked a 13-man outpost of Company A. The outpost was isolated for about an hour while heavy small arms fire was exchanged. When the firefight was over, the outpost had killed nine and captured two of the enemy without suffering any losses. On 12 January, the first section (two 3-inch guns) of the 1st Platoon, Company C, directed to destroy an enemy observation post at Forbach, fired 143 rounds in forty minutes and scored 139 direct hits.

While the enemy's Ardennes offensive (the Battle of the Bulge) was going on in the 1st Army's sector, the Germans also launched a strong offensive push in 7th Army's sector of the front lines called Operation Nordwind. This operation called for a series of surprise attacks into the Vosges Mountains. The ultimate enemy objective was the capture of the town of Saverne. The 103rd Infantry and five other divisions were tasked with preventing this. If Saverne were captured, the main supply routes for the entire American 7th Army and the 1st French Army would be severed. This enemy offensive forced the units of 7th Army to withdraw and reorganize in order to repel these forces. On 20 January 1945, when the 614th Tank Destroyer Battalion joined in a planned withdrawal of the 103rd Infantry Division to new defensive lines west of the town of Hagenau, Companies A and C remained in position in order to cover the division's withdrawal under cover of darkness. The two companies met with extreme difficulties in their own withdrawal over roads covered with snow and ice. For several hours, commanders of both companies remained behind the infantry force covering the withdrawal in an effort to salvage all possible equipment. Despite the efforts of the men of the companies not to abandon their own equipment when the roads became impassable, three guns, six half-track vehicles, and miscellaneous equipment had to be destroyed to prevent it from falling into the hands of the advancing enemy, who were expected to occupy the sector just recently vacated by the 103rd Infantry Division. The battalion took up defensive positions in the security and antitank duties of the division along the south banks of the Rothbach and Moder Rivers.

During the weeks of enemy pressure and attacks against the 7th Army, coinciding with, but less successful than the counterattacks to the north in the Ardennes region, the outposts of the 614th Tank Destroyer Battalion became as accustomed to fighting off German patrols and raiding parties as did the infantrymen. For nearly two months, the battles raged all around the mountains and in various small towns. When it was over, more than 16,000 Americans had been killed or wounded but the Germans were soundly defeated. The men of the 103rd Infantry Division had distinguished themselves at the Battle of Selestat and during the Alsace Campaign.

In the days before the planned March offensive, the 614th Tank Destroyer Battalion continued patrolling and training. A carefully trained attacking force, consisting of two officers and thirty enlisted men from the reconnaissance platoons, raided an old mill between the towns of Bischoltz and Mulhausen on 5 February, achieving perfect coordination and complete surprise. Their goal was to bring back captured enemy prisoners for interrogation. Each officer and enlisted man had been fully instructed not only in his own job, but also in those jobs of the other men. Two teams of raiders, consisting of six men each, entered the mill, while a section of machine gunners, setting up on either side of the building, covered the roads outside. Eight of the enemy soldiers were killed, and six prisoners captured. The raiding party incurred not a single casualty.

With the attachment of the 761st Tank Battalion to the 103rd Infantry Division on 12 March, each regiment of the division now had one African American tank and tank destroyer company assigned in preparation for the 7th Army's final spring offensive of the war. When the attack commenced on the morning of 15 March, all elements of the 614th Tank Destroyer Battalion were utilized in the 103rd Infantry Division's sector of responsibility. Company A laid a direct artillery barrage on the town of Kindwiller. Then, with a provisional force under the leadership of its company commander and with 30 enlisted men from the headquarters platoon, Captain Beauregard King was ordered to attack and capture the town. The dismounted force entered Kindwiller under heavy enemy fire; when Captain King, leading his men, fell seriously wounded, the platoon sergeant, Staff Sergeant Charles Parks, took command. By 1000, the force had taken the town and captured nine prisoners. Another provisional attacking force, formed with the 1st and 2nd Reconnaissance Platoons, and a platoon from Company B supporting, under the leadership of the battalion commander, Lieutenant Colonel Frank Pritchard, attacked the town of Bischoltz at 1530 and took 41 prisoners. Companies B and C continued supporting the 410th and 411th Infantry Regiments respectively with direct artillery fire. The advance continued for the next three days against light enemy rear-guard resistance until reaching the Siegfried Line towns.

The 103rd Infantry Division reached the Rhine River with the 614th Tank Destroyer Battalion still attached. The division went into an interim period of occupation and mopping up pockets of enemy resistance that were bypassed by the fast-moving armored divisions which spearheaded the attack. Elements of the 614th Tank Battalion aided in setting up military governments for the occupied towns and gathering enemy stragglers. They also trained replacement soldiers. Like the other African American combat battalions, the military leaders had not expected these units to ever be committed to combat, so there was no replacement system in place. Some replacement soldiers came from the recently disbanded 827th Tank Destroyer Battalion, while the majority were volunteers from the combat service support units in the theater. When the 103rd Infantry Division resumed its pursuit of the enemy on 21 April, the 614th Tank Destroyer Battalion, with its reorganized line companies attached to the division's infantry regiments, proceeded south toward Austria, destroying and neutralizing enemy positions and taking prisoners along the way.

By April 27, 1945, a spearhead task force composed of a battalion of the 409th Infantry Regiment, the 781st Tank Destroyer Battalion (–) using the M-18 self-propelled tank destroyers, the 614th Tank Destroyer Battalion, the 824th Reconnaissance Troop, and the 83rd Chemical Mortar Battalion, whose half-track mounted 81-mm mortars were utilized as mobile, close support artillery, had reached Schoengau, just 30 miles south of Landsberg, Austria. The 614th Tank Destroyer Battalion suffered its last casualties of the war on 2 May 1945, on the outskirts of Scharnitz, Austria, in a battle in which one officer and six enlisted men were killed while leading a task force toward Innsbruck. On 3 May, one platoon from Company C was attached to the 411th Regimental Combat Team in a dash from the town of Mittenwald toward the Brenner Pass where, on 4 May, they seized the area without opposition and went beyond to link up with elements of the 5th Army's 88th Infantry Division, approaching from Italy.[13]

Throughout the war, the 614th Tank Destroyer Battalion was attached primarily to the 103rd Infantry Division, and established a strong esprit de corps. The soldiers of the 614th Tank Destroyer Battalion lived, fought, and died side by side with white infantry soldiers of this division across France, Germany, and finally into Austria. When the war was over, it was written about this battalion: "First it proved to the world that the Negro soldier could and would fight. Other battalions had done more in this war than the 614th, but the 614th had done well everything that had been asked of it and had won the esteem and affection of the 103rd Infantry Division with which it was associated for so long. It had won respect of Corps and Army commanders and their staffs. It had merited a visit from the Commanding General of the Seventh Army, Lieutenant General Alexander M. Patch. Its exploits had been publicized in the newspapers. It had also proved that when men demonstrate their worth, racial troubles are largely ended and the colored man is accepted. No friendship could be stronger between groups of men than the friendship that existed between the colored gamecocks of the 614th Tank Destroyer Battalion and the white officers and soldiers of the 103rd Infantry Division."[14] On Wednesday, 9 May 1945, a victory parade was held in Innsbruck. The 103rd Infantry Division passed in review for civilians and senior military personnel on the River Road Drive. Portions of the infantry regiments passed, followed by the division band, then the spearheading task force, and the attached artillery units with their 105-mm and 155-mm howitzers, the 614th Tank Destroyer Battalion, and finally the 761st and 781st Tank Battalions.

With the introduction of the new M26 Pershing Tank with its 90-mm main gun late in the war, the requirement for tank destroyer battalions became obsolete.

Two other African American tank destroyer battalions were deployed to a wartime overseas theater. The 679th Tank Destroyer Battalion (Towed) was activated on 26 June 1943 at Camp Hood, Texas, and deployed overseas in March 1945 to support the 92nd Infantry Division in Italy in its final offensive push of the war. The other was the 827th Tank Destroyer Battalion (Self-Propelled). The 827th Tank Destroyer Battalion was activated on 24 April 1942, and shipped to Europe in November 1944 after its scheduled deployment to the Pacific Theater in the spring of that year had been cancelled due to training deficiencies. The eight other African American tank destroyer battalions had been disbanded beginning in August 1943, with the soldiers being sent primarily to combat service support units. Few soldiers ended up assigned to one of the three African American tank battalions. All of the disbanded African American tank destroyer battalions received higher efficiency evaluations than the 827th Tank Destroyer Battalion.

The 827th Tank Destroyer Battalion, whose training career had been plagued by inept leadership, had been recommended for disbandment by the same officers who were selected to command it. Many did not want to be assigned to an African American unit. It had trained for 2 1/2 years in the United States, but under less than optimal circumstances. From its activation in 1942, until the time it had deployed overseas, the unit had served under eight different battalion commanders. In many cases, the army would assign substandard white officers to African American units. The number of commanders passing through the 827th Tank Destroyer Battalion in this short period of time would be indicative of this policy. Each battalion commander served an average of a little more than three months in the battalion. The battalion had been reorganized under four different tables of organization and equipment (TO&E). It had been reequipped with primary weapons systems four times, but this was only normal as improvements in tactics and equipment were made throughout the war. Starting its career with towed 75-mm antitank guns, it converted successfully to self-propelled M10s. After the campaign in North African, it was decided to change to the towed M3 3-inch antitank guns. Finally, the battalion converted to the newer M18 self-propelled antitank vehicles. By August of 1944, the 827th Tank Destroyer Battalion had already failed five Army Ground Forces battalion-level tests and was never certified for having completed training. Training in indirect artillery support fire, one of the chief requirements for the secondary missions of the tank destroyer battalions, was waived entirely.

The battalion's failures were at first blamed on the lack of leadership qualities of the African American lieutenants that were assigned to the companies from Officer's Candidate School. When white officers from disbanded tank destroyer battalions replaced all of these officers, blame was then shifted to the substandard quality of the noncommissioned officers, and then to the lower army aptitude test scores of the enlisted men, which was thought to preclude any success being achieved in this battalion. Yet, these test scores coincided with the average test scores of the men of the 614th and 679th Tank Destroyer Battalions. Never did the responsibility of these failures fall to the leadership deficiencies of the white commanders or officers. Lack of confidence and trust in the soldiers of the battalion, and the inability of the officers to effectively lead and communicate with their subordinate soldiers, also led to several disciplinary problems. In addition, there was resentment from the enlisted men for having all of their African American officers replaced with white officers. Two general courts-martial involving a shooting and a murder also disrupted training in September 1944. Both cases were indicators of the lack of discipline in the unit, where neither officers nor noncommissioned officers had control of their soldiers. Soldiers that were deficient in the combat skills required for the operations of tank destroyers, or who were disciplinary problems, could not be replaced since the army was no longer training African American soldiers for assignment to these battalions. Highly qualified African American soldiers that were trained in antitank and indirect artillery support fire from the eight disbanded tank destroyer battalions could have been utilized as replacements for substandard soldiers, had they not been transferred to service and labor units. Yet, in spite of these clear deficiencies in training, discipline, and leadership, the battalion was deemed prepared for a combat deployment by the higher headquarters at the Tank Destroyer School at Camp Hood, Texas. In the latter months of 1944, tank destroyer battalions were in high demand in the European Theater of Operations, especially those equipped with the newer M18 tank destroyer vehicle.

The battalion deployed from Camp Hood in October 1944 and sailed from New York directly to Marseille, France. The battalion was the only African American armored combat unit that deployed overseas with a full complement of all-white officers. After a month in the

Delta Base Section where it readied its equipment for combat, it was assigned to proceed to a forward staging area for the 7th Army. In the five-day battalion road march from Marseille to the Vosges Mountains, undertaken over icy roads in December 1944, there were several accidents. When the battalion arrived at Sarrsbourg, its vehicles went into maintenance shops for immediate repairs. At the time, the 7th Army was adjusting its defensive lines to cover the gaps left by the departure of the 3rd Army, which had proceeded north to relieve the besieged forces of the 1st Army fighting in the Battle of the Bulge.

On 20 December, the 827th Tank Destroyer Battalion was attached to the 12th Armored Division, then being held in tactical reserve. The battalion sent one company into the line on 21 December, where it supported the 714th Tank Battalion. The 614th Tank Destroyer Battalion, then operating in the same region, offered to help orient the 827th to combat conditions, but the battalion commander declined the offer due to the 614th having African American officers that would assist in the training. The 827th Tank Destroyer Battalion remained in position for three days without encountering enemy opposition. Lack of discipline and training continued to hamper the 827th Tank Destroyer Battalion, as gun crews often left their vehicles unguarded while gathering wood to build fires, which was in violation of front-line doctrine. Soldiers leaving their vehicles would continue to be a problem during the 827th Tank Battalion's brief combat career.[15]

The 7th Army, with its defensive positions extended, and expecting a German counterattack, established alternate defensive lines for possible withdrawals. The command alerted its reserve units for use in the case of enemy attacks. On 1 January 1945, the 12th Armored Division attached one of the 827th Tank Destroyer Battalion's companies to the 92nd Reconnaissance Squadron, then maintaining a counterreconnaissance screen west of the Saar River and south of the Maginot Line. The company remained on this mission until 6 January. Requests to utilize other elements of the 827th Tank Destroyer Battalion in an indirect fire mission to increase the firepower of the division's artillery battalion were denied by the XV Corps G3, as there was a greater need to hold the battalion in reserve for their primary mission of antitank fire. On 6 January, the 7th Army released the 827th Tank Destroyer Battalion from XV Corps and assigned it to VI Corps.[16]

With Combat Command B, 12th Armored Division, the 827th Tank Destroyer Battalion deployed on verbal orders to join Task Force Wahl of the 79th Infantry Division, providing armor and tank destroyer support to counter the German offensive Operation Nordwind. Before the 827th Tank Destroyer Battalion deployed, a lieutenant and an enlisted man shot each other when the officer attempted to quell a disturbance among his soldiers. In another company, a disgruntled soldier attacked his first sergeant, resulting in the first sergeant's shooting an innocent bystander by mistake. The company that was committed for the initial deployment orders could not move out at the designated time. The company commander alleged that 75 percent of his men were missing from their bivouac area, and that many of those present were intoxicated. Another company had to be substituted and led the battalion's march to its first combat assignment.[17] This lack of discipline and leadership, which hampered the 827th Tank Destroyer Battalion's performance in training in the United States, continued to plague the unit in their combat operations.

Task Force Wahl, under the command of Brigadier General George Wahl, the 79th Infantry Division's artillery commander, comprised many different units, which had never operated together in combat. It consisted of: the 79th Infantry Division's 3/313th Infantry and the 315th Infantry Regiment (–); the 222nd Infantry Regiment (–) of the 42nd Infantry Division; Combat Command A of the 14th Armored Division; the 813th Tank Destroyer Battalion (–); and the 827th Tank Destroyer Battalion. The 242nd Infantry Regiment of the 42nd Infantry Division, the 79th Division Artillery, and the 79th Reconnaissance Troop were attached later, making this provisional task force larger than a standard infantry division.

Command and control of these combined forces was difficult, as the soldiers of the 827th Tank Destroyer Battalion had been directed to take orders only from the officers of their battalion. This procedure was enormously complicated by poor radio communication within the battalion. As a result, platoon leaders shuttled between their sections in an attempt to be everywhere at once, and the 827th Tank Destroyer Battalion's gun crews would not fire at targets on their own initiative or on orders given by officers not assigned to their battalion. The 813th Tank Destroyer Battalion, a veteran unit with over 30 months of combat throughout North Africa, Italy, and Normandy, was under the assumption the 827th Tank Destroyer Battalion was attached to them for command and control, but no written orders were ever issued.[18] Infantry officers also confused the mission of the tank destroyers with those of standard tanks, and often assigned fire missions in which the tank destroyers were not doctrinally supposed to carry out. Elements of the 827th Tank Destroyer Battalion were attached to Task Force Wahl at 0300 on 8 January. Twelve days of combat followed in which elements of the 827thTank Destroyer Battalion, in the towns of Rittershoffen and Hatten especially, were engaged in fierce and often confused fighting. German and American forces fought in the streets of Hatten for several days, with the American soldiers cut off from the Allied lines.

On 9 January, Company B of the 827thTank Destroyer Battalion, then attached to the 68th Armored Infantry Regiment in the town of Soulzsous-Forets, was dispatched to the area north of Hatten at 1325 to help halt an enemy advance. Sixteen German tanks with supporting infantry were headed for Rittershoffen and fifteen more enemy tanks approached Hatten. The Panzer tanks approaching Rittershoffen (like Hatten, a village on the open plain) were fired on by the 827th Tank Destroyer Battalion's gun crews, resulting in the destruction of eleven enemy tanks and one full-tracked assault vehicle. Upon meeting this devastating and accurate fire, the remaining enemy tanks withdrew. A joint combat team of the 827th and 813th Tank Destroyer Battalion destroyed nine German tanks at Hatten. An additional four enemy Panzer Mark IV tanks were destroyed in a counterattack on Rittershoffen. Thereafter in Hatten, isolated by day, and subject to resupply only under the cover of darkness, two tank destroyers of Company B, 827th Tank Destroyer Battalion, continued to engage in close fighting, accounting for several enemy soldiers killed and German vehicles destroyed. Another section of another platoon performed so well that the 315th Infantry Regiment's commander reported receiving excellent tank destroyer support from the 827th Tank Destroyer Battalion.

One company of the 827th Tank Destroyer Battalion was ordered to proceed to the town of Oberroedorn on 9 January to fill a request for additional tank destroyer support by the embattled 3/313th Infantry. The company arrived with only 2 out its 12 M18 tank destroyers. Icy road conditions made traveling hazardous. The company commander sent out search parties to look for the missing crews while he took refuge in an infantry pillbox for over the next three hours during a German attack. When he emerged, seven of his tank destroyers were in position and engaged in combat. Infantry officers' requests for fire support on certain targets often went unacknowledged as the enlisted men searched for the missing 827th's officers for confirmation. When they could not be found, the noncommissioned officers took the initiative and fired on the targets. Some gun crews of the company, following the example of their officers, were often found in cellars and houses, instead of with their antitank vehicles. The 3/313th Infantry commander, already annoyed with the dilatory tactics and inefficiency within the 827th Tank Destroyer Battalion, requested white gun crews to replace all of the African American tank destroyers. Crews of the 813th Tank Destroyer Battalion, which during the month had lost 19 of their 31 older M10 tank destroyers to combat, including four vehicles that were captured with the entire 2/314th Infantry, were already manning some of the 827th Tank Destroyer Battalion's M18s that had been abandoned by crews that had allegedly refused to operate them. Continuing complaints as to the combat inefficiency of the 827th Tank Destroyer Battalion finally brought the VI Corps inspector general for an investigation of training and discipline within the unit.[19]

The investigation disclosed an amazing state of affairs in the 827th Tank Destroyer Battalion. Portions of the 827th Tank Destroyer Battalion attached to other infantry elements of Task Force Wahl had performed well, especially in light of their officers' overall opinion that the unit was less than satisfactory and that they lacked any confidence in the enlisted men. Also taken into account was that the 827th Tank Destroyer Battalion was new to combat and only received partial training stateside. Meanwhile, the entire incident in question occurred while the 827th Tank Destroyer Battalion was being strafed by German jet aircraft, being tasked to attack flame-throwing tanks, and providing fire support to infantry soldiers who were themselves disorganized and confused. Nevertheless, in the investigation, every white officer of the 827th Tank Destroyer Battalion expressed doubts that their men, characterized as untrainable, slow in their reactions, or stricken by fear, would ever be dependable on tank destroyers. Some of the officers did explain that a majority of their men could be counted upon and that they had always believed that if adequate replacements could be obtained for the remainder, theirs would be an excellent unit. Replacements had not been available in the past when some of the men could have been removed while the 827th Tank Destroyer Battalion was still in training at Camp Hood. Now with the shortage of manpower and especially among trained African American tank destroyer crewmen, hope for enough new replacements to make a change in the unit was nonexistent.

While the investigation was ongoing, the elements of the 827th Tank Destroyer Battalion in Rittershoffen and in Hatten continued in combat operations. The force in Rittershoffen used its guns to shell enemy fortifications in buildings. Those fighting in Hatten destroyed two additional enemy tanks at a range of over 1,400 yards, but lost one of its tank destroyers and the entire crew when it received a direct hit from an enemy Panzer tank.

After taking testimony from only the white officers for four days, the inspector recommended that the 827th Tank Destroyer Battalion be withdrawn from front line duty, be given additional technical training that they had been lacking, and remitted to combat. The inspector general's investigators also recommended that the men that refused to operate their guns in combat be court-martialed; that the battalion commander be relieved and replaced with a more forceful officer; and that the noncommissioned officers be improved by making them perform their normal duties with their gun crews. The Commanding General of VI Corps instead, ignoring the recommendations of the Inspector General's Office, recommended that the battalion be disbanded and that its enlisted men be reassigned to appropriate combat service support units.[20] Those men who had proved themselves worthy in combat would be used as well-needed replacements for the 614th Tank Destroyer Battalion. The Commanding General of 7th Army concurred, recommending that the battalion be inactivated and that a substitute tank destroyer battalion composed of white personnel be activated within the 7th Army. White truck, medical ambulance, car and smoke generator companies could be converted to African American, to provide both white soldiers for the new battalion and service unit vacancies for the African Americans. If higher headquarters decided that a white combat unit had to be converted to African American to preserve a racial balance between service and combat soldiers, 7th Army would convert a white combat engineer battalion instead.[21]

Now began a long administrative discussion of the disposition to be made of the 827th Tank Destroyer Battalion. The simplest procedure would have been to adopt the VI Corps and 7th Army's recommendations, but the investigation supporting this recommendation had not reached the same conclusion. Tank destroyer battalions had, at this juncture in the war, returned to high priority and were in critical demand. The investigation officer had interviewed only the officers of the 827th Tank Destroyer Battalion, and a few officers of units to which its elements were attached. These did not include officers of all the units with elements of the 827th Tank Destroyer Battalion attached. The officers of the 315th Infantry Regiment, still engaged in combat at Hatten and Rittershoffen during the investigation, were never interviewed about the combat efficiency of the 827th Tank Destroyer crews. Moreover, none of the enlisted men of the 827th Tank Destroyer Battalion were deemed worthy of being questioned during the investigation. On 14 February, 6th Army Group Headquarters therefore requested that additional testimony be taken from representative enlisted men of the battalion.

In the meantime, the 827th Tank Destroyer Battalion was relieved from Task Force Wahl, with its last elements departing on 23 January 1945. The battalion returned to attachment to the 12th Armored Division, now engaged in combat operations in the Colmar Pocket Region. One platoon was attached to each of the combat commands of the division on 2 February, participating in combat during the remaining few days of the operation. On 3 February, the 12th Armored Division, then attached to XXI Corps, was committed to continue the attack to the south and east where resistance, though scattered, was intense at some points. Combat Command B launched an attack to seize Sudhoffen. The attacked progressed slowly until a task force consisting of a company of tanks, a company of armored mounted infantry, and a platoon of the 827th Tank Destroyer Battalion were committed on 4 February. They overtook the enemy strong points, destroying antitank guns and continuing the attack. On 6 February, the 12th Armored Division rendezvoused with the 1st French Army forces, sealing off the remaining Germans in the Vosges.

The remainder of the uncommitted elements of the 827th Tank Destroyer Battalion stayed with the 12th Armored Division's supply trains. On the night of 5 February, the battalion commander called upon the division asking for help. He claimed that his enlisted men were becoming increasingly difficult to handle. He alleged that they drew guns, molested civilians, and indulged in wild shootings. The division's judge advocate and inspector general conferred with the commander of the 827th Tank Destroyer Battalion. Although these allegations were never validated, the 12th Armored Division still requested to be relieved of the 827th Tank Destroyer Battalion.[22]

The 7th Army nominated the 827th Tank Destroyer Battalion for use at the 6th Army Group Headquarters for "housekeeping" duties. For the remainder of the war, the majority of enlisted soldiers of the 827th Tank Destroyer Battalion performed guard, labor, and transportation duties for the 6th Army Headquarters. Some of the enlisted men were assigned to the 614th Tank Destroyer Battalion, as they were desperately needed as replacements for that veteran unit. The white officers were either transferred to white tank destroyer battalions as replacements, or assigned temporary duties within 6th Army. The 827th Tank Destroyer Battalion remained on the active rolls with its M18 tank destroyer vehicles returned to the 7th Army supply stocks for use as replacement vehicles by other tank destroyer units. To prevent the unit's nomination for redeployment as a tank destroyer battalion, the unit was classified as one of those "surpluses to redeployment needs." This would enable the 827th Tank Destroyer Battalion to be immediately returned to the United States upon the completion of the war in Europe for deactivation.[23]

While the 827th Tank Destroyer Battalion had the opportunity to prove that it could be a valuable asset in a combat theater, inept leadership was the major factor that contributed to its failure. But the army chose not to relieve any of these officers for incompetence, choosing instead to place the blame on the African American soldiers of the battalion for its failures. As with all units engaged in combat, even when there is a lack of sufficient leadership, individual acts of bravery prevailed. There were African American noncommissioned officers and tank destroyer crewmen who performed their duties in a highly efficient manner. Having confidence in the soldiers to perform the mission was the main factor that separated the combat successes of the 614th and 679th Tank Destroyer Battalions from those failures of the 827th Tank Destroyer Battalion. The soldiers of all three battalions had the same qualifications and the same opportunities for success in a "Jim Crow Army." But the 827th Tank Destroyer Battalion for the most part was commanded by officers that did not want to be associated with that unit, were not capable of leading men in combat, and lacked the confidence and trust in their men, all traits which led to its demise.

Chapter VIII

Separate Infantry Regiments

DURING THE 1920S, MILITARY LEADERS BEGAN considering plans for the mobilization of African Americans in the event of war. Based on experiences gained in World War I, the importance of African American manpower was obvious, but it was not until the approach of World War II that concrete plans, including the types and number of units to be formed, were established. By 1940 the army leadership had decided to organize three new separate infantry regiments composed of white officers and African American enlisted men as part of the Troop Basis Protective Mobilization Plan for 1941. In November 1940, the War Department ordered the activation of the 366th Infantry Regiment at Fort Devens, Massachusetts (10 Feb 1941); the 367th Infantry Regiment at Camp Claiborne, Louisiana (25 Mar 1941); and the 368th Infantry Regiment at Fort Huachuca, Arizona (1 Mar 1941). It was later decided that the 366th Infantry Regiment would be composed entirely of African American officers and enlisted men. This would provide positions for the few senior ranking African American field grade officers (major through colonel). These new infantry regiments would draw their manpower from their respective locales, by using African American draftees and volunteers of that region. The two active regular army African American infantry regiments — the 24th Infantry Regiment stationed at Fort Benning, Georgia, and the 25th Infantry Regiment stationed at Fort Huachuca, Arizona — would provide the noncommissioned officer cadre for these new regiments. The 372nd Infantry Regiment, an African American National Guard unit with elements divided among Massachusetts, Ohio, Maryland, New Jersey, and the District of Columbia, was federalized and inducted into the regular army on 10 March 1941.[1]

The standard army infantry regiment of World War II was organized with three primary infantry battalions, comprising twelve lettered rifle companies (A-M, excluding J), an infantry cannon company (first equipped with two half-track vehicle mounted 105-mm howitzers and six half-track vehicle mounted 75-mm howitzers or guns, and later replaced with a towed short-barreled 105-mm howitzer), an antitank company (initially equipped with twelve 37-mm and later nine 57-mm antitank guns), a service company for logistic and maintenance support, and combat service support detachments. Each battalion had three "line" companies of infantrymen. Each company had three infantry platoons led by a lieutenant with non-commissioned officers as the platoon sergeants and squad leaders. The fourth platoon was a weapons platoon utilizing teams that manned the crew-served .30-caliber Browning light machine guns, bazookas, and the 60-mm mortars. The fourth company in each battalion (D, H, and M) was the heavy weapons support company, utilized for sustained fire of .50-caliber heavy machine guns, .30-caliber light machine guns, and 81-mm mortars. The regiment and each battalion also had a headquarters and headquarters company (H&H) assigned. The regimental H&H company included the intelligence and reconnaissance platoon, ammunition and pioneer platoon (A&P, responsible for light engineering duties, often employed in evacuating wounded from the battlefield, and for transporting ammunition forward to the line companies), and an antitank platoon (initially equipped with four 37-mm and later with three 57-mm antitank guns).

24TH INFANTRY REGIMENT

The 24th Infantry Regiment was the first African American infantry unit to deploy into a hostile combat zone during World War II. One of the oldest active duty infantry regiments in the army, it was created by Congress on 28 July 1866. Because of valor displayed on the Civil War battlefields, the African American soldier earned a permanent presence in the military. Relegated to serve in the remote posts of the western United States to minimize their contact with white Americans, the 24th Infantry and the other African American regiments served with distinction throughout the Indian Wars and the Spanish-American War.

With the urgent requirement for trained combat soldiers in the early part of America's involvement in World War II, the 24th Infantry Regiment was alerted for overseas deployment. Prior to the war, the regiment was stationed at Fort Benning, Georgia, performing manual labor duties in support of the Infantry School. After receiving additional soldiers from the 25th, 367th, and 368th Infantry Regiments, which brought the regiment up to full combat strength, the 24th Infantry departed the United States for the Pacific Theater in April 1942. The regiment deployed to the island of Efate in the New Hebrides Islands and on to Guadalcanal. But the theater commander, Lieutenant General Harmon, was reluctant to utilize the 24th Infantry Regiment in its primary offensive combat role. Like many of the general officers in the army at that time, prejudice and discrimination influenced his command decisions when it came to utilizing African Americans in combat.

From its arrival on 4 May 1942 as a part of Task Force 9156 (later III Island Command) until October 1942, the regiment was charged with a large part of the perimeter defense of Efate. From October to the summer of 1943, the regiment, after consolidating its three battalions, became a part of the island's mobile striking force, organized under the 24th Infantry Regiment's commander, Colonel Hamilton Thorn. While the 24th Infantry Regiment continued its training and field duties, it also performed the island's manual labor functions, including loading and unloading ships, guarding air bases, constructing roads, providing vehicle transportation, performing manual labor details for quartermaster and ordinance service units, and installing wire communications. These were to be the 24th Infantry Regiment's main contribution to the war effort in the Pacific during its early stages in the combat theater.[2]

The 2/24th Infantry was on detached duty on Guadalcanal from March to August 1943, utilized not as infantry, but as a labor force unloading ships, operating a provisional truck company, and furnishing work details to the quartermaster and ordnance supply depots. The remainder of the regiment moved to Guadalcanal in August where they also performed manual labor tasks. In the meantime, since they were not being utilized in their primary role as combat infantrymen, the regiment began to return officers and enlisted men back to the United States as cadre to form the basis of new infantry divisions. Eleven officers and 182 enlisted men left in July and 5 officers and 76 enlisted men departed in September 1943. While the 24th Infantry Regiment furnished men for local security in the outlying regions of Guadalcanal, the regiment's primary duties involved supplying work details for the Island Service Command, averaging 35 officers and 1,200 enlisted men daily.[3]

The 24th Infantry Regiment, the only African American infantry unit continuing with all white officers, remained at these tasks until the end of January 1944, when the first battalion, under the command of Lieutenant Colonel John L. Thomas, left Guadalcanal with naval Task Force 31 for Empress Augusta Bay, Bougainville. It landed on 30 January 1944 as a supporting unit in XIV Corps reserve. Upon its arrival, the 1/24th Infantry began its usual tasks of unloading ships and performing manual labor details at the supply depots at Bougainville, where marines and the soldiers of the 37th Infantry Division had landed in November 1943. The 37th Infantry Division, the Americal Division, plus two Fiji infantry battalions commanded by New Zealand officers, were still engaged in combat with the Japanese.

On 29 February 1944, two weeks after the Allied occupation of the Green Islands, to the north of Bougainville, the 1/24th Infantry was relieved of service command duties and attached to the 37th Infantry Division to become part of the regimental tactical reserves. The battalion was assigned to the western half of the 129th Infantry Regiment's reserve line. This battalion was already in position for active use against the enemy when the War Department's message urging the prompt use of Negro ground combat soldiers was sent to General Harmon. Correspondence from the enlisted soldiers of this regiment to the African American press corps, detailing how they were being utilized by the army, forced pressure on the War Department to get the theater commanders to incorporate these infantry units into combat. By 11 March, the 1/24th Infantry had been attached to the 148th Infantry Regiment of the 37th Infantry Division. It occupied the regimental reserve area. Company B was deployed forward to reinforce a weak point at the main line of resistance between the 1/148th Infantry and the 3/148th Infantry sectors. That night, Japanese forces, probing for a weak position in the defensive lines, attacked their positions. Company B repelled the enemy attack. Lost in the battle were Private First Class Leonard Brooks and Private Annias Jolly to enemy fire. These were the first African American infantry losses in combat during the war. On the night of 12 March, the 1/24th Infantry sent out its first combat patrol. Led by Second Lieutenant Henry J. McAllister, the patrol deployed several thousand yards out in front of the battalion's defensive lines. It encountered a Japanese patrol, and killed one of the enemy soldiers.[4]

Already on Bougainville upon the arrival of the 1/24th Infantry was the 2nd Battalion of the 54th Coast Artillery Regiment, an African American unit operating as field artillery. Activated during the mobilization of 1941, it was later redesignated as the 49th Coast Artillery Battalion.[5] This unit lost all of its equipment and guns when a mine off the coast of Espiritu Santo sank the cargo ship *President Coolidge* on 26 October 1942. The 2/54th Artillery, with the 172nd Regimental Combat Team of the 43rd Infantry Division, had been sent from Noumea to Espiritu Santo in anticipation of the possibility of enemy attacks upon that major base supporting operations then in progress on Guadalcanal. On Espiritu Santo, as part of the island defense, the unit operating without its organic equipment gained a wealth of experience by using borrowed 155-mm howitzers and naval artillery batteries pending the arrival of its replacement equipment due in January 1943. On 4 February 1944, 2/54th Coast Artillery deployed to Empress Augusta Bay, where it was assigned as corps artillery for the XIV Corps. Thus, they became the first African American combat arms unit to engage the enemy actively in the South Pacific.[6]

The 1/24th Infantry Battalion was utilized very sparingly in combat during those first few days while attached to the 148th Infantry Regiment. Gradually, with time, the combat efficiency of the battalion improved. By 19 April 1944, the battalion had been assigned an area along the Maravia River that was previously occupied by the 132nd Infantry Regiment. That day, a company of Japanese soldiers ambushed one of the battalion's combat patrols comprising a lieutenant and 16 enlisted men. The lieutenant ordered his men to fight their way back across the river, but he and three of his men were pinned down by heavy machine gun fire. A rifle platoon of the 1/24th Infantry, supported by a platoon of M4 Sherman medium tanks from the 754th Tank Battalion, landed from a naval landing craft tank (LCT), attacked the enemy and rescued the trapped men. Five days later, the 1/24th Infantry, supported again by tanks of the 754th Tank Battalion, cleared the area of all enemy forces. The XIV Corps commander, Major General Griswold, considered the conduct of the 1/24th Infantry to be "highly satisfactory." He concluded, "Although this battalion has been employed largely on labor duties to the detriment of its training, its work in combat here has progressively and noticeably improved." During its operations on Bougainville, the 1/24th Infantry lost 11 men killed in action, 2 who later died of wounds, and 13 wounded. It accounted for an estimated 47 Japanese soldiers killed in action and one prisoner of war.

The 24th Infantry Regiment, after the 1/24th Infantry's brief encounter with the enemy on Bougainville, returned to routine labor and guard duties for the South Pacific Base Command and for the Guadalcanal Island Command. In December 1944, the regiment deployed to the islands of Saipan and Tinian for additional garrison duty. The islands, used as air force bases for the newly arrived B-29 Superfortress bomber attacks on Japan, had been declared secure, but the surrounding jungles and caves were still occupied by Japanese forces that refused to surrender. Tinian would be the base of the 509th Composite Air Group, 20th Air Force, which would later drop the atomic bombs on Japan. The 24th Infantry Regiment was ordered to clear out all the remnants of the enemy forces, and to provide security for the air bases.

In April 1945, a survey group from the Inspector General's office led by Major General Elliot D. Cook found the 24th Infantry Regiment still clearing out pockets of stiff enemy resistance. Since it was considered a dishonor for the Japanese soldier to surrender, most of the enemy would fight fiercely to their deaths. The Inspector General reported their conduct and accomplishment to be of "such a meritorious nature" that he brought the unit's performance to the attention of the Deputy Chief of Staff. The 24th Infantry Regiment had killed or captured 722 of the enemy at a loss of only 12 of its own men killed and 20 wounded. The survey group noted the performance of the unit stating the following:

> The 24th Infantry had killed or captured an impressive number of the enemy, and even today are engaged in continuous patrolling and jungle fighting against those Japanese still hiding on the island.... It, nevertheless, conducted itself in a superior manner. Even at this late date, scarcely a day passes that members of this Regiment do not capture or kill some of the enemy and, in so doing, suffer occasional casualties themselves, yet despite all that has been accomplished by the 24th Infantry Regiment, members of this Regiment considered that they were not eligible for the Combat Infantryman's Badge, nor that provision had been made for them to be awarded a battle

clasp on the theater ribbon for the combat in which they have been engaged since assuming their task of eliminating the remaining Japanese resistance on Saipan. Nevertheless, even after three years service overseas, the morale of this Regiment is high and its discipline is well worthy of emulation and praise, as is the exemplary manner of performance in all duties to which it has been assigned.[7]

Much of the 24th Infantry's impressive record was attributed by the inspectors to the regiment's new commander, Colonel Julian G. Hearne, Jr., who had been with the unit for fours years, advancing from battalion to regimental commander. Commendations were also given to the noncommissioned officers, who formed the backbone of any unit, and many of whom had served with the unit since before the war. When the survey group informed the Commanding General, Pacific Ocean Areas, of the combat performance of the 24th Infantry Regiment, the general informed the commander of the regiment that its members were eligible for both the Combat Infantryman's Badge and a battle star for their theater service ribbon. The Combat Infantryman Badge (CIB) was established by the War Department on 27 October 1943 to recognize the sacrifice of the infantry soldier. There are basically three requirements for award of the CIB. The soldier must be an infantryman satisfactorily performing infantry duties, must be assigned to an infantry unit during such time as the unit is engaged in active ground combat, and must actively participate in such ground combat. A ten-dollar stipend was added to the monthly pay of all soldiers awarded this prestigious badge. The Inspector General requested that the group's report be forwarded to the Operations Division for consideration in the future employment of Negro troops in the Pacific theater.[8]

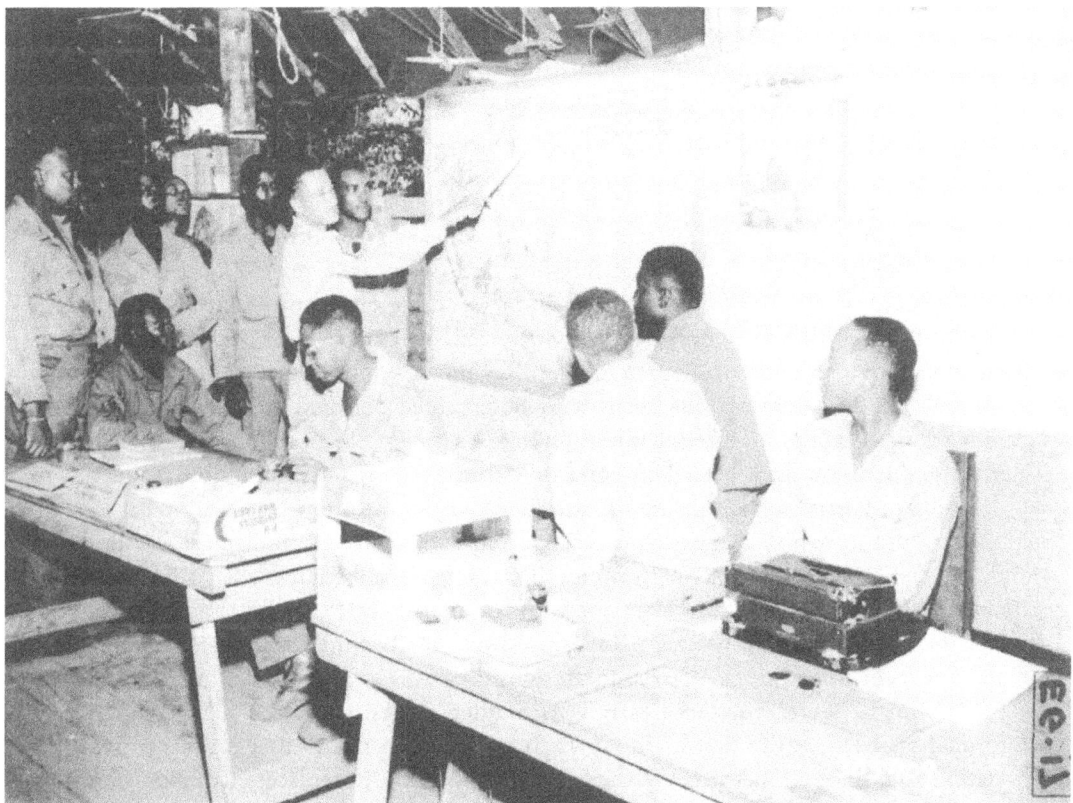

477th Antiaircraft Artillery, Air Warning Battalion, study maps in the operations section at Oro Bay, New Guinea, 15 November 1944. (National Archives 111-SC-305909)

The 24th Infantry Regiment left Saipan and Tinian in July 1945 and deployed to the Kerama Islands, west of Okinawa in the Ryukyus Islands. There, they continued clearing out the remnants of Japanese fighting forces. In early August, after the atomic bombings of Hiroshima and Nagasaki, the Japanese capitulated. On 22 August, Colonel Hearne, with representative officers and enlisted men, accepted on Aka Island the first formal surrender of a Japanese Army garrison from Major Yoshihiko Noda.

At the war's end, the 24th Infantry Regiment remained in the Pacific Theater performing occupational duties in Japan until the outbreak of the Korean War in 1950.

364TH INFANTRY REGIMENT

The regiment surrounded by the most controversy during the war would be the 364th Infantry. The 364th Infantry Regiment had been originally activated as the 367th Infantry Regiment, on 25 March 1941 at Camp Claiborne, Louisiana, under the command of Colonel Ralph C. Holliday. A team of white Regular Army officers and African American non-commissioned officers from the 24th and 25th Infantry Regiments formed the cadre, and were responsible for the training of the nearly 3,000 new recruits. This first draft of men, with no military experience, came largely from Florida, Louisiana, and Mississippi. Much of its initial basic training took place at Fort Jackson, South Carolina. Despite the usually low Army General Classification Test scores and the lack of a wide range of civilian experience, which was common among many of the African American Army ground forces units, especially those with soldiers from the South, within a year, the 367th Infantry became a well-trained infantry regiment. The men from most of these segregated, rural southern states often lacked a formal education, and were even denied the right to vote. The regiment received good reviews during its participation in the 3rd Army maneuvers in Louisiana in September 1941. But the commander of the regiment denied his soldiers access to the civilian communities for fear that there would be some form of trouble or racial disturbances.

With the Japanese attack on Pearl Harbor, and the entrance of the United States into World War II, the stability of the regiment and its training program were soon disrupted. A year after the 367th Infantry Regiment was organized, it was drastically changed as half of its personnel were transferred. The 367th Infantry Regiment, minus its first battalion, was tasked to furnish the 24th Infantry Regiment with 860 trained personnel who were qualified to deploy overseas in order to bring that unit up to full strength. The 1/367th Infantry had been alerted for duty with the Liberia Task Force in March 1942, separating from the regiment and proceeding to Charleston in April. The battalion did not sail from New York until January 1943. It would serve first in Liberia providing defense of an airfield and later in North Africa and the Mediterranean Theater performing those same airfield security duties. In the meantime, the remainder of the regiment, not knowing that its first battalion had been redesignated the 367th Infantry Battalion (Separate), waited to either refill the battalion with replacements or to rejoin the 1/367th Infantry overseas.

Due to the secrecy of those early wartime deployments, the regiment could not be informed of the 1/367th's destination or its future relationship to it. Requests to refill the battalion could not be met because there was no provision to replace a battalion in a regiment that already had three active battalions. Because the 1/367th Infantry was deployed with all its organic equipment marked as belonging to the 367th Infantry, the regiment, minus its first battalion, was redesignated the 364th Infantry Regiment. A new first battalion was organized, as the regiment would not be joining the 1/367th Infantry on their overseas movement.⁹

Although replacements were not long in coming, most received rudimentary or no basic training until they arrived at Camp Claiborne to join the regiment. The 364th Infantry Regiment, now refilled with a considerable proportion of new men from all over the United States, and faced with the task of reorganization and retraining, was assigned to the Western Defense Command's Southern Land Frontier Sector for protective guard duty. Another destabilizing factor was the change of command from Colonel Holliday to Colonel Fred Wickham in February 1942, a change that would prove both fateful and unfortunate for the 364th Infantry Regiment.

When the 364th Infantry Regiment was transferred in June 1942 to the Southern Land Frontier (a subordinate command of the Western Defense Command responsible for the security of a large area of the southwest and based at Papago Park, outside of Phoenix, Arizona), the morale situation rapidly deteriorated. In 1942 the Western Defense Command was responsible for guarding the United States from a possible attack by the Japanese. At the time the 364th Infantry Regiment was assigned to the Southern Land Frontier, sabotage in support of an invasion, or seaborne raids, seemed highly probable. The soldiers mainly performed security duties guarding bridges, dams, military sites, and enemy prisoners of war. The 1/364th and 3/364th Infantry Battalions remained in the vicinity of Papago Park; while the 2/364th Infantry was sent to the southern part of the state with its subordinate elements deployed around the cities of Tucson, Douglas, Yuma, and Nogales. The effect of this dispersion would be difficult to mitigate under the best of circumstances, and these were far from the best. Many of the men had yet to be trained in their basic combat skills. Many still lacked the proper equipment and clothing required to perform these duties.

The arrival of the regiment at Camp Papago with its inadequate facilities in all probability lowered the men's morale. The only permanent buildings were tarpaper shacks for the regimental headquarters staff, and a dining facility. The men were quartered in tents in the desert without flooring. Adding to their frustration was the mission of providing static guards and roadblocks at various installations throughout Arizona. Training did continue, but a chronic shortage of trained officers and noncommissioned officers, the dispersion of the battalions, and the lack of suitable infantry training areas hampered its effectiveness. The combined factors of boredom and isolation undoubtedly had a large effect, but the failure of the regiment's leadership in correcting these shortfalls and improving living conditions was to have even more tragic consequences.¹⁰

While stationed in Arizona, the 364th Infantry Regiment became involved in two serious racial incidents. The War Department first learned that there were serious morale problems in the regiment in a letter written in October 1942 by Chaplain (First Lieutenant) Llewellyn Thornhill to the chief of chaplains, complaining about the conditions in the camp and about the violent and racist behavior of the 364th Infantry Regiment's executive officer, Lieutenant Colonel Hugh Adair. The complaint was forwarded to the Office of the Inspector General for investigation. The investigating officer, Colonel Carl L. Ristine, recommended for Lieutenant Colonel Adair's relief.¹¹

The recommendation was not acted upon in time to prevent two incidents which led to the 364th Infantry Regiment's acquiring, perhaps unjustly, the reputation of an undisciplined and mutinous unit. The first incident occurred on the night of 13 November 1942, when soldiers in the stockade refused to obey Colonel Wickham's order to get off its roof. Yelling and catcalls from the prisoners drew a crowd of over 500 soldiers who also refused Colonel Wickham's order to disperse. Colonel Wickham later told investigators that he thought the incident was minor and that it would soon be forgotten. But it was evidently clear that the soldiers no longer respected the regiment commander and would not willingly follow his orders. The second incident was far more serious and resulted in a loss of life. It was rooted in a September 1942 change of policy by Western Defense Command that shifted the responsibility of policing soldiers on pass in the Phoenix area from the 364th Infantry Regiment to an African American Military Police (MP) company from the 733rd Military Police Battalion. Colonel Wickham realized that the Military Police would be resented by his men, who had been taking responsibility for policing themselves since arriving in Arizona, and repeatedly tried to convince Western Defense Command to change this arrangement. What ensued is usually referred to as the Phoenix Massacre.[12]

All three battalions of the regiment had returned to Papago Park after various guard details and training exercises. Colonel Wickham, in a well-meaning but ill-considered gesture, wanted the men to have a special Thanksgiving dinner on 26 November, followed by the first passes the men had in weeks. All soldiers were required to eat in their dining facilities, and a virtually unlimited quantity of beer was provided. Not surprisingly many of the men became drunk. The precipitating incident occurred when a soldier from the 364th Infantry Regiment, reportedly intoxicated, and his female companion were involved in an altercation outside a cafe in Phoenix. Military police from the 733rd Military Police Battalion arrested the man and took him into custody. A group of soldiers from the 364th Infantry Regiment, in the cafe, witnessed the arrest. A crowd formed and the military police fired one shot each into the air and one of them sent a second shot into the ground. The shot fired into the ground ricocheted and struck a soldier from the 364th Infantry. Two civilian police arrived on the scene at this time and dispersed the crowd.

The soldiers who remained at Papago Park heard an exaggerated account of the incident, and a group of them eventually secured arms and ammunition from an arms room, and returned to Phoenix. Reminiscent of the incident in Houston in 1917, several shootings between the police and men of the 364th Infantry Regiment occurred. Witness statements are confused at best, but the result was 14 people shot, with two soldiers and one civilian killed. The War Department Inspector General's Office immediately sent Brigadier General Benjamin O. Davis, Sr. (the senior African American officer in the Army and a deputy inspector general) and Colonel Joel R. Burney to conduct an investigation and to quell the violence.

The investigation concluded that the disturbance could be attributed directly to both a lack of discipline and the poor morale in the 364th Infantry Regiment as a whole. After interviewing the officers and some enlisted men of the regiment, the investigating team also concluded that it was not the result solely of the events of the night of 26 November, but the culmination of problems that had been present for some time, including the lack of adequate living conditions, clothing, and footgear for the soldiers. In short, there was a gross failure of leadership and the chain of command. Also cited was the effect of exaggerated rumors that the 733rd Military Police Battalion was shooting the men of the 364th Infantry Regiment on the streets of Phoenix. Responsibility for the shooting deaths could not be clearly established because the military police as well as soldiers from the 364th Infantry Regiment engaged in uncontrolled firing. But wrongfully removing weapons and ammunition from the arms room clearly was the fault of the 364th Infantry Regiment.

A total of 15 of the 364th Infantry Regiment soldiers were tried by courts-martial for disobeying orders, mutiny, and inciting a riot; 14 were sentenced to varying terms of imprisonment of up to 50 years. One soldier, Private Joseph Sipp, was sentenced to death. Due to an outcry from the African American press on the injustices of the court-martial procedures, President Roosevelt personally reviewed Private Sipp's case and set it aside. All the other convictions were also eventually set aside, with the soldiers returned to duty in other units. The Inspector General's investigators recommended that corrective actions be taken and that those responsible for conditions in the regiment be disciplined. The most significant step had already been taken: Colonel John Goodman assumed command of the 364th Infantry Regiment on 29 November 1942, replacing Colonel Wickham, who was relieved of his command. Colonel Goodman was a West Point graduate (Class of 1916) and an experienced infantryman. He immediately took the steps that would be recognized as the mark of a good leader. He saw to the construction of permanent barracks, adequate latrines and bathing facilities as well as proper issue of clothing and equipment. Most important, he began the infantry-training program from the ground up to correct deficiencies in soldier skills and discipline indicated by the Western Defense Command during its investigation of the 364th Infantry Regiment.

The Western Defense Command, not wanting to have a troubled African American infantry regiment with its 3,000 soldiers permanently stationed in its district, recommended that the regiment be utilized in other tasks, and specifically, that it be considered for overseas deployment, since "its long retention would produce a deterioration in its present efficiency."[13] In February 1943, it was suggested that African American soldiers of the 364th Infantry Regiment and those of the 93rd Infantry Division, then stationed at Fort Huachuca, be utilized to help harvest the cotton crop in Arizona. After the War Department's Manpower Commission advised on 24 February that Arizona's labor conditions did not warrant such a request, the movement of African American soldiers to the cotton fields was halted. But this came only after news of how African American infantry soldiers were being utilized to prepare for war was relayed to the African American press from the members of these units.[14]

In May 1943, the regiment was ordered to proceed to Camp Van Dorn, Mississippi, for retraining by the Army Ground Forces Command, a procedure usually followed for units that had served time with the defense command prior to their deployment overseas.

Camp Van Dorn, being located in one of the most segregated states in the South with its prevailing "Jim Crow" laws, was viewed by the men of the regiment as a change for the worse. It was also the most isolated large army installation in the state. The nearest town, Centreville, had a population of less than 1,200 people, and no types of facilities that admitted African American soldiers. The nearest larger towns of Baton Rouge and Natchez were 50 miles away. Some soldiers viewed the change in location as punishment for their continuing difficulties in Phoenix, which had grown distinctly cooler toward their presence as the months passed.

The 364th Infantry Regiment arrived in Centreville, Mississippi, outside of Camp Van Dorn by train in two groups on 26 and 28 May 1943. Rumors of the unit's troubles in Arizona may have preceded it, but whatever the reason, its arrival in Mississippi led to problems. The demographic make-up of the regiment had changed fundamentally from its original organization as the 367th Infantry Regiment. Most of the nearly 2,000 replacements came not from the South, as had almost all the initial group of draftees, but from throughout the entire United States. The United States, during the period prior to World War II, was very sectionalized, with the different regions operating under their unique social orders. Although some men looked forward to the move as a chance to be close to family and friends, to a majority of the soldiers, it was a trip into a virtually unknown and foreign land where a man of color often had to fear for his life. Although the army itself was segregated, it was run by rules and regulations, and therefore predictable. The official War Department policy prohibited discrimination, while unofficially accepting segregation. Many installation commanders, who were raised in the South, took the authority to establish separate facilities for the races, especially in the southern states where this practice was the norm. Added to the natural fear of not knowing where the war would take them next, this perceived lack of legal protection created a climate in which disturbances could take place. All the painstaking efforts of Colonel Goodman to improve the performance and morale were about to be undone.

On the first night the 364th Infantry Regiment arrived at Camp Van Dorn, on 26 May 1943, a group of soldiers entered an African American service club on base carrying beer, which was against the rules. They refused to leave when asked by the hostess and remained for an hour after closing time. As with so many other incidents involving the regiment, it is important to make clear that although a noncommissioned officer from the regiment identified many of the disrupting men as being from the 364th Infantry, it is not necessarily true that all the men breaking the rules were from the regiment. There were several African American units undergoing training at Camp Van Dorn during this same time period.

The following night, 27 May 1943, another incident usually associated with the 364th Infantry Regiment occurred. After a group of soldiers in Post Exchange Number 1 became noisy, the exchange officer ordered the facility closed. A crowd formed outside and began throwing beer bottles at the building. Eventually they forced their way into the exchange and helped themselves to the merchandise. The total loss was estimated to be in excess of $800.00.[15]

On Saturday, 29 May 1943, an incident took place that was once again directly attributable to the men of the 364th Infantry Regiment. Early in the evening a group of soldiers, estimated as being up to 75 in number, marched into the town of Centreville. Again, rumor is likely to have exaggerated both the numbers and behavior, but townspeople complained that the men sang obscene songs and shouted insults. The men returned to post without incident and no one was injured.

Sunday would bring both incident and injury. About 4:30 in the afternoon Sergeant Charles Hix, a Camp Van Dorn military policeman, was in town with his partner on patrol. He stopped a group of African American soldiers for a routine spot check of uniforms and passes. One soldier, Private William Walker of Company A, 1/364th Infantry, refused to button his sleeve. The military police asked him for his pass. What happened next is not completely clear, but some details are undisputed. Sergeant Hix got out of his vehicle and was reaching for his nightstick when Private Walker knocked him back into the jeep on his back and attempted to seize the military policeman's sidearm. At this point Sergeant Hix's partner failed to come to his assistance and resolve the matter quickly. Three local law enforcement officers, including Sheriff R. Whitaker of Wilkinson County, witnessed the struggle. Private Walker saw the arrival of the police and got out of the jeep. Sheriff Whitaker swore under oath that he ordered Private Walker to stop. When Walker did not, Sheriff Whitaker shot him. He never said whether he thought Private Walker was armed. Private Walker was put into the jeep and taken to the post hospital where he was pronounced dead.[16] Rumors circulated among the regiment that Walker's body had been dumped at the front gate of the post.

As was the case on Thanksgiving night in Phoenix, rumors started immediately. Several events occurred almost simultaneously. A group of soldiers started a disturbance at a post exchange located near the 364th Infantry Regiment's barracks area. Groups of soldiers having heard of the shooting began to gather in the Company A, 1/364th Infantry's area. About the same time soldiers broke into the Company C, 1/364th Infantry's arms room and took several weapons including M1 rifles and a Browning automatic rifle.

The Company C arms room was also the scene of an act of conspicuous bravery. While several men forced their way into the supply room, the supply sergeant, Technician 4 Booket Watkins, refused to surrender the keys to the locks on the rifle racks, forcing his assailants to break a rack in order to acquire only a few rifles. Despite verbal and physical assaults Technician 4 Watkins held his ground, preventing the mass theft of the weapons. For his dedication to duty and display of selfless physical and moral courage Technician 4 Watkins was awarded the Soldier's Medal. His award recommendation rightly says that his actions almost certainly prevented loss of life.[17]

Having been informed of the trouble at the post exchange, Major Jewel Suddath, Camp Van Dorn's provost marshal, sent a section of African American military police to break up the disturbance. He may have thought that following the shooting of Private Walker, white military police would seem like a provocation to the men, but he was unaware of the regiment's experience in Phoenix, Arizona, with the 733rd Military Police Battalion's African American military policemen. Some soldiers watched the arrival of the military police and began to shout, "Here they go again just like in Phoenix." Some men rushed the military police and attempted to get their weapons. The military police, in an attempt to put down the disturbance, fired several shots, one of which struck Private Raymond Johnson, an apparently innocent bystander, in the leg. Fortunately, the wound was superficial.[18]

Colonel Goodman realized something had to be done quickly before the situation got completely out of hand. Taking the regimental chaplain, Captain Elmer Gibson, with him, he went to the exchange and began talking to the men. He and the chaplain moved among them, defusing the situation. He gave orders to the battalion commanders to assemble their men and talk to them to calm the situation. The night closed without further incident.[19] It took several days of constant searching, which itself served to keep tension high, to locate and recover all the missing rifles. Citizens of the nearby town and county began to arm themselves and called for an immediate transfer of the regiment

The incidents of 27–30 May 1943 alarmed the War Department. Once again the Inspector General's Office sent Colonel Joel Burney to investigate the facts. Three separate investigations were conducted into some or all of these incidents. They were conducted by the installation commander, Colonel Robert E. Guthrie; the 3rd Army Inspector General (3rd Army was then the 364th Infantry's next higher command headquarters); and the War Department's Inspector General.

The 3rd Army conducted the most comprehensive of the three investigations. Colonel C.C. Park, the investigating officer, recommended the unit be reorganized and converted from infantry to a combat service support regiment. A belief held by many senior army officers was that African American soldiers should be utilized strictly as combat service support soldiers and were not capable of serving in infantry units. He also recommended that Colonel Goodman be relieved. Lieutenant General Courtney Hodges, 3rd Army Commander, who would later command the 1st Army in the European Theater, accepted neither recommendation. Colonel Park did recognize that the segregated facilities at Camp Van Dorn were inadequate for the 364th Infantry Regiment, and recommended improvements in the availability of goods at the post exchanges and use of post theaters, which were then off-limits to African American soldiers. These recommendations were later acted upon.

The Inspector General, Major General Virgil L. Peterson, was concerned when he read Colonel Burney's report and wrote a detailed memorandum on the 364th Infantry Regiment to the Deputy Chief of Staff, dated 8 June 1943. In this memorandum he made it clear that he believed the recent events formed a pattern and stressed the need to take firm disciplinary action and discover the identities of the "ringleaders" of the incidents. In the inspector general's investigation, as in the 3rd Army investigation, finding the responsible parties proved impossible. The Acting Civilian Assistant to the Secretary of War, Mr. Truman Gibson, was given a copy of the inspector general's memorandum for comment. He took strong exception to the report and forwarded a detailed four-page memo of his own to the Deputy Chief of Staff. In it he wrote: "Despite the very high regard and respect I have for the Inspector General, I wish to respectfully disagree with his sentiments, particularly because they represent, perhaps, the majority opinion in the Army.... the use of harsh and repressive measures against Negroes is no solution to the problem."[20]

One technique the army used to try to find the source of the problem was to infiltrate the unit with agents of the Counter Intelligence Corps (CIC), trained in countersubversion. One such agent, George F. Kennedy, infiltrated the 364th Infantry Regiment on 2 June 1943. Agent Kennedy was experienced and well regarded by his white superiors due to the fact that he normally reported what they had already perceived to be the problem associated with African American units. His report of conditions in the 364th Infantry Regiment would be widely circulated throughout the War Department and played a significant role in later decisions on the utilization of the 364th Infantry Regiment. In his agent's report, dated 12 June 1943, after being with the unit for only a few days, Kennedy referred to the men of the regiment as "a group of undisciplined delinquents." He also wrote, "Trouble will spring up spontaneously at the slightest provocation where groups are gathered." It is significant to note what he did not say: as was confirmed by later intelligence reports, that there was no evidence of subversive intent or outside agitation. These men were troubled with their present segregated environment and prevalent discrimination, and Agent Kennedy had seen them at their worst, but they were not organized in any way to promote trouble.[21]

A later intelligence report written by another CIC agent who infiltrated the regiment was circulated in November 1943. This report by Agent Homer B. Scretchings, based on his observations as a member of Company E, 2/364th Infantry, from 21 October through 7 November 1943, reinforces the conclusion that the men of the 364th Infantry Regiment were not subversive, nor were they being influenced by outside agitation, but only by the segregated conditions that were prevalent at Camp Van Dorn and the surrounding communities. His report states: "The investigation indicated that all reported incidents were not premeditated and were not inspired by any subversive influences. It appeared to be caused solely through general laxity of military discipline. It is the belief of this Agent that the reported incidents should be handled by local command action."[22]

Clearly both agents realized that while some of the men of the 364th Infantry Regiment were undisciplined and frustrated, the problem was not so great as to require the intervention of higher headquarters. The conditions associated with a segregated military force and the racial climate at Camp Van Dorn were not addressed as prevalent problems, which were attributed to the unrest.

Camp Van Dorn was not unique in having racial problems with its soldiers in the summer of 1943. Camp Stewart, Georgia; Camp Claiborne, Louisiana; and Fort Bragg, North Carolina, had far more serious racial incidents in 1943 than did Camp Van Dorn, including the loss of many lives. Chief of Staff General George C. Marshall was concerned that there would be serious damage done to the war effort if it was not abundantly clear to all commanders that they had a responsibility to seek out the causes of racial incidents and to take active steps to prevent their occurrence. His 13 July 1943 memorandum sets out War Department policy, and command responsibility, in no uncertain terms:

A study of detailed reports of many such cases indicates that there is general evidence of failure on the part of commanders of some echelons to appreciate the seriousness of the problem and their inherent responsibility. Also apparent is the lack of appreciation of the urgent necessity of continuous and vigorous action to prevent incidents of discrimination and the spread of inflammatory gossip and to take positive preventative measures to spike an impending outbreak. In some instances officers have not exercised that close supervision which is necessary to keep them aware of the pulse and temper of their unit.[23]

This letter, it should be noted, was drafted with the help of the Advisory Committee on Negro Troop Policies, the text approved by the Civilian Assistant to the Secretary of War, Mr. Truman Gibson.

Colonel Goodman now had to begin again the task of improving the morale and proficiency of his regiment. He again went back to basics with a rigorous program of training in fundamentals such as marksmanship, crew-served weapons qualification, and road marches. He also arranged for additional transportation for men on pass to be able to travel out of the vicinity of Camp Van Dorn to larger towns, which had separate segregated facilities that catered to African Americans. Morale did not improve overnight, however, and many men complained to their families or wrote to African American newspapers about what they perceived as harsh conditions at Camp Van Dorn. Several congressional inquiries into conditions at the camp were directed to the War Department.

The month of July was to bring the last incident involving the men of the 364th Infantry Regiment in a disturbance. On 3 July 1943, the hostess of the African American service club planned a dance and invited about 200 young women of color from neighboring communities. Unfortunately she advertised the dance around a camp that had 8,000 African American soldiers stationed there at the time. Naturally more soldiers arrived than could be accommodated. Military police arrived after hearing there was trouble, followed shortly thereafter by the field duty officer of the day. Believing the military police inadequate for the situation the field duty officer called for the ready battalion of the 99th Infantry Division to respond. By the time the battalion arrived, most of the soldiers had returned to their units. No one was hurt. There were several African American units at Camp Van Dorn, and it is not accurate to assign the blame for incidents of indiscipline entirely to it. But its reputation of being an undisciplined African American infantry regiment had already been established with the War Department. Memories of the Houston Mutiny incident by the 3/24th Infantry in 1917 were still prevalent with these generals.

Training in the regiment continued throughout the summer of 1943 without further incident. The regiment was going through a progressive unit training cycle to prepare to participate in the 3rd Army's fall maneuvers in Louisiana. The 364th Infantry Regiment did depart for the maneuvers as scheduled on 17 November 1943 but would not stay throughout its entirety. While the regiment had been training at Camp Van Dorn the War Department had been contemplating its future.

When the 364th Infantry Regiment departed Arizona for Camp Van Dorn, Mississippi, it was tentatively slated to be deployed to the European or Mediterranean Theater; however, by September 1943 that requirement had been deleted from the army's operational plans. The effect of the Inspector General's numerous investigations and the reports of CIC agents greatly reduced the confidence of Army Ground Forces Command and the War Department in the potential fighting abilities of the 364th Infantry Regiment. In September, Colonel Lathe B. Row of the War Department Inspector General's Office began a series of surveys on racial attitudes throughout military installations in the southern United States, beginning with Camp Van Dorn, Mississippi.

With the approach of the departure date of the alerted 99th Infantry Division, the retention of the 364th Infantry Regiment at Camp Van Dorn as the largest single unit on the post took on a new significance. Aside from small headquarters detachments, other African American units stationed at Camp Van Dorn included two quartermaster truck regiments, one service battalion, one medical ambulance battalion, and a quartermaster laundry company, totaling over 6,500 soldiers. Although no ammunition had been issued to the 364th Infantry Regiment, and the firing bolts of all rifles removed, the Inspector General felt that, "due to the attitude of civilians in this locality relative to racial matters and to the presence of large numbers of 'northern Negroes,' there exists considerable danger of racial disturbances in the general vicinity of this camp. That other than the situation [in the 364th], the outlook for generally harmonious relations between white and Negro personnel at the camp is good." The inspecting officer recommended that the unit be transferred immediately overseas.[24] Generally, it was felt by many of the senior officers that African American soldiers from the northern cities, with their liberal viewpoints and anti-discrimination beliefs, were the causes of the racial disturbances on segregated military posts.

The 3rd Army, however, was now convinced that the 364th Infantry Regiment would not be prepared for deployment overseas to a combat theater until after 1 March 1944 at the earliest. No active theater required a separate infantry regiment, especially one that had the reputation of the 364th Infantry Regiment. The Operations Division of the War Department, requested to prevent further deferment of the regiment beyond 1 March, finally arranged for the 364th Infantry Regiment to replace a white infantry regiment that was currently due to depart for the Aleutian Islands, the 140th Infantry Regiment. The War Department's G-3 (Director of Organization and Training), Major General Ray Porter, reviewed the report and wrote a short note, dated 6 November 1943, that finalized the plans for the 364th Infantry Regiment: "As you know I am most anxious to have Negro troops sent to combat; however, the 364th Infantry does not appear to fit into any practical scheme. It will not be ready for shipment prior to March 1944. Many officers have rated the regiment as a menace. Perhaps it is wise to trade it to Alaska for a good white regiment and seek to have some other Negro unit sent to combat."[25]

Once the decision had been made by the War Department, things began to progress very rapidly for the regiment. It was brought back early from the Louisiana maneuvers on 1 December 1943 and given three weeks to prepare for overseas movement. On Christmas Day 1943, the regiment entrained for Seattle to begin its journey to Alaska.

After two and a half years of training, reorganization, and turmoil in the United States, the 364th Infantry Regiment finally had a mission, the defense of several key installations in the Aleutian Islands. Although the Japanese had been defeated in a short and bitter campaign there earlier in the war, the threat remained that they might conduct attacks against American bases. This solution of what to do with the 364th Infantry Regiment seemed to meet all the requirements the War Department had set: an early departure from Camp Van Dorn, an "overseas" assignment (remote Alaska was not a state at the time), and commitment to an area where combat was not imminent. Exiled to Alaska, the regiment was to show its critics that when properly led and given a mission to accomplish, they were as capable as anyone. But this deployment to the remoteness of Alaska would ensure that the 364th Infantry Regiment would not cause any additional problems within the War Department.

Regimental headquarters was established on the island of Adak, the site of a large harbor and an air base. As in Arizona the regiment was divided in order to complete a varied number of missions: the 1/364th Infantry was deployed to the island of Amchitka, the 2/364th

Infantry was sent to the island of Shemya, and 3/364th Infantry to the island of Attu. The performance of the battalions is reflected in the reports of umpires during field exercises. For example, during a test alert on Shemya the 2/364th Infantry's umpire commented: "Staff ... was able to operate efficiently. Journal was kept properly. Speed of communications within the CP [command post] was satisfactory."[26] A similar alert exercise conducted on Amchitka with the 1/364th Infantry noted some deficiencies in command post operations, but concluded, "In spite of the miserable weather, the troops went into position and stayed there."[27]

The end of the war brought the gradual demobilization of the 364th Infantry Regiment and the return of the men to their homes and families. The regiment was deactivated in 1946. The men with remaining active service obligations were organized into two battalions: the 1/364th Infantry became the 80th Infantry Battalion, and the 2/364th Infantry was reflagged as the 81st Infantry Battalion. By this point virtually all of the men who had been drafted into the regiment at the beginning of the war had departed. Some stayed on to have successful careers in an integrated army, serving tours of combat during the Korean War and in Vietnam. Colonel Goodman relinquished command of the 364th Infantry Regiment in 1944 to become Commander of Troops Shemya, then, when promoted to brigadier general, he assumed the duties of Commander of Troops Adak. He retired in 1946 and died the following year.

366TH AND 372ND INFANTRY REGIMENTS

By mid–1943, the 366th Infantry and 372nd Infantry Regiments, both of which had been in training and on security duties at their Massachusetts and New York locations since 1941, had not been allocated for overseas deployment. The 366th Infantry Regiment had been scheduled for departure to the European Theater of Operations in February 1944, in preparations for the invasion of France. But all the European Theater's expected requirements for separate infantry regiments were canceled.[28] The requirement now was to have a full infantry division. In addition, theater commanders were not willing to accept an African American infantry regiment under their commands, especially after what had occurred with the 364th Infantry. The drain on manpower and the large number of casualties had yet to be experienced in early 1944. There had been attempts to relocate the 372nd Infantry Regiment for training since the Eastern Defense Command had released them from the security duties. The regiment, by terms of its assignment to New York, could not be relocated without the War Department's approval. The War Department was not authorized to move the regiment without authority from the White House, for the 372nd Infantry had been stationed in New York State after an agreement between President Roosevelt and Mayor La Guardia.[29] The White House, when queried on deploying the unit, replied that there was no objection to relocating the 372nd Infantry, provided it was replaced by another regiment. The 372nd Infantry Regiment therefore remained at its New York duty station for the duration of the war. It became the primary source for providing infantry replacements for the 92nd Infantry Division, which would be deployed to the Mediterranean Theater of Operations, and to the 93rd Infantry Division, which was deployed in the Pacific Theater. Yet, with no additional African American soldiers going through infantry training, it became the job of the 372nd Infantry Regiment to provide combat training for these replacement soldiers.

In November 1943, the North African Theater of Operations, which had five air base security battalions, requested 18 additional battalions or their equivalent for the 12th Air Force and the newly activated 15th Air Force. It was suggested that the air base security program be reinitialized to provide the theater with units required to prevent the increasing tide of civilian sabotage and depredations on airfields. All uncommitted air base security battalions had been disbanded and their soldiers reassigned to badly needed combat and combat support service units. It was proposed that the 366th Infantry Regiment be utilized for these duties. In addition to the 366th Infantry Regiment, the North African Theater and the Army Air Force suggested that an additional African American infantry regiment would be quite acceptable in place of the remaining air base security battalions that it required.[30] To this latter suggestion, the War Department replied that the additional African American infantry regiment was not available since the 364th Infantry was in preparation for movement to Alaska. The 65th Infantry Regiment (Puerto Rican), also segregated due to race and language differences, was to be substituted.

The 25th and 368th Infantry Regiments became the core of the 93rd Infantry Division. Along with the newly activated 369th Infantry Regiment, the 93rd Infantry Division was deployed to the Pacific Theater in January 1944. Three new African American infantry regiments were activated to form the 92nd Infantry Division: the 365th, the 370th, and the 371st Infantry Regiments, all with lineage to World War I, were deployed to Italy beginning in July 1944 in the Mediterranean Theater.

Segregation of units by race was not limited to African Americans. In addition to the 65th Infantry Regiment from Puerto Rico, there was the famous 442nd Infantry Regiment, composed of native Hawaiians and Asian Americans, that would become the most highly decorated unit in the United States Army.

65TH INFANTRY REGIMENT (PUERTO RICO)

The 65th Infantry Regiment, activated in Puerto Rico, became part of the regular army on 27 May 1908. The unit performed security duties at the Panama Canal during World War I. In June 1940, after the outbreak of hostilities in Europe, the 65th Infantry Regiment's third battalion was reactivated and an antitank company created. The regiment underwent intensive training at Salinas Training Area, Puerto Rico, until December 1942. It also performed security missions along the Puerto Rican coast and stood guard over the island's strategic military facilities.[31]

By December 1941, nearly 58,000 soldiers were stationed in Puerto Rico, Panama, and along the vast arc stretching from Surinam, north along the Antilles screen, to the Yucatan Channel. The induction of additional Puerto Rican military forces in this region allowed for the deployment of growing numbers of white soldiers to combat theaters overseas. By the beginning of 1942 17,000 Puerto Ricans were enlisted in the U.S. Army. On 7 January 1943, the 65th Infantry Regiment deployed to the Panama Canal Zone where it joined the Panama Canal Department's Mobile Force. Units of the regiment received security missions for the protection of vital installations along the canal and manned observation posts on both the Atlantic and Pacific sides of Panama. Like the majority of the African American infantry regiments, a white colonel commanded the 65th Infantry, with the majority of his senior staff being white officers. The battalions of the 65th Infantry were continuously rotated through jungle training for visiting student officers of the Latin American countries. As a result, the regiment attained a high degree of efficiency and was praised for its performance. The 65th Infantry Regiment conducted security missions in Panama until December 1943.

In January 1944, the regimental combat team embarked for New Orleans and then Fort Eustis, Virginia, in preparation for overseas deployment to North Africa. In March 1944, an advance party departed for Casablanca, French Morocco. The remainder of the regiment followed in April. The 65th Infantry Regiment remained in Oran, Algeria, in a staging area undergoing training for about two weeks, after which it relocated to Camp Port Aux Poules. The 3/65th Infantry was detached from the regiment and sent to Italy and then to Corsica to provide airfield security for the 12th Air Force. The remainder of the regiment was assigned to the 7th Army along with the Puerto Rican 162nd Field Artillery Battalion. Still in North Africa, the regiment underwent intensive training, concentrating on amphibious operations. Subsequently, the 65th Infantry Regiment, minus the 3/65th Infantry, went through the battle indoctrination course at Chanzy, Algeria. Near the end of 1944, the 3/65th Infantry rejoined the regiment and training was resumed with emphasis on village and urban combat. On 17 September 1944, Company C, 1/65th Infantry, was detached from the regiment and flown to France, where it was attached to the Special Troops Command in order to provide security for the 7th Army Headquarters. It would remain there for the duration of the war.[32]

Also in September 1944, the remainder of the regiment received orders to deploy to southern France and landed in Marseilles and Toulan early in October. The 65th Infantry Regiment then moved to a staging area near Aix-en-Provence. Company A, 1/65th Infantry took over the duties of operating the stockade of captured German prisoners of war, under the direction of the Sixth Army Group Headquarters.

The 3/65th Infantry, commanded by Lieutenant Colonel Juan Cesar Cordero-Davila, entered combat on 12 December 1944 at Peira Cava in the Maritime Alps of southern France, where it relieved a battalion of the 442nd Regimental Combat Team. On 4 January 1945, Colonel George B. Ford, the regimental commander, was killed by sniper fire while leading a combat patrol against a German strongpoint.[33] On 15 January Sergeant Angel Martinez and Private Sergio Sanchez-Sanchez of Company L, 3/65th Infantry were killed in combat, becoming the first Puerto Rican soldiers of the 65th Infantry Regiment to die in the European Theater. In all the 3/65th Infantry would suffer 47 battle casualties while assigned to this sector. The 3/65th Infantry was relieved from the Maritime Alps on 26 February 1945, and the entire regiment assembled in Lorraine for further action in southwest Germany. In March 1945, the 65th Infantry Regiment crossed the Rhine and cleared pockets of bypassed enemy resistance. The regiment remained in Germany as part of the Army of Occupation until October 1945, when it was ordered to Calais, France, for the return voyage home. The regiment arrived in Puerto Rico on 9 November 1945. Its soldiers had won a Distinguished Service Cross, two Silver Stars and 90 Purple Hearts in combat. The 65th Infantry was awarded battle participation honors for the Naples-Foggia, Rome-Arno, Central Europe, and Rhineland campaigns.[34]

Although the most prominent, the 65th Infantry was not the only Puerto Rican infantry regiment to serve in World War II. The 295th Infantry Regiment preformed security duties throughout the Caribbean in Curacao, Aruba, Surinam, Trinidad, Cuba, and Jamaica. The army utilized a platoon of volunteers from the regiment for live mustard gas tests while in Panama. The purpose of these experiments was to assess the number of casualties that could be expected in the event of Japanese use of mustard gas against American soldiers in the event of an invasion of Japan. The 296th Regimental Combat Team served in Hawaii from 8 May 1945 to 7 March 1946 and was preparing for deployment against the Japanese when the war ended.

Chapter IX

Paratroopers

By 1943, paratroopers were considered the elite branch of the United States Army. This all-volunteer force went through a more strenuous training program in order to meet the heightened physical demands of being airborne soldiers. It was during the 1930s that the Russians and Germans experimented with using paratroopers. The success of the German airborne assaults in Holland and Belgium early in the war caused the United States to develop an airborne program. A platoon of volunteers was formed in 1940 and made the first mass paratroop jump in August of that year. The first airborne regiment, the 501st Parachute Infantry Regiment (PIR), was activated in April of 1941 and the first airborne school was officially established at Ft. Benning, Georgia. On 15 August 1942, the 82nd Infantry Division was converted to the 82nd Airborne Division. It would soon be followed by the activation of the 101st and 11th Airborne Divisions, in addition to several separate airborne regiments and battalions. By the end of 1943, the 82nd Airborne Division had executed combat airborne assaults into Salerno and Sicily, and the 101st Airborne Division had been deployed to England to start preparing for the invasion of Europe.

African American representation at the airborne training facility was restricted to a service company. This unit was responsible for performing the manual labor tasks such as truck drivers transporting supplies and soldiers throughout the training areas on the post; cooks and kitchen police duties; and maintaining the cleanliness of the installation, in order to free white soldiers for other duties. The first sergeant of this service company, Walter Morris, got permission from the commander of the Parachute School to put his soldiers through the same daily physical training regimen that the white paratroopers were going through.

In September 1943, the Parachute School started recruiting African American soldiers to form a test platoon of paratroopers that would become the basis for the first unit of African American paratroopers.[1] President Roosevelt had recently visited Fort Benning and inquired as to where the Negro paratroopers were. The War Department had initially determined that African Americans lacked the stamina and physical fortitude to withstand the rigors of airborne training, and had no plans to incorporate them in this new branch of the military.

First Sergeant Walter Morris of the service company was recruited by the commander of the Parachute School to be the first member of the test platoon. Second Lieutenant Bradley Biggs, who had been an infantry officer in the 371st Infantry Regiment, volunteered as the platoon's first officer in September 1943. This test platoon of officers and noncommissioned officers would be made up of volunteers from various combat units and from the service company. On 4 March 1944, the coveted parachute wings were awarded to the first African American paratroopers. They were:

- First Lieutenant Jasper Ross — Chicago, Illinois, 1940 graduate of Howard University and commissioned through ROTC. Previously assigned to the 795th Tank Destroyer Battalion.
- Second Lieutenant Clifford Allen — Chicago, Illinois, graduate of Northwestern University and Infantry Officer Candidate School. Previously assigned to the Air Base Security Battalion, Camp Butler, North Carolina.
- Second Lieutenant Edward Baker — Chicago, Illinois, graduate of Infantry Officer Candidate School. Previously assigned to the 92nd Infantry Division.
- Second Lieutenant Bradley Biggs — Newark, New Jersey, graduate of Infantry Officer Candidate School. Previously assigned to the 710th Light Tank Battalion.
- Second Lieutenant Warren Cornelius — Atlantic City, New Jersey, graduate of Temple University and Infantry Officer Candidate School.
- Second Lieutenant Edwin Willis — Washington, D.C., graduate of Infantry Officer Candidate School.
- First Sergeant Walter Morris — Spokane, Washington, Service Company, Parachute School.
- Staff Sergeant Calvin Beal — Enlisted 21 February 1941, 371st Infantry Regiment, 92nd Infantry Division.
- Staff Sergeant Hubert Bridges — Enlisted 13 October 1940, Company C, 1/365th Infantry, 92nd Infantry Division.
- Staff Sergeant Lonnie Duke — Enlisted 1 September 1942, Company C, 1/371st Infantry, 92nd Infantry Division.
- Staff Sergeant Robert Greene — Enlisted 12 August 1941, Company H, 2/371st Infantry, 92nd Infantry Division.
- Sergeant Clarence Beavers — Enlisted 13 March 1941, Post Maintenance Detachment, Camp Indiantown Gap, Pennsylvania.
- Sergeant Ned Bess — Enlisted 27 November 1942, Company H, 2/371st Infantry, 92nd Infantry Division.
- Sergeant James Kornegay — Enlisted 3 March 1941, Cannon Company, 370th Infantry, 92nd Infantry Division.
- Sergeant Leo Reed — Enlisted 31 October 1942, Company H, 2/365th Infantry, 92nd Infantry Division.
- Sergeant Samuel Robinson — Enlisted 5 March 1942, Antitank Company, 365th Infantry, 92nd Infantry Division.
- Sergeant Jack Tillis — Enlisted 21 November 1942, Company A, 1/371st Infantry, 92nd Infantry Division.
- Sergeant Roger Walden — Enlisted 7 December 1941, Company C, 1/365th Infantry, 92nd Infantry Division.
- Sergeant Elijah Wesby — Enlisted 18 October 1941, Service Company, Parachute School.
- Corporal McKinley Godfrey — Enlisted 2 March 1943, Company I, 3/370th Infantry, 92nd Infantry Division.
- Technician 4 Alvin Moon — Enlisted 20 September 1941, Service Company, 370th Infantry Regiment, 92nd Infantry Division.[2]

This initial test platoon of 22 soldiers would form the nucleus of the 555th Parachute Infantry Company as volunteers continued to report to the parachute school. Due to the success of the test program, every enlisted member of the initial test platoon was promoted. While the remainder of the company was going through airborne training, the members of the test platoon were afforded the opportunity to receive additional training in communications, demolition, jumpmaster, pathfinding, and parachute rigging. The company was authorized with 119 enlisted men and seven officers. The command structure was:

- First Lieutenant James Porter — Commanding Officer
- First Lieutenant Calvin Cornelius — Executive Officer
- Second Lieutenant Edwin Wells — Planning Officer
- First Lieutenant Jasper Ross — Logistics Officer
- Second Lieutenant Bradley Biggs — First Platoon Leader
- Second Lieutenant Clifford Allen — Second Platoon Leader
- Second Lieutenant Edward Baker — Third Platoon Leader

The company continued to go through intensive training while assigned to Fort Benning, participating in the Advanced Tactical Divisional Training with the white paratroopers of the 17th Airborne Division. First Sergeant Walter Morris, platoon sergeants Roger Walden and Lonnie Duke, and squad leaders Timothy Armour, James Whitaker, and James McFadden attended Infantry Officers Candidate School, all receiving commissions to second lieutenant.[3]

In July 1944, at a total strength of 11 officers and 165 enlisted men, the 555th Parachute Infantry Company was transferred to Camp Mackall, North Carolina.[4] Most of the airborne units came through this installation for combat training prior to deploying overseas. With the racial segregation in the South and the influx of thousand of soldiers to this region, the members of the 555th Parachute Infantry Company were not welcomed in most of the small rural towns surrounding the camp. But the town of Southern Pines, a local resort area, welcomed the paratroopers of the company and their family members.

The company continued to train throughout the summer of 1944, but a single segregated infantry company would not be an adequate force on the battlefield. The War Department deactivated the company and activated the 555th Parachute Infantry Battalion on 25 November 1944.[5] The company commander, Captain Porter, now became the battalion commander, and all of the platoon leaders were elevated to company commanders. Additional qualified volunteers were recruited, and continued to go through airborne training. While the authorized officer strength was met for the battalion, the enlisted strength authorization was not achieved until June 1945.

In December 1944, the Germans launched their counteroffensive at a weak point in the American lines in the Ardennes Forest. American forces suffered severe casualties, especially in the airborne divisions that were utilized to halt the advance. Not quite at full strength, the battalion was alerted to provide a reinforced company of 160 men for possible deployment to the European Theater of Operations. As much as replacements were sorely needed, none of the commanders in the theater wanted these African American paratroopers assigned to their units. But as the war in Europe was coming to an end, those orders were rescinded and the battalion was ordered to proceed to Oregon on 5 May 1945.[6]

Beginning in November 1944, the Japanese had been sending silk hydrogen-filled balloons to the United States. These balloons, equipped with bombs, used what is now known as the jet stream to cross the Pacific Ocean. It was calculated that by the time the balloons reached the United States, they would have descended to an altitude where the bombs were to be automatically released. Of the 300 known balloons that reached the United States and Canada, a few drifted as far as Kansas and Iowa. The War Department surrounded these events with secrecy, but on 6 May 1945, as the 555th Parachute Infantry Battalion was en route to Oregon, a woman named Elsie Mitchell and five children from her church were on a fishing trip on Mount Gearhart near Bly, Oregon. One of the children found a strange object on the ground and the others went to investigate, while her husband the Reverend Archie Mitchell was parking the car. Suddenly the object exploded, killing the five children and Elsie Mitchell. First news reports said it was a blast of "unannounced cause." Though it remained a tightly guarded secret for a time, Elsie Mitchell and the five children had been the victims of the first intercontinental air attack on the United States.[7]

Many of these balloons dropped incendiary bombs that caused fires. This combined with the heat and unusually dry weather during the summer of 1945 caused many forest fires. The 555th Parachute Infantry Battalion was assigned to Pendleton Army Air Base in Oregon, and from there, using their skills as paratroopers, would assist the "Smoke Jumpers" of the National Forest Service to put out these fires.

The paratroopers had to be retrained with the technique of jumping into forested areas, where there were hazards such as landing on rocks and tree stumps, and the problem of getting out of their parachutes when they were hung up in the trees. They had to learn to jump with the Derry Parachute, known as the T-7 Assembly. Designed by Frank Derry, this parachute allowed the jumper to steer 360 degrees, circling while descending, in order to locate a better landing zone and to avoid hazards. The paratroopers had to learn how to suppress fires and mastered survival techniques should they become overtaken by flames. Also, specially selected men began work with bomb disposal units of the Ninth Army Service Command, receiving training on defusing unexploded ordnance. By mid–July, the battalion had completed qualifications as Smoke Jumpers. The main portion of the battalion would operate out of Pendleton Army Air Base, fighting fires in Oregon, Idaho, Washington, and Montana. Another group of six officers and 94 enlisted men operated out of Chico Army Air Base in California, where they would fight forest fires in that state.

Between 14 July and 6 October, well after the war had ended, the 555th Parachute Infantry Battalion would fight 36 fire missions, for what came to be known as Operation Firefly, with only one loss of life. On 8 August 1945, Private Malvin Brown was killed while parachuting into a forested area to suppress a fire.[8] It was later learned that the Japanese had stopped launching the balloons in April 1945 due to a shortage of hydrogen, and uncertainty that the balloons were even reaching their intended targets. The battalion also performed tactical combat jumps in participation with the navy during one of their training exercises. This would be the main contribution to the war effort for this African American airborne battalion, since they were denied the opportunity to fight in combat, but due to the secrecy surrounding the operations, very little was known of their deeds.[9]

In October 1945, the battalion was ordered back to North Carolina and assigned to the 27th Headquarters and Headquarters Special Troops, First Army, Fort Bragg. In December, the battalion was attached to the 13th Airborne Division, where it proceeded to discharge eligible "high point" personnel.

On 14 January 1946, Major General James Gavin, the commander of the 82nd Airborne Division, requested that the 350 remaining members of the 555th Parachute Infantry Battalion march with the division in their victory parade up Fifth Avenue in New York. General Gavin had heard of what the battalion had accomplished, and he knew they deserved the recognition. Now the world would see that there were African American paratroopers in the United States Army. From that time onward, the 555th Parachute Infantry Battalion would be closely associated with the 82nd Airborne Division. In February 1946, the battalion was officially attached to the recently returned 82nd Airborne Division for administration, training, and supply purposes. The division then attached the 555th Parachute Infantry Battalion to the 504th Parachute Infantry Regiment, which was commanded by Colonel William Westmoreland.[10]

With demobilization of the postwar period in full stride, the 555th Parachute Infantry Battalion was down to only 192 men. The battalion sent recruiting teams to Fort Dix, New Jersey, and Fort Jackson, South Carolina, to recruit African American soldiers that were returning to the United States from combat theaters of operation. The reputation of this elite unit would travel throughout the army, and by November 1946, the 555th Parachute Infantry Battalion had reached a maximum strength of 36 officers and 1,309 enlisted men assigned, making it the largest airborne qualified battalion in the military forces. In a segregated army, African American paratroopers could only be assigned to this single battalion.

Chapter X

2nd Cavalry and 93rd Infantry Divisions

Only three percent of the total United States combat forces during World War II were African American.

ARMY DIVISIONS

Although the four infantry and cavalry regular army regiments were the traditional type of combat units for African Americans to be assigned to in the army during the pre–World War II years, the expansion of these regiments into full divisions did not always proceed smoothly. Having an all African American combat division was still looked upon with disfavor among the heads of the military. To the army leaders, it would not be feasible to employ a whole division of over 15,000 African American men commanded by all white senior staff officers, many of which did not desire to be assigned with African American junior officers and enlisted men. To many on the General Staff, this experiment was deemed a dismal failure in World War I, and not worth the effort in this current war. In addition, trained soldiers would be required to replace the combat casualties for every job skill in that division. Earlier in the war, it was deemed that the separate regimental combat teams, consisting of approximately 3,000 soldiers, were more self-contained units that were easier to train and deploy into combat. They could be attached to other divisions for operational purposes. During World War I, the four regiments of the 93rd Infantry Division were utilized in this fashion and attached to different French infantry divisions and achieved numerous commendations for their valor in battle. But as the Second World War expanded into a global conflict, the war effort required a larger, more efficient combat force.

By the end of 1941, it appeared that the army of over 3,600,000 men that was scheduled for 1942 would have a total of 71 combat divisions, 32 of which would be the newly formed infantry and four of which would be the new armored mechanized divisions. The army would have to induct 177,000 African Americans during the year as a proportionate share of its increased military strength. The two new African American infantry divisions would not have to be developed solely from these new recruits. Separate African American infantry regiments already existed and could be incorporated as the core of these divisions. The regular army's 24th and 25th Infantry Regiments, the newly activated 366th Infantry (activated 10 Feb 1941), the 367th Infantry (activated 10 Mar 1941) and the 368th Infantry (activated 1 Mar 1941) were regular army regiments, and the 372nd National Guard Regiment (federalized 10 Mar 1941) could be utilized for this purpose.

Vernon Baker was a young man from Cheyenne, Wyoming, who enlisted in the army just prior to the outbreak of war in early 1941. In spite of the defense buildup, civilian jobs for African Americans were still nonexistent, and the military afforded Baker the opportunity to do something different with his life. For the first time he was introduced to racism and segregation in the South as he attended basic training at Camp Wolter, Texas. After basic training, he was assigned to the 25th Infantry Regiment at Fort Huachuca, Arizona.[1]

2ND CAVALRY DIVISION

In August 1940, the Department of the Army planned that the 9th and 10th Cavalry Regiments would form the 4th Brigade of the integrated 2nd Cavalry Division. The Chief of Cavalry objected strenuously to this integrated organization. He stated: "It appears to me to be obvious that such a unit nonhomogeneous — half white and half black, cannot be as effective as a homogeneous of all black or all white units. There is not only a difference in color but there is a difference in emotional reactions. The concentration of a large body of troops in one place, approximately half white and half black, involves the risk of bitter rivalries and racial clashes. I consider this to be an unwise improvisation."[2] These objections were in spite of the fact that the 9th and 10th Cavalry Regiments had fought side by side with white units throughout this country's many conflicts, and had been brigaded with the white cavalry regiments since their inception in 1866. Despite the objections of the Chief of Cavalry, the 2nd Cavalry Division was announced for organization early in 1941 at Fort Riley, Kansas. The cavalry divisions of the early 1940s had not converted to the tri-tier system that the standard infantry division had incorporated, and were composed of two cavalry brigades, each having assigned two cavalry regiments. The white 1st Cavalry Division had the 1st and 2nd Cavalry brigades assigned. The 2nd Cavalry Division consisted of the 3rd and 4th Cavalry Brigades. Its 3rd Cavalry Brigade was composed of the white 2nd and 14th Cavalry Regiments, and the 4th Brigade containing the African American 9th and 10th Cavalry Regiments. All of the rest of the organic supporting units of the division would be white with the exception of a single truck company in the quartermaster squadron.

In the spring of 1942, as the War Department decided to increase the number of armored and motorized divisions, Army Ground Forces Command recommended that one of the new divisions be provided by the conversion of the 2nd Cavalry Division, less its African American 4th Cavalry Brigade, to an armored division. This recommendation was approved with the exception that the 2nd Cavalry Division was to be retained as a cavalry division with only its 4th Cavalry Brigade remaining active while its white elements were relieved and reassigned to the new 9th Armored Division.[3] It was felt that the retention of the 2nd Cavalry Division provided for the future absorption of larger numbers of African American army inductees and the small possibility that there would be a requirement for a trained cavalry division. But the modern mechanized battlefield tactics of World War II would mean the deathblow to the old horse cavalry units of the past. In November 1942, the War Department directed that new units constituted for refilling the division be ready for activation on 25 February 1943. In the meantime, the two new African American infantry divisions, the 92nd and 93rd, had been activated.

The white 1st Cavalry Division was also converted to a standard infantry division and deployed to the Pacific Theater on 11 July 1943. The 9th Armored Division would land in France in September 1944. The division was involved in the Battle of the Bulge, but was most noted for capturing the Ludendorff Bridge at Remagen on 7 March 1945, enabling the Allied Armies to cross the Rhine River and to advance swiftly across Germany, bringing an end to the war.

On 15 July 1942, the 2nd Cavalry Division was deactivated. The 4th Cavalry Brigade with its African American 9th and 10th Cavalry Regiments, however, remained on the active rolls. With the activation of the 9th Armored Division, logistical problems were created at Fort Riley and Camp Funston, Kansas. The military installations that had accommodated only a single cavalry division were now home to a mechanized armored division and an additional separate cavalry brigade. Consequently, the 4th Cavalry Brigade Headquarters and the 10th Cavalry Regiment relocated to Camp Lockett, California. The 9th Cavalry Regiment, although still assigned to the brigade, was transferred to Fort Clarke, Texas.

As the number of African American inductees entering the army rose, the need for segregated units for these soldiers to join also increased. In November 1942 the War Department directed that the 2nd Cavalry Division would be reactivated, providing a large unit for these new soldiers to be assigned to, and that two new African American cavalry regiments, the 27th and 28th, would be activated. It was also announced that the 2nd Cavalry Division, now the army's third African American combat division, would remain divided between its two present locations in Texas and California. Construction was started at both posts since neither had the facilities to support an entire division. With the work completed, the 2nd Cavalry Division was reactivated on 25 February 1943, commanded by another southern officer, Major General Harry H. Johnson, with its headquarters located at Fort Clarke. The 9th and 27th Cavalry Regiments, active at the Fort Clark, Texas, post, were the assigned units of the newly formed 5th Cavalry Brigade. The veteran 10th Cavalry, and the newly activated 28th Cavalry Regiment, located at Camp Lockett, made up the 4th Cavalry Brigade. Support elements of the division were equally divided between the two posts.

Filled using basic recruits straight from the induction centers, the reactivated 2nd Cavalry Division spent most of the spring and summer of 1943 training its new soldiers. The division provided these men with their basic training as well as instruction in cavalry tactics. But like many other African American units commanded by white southern officers, the soldiers of the 2nd Cavalry Division were unsatisfied with the leadership it was provided. One soldier from the Medical Detachment of the Division Artillery writes to the African American press:

The Atlanta Daily World Fort Clark, Texas
April 23, 1943
Dear Editor:

I would like to know if your paper approves of a General calling his soldiers "Nigger" to their face? I think that we are in this war to fight for the rights of all minority races, the morale of this organization will be low if our soldiers are not addressed in the right manner.

Our colored chaplain was run off this post by General Johnson solely because he protested to him against using the word "Nigger" when referring to colored troops. I feel that it is my right and privilege to protest against the un–Godly way that the men of the 2nd Cavalry Division are treated by their white Texas officers.

I hope that you will see that the colored people of this nation know that these conditions exist.

Believe me that these are true statements.

A Negro Soldier[4]

The divisional training as a whole, however, would never be tested in combat. Stating that there was no intrinsic need on the battlefield for a traditional cavalry division, the War Department had devised a plan to convert the 2nd Cavalry Division. But unlike the white cavalry regiments which had been converted into either armored or infantry divisions, the 2nd Cavalry Division's personnel would provide the manpower to form needed combat service support units.[5]

By August 1943, there was a critical manpower shortage of combat service support personnel to provide the logistical support for a global war. Initially, the Army Service Force requested 14,500 African American soldiers to be utilized as replacements for these units. Thirty-one African American combat battalions — 13 antiaircraft artillery, 10 field artillery, and 8 tank destroyer battalions — contributed their personnel in this effort. The 1944 Troop Basis Plan finally abandoned any attempt to provide African American units by set quotas that were prescribed in preceding years. During 1944, all units, African American and white, were to be provided only on the basis of demonstrated and current combat requirements. "Operational demands forecast to 30 June 1945," the Assistant Chief of Staff (G-3) reasoned, "require the mobilization of a considerable additional number of service units in which Negroes can profitably be employed (port, ammunition, truck, service and dump truck companies). Generally speaking all augmentations of these types of units have been earmarked for Negro personnel. It was true that this practice had resulted in an actual decrease in the number of Negro combat units," the G-3 continued, "but enough had been retained to continue representation of Negroes in all arms and services. With the smaller number of Negro combat units now provided, careful selection of personnel should permit development of these units to the point where they will have battle value."[6]

Prior to its deployment overseas, many of the soldiers of the 2nd Cavalry Division who received training in the technical skills, such as those in the communications and medical fields, had already been transferred to other military units.

In a move to limit African American combat operations overseas, the 2nd Cavalry Division arrived in North Africa early in January 1944 only to learn that the division was to be immediately deactivated and transformed into smaller combat service support units, unloading ships, repairing roads, and driving trucks throughout the Mediterranean Theater of Operations. Most of the white officers would be transferred to other combat units. Some of veteran soldiers were disappointed by the War Department's decision to deny them the opportunity of combat duty after training for all those years; others naturally expressed relief at not having to go into battle. In the months that followed the deactivation of the 2nd Cavalry Division, the War Department circulated a survey among some of its former division members asking them if they preferred to be placed in a combat unit or to remain in their present combat service support jobs. The survey revealed that only 27 percent of the men chose combat. What the War Department survey failed to realize, however, was that the attitudinal responses of the 2nd Cavalry Division's soldiers had more to do with bouts of racism within their own ranks than anything else. One veteran, who recalled the racial dynamics in the unit during the period, stated, "We spent too much time hating and fighting our white officers to have much energy left for the Germans."[7]

The events surrounding the 2nd Cavalry Division's deactivation reflected the War Department's position of converting as many African American combat soldiers into service support personnel as possible.[8] Facing growing criticism from various sectors of African American society over the army's utilization of African American soldiers in combat zones overseas, the newly created Advisory Committee on Negro Troop Policies met in early 1943 to discuss the issue. Formed in August of 1942 and headed by Assistant Secretary of War John J. McCloy, its members included Brigadier General Benjamin O. Davis, Sr., of the Inspector General's Office; Truman Gibson, Jr., Civilian Aide to the Secretary of War for Negro Affairs; and all the directors of personnel for the Army Air Forces, Army Ground Forces, and Army Service Forces commands. After discussing the situation, the committee recommended to Secretary of War Henry Stimson that "Negro combat troops be dispatched to an active theater of operations at an early date." In the opinion of the committee, "such action would be the most effective means of reducing tension among Negro troops." Secretary Stimson, however, decided to ignore the committee's recommendation and agreed with his staff's recommendation to convert the lone remaining Negro cavalry division into the service support corps.[9] Secretary Stimson and other staff members based their secret decision on other plans that would release white combat service support soldiers for front-line duty with combat units and the growing number of technical jobs. But when New York Congressman Hamilton Fish publicly asked Secretary Stimson why Negro combat units were being converted and why the War Department had not committed Negro troops to front-line duty in the 26 months following Pearl Harbor, Stimson replied that "it so happens that a relatively large percentage of Negroes inducted into the army had lower educational classifications and many of the Negro units had been unable to efficiently master the techniques of modern weapons."[10] This would be the recurring excuse provided by the Secretary of War and the General Staff of the Army as to why there were not more African American combat units represented in the army. The few African American combat units that were available were there to placate politicians such as Hamilton Fish and the African American public, and there were no plans to actually utilize them in combat. Meanwhile in 1944, the army would start experiencing a manpower shortage within the infantry forces.

After facing a firestorm of criticism from the African American newspaper press corps, African American leaders, and national protest groups, Secretary Stimson and other War Department officials were forced to devote more attention to the problem of committing African American combat forces to operations theaters overseas.[11] It was perceived by the African American public that the military leaders were denying African Americans the opportunity to fight for their country on an equal level with white Americans. Keeping African American soldiers in combat support units, while a vital role in the war effort, equated to keeping them in the role of only being servants to the military structure. Being allowed to serve in front-line combat units on the same basis as the white soldiers would prove that African Americans had sacrificed for their country and deserved the rights that were afforded to all Americans, to be no longer treated as second-class citizens.

By the end of February 1944, the McCloy Committee had convened at Secretary Stimson's request and recommended that the Operations Division commit Negro infantry, field artillery, armor, and other units to combat.[12] A week later, Secretaries Stimson and McCloy and other directors of the War Department's agencies met to discuss the Advisory Committee's recommendation and decided to commit some of the units of the 93rd Infantry Division, then entering the Southwest Pacific Area, to combat as quickly as possible. They also agreed to create a regimental combat team of selected highly qualified soldiers from the 92nd

Newly commissioned second lieutenants outside of Theater 4, Fort Benning, Georgia, at the conclusion of the 16th Infantry Officers Candidate School graduating exercises. From left: second lieutenants Henry C. Harris, Jr., Rogers H. Beardon, Frank Frederick Doughton, and Elmer B. Kountze pin their brass bars on each other's shoulders, 29 May 1942. (National Archives 111-SC-13767)

Infantry Division and deploy it in future theaters of operations. As many scholars such as Richard Dalfiume have demonstrated, "like the drafting and assignment to units, the commitment of Negroes to combat was a reaction to pressure rather than the planned fulfillment of a need."[13]

93RD INFANTRY DIVISION

The activation of the first of the two African American infantry divisions, the 93rd, was to occur in the spring of 1942. Two of the already existing African American infantry regiments, the 25th and 368th Infantry, would form the nucleus of this new division. The newly activated 369th Infantry Regiment would make the third infantry regiment of the division. Thus, the 93rd Infantry Division would be able to provide the cadre for the formation of the 92nd Infantry Division, which was scheduled for activation in October of that same year. The officer roles would be virtually the same as those two infantry divisions had experienced in World War I. In most cases, the senior and staff officers would all be white, and the majority of the junior company grade officers, captains and lieutenants would be African Americans. No chance for advancement would cause severe morale problems and resentment for the African American officers. Many white officers considered an assignment to an African American unit degrading, detrimental to their military careers, and often sought transfers to all-white units. Rarely would a West Point graduate be assigned to an African American infantry division. During the training cycle, there would be a large turnover in the officer ranks. New African American junior officers, recently graduated from Officer Candidate Schools, would replace many of the white lieutenants and captains. But the senior staff of the division would remain unchanged. The white senior staff officers would conduct all the planning and decision-making in combat. In essence, the same leadership mistakes that plagued the African American infantry divisions during the First World War would continue to be the detriment of the divisions during this conflict.

The 93rd Infantry Division was activated on 15 May 1942 under the command of Major General Charles P. Hall. Extensive preparation was required for an infantry division to be certified combat-ready for deployment overseas. After activation, if a division had no particular types of delays, it would proceed with their training cycle. Planning in 1942 provided that a division's initial training would commence 15 days after activation. It began with 17 weeks of basic and advanced individual combat training, 13 weeks of unit training, 14 weeks of combined arms tactics, and 8 weeks of review and air-mechanized coordination. Soldiers receiving technical training in such fields as communications, logistics, and medical service, would transfer to the various military training facilities after basic training and return to the division upon completion of that training. After a year in training, an infantry division that had not been handicapped by interruptions in the training cycle or stripping of personnel, would be deemed prepared to proceed to Army Command maneuver evaluation, and then deployment to an overseas theater. In October 1942, Major General Raymond G. Lehman became the third division commander in its first five months of existence, causing numerous leadership problems.

The 93rd Infantry Division had the advantage of being able to train its entire unit at a single army post. Fort Huachuca, Arizona, the traditional home of the Buffalo Soldiers, was to be the home base for the two African American infantry divisions. The local communities had grown accustomed to having African American soldiers stationed at Fort Huachuca, and the western region of the country would not be plagued by the harsh racial discrimination that occurred on military bases throughout the South. But the post could only accommodate one full division at a time. While the 92nd Infantry Division had the continuity of the top command structure, its individual units would have to train at separate military posts throughout the United States until the 93rd Infantry Division deployed overseas. Aside from the regular army's 25th Infantry Regiment, and the 368th Infantry Regiment activated in 1941, the rest of the division would consist of newly inducted draftees. By the time the division was activated, both of these regiments also had a large numbers of new inductees in order to bring their ranks up to full combat strength authorization. Then, on 31 August 1943, the 93rd Infantry Division was responsible for furnishing the cadre for the newly activated 92nd Infantry Division. They provided 128 officers and 1,200 enlisted men.[14] But the 93rd Infantry Division was also responsible for providing many of the cadres for other new African American units that would be activated during the war. Consequently, there was a constant turnover of trained personnel within that division.

In spite of all the personnel changes, the divisions went through their scheduled training cycle and maneuvers. The 93rd Infantry's divisional level exercises were conducted in the Huachuca Mountains in March 1943. From April through June 1943, the 93rd Infantry Division participated in the 3rd Army maneuvers in Louisiana, proceeding from there to the Desert Training Center (California-Arizona Maneuver Area), where in November 1943 it went through more exercises and participated in the IV Corps maneuvers.

The 93rd Infantry Division received its final movement orders in December 1943. On 11 January 1944, their advanced party under the leadership of the division commander, Major General Raymond G. Lehman, departed San Francisco for the Southwest Pacific. The remainder of the division arrived in the Solomon Islands between then and the end of February. This would be the last time until the end of the war that the entire division would be assembled at the same location. The war in the Southwest Pacific was far different from the more famous island-hopping battles that the Navy, Army, and Marine Corps were conducting in the Central and South Pacific campaigns. The primary goal of the armies under the command of General Douglas MacArthur was to recapture the Philippine Islands. The islands of the Southwest Pacific region had a larger land mass. The enemy soldiers had more areas for concealment, and the campaigns to conquer and recapture these islands were generally longer and bloodier.

Upon their arrival in the Pacific Theater, the 93rd Infantry Division was divided into Regimental Combat Teams. These teams, in addition to the standard infantry regiment which had three infantry battalions assigned, also consisted of a separate field artillery battalion from the division artillery, a cannon company, an antitank company which could be utilized as an infantry heavy weapons company, a company of combat engineers from the division's 318th Engineer Battalion, a medical company from the 318th Medical Battalion, a scout troop of the 93rd Reconnaissance Squadron, a detachment from the 93rd Signal Company, a detachment from the 793rd Ordinance Company, and a platoon from the 93rd Military Police Company.

The 368th Regimental Combat Team proceeded onto Banika in the Russell Islands to prepare defensive positions on 7 February 1944. The 369th Regimental Combat Team, after only a few days of becoming acclimated to the tropical weather on Guadalcanal, proceeded in increments to islands of the New Georgia group. There, they relieved elements of the 43rd Infantry Division. These units of the 93rd Infantry Division began their careers as occupation soldiers, establishing guard posts, patrolling, searching for die-hard Japanese soldiers that refused to surrender, assisting the operation of ports by unloading ships, performing routine manual labor tasks, and training in jungle warfare.

The 25th Regimental Combat Team arrived on Guadalcanal on 17 February 1944. The first three weeks after its arrival was spent establishing a base camp and providing 1,000 men daily to augment the manual labor duties in the port area. In March 1944, the infantry battalions rotated through jungle warfare training, with an emphasis on scouting, patrolling, perimeter defense, weapons familiarization, and preventive malarial disease training. On 22 March, the combat team was ordered to deploy to Empress Augusta Bay, near the southern end of the island of Bougainville, where the XIV Corps was already deploying the 1/24th Infantry in combat. The Japanese, with an estimated force of 25,000 soldiers on Bougainville, were making an effort to dislodge the allied forces from the Torokina beachhead. The main attack came on 8 March with a series of poorly coordinated assaults, which resulted in heavy losses for the Japanese. The Japanese 64th Division was practically destroyed.[15]

On 28 March 1944, the 25th Regimental Combat Team, one of the four original regular army African American regiments, under the command of Colonel Everett M. Yon, arrived on Bougainville, unloading their equipment by day under intermittent Japanese artillery shelling. On 30 March, the team came under the command and control of the Americal Division for training, administration and operation. In his instructions to Major General Oscar W. Griswold, commanding XIV Corps, the theater commander, Lieutenant General Harmon, expanding the War Department's suggestion "to employ Negro troops into combat,"

Sergeant John C. Clark (left) and Staff Sergeant Ford M. Shaw clean their rifles in bivouac area alongside the East West Trail, Bougainville. They are members of Company E, 2/25th Infantry, 93rd Infantry Division, 4 April 1944. (National Archives, taken by Lt. Schuman. 111-SC-364565)

emphasized the values inherent in limited offensive operations beyond the Torokina perimeter in southern Bougainville. He suggested that the 25th Regimental Combat Team, supplemented if desired by the already available 1st Battalion, 24th Infantry, be used in these operations. A fresh one from the same regiment could replace the 24th Infantry's battalion later. The Negro units were to work with more seasoned units under experienced leaders before going on their on.[16] Each battalion of the 25th Infantry Regiment was therefore attached to one of the Americal Division's infantry regiments. The 593rd Field Artillery Battalion and the 25th Cannon Company were attached to the Americal's division artillery and other elements of the combat team to corresponding units of the Americal Division.[17] Two battalions of the Fiji Infantry Regiment, native Fijians under the command of New Zealand and Fijian officers, that had gained combat experience on Bougainville were also available to be utilized with the 25th Regimental Combat Team.

By the time the 25th Infantry Regiment had arrived on Bougainville, the main effort of Japanese resistance had been exhausted by elements of the Americal Division, the 37th Infantry Division, and the 1/24th Infantry Battalion. The 25th Infantry Regiment would come under the command and control of the Americal Division for their initial training and indoctrination into combat. Each of the battalions would be attached to a different regiment of the division. Beginning on 30 March 1944, officers of the 25th Infantry Regiment would accompany combat patrols of the Americal Division as observers. The next day, elements of the 25th Infantry Regiment, acting as ammunition bearers and pioneer platoons (responsible for keeping the main element of the fighting force supplied and evacuating wounded to the rear), were attached to the 132nd Infantry Regiment in their assaults on Hills 500 and 501. After three days of combat, the Japanese had suffered 65 soldiers killed in action. The 25th Infantry Regiment would also receive their first combat casualties with three men wounded due to enemy sniper fire. On 31 March, Private James H. O'Banner would become the first member of the 93rd Infantry Division to kill an enemy soldier in combat.[18]

Before the other battalions attached to the regiments of the Americal Division began their active patrolling, the 2/25th Infantry was temporarily detached from the 182nd Infantry Regiment and assigned to a special task force from the 37th Infantry Division, which included the 3/148th Infantry, and two battalions of the Fiji Infantry Regiment. The task force was directed to pursue and destroy the enemy elements withdrawing east and north along the Laruma River. The task force proceeded on 2 April. The 2/25th Infantry was ordered to ford the Laruma River and proceed eastward, protecting the lines of communication and securing a trail junction near the mouth of the Jaba Creek, while the 3/148th Infantry proceeded along the south bank of the river. Company E, 2/25th Infantry, while covering the river crossing, encountered and killed two Japanese soldiers. Immediately upon crossing the Laruma River, the 2/25th Infantry engaged in small skirmishes against light enemy resistance. Enemy opposition south of the river prohibited any advance on that side, and was bypassed by the 3/148th Infantry. The 2/25th Infantry placed considerable 60-mm mortar and .30-caliber light machine gun fire on these positions from their vantage point on the opposite shore.

On the next afternoon, 3 April, a small patrol under the command of the S-2, regimental intelligence officer, recrossed the Laruma River and uncovered an enemy machine gun emplacement in a pocket of fortified pillboxes. One enemy soldier was killed before intense hostile fire forced the patrol to withdraw. After machine gun and mortar preparation fire, a platoon from Company F, 2/25th Infantry, crossed the river and cleared out the machine gun positions, losing five men wounded to twenty enemy soldiers killed. Private Wade Foggie set up his bazooka (rocket launcher) under heavy fire and sent eight rounds into three enemy pillboxes, destroying them all and killing ten of the enemy soldiers. For his valor under hostile fire, he was awarded the 93rd Infantry Division's first Bronze Star medal for valor.[19]

In this manner, most of the battalions of the 25th Regimental Combat Team were introduced to the rigors of jungle combat. Patrols consisting of members of the regiment, Fijians, and members of the Americal Division, engaged in both limited and extensive missions. In the meantime, the 593rd Field Artillery Battalion joined in the fire missions along with the Americal's division artillery. The 1/25th Infantry, attached to the 132nd Infantry Regiment, received its baptism by fire on 3 April 1944. A pioneer platoon carrying ammunition and supplies to a company of the 132nd Infantry Regiment in the vicinity of Hill 500 was ambushed by an enemy patrol when a squad of the platoon was on their way back to the perimeter with a casualty. Four men of the 1/25th were instantly killed in the initial volley of gunfire. These soldiers, Privates Hugh Carrol, Oginal I. Ryan, William W. Ash and Joseph C. Mallory, were the first men of the 93rd Infantry Division to be killed in combat during the war.[20] A member of the regimental medical detachment, Technician 3 Stephen H. Simpson, Jr., was with the 132nd Infantry's patient at the time of the ambush. Staying with the wounded man, he destroyed an enemy machine gun emplacement with a hand grenade. Once he moved the patient to a safer location, he was able to dress a new wound that the man received during the firefight. He and the surviving members of the squad improvised a litter for the patient and continued toward the rear area. When darkness fell, the group was able to find their way through the jungle by following the sound of friendly artillery fire. By morning, they had reached an Americal Division outpost and delivered the patient to a battalion aid station.

Meanwhile, Company B, 1/25th took over a defensive sector of the perimeter from a company of the 132nd Infantry. On 6 April, Company C, 1/25th Infantry, operating in conjunction with Company L, 3/132nd Infantry, while on a reconnaissance-in-force patrol near Hill 500, encountered an enemy patrol. After a brief exchange of fire, the American soldiers withdrew, and called in artillery on the enemy positions.

The 25th Regimental Combat Team's indoctrination into combat had been proceeding as planned. Brigadier General William C. Dunckel, commander of the Americal's division artillery, warmly welcomed the 593rd Field Artillery Battalion, after forward observers reported the accuracy of their fire and the efficiency of their construction and occupation of their battery positions.[21] The 2/25th Infantry upon its return from attachment with the 37th Infantry Division's task force was commended by the regimental commander for its count of thirty enemy dead at a cost of four minor casualties. The 3/25th Infantry had not yet participated in any combat patrols with elements of the 164th Infantry Regiment. It had been directed to organize reserve positions for the regiment. The companies had conducted brief reconnaissance patrols without any enemy contact.

On 5 April, Company K, 3/25th Infantry, received a warning order that they were to form a trail block to impede the movement of Japanese forces approximately 3,000 yards from the base of Hill 250. A white officer, Captain James J. Curran, commanded the company with all African American platoon leaders. This would be the first company-size operation conducted by the 3/25th Infantry. Company K was noted to be the best in the 3rd Battalion during training, but was yet to be tested in combat. To augment the company, a machine gun platoon from Company M, 3/25th Infantry was attached. Company K would deploy on the morning of 6 April, and form the trail block during the night. Captain William A. Crutcher and three enlisted men of the 593rd Field Artillery Battalion accompanied the company as forward artillery observers, able to call in supporting artillery fire. The XIV Corps commander decided that this first patrol for the company would be an excellent opportunity to provide news releases for the press of the 25th Infantry Regiment in combat. An officer and enlisted man of the 161st Signal Photographic Company were attached to the patrol, and had their cameras available to record the events of the mission for press releases. To minimize the fact that this was the company's first patrol, Sergeant Ralph Brodin, a noncommissioned officer from the 164th Infantry Regiment's S-2 intelligence section, would be attached as a combination guide and liaison. He would be the only one on this mission with any previous combat experience.

Company K deployed at 0645. Its equipment and armament were standard for an infantry company, except that nine additional Browning Automatic Rifles (BAR) were substituted for nine M1 rifles for additional firepower. The weapons section had four .30-caliber light machine guns, and there was one instead of three 60-mm mortars. The unit carried two SCR-300 radios. The order of march would be: 1st platoon would provide security to the front while breaking a trail through the jungle; a light machine gun section and the company headquarters section would follow. The 2nd platoon, coming next and in column, would provide security to the flanks, sending out small reconnaissance and security patrols each time the formation stopped. Following the 2nd platoon would be another light machine gun section, with the 3rd platoon securing the rear of the formation. The company came upon an abandoned enemy hospital about 2,000 yards from their departure point. While searching the area, the first platoon sent out small reconnaissance patrols. Japanese soldiers attacked the patrols almost immediately. One of the patrols reported killing two of the enemy. Captain Curran went forward to investigate, but before he reached the dead Japanese soldiers, enemy fire erupted from around the perimeter of the company formation. Confusion spread throughout Company K as the soldiers fired in every direction. Some of the security patrols were still out on the flanks and isolated from the rest of the company. Those soldiers were caught in the crossfire between their fellow soldiers and the enemy forces. As casualties mounted, the company commander attempted to reorganize the company. First Sergeant James Gavin was ordered to get the wounded back to the battalion aid station. Throughout the firefight in the jungle, many of the casualties were a result of friendly fire from the American soldiers of Company K.

The officers and noncommissioned officers of the company tried to restore order to their platoons. First Lieutenant Oscar Davenport, the executive officer of the company and weapons platoon leader, ordered his forward light machine guns to a defensive line that was being formed adjacent to the 2nd and 3rd platoons. Lieutenant Davenport remained in the forward areas until all the surviving members of his platoon had fallen back. While crawling to the aid of a wounded soldier from the 1st platoon, he was struck by enemy fire. He continued to crawl forward until he reached the wounded soldier. Exposing himself to protect the wounded soldier, Lieutenant Davenport was killed while administering first aid. For his heroic actions, he was posthumously awarded the Bronze Star medal.[22] When Captain Curran reported his situation to the battalion command post, he was ordered to withdraw 300 yards to the rear to reorganize the company, and then counterattack the enemy forces.

The attached soldiers of the patrol would later report a total lack of any type of leadership. Sergeant Brodin of the 164th Infantry Regiment attempted to organize and encourage the soldiers. He walked calmly up and down carrying his carbine, telling the men there was nothing to worry about, and that there were only a few enemy soldiers present. First Lieutenant Charles Schuman, the Signal Corps photographer, reported: "Sergeant Brodin suggested that my sergeant and I withdraw to the rear where we ran into Captain Curran. He was running up and down the trail trying to calm the men by shouting 'Hold your fire, hold your fire.'"[23] At no time did Lieutenant Schuman observe any control being exercised over the men. Soon there was no patrol front as soldiers were lying around firing in all directions at anything that moved. By then, Captain Curran had already proceeded to the rear with his radioman, leaving most of his company in their forward firing positions. The men of the company were now aware that their commander and first sergeant had already proceeded to the rear, leaving them without any effective leadership or communications to the battalion command post. When Captain Curran reported to battalion again, he was ordered to bring his company back to Hill 250 in order to reorganize. Once the battle zone was evacuated, artillery fire was called in on the suspected enemy positions.

The first elements of the company with the first sergeant and some of the wounded arrived at the battalion's front defensive lines at 1730 that afternoon. Lieutenant Davenport and nine enlisted men were killed and twenty additional men wounded in the firefight. The dead were left behind, along with some equipment including a radio, a light machine gun, the 60-mm mortar with 30 rounds, two Browning Automatic Rifles, 18 M1 rifles, 3 M1 carbines and assorted equipment. The entire action lasted only 30 minutes. The best estimates were that there was perhaps only one squad of enemy soldiers (approximately 15 men) attacking a company of over 100 American soldiers. Many of the casualties were caused by the unit's own men in the confusion of the battle. Investigation of the incident was conducted by the Americal Division's Inspector General's Office, involving testimony from almost every available soldier of Company K that was present during the battle. The investigation lasted from 14 April until 2 May.[24]

The first sergeant and a platoon sergeant that deserted under fire were immediately relieved of their duties when the company returned to the battalion's perimeter. Often, senior non-commissioned officers were selected, not for their leadership abilities, but on how they catered to the white officers. Testimony received from the soldiers present during the battle was that Captain Curran had deserted his company and ran to the rear under fire. This belief led to confusion within the ranks and among the leadership that was left in the battle. This would not be the last time that a white commander would desert his African American soldiers when they came under fire. Lack of faith in the fighting capabilities of the soldiers that they were entrusted to lead would often cause this fear. Official military reports would not always attest to these facts, but eyewitness testimony of the African American soldiers, if even obtained, was usually ignored if it could place blame on the white officer involved. The white officer in most of these cases would be transferred, or returned to the United States without any disciplinary action. Most army leaders considered the hardships of just serving with African American soldiers to be justification for not seeking any type of disciplinary action for the failed leadership of these white officers. The question still remains as to why the 164th Infantry Regiment did not indoctrinate the soldiers of the 3/25th Infantry slowly into combat, as had the other infantry regiments of the Americal Division before it ordered Company K on this mission. These incidents may not have occurred in a more combat-seasoned unit with effective leadership.

On 7 April, a patrol from Company L was sent out to recover the dead and retrieve the abandoned equipment. The patrol ran into an ambush just short of its destination. In the battle that ensued, they lost one man killed, while another drowned crossing a river on their retreat back to friendly lines. On 8 April, Lieutenant Abner E. Jackson, the 1st platoon leader from Company K (and not Captain Curran, the company commander), along with 40 men of Company L, returned to the scene of the initial battle. Six bodies were found, but the men refused to touch or wrap the rapidly decomposing corpses exposed to the harsh tropical elements of the Bougainville jungle, and invested with maggots. Despite the threat of disciplinary actions, Lieutenant Jackson could only get two noncommissioned officers and two medical corpsmen to assist him in wrapping the bodies. At Lieutenant Jackson's request, 20 men of his own Company K, under the leadership of the new first sergeant, joined the patrol. Three of the bodies and three mattress covers full of abandoned equipment were returned to the battalion area. On the third day, another patrol with Lieutenant Jackson and led by the battalion commander retrieved the rest of the remains and equipment.

The 3/25th Infantry continued to patrol for the next two weeks without any further incidents. Most were joint patrols conducted with elements of the 164th Infantry Regiment, as were the initial patrols of the other battalions of the 25th Regimental Combat Team. On 11 April, a patrol from Company K killed two enemy soldiers, while another patrol from Company I captured a Japanese prisoner.

Individual acts of heroism would still occur throughout the regiment. The 2/25th Infantry, after its return to the Americal Division's command and control, commenced in extensive patrolling in the Torokina Valley. One of the patrols from Company F was ambushed on 8 April by a numerically superior enemy force. A member of the patrol, Private Isaac Sermon, wounded in the neck and exposed to enemy fire, returned fire with his Browning Automatic Rifle, killing at least three of the enemy soldiers, while allowing the rest of the patrol to seek cover. As Private Sermon crawled back to the patrol, he was shot three additional times, but kept moving. Private Sermon protected the retreating patrol's rear for over 600 yards before he dropped from exhaustion and the loss of blood. For his exemplary conduct under fire, Private Sermon was awarded the regiment's only Silver Star medal, the nation's third highest award for valor in combat.[25]

On the same day, the Americal Division ordered units of the 25th Infantry Regiment to occupy the new outpost defensive line. A provisional battalion composed of the antitank and cannon companies occupied positions on Hill 260, relieving the 1/24th Infantry, which was then attached to the 37th Infantry Division. The Americal Division continued to control the units of the 25th Infantry Regiment until 30 April. Then, control of the 25th Regimental Combat Team passed to a provisional brigade of the 93rd Infantry Division commanded by Brigadier General Leonard Boyd, the assistant division commander. All soldiers of the 93rd Infantry Division now on Bougainville came under his command. Their line of defense and area of responsibility would be maintained 12,000 yards beyond the American airfield, leaving it out of range of the Japanese artillery. Units of the regiment still coordinated their patrols with the Americal Division throughout the month of May. Members of the 93rd Infantry Division's 318th Engineer Battalion begin constructing roads while the 93rd Cavalry Reconnaissance Troop provided added security.

Although relations between the 25th Regimental Combat Team and the Americal Division improved as the soldiers gained valuable combat experience, the Company K incident would not only have a profound effect on the regiment, but the entire 93rd Infantry Division as a whole. Rumors quickly spread throughout the Pacific Theater that the 93rd Infantry Division (Colored) during the invasion of Bougainville had broken and run. This one incident would overshadow any other achievements that the division accomplished during the war. To the military leaders, this would justify their prejudiced reasons for not wanting to assign African Americans to combat. The two African American infantry divisions would be highly scrutinized throughout the entire time they served in a combat theater. The white leadership of these infantry divisions was never held responsible. Only the inherent combat capabilities of the individual soldiers were blamed. In addition, white officers were highly prejudicial of the leadership of African American officers, often citing that their men would not follow their orders and preferred to serve only under white officers, which was seldom the case. The men resented serving under white officers. These were the same allegations of inept leadership by African American officers that plagued the combat divisions in the First World War. After the war, the Chairman of the Joint Chiefs of Staff, General Marshall, relying on the biased reports of his senior commanders in the theater, described the 93rd Infantry as a division whose men on Bougainville "wouldn't fight — couldn't get them out of the caves to fight."[26]

The performance of the 25th Regimental Combat Team on Bougainville produced the familiar doubts in higher commands' estimate of the unit, all echoing the training experience and all tending to support the desirability of the original view of the most efficient ways to utilize an African American infantry division. The XIV Corps commander concluded after the first initial six weeks in combat:

1. It is apparent that the unit had had little "jungle training"; consequently, as individuals or as a unit, they were not prepared to handle adequately problems encountered in jungle operations. Most individuals showed willingness to learn from white troops; however, their ability to learn, and to retain what has been taught, is generally inferior to that of white troops.

2. In general, morale of all soldiers was high. However, units as a whole seemed to be unduly affected by reports of difficulties encountered by other elements of the command. Morale of the officers, especially white, seems rather low. Much of this attitude can be traced to the lack of responsibility demonstrated by their junior colored officers and noncommissioned officers.

3. In general, discipline seems satisfactory; however, there is a tendency on the part of junior colored officers to make the minimum effort to carry out instructions. This same tendency exists among the enlisted men when they receive instructions from these junior officers. As a rule, colored officers do not have control of the enlisted men. On the other hand, those units having a large proportion of white officers appear to be better controlled, trained and disciplined.

4. Initiative is generally lacking, especially among platoon commanders and lower grades. The presence of higher ranking officers, especially whites, is necessary to assure the tackling and accomplishment of any tasks.

5. Field sanitation is generally inadequate.

6. To date, the 25th Infantry, though supposedly better trained than the 1/24th Infantry has not progressively improved to the extent of the latter unit.

The combat efficiency evaluation of the 25th Regimental Combat Team was only considered fair for its infantry elements and good for the artillery units.[27]

This report by Major General Griswold contained all the stereotypes associated with African American soldiers, and lacked accuracy as to what actually occurred. It also fails to mention that it was his decision to send Company K into combat without the indoctrination by veteran soldiers in order to obtain combat photographs for a press release. Nor was there any comment relating to the fact that their commander, a white officer, deserted his company on the battlefield.

Upon receiving this report, Secretary of War Stimson made this observation about the 93rd Infantry Division: "...I do not believe they can be turned into really effective combat troops without all officers being white. This is indicated by many of the incidents herein."[28]

There could not be a fair comparison of the combat performance of the 24th and 25th Infantry Regiments. The 24th Infantry Regiment had deployed to the combat theater almost two years before the 25th Regimental Combat Team. Prior to departing the United States, the 24th Infantry Regiment was a cohesive unit composed of veteran career soldiers and all white officers. But by 1944, when the 1/24th Infantry first went into combat, many of the white junior officers had been replaced with African American lieutenants. The 25th Infantry Regiment, prior to deploying overseas, had a large changeover of personnel, losing many of their experienced noncommissioned officers to become cadres for other newly activated units. But the main underlying reason that the higher command believed the 24th Infantry Regiment was far superior in combat to the 25th Infantry Regiment was that it initially deployed overseas with all white officers, unlike the 25th Infantry, which had a race mixture of its junior officer staff. Many of the senior staff officers at the time still believed that only white officers could effectively lead African American soldiers. If the soldiers performed poorly under white leadership, then it was due to the poor combat capabilities of the men, and not to ineffectual leadership. Many of these generals believed that African American soldiers should be restricted to serve only in combat service support positions.

On 20 May 1944, it was decided by the Headquarters, XIV Corps to relieve the battalions of the 25th Regimental Combat Team from their forward defensive positions close to the Americal Division's 182nd Infantry Regiment. Patrolling continued for the 25th Infantry until 12 June, but they encountered very little enemy resistance. The 93rd Provisional Brigade was dissolved on 8 June, just as the last elements of the 25th Infantry Regiment were preparing to depart for Green Island north of Bougainville. The 93rd Infantry Division, still under the command of XIV Corps, passed to the control of the Southwest Pacific Area on 15 June after most of its elements deployed to the Treasury Islands. Battle casualties of the 25th Regimental Combat Team, as reported through 30 May 1944, totaled 26 killed, 13 seriously wounded, and 27 slightly wounded in action.[29]

When the 25th Regimental Combat Team departed Bougainville in June, it was unaware that for the duration of the war, along with that of the other regimental combat teams of the division, it would be utilized primarily in security and labor service missions. Just before orders for the relief of the 25th Infantry Regiment arrived, the results of the investigation of Company K's patrol arrived from XIV Corps, with the conclusion and recommendations: "The performance of Company K, 25th Infantry Regiment, as brought out in this report of investigation, is indicative of a lack of proper discipline, and small unit leadership. It is desired that training be instituted to correct these deficiencies, and be vigorously prosecuted in order to prevent like occurrences."[30]

Colonel Yon, the regimental commander, rebutted the report, stating "that the 1st and 2nd battalions had been indoctrinated into combat as planned with veteran units of the Americal Division, while the 3rd battalion had not, prior to Company K's patrol with only one enlisted man of the 164th Infantry Regiment. Company K had consistently been one of the three best companies of the regiment during the past two and a half years." In Colonel Yon's statement, he commented: "...had this organization been given prior instruction and been accompanied by an experienced platoon of the 164th Infantry in its initial action, the results would have been far different. The force encountered was small, but equipped with machine guns. Their men of the company inflicted the majority of our casualties. This has resulted in many instances in jungle warfare when troops were committed without proper seasoning. Early in May a company of the 182nd Infantry, a veteran of two years of jungle warfare, encountered an inferior force of the enemy east of the Saua River, became disorganized, and returned to the perimeter of the 3rd Battalion, 25th Infantry on Hill 65 after darkness. The above facts are not offered in condemnation of the failure of Company K to carry out its mission, but they were contributing causes...."[31]

Neither this opinion nor the demurrer of the 93rd Provisional Brigade's commander that the 25th Regimental Combat Team had not been adequately rated altered the course of events planned for the 93rd Infantry Division. The division was only reluctantly accepted into the Pacific Theater. The 93rd Infantry Division's initial performance in combat would be closely scrutinized, and there would be no room for error. They were to be given the same opportunity as any new division entering into combat. The units would be slowly introduced into combat under the supervision of a veteran division. But unlike the white divisions that faltered under their baptism of fire, there would be no second chances given to the 93rd Infantry Division. The rumors spread about Company K's initial performance in combat made any corps commander unwilling to utilize the division in combat. Arriving on Green Island, the 25th Regimental Combat Team relieved the 3rd New Zealand Infantry Division, where it took up duties of security, labor, and training. Like the other elements of the 93rd Infantry Division, it was to spend most of the remainder of the war moving from one Pacific island to another, relieving elements of other veteran divisions that had been engaged in combat. They took over positions that were now considered the rear areas of the battle, unloading ships and clearing out pockets of stubborn enemy soldiers that had refused to surrender. Relieving front line combat units so that they could be rested and reequipped to be deployed to other forward areas of the battlefront, were the duties contemplated by the corps and theater commanders on their acceptance of the 93rd Infantry Division into the Pacific Theater. It was only after receiving pressure from the Secretary of War to deploy African American soldiers into combat that these same commanders were forced to alter their plans for the utilization of the 93rd Infantry Division. In spite of the combat performances of the rest of the division, it was the initial combat failure of Company K, 3/25th Infantry that would dictate the use of African American combat forces in the Pacific Theater. The subsequent duties performed by the 93rd Infantry Division were essential in the war effort toward total victory, but they were not those duties that a normal combat infantry division was expected to conduct or trained to perform.

The 93rd Cavalry Reconnaissance Troop remained on Bougainville attached to the Americal Division until 25 October 1944. The skills and training of reconnaissance soldiers were highly regarded due to their ability in seek out and locate the enemy. These were usually the most highly trained and motivated soldiers in the division, and the Americal Division did not want to relinquish this valuable asset. These predecessors to the modern-day Long Range Reconnaissance Patrols (LRRP), the cavalry reconnaissance troops, engaging in mapping patrols and protecting the 318th Combat Engineers as they constructed roads and bridges, met with no enemy opposition until 16 May. On a four-day patrol on a mission reconnoitering and mapping the area between the Saua and Reini Rivers, one of its patrols, moving along a newly discovered trail leading west to the Reini River, encountered six enemy soldiers, which they then silently followed. Later, as the patrol discovered fortified enemy defensive positions, the rear security element was attacked. In a running firefight, the patrol moved to higher ground, and directed artillery fire onto the enemy-held area. The patrol continued its mapping mission the following morning, leaving its forward artillery observers and their heavy equipment within the defensive perimeter. The patrol was attacked again and engaged the enemy in firefights that lasted most of the day. The patrol leader, Lieutenant Charles Collins, was wounded in the leg, but continued to lead his patrol until he was wounded three more times and unable to continue. Three members of the patrol stayed with him and another wounded soldier. Staff Sergeant Rothchild Webb, splitting up the group, helped his partially blinded patrol leader into a nearby swamp. After three days of escaping and evading enemy soldiers in hostile territory, Staff Sergeant Webb led Lieutenant Collins to safety. For his actions, Staff Sergeant Webb was awarded the Silver Star medal.[32] The other wounded soldier and the remaining two soldiers of the patrol, who succeeded in suppressing the enemy long enough to withdraw into the jungle, spent two days evading the Japanese until they were rescued by a friendly patrol. The 93rd Cavalry Reconnaissance Troop lost three men killed and three men wounded in these firefights.

The 93rd Cavalry Reconnaissance Troop expected to rejoin the remainder of the division as it departed Bougainville. But from 20 May until 20 June it was held in XIV Corps' tactical reserve. On 20 June, it was attached to the Americal Division. From 1 July to 10 July, acting as the reconnaissance unit for the 182nd Infantry Regiment, it participated in the battle for Horseshoe Ridge on the East-West Trail of the island. The reconnaissance troop initiated coordinated attacks on the front and rear of the hill simultaneously. These attacks finally forced the enemy to withdraw from their positions. Lieutenant Glen A. Allen and his platoon occupied these positions and held off numerous enemy counterattacks until they were reinforced by elements of the 182nd Infantry Regiment. Lieutenant Allen and six enlisted members of his platoon were awarded the Bronze Star medal for their actions in this battle. The 93rd Reconnaissance Troop continued patrolling, setting up roadblocks and conducting ambushes throughout the summer of 1944, acting as the reconnaissance troop for the 164th Infantry Regiment. After seven continuous months in combat on Bougainville, the 93rd Calvary Reconnaissance Troop rejoined the 25th Regimental Combat Team.

Also remaining on Bougainville during this period was another African American ground combat unit, the 49th Coast Artillery Battalion. Between 4 February and 29 July, the 49th Coast Artillery Battalion, performing as field artillery for the XIV Corps, fired 400 missions, expending 13,113 rounds from their 155-mm guns. Missions were of all types: destruction, neutralization, harassment, and counterbattery. When the Japanese 6th Division launched its March counterattack on the Torokina beachhead, the unit functioned exceptionally well during counterbattery fire, receiving credit for the destruction of several 75-mm and 150-mm enemy artillery field pieces. One officer and one enlisted man were killed and three wounded during this action. The unit also received six Bronze Star medals, two Air Medal Commendations, and a Letter of Commendation from the XIV Corps Artillery commander, Brigadier General Leo Kreber.[33] Beginning in May, part of the 49th Coast Artillery relieved the 3rd Marine Defense Battalion in seacoast defensive positions, while Battery B remained as field artillery under the operational control of XIV Corps Artillery. This battery, attached to the 135th Field Artillery Battalion, moved to positions 1,000 yards outside of the perimeter on the Numa Numa Trail, placing artillery rounds on enemy positions in the upper Laruma Valley in support of regiments of the 37th and Americal Infantry Divisions. The 49th Coast Artillery continued with assignments on Bougainville, generally under the command of the 68th Antiaircraft Artillery Brigade, until 26 November 1944. Then, the island was taken over by Australian forces and it was relieved of tactical duties. Not until March 1945 did the unit depart Bougainville for Finschhafen, New Guinea; even then, a rear detachment remained with the unit's heavy ordnance equipment.

After Bougainville, the 93rd Infantry Division continued its mission in the Pacific, now under control of the Southwest Pacific's Eighth Army Headquarters. The 93rd Infantry Division proceeded slowly up the island chains of the Pacific toward the Philippine Islands, relieving elements of other divisions, mainly the 31st and 41st Infantry Divisions, that were moving toward the forward areas of combat. Although the 93rd Infantry Division was given oral instructions that it was to have training, fatigue, and defensive missions in exactly the same proportions as the other combat divisions in the Eighth Army, in reality, performing manual labor tasks more associated with the quartermaster or transportation branch became their primary duties. The 93rd Infantry Division was to be kept in tactical reserve in the highest state of readiness to enter combat on call, although when labor requirements at Hollandia and later on Finschhafen, New Guinea, increased sharply toward the end of 1944, the priority of missions was altered to place defense of those areas and labor details ahead of training. The 93rd Infantry Division had responsibility for the command and coordination of all labor and transportation duties furnished by the Eighth and Sixth Army units in the Hollandia area. The division would assume operational control of all Eighth Army units not involved in combat operations. Elements of the 93rd Infantry Division generally performed security, dock and warehouse labor, and patrol missions. The senior 93rd Infantry Division officer on site was often in command of the island that they occupied.

In August 1944, Major General Harry H. Johnson, the previous commander of the 2nd Cavalry Division when it was deactivated, was appointed commander of the 93rd Infantry Division. Major General Johnson was thought to be building discipline and morale, but he occupied an unenviable position. He could not complete his job if the 93rd Infantry Division followed into the footsteps of his old command of the 2nd Cavalry Division, into oblivion as a "service regiment."

Walter White of the NAACP, and a war correspondent in the Pacific Theater for the *New York Post*, sent a dispatch to the president of the United States, with copies to Undersecretary Patterson and Assistant Secretary McCloy, containing a detailed account of the career and state of morale in the 93rd Infantry Division. Mr. White reported: "The 93rd was a victim of rumor and malicious slander, all reinforced by its role as a rear echelon unit engaged primarily in labor duties. Its assignments were viewed across the Pacific as punishment for a failure on Bougainville."[34] After discussion with the division and other officers in the XIV Corps, Mr. White discovered the 93rd Infantry Division had performed its limited combat duties creditably, and the rumors about it were false. Nevertheless, the division had been the victim of improper management, and was thought to be corrected in part by the appointment of Major General Johnson as its new commander. White recommended that "the 93rd be assembled, brought to strength, relieved of fatigue and service duties except those normal to a combat division, and trained for amphibious warfare: that it be relieved of officers who were incompetent or who disliked service with Negroes; and that it be used in combat as the only means of answering reports about it and official policy current in the Pacific."[35]

General MacArthur, queried by the War Department in anticipation of a White House request for comment, replied to the War Department's brief of Mr. White's report. As requested by the War Department, he quoted General Griswold of XIV Corps as authority that on Bougainville, the artillery did good work, the engineers fair, the infantry poor; that in training, individuals were proficient in handling and maintaining their weapons; that vehicle maintenance was of high order, that the general level of leadership was poor despite a number of officer of high type and adequate qualifications, and that morale was poor. The Commanding General of XIV Corps added that under its new commander the division had taken a "new lease of life" and that under him, it would improve. General MacArthur's inspectors, at Major General Johnson's request, had investigated charges of discrimination within the 93rd Infantry Division, and their limited bias investigation had reported that these charges were without foundation in fact. No African American officers or enlisted members of the division were ever interviewed. Other combat divisions in the Southwest Pacific were all rated superior to the 93rd Infantry Division except in the matter of motor maintenance: "In this item, our inspection teams have shown it to be without peer among the units inspected."[36]

On his return to Hollandia, Mr. White found the 93rd Infantry Division preparing to deploy from New Guinea to Morotai, Dutch New Guinea. Steps were being taken to improve the division internally. Mr. White wrote to General MacArthur: "Your action in bringing the Division together in one island for the first time since the 93rd left the States will undoubtedly have immediate effect in improvement of efficiency and a sense of unity."[37] He made additional new recommendations for the readying of the division to return to combat, urging that its artillery battalions be reequipped with its own or improved guns and that its officer personnel be carefully sorted to provide better leadership both from among white and African American officers. "It is my hope," he concluded, "that neither you nor the War Department will think these recommendations by a layman presumptuous. Be assured that they are made solely with the desire that the zeal of the overwhelming majority of the officers and enlisted personnel of the grid to contribute to the speediest winning of complete victory may be utilized to the fullest degree."[38]

But sending the 93rd Infantry Division back into combat, relieving other infantry divisions so that those units could be deployed to another forward area of combat, did not curtail the internal racism and discrimination encountered between the African American and white officers. This had always been a problem within the leadership of the 93rd Infantry

Division. Major General Johnson, like many of the commanders in the army, did not feel as though African American officers were capable of leading the soldiers in combat. African American officers were continuously passed over for promotions or not allowed to perform any higher staff duties. White officers still commanded most of the companies within the division even when there were qualified African American officers that could perform those tasks. New white officers were brought into the division when there were vacancies in command and staff positions instead of allowing African American officers the opportunity to advance into positions of higher responsibility. A letter from one of the medical officers of the division reflects the frustration shared by the African American soldiers.

Mr. P.B. Young   July 27, 1945
The Norfolk Journal and Guide

My dear sir:

We are writing first to assure you of the general attitude of the personnel of the Division representing you in the Pacific and to simultaneously express concurrence in thought as expressed in your opinion of the Conference at San Francisco [the first meeting of the United Nations]. We see no logic in such conferences when within the hearts of our contemporaries there remains that discrimination against race, which nullifies the acts put in for a show of the future. There's no use in holding the penny before the or our eye — we must exert more and constant pressure through existing and future contacts and channels to correct the practices going on here — now. There is an increased fervor to depress, discredit and criticize the Negro Officer — and a direct disregard for the ability of Medical and Dental Officers of color to handle the Division Surgeon's Office. The members of the Medical Department are 97% of the force now in the division with a pending and possible reduction of that percentage by one.

The Senior medical and Dental Officers of our race have not been given the ordinary privilege of assuming leadership in either the Division Medical Staff vacancies. A general influx of white officers of company and field grades of most all components arrive in large numbers, and to all intents and purposes have usually, with few exceptions proved to be washouts from white organizations now at the front or desk workers fresh from the states.

The length of time in service for many of the colored officers dates to the period before Pearl Harbor. These officers are passed over, given ratings of efficiency below their merits, are placed on prearranged flop assignments in order to discredit them or have apparent cause for action being brought against them.

Neglects on the part of the various staffs (white) — regimental and higher — have telling effect on the morale and function of troops of our racial strain.

Aside from being a slap-in-the-face to the Negro Medical and Dental professions, the recent arrival of a white Surgeon to direct the service, permits us no alternative in thought; either we are not considered competent to assume the office and its responsibilities or the Division Staff cares to have only a lily-white Staff — which has the spectra of racial superiority or prejudice as the cause. We are not fighting to preserve that ideology. The office of Dental Surgeon has been vacant for four months, the Surgeon's Office for over a month. No attempts were made to turn these offices over to the senior Medical Dental Officers of the Division. The enlisted personnel feel these acts keenly. We cannot stand idle. We need outside help.

We therefore solicit your good offices and unbiased opinion on the matter. Request that if you find our problem sufficiently important to the race as a whole, that segment of service we represent, then contact the War Department with all the fervor of that race, through all available channels now open or to be opened.

The Division Psychiatrist now one of our officers has not been given his proper rank of Major since his appointment but several white officers have been brought in and given priority of colored officers who have been holding particular assignments without prejudice and competently.

These are only a few of the facts, if we can get them to you, for your appraisal and liquidation if possible, with a more favorable outlook for the Negro Officer in a Negro Division —(so called) but with lily-white staffs to which we must pay homage or get the benefits of a Court-Martial whose members' minds were formed and trained in Texas, Alabama, Arkansas and Georgia.

We think that all agents should set about, *together*, and at once to curb this action.

Yours very truly,
The Officers of the 93rd Infantry Division[39]

Meanwhile, the other regimental combat teams of the division had only minor encounters with enemy forces during 1944. The 2/368th Infantry on the island of Vella Lavella made several contacts while charged with the security of that island from February to June. The 369th Regimental Combat Team, while stationed at Munda and the other islands of the New Georgia group, encountered no hostile forces at all. They engaged in training and established a jungle patrol leaders' school whose attendance was required for all officers and noncommissioned officers of the regiment. In addition, 50 officers and petty officers of the 73rd Naval Construction Battalion (Seabees), and selected officers and noncommissioned officers of the 368th Infantry Regiment also attended the course. Only at the end of 1944 did elements of the 369th Infantry Regiment have any contact with the enemy. At Wardo on the island of Biak, a small detachment from the 369th Infantry originally consisting of 15 enlisted men and one officer, later augmented by 27 additional enlisted men and another officer, were sent to provide security for a radar installation located there. Between 6 November and 16 December, the detachment killed 38 of the enemy and captured one soldier. On 31 December, a similar detachment at Wari Island killed ten enemy soldiers in a firefight. By the time the 369th Regimental Combat Team departed Biak on 31 March 1945, 74 Japanese soldiers had been killed and 34 captured, with no casualties suffered by the American forces. The 2/369th Infantry remained at Biak after the war's end until 1 October 1945 as occupation soldiers, performing labor duties, training, routing out die-hard Japanese soldiers, and performing security missions.[40]

These were to become the routine activities of the elements of the 93rd Infantry Division. Some men would be out on patrols, providing security, and attempting to locate enemy forces, while the majority of the soldiers were on the docks, warehouses, or other manual service details. When the 25th Regimental Combat Team arrived at Finschhafen, New Guinea, from the Green Islands on 30 October 1944, in addition to providing local defense, they were utilized for work in the warehouses and dock operations. Finschhafen at the time was a major supply depot for the entire Southwest Pacific area. Infantrymen were retrained as winch operators, signalmen, and checkers. They worked solely in this capacity for four months, in essence, losing their combat efficiency.

Occasionally, there would be a requirement to utilize the combat abilities of the infantry division. The 368th Regimental Combat Team was tasked to provide amphibious combat landing teams to provided perimeter guards at the island of Toem, in the Maffin Bay area in February 1945. Here, they provided local security forces, evacuated supplies, and disinterred bodies from the American cemetery in preparation for closing out the installation. Continuous patrols were deployed, and Battery C of the 594th Field Artillery Battalion harassed the enemy by firing on area targets. When all the remains were removed from the cemetery, and all the bridges and non-portable structures destroyed by the engineers, the landing team of the 368th Infantry moved on to the island of Wakde, four miles away. From Wakde Island, patrols to the Toem mainland continued to operate for months. Company K, 3/368th Infantry, occupied Wakde until after the conclusion of the war on 2 October 1945. Often, its patrols would engage in firefights with enemy forces that refused to surrender and remained in the Toem area. The remainder of the 93rd Infantry Division that was not presently involved in occupational duties was deployed to the island of Morotai on 12 April 1945.

An estimated 600 Japanese soldiers remained on Morotai. On the nearby island of Halmahera, there were 40,000 more enemy soldiers. The 93rd Infantry Division relieved elements of the 31st Infantry Division on Morotai on 13 April 1945, assuming responsibility for the defense and operation of all the Eighth Army installations on the island. It had air support from the 80th Wing, Royal Australian Air Force, and sea support from the Naval Task Unit 701.2, Patrol Torpedo Boats (PT). Combat soldiers of the division were instructed to kill or capture all the remaining Japanese forces.[41] The mission of the division was to keep the Japanese from reorganizing into units capable of inflicting damage to the Eighth Army units. Operations on the west coast of Morotai were intensive, with combat patrols covering a vast area. The Japanese force, under the command of Colonel Kisou Ouchi of the 211th Infantry Regiment, was a composite force, composed of the remnants of several scattered Japanese units. After months engaged in combat with the 31st Infantry Division, and unable to be resupplied, the enemy could offer little organized resistance to the Allied forces. The 93rd Infantry Division's mission became one of mopping up these remaining forces. Halmahera, a major Japanese strong point, would be bypassed on the drive toward the Philippines.

Patrols commenced on 15 April. By 21 April, the 369th Infantry Regiment had captured their first prisoner. The 25th Infantry Regiment, then being kept in reserve, performed port duties on Morotai in support of the Australian forces' invasion of oil-rich Borneo. From 10 April to 10 July, the soldiers of the 93rd Infantry Division, working side by side with Australian dockworkers, discharged and unloaded 311,552 tons of supplies and equipment, moved thousands of Allied soldiers from transport ships to staging areas and improved harbor facilities, roads, and campsites.

The Japanese had orders to conduct raids against the Eighth Army installations. The Japanese stayed close to the native gardens in the western region of the island, as that became their primary source of food. Supply barges had previously come to Morotai from Halmahera, landing near the mouth of the Tijoe River. But the PT boat squadrons now prevented this bulk resupply or the evacuation of enemy forces from Morotai. Enemy barges were able to resupply their forces only once while the 93rd Infantry Division patrolled the area. On 13 May, PT boats sank two of the four enemy barges attempting to deliver supplies, while the other two escaped to the Tijoe River. One was sunk on the way back to Halmahera and the other one was destroyed by a combat patrol from the 93rd Cavalry Reconnaissance Troop. There was no organized resistance or offensive action on the part of the Japanese forces. The mission for the patrols of the 93rd Infantry Division was to prevent the consolidation of the remaining Japanese forces that might yet engage in harassing actions against the Allied bases on Morotai, and to search out and kill or capture all enemy forces.

By 24 May, all three regimental combat teams of the division had patrols deployed along the western and northern coast. The division artillery provided harassing and interdiction fire. A patrol led by Lieutenant Richard L. Crawford of Company F, 2/368th Infantry, tracked down, ambushed and killed six members of an elite Japanese Kempoi party, the dual-functioning military police and intelligence personnel who had recently come to Morotai from Halmahera in an attempt to organize enemy resistance. The 93rd Infantry Division also employed psychological warfare in an effort to get the enemy forces to surrender. Many of the captured prisoners, suffering from a lack of food, carried propaganda leaflets that had been dropped into enemy territory. They also used loudspeaker broadcasts in an effort to get the

Japanese to surrender. Intelligence gathered from these prisoners pertaining to the enemy's status and location became invaluable. From the information gained, it was decided to attempt to capture Colonel Ouchi alive. This task fell primarily to the combat veterans of the 93rd Cavalry Reconnaissance Troop.

On 31 July 1945, a 12-man patrol set out to capture Colonel Ouchi. PT boats in the Tijoe River region landed the patrol. After moving inland from the coast, the patrol came upon two enemy soldiers, one of whom they wounded and captured. The wounded prisoner informed the patrol through a Nisei translator that a camp of higher-ranking officers was not far away. After administering first aid to the wounded prisoner, and leaving one guard behind, the patrol located a three-hut camp with six enemy soldiers. In the ensuing firefight, one enemy soldier was killed, but the other five escaped into the jungle. The three huts were well supplied with rice, ammunition, blankets, and grenades. After destroying the supplies, the patrol continued to scout the area. On 2 August, they spotted four huts in a clearing in which several Japanese were sleeping. The patrol then surrounded the area and ordered the Japanese to surrender. The enemy soldiers attempted to escape. Five of the Japanese were killed; two escaped into the jungle, and one was captured. The prisoner turned out to be Colonel Ouchi. He was one of the highest-ranking Japanese officers captured before Japan formally surrendered. The soldiers on the patrol received the following awards: Sergeant Alfonzia Dillon, the Silver Star medal; Technical Sergeant Albert Morrison, Private First Class Robert A. Evans, and Private First Class Elmer Sloan were awarded the Bronze Star medal.[42]

In the last days of the war, the 93rd Infantry Division had charge of more than 1,500 enemy patients and the crew from the Japanese hospital ship *Tachibana Maru*. This ship had been intercepted by two American destroyers, the USS *Conner* and the USS *Charette*, and delivered to Morotai on 6 August. The patients on the ship had been evacuated from a Japanese general hospital on New Guinea. Most had been suffering from beriberi, malaria, and other tropical diseases. After the patients were removed from the ship and interned, a boarding party of 93rd Infantry Division personnel discovered hundreds of mortar shells packed in boxes marked with red crosses, plus rifles, machine guns, ammunition, and grenades hidden throughout the ship. Also found were 45 knee mortars and four 8-cm field howitzers.[43]

When the hostilities ceased on 15 August 1945, the 93rd Infantry Division was made responsible for the surrender of all the Japanese forces in the Moluccas Island Group. Via broadcasts on the local Armed Forces Radio Station, WVTL, the Japanese on Halmahera were given instructions to meet with the division staff. After a preliminary meeting on a PT boat off the shores of Halmahera, the commander of the Japanese forces and his staff were brought over to Morotai to sign the instrument of surrender for the 40,000 enemy soldiers. Another 660 stragglers were collected on Morotai. Formal surrender of the Japanese in the Moluccas Islands was made to the Australian military forces commander, with the 93rd Infantry Division assisting, on 2 September 1945.[44] Also in September, Brigadier General Boyd assumed command of the 93rd Infantry Division from Major General Johnson.

In October, the 93rd Infantry Division, minus the 368th Regimental Combat Team, which had already deployed forward, proceeded to the Agusan-Del Monte Area on Mindanao in the Philippines. There, it relieved the 31st Infantry Division of its mission. The 93rd Infantry Division controlled the supply depots at Agusan and Davao, assumed command of all soldiers previously attached to the 31st Infantry Division, and reassumed command of the 368th Infantry Regiment and its attached soldiers at Zamboanga on Mindanao and on Jolo, Sanga Sanga, and Palawan. Under the discharge and transfer program available at the close of the war, the 93rd Infantry Division was responsible for the readjustment and discharge of

25th Regimental Combat Team knee deep in mud on a trail to Hill 165, Bougainville, 15 April 1944. (National Archives)

all soldiers that had achieved enough combat points to return to the United States. Combat points were accrued based on time in a combat zone, military awards, and wounds suffered. The division was also responsible for the defense and security of Mindanao, and the collecting, guarding and evacuating of Japanese prisoners of war. As of 20 October 1945, the 93rd Infantry Division had over 30,000 Japanese prisoners, including civilians, locked in its stockade. The supervision, training, and supplying of all Philippine Army units, to include the 6th Philippine Infantry Division, also came under the responsibility of the 93rd Infantry Division. On 15 November, it acquired all of the Southern Islands Area Command's missions; the Mindanao-Sulu-Morotai area thereupon became the 93rd Division Area Command.[45] Thereafter the 93rd Infantry Division supplied the 6th Philippine Infantry Division, gathered up remaining Japanese stragglers, furnished psychological leaflets to be dropped on areas suspected of harboring Japanese forces, furnished transportation for Philippine Army patrols to distant locations, and operated prisoner of war collecting points throughout Mindanao. Processing and evacuating the Japanese, processing American soldiers for return to the United States or transfers into other units, classifying and storing surplus equipment, and operating supply depots were the division's last missions of the war before deactivation.

The 93rd Infantry Division would perform these logistical and command duties until 1 February 1946 when the remaining members of the unit returned to the United States. The division was unceremoniously deactivated on 3 February 1946. The 93rd Infantry Division would serve the United States as a segregated unit, commanded by white officers during two world wars. In spite of the derogatory rumors that would be spread about the African American combat forces, the discrimination encountered, and being made to perform non-combat duties, the 93rd Infantry Division served overseas for more than two years throughout the Pacific Theater, performing all tasks which they were assigned in a highly creditable manner. During that period, the division and its personnel would be awarded the following decorations.[46]

Battle Campaign Streamers	New Guinea, Northern Solomons, Bismarck Archipelago
Distinguished Service Cross	1
Distinguished Service medal	1
Silver Star medal	5
Legion of Merit medal	5
Bronze Star medal	686
Air Medal	27

Chapter XI

92nd Infantry Division

THE 92ND INFANTRY DIVISION WAS REACTIVATED for duty in World War II on 15 October 1942, less than a year after the attack on Pearl Harbor. The division, one of the two African American infantry divisions that fought in France during World War I, was known as the Buffalo Division, and drew its name from the heritage of the four original African American regiments that were activated by Congress in 1866. Controversy would remain with this division throughout its active service during World War II.

Immediately after activation, the 92nd Infantry Division Headquarters and its subordinate units were distributed among four military installations: Fort McClellan, Alabama; Camp Atterbury, Indiana; Camp Breckinridge, Kentucky; and Camp Robinson, Arkansas. Seven months later, all components of the division arrived at Fort Huachuca, Arizona, to continue training before deployment overseas. The division was composed of African American enlisted personnel and a combination of African American and white junior officers. Initially, over 63 percent of the officers that were assigned or attached to the division were African Americans. This encompassed all ranks from second lieutenant through lieutenant colonel. The 597th and 600th Field Artillery Battalions, and the later attached 366th Infantry Regiment, had all African American officers within their command structure.[1] But for the rest of the division, the highest-ranking African American officer would be a captain, and this would only occur when there were no white lieutenants subordinate to them in the chain of command. The unwritten rule was that no African American officer would ever have any white soldiers serving under his command. No African American field grade officer (major and above) would serve on the division headquarter staff during Major General Almond's tenure. This would cause much discontent for the African American officers of the 92nd Infantry Division for the duration of the war. One noncommissioned officer would be prompted to write one of the nation's African American newspapers of the mistreatment of the officers and enlisted men of the division.

Mr. C.A. Scott
General Manager
Atlanta Daily World
Dear Sir:

ENROUTE TO FORT HUACHUCA, AZ
A Noncommissioned officer in the 92nd Div.
November 23, 1943

May I extend my heartfelt congratulations to you and your paper for the article printed awhile back concerning the 92nd Division. It really pictured quite a few existing evils that the Negro soldiers and officers are forced to come in contact with. A thousand congratulations to you. May I add that the conditions are really appalling? This outfit is the most rotten outfit in the world. We have no program — we only walk, walk, walk. These daily hikes are made only to keep us away from the garrisons, because the program made out by Colonel Bailer's Chief of Staff, is really unfit for an inductee.

The colored officers are fed up with it. They know that they are not being treated fairly, but there is nothing they can do. Whenever they go over bounds, they are simply re-classified. Though we have some brilliant Negro officers, they are never promoted. Some of these officers hold degrees from the nation's outstanding universities, while white officers come from Fort Benning, ignorant as the days are long. In a few months they are captains. The poor colored officer, who is his superior in service, tact, etc., is still a second lieutenant.

General Almond is rotten. Possibly the news never reached you but there are several rumors that he has been fired at by soldiers who despise him. Whenever he is introduced, there is the usual "boo."

When General Davis inspects the physical training unit, our cripples are hidden. These are men who are walked "to death" and are physically unfit to carry on. They are really sapping the life out of the fellows. The morale is at as low ebb as in a whorehouse. Nobody gives a damn about what happens. Unless something is done, there will be an internal revolution. They are afraid for us to have rifles after we leave the field. They search daily for ammunition. I swear to God, it is pathetic.

It is true that I am a noncommissioned officer in the outfit, but I shall withhold my name because it will only get me "busted" and a term in the guardhouse. I ask that you even destroy this letter after reading it.

One who desires you to know[2]

The 92nd Infantry Division included the following units:

Headquarters and Headquarters Company
92nd Cavalry Reconnaissance Troop, Mechanized
365th Infantry Regiment
370th Infantry Regiment
371st Infantry Regiment
92nd Division Artillery, Headquarters and Headquarters Battery
    597th Field Artillery Battalion (105-mm Howitzer)
    598th Field Artillery Battalion (105-mm Howitzer)
    599th Field Artillery Battalion (105-mm Howitzer)
    600th Field Artillery Battalion (155-mm Howitzer)
317th Engineer Combat Battalion
Headquarters Special Troops
    92nd Signal Company
    92nd Quartermaster Company
    92nd Ordnance (Light Maintenance) Company
    92nd Military Police Platoon
    92nd Infantry Division Band
317th Medical Battalion

Early in 1944, after the 93rd Infantry Division had deployed to the Pacific Theater, the 92nd Infantry Division was able to consolidate all of its forces in one location at Fort Huachuca, Arizona. There, it completed its entire training program prior to movement overseas. It participated in the Sixth Louisiana Maneuvers from February to April 1944, receiving a satisfactory rating. Headquarters XVIII Corps, the 8th and 11th Armored Division, and

A squad of noncommissioned officer cadres of the 92nd Infantry Division gets a refresher course in charging through smoke, Fort McClellan, Alabama, November 1942. (National Archives, 111-SC-14799)

the 44th and the 75th Infantry Divisions also participated in the exercise. Before departing from Louisiana, the 92nd Infantry Division received the news that, in accordance with the War Department's decision, as a result of pressure from the African American public through its newspapers to deploy combat units into the war theaters, one regimental combat team would begin preparations for overseas movement upon returning to Fort Huachuca.

The 92nd Infantry Division's combat readiness was hampered when it transferred many of its soldiers to the 93rd Infantry Division, the 2nd Cavalry Division, and the 364th Infantry Regiment as these units deployed overseas. The 92nd Infantry Division received replacements from the 372nd Infantry Regiment, other stateside African American units, and new inductees in order to bring its personnel strength up to 100 percent in preparation for its deployment. This was a normal procedure for any unit preparing for deployment into a combat zone. By May 1944, the division was over-strength in both officer and enlisted personnel.[3] Extra enlisted men were required to replace men who were not physically or mentally capable to endure the rigors of combat. The division had over 1,000 of these soldiers, not fit for combat, which had to be replaced. During the period of preparation for deployment, the division was visited and inspected by the Chief of Staff, General George C. Marshall, Undersecretary of War Patterson, Major General Ray Porter and members of his G-3 staff, General McNair and his Ground Forces staff, Major General John P. Lucas and members of his 4th Army staff, Major General Louis Craig and his XXIII Corps staff, and visiting generals of the Mexican Army.[4] It was

Lieutenant B. Holmes (foreground) instructs cadres in the art of parry and long thrust in bayonet practice. Left to right: Sergeant First Class Leroy Smith, Private George W. Jones, and Sergeant Leo Shorty, observe. 92nd Infantry Division, Fort McClellan, Alabama, November 1942. (National Archives 111-SC-14797)

their impressions that the division commander, Major General Almond, had done an outstanding job in preparing the 92nd Infantry Division for combat. Also, being the brother-in-law of General Marshall did not hurt his stature in the politics associated with the army leadership during this period.

But the African American officers and enlisted men of the 92nd Infantry Division had a far different opinion of their commanding officer. Most white officers assigned to African American units were not the brightest or the best. Many commanding generals thought that southern white officers were the best to be assigned to African American units because they normally had more interactions with blacks. But the racial prejudices that these white officers brought to these units were a recipe for failure. It also was a tradition. A similar army strategy had clearly failed more than two decades earlier, when all-black infantry units went to France during World War I under the direction of white southern commanders. General Almond's credentials were impeccable, considering the same false qualifications for commanding African American combat soldiers persisted during World War II. He was the part of the Virginia aristocracy, a graduate of Virginia Military Institute, and married to the sister of General George C. Marshall. That was no small connection considering Marshall was the highest-ranking general in the army. Almond commanded a battalion of all-native soldiers in the Philippines for three years during the 1930s, perhaps adding to his supposed talents for handling nonwhite soldiers.

In preparing itself for service in Italy, the 370th Regimental Combat Team, commanded by Colonel Raymond Sherman, went through a complete reorganization prior to becoming the advanced representative of the 92nd Infantry Division overseas. The combat team was organized on 4 April 1944, upon its return from the Louisiana training exercises.[5] During this period of intensive training in preparation for combat, many substandard soldiers were transferred out and replaced with a higher quality of men, many of whom volunteered. The pace and tempo of training was increased, with the emphasis on physical conditioning, basic weapons proficiencies, and improvement of leadership and teamwork tactics. Late in the spring of 1944, all the African American officers of the 370th Infantry Regiment were ordered to the division headquarters. The Division Chief of Staff, Colonel Frank E. Barber, informed the officers that a regimental combat team was being formed utilizing the best officers and enlisted men from within the division. Nothing was said about the destination. The Chief of Staff stated: "All these years, our white boys have been going over there and getting killed. Well, now it's time for you black boys to go get killed."[6] With those words from the Chief of Staff, many of the officers requested transfers. The regimental combat team consisted of:

1/370th Infantry Battalion
2/370th Infantry Battalion
3/370th Infantry Battalion
598th Field Artillery Battalion
Company B, 317th Combat Engineer Battalion
Company B, plus one platoon from Company D, 317th Medical Battalion
Detachment 92nd Ordnance (Light Maintenance) Company
Detachment 92nd Quartermaster Company
Detachment 92nd Signal Company
Detachment 92nd Military Police Platoon

The combat team departed Hampton Roads, Virginia, on 15 July 1944 via Oran, Algeria, finally arriving at Naples, Italy, on 30 July. When the 370th Infantry Regiment arrived in Italy, the 5th United States Army had advanced to the south bank of the Arno River. Their units were disposed along an 85-mile front extending east from the Tyrrhenian Sea. The 5th Army was now involved in reorganizing in preparation to attack the German defensive Gothic Line on the southern slopes of the Northern Apennines Mountains before the harsh Italian winter weather caught the Allied forces in another stalled mountain campaign. Between May and the end of July, the 5th Army had lost seven veteran infantry divisions that would be utilized in the 6th Army's invasion of southern France in August. The force also included the four infantry divisions of the French Expeditionary Corps, and the United States' IV Corps consisting of the veteran 3rd, 36th and 45th Infantry Divisions, the 442nd Regimental Combat Team, the 517th Parachute Infantry Regiment, the 509th Parachute Infantry Battalion, and the First Special Service Force, as well as supporting combat engineer, armor, artillery, and other essential elements. These were the best and most experienced units in the theater. As France and the push through Western Europe became the primary focus of the main Allied offenses in Europe, the fighting in Italy assumed a secondary role. If a major Allied offensive were to be launched, additional soldiers would be required, and American combat forces were beginning to experience a shortage in manpower. The addition of the 92nd Infantry Division to this theater was viewed as a welcome relief. Six German divisions opposed the United States 5th Army, and 14 opposed the British 8th Army. Lieutenant General Jacob L. Devers and General Sir Henry M. Wilson expressed themselves as being "delighted to have the 370th Infantry Regiment and as many more units as could be spared. The regiment would be put into action as quickly as possible."[7]

Private Jonathan Hoag of a 5th Army Chemical Battalion is awarded the French Croix de Guerre by General Alphonse Juin, commanding general of the French Expeditionary Corps, for courage shown in treating wounded under fire, even though he, himself, was wounded. Pozzuoli area, Italy, 21 March 1944. (National Archives 111-SC-188939)

At the beginning of August, IV Corps, located on the left flank of the Allied lines, under the command of Major General Willis D. Crittenberger, had the arduous task of defending the greater part of the 5th Army front lines, while II Corps, on the right, prepared for an attack on the Gothic Line to follow a British 8th Army assault to the east along the Adriatic Sea. The IV Corps held the western 30 miles of 5th Army's front lines along the south bank of the Arno River. Its Task Force 45 was on the left and the 1st Armored Division on the right.[8] Task Force 45, formed from antiaircraft soldiers of the 45th Antiaircraft Artillery Brigade and attached soldiers, was itself symbolic of the weakened infantry strength of 5th Army. As the Allied air forces gained air superiority of the skies from the German Luftwaffe, the requirement for so many antiaircraft artillery batteries lessened. These antiaircraft artillery units were reequipped with infantry weapons on 26 July 1944, received minimal training in infantry tactics, and started to relieve elements of the 34th Infantry Division on the left flank of IV Corps. The antiaircraft artillery battalions were still undergoing infantry retraining, rotating some elements to the front lines while others were given training in the rear. Task Force 45, originally formed as a task force and later redesignated as the 473rd Infantry Regiment, had close relation with elements of the 92nd Infantry Division. It described itself as "a polyglot task force of American and British antiaircraft gunners acting as infantry with Italian Partisans, Brazilians and colored American troops fighting by their side ... [which] learned that different peoples can fight well together."[9]

When the 370th Regimental Combat Team arrived in the 5th Army sector, it was attached

Members of a mortar platoon of the 92nd Infantry Division pass the 81-mm ammunition and fire it at the Germans in an almost endless stream near Massa, Italy. This platoon was credited with liquidating several enemy machine gun emplacements. (National Archives)

to IV Corps. As the 370th Infantry Regiment entered the army area, small groups of officers and enlisted men were attached to the 1st Armored Division's infantry and artillery battalions. One small group of 20 officers and 23 noncommissioned officers spent several days with the 85th Infantry Division for combat orientation. The combat team was attached to IV Corps on 17 August, and then to the 1st Armored Division on 18 August. The 3/370th Infantry, commanded by Lieutenant Colonel Clarence Daugette, entered the front lines on the night of 23–24 August, relieving the 14th Armored Infantry Battalion near Pontedera. On the next night, the 2/370th Infantry, commanded by Lieutenant Colonel George Weber, relieved the 6th Armored Infantry Battalion south of the town of Pontedera. On 26 August, the 1/370th Infantry, commanded by Lieutenant Colonel Ernest V. Murphy, Jr., moved up to the reserve position behind the other two battalions. As the 598th Field Artillery Battalion, under the command of Lieutenant Colonel Robert C. Ross, moved into their firing positions on 28 August, the 370th Regimental Combat Team began its battle indoctrination. Key officers and noncommissioned officers of the relieved units remained in the line with the men of the 370th Infantry for the first 24 hours to ensure they were familiar with the terrain and possible enemy forces that opposed them.[10]

As the 370th Infantry Regiment was the first African American infantry unit in the theater that would be utilized in combat, they received a series of distinguished visitors, including British Prime Minister Winston S. Churchill. When the 370th Infantry Regiment deployed into their combat positions, Brigadier General Benjamin O. Davis Sr. and a motion picture team arrived and began filming the unit for the film *Teamwork*. Lieutenant General Mark Clark, the 5th Army commander, visited the 370th Infantry Regiment, anxious to welcome the 92nd's soldiers for he understood that General Marshall desired to give them an opportunity to prove the ability of Negro troops in battle.[11]

The IV Corps was readying for its part in the 5th Army's renewed offensive. IV Corps now assumed command of a larger sector extending inland 55 miles, nearly to Florence, thus enabling II Corps on its right flank to concentrate greater strength on a reduced front to break through the Gothic Line north of Florence. IV Corps would simulate a crossing in conjunction with II Corps and the British 13th Corps and be prepared, at any time after the initial attack, to follow up an enemy withdrawal across the Arno River.

The 370th Infantry Regiment, in the Pontedera area along the Arno River, began its baptism by fire. During the night of 27 August, enemy aircraft bombed the 3/370th Infantry's command post. Antipersonnel bombs caused several casualties. One platoon drove off two enemy patrols, which attacked with machine gun support from across the river. Battery C, 598th Field Artillery Battalion, fired its first rounds into the enemy lines on the morning of 29 August. Combat patrols of the 370th Infantry joined with those of other units along the Arno River in moving into the enemy-held areas across the river. One 22-man patrol from Company F, 2/370th Infantry, led by Lieutenant Jake Chandler and accompanied by the company commander, newly promoted Captain Charles F. Gandy, crossed the Arno River on 30 August and proceeded to the village of Calcinain, where it destroyed a machine gun emplacement and captured two German prisoners, the first captured by African American infantrymen in Europe. Both prisoners attempted to escape, but enemy fire killed one and wounded the other. This was the first patrol that 5th Army had put across the Arno River. It was determined that although the area was heavily fortified with mines, automatic weapons, and heavy armor, enemy strength was relatively light. As a consequence, General Clark directed 5th Army to resume the offensive.

But the inexperienced soldiers of the 370th Infantry also made mistakes in combat that veteran soldiers would not make. A German first lieutenant from the 1st Parachute Division, captured after the war, stated in an interview at a prisoner of war enclosure at Leghorn, Italy, in September 1945: "I was a company commander in the 1st Parachute Division. In September 1944, we were withdrawing from north of Montignoso in the vicinity of Prunetta when the Negro troops moved into that area. Your advance was too rapid. I saw you come forward in trucks, dismount, and advance. I requested artillery but our artillery ammunition was so low that strict orders had been issued to fire only in the event of a determined attack. That night as we continued the withdrawal, I lost contact with the company on my right, which was a part of another regiment. You sent out a 12-man patrol that moved into the gap. Personnel of my company thought it was a company on our right and paid no attention to it for some time. However, later some of my men challenged and your patrol answered with fire. We knew immediately that they were American personnel. I stopped the withdrawal of my company, closed the gap, and captured all 12 of your men. Had they not answered by fire, we would probably not have paid any attention to them. You would then have been able to move in a sufficient force to cut off the withdrawal of my company."[12]

If the situation were favorable after crossing the Arno River, IV Corps was to occupy Mount Albano and Mount Pisano, the two major hills on the Arno Plain. Mount Pisano lay between the 370th Infantry Regiment's positions and the town of Lucca. The 370th Infantry Regiment was ordered to join with other IV Corps units to cross the Arno River at 1000 on 1 September. With the 3/370th Infantry on the left flank, the 2/370th Infantry in the center, and the 1/370th Infantry (minus Company C) on the right flank, the regiment crossed the river as ordered. By nightfall, the battalions had moved three miles north of the river. Company C crossed with Combat Command B of the 1st Armored Division, to which it was attached. Sniper fire and mines caused light casualties. By 0300, 2 September, the combat team's engineers had bridged the Arno River with an armored force treadway bridge. They and the 1st Armored Division's engineers had already cleared mines and improved fords so that armored vehicles might cross.

Combat Command A, 1st Armored Division, with the 370th Regimental Combat Team as its infantry component and the 1st Tank Battalion in support, deployed toward Mount Pisano. The 3/370th Infantry, on the left flank, moved around the west side of the mountain and at 2200 on 2 September, elements of the battalion reached the Serchio River at Papiana, five miles north of Pisa. The enemy showed no sign of offering more than local rear guard opposition. The soldiers deployed so rapidly that by the time the 1st Tank Battalion moved its three medium tank companies into positions south of the river and registered their guns, it was unsafe to fire. In the next three days, the advance continued without enemy opposition, as the German 65th Grenadier Division retreated toward their defensive positions on the Gothic Line. The 2/370th Infantry moved northwest across Mount Pisano on 3 September, reorganized, and attacked toward Lucca. On that same day, one of many gallant acts that occurred resulted in the award of the Silver Star to Captain Allen L. Johnson, of the Chaplain Corps. The citation reads:

> For gallantry in action, on 3 September 1944, in the vicinity of Vorno, Italy. A patrol ran into an enemy machine gun emplacement and was forced to withdraw. One of the members of the patrol was seriously wounded and given first aid, but had to be left behind on the field of battle when the enemy started a concentration of machine gun and artillery fire on their position, making it impracticable to evacuate the wounded man. Captain Johnson called for a medical aid man and the two of them ran approximately four hundred and fifty yards over an exposed area to the aid of the wounded man. After administering the first aid, although under continuous enemy artillery fire, Captain Johnson instructed the medical aid man to leave and have a vehicle ready to meet him at the nearest covered position. He then placed the wounded man on his shoulders, and although still under fire from the enemy, carried him to a place of safety from where he was evacuated. Captain Johnson's gallant act in all probability saved the wounded man's life and was in keeping with the highest traditions of the Chaplain Corps of the United States Army.[13]

Major A.R. Biggs, the regimental executive officer, was killed on 4 September by enemy artillery fire in the vicinity of Ripafratta. On 5 September, Company E, 2/370th Infantry entered the town of Lucca, followed by Company F, 2/370th Infantry. The 3/370th Infantry cleared the road from Pisa to Lucca of small pockets of enemy resistance. On the left and right flanks of the 370th Infantry Regiment and Combat Command A, Task Force 45 and Combat Command B moved less rapidly. Task Force 45, which also included the 100th Infantry Battalion of the heroic Japanese-American soldiers who had been fighting in Italy since 1943, had yet to deploy to southern France with the 442nd Regimental Combat Team, and were held up by extensive minefields. Combat Command B met stiffer German resistance along their line of advancement.

Once Lucca was secured, General Clark directed that IV Corps regroup its forces, consolidate its positions, maintain contact with the enemy, be prepared to move forward in the event the enemy continued to withdraw north, and form a task force of armor and infantry for possible employment under II Corps control. The rapid advance by IV Corps had not been anticipated. A temporary halt was called in order for II Corps, the army's main effort, to initiate its offensive. The general advance of 5th Army toward the Gothic Line began the morning of 10 September. The 2/370th Infantry, deployed on the left flank, crossed the Serchio River and moved north along its west bank.

The mountain barrier facing 5th Army, known as the Northern Apennines, extends from the Ligurian Alps, south of Genoa, southeast across the Italian peninsula, nearly to the Adriatic Sea. Late in September, the fall rains begin, mountain streams, virtually dry during the summer months, change to raging torrents in a few hours, and fog and mist reduce visibility to near zero. By late October, snow begins to fall on the higher peaks, and in midwinter, the mountain passes are sometimes impassable. The German name for their fortification of these mountain ranges was called the Gothic Line. Construction of these defenses began after Italy's capitulation in September 1943. This line of defense extended approximately 170 miles across the entire Italian peninsula. The Germans intended to hold the Gothic Line to prevent the Allies from occupying the Po Valley and the industrial and agricultural northland of Italy.

On the morning of 10 September, the entire 5th Army front erupted in an offensive against the main defenses of the Gothic Line. The 2/370th Infantry began clearing hills on the west side of the Serchio River, while the 1/370th Infantry pushed north over the last few miles of plain on the east side of the river. The 3/370th Infantry was placed in reserve south of Lucca. The 598th Field Artillery Battalion, with the Cannon Company, 370th Infantry Regiment attached, redeployed to positions north of Lucca in order to provide supporting fire.

As the 42nd Jaeger Division withdrew, major obstacles were created by the destruction of bridges, blown roads on the sides of mountains, and other types of roadblocks. The advance was marked by frequent sharp encounters with small groups of the enemy acting as a rear guard delaying force. On 16 September, IV Corps ordered a renewed effort to prevent the enemy from withdrawing soldiers from the front. The 370th Infantry Regiment commenced its attack on 17 September. After a number of close-range firefights, it advanced to the vicinity of the towns of Ponte della Maddalena and Bagni di Luca. At 1535 on 18 September, Companies K and L, 3/370th Infantry commenced an attack on Mount Castellaccio. Lieutenant Ralph G. Skinner, a platoon leader from Company L, led his men through a breach in the wire and surrounded a church which the Germans were using as a defensive position for several machine gun emplacements. A vicious close-range firefight involving the three leading platoons drove the Germans from the church. German fixed emplacements on the ridge were attacked and destroyed by two of Company K's platoons. During the savage battle for the mountains, several officers and enlisted men distinguished themselves. The citation for the Silver Star for Private Charles J. Patterson states:

> For gallantry in action on the morning of 18 September 1944 in the vicinity of Colletta, Italy. At approximately 0930 hours the squad of which Private Patterson was a member, was fired upon by an enemy machine gun emplaced in the wall of a church. The squad continued to advance in spite of the machine gun fire until it was pinned down by another enemy machine gun, which opened up from the right flank of the squad. Seeing the imminent danger that the squad was in, Private Patterson started crawling forward up a hill to attack the machine gun that was firing from the front of the squad and holding up their advance. Private Patterson worked his way to the right of the machine gun emplacement and dropped a grenade into the emplacement killing two of the enemy and forcing the remainder to retire. During this time, an enemy artillery shell injured the squad leader. Upon observing this, Private Patterson made his way back to the squad, took command of it, and led it forward up the hill. Private Patterson's gallant act enabled the platoon to reach its objective and was within keeping of the highest traditions of the United States Armed Forces.

Sergeant William H. Harrison and Private John E. Toney also were cited for heroic achievements in this attack and received the Bronze Star medal. Sergeants Henry Powell and Eugene Larkins were severely wounded during the fighting for the mountains, and were evacuated.[14]

On 21 September, the 1/370th Infantry relieved the 14th Armored Infantry Battalion. By 24 September, the 2/370th Infantry was shifted to replace the 6th Armored Infantry Battalion, which was being pulled out of the front lines. The 1st Armored Division, less Combat Command B (CCB), was transferred from IV Corps to II Corps.

Command of the 370th Regimental Combat Team and Combat Command B, together with responsibility for the sector of the 1st Armored Division, was passed to Task Force Wood, commanded by Brigadier General John Wood, Assistant Division Commander of the 92nd Infantry Division. His staff comprised a small advance group from the 92nd Infantry Division Headquarters. The 3/370th Infantry relieved elements of Combat Command B in the vicinity of S. Marcello, and on 29 September, deployed north to the town of La Lima. The 1/370th Infantry and 2/370th Infantry continued moving forward through the mountains, north of Mount Prano, west of the Serchio River to the vicinity of Bagni di Lucca. Task Force Wood was reduced to the 370th Infantry Regiment with a zone 20 miles wide. On 5 October, Task Force Wood became Task Force 92 under the command of Major General Almond, with responsibility for the coastal sector extending from Forte dei Marmi on the west coast to the left boundary of the 1st Brazilian Division.

The 370th Regimental Combat Team had been on the front lines for 42 straight days. It had sustained 263 casualties: 19 killed, 225 wounded, and 19 missing. It had advanced almost 30 miles against resistance that included small arms, machine guns, and automatic weapons in fixed positions and heavy artillery fire. They had penetrated the Gothic Line and cleared the east-west portion of Highway 12 in front of IV Corps. The 370th Infantry Regiment's combat performance was on a par with any other unit's introduction to combat. Mistakes made could be attributed to inexperience. Over time, these inefficiencies would be overcome. But casualties among its junior officers and noncommissioned officers, many who had been with the division since its activation, would have detrimental affects.[15]

Task Force 92 was formed in the vicinity of Viareggio, Italy, on 5 October. This task force included the 370th Regimental Combat Team, the 2nd Armored Group with the 434th and 435th Antiaircraft Battalions fighting as dismounted infantry, the 751st Tank Battalion, the 894th Tank Destroyer Battalion, the 179th Chemical Smoke Generator Company, Battery C 450th Antiaircraft Artillery Battalion, and the 2nd Company 23rd Engineer Battalion (Italian). These integrated formations would become prevalent in future combat operations within the 92nd Infantry Division.

On 3 October 1944, Colonel Frank E. Barber, the Chief of Staff who had addressed the African American officers of the 370th Infantry before deploying overseas by stating, "It's time for you black boys to get killed," was shot while en route to survey the damage of a recently demolished bridge. German machine gunners killed both him and his driver. This was his third day in Italy.[16]

On 6 October, Task Force 92 launched its first concerted effort to capture Mount Cauala as an initial objective for the capture of Massa. The 1/370th Infantry and the 2/370th Infantry attacked Mount Cauala with battalions abreast after a two-hour artillery preparation that commenced at 0600. The 434th and 435th secured the left flank between Highway One and the sea. The 2/370th Infantry secured the upper slopes of Mount Cauala after being repulsed by mortar and artillery on 9 October. That afternoon, heavy enemy artillery and mortar fire forced a second withdrawal. On 11 October, the 2/370th Infantry and 3/370th Infantry secured Mount Cauala, only to be driven off again by heavy artillery fire. No further effort was made to secure the mountain until 18 October when a patrol fought its way to the crest of Mount Cauala. Their positions were further reinforced and the road to Seravezza was opened for vehicle traffic.

During this offensive, Company C, 1/370th Infantry was involved in securing positions on the attack of Mount Cauala. The battalion commander's eagerness to capture a hillside house pushed the company commander, First Lieutenant Montjoy, to deploy a platoon to attack it. First Lieutenant Alonzo Frazier led his platoon through one end of the village, over the remains of a demolished bridge, and toward the top of the high valley wall. The lieutenant barely made sight of the house when he was killed by machine gun fire. Several members of his platoon were killed or wounded. Lieutenant Frazier was the first officer killed in Charlie Company. Even with this lesson, the battalion commander insisted that soldiers continue trying to capture this objective with frontal attacks in daylight.

As Lieutenant Frazier lay mortally wounded, he refused a medic's offer to evacuate him to the rear, and instead ordered him to return and have the rest of the platoon to come up and cover the gap between the wires. The medic could only locate three sergeants and a private. One was wounded on the return trip back up the slope. The rest of the platoon had retreated across the river. The remainder of the company, then under heavy fire on the far side of the river, did not advance at all.

Lieutenant Vernon Baker and his platoon would assault the house next. With his platoon in tow, he chose an alternative route to the house. German snipers killed one of his men en route. As Lieutenant Baker and his new replacement squad leader, Sergeant Belk, crossed the remains of a partially destroyed bridge, pre-sited enemy mortars fired on the platoon's path. One of the riflemen was hurled from the bridge and into the stream below, the force of the explosion tearing off his left arm and propelling it, end over end, to an unknown location. Additional mortar rounds killed another soldier in the middle of the bridge. The remaining soldiers scattered back to the village. Lieutenant Baker and Sergeant Belk lay stranded on the German side of the bridge. Once nightfall provided the cover of darkness, the two soldiers were able to make it back to safety. The platoon attempted another attack around three o'clock in the morning. Lieutenant Baker and platoon sergeant Jacy Cunigan circled the house to the right. In the ensuing firefight, five German soldiers were killed inside the house. The rest of the platoon was fired on by an enemy machine gun emplacement, which killed two more of the soldiers before it was destroyed by grenades. Wounded in the arm during the firefight, Lieutenant Baker was evacuated to the 64th General Hospital near Pisa.

With the house secured, Lieutenant Montjoy continued to push his company to secure Mount Cauala. As they proceeded up the hill, they encountered light machine gun fire, and the majority of the company streamed back through the wire across the Sera River. By morning, only two officers and ten enlisted men remained dejectedly alone across the river, opposite their objective. The company had to be rounded up and reorganized. On the night of 12 October, when other units using scaling ladders had secured Mount Cauala, Company C could only get 30 men started on the attack. Of the four companies that assaulted the hill, only two remained after severe enemy counterattacks. Company F, 2/370th Infantry and Company I, 3/370th Infantry remained in their positions though they were pinned down. Captain Gandy, commander of Company F, though mortally wounded, led the stand until 0300 the following morning, when ordered to withdraw.

During the later part of October, the remainder of the 92nd Infantry Division arrived in Italy and staged out of the port city of Leghorn. Unlike the 93rd Infantry Division, which had been utilized in "mopping up" operations with regimental combat teams and in labor duties throughout the Southwest Pacific Theater, the 92nd Infantry would be utilized as a standard infantry division with front-line combat duties. Beginning on 31 October, elements of Colonel James Notestein's 371st Infantry Regiment, which arrived at Leghorn on 18 October, deployed forward to replace the 370th Infantry Regiment on the line. The 1/371st Infantry, commanded by Lieutenant Colonel Theodore Kimpton, relieved the 3/370th Infantry under the cover of darkness on 31 October. Major John Hazel's 3/371st Infantry was also committed to the front lines on 31 October, and Major George Pinard's 2/371st Infantry took up positions as the regimental reserve. The 370th Infantry Regiment, after reorganization and replenishment with new replacement soldiers, was shifted to the east to replace the 1st Brazilian Infantry Division in the Serchio Valley.

The common soldier's view of the war differed somewhat from that of the white officers that staffed the division headquarters. An infantryman from the 370th Infantry Regiment stated: "Somewhere in October, the glory of war began to dissipate in earnest throughout the regiment. Our mood darkened with the departure of the agreeable weather, the arrival of General Edward M. Almond to command the 92nd Infantry Division, and a rising number of casualties. Our regiment, the 370th was reassigned from the 1st Armored Division to the 92nd. To round out this cheery picture, we faced nothing but wet, slippery, steep terrain. That, combined with the impenetrable German defenses, stymied our attempts to press into the mountains. It took a month to move from Pietrasanta to Seravezza, four kilometers by way of a road the Germans controlled, and a hell of a lot farther sliding up and down ravines, terraces, gullies, and steep, mountain passes to get around the Germans. More and more of our energy focused on keeping our feet dry and our hands warm. Fires were forbidden. During the day, the curling wisps of smoke alerted the Germans to our exact position. At night, the flames became even more efficient homing beacons for German artillery observers. Eventually my platoon learned to dig a special foxhole, with a deep pit at the front, and built a small nighttime warming fire that wasn't visible for any distance. The fires were more psychologically heartening than physically warming. It was a small moral victory to outsmart both our commanders and the Germans. And anything that improved morale was a bonus."[17]

During the month, casualties reported from Task Force 92 were 32 killed, 223 wounded, and 110 missing in action. A total of 124 enemy prisoners of war had been captured.[18]

By the end of October, the enemy had massed its strength to cover Bologna against the attack of 5th Army. As a result of this and the oncoming winter weather of torrential rains, which turned supply routes into mud-clogged roads, 5th Army's drive to Bologna came to a halt. On 2 November, the army assumed a posture of an active defense, while regrouping and preparing for the resumption of the winter offensive in December. On 4 November, the 92nd Infantry Division fell under the direct control of 5th Army. It was responsible for the defense of a 23-mile-wide coastal sector. With the 92nd Infantry Division covering such a large front, it permitted the concentration of other elements of 5th Army for the resumption of the offense.

While the soldiers of the division were enduring the hardships of the beginnings of the harsh Italian winter on the front lines, the staff officers established the Division Command Post at the small city of Viareggio, with the Division Forward Command Post under the leadership of Brigadier General Wood, in the location closer to the front line in the Serchio Valley. The Division Command Post, responsible for the command and control of maneuvers and operations of the division, was set up next to the Principe de Piemonte Hotel, with most of the white staff officers billeted there. The commanding general's mess for General Almond and the white officers of his staff was established in a casino across the street. The 92nd Division Band played soft dinner music each evening. An officers' club for the white officers of the division was operated in the Principe de Piemonte Hotel. The Division Rear Command Post, mainly responsible for the logistical support of the 92nd, was set up in another hotel a few blocks away in Viareggio. An officers' club with a bar operated out of that hotel was established for the white officers. From these relatively comfortable surroundings, the staff officers of the division controlled the daily combat operations of the soldiers in the field, far removed from the rigors and hardships of war. This distancing of the command staff from the soldiers would hamper decision-making, and cause severe morale problems within the 92nd Infantry Division until the conclusion of the war. This environment emphasized the social distinction between the white officers and the African American officers and enlisted men of the division.

In early November, the initial reports of the combat efficiency of the 92nd Infantry Division were reaching the War Department. Truman Gibson, on behalf of the Advisory Committee for Special Troop Policies, asked Major Oscar J. Magee of the Intelligence Division, Army Service Forces, then about to depart on a mission to Italy, to bring back factual data on the progress of the division. Major Magee, after visits to Allied Force Headquarters, 5th Army, and the 92nd Infantry Division between 15 November and 2 December, returned with his impressions.

"The 92nd at this time was carrying out its assigned missions, maintaining pressure so that the enemy could not shift forces elsewhere and protecting the left flank of the 5th Army. As a result of its recent arrival, small losses of materiel, and favorable coastal positions in the line, it was very possibly the best fed, clothed and equipped division in the 5th Army. Its combat capabilities were still in process of being ascertained. Generally speaking, the work of the various components of the division has been satisfactory since its arrival overseas, with two exceptions: infantry patrol and assault.... In regard to assault by the infantry and observance of the rule, 'Close with the enemy and destroy him with cold steel' tenacity. Too frequently the infantry 'melts away' under fire and an abnormal number of men hide in cellars until they are routed out by their officers. The infantry was being 'nursed along' to give it confidence, but to date, results had been disappointing. General Almond believed the 'true evaluation' of the Negro soldiers' capabilities would have to await the end of the war. But the true evaluation of the 92nd would be obtained when the division is fiercely attacked by or is thrown into an all-out offensive against German, not Fascist (Italian) troops. Efficiency and morale, were not appreciably affected by racial problems: Racial sensitivity is strongly evident in the typical Negro officer, while distrust of a Negro's capabilities is present but less evident in the typical white officer. Yet these attitudes did not affect the work at hand. No report of racial discrimination within the division should be accepted as 'the true reason for any tactical or administrative action taken by the divisional leadership.' Complete trust should be placed in the 'integrity, ability and impartiality of the Generals and policy-making officers whose decisions affect the 92nd Infantry Division.' Mr. Gibson should accept the informal invitation of Lieutenant General Mark W. Clark delivered through me, to 'Come and see us.'"[19]

Lieutenant General Clark, reflecting early reports from the 92nd Infantry Division, reported shortly thereafter in a similar vein to General McNarney. "Allowing for the short period of actual combat, they have performed excellently in supply and administrative matters and in such tactical operations as do not require sustained demonstration of initiative and aggressiveness on the parts of junior leaders and of the rank and file. The division's commander

Major General Edward M. Almond, commanding general of the 92nd Infantry Division in Italy, inspects his soldiers during a decoration ceremony, March 1945. (National Archives, 208-AA-47Y1)

and his senior subordinates found it necessary 'to lead and supervise their troops much more in detail than is normally the case.' The division had been well prepared for commitment; it entered combat 'under no handicaps.' It was true that the division's combat experience was still too brief for conclusive impressions. Its combat value still had to be demonstrated: 'It is my intention to give the division increasing opportunity to assume combat responsibility and to demonstrate its ability to carry a full load in offensive operations. A further report on this subject will be submitted on the basis of future experience." General McNarney, forwarding this report, concurred.[20]

The Magee Report, while revealing, omitted most of what was discussed informally between Truman Gibson and Major Magee. Magee reported: "The white officers in the 92nd Infantry Division generally disliked their assignments, had no confidence in their men, and believed that the experiment of using Negroes in combat would fail." One key officer on the division staff told Major Magee "that although there had been many examples of individual heroism on the part of Negro officers and soldiers in the 92nd, it was his belief that the Negro generally could not overcome or escape his background of no property ownership, irresponsibility, and subservience. The Negro is panicky and his environment has not conditioned him to accept responsibilities." Said another high-ranking white officer on the division staff: "I don't like my assignment because I don't trust Negroes. White officers who work with them have to work harder than with white troops. I have no confidence in the fighting ability of Negro soldiers." A third officer on the division staff declared that "the 93rd Division was the first out, the 2nd Cavalry Division the second, and now the 92nd Division is at bat with one strike already against us."²¹ These were some of the same attitudes of the white officers who led the division to failure in World War I.

Mr. Gibson declared that he did not believe that these attitudes were consciously developed or viciously applied, but the report on them "more than justified [the] trip because they show the nature of the problem ahead and the necessity of exercising great care in evaluating all reports from this and other Negro organizations. In the instant cases, the conclusions reached completely overlooked the effect on the men of the attitudes of the officers. Soldiers generally know how their officers feel. If they know their officers dislike them, have no confidence in them, or feel that they will not stand up under combat, the likelihood is that they will fail.... The problem is one of getting in the whole story and not the segments that go to prove a conclusion. Enough exists in any Negro unit to prove just about anything."²²

Any conclusions about the combat performance of the 92nd Infantry Division were determined by the general staff and white officers of the division long before the unit deployed overseas.

As the remainder of the division arrived in Italy, they were deployed to forward combat positions. Lieutenant Colonel Marcus Ray, the highest ranking African American officer in the 92nd Infantry Division, and his all African American 600th Field Artillery Battalion with their larger 155-mm howitzers occupied its initial supporting fire positions on 2 November 1944. The 317th Engineer (Combat) Battalion, commanded by Lieutenant Colonel Edward Rowney, was in positions to provide engineer support to the division by 8 November. The 365th Infantry Regiment, commanded by Colonel John Armstrong, arrived in country on 29 October. The 2/365th Infantry, commanded by Lieutenant Colonel Howard Schwarz, relieved the 435th Antiaircraft Battalion from its infantry duties. Major Jesse Johnston's 1/365th Infantry deployed to the front lines on 13 November, and the 3/365th Infantry, led by Lieutenant Colonel Lawrence Lashley, took up positions as the regimental reserves. In accordance to standard infantry operating procedures, the 92nd Cavalry Reconnaissance Troop also deployed to the front lines on the same day, with the mission of protecting the division's right flank and maintaining contact with the allied units located there. Later the 92nd Cavalry Reconnaissance Troop was shifted to occupy the central portion of the division front, a sector 8,000 yards in width, in extremely mountainous terrain. To augment the lack of radio communications in these mountainous regions that often blocked transmission signals, four pigeon lofts of the 209th Signal Pigeon Company were attached to the division. To facilitate operations in the mountains that were not always accessible to vehicle traffic, a four-company, 92nd Division Pack Battalion (Provisional) was organized under the command of Lieutenant Hugh Hanley. Italian mules were requisitioned, and local Italians were utilized as muleskinners. Both Italian men and women were used as porters to transport rations and ammunition in these regions.

The 92nd Infantry Division was now deployed with the 365th Infantry Regiment on the coastal plains, the 371st Infantry (less the 3/371st), in the foothills just west of the coastal sector, and the 370th Infantry Regiment with the 3/371st attached, in the Serchio Valley. On 15 November, the 92nd Cavalry Reconnaissance Troop entered combat for the first time, setting up the Troop Command Post at Coreglia, with the mission of protecting the division's right flank and maintaining contact with Task Force 45.

On the morning of 16 November, the 370th Infantry Regiment launched an attack to capture Castelnuovo, a key road and rail center in the Serchio Valley, and the high ground dominating it. The 3/371st Infantry deployed forward against light resistance and seized the town of Grottorotondo and remained there until the end of the day. Company B, 1/370th Infantry's objective was to seize the town of Brucciano, then move against two hills to the north, with the attack to be supported by fire from Company A, 1/370th Infantry, and Company D, 1/370th Infantry, the heavy weapons support company. Once this objective was taken, Companies A and B together were to attack to the north, seizing Mount Altissimo, and then drive to the high ground of Le Forche. The attack of these last two objectives was to be supported by the covering fire of Company C, 1/370th Infantry from the town of Cascio. This ambitious, complex plan did not develop as envisioned by the planners on the regimental staff. The 1/370th Infantry Regiment commenced the attack on schedule, but Companies A and B came under heavy shelling from enemy artillery, mortars and small arms fire, stopping the attack as soon as it begin.

On the right flank, the 3/370th Infantry had as its objective the formidable Lama Ridge running from Lama di Sotto southwest of Monte San Quirico. Company L was to climb up the ridge and seize Lama di Sotto; Company K was assigned the ridge to the north near Colle, while Company I was assaulting Monte San Quirico. Company M would provide fire support with their 81-mm mortars and heavy .50-caliber machine guns. Company L scaled the slopes and reached Lama di Sotto. Company K achieved part of their objective, and Company I had advanced to a point just north of Castelvecchio and Caproni by nightfall.

The first day's fighting gave indication that the German command intended to vigorously defend its present positions in the 92nd Infantry Division's sector of the front. Minefields abounded at all approaches to prospective objectives; scores of enemy machine guns and mortars were pre-sited to fire on the approaching roads, trails, and draws, and were positioned to deliver mutually supporting interlocking fire. Supporting enemy artillery was available to deliver suppressing fire on call. The German artillery observers, positioned high on the ridges and mountaintops, must have been completely amazed to look down and clearly see three battalions of American infantry exposed in the open, and advancing during the daylight. They concentrated their artillery fire on these formations.

At daybreak on 17 November, the 3/371st Infantry resumed the attack, with Company I moving up Hill 832. Near the base of Monte d'Anima, Company L, 3/371st Infantry, came under attack from extremely heavy and pre-sited mortar fire, while enemy heavy machine gun fire from the slopes above inflicted large numbers of casualties. The company commander, Lieutenant Magellan C. Mars, leading the assault, was killed, and over half of his command was either killed or wounded. At the same time, Company I on Hill 832 was hit by a strong enemy counterattack, preceded by heavy mortar fire, which drove it from the hill. Company K, 3/371st Infantry, was also counterattacked and subjected to a heavy concentration of mortar fire, but held on to Hill 1031. Lieutenant Mars was posthumously awarded the Silver Star for his efforts to accomplish his objective and to save his company. His citation states:

> Lieutenant Mars' company, while deployed in a sector of mountainous terrain, became the object of an intense enemy mortar attack. Without thought of personal hazard Lieutenant Mars moved among his men adjusting counter-fire and insuring that each man was in protected position. When the severity of the hostile mortar barrage forced the supporting right flank unit to withdraw, Lieutenant Mars' company immediately became chief target for a concentration of enemy machine gun fire, In spite of this, he continued to expose himself until he was killed by hostile fire.[23]

Technical Sergeant David Harris, Company L, 371st Infantry, was also awarded the Silver Star for gallantry in action on that day in Italy.

> Under a severe enemy counter-attack, Sergeant Harris's company was forced to withdraw. The Company Commander having been critically wounded, Sergeant Harris took charge of the immediate situation, deployed his platoon into a defensive position and then without regard for

personal safety, went back to the enemy exposed area to aid his wounded Company Commander. The officer died in his arms. Sergeant Harris then voluntarily returned to the area four more times, each time bringing back a seriously wounded soldier.[24]

The battalion commander, Lieutenant Colonel Arthur H. Walker, also was awarded the Silver Star posthumously, for his gallantry in action on 18 November 1944.

> When one of the companies became disorganized in an attack after its commander was killed, Lieutenant Colonel Walker, the Battalion Commander, immediately went forward to personally reorganize the company and direct its continuation of the attack. All afternoon, he exposed himself to intense small arms fire as he encouraged the men to improve their position and adjusted their fire on the enemy. The next day, Lieutenant Colonel Walker, with the aid of an enlisted man, crossed approximately 300 yards of enemy territory under hostile small arms fire, and recovered the body of the Company Commander and evacuated a severely wounded soldier whom they discovered.[25]

By 19 November, all front-line companies had completed their reorganization and consolidation of positions substantially as they were before the attack began. For the next few days, strong patrolling was resumed and the artillery continued to harass the enemy. The 370th Infantry Regiment began planning immediately for yet another frontal attack to gain the high ground, with the specific objective still being to drive the Germans from Monte d'Anima.

The attack of the 1/370th Infantry was to be in the center of the 370th Infantry Regiment's sector to capture the mountain villages of Eglio and Sassi. The plan called for a coordinated attack on 27 November of the 1/370th Infantry from the south while partisans forces of approximately 1,000 men, led by Major John Oldham of the British Special Air Services, assaulted from the north. But parachute supply drops of equipment and arms to the partisans in the days leading up to the attack alerted the Germans that an assault was imminent. The Germans began gathering up suspected partisans. Those not captured, scattered into the surrounding hills, and their coordinating assault never occurred. Still, the 1/370th Infantry was ordered to attack during daylight as planned. They encountered extremely strong enemy resistance, suffered high casualties, and by nightfall had been unable to make any progress. Later reports revealed that spies in Major Oldham's unit had issued false orders directing the majority of the partisans to return to their assembly area. When the attack commenced, Major Oldham had only about 60 men. To their credit, they succeeded in getting atop Monte d'Anima at 1000, but were driven off by a heavy counterattack of enemy advancing from three directions.[26]

During the month of November, the 92nd Infantry Division had sustained 64 men killed in action, 318 wounded, and 115 listed as missing in action.[27] The critical impact of these casualties lies not only on the number of casualties, but in the fact that they included many outstanding junior officers and enlisted men who had distinguished themselves in battle. Particularly in small unit tactics at the squad, platoon, and company level, where bold, imaginative leadership and visible courage and initiative were required, these losses were irreplaceable. Just like in other African American combat units deployed in the various theaters of war, the replacement measures utilized were not satisfactory. The army never envisioned utilizing large formations of African American soldiers directly in combat and had never prepared a replacement system. Had the military not been segregated, the 92nd Infantry Division could have just drawn from the replacement pool of trained infantry personnel. Transfers were made of officers and noncommissioned officers among the platoons, companies, and battalions to fill leadership shortages. Often, the soldiers did not know who was in command.

Noncommissioned officers often replaced platoon leaders, as the casualty rate for lieutenants was usually higher in infantry divisions. Some qualified replacements came from the stateside 372nd Infantry Regiment, but never enough to fill the void. Unlike the other combat divisions, who often awarded battlefield commissions of lieutenant to deserving enlisted soldiers who showed an aptitude for leadership in battle, none were ever recorded in the 92nd Infantry Division. Instead, new white officers were brought in to replace officer casualties.

On 30 November, in preparation for a new winter offensive, the 365th Infantry Regimental Combat Team was withdrawn from the coastal sector and transferred to the Bologna front and was attached to the 88th Infantry Division, which was located on the extreme right of the 5th Army front lines. The coastal sector had been relatively quiet up to this point. The 365th Infantry would remain with the 88th Infantry Division until January 1945. This left a large void in the 92nd Infantry Division's 23-mile sector. The 2/370th Infantry was attached to Task Force 45, and did not return to the division's control until 18 December. The 3/370th Infantry remained attached to the South African 6th Armored Division in another sector. This left the 370th Infantry Regiment with only one battalion in the Serchio Valley. The 371st Infantry Regiment shifted its defensive lines to the coastal sector recently vacated by the 365th Infantry.

366TH INFANTRY REGIMENT

With 5th Army's concern about the 92nd Infantry Division being able to defend its entire sector of responsibility and maintain pressure on the enemy forces with only four battalions, it was decided by the commanding general to attach the 366th Infantry Regiment to the division. The 366th Infantry was an all African American regiment that arrived in Italy in May 1944 in order to provide security forces to the Army Air Force installations in the theater. The 366th Infantry Regiment was a proud unit that had been together longer than the 92nd Infantry Division, and performed all its assigned duties in an exemplary manner. With its all African American officers, there was a certain pride in the unit that was not experienced throughout the rest of the 92nd Infantry Division. There was an element of trust between the officers and enlisted men that was lacking in the 92nd Infantry Division. Initially denied the chance to fight as a combat unit, they realized this as an opportunity to show what African American soldiers were capable of achieving. Although 15 company grade officers had attended a three-week leadership and battle-training course in September, the majority of the regiment had not trained in infantry tactics since deploying to the theater. Due to the regiment's prolong exposure to security duties, its operation readiness suffered. Prior to being deployed to the North African and the Mediterranean Theater, the 366th Infantry Regiment also performed security duties in Massachusetts. Yet the 366th Infantry Regiment desired to enter into combat, no matter what the circumstances may have been.

The 366th Infantry Regiment, coming from various locales throughout Italy, arrived at the staging area in Leghorn on 28 November expecting to receive three months of intensive combat training before being deployed to the front lines. Instead of being utilized in the same manner as the other regiments of the division, as a combat team with its own internal command structure, the units of the 366th Infantry were individually attached to other units within the division. General Almond, determined to disrupt the esprit de corps of the 366th Infantry Regiment, decided to attach the individual units piecemeal to the regiments of the 92nd Infantry Division in order to minimize the command and control powers of the 366th

Regimental Headquarters staff. Since all of the regimental commanders and the vast majority of the battalion commanders were white, this ensured that the members of the 366th Infantry Regiment would always be subservient to a white command structure. Like the division staff, all of the officers working on the three regimental staffs were also white. Beginning on 30 November, the units of the 366th Infantry Regiments were attached as follows:

30 November — Company E, 2/366th Infantry attached to the 3/371st Infantry on the coastal sector.

1 December — Intelligence and Reconnaissance Platoon attached to the 92nd Reconnaissance Troop.

2 December — 2/366th (-Co. E) attached to the 370th Infantry Regiment in the Serchio Valley.

5 December — Company I, 3/366th Infantry attached to the 370th Infantry Regiment.

9 December — Cannon Company and the Antitank Company attached to the 371st Infantry.

11 December — Company K, 3/366th Infantry attached to the 370th Infantry Regiment.

12 December — 1/366th relieved 3/371st under the operational direction of the 92nd Infantry Division.

14 December — Regimental Headquarters deployed to Forte dei Marmi and was responsible for the 1/366th Infantry. The 3/366th Infantry (-Co. K) remained in the division training area in reserve.[28]

Despite the urgent requirement for additional infantry units in the sector, there was evidence to indicate General Almond did not welcome the 366th Infantry Regiment's attachment to the 92nd Infantry Division, especially with its senior African American officers. The officers and enlisted men found little comfort in his welcome speech upon their arrival in the combat zone. Lieutenant Sidney Thompson recalls General Almond's speech as being negative and stating that "we were not assigned by his wish."[29] Lieutenant John T. Letts remembers General Almond stating: "Your Negro newspapers have seen fit to cause you to be brought over here; now I'm going to see that you suffer your share of casualties."[30] There were many concerns in the 366th Infantry with General Almond's displeasure of the regiment. Some felt it was due to the number of high-ranking African American officers. The regimental headquarters was visited daily by General Almond to check on the status of the 366th Infantry. Colonel Howard D. Queen, the regimental commander of the 366th Infantry, requested relief from command on 11 December 1944, alleging:

"1. Respectfully request that I be relieved from assignment and command of the 366th Infantry Regiment for the following reasons:
   a. The treatment the regiment and myself have received during the period of the attachment to the 92nd Infantry Division has been such as to disturb me mentally and has not been such as is usually given an officer of my grade and service.
   b. To keep my record clear and up to normal expectations, before I break under the present strain as I am now physically and mentally exhausted.

2. I have been in command of this unit since 31 January 1943, and have at all times subscribed fully to the policy of higher authority and previously have received the proper courtesy and respect in return."[31]

The initial impressions of mutual dislike, mistrust, and misunderstanding between General Almond and the 366th Infantry Regiment continued, unresolved, throughout the period of its attachment to the 92nd Infantry Division. On 11 December, the 366th Infantry Regiment found itself without the leadership of the professional soldier who had led them since 1943. He represented a great loss to all the officers and men of this proud regiment of African American soldiers, especially during such a critical moment in its history. His mistreatment and disrespect at the hands of the 92nd Division Staff would never be forgiven. The division staff even reported that Colonel Queen reported to the division commander on the morning of 15 December, as a result of the 366th Regimental Headquarters having been subjected to heavy concentration of hostile artillery fire from the large caliber coastal guns at La Spezia. Lieutenant Colonel Alonzo Ferguson, the 366th Infantry Regiment's executive officer, assumed command of the regiment.

In December, an analysis of ammunition stocks indicated that sufficient supplies were on hand to support a 15-day attack during the month, but such consumption would result in the inability to carry out further offensive actions until the end of January 1945. By that time, receipt of scheduled allocations would again boost the reserve supplies to a point which would allow full artillery support to any operations. Allotments of artillery ammunition were greatly reduced, and the Italian front was now a secondary theater in the European campaign. Limitations of 15 rounds per day for each 105-mm howitzer, 18 rounds per day for the 155-mm howitzer, and 11 rounds per day for the 155-mm gun were initially imposed. Later in the winter, allocations were reduced even further. Drastic reductions were also made in infantry supporting ammunition, which included 81-mm and 60-mm mortars, as well as .30 caliber rifle rounds.

With artillery being in short supply, the 92nd Infantry Division amassed all of its .50 caliber machine guns, 37-mm and 57-mm antitank guns, and later British 40-mm Bofors antiaircraft guns to harass the enemy. Known as infantry weapons shoots, all weapons were fired simultaneously at a specified time, in the place of artillery harassment and interdiction (H&I) fire.

A captain from the German 101st Cavalry Reconnaissance Battalion describes the effectiveness of these "weapons shoots" as a prisoner after the war ended, in September 1945 in Leghorn, Italy: "The 101st Cavalry Reconnaissance Battalion was attached to the 148th Grenadier Division for observation duty as directed by the Division G-2. Your massed fire from very heavy machine guns was terrific. They were not only casualty producing, but also very demoralizing. This tended to restrict movements in the forward areas and in some cases caused us to withdraw from some of our most forward blocking positions."[32]

DECEMBER OFFENSIVE

In early December, it was decided to again attempt to seize and secure Mount Cauala, a part of it referred to as "Maine" by the soldiers of the 371st Infantry Regiment. At 0400 on 4 December, the 2/371st Infantry, commanded by Major George E. Pinard, attempted another frontal daylight attack with Company B, 1/366th Infantry, on the left flank, Company F, 2/371st Infantry in the center and Company G, 2/371st Infantry, securing the right flank. Immediately, Company G was deluged with massed enemy fire, as all movement on Maine was exposed to enemy observation. The company was forced to halt its advance. Company F ran into overwhelming enemy resistance and withdrew back to its initial positions.

Company B, 1/366th Infantry, commanded by Captain Walter E. Dabney, moving steadily forward, was on top of a hill codenamed Alaska, one of the several small hills on the left of the sector. They found themselves subjected to heavy enemy mortar, machine gun and small arms fire from the direct front and right flank. The enemy firing positions could not be located, and Major Pinard, believing the position untenable, requested permission to withdraw the company, but the regiment refused. Orders were to hold the position during daylight unless forced to withdraw by overwhelming physical contact. Company B, 1/366th Infantry, continued to be fired upon by unrelenting enemy fire and the company became somewhat disorganized as a result. Captain Dabney moved about valiantly, reorganizing his unit, and accurately directing fire in spite of his also being wounded. Several of the enemy were killed attacking his position including a German officer, and 12 prisoners were captured. When finally ordered to withdraw, Captain Dabney ensured the wounded were evacuated first, and he was among the last to depart. For his gallant actions, Captain Dabney would be awarded the first Silver Star medal for the 366th Infantry Regiment.[33]

On 4 December, enemy activity also increased in the 370th Infantry Regiment's sector of responsibility in the Serchio Valley. The Antitank Company deployed in and around the town of Vergemoli, and was attacked at 0830 by a full company of Italian Fascist soldiers led by German officers and noncommissioned officers. Throughout the duration of the fighting, 300 to 400 artillery and mortar rounds landed in the vicinity of Vergemoli. The 370th Antitank Company held its positions, effectively employing their 57-mm antitank weapons against the advancing soldiers, withstanding both heavy enemy fire and the determined attack. When the fighting ceased at nightfall, the Antitank Company's positions were still secure. At one time, enemy soldiers had advanced to within ten feet of their defensive positions. The Antitank Company suffered two killed while inflicting over 30 enemy casualties. First Lieutenant Roland Fraser was awarded the Silver Star for his heroic actions on that day. Under a continuous rain of enemy fire, Lieutenant Fraser constantly exposed himself by moving between the defensive fighting positions that were under his direct command, establishing fields of fire, encouraging his men, and replenishing ammunition.[34]

While the battle was raging at the front, several major changes in the Allied Command structure occurred in mid-December. British Field Marshal Wilson relinquished his command of the Mediterranean Theater to Field Marshal Alexander. On 16 December, while 5th Army was resting and refitting its forces for a renewal of the offensive, Lieutenant General Mark Clark left his 5th Army Headquarters at Futa Pass to assume command of the newly formed 15th Army Group. Lieutenant General Lucian K. Truscott, Jr., replaced him as the commander of the 5th Army.[35]

During the next few days, the German front lines became relatively quiet. Artillery and mortar fire continued to fall. Meanwhile, the 370th Regimental Combat Team continued to prepare for a possible enemy attack. The 5th Army was aware of reports of additional enemy soldiers in the Serchio Valley Sector. There were Italian partisan reports of a possible enemy offensive emanating from the Castelnuovo di Garfagnana area, in addition to reports confirmed by patrol and air reconnaissance of road and bridge repairs on routes leading into Castelnuovo. This offensive would coincide with the Germans' Ardennes Forest counteroffensive being conducted in the European Theater. Germany was hoping that an all-out attack in the American and British sectors along the Western European and Mediterranean Theaters might force the Allies to sign a separate peace treaty and the German military forces could then divert all their attention to the rapidly advancing Soviet forces.

Another indication of a possible attack was the buildup of enemy forces in the western section, which greatly exceeded the normal defensive requirements of that region. In addition to the Monte Rosa and San Marco Italian Division, and two regiments of the German

148th Grenadier Division that had been opposing the 92nd Infantry Division for some time, the German 157th Mountain Division, which was stationed in Northeastern Italy, was dispatched to the La Spezia area on 15 December. The third regiment, the 285th of the 148th Grenadiers, was deployed from Genoa. The Italia Division, purportedly ready for employment in the counterattack role in support of German units, which had previously been concentrated in the Parma area, was moved to the La Spezia area. There was also the possibility that the 16th SS Panzer Grenadier Division and the 26th Panzer Division, which were currently in reserve, would also be utilized in any offensive deployments. In evaluating the buildup of enemy forces in the western sector, there was the possibility that an offensive force of five divisions could attack the thinly held front of the 92nd Infantry Division. The 92nd Infantry Division was the only force between the enemy lines and the 5th Army logistical and supply center located at Leghorn, Italy.

The 370th Antitank Company, now trained in infantry tactics, was also equipped with additional rifles, .30-caliber light machine guns, and Browning automatic rifles in addition to its organic 57-mm antitank weapons. Now performing the duties of a provisional heavy weapons infantry company, it was assigned to a blocking position in the vicinity of Vergemoli, on the regiment's left flank. Early on 22 December, the company was attacked by a German patrol. As the fighting became intense, suddenly some of the Germans started fighting other Germans. When the fighting subsided and the hostile forces withdrew, the 370th Antitank Company discovered that they had captured a platoon of 16 Russians, who had been forced to join the German army and had suddenly changed sides. These men proved to be invaluable in locating minefields and other obstacles that impeded any advances that would be made by the 370th Infantry Regiment. The regiment requested that they be allowed to stay and fight with them, but 5th Army ordered that they be turned over to the Prisoner-of-War (POW) holding cages. From there, they were turned over to a Soviet Liaison Officer, who promptly had them executed as traitors.[36]

As early as 22 December, 5th Army Headquarters began procedures to reinforce the 92nd Infantry Division sector. The 760th Tank Battalion, commanded by Major Clair Curtis, was attached to the 92nd Infantry Division. The 339th Regimental Combat Team of the 85th Infantry Division was deployed to IV Corps, and the 337th Regimental Combat Team of the same division, commanded by Colonel Oliver Hughes, was attached to the 92nd Infantry Division. The 6th South African Armored Division reverted to United States Army control and was directed to be prepared to reinforce the 92nd Infantry Division if needed. The 19th and 20th Brigades (Gurkhas and Sikhs) of the British 8th Indian Division were also placed under "operational control" of the 92nd Infantry Division.[37]

The fact that the German commanders were fully aware of the situation in the 370th Infantry Regiment's sector was demonstrated in a postwar interrogation conducted by Lieutenant Colonel Arnold, G-3, 92nd Infantry Division. Brigadier General Fretter Pico, commanding general of the 148th Grenadier Division, stated: "The weaknesses of your deployment in the Serchico Valley in December 1944 were that your troops were deployed on a front which was too long for the number of troops available, and your reserves were too far in the rear area which prevented their being deployed immediately."[38]

The enemy launched a predawn attack on 26 December following a series of probing thrusts by patrols the previous night. The enemy struck the 92nd Infantry Division at several points in the rugged mountains, on a six-mile front astride the Serchio River. A very heavy mortar barrage and about 800 rounds of enemy artillery in the coastal sector preceded the attack. West of the Serchico River, elements of the German 2nd Battalion, 285th Grenadier

Regiment, 148th Grenadier Division, and the Brescia, Alpine Battalion of the Italian Monta Rosa Division, struck the 1/370th Infantry near Molazzana, four miles south of Castelnuovo, and Company G, 2/370th Infantry, at Calomini, south and west of Molazzana. East of the river, large elements, identified as belonging to the 2nd Battalion, 285th Grenadier Regiment, and the 2nd Battalion, 286th Grenadier Regiment, attacked the village of Sommocolonia, held only by a platoon of Company E, 2/366th Infantry, artillery forward observers, and Italian Partisans. Hand-to-hand fighting in the streets developed. The enemy was estimated to be attacking in strength of about one reinforced regiment on each side of the river in the initial assault.

At 0414, the 1/370th Infantry reported machine gun fire on Companies A and C in the vicinity of Molazzano. A platoon of the 92nd Reconnaissance Troop at Bebbio on the extreme right flank, reported hearing small arms and artillery fire in the vicinity of the town of Sommocolonia. At 0455, the 2/366th Infantry confirmed this report, stating the fire was coming from directly north of Sommocolonia. At 0530, an enemy squad appeared at the draw north of Sommocolonia and Italian partisan soldiers met them head-on in a fierce firefight, driving them off with the aid of supporting small arms, light .30-caliber machine guns, and 60-mm mortar fire from the platoon of Company E, 2/366th Infantry. However, a larger enemy force comprising Austrians and Fascist Italians, some dressed as friendly partisans, drove the defending force back into Sommocolonia, and by 0730 had surrounded them. Hand-to-hand fighting ensued, and the platoon leader, Lieutenant Graham Jenkins, sent a radio message that they were being attacked in large numbers and needed assistance, informing his battalion: "Don't worry about anything, my men will hold."[39] The battalion commander dispatched an additional platoon from Company E to reinforce the platoon already engaged in the fighting. All weapons against the enemy forces at Sommocolonia were employing defensive fire. Meanwhile, enemy artillery and mortar fire continued to fall accurately on all front-line positions on both sides of the river.

As the small force of approximately 60 men, comprising Italian partisans and the single platoon of Company E, 2/366th Infantry, fought desperately in Sommocolonia, the 92nd Cavalry Reconnaissance Troop's platoons in Bebbio and Scarpello began to experience enemy movement in their sectors. Their alerted outposts observed 50 enemy soldiers on Lami di Sotto and called down artillery fire on them with excellent effect. They also observed enemy soldiers with approximately 30 mules attempting to resupply their fellow soldiers attacking Sommocolonia. Again, artillery fire was directed on the mule train with heavy casualties to men and animals observed. At 0820, a wounded partisan reported to the 370th Infantry Regimental command post that approximately 300 enemy soldiers were in Sommocolonia and fighting their way house to house.[40]

Late in the morning, over 200 German soldiers from the veteran Austro-German Mittenwals Battalion poured down the sheltered draws between the towns of Bebbio and Scarpello, led by Italian guides familiar with the terrain. Despite the overwhelming odds, the small force of cavalry troopers fought bitterly before being forced to withdraw to the Cavalry Reconnaissance Troop command post at Coreglia, in accordance with their contingency plans. The Silver Star medals awarded to Staff Sergeant William Morris and Technician 5th Class Jefferson Hilliard reflect the courage and tenacity of these embattled soldiers.

> Staff Sergeant Morris commanded several platoon strong points from which he directed artillery fire on two enemy columns, causing at least 35 casualties. When his position was vigorously attacked with heavy mortar, automatic weapons and small arms fire, he quickly coordinated effective counter fire that caused more casualties and repulsed the attack. The enemy then reor-

ganized, attempting to envelope the strong point from all sides at once with a numerical superior force. Staff Sergeant Morris, personally manning one of his weapons, directed his fire, maintained contact with his company until his radio went out and the enemy had cut off and partially overrun his position from three sides. Then he ordered his men to proceed through the remaining exit to a previously prepared position. During this activity, Staff Sergeant Morris was wounded, but, despite his injuries, he reached his men who had discovered the enemy occupying the position they now sought. He then safely led his men around the hostile force to a new position where he remained under an intense mortar concentration until recalled by his company.

Technician 5th Class Hilliard manned a machine gun in a strong point under vigorous enemy attack. For two hours his position was one of two main enemy objectives. During this activity, he accounted for at least 12 enemy casualties while he and his assistant gunner were the target of an intense mortar concentration. When maneuver and superior forces of the enemy made his position untenable, T/5 Hilliard was ordered to cover the withdrawal of the other men. He removed the machine gun from its tripod, and fired from the hip, carrying the ammunition belt on his shoulder while his assistant carried the tripod. He fired in this manner until his ammunition was exhausted, accounting for at least two more enemy casualties.[41]

By noon the troopers of the 92nd Cavalry Reconnaissance Troop were forced to withdraw to Coreglia. Their vacated positions at Bebbio, the key terrain feature with a commanding view of the entire 2/370th Infantry sector, made the right flank of the front lines vulnerable and exposed. The 2/370th Infantry's command post was never told of the 92nd Cavalry Reconnaissance Troop's withdrawal, thus leaving their right flank totally exposed and unprotected.

Bitter fighting continued within the village of Sommocolonia. The valiant band of Company E, 2/366th Infantry's soldiers and the Italian partisans fought desperately to repel the enemy swarming through the streets. First Lieutenant John R. Fox, Cannon Company, 366th Infantry Regiment, was acting as the forward artillery observer for the supporting 598th Field Artillery Battalion. Lieutenant Fox initially joined the army as an enlisted man in the 372nd Infantry Regiment, which was a National Guard unit in 1940. He received his officer's commission through ROTC at Wilberforce College and was assigned to the 366th Infantry Regiment in 1941. His heroic actions were described dramatically in the *Field Artillery Journal*, January 1946 edition.[42]

> One of the forward observers showed unbeatable heroism. Lieutenant Fox and his party had ample time to pull out. They remained on the second floor of a house directing defensive fires until only a handful of defenders remained. As the enemy closed in, Lieutenant Fox called for artillery fire increasingly close to his own position. One of his last requests for fire included a target only 60 yards from him. The enemy continued to press forward in large numbers. When the house ... was entirely surrounded, he called for fire directly on it. He was questioned as to whether the mission was safe to fire it. He answered, 'Fire it! There's more of them than there are of us.' He was recommended posthumously for the Distinguished Service Cross.

No further word came from Lieutenant Fox. His body was discovered in the demolished observation post days later, along with the remains of over 100 enemy soldiers that he had taken with him. On 1 April 1982, nearly 39 years later, Lieutenant Fox was finally awarded the Distinguished Service Cross, this nation's second highest award, posthumously for extraordinary heroism in action. The citation concluded:

> As the Germans continued to press the attack towards the area that Lieutenant Fox occupied, he adjusted the artillery fire closer to his position. Finally he was warned that the next adjustment would bring the deadly artillery right on top of his position. After acknowledging the danger, Lieutenant Fox insisted that the last adjustment be fired, as this was the only way to defeat the attacking soldiers. Later, when a counter attack retook the position from the Germans, Lieuten-

ant Fox's body was found along with bodies of approximately 100 German soldiers. Lieutenant Fox's gallant and courageous actions, at the supreme sacrifice of his own life, contributed greatly to delaying the enemy advance until other infantry and artillery could reorganize to repel the attack. His extraordinarily valorous actions were in keeping with the most cherished traditions of military service, and reflect the utmost credit on him, his unit, and the United States Army.[43]

As the situation in Sommocolonia increasingly worsened, enemy forces attacked all front-line companies with an estimated two reinforced infantry battalions supported by artillery, mortars, and machine guns. The main thrust of the attack was directed at Company G, 2/366th Infantry. The battalion commander ordered the weapons platoon from Company E to support Company G, while the final platoon of Company E was ordered to deploy forward to relieve the beleaguered forces at Sommocolonia. The commander for the 370th Infantry Regiment countermanded that order and deployed those forces to occupy positions on Mount Vano to secure the right flank, which had been abandoned by the 92nd Cavalry Reconnaissance Troop. At 1015, another wounded partisan evacuated from Sommocolonia reported three enemy companies were in the village, but that the platoon from Company E continued to offer stiff resistance.

Shortly thereafter, the Company E platoon, originally dispatched to assist the beleaguered forces in Sommocolonia, reached the edge of town, but were immediately overtaken by a numerically superior force of enemy soldiers. First Lieutenant Lewis Flagg III, Company H, 2/366th Infantry observed: "The relief should have been a full company, not a platoon. The small group got caught in machine gun crossfire. The man in front of the lieutenant and the man behind him were cut down in the first burst of fire and the platoon never had a chance. They tried to fight on, but heavy casualties forced them to retire."[44]

At 1145, the Sommocolonia force was ordered to withdraw, as relief would not be possible. But by then, the small force was surrounded. Unable to extricate itself, the force was directed to hold until dark, and then proceed to the prepared defensive positions along the Mount Vano-Barga Ridge. Of the approximately 60 Americans and Italian partisans still fighting in Sommocolonia, only one officer and 17 enlisted men were able to withdraw. They did so, fighting every step of the way, still inflicting casualties on the enemy. The Silver Star medal was awarded to First Lieutenant Graham H. Jenkins for his profound leadership and gallant actions on that day:

> Lieutenant Jenkins' platoon was on an exposed hill. After a 24-hour artillery and machine gun barrage, the enemy launched a deadly offensive at the battalion positions with a numerically superior force. Lieutenant Jenkins, with outstanding personal leadership kept his men in position, without food and with limited amounts of ammunition. Resisting the enemy with fierce determination, Lieutenant Jenkins killed several enemy soldiers who attempted to storm his position during a lull in the artillery fire, and exposed himself to help drag three of his wounded machine gunners to comparative safety. Upon being ordered to withdraw, Lieutenant Jenkins refused to leave the unevacuated wounded which now numbered over 50 percent of his platoon unable to walk. He continued to direct counter-fire and care for the wounded until his ammunition was exhausted and every man in the platoon but one had become a casualty, and he himself wounded. When the enemy closed over his position, he was still trying to comfort a severely wounded soldier; First Lieutenant Jenkins' intrepid valor in the face of overwhelming odds exemplifies the conspicuous gallantry of the American soldier.[45]

German fire was now falling on the regiment and battalion command posts. The IV Corps commander, Major General Crittenberger, with members of his staff, arrived at the 370th Infantry Regiment's command post in the afternoon, discussed the situation with Colonel Sherman, approved steps taken by the regiment, and informed the regimental commander that the 8th Indian Division was on its way to take up defensive positions behind the 370th Infantry's defensive lines. The 2/366th Infantry was reinforced with Company F, 2/370th Infantry, which was withdrawn from the west bank of the Serchio River when the main attack shifted to the 2/366th Infantry's sector.

At 1245, civilians reported citing large numbers of German forces approaching the town of Barga from Bebbio.[46] At 1400, the enemy attacked the 2/366th Infantry positions around Barga with a large force preceded by a massive artillery barrage. The enemy assault units attacked Company G, 2/366th Infantry, supported by artillery and mortars. Initially, the company resisted stubbornly, inflicting heavy casualties, but under the intense pressure of the onslaught of advancing enemy soldiers, Company G retreated, leaving an exposed gap on the east bank of the Serchio River to the Barga Ridge. With their flanks exposed, other elements of the 2/366th Infantry withdrew to a new defensive line to avoid being encircled. A German company took advantage of the breach in the line and moved to the south unopposed.

By 1630, the 92nd Cavalry Reconnaissance Troop reported an estimated two enemy companies in the village of Tiglio, on the extreme right flank. At 1730, the 2/366th Infantry reported to the 370th Regimental Headquarters that Company G on the left flank was reeling under the constant heavy artillery shelling and infantry assaults for over four hours, and was withdrawing. By nightfall, the enemy had forced its way through the company's depleted perimeter along the river road and was proceeding toward the 370th Infantry's Regimental Command Post at Fornaci. All command post personnel, including cooks, clerks, and staff officers, and a platoon from Company F, 2/370th Infantry, hastily organized under the leadership of the regimental executive officer, deployed forward to meet the enemy assault. A platoon of four Sherman medium tanks from the 760th Tank Battalion was ordered to fire down the river road. The force found no traces of the enemy.

Battery C, 598th Field Artillery Battalion, redeploying to another position further to the rear, received orders to fire 100 rounds of 105-mm high explosive ordnance per gun straight down the road just west of the command post. The enemy attack never reached the command post. When breaching the perimeter previously held by Company G, 2/366th Infantry, the enemy forces failed to exploit their gains in attacking the vulnerable regiment command post. At 1840, the regiment's defenders and the platoon of tanks moved to the north end of Fornaci and set up a defensive perimeter. There was no further contact with the enemy that night on the east side of the Serchio River. The regiment command post deployed back to the village of Osteria and the 598th Field Artillery Battalion had completed displacement of its command post with its vital Fire Direction Center. On the west side of the river, Company G, 2/370th Infantry, in the village of Calomini, reoccupied its heavy weapons' positions after pinning down the enemy with machine gun fire. The battered companies of the 2/366th Infantry, 2/370th Infantry, and the 92nd Cavalry Reconnaissance Troop reorganized and prepared for additional enemy attacks that night.

Throughout the battles, during the morning hours, enemy artillery and mortar fire fell continuously on 1/370th Infantry's defensive positions in Calomini, Molazzana, and Vergemoli. These soldiers repelled enemy attacks, sometimes from as many as three sides simultaneously. Repeatedly, defensive artillery and mortar fire was called down on the onrushing enemy. In addition, mines laid by the 1/370th Infantry along the approaches were responsible for many of the enemy casualties. Heavy shelling continued, and at 1655, the commanding officer, 1/370th Infantry, realizing that they would not be reinforced, ordered the battalion to consolidate their defenses. The 370th Antitank Company at Vergemoli was redeployed back to Trassilico, to better protect its flank; Company A, with one platoon of Company B attached, was maneuvered laterally, thus abandoning positions under current observation and fire by the enemy in Promilano. The withdrawal of Company G, 2/366th Infantry, on the east bank of the river left the right flank of the forces on the west side uncovered. The 370th Regimental Command Post ordered 1/370th Infantry on the west bank to fall back to high ground to occupy previously reconnoitered defensive positions on the south side of the Gallicano Stream by dawn.

On the morning of 27 December, at 1000, Sherman tanks from Company B, 760th Tank Battalion, reported to the 370th Regimental Command Post on hearing small arms and automatic weapon fire. A few minutes later, 2/366th Infantry reported that Company G had withdrawn to the battalion command post at Pedona. Under the control of the battalion staff were two depleted platoons of Company E, and many other soldiers from various units who had become separated in the confusion of battle during the night. Some of the men from Company F, 2/370th Infantry were also among this mixed group. While defensive positions were being organized, the battalion was attacked by a numerically superior enemy force advancing from Barga towards Pedona. The remaining platoons of Company E defended the road between Barga and the battalion command post at Pedona when the attack began. The enemy with devastating force used one of the battalion's own 57-mm antitank guns, which was abandoned in Barga, against the two platoons. The platoons of Company E were nearly decimated by this accurate fire. The 2/366th Infantry was forced to withdraw once again to more defendable positions. The remainder of the battalion was reorganized on the bluffs in the rear of Pedona where they were finally able to halt the enemy advance.

It was for his actions during that portion of the battle that the executive officer of the 370th Infantry Regiment, Lieutenant Colonel John J. Phelan, was awarded the Silver Star for reportedly taking to the field and reorganizing the retreating forces to establish a firm defensive line on the bluffs just in the rear of Pedona. But postwar interviews with the soldiers of 2/366th Infantry never witnessed Lieutenant Colonel Phelan anywhere near the battlefield on that day. Captain Samuel Tucker, S-2, 2/366th Infantry, in a letter written in July 1980, states: "I met Colonel Robinson (Battalion Commander) near Pedona, leading his troops. There was no panic, I do not doubt that there was some disorganization, but I do not recall not knowing, generally, the location of our three rifle companies. The suggestion of a rout is news to me. I do not recall seeing Lieutenant Colonel Phelan."[47] This was common practice for soldiers assigned to regimental staffs in the rear to fabricate reports and award recommendations in an effort to advance their careers.

Further to the east, German mountain soldiers, clad in white camouflage winter uniforms, descended in force on the villages of Tiglio Alto and Tiglio Basso, both a few kilometers from Coreglia, which was being defended by the 92nd Cavalry Reconnaissance Troop. The 2/370th Infantry, minus Company F, with a company of the 19th Indian Brigade attached, deployed eastward to meet this new threat. However, by this time, the 2/366th Infantry at Pedona had successfully halted the main enemy assault, although the 92nd Cavalry Reconnaissance Troop had abandoned Coreglia.

At 1300, Major General Dudly Russell, commander of the 8th Indian Division, assumed command of the entire Serchio sector, and directed the soldiers of the 370th Infantry Regiment and its attached units including the 2/366th Infantry to withdraw from the east bank through the lines of the Indian soldiers, then in position behind the combat team. It was then to deploy to the west bank of the Serchio River to reinforce the 1/370th Infantry. At 1530, orders were issued and the 370th Regimental Combat Team, minus the 598th Field Artillery Battalion, crossed to their new positions. The 598th Field Artillery Battalion was retained on the east side of the Serchio River to provide mutual artillery support to both the 8th Indian Division and the 370th Infantry Regiment. The 370th Regimental Command Post was moved to Pian della Rocca. Throughout the afternoon, fighter-bomber aircraft support from the XII Tactical Air Force attacked the areas now occupied by enemy forces. Over 200 air sorties were flown that day against Sommocolonia, Barga, and Vergemoli.

By the evening of 27 December, the air strikes, coupled with accurate artillery, and the additional forces of the 8th Indian Division, halted the enemy advance. Barga was cleared by the 8th Indian Division on 29 December, and Sommocolonia on 30 December. Allied patrols entered Bebbio, Gallicano, and Molazzano against weak rear-guard enemy resistance. By 1 January, the 2/366th, the 1/370th, and the 2/370th Infantry Battalions had been reorganized and reequipped on firmly established defensive positions along the west side of the Serchio River. On 10 January 1945, the 8th Indian Division was withdrawn from the Serchio Valley, and the 370th Infantry Regiment returned to the command and control of the 92nd Infantry Division, with Brigadier General John Wood assuming command of the Serchio sector.[48]

That same day, the 365th Infantry Regiment, which had previously been attached to the 88th Infantry Division on the Bologna front since 2 December, returned to the 92nd Infantry Division's control. The 365th Infantry Regiment promptly relieved any of the remaining elements of the 370th Infantry Regiment still positioned on the eastern side of the Serchio River, with the 1/365th and the 2/365th Infantry deploying into positions in the vicinity of Barga, and the 3/365th going into tactical reserve in the vicinity of Coreglia. The 365th Regimental Command Post was headquartered in the town of Ghivizzano.

Recriminations and accusations came quickly from the Army Command Headquarters. Both Generals Clark and Truscott concluded that the German attack had caused serious disruption of the 5th Army's soldiers' dispositions and consequently tended to cast blame upon the 92nd Infantry Division for the abandonment of plans to renew the winter offensive. But it was actually the battle that convinced Allied commanders that conditions along the front lines were not favorable for a winter offensive. The enemy had made a clear point of defending its Gothic Line positions. The harsh winter weather, the rough terrain, the depleted ammunition stocks, the lack of replacements, and the physical and emotional condition of the soldiers, all dictated postponement of the attack. Yet, the 92nd Infantry Division drew the brunt of the blame. General Clark stated in a postwar book: "It [92nd Infantry Division] did not come up to the test, and when the Germans struck down the Serchio Valley, the Regimental Commanders were unable to exercise sufficient control over their troops in an emergency."[49] General Truscott also stated after the war: "The Germans launched several limited objective attacks in the Serchio Valley, with forces involving five or six battalions which struck the 1/370th Infantry and the 2/366th Infantry, both of which 'melted away'—a term which was to be frequently used in describing actions of colored troops."[50]

Major General Almond agreed with the assessment of his superiors and offered nothing in defense of his "own" soldiers. Neither he, nor his divisional staff, nor the 370th Regimental Commander and his staff, were blamed or criticized for the events which occurred during the battle. All the blame was placed upon the African American junior officers and enlisted men, many of whom felt they were thrust into an impossible situation because of inadequate preparation, lack of reliable intelligence reports, and poor planning by the command staff. The actual cause for the 92nd Infantry Division's failure to maintain the defensive posture in this sector of the front lines was inadequate assessment of the enemy forces opposing them and the insufficient number of soldiers to protect this vast area. Unlike the white infantry divisions, where the commanding officers take responsibility for all the actions of the soldiers entrusted to their leadership, white officers in command of African American soldiers, while given credit for any successes, were not held liable for their failures. This was attributed to the feelings among most of the military leaders at the time that the African American soldier was far inferior to the white soldier when it came to combat capabilities. Any individual heroic deeds or acts of bravery on the part of the African American soldiers were to be considered the exceptions to the rule.

Colonel Sherman, the commander of the 370th Infantry Regiment, in an After Action Report of the battle submitted to General Almond on 4 March 1945, attempted to explain his shortcomings: There were several factors militating against a really sound defensive set up against a major enemy effort.

> Due to the small number of troops available and large frontage assigned, both flanks of the position were open except for a reconnaissance screen. The Combat Team was itself under orders to launch an attack as part of a larger effort on December 25. The planning for this effort and the consequent disposition of troops naturally limited defensive preparations. Word that this attack was being postponed did not reach Combat Team 370 until the evening of 24 December 1944. The mission of the Combat Team at all times had been to maintain constant offensive pressure against the enemy to prevent the shifting of more troops to the Bologna front. Accordingly, the Combat Team had pushed forward to the lower slopes of ridges held by the enemy. This mission had been further amplified by a directive that in the event of attack the Combat Team was to *hold* its present position at all costs.[51]

In spite of the allegations of "melting away," and of the inferior combat capabilities of the African American infantryman, there were several heroic acts in the face of overwhelming forces during the battle. The Silver Star medal was awarded to the following:

> William E. Porter, First Lieutenant, Infantry. Lieutenant Porter's platoon was attacking a strong enemy position. The enemy's automatic weapons fire pinned down the platoon. Lieutenant Porter alone, advanced on an enemy machine gun nest, killed the German officer in charge and forced the enemy to surrender, thus facilitating the advance of his company. Later in the day, after his platoon had been completely surrounded by superior enemy forces he constantly exposed himself to hostile fire in moving back and forth between platoon positions maintaining contact, directing fire, encouraging his men, and leading them in fighting their way out of the enemy trap.
>
> (Posthumous) John A. Williams, Staff Sergeant, Infantry. On December 26, 1944, when the enemy counter-attacked and infiltrated a town held by our troops and forced a withdrawal, Staff Sergeant Williams, a platoon guide was ordered to take a squad of men to cover the withdrawal. The squad encountered a sniper while moving into position and Staff Sergeant Williams personally maneuvered to an advantageous point and fired upon the sniper thus enabling the squad to proceed. Subsequently, when the enemy fired an intense concentration of artillery on the entire area, Staff Sergeant Williams and two other men became separated from their squad. Finding a soldier in OD uniform guarding a house, they went to inquire the whereabouts of their unit. As they approached closer they discovered that the soldier was one of the enemy dressed in an American uniform. The enemy attempted to fire upon them, Staff Sergeant Williams made a blind tackle, the enemy wounded him mortally but his grappling with the German enabled his companions to escape to safety. Staff Sergeant Williams' aggressiveness and self-sacrifice was a heroic exemplification of the fighting spirit of the American soldier.
>
> Melvin W. Walker, First Lieutenant, 366th Infantry. On December 30, 1944, the raiding party of which first Lieutenant Walker was a member, was assigned the mission of crossing an enemy-observed canal, penetrating enemy lines, capturing prisoners and locating and destroying hostile installations. First Lieutenant Walker proceeded under cover of smoke across a heavily

Lieutenant General Joseph T. McNarney, Deputy Supreme Allied Commander, Mediterranean Theater, inspects Honor Guard of Military Police during his tour of the 5th Army front at the 92nd Infantry Division Sector, 4 January 1945. (National Archives 111-SC-380271)

mined beach and through icy water while subjected to intense enemy artillery, mortar, and automatic weapons fire. After crossing the canal, he assisted in directing the fire fight and, in spite of finding that his own weapons would not fire because of exposure to water and sand he repeatedly exposed himself to draw enemy fire. When the company returned from the raid, he assisted in the evacuation of the wounded at the canal and led the group through withering hostile fire back to safely.[52]

Throughout January, the 92nd Infantry Division, like the other units on the 5th Army front lines, continued an active defense of their positions. At the end of December, the 758th Tank Battalion (Light), the first of the three African American tank battalions activated for military service in 1941, arrived in the Mediterranean Theater. Its three companies, equipped with the M5 Stuart light tank, were, by this time in the war, no match for the German armored forces. But this tank, manned by a crew of four, with its 37-mm cannon main gun, and .30-caliber light machine guns, was an excellent platform for armored screening operations and attacking fortified enemy positions. The 758th Tank Battalion had a long association with the 92nd Infantry Division during maneuvers in the United States, and on 29 and 30 December, its companies were attached to the 760th Tank Battalion for command and control.

Early in January 1945, Lieutenant Vernon Baker, having just returned to Company C, 1/370th Infantry from the hospital, was made the executive officer. The commander, First Lieutenant Montjoy, had been replaced by Captain Booker T. Matthews in his absence. All the other officers of the company had been wounded or killed in combat. During a mortar attack, Captain Matthews was severely wounded, losing his right arm. This left Lieutenant Baker as the sole officer in Company C, 1/370th Infantry.

On 9 January 1945, 5th Army announced the postponement of further large-scale offensives by the 15th Army Group. It directed its units to prepare for the resumption of offensive operations on or about 1 April 1945. In the meantime, units of the army were to train and rest in preparation for a major spring offensive. The IV Corps, holding its 75-mile-long front with only the 92nd Infantry Division, the Brazilian Expeditionary Force, and the equivalent of one regimental combat team (Task Force 45), was directed to plan a limited objective attack with its available soldiers to improve tactical positions, especially in the 92nd Infantry Division's sector. Throughout the period, the 5th Army units were to continue to harass the enemy in order to prevent the withdrawal of German units from the IV Corps front.[53] High-level intelligence reports, which later turned out to be false, indicated German intentions to withdraw from Italy to Germany, and to replace German soldiers with Italian military forces. Even then, elements of three Fascist divisions, still loyal to the Germans and Mussolini, were operating in the coastal sector and in the Serchio Valley. These were the Monte Rosa, the San Marco, and the Italia Divisions. In at least one instance it was believed that such a relief was already in progress. Colonel Donald M. MacWillie, the G2/intelligence officer of the 92nd Infantry Division, reported: "The introduction of the Second battalion, Bersaglieri Regiment of the Italia Division to *replace* the Second Battalion, 286th Regiment (German), east of the Serchio, *seems* certain now."[54]

OPERATION FOURTH TERM

Operation Fourth Term, developed by Major General Almond and the 92nd Infantry Division staff, was an ambitious plan designed to explore the extent of a possible enemy withdrawal. It was not designed as a full-scale, long-range offensive action, but as a limited-objective attack. The plan was envisioned to improve the division's defensive positions, to seize the Satrettoia hill mass, which dominated the coastal plain north of the heavily mined Cinquale Canal, and to advance the Serchio Valley positions to the Lama di Sotto Ridge, overlooking the town of Castelnuova di Garfagnana two miles beyond.

The IV Corps commander approved Plan Fourth Term, but limited the operation's objective to the line along the Magro Canal-Montignoso-Mount Folgorito. The five-mile sector from the sea to the mountains east of Highway 1 was to be the battleground. First, the enemy was to be driven from their strategic positions in Strettoia Hills, and the higher peaks along the Mount Cerreta-Folgorito Ridge line. Thus, the soldiers attacking on the coastal plain and along Highway 1 would be protected from observation and fire from these hills and peaks. This would open the way for the drive to Massa, and enable allied artillery to be positioned within range of La Spezia, the Italian naval base with its long-range 152-mm coastal guns.

Prior to the main attack, a major diversionary operation was to be made in the Serchio Valley. In addition to drawing enemy reserves from the coastal region, while holding the maximum number of enemy soldiers in the Serchio Valley, it was also hoped to clear the Lama di Sotto Ridge of the enemy forces, thus assuring direct observation of Castelnuovo di Garfagnana, the huge German supply and communications center.[55]

The operations order called for a crossing to be made at the Cinquale Canal, near the sea. Brigadier General Wood would continue to command forces in the Serchio Valley sector. Two brigades of the 8th Indian Division would be in reserve, one for the Serchio sector and one for the coast. One battalion of medium tanks (760th) and two companies of light tanks (758th) would support assaulting units, with the principal effort being directed at the Cinquale Canal crossing. In addition to the 92nd Division Artillery battalions, two battalions of reinforcing IV Corps medium artillery and one battalion of heavy artillery were to be provided. Two medium bombardment squadrons and two fighter-bomber squadrons would provide tactical air support.[56]

The plan itself acknowledged two significant disadvantages. The first was that the enemy positions were heavily mined, fortified and, from a terrain standpoint, very strongly defended. Secondly, offensive actions in the directions indicated would not be decisive and would cause only small immediate difficulties to the enemy. The plan called for the 371st Infantry Regiment to attack on the right flank, through the high grounds in a column of battalions. The 370th Infantry Regiment would attack the center with its battalions in column. The 3/366th Infantry was to make the main thrust in a combined armored/infantry task force at the mouth of the La Foce (Cinquale) Canal. The goal was to reach phase line 1 on the afternoon of the second day.

Diversionary Attack

On 4 February, the diversionary attack was launched in the Serchio Valley on both sides of the river by the 365th Regimental Combat Team with the 366th Regimental Combat Team (−3/366th Infantry) attached. West of the river, Company C, 1/366th Infantry, occupied Gallicano and pushed patrols forward to probe enemy positions. On the east side of the river, the 2/366th Infantry's companies moved into the villages of Albiano and Castelvecchio, at the foot of the Lama di Sotto Ridge. On 5 February, the 3/365th Infantry attacked to the north with the mission of seizing and holding Lama di Sotto, Mount Della Stella, and Hill 906.[57] Companies I and L, 3/365th Infantry, attacked abreast, and by 0750, Company L had reached the summit of the hill after some bitter fighting and suffering 30 casualties. Company I had encountered stiff enemy resistance, but drove the enemy from Lama di Sotto, capturing 4 German and 8 Italian soldiers. At 0750, a platoon from Company K had captured Mount Della Stella. During the day's action, the 3/365th Infantry Regiment suffered 54 casualties, while capturing 35 enemy soldiers and inflicting heavy enemy losses. As a result of their actions, the front lines were advanced 2,000 yards. The 365th Infantry Regiment, with its determined, well-coordinated, and swift attack had achieved complete surprise and was able to reach initial objectives quickly. Due to the strategic importance of the Lama di Sotto Ridge, the enemy could not afford to let the American soldiers occupy defensive positions there.

On 6 February, the 2/365th Infantry attacked at 0645 with Companies F and G abreast and Company E in reserve at Albiano. At 0850, Company G reached its objective on Hill 608, but Company F encountered fierce enemy resistance, resulting in heavy casualties. When Captain Bernard Yolles, the company commander, was killed, the attack was stalled. Company E, commanded by Captain William Banks, Jr., was ordered to continue the mission of Company F and to seize the objectives before dark. By 1745, after several hard-hitting assaults, Company E had seized that objective and was in the process of consolidating their positions. The 2/366th Infantry (−Company F) was attached to the 365th Infantry Regiment at Fornaci.

On 7 February, at 1400, the 1/365th Infantry (−Company A) moved near Barga to relieve the 3/365th Infantry. The 365th Infantry Regiment's command post deployed forward from Ghivizzano to Fornaci in proximity to the 2/366th Infantry. Elements of the 1/365th and 2/365th Infantry were astride or near the regimental objectives of Lama di Sotto, Mount Della Stella, and Hill 906. The 3/365th Infantry, having been relieved, had moved to an assembly area near Barga, resupplied with ammunition and reorganized for any future assaults. The regiment had captured 4 more enemy soldiers and suffered another 58 casualties in counterattacks launched by the Germans.

On the night of 7–8 February, the 2nd Battalion, 286th Grenadier Regiment of the 148th Division counterattacked. The first assault, just before dawn, was in company strength and repulsed. During the afternoon, Companies B and C, 1/365th Infantry, received three counterattacks, the third coming at 1715 in battalion-size strength. The companies were attacked on three sides, and they were finally forced to withdraw 500 yards from Lama di Sotto and Mount Della Stella to a position just north of Sommocolonia. Enemy pressure continued to increase on 9 February. At 0720 Company G, 2/365th Infantry was counterattacked on the left flank. At 0810, Company E, 2/365th Infantry received counterattacks on their front and left flanks simultaneously. All attacks were driven off. On 8–9 February, ten enemy counterattacks had been thrown against the 365th Infantry and 75 additional casualties were sustained.

That night, the division staff ordered the 365th Infantry Regiment to recapture and consolidate the Lama di Sotto Ridge. At 0630, on 10 February, the 365th Infantry Regiment resolutely deployed forward with three battalions abreast, the 2/366th Infantry, 1/365th Infantry, and the 3/365th Infantry. The 2/365th Infantry was on the extreme left sector, protecting the flank and consolidating positions. The enemy was prepared for a counteroffensive assault, and their defensive artillery and mortar fire, pre-sited on possible avenues of approach, was accurate and devastating. Company B, 1/365th Infantry seized Hill 906 and began to dig in. Company A, 1/365th was unsuccessful in their attempt to retake Hill 1048 and were forced to withdraw to Sommocolonia. Companies E and G, 2/366th Infantry, suffered heavy casualties in their advance and were forced to halt. The 3/365th Infantry's advance was slowed by heavy resistance and they were ordered to fall back and occupy Mount Della Stella.

The following day, Company B, 1/365th Infantry, fought off several enemy counterattacks but was also finally forced to withdraw at 1835 to the vicinity of Sommocolonia. At this point Company I, 3/365th Infantry, which had been ordered up to aid Company B in holding Hill 906, was caught in the open and subjected to heavy enemy artillery, mortar, and machine gun fire and forced to halt. After reorganizing, Company I took up defensive positions on Trebbio Ridge.

Even though the Lama di Sotto Ridge remained in enemy hands, their hold on it was tenuous, and it continued to be subjected to attacks, strong patrol actions, and continuous artillery and heavy weapons fire from American forces. As a result of the attacks by the 365th and 366th Infantry Regiments in the Serchio Valley sector, the American positions lost in the December 26–28 German attacks were retaken. A well-executed and extremely effective attack by these units went relatively ignored because this was only intended to be a diversionary attack. There were countless instances of great courage during the battle. A total of 288 enemy prisoners were taken during the battle, and one entire Italian infantry battalion, the 2nd Battalion, 1st Bersaglier Regiment, Italia Division, was completely neutralized. Heavy casualties were also inflicted on the 1st and 2nd Battalions of the 286th Grenadier Regiment, 148th Division (German).

American Casualties

Wounded in Action	241 Enlisted Men	8 Officers
Killed in Action	52 Enlisted Men	1 Officer
Totals	293 Enlisted Men	9 Officers[58]

The Main Attack

The positions held by the enemy in the Serchio Valley and along the jagged Mount Folgorito — Mount Cauala Mountain Ridge, as well as the flat coastal plain, were among the most formidable defenses in the entire 200-mile-long Gothic Line. The German loss of these positions would clear the way for the 5th Army forces to capture the naval base of La Spezia, and then permit access to key enemy installations in mid-northern Italy, and the industrial Po Valley.

The American units attacked on 8 February at 0600 along a five-mile front. The 370th Regimental Combat Team was to attack over its narrow front (200–500 yards), in a column of battalions, with the 3/370th Infantry leading the assault, followed closely by the 2/370th Infantry. The 1/370th Infantry was to be held in reserve, to be committed to combat only on the division staff's orders. The hills to the immediate front of the 370th Infantry's sector, designated X, Y, Z, and Aghinolfi, were part of the Strettoia Mountain mass overlooking the town of Strettoia. Hill X, the lowest, was 450 feet high, and somewhat round, surrounded by ridges. Hills Y and Z were similar in appearance but were 600 feet high, and were further beyond and looked down on Hill X from two sides. All these hills were studded with a series of enemy strong points, which included interlocking and mutually supporting steel and concrete fortifications for machine guns, mortars and observation posts. Barbed and concertina wire was strung out among the hundreds of carefully planted mines covering all anticipated approach routes.

The mountain leading to Castle Aghinolfi was strongly fortified from its base to the four-foot-thick mortar and stone fences, which encircled the castle at different levels. Minefields, concrete and reinforced steel bunkers and dugouts interconnected laterally, allowing access through protected cover and flexibility of movement for the defenders. Enemy machine guns were placed to deliver devastating mutually supporting interlocking crossfires. These emplacements also hid artillery and mortar observation teams with communications directly to the gun batteries, who had an unobstructed view of the frontally advancing 370th Infantry Regiment, the 3/366th Infantry which was attacking along the coastal plains, and the 371st Infantry Regiment, whose objectives were the dominating peaks of the Cerreta Ridge, a few hundred yards to the east. The thick, centuries-old fences and walls around the massive castle were impervious to Allied air attacks and all calibers of artillery and mortars. Barbed and concertina wire entanglements and extensive minefields covered by trip flares were emplaced in all approaches to the castle.

As the main force of the 370th Infantry Regiment was advancing through the hills, another regimental strike force of volunteers, labeled the "Raiders," was to move up the coastal Highway 1. This left flank force on Highway 1, consisting of a company of light tanks from the 758th Tank Battalion, a company (–) of medium tanks from the 760th Tank Battalion, a platoon of tank destroyers from the 701st Tank Destroyer Battalion, attached soldiers from the 317th Engineer Battalion for clearing mines and filling obstacles, plus the 370th Infantry Regiment's "Raider" unit made up of 60 enlisted men and three officers, were to make a diversionary attack. The Raiders had been carefully selected and had been in specialized training for two weeks. The intent was to divert enemy attention away from the main attack of the 370th Infantry Regiment and to capture and control a portion of the Montignoso Road overlooking the Magro Canal west of Highway 1.

On the right flank, it was the mission of the 371st Infantry Regiment to capture the high ground of Mount Cerretta and Mount Folgorito, where some of the crests along the rugged ridge rose to 4500–5000 feet. The 1/371st Infantry and the 2/371st Infantry would advance abreast of each other, while the 3/371st waited in reserve near Pozzi, with its Company K protecting the left flank and maintaining contact with the 370th Infantry Regiment.

Attacking along the left flank, along the coastal plains, were the 3/366th Infantry, commanded by Major Willis D. Polk; Company C, 760th Tank Battalion; a platoon of tank destroyers from Company B, 701st Tank Destroyer Battalion; the 27th Armored Field Artillery Battalion (–Company C) of the 1st Armored Division; a platoon of Company A, 984th Chemical Mortar Battalion; and a platoon of Company B, 317th Engineer Battalion. This combined assault team was designated Task Force 1 under the leadership of the commander of the 317th Engineer Battalion, Lieutenant Colonel Edward Rowney. Normally, the senior infantry officer on the ground would be given command of such a task force, with his staff being well trained in coordinating such a combined arms force. But since the senior infantry commander was the African American officer in charge of the 3/366th Infantry, General Almond instead chose his division's engineering officer, who was white, and not trained in infantry tactics, to lead this combined arms task force.

The plan called for infantrymen and engineers, mounted on medium Sherman tanks, to move forward along the sea's edge during daylight, and cross the mouth of the knee-deep, 90-foot wide Cinquale Canal, under the cover of the artillery preparation. Once clear of the canal, the soldiers were to dismount, with the platoon of engineers proceeding to clear minefields and other obstacles ahead of the armor and the infantry, with the supporting firepower of the tanks to provide cover for the engineers. Once the obstacles had been cleared, the tanks, closely followed by the infantry for protection, were to deploy forward and attack towards Montignosa. Meanwhile, the platoon of tank destroyers was to provide direct supporting fire when needed from positions on the south side of the canal against flank attacks or enemy counterattacks.

The 92nd Infantry Division Staff had planned a full frontal daylight attack along the length of its entire sector. H-hour was 0600 on 8 February 1945. This strategy obviously contained many flaws and poor planning by the division staff, who for the most part remained far removed from the main line of battle. They clearly underestimated the ability of the enemy forces to mount strong counterattacks on their own terrain. Also, not taken into account was the highly accurate and effective fire of the long-range enemy naval artillery batteries at Punta Bianca. At this stage of the war, with the shortage of available Allied artillery ammunition, any artillery preparation fire usually alerted the enemy that an attack was imminent in that sector. Intelligence failed to report that artillery preparation fire had a nominal effect on well-entrenched, fortified enemy defensive positions. Also underestimated was the devastating effect that land mines would have, and the lack of sufficient trained combat engineers to locate and clear these obstacles on such a wide frontal attack.

Day One

The attack was preceded by an artillery preparation by all of the 92nd Infantry Division Artillery, and attached artillery batteries, amplified by all supporting infantry weapons, tanks, and tank destroyers. Aircraft from the 86th Fighter Squadron supported the attack by bombing and strafing suspected enemy positions in the hills and the coastal gun batteries at Punta Bianca. Chemical mortars and artillery smoke shells pounded the immediate front of the advancing infantrymen in an effort to conceal the movement of tanks and infantry as they advanced toward their objectives.

The 370th Infantry Assault

In the 370th Infantry's sector, engineers were attempting to clear the way through the mine fields, while suffering heavy casualties from small arms fire. At 0650, Companies I and K, 3/370th Infantry, moved swiftly through the outer German defenses. By 0705, Company L, 3/370th Infantry was a half-mile into the hills, but was temporarily held up by increasingly heavy machine gun and small arms fire. The forward artillery observer attached to that company called for supporting mortar and artillery fire missions, and by 0930, the western half of Hill X had been secured. In heavy fighting, two machine gun emplacements were overrun, and several German prisoners were captured. By 1030, Company L had seized their objective atop Hill Z and began to fortify their positions. At this point, Company I was ordered to pass through Company L's positions and secure Hill Y. By 1500, this objective was also secured, with the company capturing nine additional prisoners, destroying several machine gun positions, and inflicting heavy casualties on the enemy. In one quick violent thrust, a group of the enemy was driven into one of the caves and fired on from bazooka teams from Company M when they refused to surrender.

By now, the German defenders were fully aroused and aware of all the attacking 92nd Infantry Division forces along the front. The huge 152-mm coastal gun batteries began to fire on all positions. Despite continuous attacks by Air Force bombers and attack fighters, these heavy caliber guns fired without interruption throughout the four-day battle. The same was true of enemy mortars and artillery, which were devastatingly accurate, heavy in volume, and almost always delivered timely on soldiers exposed in the open, despite counterbattery efforts of American artillery. American artillery was not within range of the long-distance coastal gun batteries, which had the most devastating effects on the 92nd Infantry Division's attacking forces. As the battle progressed, it became evident that the G-2 Intelligence Reports relative to that fact, issued daily up to February 8th, were highly unreliable.[59]

By 1600, all the companies of the 3/370th Infantry were being counterattacked by enemy forces. Company K, on Hill Z, was attacked and forced to withdraw to the lower portion of the hill. Here, they remained under heavy machine gun fire from both flanks. Throughout the four days of fighting, Company K repelled all enemy assaults. The 2/370th Infantry had been ordered to reinforce positions on Hill Y adjacent to Company I on the left flank. Company F, 2/370th Infantry was fighting their way toward Hill Y, just as Company I was repelling another enemy counterattack. At 1730, forward observers of the 598th Field Artillery Battalion, attached to the 2/370th Infantry, reported: "At this time the Third Battalion received a tremendous barrage of mixed heavy mortar and artillery fire estimated to be between 400 and 500 rounds."[60]

This devastating barrage inflicted numerous casualties in Company I, 3/370th Infantry. Two officers were wounded and the commander was killed. Many of the enlisted men, including most of the noncommissioned officers, became casualties, and in the immediate terror and panic of a devastating artillery barrage, many men began to retreat from the hill and the inferno. First Lieutenant John Madison, now acting commander of Company I on Hill Y, resolved to remain and repulse any enemy attacks. A few men withdrew to Hill X, but the majority returned back to the original line of departure.

Companies F and G, 2/370th Infantry, reached Hill Z just in time to be victims of the same intense artillery barrage. Company F proceeded towards the objective, but came under heavy machine gun fire which pinned them down just as they arrived on Hill Y. Company G discovered that due to the mortar barrage, the rear half of the company had scattered to take cover, but 60 men remained on Hill X. Shortly after the barrage, Lieutenant Madison, with the remnants of Company I, 3/370th Infantry, was ordered to withdraw. Company L, 3/370th Infantry, was ordered to secure the eastern portion of the hill, but as they advanced, they were also attacked with pre-sited mortars and machine guns. Company L became disorganized and, under heavy enemy artillery fire, proceeded off the hill. By 2000, no 92nd Infantry Division soldiers remained on Hill Y. The remnants of the 2/370th Infantry remained on Hill X despite their depleted ranks due to heavy casualties. Company K, 3/370th Infantry was still intact on the eastern slope of Hill X.

Companies G and F and part of Company E dug in on Hill X in a perimeter defensive position. Throughout the night, the enemy shelling never ceased and caused many additional casualties, mainly from tree bursts. A barrage would cease briefly, and when the surviving infantrymen would go out and attempt to pull the wounded men to safety, they would be caught in another artillery barrage, which inflicted additional casualties. Lieutenant Miles, commanding Company F, and Captain Thayer, commanding Company G, reported that they had run into minefields on Hill X and the reverse slope of Hill Y, causing many additional casualties. These minefields also caused extreme difficulty in evacuating the numerous wounded and hampered being resupplied from the rear. The one route cleared by the engineers was subjected to heavy concentrations of artillery and mortar rounds. During the night, the officers and noncommissioned officers worked at reorganizing the remnants of the 370th Infantry Regiment to be prepared to resume the attack on Hill Y at 0600 the next morning. For his courage and leadership throughout the night, Lieutenant Aurelius Miles was awarded the Silver Star medal.

Silver Star, Aurelius A. Miles, First Lieutenant, Infantry, United States Army, for gallantry in action on 8 February 1945, in Italy. The enemy launched a counterattack against Lieutenant Miles' company as it moved into a new position on a hill under cover of darkness. The pressure of the hostile attack forced his company to withdraw and brought much confusion to five other companies, which then occupied the hill. Lieutenant Miles, realizing the situation, gathered all the men he could see and led them under withering enemy fire and over heavily mined terrain to defensive positions along the base of the hill. All night he personally checked the positions and rearranged the lines. During the next day, he constantly exposed himself in keeping control of his sector of the hill. He left the safety of his foxhole during an artillery barrage to personally supervise the evacuation of two casualties and maintained his command post in a foxhole, only 20 yards from the front line until he was wounded.[61]

During the day, the diversionary force of the 92nd Raiders and their supporting armor met with little success on Highway 1. The engineers and a mine-clearing platoon were to remove three obstacles on the highway north of the village of Querceta. The town of Porta was to have been shelled, then reduced by tanks and tank destroyers beginning at 0500. After completion of the operations, during which the Raiders were to provide local security, they were to extinguish all resistance in the vicinity of Porta. After securing Porta, the infantrymen and engineers would then mount the tanks for the drive to the Montignoso Canal.

One tank was disabled by a mine as soon as the force left the line of departure. After some delay to remove the tank that was blocking the road, the force proceeded up Highway 1. The fully alerted enemy forces halted the armored convoy short of Porta with heavy machine gun and small arms fire from their front and from fortified positions on the forward slope of Hill X. The enemy kept them pinned down most of the day under this withering fire and that of artillery and mortar rounds.

The 371st Infantry Assault

On the extreme right flank, the 371st Infantry Regiment crossed the line of departure and proceeded to their formidable objectives of Mount Cerretta and Mount Foggorito. Due to the shortage in artillery ammunition, only a 10-minute preparatory artillery barrage could be delivered by the 599th Field Artillery Battalion. The division G-2 had failed to provide any information on the extensive enemy fortifications that awaited the 371st Infantry Regiment in their sector. In addition to the advantage provided by the height and ruggedness of the terrain, the Germans had constructed an excellent system of fortifications all along the ridgeline. Weapons were concealed and protected by concrete and steel bunkers or were placed in positions blasted out of the solid rock walls of the mountains. All of the defensive positions were mutually supporting and connected by lateral trails, trenches, or tunnels. In all firing positions, the weapons had been pre-sited, and prepared to fire on any targets approaching them. Concertina wire was placed throughout, with trip flares, and extensive minefields carefully planted on all avenues of approach. Tank barriers and demolitions impeded and channeled the movement of tanks and motorized vehicles to trails that had been pre-sited by the enemy artillery batteries.

Once the short artillery preparation had been completed, the 1/371st Infantry advanced to their first objective, a mountain ridge code-named Maine. The 2/371st Infantry advanced toward their objective code-named Rocky Ridge, on the left flank of their zone. Assaulting units of the 1/371st Infantry deployed quickly up the vertical approaches to Maine, overpowering the enemy resistance. Other units quickly advanced to other mountain ridges code-named Florida and Georgia. Company A, 1/371st Infantry, had a platoon near the peak of Georgia, but was held up by a minefield and snipers. But by 1015, Company A, under the intense artillery and automatic weapons fire, was forced to withdraw to the northeast edge of a wooded area. Company B had advanced only 100 yards north of the woods, while Company C was passing around the mountain to the left flank of Company B. All three companies of the 1/371st Infantry were advancing near the top of Georgia.

The 2/371st Infantry assaulted formidable positions on Rocky Ridge with two companies abreast. Company E, commanded by Captain Winston D. Wetlaufer, was on the left flank. Company G, led by Captain William E. Cooke, was on the right flank, while Company F, commanded by Captain Edmund Essholm, was held in reserve. Company E discovered they were in the midst of an extensive minefield, and the stalled company, while exposed in the open, fell victim to heavy concentrations of artillery, mortar, and machine gun fire. In spite of their many casualties, the company, while fighting off several enemy counterattacks, began clearing a path, and slowly advanced forward. Meanwhile, as Company G was advancing up the steep slopes of Rocky Ridge, they were suddenly bombed and strafed by friendly American aircraft, resulting in a number of casualties, including the company commander. The aircraft support had been called in by the 371st Infantry Regiment's command staff, who had not received accurate information pertaining to the advancements of their companies.

The immediate result was panic and some disorganization. Company F was deployed forward to maintain the momentum of the attack, and to cover the reorganization of Company G. Company F, fighting desperately, captured 25 enemy prisoners, while inflicting casualties on the retreating German and Italian forces. By 1030, the enemy started a series of counterattacks, supported by accurate artillery and mortar fire. Meanwhile, Company E, still intact, was clearing its way out of the minefields, and fighting off enemy counterattacks. With enemy resistance stiffening, the 371st Infantry Regimental Commander halted all advances in order to permit reorganization along the line.

At 1350, Company E had cleared two minefields, evacuated many of the wounded and continued their advance. Company G, now recovered after being attacked by their own aircraft, deployed to the northeast to make contact with the 1/371st Infantry, and to continue the advance, which was scheduled to resume at 1400. At 1425, Company E ran into another minefield. In spite of receiving heavy fire from the upper reaches of Rocky Ridge, the company held its ground, repelled an enemy counterattack and continued its advance.

At 1800, all elements were ordered to dig in and plan to continue the attack at 0630 the next morning with the ridges Georgia and Ohio 1 as their next objectives. At 1912, Company E, still fighting out of minefields, reported capturing two additional enemy soldiers, killing nine, and capturing two machine gun emplacements. For his leadership on that day, Captain Wetlaufer was awarded the Silver Star medal. He had previously received the Bronze Star medal for heroic achievements in battle on 4, 9, and 11 January.[62]

During the first day of the battle, the 371st Infantry Regiment lost some of its finest officers and enlisted men. On this day, Lieutenant Theodore O. Smith was posthumously awarded an Oak Leaf Cluster to the Silver Star medal that he had won for heroic actions on 11 January 1945.

> Lieutenant Smith was the leader of a squad committed to assist in taking his company's initial objective. Passing through one platoon, which had suffered numerous casualties, he seized his objective under heavy enemy artillery and machine gun fire. Using the balances of his platoon, he then captured nine enemy soldiers from well-fortified positions, which commanded the ridge of approach. Still under increasing enemy fire, Lieutenant Smith then used another squad to capture a second enemy position, which yielded numerous small arms threatening the entire left flank of the company's objective. His intrepid determination in his desire to close with the enemy and destroy exemplified the highest gallantry of the American soldier.[63]

Task Force One

Task Force One attacked in the coastal sector at the same time the 370th and 371st Infantry Regiments were commencing their attacks in the hills and mountains to the east. Initially, the Germans were taken by surprise, but it soon became evident that they were determined to hold and defend their positions along the Gothic Lines. One of the many mistakes of the plan designed by General Almond and his staff quickly became clear to the officers who would lead their soldiers in battle. It was a full frontal attack on three fronts, dividing their resources, instead of first utilizing sufficient forces to seize a hold the mountainous sector, thus securing the high ground. This would provide a secured flank for the main assault along the coastal plains. It became evident early in the battle that as long as the Germans controlled the mountains, it would be impossible for American forces to succeed along the coastal plain.

Facing Task Force One was an array of Fascist Italian soldiers, German soldiers from the 148th Fusilier Battalion, supported by many previously unknown or inactive artillery battalions, the dreaded self-propelled 88-mm guns, mortars, fortified machine gun emplacements, and several coastal batteries of heavy, long-range guns emplaced in the rocky cliffs at Punta Bianca. These huge guns, designed for coastal defense against possible sea attacks by Allied naval elements, were utilized to fire on the soldiers of Task Force One, and were never silenced for the duration of the battle. To many of the survivors, the continuous fire from these guns was one of the most terrifying and destructive weapons in the enemy's arsenal. Lieutenant Dennette Harrod of the 3/366th Infantry stated: "The sound of gunfire from Punta Bianca never ceased and the sound and the sight of heavy shells falling and exploding among us was terrifying, but we stayed there until ordered back."[64]

Even effective fire support from Allied Naval Forces that were available at the time was nullified in this attack due to destroyers' having to remain over 30,000 yards from these coastal defense guns, which out-ranged the 5-inch main gun of these ships.[65] As a result, the enemy ground forces were able to deploy reinforcements and mount counterattacks utilizing coastal roads with relative impunity.

The beaches were heavily mined, even out beyond the surf and up to the coastal road. The 317th Combat Engineer Battalion's companies, assigned to each of the three attacking forces, attempted, usually under heavy enemy fire, to remove and clear routes through the thousands of mines. But this task was usually too massive for the 317th Engineers to perform alone. On the night of 6–7 February, a platoon of engineers glided stealthily along the beach to clear mines from a wide lane to the sea that would enable the tanks a path past the mouth of the Cinquale Canal. On the following night, a different platoon of engineers rechecked the path to ensure all mines were cleared and that the enemy did not plant additional mines during the day.

At 0545, the 27th Field Artillery Battalion began firing its artillery concentration from its self-propelled howitzers, muffling the sounds of tank engines as they maneuvered along the shore of the sea, around the mouth of the canal. These tanks were mounted with soldiers from Company L, 3/366th Infantry. As the ten-minute artillery preparation wound down, the chemical mortars and the artillery fired smoke shells all along the front to mask the forward movement of the 3/366th infantrymen. Artillery fire was then called down on machine gun emplacements, located by the forward artillery observers who were moving alongside the infantry and armored forces.

The tanks, with Company L, 3/366th Infantry and the 317th Engineers mounted aboard, maneuvered across the beach and around the mouth of the canal as planned. They turned inland at 0730, at a point approximately 500 yards north of the Cinquale Canal. Two of the tanks were soon disabled right at the canal mouth. One had struck a mine, and the other's engine stalled out in the canal's water. As the other tanks continued forward, these two disabled tanks provided supporting fire for the soldiers moving across the canal for the duration of the day. By 0700, the enemy had responded to the attack with artillery, mortars, and machine gun fire. The coastal batteries at Punta Bianca began to fire all along the front, with several shells landing in the mouth of the canal. Lieutenant Colonel Rowney, the commander of the Task Force, reported: "The first one hit squarely in the middle of my little command group and when I looked around there were only two others who had not been hit. The shell had killed seven. The entire mouth of the canal appeared to turn red with blood."[66] Enemy forward artillery observers often would target white soldiers that were with the 92nd Infantry Divisions, realizing that they were most likely officers.

Six more tanks were quickly disabled due to mines as they begin to turn inward toward the coastal road running north and south, just to the west of Highway 1. By 0820, the lead elements of Company L, advancing through heavy fire, reached its objectives near the Magro

Canal. Company I was also nearing its initial objective. By 0930, all of the committed forces of Task Force One had crossed the waterway and were involved in heavy fighting north of the Cinquale Canal. By 1000, eight of the ten tanks involved in the crossing had been disabled. They blocked the lanes which had been cleared by the engineers, and this necessitated the clearing of mines from an alternate route. Heavy artillery and mortar rounds had disrupted wire and radio transmission communications to the division command post. This failure of communications, and the casualties among the Task Force command group, caused severe problems with the command and control of the attacking forces.

The engineers, having dismounted the tanks, begin clearing an alternate route. They immediately suffered many casualties caused by the accurate artillery and machine gun fire. Two tanks managed to maneuver from the beach area, one reaching a point 25 yards away, the other only 15 yards away. Many of the infantrymen and engineers, having dismounted the disabled tanks, attempted to dig in. Lieutenant Colonel Rowney describes the situation: "The enemy had brought small arms fire on the point of break-through, and I noticed a half-dozen engineer soldiers laying dead or wounded at this point. Artillery and mortar fire were falling on the dispersed tanks and it was obvious that their exposed position was the worst possible place they could be. I gathered a handful of engineers and had them prod for mines with bayonets. Then I instructed the commander of the second tank to try to pass the first tank. It worked. We now had one disabled tank 25 yards in from the beach, and a good one about 60 yards from the beach."[67]

With none of the tanks moving, the infantry begin to fight their way inland. Company L, 3/366th Infantry, commanded by Captain Wejay S. Bundara, made good progress as he pushed his first platoon, weapons platoon, and the headquarters section toward the battalion's objective, and began to organize defensive positions just south of the Magro Canal. Company M, the heavy weapons support company, followed and set up their supporting mortars, bazookas, and machine guns. Company I, commanded by First Lieutenant Melvin Walker, had orders to pass through positions occupied by Company L and place its easternmost elements about 700 yards inland. However, Company I, in its advance across open and exposed terrain, was caught in heavy artillery and mortar concentrations which halted all forward movement. Elements of the company were forced to fall in line with Company L and maintain defensive positions there.

Many of the tank crews remained with their disabled tanks, for those steel hulks provided the only cover on the exposed beach. They continued to deliver close-in direct support artillery fire with their 76-mm and 37-mm main guns. Their machine guns were successful in deterring several enemy counterattacks, while providing supporting grazing fire for small unit attacks by the surviving infantrymen and engineers. Company K, also subjected to increasingly heavy artillery fire, deployed to the east, and organized defensive positions to the rear of the other two companies, about 350 yards north of the Cinquale Canal.

First Lieutenant Dennette Harrod, commanding the first platoon, Company I, describes the battle he encountered that day: "The tanks had stopped on the beach, some hit by artillery, some knocked out by mines. Heavy shells from Punta Bianca and La Spezia were falling on us all over the area. I don't know how we did it, but we kept moving up through all that shelling and mortar and machine gun fire, losing killed and wounded every step of the way. We had advanced about 400 yards beyond the canal, when I got hit in both legs by artillery shell fragments, and I went down. Company L had about 50 prisoners lined up against a farmhouse. I don't know how I came out of it alive. Lieutenant Walker [commanding officer of L Company] was also wounded about the same time and carried out. The fire from Punta Bianca came at us all morning."[68]

First Lieutenant John T. Letts, the acting 3/366th Infantry's Intelligence Officer/ S-2, was also seriously wounded and evacuated. The battalion commander, Major Willis D. Polk, and his Operations Officer/S-3, Captain George Welch, were both killed during the initial moments of the battle by the devastating enemy fire. The citation for the posthumous Silver Star medal reflects the courage of Major Polk on this day.

> Major Polk was in command of an infantry battalion participating in a task force operation of infantry, tanks, and engineers in an offensive against the enemy, during the planning of the attack; he displayed great initiative and zeal, and had his men in a high state of willingness to close with the enemy before jump-off time. Shortly after launching of the attack, the battalion sector was subjected to intense enemy artillery and mortar fire. Major Polk then personally went out to encourage the troops and while doing this was hit by artillery fragments. Despite his wounds, he refused to be evacuated, and remained with his troops. As he personally led them toward their objective, he was hit and killed by an enemy sniper.[69]

These losses in the command staff of the 3/366th Infantry left the battalion virtually leaderless. Captain Raymond A. Diggs, the battalion executive officer, was summoned forward from the rear of the formation, and he assumed command of the battalion. After making a quick assessment of the situation, he ordered all units to continue the advance.

At 1030, the enemy launched a strong counterattack straight down the beach toward the disabled tanks of the 760th Tank Battalion. Lieutenant Colonel Rowney recalls these initial phases of the battle: "Major Willis D. Polk, the battalion commander, came toward me. I noticed that he had been shot in the shoulder. He told me that he wanted to reassure me that he was up forward doing everything that he could to get the men into position and that he would have to be hit harder that he was to make him stop. There was no bravado in his voice — it was filled with sincerity. Later that afternoon, I found him lying in the vicinity of the lead tank with a bullet hole between his eyes.

"While organizing the defensive position in the east-west line, I could hear the sound of German burp guns building up off to the left flank. An enemy counterattack of perhaps platoon strength was coming straight south down the beach. Several of the tank commanders had huddled together and were debating what to do about it. They seemed to agree on a solution collectively which no individual would want to dispute: to stay where they were and repel the counterattack. Returning from the beach, I found Lieutenant Thomas Johnson, the engineer platoon commander, who with a force of 20 or 25 men moved to a knob of the high ground on the left front overlooking the beach. His mission was to fire in the general direction of the sea and to be prepared to repel the counterattack should it come further down the beach. The tank commander called for artillery using his grid system and the artillery came down promptly right in front of the advancing enemy. Continued artillery fire and machine gun strafing from the tank, plus the fire which was coming from the platoon, broke up the counterattack."[70]

Shortly after noon, Lieutenant Colonel Arnold, the division G-3, made a personal reconnaissance of the leading elements north of the Cinquale Canal. There amid continuous hostile small arms fire, he conferred with Lieutenant Colonel Rowney. He was informed that the 3/366th Infantry had sustained heavy casualties, which included the battalion commander, the S-2 intelligence officer, and the S-3 operations officer. After spending the afternoon observing the operations, the division G-3 concluded that if the initial success of establishing a beachhead north of the Cinquale Canal was to be exploited, reinforcements would be required. Based on Lieutenant Colonel Arnold's recommendations, Company B, 1/370th Infantry, was to be attached to the 3/366th Infantry Battalion.

Efforts to move tanks, infantry, and engineers inland into the wooded area north of the canal continued and by 1500, most of the survivors of Companies I, K, and M were deployed into defensive positions. At 1700, Company B, 1/370th Infantry arrived. After being briefed by Lieutenant Colonel Arnold of the current situation, the company commander decided to use a ditch on the west side of the coastal road as a line of departure. Captain Diggs had ordered Company B to organize a defensive position to the left of Company L from the east onto the outer coastal road utilizing its first and second platoons, and to send the third and weapons platoon to protect the battalion's forward command post. As the company commander was about to give orders to move out, an artillery barrage from the large coastal guns at Punta Bianca landed directly in front of the ditch. An observant enemy forward artillery observer found the large concentration of soldiers an ample target. Despite the disorganization and large number of casualties, the remainder of Company B, 1/370th Infantry, managed to establish the defensive line as ordered.

Throughout the first day of the battle, the engineers valiantly went about their functions of clearing mines and obstacles, usually under heavy concentrations of artillery and mortar fire. At 1115, efforts were made to operate an infantry support raft across the Cinquale Canal near a demolished inner coastal bridge. This would allow the evacuation of wounded, and the resupply of ammunition and supplies to the soldiers along the front lines. Heavy mortar fire directly on the site prevented construction of this raft. In attempting to clear a path for tanks across the beach from the surf to the woods, difficulty was encountered in locating mines. The task was made much more difficult after the tanks were disabled from mines and incoming artillery, and the engineers sought cover on the exposed beach. The engineers also were unable to clear a lateral road from the outer coast road to the inner coast road due to the prevailing presence of enemy snipers.

Lieutenant Colonel Rowney recalls: "I issued instructions to the tank commander to get more of his tanks off the beach and into the east-west line. However, I did not spend much time with the tanks, as I felt that organizing the infantry positions before dark were more important. Several of the tanks managed to come into the line and by dusk, six or seven of the tanks were deployed along the beach-half of the defense line. In the lull before dark, I was able to talk to most of the officers and formulate plans for the night. We had feeble radio communication with the rear. The radio had gone completely dead. Both telephone lines had been repeatedly blasted out by artillery which was still landing all along the beach. I knew that it was useless to count on it being repaired. As night came on, I had a short-lived feeling of confidence. The unit had reached its position and had stayed all day. That was something. And while the small arms fire was light, that area had taken the greatest concentration of enemy artillery fire I had ever seen. (Later I learned from information furnished us by 5th Army Headquarters, that this area received the greatest single concentration of artillery fire of the entire Italian Campaign. Looking back on it now, I can well believe it. There did not seem to be a single patch of ground anywhere that was not covered with artillery fragments.) About 150 men, all that was left of the battalion, were dug in to what seemed to be a tenable defense. Several of the soldiers digging in struck mines. This added to the number of casualties. The main line was about 100 yards forward of the east-west road. In the center and on the south side of this road I had established my command post in a small one-story concrete building, Fifty soldiers, under Lieutenant Johnson, dug in at the rear of the Command Post, where I could reach them if I needed a reserve."[71]

At 2130, IV Corps, not having any faith in the engineers of the 92nd Infantry Division to bridge the canal, ordered its 337th Engineer Battalion (IV Corps) to construct a pneumatic treadway bridge across the Cinquale Canal at the inner coast road. Commencing at midnight, Company B, 317th Engineers, moved the bridge equipment to the site. By 0235, the S-3 operations officer of the 337th Engineers reported to IV Corps that his unit had been driven from the site by heavy mortar fire, and that construction of a bridge under existing conditions was impossible.[72]

The night of 8–9 February brought three enemy counterattacks on the beleaguered task force, with each succeeding attack increasing in force and intensity. Shortly after dark, enemy flares appeared above the frontline areas, immersing the east-west road and buildings in persistent bright light. A strong enemy force firing automatic weapons swept forward towards the sea. Infantrymen from the 3/366th Infantry were deployed in front of the tanks to protect them from enemy "Panzerfaust" fire. The tank farthest east opened fire with cannon and machine gun fire; the combined tank and small arms fire from the infantry repelled the counterattack with numerous casualties inflicted on the enemy. Two hours later, at midnight, another counterattack was repulsed, but not before they had advanced past the task force command post. The third counterattack of the night came exactly two hours later, advancing all the way to the beach, with small arms, machine guns, and grenades taking their toll on the enemy.

Lieutenant Colonel Rowney remained in the protective shelter of his command post during the first night of fighting. He recalls the fighting that took place: "Shortly before 2200, a steady increase in the sound of burp guns came from the east down the east-west road. The tank furthest to the east was instructed to fire to the east. A half dozen men were placed about a hundred yards forward of the tank in order to make sure that no Germans would attack the tanks with bazookas. The sound of the burp guns came closer and closer and then the fire from the tank stopped. There seemed to be very little firing coming from our side. The suspense became unbearable. I issued instructions to the tiny reserve near my Command Post to deploy across the east-west road. After some confused exchange of shots, quite a few of them ricocheting off the building, the enemy fire stopped. The Germans could have taken the Command Post, but for some unknown reason they backed off. A few minutes before midnight another counterattack of the same type occurred. Again there was some confusion and this time the enemy came down the road and passed the Command Post. And again, after an exchange of fire they withdrew. We were sure that at 0200 the performance would be repeated. The tension mounted and praying and moaning became audible. Another counterattack came down the east-west road promptly on schedule, at 0200. This time, the Germans must have gone all the way to the beach. We could hear them talking and shouting. Several voices came close to the building, there was an exchange of fire, several grenades went off against the side of the building, and again they moved away. The next morning, we found two Germans dead in the doorways of the Command Post. As dawn broke, I began to look around to see what was left. Only a handful of men were in their defensive positions. Several had been wounded and others had remained. The others had drifted toward the rear."[73]

During the battle, the entire 317th Engineer Battalion was deployed in action in the coastal sector, leaving the 365th Infantry Regiment and the 2/366th Infantry without engineer support in the Serchio Valley. Engineer detachments removed mines and cleared jeep supply roads on the southern slopes of Mount Cauala for the 371st Infantry Regiment. Company A, 317th Engineer Battalion, attached to the 370th Infantry Regiment, and working in conjunction with the "Raider" Company, opened and swept Highway 1 clear of mines and obstacles, often under enemy fire. When not clearing mines, the engineers fought as infantrymen. Several awards of gallantry were awarded to members of the 317th Engineers for their deeds on that first day of the attack. The Silver Star citation for Private John Q. Mitchell highlights the dangers and difficulties the engineers encountered while completing the tasks.

> Private Mitchell, a combat Engineer attached to a rifle company, was assigned the mission of blowing hostile barbed-wire entanglements that impeded the company's assault. Under withering small arms fire, he crawled to the wire, placed his bangalores and blew the entanglements. Additional enemy machine gun and sniper fire then held up the infantry assault by pinning down the Company Commander. Private Mitchell spotted the sniper's position, moved to a more advantageous point, and killed the enemy soldier. From that position, he spotted a machine gun nest, and, wounding the enemy gunner with his first shot, he then rushed the position and captured the enemy. The machine gun and the sniper thus silenced, the infantry was able to advance.[74]

Throughout the night, constant shelling of the Cinquale Canal, particularly at the crossing point near the beach, disrupted all normal supply functions. With no bridge available, vital supplies had to be carried by men across the canal. The wounded were evacuated to the battalion aid station in the same manner. Being under direct observation from the enemy forward artillery observers located at high points in the mountains, the exposed soldiers were immediately fired upon by all types of weapons.

Day Two

The declining winter weather, combined with the formidable terrain and the increasingly stubborn German resistance, presented more discouraging problems for the American forces on the second day of the battle. The inclement weather prevented the operation of Allied aircraft and all the commanders felt the loss of this support. Although the division and corps artillery were available to support the attack, poor visibility hampered both ground and aerial observation. The ammunition shortage continued to curtail the length of artillery barrages delivered on suspected enemy positions.

370th Infantry Regiment

Day two of the battle was a day of regrouping and reorganization for the 370th Infantry Regiment. The 92nd Infantry Division staff classified missing men as "stragglers." Events would indicate that most of these men did not just desert the battlefield. Many men were separated from their units and leaders during the confusion of battle and in the frantic search for cover and concealment from the fierce uninterrupted enemy artillery fire, which often blanketed their positions with flying shell fragments. Men searching for their units in darkness often wandered into minefields, tripping flares and bringing more firepower on their positions. The wounded often lay in minefields in fully exposed positions for hours or even days since evacuation was improbable. The devastating effects of an artillery barrage often made locating the remains of the missing impossible. Some defensive positions were overrun by enemy counterattacks, and the soldiers taken prisoner by the Germans. Men of the ammunition and pioneer platoon of the 2/370th Infantry were designated as stretcher-bearers, but only one dangerous trail could be utilized for evacuation and resupply. Because of the high rate of battle casualties among the officers and non-commissioned officers, soldiers often wandered, leaderless, down the treacherous slopes, joining others who found cover in houses, cellars, and caves.

All 3/370th Infantry soldiers still on Hill X were attached to the 2/370th Infantry. Officers not involved in the battle would reorganize the dislocated men. As soon as a sizeable force was established, it would rejoin the fighting on the hills. Captain Thayer assumed command of all soldiers located and began to assemble them near Querceta in the early morning hours of 9 February. At 0430, Captain Thayer reported that he had only 40–50 men in position representing the officers and men from the companies of the 2/370th Infantry. The attack planned for Hill Y at 0600 was then delayed after consultation with the Regimental Commander, and a secondary defense line was established near the base of Hill X. Elements of Companies E and G, 2/370th Infantry went back into positions on the hill during the day.[75] Company K, still holding out on Hill Z, but under constant enemy machine gun fire from both flanks, was attached to the 2/370th Infantry.

The 3/370th Infantry continued its reorganization, and reported by the evening of 9 February that Company I had 113 men, Company L 136 men, and Company M, the heavy weapons support company, was intact. Company K still remained in positions on Hill Z.[76] Throughout the day, the 2/370th Infantry and 3/370th Infantry made limited gains but managed to hold them against several enemy counterattacks. Company I, with limited resources, made an advance toward Hill Y but was again forced to withdraw under heavy and accurate enemy artillery fire. The remainder of the 3/370th Infantry in reserve at Querceta was ordered to deploy to Hill X during the night in preparation to join in on the attack on Hill Y the next morning. The 3/371st Infantry was also attached to the 370th Infantry Regiment for this attack. During the night, the 371st Infantry's cannon and antitank companies, equipped with infantry weapons, were attached to the 370th Infantry Regiment with the mission of securing Hill X and relieving the 2/370th Infantry the next day.

Also that night, Lieutenant Miles, commanding Company F, 2/370th Infantry was seriously wounded and evacuated, leaving the hard-hit company without any officers, as three of its officers had been killed and one wounded. The company's first sergeant had also been killed. Captain Thayer was then ordered to absorb the remainder of Company F's soldiers into his provisional Company G.

During the day, some other significant attachments and adjustments were made by the 92nd Infantry Division Headquarters, which did little to aid the predicament of the 2/370th and the 3/370th Infantry. Company C, 1/370th Infantry reverted to the Division reserve; one platoon of tanks from the 760th Tank Battalion was attached to the regiment; and at 1345, Lieutenant Colonel Harold R. Everman, the new commanding officer of the 1/370th Infantry (in Division Reserve) was ordered to relieve the commanding officer of Task Force One (Lieutenant Colonel Rowney), and to deploy Company A, 1/370th Infantry into the Task Force One sector with him. Company B, 1/370th Infantry was already attached to Task Force One.

Throughout the night of 9–10 February, efforts to increase the amount of forces on Hill X continued. During the two days of fighting, the 370th Infantry Regiment suffered heavy casualties, many of them to key officers and noncommissioned officers, who were always at the forefront of the battle, leading their men. These losses in leadership and men could not be replaced, and had a demoralizing effect on the men. In spite of these losses, the 370th Infantry Regiment prepared for the offensive the next day.

Casualties for the 370th Infantry Regiment during the first two days of the battle[77]:

Officers	*Enlisted Men*	*Non-Battle*
13	170	33

371st Infantry Regiment

On the second day of battle, the heavy rainfalls and the rugged terrain made operations even more difficult for the 1/371st and 2/371st Infantry, as they prepared to assault the mountainous sector. The 1/371st Infantry continued its attack against well-fortified enemy positions along the jagged peaks. The 2/371st Infantry was preparing to dislodge the enemy from their defensive positions on Rocky Ridge. Meanwhile, the antitank company, which had dug in during the night, had failed to make contact with the 370th Infantry Regiment that was positioned on their left flank.

The 598th Field Artillery Battalion fired 225 rounds in a preparatory barrage on suspected enemy-held positions at 0630, as both infantry battalions deployed forward. Accurate enemy artillery and mortar fire still plagued the advance of the assaulting soldiers. As the soldiers of the 1/371st Infantry advanced slowly through the ever-present minefields, enemy soldiers of the First Company, 281st Grenadier Regiment, 148th Grenadier Division, abandoned their positions. Accurate fire from the 598th Field Artillery Battalion had caused many enemy casualties in this sector.[78]

In the 2/371st Infantry sector of operations, Company E was still engaged in a firefight from the minefields. Company G pulled back temporarily to permit the artillery, tanks, and tank destroyers to concentrate fire on the enemy positions to their front. At 0745, only one platoon of Company G remained in its forward position. The battalion commander then committed Company F to deploy forward between Company E and the platoon of Company G, with the mission of attacking Rocky Ridge.

At 1350, the 1/371st Infantry was forced to halt its advance due to several casualties, and dug in planning to resume the attack after reorganization. Company F continued to make significant advances against Rocky Ridge. At 1700, Company B, 1/371st attacked the peaks of Hill Georgia. By 1930, they had established fortified defensive positions on the north slope, while Company A had advanced and occupied positions along the south slope. A platoon of the antitank company, after engaging in firefights with the enemy, made contact with the 370th Infantry Regiment. The 371st Infantry Regimental Commander ordered all companies to dig and to resume the attack the next morning. That evening, the 3/371st Infantry, then in reserve, was attached to the 370th Infantry Regiment to reinforce its attack on Hills X and Y the next morning.

Casualties for the 371st Infantry Regiment for the first two days of battle were:

Officers	*Enlisted Men*	*Non-Battle*
3	63	42

Task Force One

February 9 brought no progress for the beleaguered soldiers of the 3/366th Infantry, as fierce enemy resistance continued along the coastal sector. The contested area extended 1,000 yards north of the Cinquale Canal, and 600 yards inland. Intense enemy shelling continued throughout the night, severing wire communications with the division headquarters and disrupting any efforts by the engineers to bridge the canal. Radio communication was nonexistent between division and the task force commander. Messages had to be relayed through the 760th Tank Battalion. Lack of leadership or any communications from the task force commander throughout the night led to confusion and a lack of any coordination for the combined infantry/armored/engineer task force in repulsing enemy counterattacks.

The Division G-3, Lieutenant Colonel Arnold, again visited the task force area about mid-morning. After assessing the situation, with the high number of casualties suffered in the 3/366th Infantry, which left some companies totally ineffective, and the apparent lack of command and control, Lieutenant Colonel Arnold concluded that another battalion headquarters and headquarters company would be required. The 1/370th Infantry was ordered to deploy its battalion staff and Company A to the coastal sector to relieve Lieutenant Colonel Rowney, and to take over command of Task Force One. Lieutenant Colonel Rowney returned to division headquarters, and nothing else was said about the leadership fiasco in the coastal sector. Tanks from the 758th Tank Battalion were attached to ferry Lieutenant Colonel Everman and his headquarters across the Cinquale Canal. Major Richard G. Tindall, the 92nd Infantry Division Signal Officer, was also on the beach that morning attempting to reestablish wire and radio communications with the division headquarters. He, a white soldier in an exposed open field, was later killed by enemy artillery fire.[79]

The enemy attempted several counterattacks in the coastal sector that morning. Company L, 3/366th Infantry reported a strong enemy counterattack had begun, and that their ammunition supply was virtually exhausted. Bayonets were fixed for hand-to-hand combat. Defensive fire was called in, and artillery concentrations, combined with heavy .50-caliber machined gun and 76-mm cannon fire from the tanks, broke up the attack. At 0800, another counterattack drove back elements of Company I, 3/366th Infantry, which exposed the extreme left flank of the defensive line.

Company B, 1/370th Infantry, sent out patrols to recapture those positions which had been abandoned by the survivors of Company I, 3/366th Infantry and occupied by enemy forces. Exposed and crossing open ground, half the members of the patrols were either killed or wounded, as this mission was doomed to failure from its inception.[80] With total disregard for the safety of the men, Lieutenant Colonel Rowney ordered these patrols to advance on open, exposed ground, with little space for maneuver, and with no attempt at deception, straight into the face of the determined enemy defenses.

By this point in the battle, the offensive operations had turned into a defensive mission. Tanks remaining on the beach assumed defensive positions in order to repel enemy counterattacks by either infantry or armor. Three medium Sherman tanks were positioned at the junction of the Montignoso and inner coastal roads to suppress any attacks or patrols that bypassed the thinly held infantry lines. Tanks near the command post were prepared to repel any attacks that ventured in that vicinity. In at least two attacks the previous night, the devastating cannon and heavy machine gun fire was responsible for repulsing enemy counterattacks while inflicting heavy casualties.

Continuous artillery and mortar shelling of the canal, especially at the crossing near its mouth, interrupted all resupply efforts. Neither the 317th Engineers, nor the 337th Engineers (IV Corps) had been able to successfully complete the construction of two bridges that were vital to accomplish the operations due to accurate artillery fire. The lack of these bridges hampered evacuation of the wounded, hindered resupply of ammunition and medical supplies, and disrupted communications. North of the canal, heavy minefields restricted the use of tanks, which the infantry desperately needed if an offensive operation was to be staged.

Three medium and ten light tanks were dispatched to carry soldiers of Companies A and D, 1/370th Infantry across the Cinquale Canal. Sergeant Jefferson Hightower of the 758th Tank Battalion recalls the crossing of the canal on that day.

> There was a canal that went down to the Mediterranean Sea. 758th, A Company, First Platoon, which I was a part of, was given the job of crossing that canal and picking up the infantry and making an advance up the coast. I was in tank number 3, and Lieutenant McLain was in tank number 1. When he hit that canal, he turned over and all of them jumped out into the cold water and made it back to the beach. Tank number 2 tried to pass him and they turned over too.

I'm in tank number 3 and I am sure he is going to tell me to turn around and go back. He is lying there in the sand on the beach cursing and waving me to go across. My driver, who was very good, went around those two tanks and kept his foot on the gas long enough to keep water from sucking up into the engine and we made it across. Tank number 4 turned over and tank number 5 commanded by Sergeant Seymour Miller of New York made it across. As soon as we made it across, some officer from the 92nd told us to go back. "We can't go any farther right now and all you guys do is draw fire." He was right, we were drawing fire. We drew fire from those big naval 12 and 14-inch guns. We stayed around and did a little bit of firing and then the officer insisted that we go back because he had infantry out there and he didn't want their positions given away. We made it back across that canal by taking the same route. I will never forget that because the shells were coming so close to us that I could see fire coming out of the tail ends. They came right at us and we had to maneuver through them. If they caught you — you were gone![81]

While all the confusion in orders was taking place, the men of Companies A and D sought whatever cover they could from the enemy shelling and waited for someone to give some orders that made sense to them. Enemy forward observers would key in with heavy artillery concentrations on any formations of soldiers. During that period of heavy shelling, the new white commanding officer of Company A was evacuated for "battlefield neurosis," a term used to often used to describe the mental breakdown of someone exposed to combat. Only two lieutenants remained with the company.

Lieutenants Henson and Harris of Company A commenced organizing the soldiers of their command and the remaining soldiers of Company B, which were located in fighting positions along the beach extending to the coastal road. One squad of Company B, along with members of the 3/366th Infantry, had been deployed in fighting positions in and around Task Force One's command post.

Communications were still difficult between the command post and the forward deployed companies across the canal. The division signal officer had been killed earlier that day in an attempt to reestablish communication lines. The division headquarters ordered the task force to get wire communications across the canal and attached extra men from the 92nd Signal Company to perform this task. Within 10 minutes of the wire being laid, German artillery observers directed fire and destroyed the connection. One wire-laying team, while attempting to cross the canal that night, was illuminated with flares, and shot down by enemy interlocking machine gun and mortar fire. No other attempts would be made to install wire or land line communications.[82]

During the night, the 317th Engineers continued to attempt to build a footbridge across the canal. Shortly after midnight, Company C, 317th Engineer Battalion, utilizing one platoon for security and one platoon to transport the bridging equipment, came under enemy fire and were halted after reaching the far side of the canal. Enemy mortar fire forced the engineers to abandon this task. The engineers continued their efforts to clear routes of mines for movement of tanks and infantry.

Shortly before dark, Lieutenant Colonel Everman had Company A, 1/370th Infantry, deployed in defensive positions, and he took the command of the remnants of the original task force, with the 3/366th Infantry attached. Now with both Companies A and B, 1/370th Infantry in place, orders were issued that the attack be resumed at 0630 the next morning. Major Helmuth Foreschle, the executive officer of the 760th Tank Battalion, was appointed Task Force One executive officer in an effort to better coordinate infantry/armor combat tactics. During the night, a platoon from Company C, 1/370th Infantry, was also attached to reinforce the task force.

Throughout the night, the task force continued to receive counterattacks. The battalion command post continued to be the target of several attacks, as they received mortar and small arms fire. At one point, Panzerfaust fire from a wooded area east of the command post destroyed one of the tanks. Lieutenant Bracey of Company B, 1/370th Infantry, successfully led a squad on an assault of two houses near the command post which had been occupied by enemy forces, and routed the German soldiers.

Day Three

Offensive operations were again ordered for all three sectors of the 92nd Infantry Division. Early in the morning, Lieutenant Colonel Rowney assumed command of all the soldiers south of the Cinquale Canal, with the mission of organizing a defensive line and to aid in resupplying and communications with the 1/370th Infantry.

370th Infantry Regiment

On the morning of 10 February, the 370th Infantry Regiment resumed the attack on the heavily mined Strettoia-Sera Sector, after spending the night reorganizing the remnants of their remaining forces. Elements of Company G, 2/370th Infantry and Company K, 3/370th Infantry, were firmly entrenched on Hill X. At 0630, Companies I and L, 3/370th Infantry, commenced their attack on Hill Y, but were halted by heavy enemy artillery fire. At 1000, the 3/371st Infantry began their attacks on Hill Y, advancing through positions held by Company G, 2/370th Infantry, and by 1025 had secured a foothold on Hill Y as well as the western slope of Hill X. By 1300, Companies I and L, 3/370th Infantry, formed into a command group under Lieutenant Madison, proceeded to the woods west of Hill Y to provided left flank protection for the 3/371st Infantry. Three officers from the 371st Infantry were attached to this command group to replace the officer ranks, which had been depleted by casualties.

The companies of the 3/371st Infantry did not find it easy to advance through the badly hit soldiers of the 370th Infantry beyond Hill X to reach their objective on Hill Y. Company L, 3/371st Infantry, leading the advance, drove through enemy resistance and continued to press on the attack. At 1100, Lieutenant Colonel Walker, the battalion commander, who was with the forward elements of the advance, was killed by mortar fire. The battalion Executive Officer and the S-3 Operations Officer immediately moved forward and took command of the assault. Company I, 3/371st Infantry was halted by an enemy counterattack, but after regrouping, and some accurately placed supporting artillery fired by the 598th Artillery Battalion, they were able to drive off the attackers.

At 1500, Lieutenant Madison's detachment had proceeded to Hill Y, where they made contact with the left flank of the 3/371st Infantry. The detachment had captured seven prisoners en route, while destroying two machine gun emplacements and two enemy dugouts. By 1800, the 3/371st Infantry's position on Hill Y was well organized, with the flanks reinforced by three sections of heavy machine guns from Company M, 3/371st Infantry, and both wire and radio communications were functioning.[83]

At 2045, all elements of the 2/370th Infantry except Company E were relieved by only two platoons of the antitank company, 371st Infantry Regiment. During the night of 10–11 February, heavy rains fell, and the soldiers on Hills X and Y were prepared to repulse any enemy counterattacks.

371st Infantry Regiment

The assault for the 371st Infantry was planned for 0630. Problems continue to plagued the regiment before initial attack. For the 1/371st Infantry, supplies, badly needed, had not been moved forward, curtailing its ability to coordinate the offensive with the 2/371st Infantry, which was preparing to attack hills Rocky Ridge and Maine. Shelling throughout the night had decreased the already depleted ranks with a number of casualties and missing soldiers. At 0600, the Division Commander issued this directive to the Regimental Commander:

> 371st Infantry will push towards its objective. The 3/371st Infantry minus Company K will be attached to the 370th Infantry, and the 370th will have priority on all artillery. If 370th does not go forward, the attack will be called off. 371st will transfer three line officers to the 370th immediately.[84]

All priorities were given to the 370th Infantry Regiment so that they could secure the high ground to protect the coastal sector to the west. The division staff now realized that their original plan was flawed by not securing the high ground prior to the coastal assault, and attempted to make corrections during the heat of battle. But by now, too many casualties had been suffered, and the attack was pressed on with under-strength units.

At 0630, the 599th Field Artillery Battalion fired its preparatory concentrations on hills Ohio 1, Ohio 2, and other specified enemy targets. Company A, 1/371st Infantry deployed around the left of Hill Georgia. Company B, 1/371st drove straight up Hill Georgia from the north and west, while Company C, 1/371st Infantry, was facing north into the Georgia woods to protect the flanks. By 1055, the 1/371st Infantry had halted their assault on Hill Georgia, and were bypassing the hill. As they attempted to assault the Ohio hills, mines and heavy enemy fire halted that advance. The battalion was then ordered to attempt another assault on Hill Georgia. Their ranks' being depleted even more due to additional heavy casualties caused the companies of the 1/371st Infantry to become ineffective fighting forces.

The reorganized Company G, 2/371st Infantry, along with the remaining two platoons of the antitank company, constituted the regimental reserves.

In the 2/371st Infantry's assault, minefields and machines gun positions slowed their advance. By nightfall, both battalions consolidated their position and reorganized for another anticipated attack in the morning. But the steady pressure of the 371st Infantry Regiment had caused the enemy to abandon their positions on Hill Georgia. A captured German prisoner stated that his company, which had been left to defend Hill Georgia, had evacuated their positions.[85]

Task Force One

At 0400, Lieutenant Colonel Everman ordered the battalion to commence an attack at 0600 along the Montignoso Road to Highway 1. The assault force would consist of five Sherman tanks from Company A, 760th Tank Battalion, two companies of engineers from the 317th Engineers, and the platoon of infantry from Company C, 1/370th Infantry. But without communication, at 0600, only one platoon each of infantry and engineers was all that was available.[86] The small force moved out and was immediately met by a strong enemy counterattack supported by heavy artillery, mortar, Panzerfaust, and machine gun fire. With the high ground still being controlled by enemy forces, artillery observers could direct fire down on the beleaguered task force. The engineers and infantry were pinned down and forced to make a limited withdrawal, as the tanks assumed defensive positions around the command post, and fired on the enemy forces. At 0730, another enemy counterattack by approximately 50 enemy soldiers was driven off. At 1100, a strong enemy counterattack was repulsed by the combined small arms and tank fire. Artillery was also called in on the attacking forces. Now, again on the defensive, the American soldiers continued fighting throughout the morning, with the enemy finally withdrawing at 1330.

Another attack was ordered for 1630 utilizing a platoon each from Company A and Company B, supported by tanks and artillery. Artillery fire was to be directed at enemy positions located near Company B's defensive locations. Inaccurate coordinates by the forward artillery observer caused the friendly artillery fire to fall on Company B, causing several casualties.[87] The tanks, stationary after being disabled by mines, continued to provide supporting fire with their cannons and machine guns. Company B withdrew with their wounded after the errant artillery strike.

At 1730, Company K, 3/366th Infantry, positioned just north of the battalion command post, reported a heavy counterattack in their sector. With their depleted ranks and nearly out of ammunition, they were forced to withdraw to the command post. By 1800, enemy pressure continued to increase, as weak points along the line were exploited. The task force was forced into a defensive posture.

Meanwhile, south of the canal, the task of reorganizing remnants of the 3/366th Infantry proceeded despite heavy harassing enemy fire. As men from Companies I and L were identified, they were sent to small group concentration points, where they were reequipped with clothing, new weapons, and ammunition, and assigned under the control of Company L. By 1500, they were preparing to rejoin the battle on the north side of the canal, when reports were received of an enemy counterattack south of the canal. They were immediately ordered to a reserve position instead.

It was now apparent that any further attacks on the enemy would be futile, and Major General Almond ordered a full withdrawal. Lieutenant Colonel Everman was then ordered to redeploy the task force south of the Cinquale Canal. Company B, 1/370th Infantry would cover the withdrawal, and details were set up to assist in the evacuation of the wounded. A night withdrawal was ordered to minimize the effects of the enemy artillery fire. Lieutenant Colonel Everman and his command staff reached the rear command post at Forte Dei Marmi at 0300, 11 February 1945. The reconstituted force of the 3/366th Infantry was also ordered to withdraw. All tanks and tank destroyers still operational south of the canal were ordered into defensive positions to repel enemy forces reported to be attacking across the canal.

Day Four

371st Infantry Regiment

At 0600, the commander of the 1/371st Infantry reported to the regimental command post that he had seized Hill Georgia and were occupying the bunkers.[88] During the night, their positions were fired on by enemy artillery and mortar concentrations. The two battalions consolidated their positions, received badly needed supplies and evacuated their wounded. Field Order #8 had been received from Division Headquarters, and the 371st Infantry had received orders to seize and set up defensive positions on the Ohio Ridge.

By nightfall, the 1/371st Infantry were unable to dislodge the enemy from their well-fortified positions on Hill Ohio 1. The battalion formed a defensive line on Hill Georgia. The two platoons of the antitank company were attached to the 1/371st Infantry, and took up defensive positions on Hill Florida, constituting the battalion reserve.

The 2/371st Infantry outposted its existing positions with platoons from Companies E and F. Company G was ordered into the regimental reserve south of Ripa. The remainder of the battalion established the main line of resistance on the Georgia Ridge, tying in with the 1/371st Infantry on their right flank and the 370th Infantry Regiment on the left.

370th Infantry Regiment

The attached 3/371st Infantry, now under new leadership after losing its battalion commander, was charged with the responsibility of the central sector. Company L, 3/371st Infantry, occupied positions on Hill Y, and the other two platoons of the antitank company took up positions on Hill X. Company E, 2/370th Infantry, also remained on Hill X, while the remainder of the 2/370th Infantry moved to the assembly area near Ripa to reorganize its forces. The detachment formed by elements of Companies I and L, 3/370th Infantry, commanded by Lieutenant John Madison, protected the left flank on Hill Z.

Enemy artillery and mortar fire continued to fall throughout the night. In the early morning hours, a strong enemy counterattack was launched against the left flank on Hill Y. The soldiers of Company L, 3/371st Infantry held the line, but when supporting artillery fire did not arrive from the 598th Field Artillery Battalion, the determined and numerically superior German soldiers drove them back to positions on Hill X. At the time of the attack, the forward artillery observer was out of contact with his artillery battalion, as the wire lines had been cut by enemy artillery fire, and his radio was inoperable. By the time fire support was requested via infantry radio channels, it was too late to assist the soldiers.

The units on Hill Z, seeing Company L, 3/371st Infantry retreating, began withdrawing also without orders, as their flank was now unprotected. Lieutenant Madison, with his small detachment, remained in position until the last possible moment, inflicting heavy casualties on the enemy. When the order for a general withdrawal came, his men then fell back. But by then, Lieutenant Madison had been mortally wounded. His posthumous citation for the Silver Star medal reflects his courage and determined fighting spirit:

> Silver Star (Posthumous). John M. Madison, First Lieutenant, Infantry. For gallantry in action on 8 and 10 February 1945, in Italy. Lieutenant Madison's company had taken its objective against light enemy resistance. Immediately thereafter, the enemy subjected the position to terrific artillery and mortar fire, which killed or wounded all officers except First Lieutenant Madison. Extremely heavy casualties and the lack of leadership disorganized the company and it sought to withdraw. Lieutenant Madison gathered the remaining fifteen men and regardless of continuing enemy fire, put them into positions to hold the hill. By sheer personal courage and disregard for his own life, Lieutenant Madison inspired his men to repulse three separate enemy counter-attacks aimed exclusively at their position. He withdrew, only upon orders. Two days later, he captured seven enemy soldiers while leading his company in an attack through an extensive unmarked minefield.[89]

Company K, 3/370th Infantry was still in positions on Hill Z, but regimental headquarters ordered their withdrawal. Under the cover of smoke, they moved back in good fashion, and by 1020, were in positions on the newly formed defensive line extending from Highway 1.

Captain Jesse Jarman was one of many who would be awarded posthumous medals of valor. His citation for his heroic deeds states:

> Jesse E. Jarman, Captain, Infantry (Posthumous), Silver Star. On 8 February 1945, Captain Jarman personally led his company over difficult mountain terrain in an attack on an enemy hill.

Under the pressure of intense enemy mortar, artillery and small arms counter-fire, he encouraged and exhorted his men to continue their aggressive advance by personal example. After each desperate burst of withering small arms fire, he positioned his men more advantageously and pushed forward with zeal and fortitude. With total disregard for snipers, Captain Jarman continually exposed himself to strengthen his position, undaunted in the face of the enemy. His capture of the hill yielded 15 prisoners and two machine guns. The company held their position against many vicious and determined enemy counter-attacks and inflicted numerous casualties on the enemy. His courageous initiative in extreme combat hazard exemplifies the American soldier's highest standard of fidelity to duty.[90]

By the end of the day, the 3/371st Infantry had been relieved and reverted back to the control of their parent regiment. The 370th Infantry Regiment, minus the 1/370th Infantry, organized positions near their original line of departure on the first day of the attack. The enemy made no attempts to reoccupy Hill X or to engage the 370th Infantry's front lines.

The 92nd Infantry Division's limited objective attack achieved a slight improvement of frontline positions, but the main contribution was that they had kept enemy forces occupied in this sector and served to keep the enemy confused as to future Allied intentions. A considerable amount of information as to hostile strength and disposition, which was highly inaccurate before the battle, was developed. This would prove to be of considerable value during the spring offensive. However, the four-day attack, with minimal advance of the defensive lines, was extremely costly for the 92nd Infantry Division. The number of casualties is listed below.[91]

Officer Casualties

Killed in Action	Wounded in Action	Total
9	47	56

Enlisted Casualties

Killed in Action	Wounded in Action	Missing in Action	Total
73	740	260	1073

The 3/366th Infantry suffered the heaviest casualty ratio. In addition to losing their commanding officer, they suffered a total of 329 casualties (not included in the above figures), approximately half of their strength. The high casualty rate should have dispelled the notion that the soldiers left the battlefield. Also lost during the battle were 24 tanks and other pieces of equipment.

Brigadier General Otto Fretter-Pico, Commanding General of the German 148th Grenadier Division, reacted to the 92nd Infantry Division's attack in a postwar interview: "My initial reaction to the attack of the 92nd Division on 8 to 11 February 1945 was that of not too much concern as I knew that the 92nd Division had not received front line replacements for this attack. I did not consider this action as a major offense, but only as an attack to relieve the fight at the main front. I was right in that the attack was halted and no other attacks followed immediately." [92]

Within only a few days of the battle, the 92nd Infantry Division Headquarters was directed to obtain detailed reports from the commanders of all units involved. Most reported by 21 February 1945. The most condemnatory "official" report written about the battle conducted on 8–11 February was written on 5 March 1945, by Lieutenant General Lucian K. Truscott, Jr., Commanding General of 5th Army. He concluded that:

The failure of this operation is marked by the failure of the infantry and engineers of the 92nd Division. The Negro has clearly demonstrated that, in spite of excellent and long training, excellent physical condition, superior support by artillery and air, the infantry of this division lacks the emotional and mental stability necessary for combat. I do not believe that further training under present conditions will ever make this division into a unit capable of offensive action.[93]

General Truscott's conclusions came as no surprise. He had expressed similar disillusionment in reference to the Serchio Valley attack by the Germans in December 1944. In his autobiography, he coined a phrase, which stigmatized not only the African American combat soldiers in Italy, but in all theaters of war. His were the opinions that were prevalent in most of the army leaders in regard to African American soldiers.

"German launched ... attacks ... which struck the First Battalion, 370th Infantry, and the Second Battalion, 366th Infantry, both of which 'melted away.' (A term which was to be frequently used in describing action of colored troops.)"[94]

Command and staff from higher headquarters concurred with General Truscott's report and negative conclusions about the 92nd Infantry Division. They also recognized that the 5th Army must be able to maintain an offensive attitude on the west coastal sector and be powerful enough to capture La Spezia, Carrara and other key tactical objectives. There was considerable doubt that the 92nd Infantry Division could obtain these goals. Yet considering the constant reductions of forces available in the Italian Theater, and the high combat and attrition losses during the winter campaigns, it was decided that the division was too much needed to justify removing it entirely from the line.

In spite of all the criticism, the 92nd Infantry Division had continuously been employed in frontal attacks on the enemy, and had repeatedly shown individual acts of bravery among its soldiers. The 2/366th Infantry, although accused of "melting away" during the February offensive to take the Cinquale Canal, suffered over 50 percent casualties including the deaths of the Battalion Commander and the S-3 operations officer. All initial objectives by the battalion were seized and held. Only depleted ranks due to numerous casualties and exhausted ammunition resources forced the eventual withdrawal, which was ordered by the division commander. The 317th Combat Engineer Battalion continued to attempt to bridge the canal and to clear lanes for the tanks and infantry, while the white 337th Engineer Battalion from IV Corps assessed the mission impossible after only being in the battle for three hours.

REORGANIZATION

While the 92nd Infantry Division was involved in the February offensive, the 1st Canadian Corps was alerted for departure from Italy to join other Canadian forces engaged in combat in Germany, France, Holland, Belgium, and Luxembourg. The loss of the Canadian Corps was partially compensated for by the arrival of some new units. The main body of the 10th Mountain Division arrived from the United States in January. This was a unit composed of volunteers that were specially trained in mountainous terrain warfare. The famed Japanese-American 442nd Regimental Combat Team was also scheduled to return to Italy from combat duties in southern France.

Being critically short of infantry soldiers in the theater, in January 1945, Headquarters, 2nd Armored Group, the 434th, 435th, 532nd, and the 900th Antiaircraft Artillery Automatic Weapons Battalions were deployed to Montecantini, and reorganized as the 473rd

Infantry Regiment. Colonel Willis D. Cronk, who had commanded the 2nd Armored Group, assumed command of the new regiment. The 1/473rd Infantry was commanded by Lieutenant Colonel Peter Urban, the 2/473rd Infantry by Lieutenant Colonel Hampton H. Lisle, and the 3/473rd Infantry by Major Paul Woodward. After receiving 31 days of intensive infantry combat training, the regiment was committed in a defensive role on the night 15 February, on the right flank of the 92nd Infantry Division. The regiment fell under the command and control of IV Corps. Feeling the regiment needed an experienced combat infantry leader, 5th Army relieved Colonel Cronk, who was assigned to 5th Army headquarters, and assigned Colonel William P. Yarborough, of the airborne infantry, as its new commander.

Following the 92nd Infantry Division's failure to capture its objective of the city of Massa during the February offensive, Major General Almond began to search for ways to increase the combat effectiveness of his infantry units. Further, General Clark sought ways to make up for the losses of five infantry divisions from 15th Army Group, and was of the opinion that it was vital for the success of the capture of Bologna for 5th Army to maintain an offensive posture on the western coastal sector, and to be capable of capturing the strategic town of La Spezia with its long-range coastal artillery weapons. This led to a series of discussions and correspondence between Generals Marshall, Clark, Truscott, Crittenberger, and Almond. Replacement stocks of trained African American infantry soldiers would not be sufficient to sustain the 92nd Infantry Division through any additional major offensive.[95] Finally, General Marshall proposed that the most reliable elements of the three infantry regiments of the 92nd Infantry Division be combined into one regiment, and that the 473rd Infantry (white) and the 442nd Infantry (Japanese-American) Regiments be attached as the other two infantry regiments of the division.

Over a three-week period, from 24 February to 17 March, 70 officers and 1,359 enlisted men, supposedly holders of decorations and/or Combat Infantryman Badges, were transferred into Major General Almond's favored 370th Infantry Regiment from the 365th and 371st Infantry Regiments. From the 370th Infantry Regiment, 52 officers and 1,264 enlisted men were transferred out.[96] There would not be any African American officers over the rank of first lieutenant assigned to the 370th Infantry Regiment, as all the company commanders would now be white. As in World War I, it was felt by General Almond that only white officers could effectively lead African American soldiers, and that the failures in battle were directly attributed to the combat inefficiency of those African American officers, many of whom had given their lives for their country.

Under Lieutenant General Truscott's planning, the untested 473rd Infantry Regiment would be attached to the 92nd Infantry Division in its present Cutigliano Sector on the division's right flank. The 365th Infantry Regiment would then gradually relieve the 473rd Infantry, and the 366th Infantry Regiment, which were holding defensive positions in the Serchio Valley. Major General Almond had wished to utilize the 365th Infantry Regiment as a source of replacements for the division, but General Truscott felt the 365th Infantry Regiment, with their stellar record in combat, would be better employed as available infantry under the command and control of IV Corps. The 371st Infantry Regiment, with its ranks badly depleted, was currently securing the coastal sector of the division's lines and would remain in place to conceal the identity of the 473rd and 442nd Infantry Regiments when the spring offensive commenced. Then it would fall under the command and control of 5th Army. The reconstituted 370th Infantry Regiment would be utilized in the spring offensive attack.

The 366th Infantry Regiment was then to be detached from the 92nd Infantry Division's control, and it was recommended that that the regiment be converted into a general service engineer unit. The possibility of any soldiers from the 366th Infantry Regiment returning to the 92nd Infantry Division as replacements, was also nullified. General Truscott shared General Almond's animosity toward this all African American infantry regiment. He stated: "Possibly, the designation '366th Infantry' might be preserved. By organizing two general service regiments, all personnel of the 366th could be used, thereby avoiding returning any to replacement depots from which they might be routed individually back to the 92nd Division."[97] This was to be done in spite of the fact that the theater was in dire need of trained infantry soldiers.

Additional controversy would hamper the reputation of the 92nd Infantry Division. Arriving on 26 February 1945, Truman Gibson, special aide to the Secretary of War on Negro Affairs, went directly to General McNarney's Mediterranean Theater headquarters where, after discussions of field commanders' recommendations that the 92nd Infantry Division be relieved of front-line duties, he was shown the latest after action reports, written by white officers, on the division's career in combat. Some information on the 92nd Infantry Division's combat reverses had already reached the United States through newspaper correspondents. The December counterattack was the main news of the day from Italy. The *New York Times*' Milton Bracker, after reporting the halting of the February attack, observed that the official report from 15th Army Group was "unusually detailed and candid." He concluded that the Army Group was trying to solve its public relations problem on the division "in view of the super-sensitivity of some Negro papers at home, which have unquestionably tended to overemphasize the division's accomplishments ... Negro correspondents in the theater as well as their white colleagues," Bracker continued, "were sometimes embarrassed by their papers' handling of dispatches. The general feeling here today was that the 15th Army Group was taking no chances on the distortion or false play of the story of the 92nd's operation," he reported.[98]

Mr. Gibson, after visiting Generals Clark, Truscott, and Crittenberger, visited the 10th Mountain Division's sector, Leghorn, Viareggio, and the 92nd Infantry Division with Major General Otto L. Nelson, the deputy theater commander. He talked with about 800 officers, hundreds of enlisted men, and then with the higher staff officers of the 92nd Infantry Division. Biased and often inaccurate reports, written by white officers far removed from the actual battles, shown to him, he observed to General McNarney, placed complete responsibility for the 92nd Infantry's combat performance solely on the African American officers and enlisted men, failed to examine any underlying causes, and made it seem that "everything possible had been done for the 92nd Infantry Division and yet, notwithstanding this, complete failure had resulted." He set out therefore to determine not only the facts but, where possible, the reasons behind these facts.

Mr. Gibson felt that no extended discussion of certain facts was necessary. One of these was the allegation of melting away, or leaving the battlefield. "It is a fact that there have been many withdrawals by panic stricken infantrymen. However, it is equally evident that the underlying reasons are quite generally unknown in the division. The blanket generalizations expressed by many, based on inherent racial difficulties, are contradicted by many acts of individual and group bravery." In the 365th Infantry Regiment, before large numbers of men were transferred to the 370th Infantry, certainly the generalizations do not hold. Other facts which he regarded as similarly in no need of extended discussion were: the "unsatisfactory promotion policy for Negro officers, mentioned by both white and Negro officers, and the racial attitudes of the command, expressed by those white officers who commented upon it as one in which any type of close association with Negro officers is discouraged." This policy was symbolized, Mr. Gibson felt, "by the establishment of an officers' club in the attached white 894th Tank Destroyer Battalion, whose rules of attendance by invitation only were intended to exclude Negro officers."[99]

On 14 March 1945, Mr. Gibson said much the same in a press conference arranged in Rome by the public relations officer of the theater at the request of war correspondents in the area. "I agreed to participate in the conference only after being advised by officers of the theater command that there would be no objection to my engaging in a frank discussion of conditions as I observed them during my visit to the 92nd Division," Gibson later told Assistant Secretary McCloy. "The fact that the reporters knew of the failure of the division but not the underlying reasons therefore was largely responsible for my decision to talk to the reporters," he continued.[100] Mr. Gibson's views were taken "most seriously because he is the official representative of the War Department and is a Negro," the *New York Times*' correspondent reasoned. "He also is the first government official to make a candid publishable appraisal of the situation," the dispatch continued.[101]

But Mr. Gibson's "candid" appraisal of the situation and the heavy emphasis of the press on his figures on low literacy and on "melting away" brought down upon him the wrath of a powerful portion of the African American press in the United States, already objecting to the *New York Times* correspondent's surmise that its emphasis on the 92nd Infantry Division's accomplishments and its "super-sensitivity" had brought forth the 15th Army Group's detailed account of the February attack and embarrassed their own correspondents. It did not matter that Mr. Gibson had said: "If the division proves anything, it does not prove that Negroes can't fight. There is no question in my mind about the courage of Negro officers or soldiers and any generalization on the basis of race is entirely unfounded; nor that, after admitting that there had been more or less panicky retreats, particularly at night when the attitude of some individual soldiers seemed to be 'I'm up here all alone; why in hell should I stay up here?'" He had added, "not all straggling and running has happened in the 92nd Division." African American newspapers adopted a stand ranging from calls for Mr. Gibson's immediate resignation to a quiet plea that Gibson's analysis be looked at more closely for the profits which might be derived from it. "Somebody's Gotta Go!" the *Chicago Defender* editorialized: "Negroes have fought bravely and valiantly in all American wars without the generalship of Truman K. Gibson Jr.... Yet no sooner does Truman Gibson Jr. come upon the scene, the Negro troops start 'melting away' in the face of the enemy.... It is enough our boys have to fight Nazis and Dixie race haters without having to face the venom and scorn of Uncle Toms."[102] To the *Michigan Chronicle*, the Gibson statement was interpreted as "The Gibson Folly." To Congressman Adam Clayton Powell's *New York People's Voice* it was a "smear" on the 92nd Infantry Division.[103] To one columnist the Gibson Report and the state of affairs in the 92nd Infantry Division was nothing that should not have been expected in light of army policies: "Gibson knows all these things and knew them when he stayed on and succeeded William H. Hastie when the latter could no longer stomach Army Jim Crow policies. He has been an appeaser and one of the NOUVEAU Uncle Toms since taking office. He should resign at once."[104]

Two others of the larger papers, both with their own correspondents in Italy, took the interview more philosophically. "What Mr. Gibson said about the 92nd is not new," the *Baltimore Afro-American* informed its readers. "Those newspapers having correspondents with the division had such reports long before Mr. Gibson went overseas. The men in the line are certainly in a better position to know the facts than are armchair warmers back home." "The term [melting away] may prick us painfully," the *Norfolk Journal and Guide* observed, "but Mr. Gibson might not have been as wrong as some would like to believe that he was. According to news reports, at times certain units of the division, or its attached units, have 'melted away' before enemy pressure just as units of white divisions have frequently 'melted away.' Situations arise on battlefields where it seems the only thing left to do, especially to inexperienced troops. Army news releases, however, carefully refrain from the use of such terms as 'melting away.' Instead, the official communiqué would read that 'our troops withdrew to lines they could better defend,' or something of that tactful nature."[105] The *Baltimore Afro-American* had earlier given its advice to the soldiers and called for a new commander for the 92nd Infantry Division: "[Gibson] didn't bite his tongue on his tour of the war front last week.... The *Afro-American* advises all soldiers overseas to fight the enemy and let us at home battle the segregation. It is plain that the 92nd doesn't take our advice. It had no intention of fighting for General Almond, his lily-white staff and clubhouses. General Almond should be removed, quickly."[106]

Some of the African American correspondents in Italy protested that the criticism of Mr. Gibson was unfair.[107] Mr. Gibson, back in Washington, observed, "It is hard for me to see how some people can, on the one hand, argue that segregation is wrong, and on the other hand, blindly defend the product of that segregation."[108]

Following its relief from the division on 28 February, the 365th Infantry Regiment deployed to the east and assumed responsibility for the Cutigliano sector under IV Corps. The 366th Infantry Regiment moved to the Division Training Area south of Viareggio. There it turned in all of its infantry equipment and crew-served weapons. On 29 March, the regiment was relieved from division control and converted into two general service engineer regiments, less one battalion: the 224th General Engineer Service Regiment, commanded by Lieutenant Colonel Otto J. Rhode, and the 226th General Engineer Service Regiment, commanded by the former commander of the 366th Infantry Regiment, Lieutenant Colonel Alonzo Ferguson.[109] These were the manual labor units of unskilled workers who were assigned the most menial labor tasks in the theater. This was a devastating blow to a once proud and highly trained infantry regiment. With the shortage of infantrymen, not only in the theater, but throughout the army, the only feasible cause for this action was the racial prejudice that was prevalent in American society at the time "to keep the colored in his place," and to enforce the notion that African American officers were not capable of leading soldiers in combat.

On 17 March, the reorganized 370th Infantry Regiment began preparation for the next offensive. The 442nd Infantry Regimental Combat Team and the 23rd Engineer Company (Japanese-American), under the command of Lieutenant Colonel Virgil R. Miller, arrived in Leghorn from combat duties in France after a tiring trip in open landing craft. The 442nd Infantry Regiment comprised the 100th Infantry Battalion, the 2/442nd Infantry and the 3/442nd Infantry.[110] The regiment's 552nd Artillery Battalion remained in combat in Germany. The 442nd Infantry, a battle-hardened combat regiment, had served with distinction both in Italy since 1943 and in southern France, and were feared by the Germans for their tenacity in combat. These units moved to a training area north of Lucca and were attached to the 92nd Infantry Division on 25 March. Here, they received the same infantry equipment which was being turned in by the 366th Infantry Regiment.

After the defeats and the large numbers of casualties in the February offensive, the morale of the soldiers of the 92nd Infantry Division plummeted. Many soldiers felt as though the white commanders were just using them as cannon fodder, sending them to their deaths in daylight frontal attacks on fortified positions. White senior officers of the division blamed the black officers for the lack of success, and continued to plan these assaults from the relative safety of the rear areas. General Almond planned to replace all the African American company commanders with untested white officers. To make up for the large number of lieutenants that had been wounded or killed in battle, Almond planned to replace them with white officers also. The enlisted soldiers of the division grew to resent this and became mistrustful of their new leadership.

In March 1945, three white officers reported to Company C, 1/370th Infantry. Vernon Baker, still a second lieutenant after two years, had been running the company since Captain Matthews had been wounded in a mortar attack. General Almond was not going to leave an African American officer in charge of one of his infantry companies, and brought in Captain John F. Runyon to take command. None of the new white officers had any combat experience.

OPERATION SECOND WIND

The last month of fighting in the Italian campaign during World War II would see some of the harshest combat of the war. The American 5th and the British 8th Armies' strategy was developed, as in earlier offensives, to:

1. Hold steadfast against any enemy offensive gestures.
2. Force the maximum of enemy forces to remain in Italy.
3. Seek, find, and completely destroy the enemy on the ground.[111]

The 8th British Army, attacking from positions along the Adriatic Coast, and the United States 5th Army moving forward along Highway 64, were to converge on and capture Bologna. Army group's planning called for the 92nd Infantry Division to launch a diversionary attack four days before 5th Army's main attack toward Bologna. This attack might draw in the enemy's reserves in the coastal area and, at the very least, would occupy the attention of the German 148th Grenadier Division opposite the 92nd Infantry Division's lines. The 442nd Regimental Combat Team would be prepared by 1 April. The attack would be carried out shortly thereafter in time to permit some of the supporting soldiers to be diverted, if necessary, to the main front in time for the attack there.[112]

By the time of the 92nd Infantry Division's spring offensive, given the symbolic code name Second Wind, the 92nd Infantry was no longer an all African American combat division. The division was composed of the following:

370th Infantry Regiment (reorganized with all company commanders being white)
442nd Infantry Regiment (Japanese-American)
473rd Infantry Regiment (converted from white anti-aircraft artillery battalions)
Organic artillery and service units of the 92nd Infantry Division

Attached units for the offensive included:

758th Tank Battalion (Light) (African American)
760th Tank Battalion (-) (Medium)
679th Tank Destroyer Battalion (Towed) (African American)[113]
894th Tank Destroyer Battalion (-)

Both the 760th Tank Battalion and the 894th Tank Destroyer Battalion had two of their companies deployed elsewhere for the offensive. The 679th Tank Destroyer Battalion, the third of the three African American tank destroyer battalions, arrived in Leghorn, Italy, on 1–2

March 1945, deploying into combat positions in support of the 92nd Infantry Division on 17 March. It was equipped with the towed 76-mm high-velocity antitank guns. British and American artillery, air, and naval support would also be available. The division's 371st and 365th Infantry Regiments, scheduled to occupy the Serchio and Cutigliano sectors, would operate under IV Corps command and control while the 92nd Infantry Division operated directly under 5th Army control for the attack. The two detached regiments were expected to maintain defensive positions and have a follow-up role in IV Corps' later attack.

The immediate objective for the 92nd Infantry Division's diversionary attack was the town of Massa. To avoid the heavy, long-range coastal guns at Punta Bianca, whose fire had largely been responsible for smashing the February attempt to cross the flat Cinquale Canal and stream-crossed plain before Massa, this attack would be made to the east of the Mount Cauala / Mount Cerreta mountain ridge along the line from Mount Folgorito through Mount Belvedere and on north to Mount Brugiana. Once these mountain ridges were cleared, the enemy on the Mount Strettoia hill mass might be driven out, forcing an evacuation of the heavily mined plain before Massa. The attack would then proceed to La Spezia.

The 442nd Infantry Regiment, with the indirect supporting fire of the 599th and 329th Field Artillery (85th Infantry Division) Battalions, one platoon of the 894th Tank Destroyer Battalion, and a company of the 84th Chemical Battalion's 4.2-inch mortars, would play a major part in the attack. The 758th Tank Battalion, providing armored reconnaissance support, was to drive up and around the mountains overlooking the coastal plain in order to bypass Massa and seize Mount Brugiana beyond. The 370th Infantry Regiment, with the 597th and 598th Field Artillery Battalions and guns of the 894th Tank Destroyer and 760th Tank Battalions in support, would push through the lower hills in column of battalions, branch off to the sea above the Cinquale Canal, and drive on through Massa to the Frigido River. In division's reserve on the quiet right flank in the Serchio valley, the untested 473rd Infantry Regiment was to be prepared to support either the attack of the 370th or the 442nd Infantry Regiments.

D-Day in the 92nd Infantry Division's sector was 5 April 1945. In the pre-dawn hours, units of the newly reconstituted division moved silently towards assembly area in front of their initial objectives. The 370th Infantry Regiment, with all new white company commanders which had been assigned for less than a month, would again assault those objectives which it failed to hold in the February offensive.

In the 370th Infantry's sector, the 1/370th Infantry and the 3/370th Infantry were in position to assault the familiar high ground east of Highway 1. The 2/370th Infantry, moving up behind the 1/370th Infantry, planned to cut sharply to the west onto the coastal plain after reaching the town of Porta, with the objective of seizing the flat lands north of the Cinquale Canal, then clearing out the enemy south of the Frigido River. The 3/370th Infantry was to drive on Strettoia an hour after the initial attack, then advance to the high ground overlooking Montignoso.

The 1/371st Infantry was positioned in the Serchio Valley. The 2/371st Infantry was widely dispersed along the coastal sector. They were to feint an attack on the Cinquale Canal once the assault began in order to confuse the enemy as to what was to be the main objective. The 3/371st Infantry was still in defensive positions on the Mount Cauala-Florida Ridge Line, where the 100th Infantry Battalion relieved it on the eve of the battle.

The 442nd Infantry Regiment had free rein to plan and coordinate their operations and was not controlled by the 92nd Infantry Division Headquarters' staff. Upon arrival back in Italy, the 442nd Infantry's staff read all the after actions reports of the 92nd Infantry Division and their assaults on the Gothic Line. Assessing that the frontal attack tactics employed by the 92nd Infantry Division would not be feasible in breaching the German defenses, the 442nd Infantry Regiment planned to attack their objectives from the front and simultaneously from the rear. During the night of 3–4 April, the 3/442nd Infantry entered the town of Azzano after a five-hour climb up steep, rocky trails and in drizzling rain. This town, located on a peak in the Mount Cavallo hills, was separated from the battalion's objective, the 2,500-foot high Mount Folgorito, by a narrow valley, and was under direct enemy observation. All day on 4 April, the 3/442nd Infantry lay hidden in houses, unseen by the enemy. The next night, the 100th Infantry Battalion relieved the 3/371st Infantry on Hill Florida, just south of the enemy-held Hill Georgia. Simultaneously, the 442nd Cannon Company moved to the town of Vallechia and tied into the fire direction center of the 599th Field Artillery Battalion. At 2200 on 4 April, the 3/442nd Infantry deployed two companies and a machine gun platoon, under the cover of darkness, between Mount Folgorito and Mount Carchio. From here, an assault was to be launched against Mount Folgorito from the rear; at the same time the 100th Infantry Battalion would mount a frontal attack against Hill Georgia. The 2/442nd Infantry was held in mobile reserves.

The 1/473rd Infantry and the 3/473rd Infantry were in defensive positions in the Serchio Valley, having relieved the 365th Infantry Regiment, which had been sent to the Cutigliano Sector. The 2/473rd Infantry was held in division reserve in the coastal sector on 5 April.

Opposing the 92nd Infantry Division, under the command of Brigadier General Fretter-Pico, were the 148th Grenadier Division and the Italia Division, together with two additional German battalions and five additional Fascist Italian battalions. All of them were on commanding terrain, in well-fortified defensive positions. Defending the Serchio Valley was the 268th Grenadier Regiment with the Reconnaissance Battalion, Italia Division; 1st Battalion, 1st Bersaglieri Regiment; 2nd Battalion, 2nd Bersaglieri Regiment; and 3rd Battalion, 3rd Bersaglieri Regiment attached. Defending the coastal sector were the 281st Grenadier Regiment; 2nd Battalion, 285th Grenadier Regiment; Fusilier Battalion, 148th Grenadier Division; Kesselring Machine Gun Battalion; 4th Mountain Battalion; 101st Cavalry Reconnaissance Battalion; and the Intra Alpine Battalion, Monte Rosa Division. Available as local reserve were the 285th Grenadier Regiment (minus one battalion), and the possible use of sailors on duty at La Spezia. General Fretter-Pico was apprehensive of an amphibious operation on his right flank. In a postwar interview, he stated: "My principal worry, prior to the April attack, was the possibility of an attack from the sea. Such an action would have made my position untenable."[114]

At 0500 on 5 April, the 92nd Infantry Division began their attack. In the center, the 370th Infantry Regiment moved forward. Initially, the attack went well, catching the enemy by surprise. With the influx of new company commanders and platoon leaders, most of the soldiers had no idea who was leading them. This would cause severe problems within the 370th Infantry Regiment later in the battle. The Germans knew most of the officers of the division were white. It was routine for snipers to try to kill the leaders, thereby sowing confusion and panic among the rest of the troops. However the enemy reacted quickly once they discovered the 92nd Infantry Division's plan of attack was along the same terrain and routes as the February assault. Enemy pre-sited artillery and mortar fire fell onto the 370th Infantry Regiment's ranks throughout the day.

Shortly after Company A, 1/370th Infantry had frontally attacked Hill X, the commanding officer, Captain Doiranoff, could not be found and the attached forward artillery observer had become separated from his radio operator.[115] It was later discovered that Captain Doiranoff had been killed. By 0730, the remnants of Company A had secured Hill X, but were under heavy fire. Company B, 1/370th Infantry moved up to reinforce Company A, and then proceeded to assault Hill Y. Heavy machine gun fire from enemy positions on Hill Y and continual mortar and artillery fire caused several casualties, including the company commander, First Lieutenant Bailey, who was killed just short of the top of Hill Y.

In the meantime, Company C, 1/370th Infantry, deployed forward on the western slope of Hill X before dawn, surprising the enemy. They were halted temporarily, while a detail of infantrymen cleared a path through a minefield. When they resumed the attack, the enemy had become aroused and bombarded the company with mortar and machine gun fire. As they continued forward, the fire increased and anti-personnel mines caused additional casualties. Elements of two platoons and the mortar section were cut off and the radio operator became separated from the company commander, Captain John F, Runyon. Nevertheless, he ordered the company forward. He, four officers and approximately 25 enlisted men set out along the Porta Ridge to within 250 yards of Castle Aghinolfi.

In a 2006 interview for the History Channel, Lieutenant Baker vividly recalls the events of that day and what transpired in his eyewitness account. After reaching their objective under intense enemy fire, he organized the remnants of two platoons, 26 men, into defensive positions. He then personally destroyed camouflaged enemy machine gun emplacements and dugouts killing several German soldiers. After again coming under enemy fire, Captain Runyon volunteers to evacuate several wounded soldiers and leaves Lieutenant Baker and his men promising to send reinforcements. After several hours of battle, running low on ammunition and without any communications since Captain Runyon took the last working radio with him, Lieutenant Baker orders the surviving soldiers off the hill. In a running gun battle, Lieutenant Baker and men retreat down the hill, firing what is left of their ammunition. Baker stops by every dead soldier to remove their dog tags to identify the casualties of battle. When the men reach the bottom of the hill, there are only six soldiers and Lieutenant Baker. With him, Lieutenant Baker caries 18 sets of dog tags.[116]

After debriefing his battalion commander, Lieutenant Colonel Murphy, Lieutenant Baker headed to the 370th Infantry Regimental Headquarters with the arduous task of delivering his dead comrades' dog tags. In his briefing to his battalion commander, Lieutenant Baker left out the details of Captain Runyon's desertion of the company and not sending up reinforcements. He would learn after the war that the reason no reinforcements were sent was that Captain Runyon told Lieutenant Colonel Murphy not to worry about the men left on the ridge because they were wasted. This, in an effort to eliminate any eyewitness accounts to his cowardly performance. Upon reporting to Regimental Headquarters, Lieutenant Baker, after being thoroughly chewed out by Colonel Sherman for not wearing his helmet in combat, was informed that he would be leading the 473rd Infantry Regiment the next day to the castle.

The remnants of Company A, 1/370th Infantry, secured defensive positions on Hill X. After their withdrawal, Company C began reorganizing near the base of the hill. The 1/370th Infantry made no more advances on the first day of battle. Two of their new rifle company commanders had been killed, and Captain Runyon would not return to Company C, being administratively relieved and attached to the 473rd Infantry Regiment. With him deserting his company under fire, and leaving the remaining soldiers to die on the hill without sending reinforcements or leaving any means of communication, would have warranted a court-martial had this been a white infantry regiment. Yet, for white officers assigned to an African

American unit during World War II, this behavior was tolerated. There was already a preconceived notion that African American soldiers would "melt away" as soon as the battle began. The white officers, who wrote the official records of the battle, guaranteed that this false notion of cowardice among the African American race remained for over fifty years.

In an after action report of the battle, dated 12 April 1945, and written by Captain Runyon, the official records differ highly from the eyewitness accounts as to what occurred on 5 April 1945. Obviously, this was an effort the place blame elsewhere for his lack of leadership, his failure to achieve the objective, and his cowardice under fire. "There were individual derelictions in Company C, particularly in the rear platoon that lost its leader early," causing Captain Runyon to observe that "The ideal situation with colored troops would be to have noncommissioned and commissioned officers who would never become casualties." Captain Runyon also falsely stated that if he could have had every man in Company C at the castle, he could have held. "I also feel quite certain," he added, "that if other companies of the 370th Infantry were imbued with the determination that those members of C Company possessed, the high ground above Montignoso could have been taken without the assistance of the 473rd Infantry." And, he continued, "Using hind sight, I am thoroughly convinced that if reinforcements had been sent up on the 5th of April and had been kept moving forward, the ground above Montignoso could have been taken with one quarter of the casualties sustained by the 473rd Infantry, and that the 370th Infantry could have done the job alone." By now, approximately 60 percent of Company C's advanced group, including one officer, were casualties. With his artillery radio, his only means of communication, fading out, Captain Runyon claimed he decided to pull back five hundred yards to prepare a defensive position. To the men remaining, the order to withdraw was "a big disappointment ... but we all knew that we were too small to hold out any longer in that exposed position. Though the withdrawal was orderly, once it began many men of the company reverted to general 370th practices. The loss of platoon commanders — two were wounded, one in the advance group at Castle Aghinolfi and another with his platoon on one of the hills to the rear — resulted in disorganization, largely because men paid little attention to their platoon sergeants' orders. Despite pleas and orders, the men bunched up, making excellent targets. To one order to spread out, a private, paraphrasing an old spiritual, replied that he preferred to die with his friends rather than be killed alone."[117]

The 370th Infantry Regimental Commander, Colonel Sherman, also contributed to the inaccurate reports of the battle in his narrative of the actions that transpired on 5 April 1945. In his report he states: "The company's lines, with an exposed right flank, came under machine gun and mortar fire from the castle atop the hill. Reinforcements from the remainder of the units supposedly behind the lead company were called for. At first the regimental S-3 refused to accept the forward observer's word for the company's position; the 370th had not been changed enough by reorganization to believe that one of its units could move out as planned and once again Company C had to convince the regiment that it had moved as far as it had. Then the regimental executive officer informed Captain Runyon not to expect reinforcements for a long time, perhaps for days. The 370th was having trouble getting its other units to move and hold. In its 1st Battalion, the commanders of the other two rifle companies were both dead by midday and their companies were straggling away."[118] This in an effort to keep from reporting what had actually occurred.

At 1040, the 2/370th Infantry, then being held in reserve, moved through the 1/370th Infantry's lines. Smoke initially covered their advance, but heavy enemy artillery and machine gun fire caused many casualties and disorganization as the battalion assaulted Hill X. By 1410, Company E, 2/370th Infantry had secured positions on Hill Y.

The night of 5–6 April found two rifle companies of 2/370th Infantry atop Hill Y, and the other rifle company with elements of the 1/370th secured on Hill X.

The 3/370th Infantry, located on the right flank, moved out against Strettoia and Hill Z, located just beyond a jagged ridge line above the west of the heavily defended town. Massive enemy artillery strikes forced Company K, 3/370th Infantry to halt their advance. While Company K attempted to reorganize, Company I, 3/370th Infantry advanced through their lines, supported by the heavy weapons of Company M, 3/370th Infantry. Company L, 3/370th Infantry meanwhile began its assault on Strettoia, supported by a platoon of tanks, but was also halted by intense automatic weapons and mortar fire from the town and Hill Z. After mines neutralized three of the tanks, a small group of infantrymen remained in their positions for the rest of the day, supported by the firepower of the Sherman tanks.

While the remainder of the 370th Infantry Regiment was trying to get fully underway, the 442nd Infantry to the right, with its 100th Infantry Battalion attacking frontally and its 3/442nd Infantry making an enveloping move around Mount Folgorito from the east, took the ridge between Mount Folgorito and Mount Carchio on the first morning. One company of the 3/442nd Infantry turned south to take Mount Folgorito. Then, cutting the supply line of the enemy on Mount Cerreta where the 100th Infantry Battalion, approaching from the south, was methodically destroying bunkers one by one with bazookas and grenades, another company pushed northeast from the ridge to occupy Mount Carchio. The 442nd Infantry suffered 20 killed and 123 wounded in the first day of battle.[119]

On the morning of 5 April 1945, the 442nd Infantry Regiment began their assault. The American artillery rounds of the 92nd Infantry Division pounded Hill Georgia. In their fortified positions, the enemy took cover from the fierce shelling. At 0500 the artillery barrage began to let up. As the enemy tried to regroup they were faced with a sight they had not expected to see. Hundreds of Japanese-American soldiers were making a frontal assault on the hilltop the Germans had held for months. The "Go For Broke" Regiment had returned to Italy, and their presence was no longer a secret. Quickly the enemy began to recover from the shelling to rain machine gun fire on the advancing Nisei. As Company A, 100th Infantry Battalion, attacked, Private First Class Munemori watched his squad leader fall, wounded by German grenade fragments. He then took command of the squad, leading them unobserved through the enemy's protective minefield to within 30 yards of the first machine gun emplacement. The Germans turned their MG42 machine guns on the advancing squad. Quickly the men, many of them replacements, exposed to combat for the first time, took defensive positions in the protection of the craters the earlier artillery barrage had created on the hilltop. The continuous fire from two enemy gun emplacements had them pinned down. Private First Class Munemori was gathering grenades from the men of his squad when an enemy soldier stealthily approached their position and tossed a grenade. Quickly the young private dove on top of the grenade, covering it with his body as it detonated. The two soldiers with Munemori survived due to the young soldier's ultimate sacrifice.

Two years almost to the day later, on 7 April 1947, a quiet but dignified ceremony was held to honor an American hero. On that day Sadao Munemori's mother accepted his Medal of Honor for the ultimate sacrifice that he made on that Italian mountain while attached to the 92nd Infantry Division. For over 50 years it would remain the only Medal of Honor awarded to a Japanese-American for heroism in World War II, or to any member assigned or attached to the 92nd Infantry Division during the war. (Sadao Munemori's Medal of Honor is now on public display at the Smithsonian in Washington, D.C.)[120]

All along the slopes of Hill Georgia, other soldiers of the 100th Infantry Battalion continued the assault. Half an hour later the shooting began to subside as the enemy forces retreated. In just 30 minutes, the 100th Infantry Battalion had taken Hill Georgia, the opening steps in the month-long campaign to end the war in Italy.

To the northeast, 3/442nd Infantry had spent the previous night climbing towards Mount Folgorita. At 0600 Company L launched the attack on its objectives. The enemy alerted the coastal batteries at La Spezia and German artillery and mortars began to create a steel curtain between the Nisei and the well-fortified Germans. Heedless of the explosions that ripped the mountainside, the soldiers of Company L pressed forward, often engaging the enemy in hand-to-hand combat. Meanwhile Company K, 3/442nd Infantry, reinforced by Company M's mortar platoon, began a daylight climb towards the crest of Mount Folgorita. From their high vantage point on Mount Altissimo, the enemy fired accurate mortar rounds on the brave Nisei, killing 17 and wounding 83. Yet, the company continued its assault, destroying one enemy strong point as they advanced.

That night the Germans launched a counterattack on the 100th Infantry Battalion in a strong effort to retake their strategic positions. Despite the fact that the men had been nearly two days without sleep, they fought back valiantly and repulsed the enemy. The sudden appearance of the Japanese-American regiment had stunned the enemy, both by its presence and by the ferocity of its fighting men. In the first day the Germans lost 30 men killed in action, with more wounded or captured. Also lost were a dozen well-fortified bunkers, 17 machine gun emplacements, and three artillery howitzers. But the 442nd Infantry Regiment paid a high cost for their victories. There were over 100 casualties for Company K, 3/442nd Infantry alone.

The next morning, Lieutenant Baker led a company of the 473rd Infantry Regiment back up to the castle on Hill X. On his trek back up the hill, no enemy soldiers were encountered. Only the bodies of dead African American soldiers remained on the hill, all of them barefoot. The Germans had robbed them of their boots and socks before withdrawing.

The 370th Infantry Regiment, after reorganizing during the night of 5–6 April, prepared to resume its attack at 0600 in a column of battalions with its 2/370th Infantry leading. The enemy, having intercepted radio messages giving the time of the attack, laid down heavy mortar concentrations on the hills. The attack was postponed until 0800. Radio monitors then intercepted a message from a German commander who said that his position was to be attacked at eight and that if given reinforcements he could hold. The 2/370th Infantry deployed forward but a second mortar barrage halted its advance. Its companies began to move out of their positions. The 1/370th Infantry, ordered to move through the rapidly disintegrating 2/370th Infantry's lines, replied that it could not move because of heavy mortar fire. The 3/370th Infantry was alerted for movement. A small enemy counterattack at noon was repulsed. Any further attacks by the battalions of the 370th Infantry Regiment were postponed until the afternoon. At 1400 Company C was ordered to rejoin the 1/370th Infantry for another assault on the Strettoia hill mass. The 71 men remaining were called out and given instructions. Lieutenant Baker and yet another newly assigned white company commanding officer tried to work their men through a smoke screen across an open plain. Each rifle company of the 1/370th Infantry had now lost the commander with which it had begun the attack the previous day, two by death and one by administrative action. By 1455, the first of the replacement commanders was killed.

General Almond's plan of relieving combat experienced company commanders based solely on race, and replacing them with inexperienced white officers, was a dismal failure. The commander of the 3/370th Infantry stated of the companies in his command: "One company commander was 'discouraged,' and asked to be relieved. The company commander of I Company was evacuated for 'shell shock,' and the executive officer was wounded, leaving a second lieutenant in command. The zone assigned to the battalion initially was such that it made one of the attacking companies subject to fire from both flanks as well as the front."[121]

On 6 April, the 2/442nd Infantry and the 3/442nd Infantry completed the task of clearing all resisting enemy forces from Mount Carchio, Mount Folgorito, and Mount Cerretta, and were preparing to move on to Mount Belvedere. The 100th Infantry Battalion fought against the well-entrenched enemy on the Ohio peaks for two hours without making any gains.

By midday the Nisei had secured the area all the way from Mount Georgia to Mount Folgorita. Only Hills Ohio 1, 2 and 3 remained with any measured resistance, as many of the enemy were now cut off from the rest of their command. Throughout the day, the 92nd Infantry Division's artillery fired on the last defenders, effectively nullifying their impact on the advance through the mountains. Meanwhile, Company L, 3/442nd Infantry assaulted and took control of Mount Cerreta and Company F, 2/442nd Infantry and Company I, 3/442nd Infantry obtained control of Mount Carchio in the shadow of Mount Belvedere and Mount Altissimo. The latter were the only remaining major enemy positions between the 442nd Infantry Regiment and a complete breach of the Gothic Line. While the fighting had raged on the ridgelines from Mount Georgia to Mount Folgorita, the 2/442nd Infantry had been positioning itself for the assault on the all-important Mount Belvedere overlooking Massa and the Frigido River. During the day, the 442nd Regimental Combat team suffered an additional 13 men killed in action and 60 more wounded.

On the morning of 7 April, the now ineffective 1/370th Infantry was withdrawn from the lines, and redeployed back to the Serchio Valley. The 2/370th Infantry, still in its positions after the 1/370th Infantry withdrew, waited patiently as elements of the 2/473rd Infantry passed through their lines on the way to the Porta Ridge line. The movements were made without artillery preparation and under complete pre-dawn darkness. The 2/473rd Infantry advanced through minefields and harassing enemy artillery as they bypassed Strettoia and Porta Ridge. Its three rifle companies, supported by the weapons company, were deployed along a line running east from Porta, to the left front portion of Hill Y by 0900.

The 2/370th Infantry continued to fight the enemy as they advanced to secure Hills Y and Z. By 0800, they had taken Hill Z, and after bitter, hard fighting had by 1730 reduced all enemy resistance on Hill Y. The 3/370th Infantry, supported by an armored force consisting of elements of the 894th Tank Destroyer Battalion and the 758th and 760th Tank Battalions, was alerted to deploy down Highway 1 and to seize the area south of the Magro Canal. With Hills X, Y, and Z now secured, it was expected that this armored mechanized force would encounter no difficulties proceeding to their objectives. But minefields, increased fire from enemy artillery and mortars, and German machine gun fire to their immediate front, halted the advance. The battalion command post ordered a reinforced platoon from Company K, 3/370th Infantry to secure the village of Porta, and later to be followed by the rest of the company. South of the village, the force was halted by heavy artillery and machine gun fire from the Porta Ridge, and efforts to outflank the enemy failed. By 2315, Company K, 3/370th Infantry, had moved to within 400 yards of Porta.

Mount Belvedere was the one remaining major obstacle facing the advance of the 442nd Infantry Regiment, and 2/442nd Infantry attacked from the heights of Mount Folgorita. The battalion had spent the previous night hiking up mountain trails in order to get into position, and then already exhausted and without sleep, they attacked at dawn. One unfamiliar with the terrain might envision a series of individual mountains among the dominant peaks stretching along the Gothic Line. In fact, it was more a series of peaks along a continuous ridgeline, each separated from the next by a low-lying saddle. The approaches varied from dense forests to dangerous open expanses of loose shale. Embedded on all approaches were the hidden, well-fortified machine gun emplacements of the battle-hardened Kesselring Machine Gun Battalion.

Darting from boulder to boulder, the soldiers of the 2/442nd Infantry advanced on the Germans entrenched on Mount Belvedere. Mortar fire began to fall among the ranks of the battalion as the enemy struggled to hold their last bastion in the chain of mountains that sheltered Massa and the Frigido River. Company F, 2/442nd Infantry was moving forward when three enemy machine gun emplacements opened up on one of its platoons in a deadly crossfire that halted the advance and sent the men seeking cover. Technical Sergeant Yukio Okutsu watched the deadly interlocking machine gun fire cross the hillside. Slowly he began to crawl towards the first enemy position, moving within 30 yards. Then he raised up, throwing two grenades. The enemy gun fell silent, the grenades killing the men who had manned it. Sergeant Okutsu moved on. Locating the position of the second machine gun, he maneuvered from rock to rock, and then hugged the barren ground to crawl from one vantage point to the next. Again he raised up to throw a well-aimed grenade in the direction of the enemy. The second position fell silent, with two of its gunners wounded. The remaining enemy soldiers at that position quickly surrendered. A third MG42 machine gun position continued to fire. Bullets ricocheted off the hard shale of the hillside as Sergeant Okutsu continued his one-man assault. Suddenly the brave sergeant staggered from the impact of a hard blow to the head. As Sergeant Okutsu staggered, his men could hear the sound of the impact on his helmet. Fortunately, the steel helmet deflected the round and, recovering quickly, Sergeant Okutsu rushed the enemy position with his submachine gun firing. Under the unrelenting charge, the enemy withdrew. Sergeant Okutsu's men were spared, able to rise up and move forward.[122]

The Nisei of the 2/442nd Infantry spent the day attacking the fortified positions of some of Germany's finest machine gunners. By 1800, the 2/442nd Infantry had overcome enemy resistance on Mount Belvedere and on the night of 7–8 April, a strong enemy counterattack was repulsed with severe enemy losses inflicted. The Kesselring Machine Gun Battalion was, for all practical purposes, not only nullified, but also rendered useless for the remainder of the war.

The 100th Infantry Battalion cleared its sector of enemy forces and improved their defensive positions along the ridge from Mount Cauala to Mount Cerretta. A combat patrol from Company B moved into the town of Strettoia, below Rocky Ridge, and occupied it without opposition. The 100th Infantry Battalion was now in control of Strettoia, and the Mount Cauala/Mount Cerreta Ridge.[123] The 3/442nd Infantry prepared to attack German strong points along the Colle Piano ridge line and seize Montignoso.

In the center of the 92nd Infantry Division's offensive sector, the 2/473rd Infantry and the 2/370th Infantry had driven the enemy from the Strettoia Hills X Y, and Z, and from around Castle Aghinolfi. On the plains below the Porta Ridge, the 3/370th Infantry, along with its supporting armored force, was preparing to resume its advance up Highway 1. The 3/370th Infantry was attached to the 473rd Infantry Regiment for command and control, as the 1/473rd was deploying forward to the assemble area near Pietrasanta. The 3/473rd Infantry was still in the Serchio Valley. Along the coastal sector, Company E, 2/370th Infantry relieved the 2/371st Infantry, which was occupying defensive positions near the Cinquale Canal. The 2/371st Infantry then rejoined the rest of its regiment, which was deployed east of the 92nd Infantry Division's sector under the command and control of IV Corps.

Company K, 3/370th Infantry, finding no enemy in the town of Porta or the hills immediately due east of there, proceeded up Highway 1, and by 1120 had reached the road junction of Highway 1 and the Montignoso Road beyond the castle. The 473rd Infantry Regiment was then given control of the coastal sector, and the 370th Infantry Regiment, minus 3/370th Infantry, resumed control of the Serchio Valley.

On 8 April, the 3/370th Infantry resumed their attack, and by 0900, Company L, located on the western sector, had advanced to within 200 yards of the Frigido River. Company I, in the center, was delayed by three machine gun emplacements. Elements of the company attacked, neutralizing the positions, but suffering 11 wounded, including the acting company commander. They captured four enemy prisoners and continued their assault, advancing slowly under continued heavy fire from all available German weapons. Several light tanks from the 758th Tank Battalion were sent through Company L's sector to silence fortified enemy machine gun emplacements located in several buildings to the company's immediate front. That night, after fighting the stubborn enemy for five days, the 3/370th Infantry was deployed to the east side of the Serchio River, where it rejoined the 1/370th Infantry under the command of the 370th Infantry Regiment. The 2/370th Infantry was the only original infantry battalion of the 92nd Infantry Division still involved in the fighting in the coastal sector. After clearing Strettoia, the soldiers moved through the town of Montignoso and maintained security of the right flank in the coastal sector.

So swiftly had the 442nd Infantry Regiment taken their objectives, it was often hard for the supporting supply lines behind them to keep up with the advancing soldiers on the front. While 2/442nd Infantry had been assaulting Mount Belvedere the previous day, Company K, 3/442nd Infantry, had been moving so swiftly they had actually moved beyond their initial enemy-held objective. Turning back, they approached their assigned position from the rear, catching the enemy unprepared and quickly capturing 20 German soldiers. The 3/442nd Infantry advanced down the Colle Piano ridgeline, capturing an additional 16 enemy prisoners as they occupied Montignoso. The 2/442nd Infantry attacked Colle Tecchione, another ridge of Mount Belvedere, and immediately came under constant artillery fire. In a three-hour firefight, eight Germans were killed and six taken prisoner, and three machine gun emplacements destroyed.

Major General Almond was not pleased with the advance of the battalions of the 473rd Infantry Regiment. They proved to be no better than the battalions of the 92nd Infantry Division when making frontal attacks against well-fortified enemy positions, dispelling the belief that the white soldiers' combat capabilities were superior to the African American soldiers.' Not wanting to have blame placed on his leadership for the 473rd Infantry Regiment's failures, Major General Almond relieved two battalion commanders, and four rifle company commanders, replacing them with infantry officers selected from his staff. Lieutenant Colonel John J. Phelan, executive officer of the 370th Infantry Regiment, assumed command of the 1/473rd Infantry. Major Robert H. Kirkwood of the division headquarters staff assumed command of 2/473rd Infantry Battalion.

The 1/473rd Infantry fought all night on 8–9 April, supported by tanks of the 760th Tank Battalion. By dusk on 9 April, they had reached the outskirts of the town of Massa. Tanks of the 758th and 760th Tank Battalions reached the center of town, but were forced to withdraw due to heavy antitank fire. The coastal artillery guns continued to fire on the entire coastal sector front-line units, despite aerial and naval bombardment. Ten armored vehicles were lost to the devastating fire from these coastal guns. The 3/473rd Infantry continued to advance towards Rocca, east of Massa, coming on line with the 1/473rd Infantry.

The 2/473rd remained in division reserve. Eventually, all elements of the 473rd Infantry Regiment would be reunited for the final offensive push in the coastal sector.

On 9 April, the 2/442nd Infantry became engaged in a bitter battle for the town of Pariana. Infantry elements secured Altagnana and Pariana after heavy fighting. The latter was a small village to which the survivors of the battered Kesselring Machine Gun Battalion had withdrawn. All day and into the night, Companies E and F, 2/442nd Infantry took the battle to the 150 survivors of the infamous German battalion. By 10 April, of the 150 enemy soldiers trapped in the village, 65 were killed and 62 were captured. Twelve enemy mortars and 8 enemy machine guns were secured as well in the fierce fighting. The 2/442nd Infantry then advanced on to the Frigido River line where they secured defensive positions along the southern bank. The 3/442nd Infantry moved northwest along the slopes of Mount Belvedere against stiff resistance. The 100th Infantry Battalion, which had been protecting the regimental right and rear flanks on Mount Folgorito, Mount Carchia, and Mount Belvedere, were relieved by the 2/370th Infantry (minus Company E). The 100th Infantry Battalion then assembled in the vicinity of Altagnana as the regimental reserve.

When Massa was outflanked from the hills on the east, the enemy evacuated the town. The 1/473rd Infantry, supported by elements of the 758th and 760th Tank Battalions, fighting against M42 machine gun emplacements and snipers left as a rear guard, reached the center of the city. Fighting continued throughout the day as pockets of resistance were eliminated. The 2/473rd Infantry advanced on the left flank to the south bank of the Frigido River.

On 10 April, the 442nd Infantry Regiment continued its advance as it crossed the Frigido River and proceeded 3,000 yards north to occupy the high ground before the marble mining center of Carrara, a city of about 50,000 people. The 2/442nd Infantry seized the 3,000-foot Mount Brugiana, which overlooked the city. Elements of the 100th Infantry Battalion occupied the town of Ancona on the eastern flank of the regiment while the regiment's antitank company blocked the road leading into Massa from the east.

With the success of the 92nd Infantry Division's advance along the coast, the Germans were forced to risk weakening the Serchio Valley by removing two battalions from there. This left only enemy Italian forces in the Serchio Valley. These measures proved to be insufficient, and eventually the 361st Panzer Grenadier Regiment of the 90th Panzer Grenadier Division in Bologna area were sent to the west coast. With the success of their advances, General Truscott authorized the 92nd Infantry Division to continue its attack to secure the port of La Spezia. The American 5th and the British 8th Armies commenced their attacks as planned on the 10th of April.

Having finally breached the Gothic Line, the 92nd Infantry Division now faced the next line of defense, the Green Line defenses. The Germans developed a series of well-fortified defensive lines that they were able to fall back to throughout Italy. In addition to the 281st and 285th Grenadier Regiments, the coastal sector was defended by at least one battalion of the 286th Grenadier Regiment, the 4th High Mountains Battalion, the 1048th Engineer Battalion, the 907th Fortress Battalion, the 1st Battalion, 361st Panzer Grenadier Regiment, plus marines, sailors, and service soldiers from La Spezia supported by the coastal guns of Punta Bianca.

In order to speed the advance, an armored task force under the command of Lieutenant Colonel Claire Curtis was formed. It consisted of the 758th Tank Battalion (minus Company A); Headquarters and Company B, 760th Tank Battalion; Company A, 894th Tank Destroyer Battalion; Company E, 2/370th Infantry; and the Antitank Company, 473rd Infantry Regiment. Task Force Curtis was given the mission of clearing the coastal sector west of Massa.

The 1/473rd Infantry and the 2/473rd Infantry were ordered to continue the attack and capture the port of La Spezia. The 442nd Infantry Regiment was directed to continue its attack and capture the important road junction of Aulla, northeast of La Spezia. The 370th Infantry Regiment (minus 2/370th Infantry), with the 3/473rd Infantry attached, was directed to hold its position in the Serchio sector, patrol aggressively, and follow any enemy withdrawal. The 2/370th Infantry with the attached 1st Platoon of the 92nd Cavalry Reconnaissance Troop was to fill the mountainous gap between and the 442nd and 370th Infantry Regiments.

Attempts by the 473rd Infantry Regiment to cross the Frigido River on the afternoon of 10 April were fiercely contested until the 2/473rd Infantry brought up a platoon of the 894th Tank Destroyer Battalion, and had them fire throughout the afternoon on the numerous enemy gun emplacements in the houses along the north bank. The battalion was able to complete its crossing under the cover of darkness, and immediately repulsed an enemy counterattack. The 1/473rd met strong resistance, so its efforts to cross the Frigido River were delayed until noon on 11 April. Despite Allied aerial bombing, the Punta Bianca heavy coastal artillery guns shelled the river crossings and the town of Massa continuously.

The 370th Infantry Regiment continued active patrolling in the Serchio sector, being denied the opportunity to participate in the main assault. Task Force Curtis proceeded slowly forward as it was subjected to heavy fire from the high ground on the right flank and from enemy guns at Punta Bianca. Resupply became critical for the 442nd Infantry, as they had advanced far beyond their logistical support lines, and to a lesser extent for the 473rd Infantry. The Massa-Carrara road was rendered impassable due to mines laid, craters, roadblocks, and constant artillery fire. Four bulldozers of the 232nd Combat Engineers, attempting to repair the road on 11 April, were destroyed by mines and artillery fire. The harsh terrain and enemy artillery fire prevented movement of carrying parties, making it necessary to resupply via airdrops.

The units of the 92nd Infantry Division now came up against the next of the enemy's strong defense lines, running behind Carrione Creek. The Germans had begun to commit their available reserves. A company each of the 1048th Engineer Battalion and the 907th Fortress Battalion were already committed and virtually destroyed.[124] On 14 April, a battalion of the 90th Panzer Division, one of the two reserve divisions available to the German Fourteenth Army, was committed.

Lieutenant Colonel Phelan started his 1/473rd Infantry in the attack against Hill 366, with Company B assaulting the left, and Company A on the right. Heavy enemy resistance forced Company C to be committed from battalion reserve on 13 April. The final assault through heavy fire netted Sergeant Antonio Tanas and his squad 52 enemy prisoners. But before the position was completely consolidated, the hill was saturated with a mortar and artillery barrage. One round landed in the doorway of a church being utilized as a the battalion command post, killing Lieutenant Colonel Phelan, several members of his command staff, and some of the prisoners of war. From 14 through 19 April, the stiffening resistance of the reinforced enemy slowed the advance of the 92nd Infantry Division, but the attack had achieved its purpose. Its primary objectives had been secured, the enemy on its front had been badly mauled, and all reserves the enemy dared use had been committed just in time to prevent their use against the main attacking force of 5th Army.

The 2/442nd Infantry moved five miles north of Carrara, passing by the towns of Gragnana and Castelpoggio and pursuing the retreating enemy. Just as 2/442nd Infantry reached the base of the mountain, the German gunners commenced firing. The battalion was quickly pinned down, as was the 100th Infantry Battalion slightly a mile behind them. The advance halted and casualties began to mount. The enemy had been retreating in disarray, but quickly reorganized in new defensive positions. The heavy enemy coastal guns at La Spezia fired upon both American battalions, while also dropping artillery on 3/442nd Infantry being held in reserve at Carrara. For the Americans, there was no friendly heavy artillery fire support. So quickly had the 442nd Infantry Regiment advanced, their supporting artillery could not maintain the pace to keep up with them. Under cover of darkness that night, Company B, 100th Infantry slipped quietly into Castelpoggia to support the 2/442nd Infantry's command group. Meanwhile, also during the night, the Allied artillery deployed its big guns forward to lend fire and counterbattery support. On the morning of 14 April, the Germans sent a battalion to attack Castelpoggia. They were caught unprepared by the developments of the dark hours of the previous night. In the bitter fighting that followed the enemy was thrown back with many casualties. The 442nd Infantry Regiment suffered five of their own comrades killed in action, and five more were wounded.

Brigadier General William Colbern, commander of the 92nd Division Artillery, coordinated the use of his 155-mm guns of the 600th Field Artillery Battalion in suppressing hostile antiaircraft batteries protecting the coastal guns at Punta Bianca. The daily aerial attacks had no effect on the operations of the well-fortified naval guns. By 14 April, leading elements of the attacking forces had advanced sufficiently to permit Allied artillery to come into range. The task of eliminating these enemy guns fell to the soldiers of the 679th Tank Destroyer Battalion. The battalion utilized all 36 of its towed 76-mm guns in neutralizing these naval guns. The ports of the coastal guns were covered by steel doors and were opened to permit the guns to fire. Each time an enemy gun fired, it received 60 to 180 high velocity rounds, aimed at the ports, from the tank destroyer crews. Enemy self-propelled guns, which attempted to duel with the tank destroyers, were quickly silenced. By 19 April, all of the guns on the east side of Punta Bianca had been destroyed.[125]

The 5th Army launched the main attack on 14 April. The IV Corps attacked with its three divisions and the two infantry regiments of the 92nd Infantry Division. In II Corps, the 88th Infantry Division and the 6th South African Armored Division's main objective was the capture of Bologna. On the IV Corps front, on the right of the 92nd Infantry Division, was the 365th Infantry Regiment in the Cutigliano sector, and the 371st Infantry Regiment, which on 9 April had taken over part of the Brazilians' sector, thinly held the left half of the IV Corps' line. These units, now under IV Corps command and control, were expected to continue patrolling and to harass the enemy with artillery fire while the divisions to their right made the main thrust into the Po Valley. The 371st Infantry patrolled in company strength, its units engaging in successful firefights on 14 April and reaching the Leo River on 16 April. Their reconnaissance patrols crossed the river and attacked the enemy's main line of resistance. Because there was no advantage in consolidating positions in low plains, the 371st Infantry Regiment ordered its companies in. The regimental commander, Colonel James Notestein, now fully realized something that he and the whole command of the division had sensed all along but could not demonstrate: that missions are best performed when units know what the objectives are and believe that they can be accomplished.[126] Patrols continued forward from both the 365th Infantry and the 371st Infantry Regiments. The 371st Infantry Regiment assumed control over more of the Brazilian Expeditionary Force's sector on 18 April as the Brazilians moved out on the right. Against little resistance, and most of that from rear guard detachments and bypassed elements of the withdrawing enemy, both regiments moved forward. On 25 and 26 April, they began guarding the many prisoners of war, with the 1/371st Infantry (–) moving to Bologna on 27 April to relieve the Italian Legnano Group.

Task Force Curtis crossed the Carrione Creek on 15 April, and their tanks began to roll on the afternoon of 16 April. In the Serchio sector, the 370th Infantry continued active patrolling, occupying Fiattone without opposition. Indications were that the enemy had stealthily withdrawn from this sector, and combat patrols occupied Campo and Bechelli on 17 April. On 19 April, patrols deployed forward, and the important road junction and communications center of Castelnuovo was occupied. The 3/473rd Infantry was detached from the 370th Infantry Regiment and returned to its parent unit. The 2/370th Infantry, operating in an area between the coastal plains and Serchio sectors, occupied Mount Antona and Mount Altissimo on 20 April. On 19 April, the regiment began a wide enveloping action through the mountains to meet the 442nd Infantry Regiment at Aulla and to block further movement of enemy troops in an east-west direction, thus preventing the formation of another German line. On the morning of 20 April soldiers of the 370th Infantry entered Castelnuovo di Garfagnana and continued the pursuit northwest along the main road to Aulla. Demolished bridges and road craters made the movement of vehicles and supplies difficult. All advances were on foot. With wire communication next to impossible, radio and runners were relied on completely.

The remainder of Company C, under the command of yet another nameless, forgotten captain, slowly regrouped after those brutal days in early April and slogged north for the remainder of the war. The Germans ran. The remaining Italian Fascist troops disintegrated.

In the week that followed, the Allied advance continued at a furious pace. On April 17th the Germans destroyed their railroad guns at La Spezia, pulling back to concentrate their forces in and around Aulla in the Po Valley. For three days the enemy continued to destroy their fortifications to keep them from falling to the Allies, while pulling all their manpower into a tight last-ditch defense of Aulla. To take Aulla the 442nd Infantry Regiment battled their way over Mount Pizzaculo and Mount Grugola stretching along the coast from Castelpoggio to Aulla. Along the way they entered the small town of San Terenzo. From there, the attacks would be launched to take Aulla. Task Force Fukuda, consisting of Company B, 100th Infantry and Company F, 2/442nd Infantry, would launch their assault from the coast, while the 100th Infantry and 3/442nd Infantry Battalions would be attacking from the inland side. In their path loomed the towering heights of Mount Nebbione southeast of Aulla, the last high ground to protect the Germans fighting for survival in Italy. On April 19th, the 2/442nd Infantry and the 3/442nd Infantry Battalions assaulted Mount Nebbione. After a day of fierce fighting, the enemy held and the Nisei pulled back to recover and plan for a renewed effort. On their flank the 100th Infantry Battalion was lending support by taking the towns of Marciaso and Posterla. Next in line for the 100th Infantry Battalion was the town of Colle Musatello.

The 370th Infantry continued its advance to the northeast against light resistance. Numerous mines and obstacles along the road slowed the advance. On 22 April, the 1/370th Infantry encountered stiffer resistance in the vicinity of Camporgiano. A captured enemy field order detailed the new line of German resistance that was being organized. Under the cover of darkness on 23 April, the 3/370th Infantry deployed to the town of Gramolazzo and along the enemy's next planned line of resistance before they could get there. Moving on to Casala, the battalion defeated the German garrison after a brief firefight, capturing two German officers and 24 enemy enlisted soldiers. The 2/370th Infantry, after a two-day road march, rejoined their regiment and moved on to Gragnola.

On 20 April, the 3/442nd Infantry encountered stiff enemy resistance in the vicinity of Fosdinovo and Tendola. On 21 April, both the 100th Infantry Battalion and the 2/442nd

Infantry attacked along the Colle Musatello ridgeline. Fresh soldiers of the 3rd Battalion, 361st Grenadier Regiment, 90th Panzer Grenadier Division defended the ridge. By now, the 442nd Infantry Regiment had been fighting nonstop for nearly two weeks in the rugged terrain of the high North Apennines Mountains.

Lieutenant Daniel Inouye positioned his platoon for the assault in the early morning darkness. With the first rays of sunlight, his rifle platoon would join two others in the assault on the heavily defended ridge that was Colle Musatello. Daniel Inouye had trained with the 442nd Infantry Regiment at Camp Shelby, Mississippi, shipped out with the Regimental Combat Team to Europe, and arrived a year earlier at Naples. Promoted en route to Italy to sergeant, he was transferred to the 100th Infantry Battalion as a replacement, and had fought through the first assault north to the Arno River. He served valiantly in Italy and in the Vosges sector in France. For his outstanding leadership in combat, he received a battlefield commission to second lieutenant. Two rifle platoons would attack Colle Musatello from the front while Lieutenant Inouye's third platoon would encircle and assault the hill from the rear.

At the first sounds of gunfire from the other two platoons, Lieutenant Inouye led his own men forward, rapidly encircling the enemy. His third platoon quickly defeated an enemy patrol, captured a mortar position, and moved to within 40 yards of the main defensive force the Germans had emplaced on Colle Musatello. So well had the attack been coordinated by the third platoon, that it was in position to assault the main fortifications while first and second platoons were still struggling to make their way through enemy defenses further down the ridge. As the platoon began their assault on the last German stronghold, three enemy M42 machine guns began firing at the advancing soldiers, forcing them to take cover. The platoon was pinned down in a crossfire from the three guns. Lieutenant Inouye crawled to within five yards of the closest machine gun and threw two grenades into the emplacement. He then stood up and destroyed the second gun crew with fire from his Thompson submachine gun. He was wounded in the abdomen by a bullet, which exited through his back. Ignoring the pain, he continued to press his attack. Approaching another machine gun emplacement, he destroyed it with two grenades. Inspired by their lieutenant, the third platoon attacked another German machine gun fortification.

The platoon's assault monopolized the attention of the enemy at the last machine gun fortification. Lieutenant Inouye used the diversion to his advantage, crawling unseen along the enemy flank. As he pulled the pin on his last grenade, one of the enemy soldiers discovered him and quickly fired a rifle grenade in his direction. The explosion nearly severed his right arm, which remained in place by only a few tendons. Clutched in the nearly detached hand that could no longer respond to impulses from the brain was the grenade. With his one good hand he pried the grenade from the frozen fingers of his useless right hand and threw it at the enemy. Then, stumbling to his feet and firing his submachine gun left-handed, he continued to advance through the smoke and dust of the grenade's explosion to kill all but one of the German defenders. The last survivor sent a burst of fire in the direction of the Lieutenant Inouye, striking him in his right leg and finally halting his advance. Lieutenant Inouye would spend the next 20 months in army hospitals after having his right arm amputated. In the attack, 25 German soldiers were killed and eight enemy prisoners captured. For his heroic acts, Lieutenant Inouye received the Distinguished Service Cross.[127] On 21 June 2000, Inouye and 21 other Asian-American veterans of World War II would be awarded the Medal of Honor.[128]

After recovering from his wounds, Daniel K. Inouye in 1959 was elected to the United States House of Representatives as Hawaii's first congressman and later, in 1962, was elected to the United States Senate. He would have this to say about the men of the 92nd Infantry Division: "I and other men of the 442nd Infantry Regimental Combat Team held the highest respect for the 92nd Division. In addition to being comrades in arms against Nazism, we were also fighting another battle — one against racism and bigotry. Sad to say, this battle goes on today. I have a special, personal memory of the 92nd. In the hours after I was wounded and doctors were treating me at the field hospital, I remember a nurse showing me a bottle of blood. It had a name on it — Thomas Jefferson Smith, 92nd Division — and while they were rigging it for transfusion into my left arm, I realized that fighting men did more than fight, that they cared enough about each other and the men assigned to their sector to donate their blood for the time when somebody would need it to sustain life. I was to have 17 transfusions in that first week alone. I am very, very grateful for it, and perhaps this is a fitting time to extend my thanks to every man in the 92nd Division who donated blood that helped save my life."[129]

On the same day that Lieutenant Inouye assaulted those enemy gun emplacements, and as Company E, 2/442nd Infantry was preparing for their assault on Colle Musatello, the 3/442nd Infantry had advanced to within ten miles of Aulla. Company K, 3/442nd Infantry was attacking along the hillsides above Tendola when enemy machine gun fire halted their advance and inflicted several casualties. Private First Class Joe Hayashi, an acting squad leader, moved his men within 75 yards of the enemy before they fell to the enemy fire. Despite the heavy enemy fire, Private Hayashi dragged his wounded comrades out of harm's way. Then he returned to the center of combat, boldly advancing alone and in full view of the enemy, to direct and adjust supporting mortar fire. When the bombardment began to subside, Private Hayashi took command of what remained of his platoon and led them forward to capture the hilltop. In that action, because of Private Hayashi's courage in standing openly in the field of battle to direct the fire of the mortar crews, three machine gun emplacements had been destroyed and 27 enemy soldiers killed. Throughout the remainder of 20 April and into the following day, as the 100th Infantry Battalion battled to secure the San Terenzo area, the 3/442nd Infantry fought to claim each of the hillsides above Tendola.

Private Hayashi's squad was assigned to secure a steep hillside above Tendola. On 22 April, Private Hayashi deployed his squad up the steep, terraced hillside to within 100 yards of the enemy. As the Germans opened fire on the advancing soldiers with their machine guns, Private Hayashi crawled forward alone until he was able to destroy the closest enemy position with a grenade. While pursuing the surviving retreating enemy, Private Hayashi noticed other elements of his platoon being fired upon by four additional enemy positions. Hayashi threw a grenade at the next machine gun emplacement, destroying it. Then he crawled to the right flank of another, killing four of the enemy gunners and forcing the remaining enemy to abandon the position. As he attempted to pursue the fleeing enemy soldiers, Private Hayashi was mortally wounded. For his valor on these two occasions, he was posthumously awarded the Distinguished Service Cross.[130]

After the 3/473rd Infantry completed its move from the Serchio sector on 20 April, the 1/473rd Infantry, having lost its battalion commander, moved into regimental reserve to reorganize. The 2/473rd Infantry and the 3/473rd Infantry continued the attack against strong enemy resistance south of Sarzana. Little progress was made for the next two days, and the refitted 1/473rd Infantry relieved the 2/473rd Infantry on 22 April. Despite heavy concentrations of enemy artillery, the advance continued and the towns of Sarzana, S. Stefano, and Caprigliola were occupied as the Germans were in full retreat. The tank-infantry force of Task Force Curtis, with Major Lawrence Becnel's 758th Tank Battalion and reinforced with Company E, 2/370th Infantry, crossed the Magra River into Po, deployed up Highway 1, and onto Punta Bianca on 22 April. The I and R Platoon, 473rd Infantry, led by First Lieutenant Earl Heggett, in their armored scout cars leading the advance, was suddenly met by a delaying enemy force, and the task force was halted at the southern outskirts of S. Stefano. The Germans delayed the force for a few hours before retreating to Aulla on the evening of 23 April.

San Terenzo fell on 23 April, with the 2/442nd Infantry killing 40 enemy soldiers and capturing 135. Meanwhile, the 3/442nd Infantry finally took Mount Nebbione and Mount Carbolo, and Major Mitsuyoshi Fukuda led his Task Force Fukuda to control the important road junction that was the German lifeline to Aulla. On 24 April, the 1/370th Infantry secured Fivizzano and pushed on against light resistance to Lucciana. On 25 April, Aulla fell, with the 2/442nd Infantry and Task Force Fukuda advancing into the town in a pincer movement that cut off all hope for the enemy to withdraw. The 3/370th Infantry relieved elements of the 442nd Infantry in Aulla, and deployed forward to occupy Terrarossa.

Elements of the 92nd Infantry Division on the west coast, now under temporary control of General Clark and the 15th Army Group, entered La Spezia on 24 April. With the enemy in full retreat, the 92nd Infantry Division was ordered to pursue the enemy with all speed. That afternoon, the 92nd Infantry Division Field Order 11 directed Combat Team 370th Infantry, consisting of the 597th Field Artillery Battalion; the 111th (British) Field Artillery Regiment; 1st Platoon, Company A, 758th Tank Battalion (Light); and the 1st Platoon, Company A, 894th Tank Destroyer Battalion, to pursue the enemy north on Highways 62 and 63 to the limit of the Cisa Pass and Cerreta Pass. Combat Team 473rd Infantry, consisting of the 598th Field Artillery Battalion; Company C, 760th Tank Battalion (Medium); Company A, 894th Tank Destroyer Battalion (minus 1 platoon); Company B, 317th Engineer Battalion; Casualty Collecting Company, 317th Medical Battalion; and the Assault Gun Platoon, 758th Tank Battalion (Light), was to pursue the enemy west and seize Genoa. The 92nd Reconnaissance Troop was to reconnoiter in zone, bypassing enemy resistance and report crossing phase lines. The 442nd Regimental Combat Team was to assemble at the 92nd Division Reserve, and be prepared to make an amphibious envelopment. Lieutenant Colonel Arnold was relieved of his duties as Assistant Chief of Staff, G-3 and placed in command of the 598th Field Artillery Battalion. Lieutenant Colonel Edward Rowney became the new Assistant Chief of Staff, G-3.[131]

As the 473rd Combat Team entered the eastern edge of Chiavari, their advance was stopped by hostile enfilade fire and heavy artillery concentrations from 135-mm coastal defense guns above the hillside tunnel at Chiavari, 152-mm coastal defense guns at Porto Fino, and field artillery batteries of 88-mm guns. Major Robert Crandall, the commander of 2/473rd Infantry, was killed, along with Captain Murray Steinman, commanding officer of the 92nd Reconnaissance Troop. In addition to the personnel losses, reconnaissance vehicles, 12 jeeps, several trucks, and other equipment were destroyed. Captain David Streger assumed command of the 2/473rd Infantry. Due to the rapid advance of the column, it had outdistanced the range of its supporting artillery. The only supporting fire available were the 75-mm main guns of two tanks of the 760th Tank Battalion. The 598th Field Artillery Battalion, also subjected to heavy artillery concentrations on the road from Sestrilevante to Lavagna, occupied firing positions between Lavagna and Chiavari, and by dusk had silenced four 135-mm batteries and destroyed one six-inch battery.

The 473rd Regimental Combat Team entered Genoa on 27 April. The last enemy pockets of resistance to surrender at Genoa were the harbor defense guns high up on Mount Maro. On the moonless, rainy night of 27 April, in blackout conditions, Company A, 679th Tank

Destroyer Battalion, moved its twelve guns up steep streets barely wide enough for a half-track vehicle. When the half-tracks failed to make the final turn, the guns were manhandled into position, where by daylight they were prepared for direct fire at 400 yards on the enemy concrete emplacement openings where two 381-mm, three 152-mm, and four 88-mm guns looked down on the city. The enemy gun tubes could not be depressed to fire on the 679th Tank Destroyer's guns. At 1430, on 28 April, the enemy on Mount Maro surrendered.

While the 473rd Infantry Regiment was advancing on Genoa, the 370th Infantry was advancing toward the Cisa Pass and Cerreta Pass on Highways 62 and 63. The 148th Grenadier Division and the Italia Division retreated to the north to avoid being captured. At Reggio, the 370th Infantry Regiment established contact with the Brazilian Expeditionary Force. The 3/370th Infantry advanced north on Highway 62 and reached Pontremoli and the Cisa Pass on 26 April. With the assistance of 1,000 Italian partisans, the enemy was driven from the city on 28 April. On 29 April, the 148th Grenadier Division surrendered to Major General Mascarenja's Brazilian Expeditionary Force. On that same day, the 2/370th Infantry assumed the security of all tunnels on Highway 1 between Sestrilevante and Genoa.

On 27 April, the 442nd Infantry Regiment moved from its Division Reserve positions to Chiavari and then proceeded to outflank Genoa from the north. Lieutenant Colonel Alfred A. Pursall's 3/442nd Infantry made contact there with the 473rd Combat Team. The 100th Infantry Battalion continued its march to the northwest and reached Busalla in the mountain pass which led from Genoa to the Po River, where patrols were deployed. Isola del Cantone was outposted with tanks and infantry. The 2/442nd Infantry continued its advance to the north and northwest mounted on tanks and riding in trucks. It made contact with elements of IV Corps in Pavia and with the Brazilian Expeditionary Force in Alessandria. On 30 April, the 442nd Intelligence and Reconnaissance Platoon, led by Lieutenant Robert I. Wakuya, and a machine gun section from Company H, 2/442nd Infantry, accompanied by Colonel William McCaffrey, the Chief of Staff, 92nd Infantry Division, made a 75-mile trip to Torino; however, the German 75th Corps refused to surrender to such a small force.

On 29 April, Benito Mussolini was captured and executed by partisans in the mountains of northern Italy while attempting to escape the country. His body, together with that of his mistress, Clara Petacci, was brought to Milan and hung upside down in a service station in the Piazza Loreto. The 92nd Infantry Division and its attached units captured a total of 13,630 enemy prisoners of war in the month of April.[132]

Also on 29 April, two German officers, a lieutenant colonel acting on behalf of General Heinrich von Vietinghoff, Commander-in-Chief, Southwest, and a major representing SS General Karl Wolff, Supreme Commander of SS and Police Troops and Plenipotentiary General of the Wehrmacht in Italy, signed the surrender agreement at Allied Force Headquarters in the Royal Palace at Caserta, Italy. In accordance with the agreement, the war in Italy ended on 2 May 1945.

On 2 May, the 92nd Infantry Division reverted from the control of 15th Army Group to that of 5th Army and IV Corps. On 4 May, General Von Senger und Etterlin, commanding the XIV Panzer Corps, representing Colonel General von Vietinghoff, Commander-in-Chief, German Armies Southwest, presented himself to General Clark at his 15th Army Group Headquarters to receive his orders for the surrender of his armies. The problems of feeding this captured army, totaling close to one million soldiers, presented a formidable logistical problem.

The 92nd Infantry Division was assigned the mission of maintaining order in the Ligurian area, clearing all of the enemy forces from its zone west to the Italian-French border, collecting prisoners of war, and administering to displaced persons. The 442nd Infantry Regiment was directed to maintain roadblocks and prevent the enemy from infiltrating toward the Italian-French and Italian-Swiss borders. The 473rd Infantry Regiment was ordered to secure roadblocks, prevent enemy infiltration toward the Italian-French border, and to maintain contact with French forces along Highway 1. On 10 May, the 365th Infantry Regiment and the 371st Infantry Regiment returned to the control of the 92nd Infantry Division. The 442nd and 473rd Infantry Regiments were detached from the 92nd Infantry Division and returned to 5th Army. The 365th Infantry assumed the occupation duties of the 442nd Infantry, north and west of Genoa. The 371st Infantry assembled in the vicinity of Acqui. The 370th Infantry assumed the security duties of the 473rd Infantry in Genoa and west to the French border.

The 366th Infantry Regiment remained in training as the 224th and the 226th Engineer General Service Regiments, both earmarked for redeployment to the Pacific Theater, where the war still raged on. The combat careers of both the 92nd Infantry Division and the 366th Infantry Regiment became major ingredients in the considerations for the future utilization of African American combat forces. Enlisted men and officers of both units had dimming views of both the future and the past. One private wrote to the *Stars and Stripes* that the men of the 92nd Infantry Division had been wondering and arguing among themselves as to why the 473rd and 442nd Infantry Regiments had displaced the division's own regiments. Views and opinions differed, he said, "Yet all of us agree that it was a profound shock to us." For himself, he wanted to know "whether this was to prove that Negroes can't fight together, without the so-called inducement of a white regiment to sting us into activity; or was it to prove (after certain unfortunate setbacks, like the setback in the Serchio Valley, where we had one regiment, yet the entire division was ridiculed), that we were too illiterate to fight; or that Mr. Truman Gibson's illiterate Negroes were afraid of the big bad Germans, and that we would run every time we saw one of the master race." Whatever was proved, he continued, "the men of the 92nd were sure that they were not sharing in the glory of the defeat of the Germans in Italy. Thank God the men who died did not know this. We are sorry we did not live up to the expectations of the newspapers and magazines (such as News Week) as a political division. We will try to do better next time."[133]

One of the few senior African American officers assigned to the 92nd Infantry Division, Lieutenant Colonel Marcus H. Ray, commander of the 600th Field Artillery Battalion, one of the two artillery battalions with a complete cadre of all African American officers in the division, summed up the feelings of the officers in the division in a letter written to Truman Gibson:

> Your findings on the state and training and morale of the Division were accurate but enough space was not given to the causes therefore. I realize that your release suffered 'clever' editing. It is my considered opinion that the 92nd, at the best, was doomed to a mediocre performance of combat duties from its very inception. The undercurrent of racial antipathies, mistrusts and preconceived prejudices made for an unhealthy beginning. The failure to promote worthwhile Negroes and the giving of preferred assignments to white officers made for logical resentments. I do not believe that enough thought was given to the selection of white officers to serve with the 92nd and further, that the common American error was made of assuming that Southern white men understand Negroes. Mixed units, as we have known them has been a dismal failure. In white officered units, those men who fit into the Southern pattern are pushed and promoted regardless of capabilities and those Negroes who exhibit the manliness, self-reliance, and self-respect which are the 'sine qua non' in white units, are humiliated and discouraged. In the two Artillery Battalions of the Division, officered by Negroes, it was necessary to reduce large num-

bers of noncommissioned officers because they held rank only because they fitted the 'pattern.' Their subordinates resented and disrespected them — justly so. I was astounded by the willingness of the white officers who preceded us to place their own lives in a hazardous position in order to have tractable Negroes around them.

In the main, I don't believe the junior officers guilty of faulty judgment or responsible for tactical failures. Soldiers do as ordered but when plans sent to them for execution from higher headquarters are incomplete, inaccurate, and unintelligible, there is inevitable confusion. The method of selection and the thoroughness of the training in the Officer Candidate Schools weeded out the unfit and the unintelligent with but rare exceptions but the polishing of the officer after graduation was the duty of his senior officers. In mixed units, this, manifestly, has been impossible. I believe that the young Negro officer represents the best we have to offer and under proper, sympathetic and capable leadership would have developed and performed equally with any other racial group. Therefore, I feel that those who performed in a superior manner and those who died in the proper performance of their assigned duties are our men of the decade and all honors should be paid them. They were Americans before all else. Racially, we have been the victims of an unfortunate chain of circumstances back grounded by the unchanged American attitude as regards the proper 'place' of the Negro... Perhaps, from your vantage point, where you see the worldwide picture, it is not as dismal as my rather restricted view based mainly on the 92nd Division. I do not believe the 92nd a complete failure as a combat unit but when I think of what it might have been, I am heartsick....[134]

After the war, Lieutenant Colonel Ray succeeded Truman Gibson as the Civilian Aide to the Secretary of War on Negro Affairs in November 1945.

In view of the limited requirement for occupation forces, most of the American personnel and materiel in Italy were to be shipped out either to the Pacific Theater, or back to the United States. During the period 10 to 17 June, the 92nd Infantry Division moved from the Genoa area to the Viareggio Redeployment Training Center. There, soldiers who were eligible to return to the United States were prepared for redeployment. Replacements were brought into the units. The 92nd Infantry Division was being prepared for deployment to the Pacific Theater. Second Lieutenant Vernon Baker, having been passed over for promotion for two years, was finally advanced to the rank of first lieutenant at the conclusion of hostilities.

As the war had now ended, many of the senior white officers, who were career soldiers, sought positions in all-white units. On 30 June, Brigadier General William Colbern, the commander of the 92nd Division Artillery, and Colonel William McCaffery, the division Chief of Staff, departed for assignments in the United States. Colonel Sherman, the commander of the 370th Infantry Regiment, assumed duties as the division Chief of Staff.

On 4 July 1945, the 92nd Infantry Division held an awards ceremony. First Lieutenant Baker was awarded the Distinguished Service Cross, this nation's second highest award for valor, for his heroic deeds on 5 April.[135] Ironically, also given awards that day in the ceremony were Captain Runyon and Major General Almond. Both were receiving the Silver Star. Captain Runyon was receiving this nation's third highest award for the same battle in which he deserted his company at Castle Aghinolfi. General Almond, ignoring military protocol, took the position of honor, which should have gone to Lieutenant Baker for receiving the highest award. Lieutenant Baker would later be awarded the Italian *Croce di Guerra al Valore*, the Cross of Valor in War, and the Polish Cross of Valor, making him the most highly decorated African American soldier in the Mediterranean Theater.

On 15 August, Major General Almond departed Italy to assume command of the 2nd Infantry Division, which had departed Germany and was now training in Texas in preparation for deployment to the Pacific Theater. The dropping of the atomic bomb, and the surrender of Japan, would curtail any further assignments of units being deployed to the Pacific

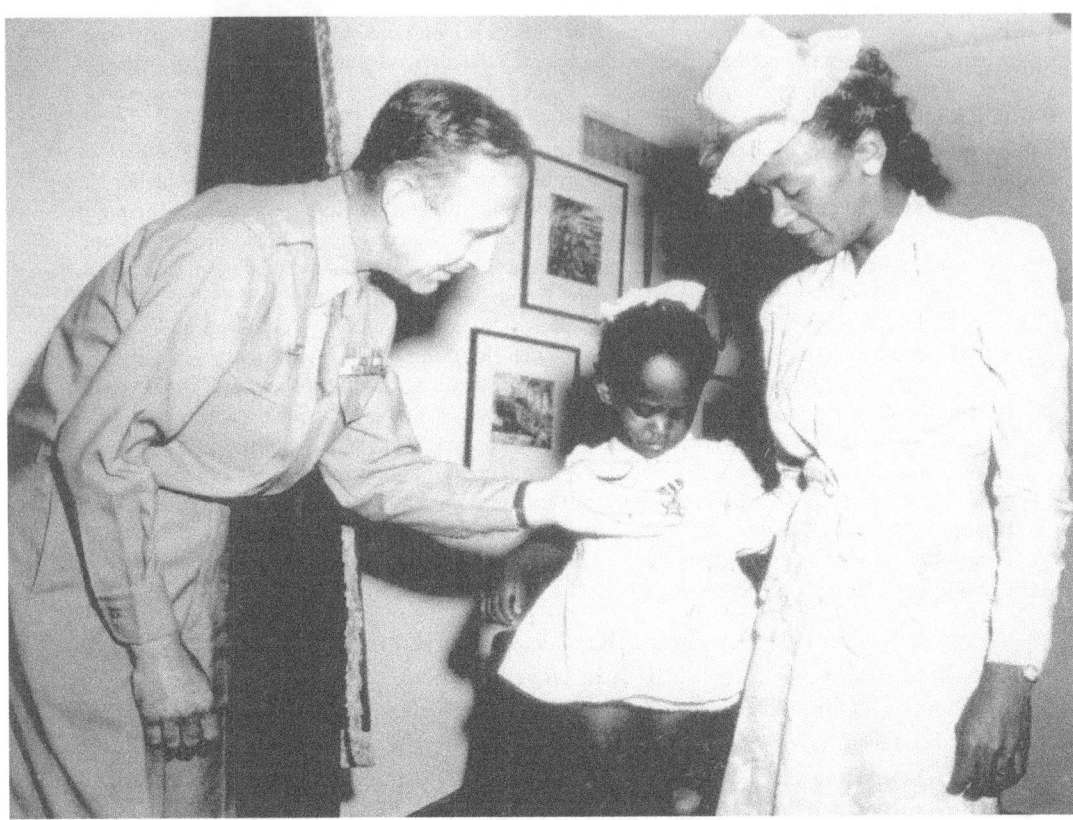

Brigadier General Robert N. Young, Commanding General of the Military District of Washington, assists Melba Rose, aged 2, daughter of Mrs. Rosie L. Madison, in viewing the Silver Star medal posthumously awarded her father, First Lieutenant John W. Madison, of the 92nd Infantry Division, who was killed in action in Italy, 1945. (National Archives 208-AA-139B-1)

Theater. Brigadier General Wood assumed command of the division and Colonel Sherman was designated Assistant Division Commander.

On 19 October, King Umberto II of Italy awarded the 92nd Infantry Division the Cross of Merit in War. Similar Italian awards were presented to 38 officers and enlisted men of the division. On 16 November 1945, the remainder of the 92nd Infantry Division departed Italy for the United States. On 28 November, the 92nd Infantry Division was unceremoniously deactivated at Camp Kilmer, New Jersey. The experiment had ended, and the facts were still in dispute as to the performance of African American soldiers in combat. This would be the last African American infantry division to ever see combat operations in a theater of war.

Italy had proved to be one of the hardest fought campaigns of World War II. The German and Italian Fascist forces had not been soundly defeated by any Allied division. When the war ended, the German forces were pulling back to their next line of defense to continue the battle.

92nd Infantry Division Awards136

3 Distinguished Service Crosses
1 Distinguished Service Medal
16 Legion of Merits
145 Silver Stars and
33 Expert Infantryman Badges
670 Driver's Badges
126 Mechanic's Badges
205 Division Commendations

92nd Infantry Division Awards136

47 Oak Leaf Clusters
6 Soldier's Medals
723 Bronze Stars and
30 Oak Leaf Clusters
31 Air Medals and
36 Oak Leaf Clusters
1891 Purple Hearts and
19 Oak Leaf Clusters
410 Combat Medical Badges
7996 Combat Infantryman Badges

4 Meritorious Service Unit Plaques
8 Orders of the Crown of Italy
17 Military Crosses for Military Valor (Italian)
22 Military Crosses for Merit in War (Italian)
1 Military Cross for Merit in War (Italian)
92nd Infantry Division Colors
1 War Medal (Brazil)

Chapter XII

Combat Infantry Replacements

By late 1944, the army was suffering a severe manpower shortage in the infantry and armored divisions. Plans to expand the army to 213 combat divisions could never be met and it was proving difficult to maintain the 89 infantry, airborne, and armored divisions then in existence, even though almost one-quarter of them had yet to be deployed to an overseas theater. Furthermore, the prewar planning for replacement personnel was found to be totally inadequate. The causes were manifold: the United States industrial and agricultural demands could only be partially met by bringing women into the workforce; the Women's Army Corps did not release as many male soldiers to combat duties as originally anticipated; the army was fighting a multi-front war; fear of the German Blitzkrieg had resulted in an over-expansion of the antiaircraft artillery and tank destroyer forces; the requirements of the massive expansion of the combined United States Armed Forces in general had reduced the manpower pool; and, perhaps worst of all, segregation meant that a large percentage of the available manpower, African Americans, were restricted to duty in combat service support organizations, two infantry divisions, three separate infantry regiments, and a few token armored, tank destroyer, airborne, and field artillery battalions.

The original War Department replacement-planning factor for infantry was 64.3 percent of the total casualties. Following continued pleas from the European Theater of Operations Command, and due to the large numbers of casualties suffered in the Mediterranean Campaign, the factor was raised to 70.3 percent in April 1944. However, the harsh combat associated with the Normandy invasion on 6 June 1944 soon proved that this figure was still below what it would take to replace all the battlefield casualties. By mid–July the European Theater of Operations estimate was that 90 percent of its total casualties occurred in the infantry. Infantry divisions incurred nearly 100 percent losses in rifle company strength in the two months after D-Day. The lack of infantry replacements soon approached near disastrous proportions. For example, on 8 December 1944, the United States 3rd Army was short 11,000 infantrymen. This was only about four percent of the 3rd Army's total strength, but was the equivalent of 55 rifle companies or the same rifle strength of two infantry divisions. This was approximately 15 percent of the infantry forces of General Patton's 3rd Army.[1]

The infantry further suffered from the army's personnel policy, which normally allocated the most highly qualified and intelligent people to a specialist arms branch of the service (Airborne, Ranger, Artillery, Armor, and Engineers). The infantry was filled with men who had lower average scores on the Army General Classification Test, the intelligence and aptitude test, which was a determining factor on which branch of the army a soldier was classified into. Although African American soldiers were tested, they would just be assigned to wherever there was a shortage, regardless of the aptitude to perform technical skills. The elimination of the Army Specialized Training Program, which allowed selected enlisted men to gain a college education while deferring induction into the army and the reduction of specialized units, especially antiaircraft artillery battalions, had remedied matters to some degree by the end of 1944.

Adding to the problem for a swift remedy to the manpower shortage was the policy of segregation. In the 1940s Jim Crowism was rampant in the United States. Racism and segregation affected all aspects of society. The effect was that more than 10 percent of the nation's military manpower was not being utilized where it was most needed. It was thought that assigning African Americans to these labor-intensive duties would free white combat support soldiers for the infantry.

In early December 1944, shortages of infantry replacements in the European and Mediterranean Theaters reached the critical stage. Since the invasion of Normandy, large numbers of casualties among front-line soldiers left many combat units operating with the minimum number of personnel. Both theaters actually began experiencing shortages in July 1944, and the Ground Force Replacement Command had been engaged in a training program to convert basic privates from other military occupational skills to infantrymen.[2] In the Italian Campaign, with the transfer of several infantry divisions to the new 6th Army Group in southern France, the command took entire antiaircraft artillery battalions and retrained them as infantrymen. In December 1944, the forecast of shortages increased rapidly as the availability of infantry replacements from the United States declined. By then, 50 percent of all draft-age men in the United States were already in the armed forces supporting the various theaters of operation. As of 8 December, a week before the beginning of the German counteroffensive in the Ardennes Forest caused further manpower depletions, the European Theater command estimated that there would be a deficiency of more than 29,000 infantrymen by the end of the month. Such a deficiency would effectively curtail plans for pressing a winter offensive against Germany. Only the veteran 82nd, 101st, and the newly arrived 17th Airborne Divisions were held in reserve in Europe. By the beginning of the Ardennes counterattack, it had already been planned to convert to infantry as many physically fit soldiers from combat service support units as possible. Basic infantrymen from new divisions were already being diverted to fill vacancies in the infantry battalions of veteran divisions. Lieutenant General John C.H. Lee, commander of the Communication Zone in the European Theater, planned to release and train 20,000 service support personnel as additional infantry riflemen.[3]

Lieutenant General Lee, after consulting with General Eisenhower and other army commanders, proposed adding to this number the physically qualified men from the Communications Zone's African American combat service support units. General Eisenhower, General Bradley, and the army commanders agreed. General Lee then consulted with Brigadier General Henry J. Matchett, commanding the Ground Force Reinforcement Command, and Brigadier General Benjamin O. Davis, then Special Advisor and Coordinator to the Theater Commander on Negro Troops. General Davis, seizing this as an opportunity for integrating African American soldiers into all-white units, responded enthusiastically. On 25 December 1944, General Davis, General Matchett, and the head of Ground Forces Reinforcement Command's personnel section, G-1, drew up a plan to train African American volunteers as individual infantry replacements to serve in white combat divisions.[4] General Lee had already prepared a call for volunteer soldiers, which went out to his base and section commanders on 26 December with instructions that it be reproduced and disseminated to soldiers within 24 hours. It read:

1. To this end the Commanding General, Com Z, is happy to offer to a limited number of colored troops who have had infantry training, the privilege of joining our veteran units at the front to deliver the knockout blow. The men selected are to be in the grades of Private First Class and Private. Non-commissioned officers may accept reduction in order to take advantage of this opportunity. The men selected are to be given a refresher course with emphasis on weapons training.

2. The Commanding General makes a special appeal to you. It is planned to assign you without regard to color or race to the units where assistance is most needed, and give you the opportunity of fighting shoulder to shoulder to bring about victory. Your comrades in the front are anxious to share the glory of victory with you. Your relatives and friends everywhere have been urging that you be granted this privilege. The Supreme Commander, your Commanding General, and other veteran officers who have served with you are confident that many of you will take advantage of this opportunity and carry on in keeping with the glorious record of our colored troops in our former wars.

3. This letter is to be read confidentially to the troops immediately upon its receipt and made available in Orderly Rooms. Every assistance must be promptly given qualified men to volunteer for this service.[5]

Before the plan could be initiated, a number of changes, some resulting from misunderstanding and others from apprehension, occurred. The plan itself represented a major break with traditional military policy, for it proposed mixing African American soldiers into white units neither on a quota nor a smaller unit basis but as individual replacements to be utilized where the requirement was the greatest. General Eisenhower personally rewrote the directive, changing all but the first two sentences and making dissemination permissive instead of mandatory. The new directive, officially approved by both General Eisenhower and Lieutenant General Lee, appeared over Lieutenant General Lee's signature with the same date, file number, and subject as the earlier directive, under a cover letter ordering return and destruction of all copies of the original version. The substitute letter read:

1. The Supreme Commander desires to destroy the enemy forces and end hostilities in this theater without delay. Every available weapon at our disposal must be brought to bear upon the enemy. To this end the Theater Commander has directed the Communications Zone Commander to make the greatest possible use of limited service men within service units and to survey our entire organization in a effort to produce able-bodied men for the front lines. This process of selection has been going on for some time but it is entirely possible that many men themselves, desiring to volunteer for front line service, may be able to point out methods in which they can be replaced in their present jobs. Consequently, commanders of all grades will receive voluntary applications for transfer to the Infantry and forward them to higher authority with recommendations for appropriate type of replacement. *This opportunity to volunteer will be extended to all soldiers without regard to color or race, but preference will normally be given to individuals who have had some basic training in Infantry.* Normally, also, transfers will be limited to the grade of Private and Private First Class unless a noncommissioned officer requests a reduction.

2. In the event that the number of suitable Negro volunteers exceeds the replacement needs of Negro combat units, these men will be suitably incorporated in other organizations so that their service and their fighting spirit may be efficiently utilized.

3. This letter may be read confidentially to the troops and made available in Orderly Rooms. Every assistance must be promptly given qualified men who volunteer for this service.[6]

The revised letter could be interpreted in a number of ways. There were no African American infantry units in the European Theater of Operation, only in the Mediterranean and Pacific theaters. The theater had long been concerned with replacements for its African American artillery, tank, and tank destroyer battalions, for it had already been told that none were available from the United States. There had been no plans to ever deploy these African American armored and artillery units into a combat theater. Most senior military leaders had no faith in the combat capabilities of African American soldiers, and believed these units were established to placate the first lady, Eleanor Roosevelt, who in her tours of military bases would inquire where the Negro combat units were. These battalions were established, but without a replacement contingency for personnel. The urgent requirement for this type of unit in the European Theater superseded the "unwritten" policy of not deploying well-trained African American armored and artillery units overseas. If African American volunteers from service units were to be retrained for combat use, the greatest immediate need was to place priority for replacements to units such as the 761st and 784th Tank Battalions, the 614th Tank Destroyer Battalion, and the 333rd Field Artillery Battalion, whose losses without replacements threatened their combat efficiency and, in the case of the 333rdArtillery, threatened their total existence. The African American volunteers would have first priority to be utilized for these units. But the Ground Forces Reinforcement Command could only instruct infantry replacements and was not equipped to train individuals in those more technical military skills. Those African American armored and artillery battalions were already operating under a system of retraining their own replacements of volunteers from service units.

By February 1945, 4,562 African American soldiers had volunteered, many of them non-commissioned officers who had taken reductions in rank to private in order to be accepted for training.[7] These men had volunteered for military service to fight for their country, only to be used as truck drivers, laborers, and cooks because of their race. Now, they were being afforded the opportunity to prove that they were just as capable as white soldiers. Thus, they gave up the relative safety and comfort of the rear echelon, to face the rigors and the dangers of front-line combat service. The first 2,800 men reported to the Ground Force Reinforcement Command in January and early February, after which the flow of volunteers was halted. The service branches from which these men came paralleled the ratio of African American soldiers in the Army: 38 percent from the engineer branch, 29 percent from the quartermaster branch, 26 percent from the transportation branch, 3 percent from the signal corps, 2 percent from the ordnance branch, and the remaining 2 percent from all other branches. Infantry training was conducted at the 16th Reinforcement Depot at Compiegne, France, which had been retraining white combat service support and antiaircraft artillery personnel as infantrymen since November 1944. The African American infantry trainees were organized into the 47th Reinforcement Battalion, 5th Retraining Regiment, under the command of Colonel Alexander George. The training staff reported that the African American volunteers were highly motivated and willing to learn. There were proportionately fewer absentees and fewer disciplinary problems among the volunteer African American trainees than among the non-volunteer white soldiers being reclassified as infantrymen. In many cases, the white soldiers were not volunteers, as the combat service support unit to which they were assigned was completely converted over to infantry.

Under the guidance of the new deputy theater commander, Lieutenant General Ben Lear, it was decided to form the African American replacements into over-strengthened platoons to compensate for the expected lack of any future replacements at the conclusion of this test program. The first 2,253 men were trained and available by 1 March 1945. They were organized into 37 platoons, of which 25 were assigned to the 12th Army Group, and 12 platoons to the 6th Army Group, the two major army groups in the theater. A second group was distributed later with 12 additional platoons being assigned to 12th Army Group and 4 platoons going to 6th Army Group. The infantry and armored divisions to which these soldiers were being assigned sent one platoon leader (lieutenant) and one platoon sergeant to meet each platoon at the 16th Depot. The possibility of receiving new replacements, regardless of race, in early March at the start of the spring offensive and the crossing of the Rhine River was readily accepted by most of the combat-weary divisions, which had taken huge losses during the Battle of the Bulge and other winter offensives conducted by the German forces.

In the 12th Army Group, the platoons were assigned three per division, with the divisions usually assigning one to each infantry regiment. The regiments would then select a company in which the platoon would act as an additional fourth rifle platoon. In most of the divisions, the platoons were provided additional instruction periods of varying lengths before commitment into combat. In others, such as the divisions involved with the assault in the Remagen Bridge sector, the platoons arrived just in time for immediate use in combat. These platoons, made up entirely of volunteers, and previously denied the opportunity to fight for their country, were anxious to prove their worthiness in combat alongside the white soldiers. Where the period of the African American platoon's arrival coincided with a period of heavy fighting, their welcome as fresh replacements was warmer than in units that were not yet engaged in combat. But divisional training periods of indoctrination to combat were valuable both to the platoons and to the divisions' attitude toward accepting these new African American soldiers. The assistant division commander of the 104th Infantry Division explained: "They had had some sort of training before they joined us, but we wanted to make sure they knew all the tricks of infantry fighting. We assigned our best combat leaders as instructors. I watched those lads train and if ever men were in dead earnest, they were."[8] In some cases the platoons were given the division patch and a brief indoctrination in the division's history and accomplishments, in addition to personal welcomes by either the division or assistant division commander. This reinforced the position of the platoon's acceptance into the division.

In most instances, the platoons quickly identified themselves with the more than three dozen battalions and companies to which they were distributed. They were utilized just as any other rifle platoon within their companies, a point frequently noted by their regiments. Veteran white platoon sergeants and lieutenants led these test platoons. Some platoons were assigned to veteran regiments, which, like those of the 1st and 9th Infantry Divisions, had fought in North Africa, Italy, and France. Others went to newer units in the theater like the 12th and 14th Armored Divisions, and the 69th, 78th, 99th, and the 104th Infantry Divisions. These divisions played varying roles in the concluding months of the war. Some still met hard fighting in their marches across the Rhine River and the battles through Central Germany. Others found resistance collapsing all around them and spent the last weeks of the war rounding up the bypassed pockets of enemy resistance and establishing provisional military governments.

As this was only a test program, army and theater headquarters were considerably more interested in the performance of these African American platoons assigned to all-white combat divisions, than were the units which, having accepted them, proceeded to utilize them as they would have any other platoon. Selected divisions were required to report weekly on the strength and casualties of the platoons. Their casualties were usually proportionate and in some instances relatively higher than those of comparable platoons in the same company. Army headquarters finally determined that the platoons would be authorized to have noncommissioned officer ranks since the African American infantrymen were not to be integrated into the white platoons. Many of these new infantrymen were noncommissioned officers in their combat service support units. In most instances, authority for these promotions did not arrive in time to affect the organizations of the platoons. Most of the platoons, including those organized as provisional companies with the armored divisions, finished the war without those higher grades, as the war would end in early May 1945. But in these cases, it was not uncommon to have a private first class serving as a squad leader, a position normally held by a sergeant.

The 104th Infantry Division, whose platoons had joined them while the division was defending the west banks of the Rhine River at Cologne, commented: "Their combat record has been outstanding. They have, without exception, proven themselves to be good soldiers. Some are being recommended for the Bronze Star Medal."[9] One of these outstanding soldiers was Private Willy F. James, Jr., assigned to Company G, 2nd Battalion, 413th Infantry Regiment. He was the lead scout during an attempt to capture a vital bridge near Lippoldsberg, Germany, on 7 April 1945. This Kansas City, Missouri, native was the first American soldier to draw enemy fire in this battle and was pinned down for more than an hour. He used this time to observe enemy positions in detail. Private James managed to eventually get back to rejoin his platoon, where he helped develop a plan of attack, and then led the lead squad in the assault, accurately designating targets as he advanced. Private James was killed by a German machine gunner a short time later while attempting to go to the aid of his wounded platoon leader, First Lieutenant Armand J. Serrabella. For his valor, he was posthumously awarded the Purple Heart and the Distinguished Service Cross medals.[10]

When General Benjamin O. Davis stopped at 12th Army Group headquarters on his way to observe the platoons a month after they had joined their units, he found that General Bradley was well satisfied with his status reports of the performance and conduct of the of the African American replacement infantrymen. The 104th Infantry Division's G-1 noted in the report that he gave General Davis. "Morale: Excellent. Manner of performance: Superior. Men are very eager to close with the enemy and to destroy him. Strict attention to duty, aggressiveness, common sense and judgment under fire has won the admiration of all the men in the company. The colored platoon after initial success, continued to do excellent work. Observation discloses that these people observe all the rules of the book. When given a mission, they accept it with enthusiasm, and even when losses to their platoon were inflicted the colored boys accepted these losses as part of war, and continued on their mission. The Company Commander, officers, and men of Company F all agree that the colored platoon has a caliber of men equal to any veteran platoon. Several decorations for bravery are in the process of being awarded to the members of colored platoons."[11]

In the 60th Infantry Regiment, 9th Infantry Division, the African American platoon saw its share of combat. On 9 April, Private First Class Jack Thomas would be awarded the Distinguished Service Cross, the nation's second highest award for valor, for leading his squad on a mission to destroy an enemy tank that was providing heavy weapons support for a fortified roadblock. Thomas deployed his squad into defensive positions that would provide adequate covering fire as he advanced upon the enemy. Once well within range of the enemy positions, and not being detected, he threw two grenades, wounding several German soldiers, and then kept them pinned down with fire from his Thompson submachine gun. As his squad commenced firing, German soldiers that had outflanked them wounded the two men at the bazooka position. Thomas was able to avoid enemy fire and recovered the bazooka. He then fired rockets at the Germans, preventing them from manning the tank. Private Thomas then picked up one of the seriously wounded members of the bazooka team, and through a barrage of small arms and automatic fire, carried him to safety.[12]

The platoons attached to the three regiments of the 1st Infantry Division illustrate the range and circumstances of the utilization of African American reinforcements within a single division. The 26th Infantry Regiment's platoon was continuously engaged in combat form 12 March until 8 May at the war's end. They took their turn at every assignment within their company: patrolling, outpost duties, assault platoon, support platoon in attacks, and rifle platoon on the defensive. While there was little time available for training, the regiment estimated that the combat efficiency improved from 30 percent to 80 percent by the end of their second week. Efficiency increased further in the next few weeks as the platoon was involved in its full share of almost continuous combat.[13] Initially, replacements kept this platoon operating as an entity, but the platoon assigned to Company B, 16th Infantry Regiment had 30 men wounded and 9 men killed in action. By the end of the war, they only had 15 men remaining present for duty. When the platoon's strength fell too low to operate as a platoon, the African American infantrymen were used as squads within the white platoons. They would also participate in every battle from 12 March to the end of the war. Despite suffering high casualties, their success achieved in battle was excellent and they took their assigned objectives in an aggressive manner. The platoon with Company B, 18th Infantry Regiment kept unit strength of between 20 and 43 men. It was utilized in the same manner as any other rifle platoon in the regiment. From its first contact with the enemy on 18 March near Eudenbach in the Remagen bridgehead sector, it participated in all company combat engagements until the hostilities ceased. When the white platoon sergeant was wounded, he was replaced by one of the African American infantrymen who performed "all the duties of a platoon sergeant, in and out of combat, in a superior manner."[14]

The African American platoons of the 99th Infantry Division were all utilized just as any other rifle platoon without preferential treatment. The division commander noted that they had "performed in an excellent manner at all times while in combat. These men were courageous fighters and never once did they fail to accomplish their assigned mission. They were particularly good in town fighting and [were] often used as the assault platoon with good results. The platoon assigned to the 393rd Infantry Regiment is credited with killing approximately 100 Germans and capturing 500 more. During this action, only three of their own men were killed and fifteen wounded."[15] One platoon, when faced with heavy automatic weapons fire from outlying buildings in a town which another white platoon was already supposed to have taken, made a hasty estimate of the situation and, realizing that its only safety was in the buildings from which its men were receiving fire, broke into a run with all weapons firing, raced 300 yards under "a hail of enemy fire," took the buildings and, in a matter of minutes, the entire town. The battalion commander concluded: "I know I did not receive a superior representation of the colored race as the average Army General Classification Test was Class IV. I do know, however, that in courage, coolness, dependability and pride, they are on a par with any white troops I have ever had occasion to work with. In addition, they were, during combat, possessed with a fierce desire to meet with and kill the enemy, the equals of which I have never witnessed in white troops."[16] Statements like this dispelled the theory behind low-test classification scores being associated with not being able to withstand the rigors of combat.

There was less initial satisfaction with the African American infantrymen assigned to the 7th Army. The 6th Army Group and 7th Army had not been included in the original test plan to utilize African American soldiers as reinforcements. On the decision of General Patch, commander of the 7th Army, the 12 African American infantry platoons assigned were organized into provisional companies and assigned to the 12th Armored Division, whose armored infantry battalions had greater shortages of men than the standard infantry regiments. The armored divisions of World War II were used to spearhead the thrust of the Allied armies' advance into Germany. These new armored divisions coming into the theater were organized into two armored regimental combat teams with the infantry providing support, and a third combat team that was normally held in reserve, but could augment any of the armored combat teams. It was the job of the infantry to protect the tanks from enemy infantry forces, usually equipped with antitank and Panzerfaust weapons. The American M4 Sherman medium tank was highly vulnerable to these weapons.

The African American platoons receiving the minimum amount of training in squad and platoon tactics had not been afforded the opportunity for any training in company level combat tactics. The divisions felt that there was little time to equip and train them before their next battle. The 12th Armored Division had also received unsatisfactory support from the African American 827th Tank Destroyer Battalion in the previous months, and objected to having to use these new infantrymen. The 12th Armored Division's African American infantry companies were known as the 7th Army Provisional Companies 1, 2, and 3, not really being assigned to the division, but as attachments from higher headquarters. When they were attached to one of the infantry battalions, they were known as Company D. Infantry companies of World War II were organized with three rifle platoons and one weapons support platoon equipped with crew-served 60-mm mortar teams, bazooka teams and .30-caliber light machine gun teams. The African American infantry replacements had not received any training with crew-served weapons, as it was planned that they were to be utilized strictly as basic rifle platoons incorporated into veteran infantry companies. By forming the platoons into separate companies, it minimized their exposure to other white infantrymen. A veteran white captain, with white platoon sergeants and lieutenants, led the provisional companies.

All of these companies were used as armored infantry in support of tanks or with tank support, but their unit organization differed. One company was composed of four platoons, each organized into one light machine gun and three rifle squads. The other two companies had three platoons; each with two 60-mm mortars and several light machine guns. The companies attacked dismounted or mounted on tanks or armored half-track vehicles. Their initial combat performance was considered very satisfactory, improving as experience made up for their lack of training time with machine gun and mortar crews.

One of these new infantrymen to this division was Sergeant Edward A. Carter Jr. Born in Los Angeles, he was raised in China by missionary parents and fought in the Spanish Civil War with the American Lincoln Battalion. When he enlisted in the United States Army in 1942, in spite of having combat experience, he was assigned the duties of a cook. He quickly rose to the rank of staff sergeant, but took a reduction to private in order to be assigned to an infantry unit. His leadership skills and experience in combat got him assigned as a squad leader and quickly re-promoted to sergeant. Originally assigned to the 69th Infantry Division, Sergeant Carter had recently been transferred to Company D, 56th Armored Infantry Battalion, 12th Armored Division. He had been assigned to the division less than two weeks, when on 23 March, near Speyer, Germany, Sergeant Carter, while riding on a tank, came under intense fire from enemy Panzerfaust and MG42 machine gun fire. Sergeant Carter jumped from the tank and volunteered to lead a patrol of three other men across 150 yards of open field. Two of the men were killed immediately from the devastating fire, and the third man was seriously wounded. Sergeant Carter sustained three wounds in his left arm from a machine gun, but determinedly continued forward, in spite of the fact that the tanks were not following him. He charged the machine gun emplacement and immediately silenced it with a grenade. Two additional grenades put a German mortar crew out of commission. Still charging forward, Sergeant Carter was knocked down by bullets number four and five. Before he could see which direction the enemy fire was coming from, bullet number six slammed into his shoulder. As he lay wounded on a narrow slope, bullet number seven struck his left hand as he attempted to drink water from his canteen. After he lay in this position for several hours, eight enemy soldiers believing him to be seriously wounded or dead came forward to investigate. Sergeant Carter killed six with his Thompson submachine gun after firing off three magazines of ammunition, and captured the other two. He retreated using his prisoners as a shield. An artillery barrage caused wound number eight, as a German 88-mm shell slammed into a building, sending splinters into his legs. Although the attacking German soldiers killed one of the prisoners, and the severity of his wounds limited his movement, Sergeant Carter continued toward his lines. He killed three more German soldiers with his submachine gun who were attempting to capture him. Members of his battalion could not believe it when Sergeant Carter emerged from a cloud of smoke with his prisoner. Because he was able to speak German, Sergeant Carter received valuable intelligence information from the prisoner on the location of other enemy positions. His commander, First Lieutenant Russ Blair, would ensure that Sergeant Carter was awarded the Distinguished Service Cross and Purple Heart medals for his heroic deeds.[17]

The 6th Army Group's four supplementary platoons arrived on 26 March and were similarly assigned to the 14th Armored Division, which took them with it when they were attached to General Patton's Third Army on 23 April 1945.[18] In the 14th Armored Division, they were known as 7th Army Provisional Company No. 4, or since they were attached to the Combat Command Reserve, as CCR Rifle Company. The Combat Command Reserve was normally utilized in a role of reinforcing elements of the division as needed. The 240-man company remained in combat from 5 April to 3 May. The 14th Armored Division was advancing south through Bavaria along the Bayreuth-Nurnberg Autobahn. The Combat Command Reserve rifle company was mainly utilized in attachment to the 25th Tank Battalion, which was held in the Combat Command Reserve.

The company's baptism by fire came at Lichtenfels, where two platoons crossed the Main River, and after a bitter fight, secured the town.[19] On 15 April, the 94th Reconnaissance Squadron entered the town of Creussen, the site of a weapons factory, when enemy tanks and infantry surrounded them. A call for reinforcements led two platoons of Sherman tanks from the 25th Tank Battalion and a platoon of infantry from the CCR Rifle Company toward the town. At 1145, near the town of Gottsfeld, the tanks were fired on by German antitank guns. Four tanks were hit, with two being destroyed. The remaining tanks withdrew, and the dismounted infantry were summoned to enter the town. The retreating Germans called in artillery on the town, but by 1500, the infantry platoon had cleared the town. The remaining tanks then proceeded in, and the tank/infantry force continued toward Creussen. Before reaching

Volunteers for Combat Infantry Training, France, January 1945. (National Archives)

their objective, the American M4 Shermans destroyed five German Mark IV Tiger tanks which came out into the open fields to attack the relief force. Due to the action in Gottsfeld, enemy resistance had been reduced at Creussen. For the next two days, platoons of the CCR Rifle Company patrolled the vicinity around Gottsfeld and Creussen, clearing pockets of bypassed enemy resistance and capturing German prisoners.

As the war drew to an end in Europe, opinions varied as to the performance of the African American reinforced infantrymen. When utilized as they were trained, as basic combat infantrymen in rifle platoons, their evaluations were mainly excellent. They operated in cohesion with the veteran white platoons of their companies, and gained valued combat experience under their tutelage. When they were used as provisional companies, the results were initially not as impressive. The African American riflemen had not received any training on crew-served weapons, or in company-strength combat tactics due to the urgency of getting them to the divisions that desperately needed replacements. But they quickly adapted, and within a short amount of time had become proficient in these tactics.

With these replacement infantry platoons, the utilization of the African American soldiers moved the farthest from the traditional army patterns of that time. Despite a multitude of problems which the army was faced with in the use of African American soldiers in segregated units during World War II, at the war's end, a greater variety of experiences existed than had ever before been available within the American military establishment. For African American soldiers had been used in larger numbers, over a longer period of time, than in any previous war. They had been used in more branches and in a greater variety of units, ranging from divisions to platoons in size. They were used in every theater of war in a wider range of geographical, cultural, and climatic conditions than was believed possible in 1942. Due to the short span of time in which these test platoons were utilized in combat, it is hard to determine the overall success it had. It was obvious in the units to which they were assigned; the commanders had nothing but praise for these new volunteer infantrymen. The sacrifices of these men and other African American soldiers who served in combat, would forever change those opinions that they were incapable of fighting for their country.

Chapter XIII

Armored Forces

It was often claimed that Eleanor Roosevelt, representing her husband, would tour various military installations, and ask where were the Negro soldiers, and what were they doing. Like the other branches of the United States Army, with the buildup of military forces commencing in 1940, there was strong resistance to incorporate African American soldiers into the Armored Forces Corps. Late in 1940, the Armored Forces had been directed by the War Department to make provisions for African American units. All branches of the segregated army were to have representation by African American soldiers, even if the representation was a token effort to appease the politicians. The Armored Forces suggested that its token representation be provided by using African Americans in lieu of white soldiers in their service detachments at the Armored Forces School and Replacement Center. These two detachments, to include 574 and 403 African American soldiers, respectively, would be used to provide the manual labor force, performing menial jobs such as chauffeurs, janitors, firemen, cooks, basics (an enlisted man with the minimum essentials of military training, assigned to tasks requiring little experience and no specialized skills), and bandsmen.[1]

The commanding staff of the Armored Forces claimed that "it was too busy with the problems of welding a new unified armored mechanized force out of what was essentially a combination of the combat arms to have time for the activation and training of experimental Negro armored units."[2] The Chief of Staff G-3 pointed out that the Armored Force functioned as a separate branch of the army and was accepted by the public as such. It therefore recommended that the Armored Forces, in addition to the two proposed African American service detachments, activate the 78th Light Tank Battalion at Camp Claiborne, Louisiana, with African American personnel.[3] This battalion was to be activated on 1 June 1941, with 32 white enlisted instructors temporarily attached to compensate for the lack of trained African American noncommissioned officer cadres.[4] The Armored Forces strongly objected to having to instruct African American soldiers to become tank crewmen, mechanics, and other support personnel.[5] In spite of the Armored Forces' objections to the War Department's initial request, two additional African American tank battalions were also scheduled for activation. The 761st Tank Battalion was to be activated on 1 April 1942 and the 784th Tank Battalion a year later on 1 April 1943.

The War Department also activated five armored groups in 1942, each comprising three tank battalions. The army at the time operated on a new tri-tier basis. Each corps was assigned three infantry divisions. Each infantry division had three infantry regiments. Each regiment had three infantry battalions, etc. In theory, by activating only three African American tank battalions, they were able to keep these units totally segregated under the command and control of a single armored group. These three tank battalions, with the 78th later redesignated as the 758th Tank Battalion, formed the 5th Armored Group, which would be activated on 23 May 1942, and commanded by Colonel Leroy Nichols. White officers and African American enlisted men would staff the headquarters element of the 5th Armored Group. The armored group was responsible for the command and control of their assigned and attached tank battalions.

In March 1941, the first 98 African American volunteer enlisted men reported to Fort Knox, Kentucky, from Fort Custer, Michigan, for armored warfare training with the 78th Tank Battalion (Light). The pioneer tank crewmen trained continuously as additional enlisted men from other army installations joined their ranks. The battalion trained in armored operations, mechanics, and related phases of the new mechanized warfare. The authorized strength of the battalion was to be 36 officers and 593 enlisted men.

The 78th Tank Battalion (Light) would be composed of three line companies designated, A, B, and C, a headquarters company, and a service company. The "Light" designation indicated that the battalion operated the M5 Stuart light tank. Each tank carried a crew of four consisting of a driver, assistant driver, gunner, and the tank commander/loader. The M5 was powered by twin, 220-horsepower Cadillac V-8 engines, capable of a maximum speed of 40 miles per hour, and an open road cruising range of 172 miles. It was armed with a .30-caliber light machine gun mounted to fire along the same axis as the main armament, a 37-mm antitank cannon. When tracer bullets from the .30-caliber machine gun indicated they were on target, the cannon could be fired for a direct hit. The M5 was also armed with two additional .30-caliber machine guns. One was located on top of the turret, which was operated by the tank commander, and one in the bow operated by the assistant driver. The M5 Stuart tank was designed to provide firepower, mobility, and crew protection in screening and reconnaissance missions. By the time of the United States' entry into World War II, the M5 was too lightly armored to directly oppose the main German Panzer tanks.

Each of the line companies contained three tank platoons, each with five M5 tanks. A lieutenant was in command of each platoon, and a noncommissioned officer commanded each tank. Two additional M5 tanks were maintained in the headquarters platoon for the company commander and executive officer. The headquarters company had a reconnaissance platoon, an armored 81-mm mortar platoon, and an assault gun platoon, which contained four armored, self-propelled 75-mm howitzer canons. The headquarters company also operated and maintained the tanks that were utilized by the battalion commander and his staff. The service company was responsible for logistics, maintenance, ordnance, and the administration support duties of the battalion. Later, with America's entry into World War II, a medical detachment was added. A tank battalion was designed to be a separate, self-contained unit, capable of supporting any infantry division. The standard infantry and airborne divisions did not contain any organic armored units. When a tank battalion was attached to an infantry division, one of the three line companies would usually be assigned to support one of the three infantry regiments. One tank platoon would be assigned to support one of the three infantry battalions that were assigned to the regiment. When combined with the armor of a medium tank battalion, equipped with the heavier M4 Sherman tanks, and a tank destroyer battalion, this would provide ample armor support and firepower for the infantry soldiers.

The 758th Tank Battalion continued their training as a unit at Camp Claiborne, Louisiana, once they completed the initial training at Fort Knox. Early in 1942, Second Lieutenant David J. Williams was assigned to the battalion. As a white officer assigned to an African American tank battalion, he recalls his arrival to Camp Claiborne and the welcome he received from his company commander: "Captain Barnes sat me down and said, 'Boy, I'm gonna teach you about Nigras.' I didn't know what to say. Then he said, 'You're down here with Eleanor Roosevelt's niggers, boy! These people you've got to handle different. You're young and you're from up East.' My dad's friend, Ira Lewis, put my face on the front page of the *Pittsburgh Courier* (an African American newspaper) with the headline: 'Pittsburgh Industrialist's Son and Politician Goes With Race Troops.' Captain Barnes had this and said, 'Your old man has influence. These Nigras ain't gonna fight. Your old man put you in a safe place.' Imagine, telling me this. This was the greatest war in history, and everyone wanted to fight. We had two enemies to fight, Hitler and Hirohito. Who needed better enemies? So, I'm sitting there and Captain Barnes is saying 'You're not going nowhere, we're just marking time down here.' Then First Sergeant Sam Turley came in. He said, 'Turley, I want you to meet our new second lieutenant from up East, from the uppity college, Yale University.' So I shook hands with Sam Turley. Captain Barnes said, 'Turley, get out of here!' He stuck his finger out at me and said, 'Boy, don't you ever put yourself on the same level with a Nigra!' Well, my first sergeant from the 70th Tank Battalion, where I went to OCS (Officers Candidate School), our captain and colonel had us both for dinner. I said first sergeants run the army; they command respect. He said: 'Boy, you don't know nothing! You're up in that college and the only Nigras you see up there are sheltered.' So, two weeks later he called me and said, 'I'm getting rid of you. April Fool's Day they created another Nigra tank battalion, the 761st.' So he kicks me and Turley out and said, 'Boy, you done ruined my best first sergeant.'"[6]

This was the plight of many of the white officers that were assigned to the African American units during the war. It was perceived that African American combat units would never be deployed overseas to any of the front-line wartime theaters. That was the reason that it was never planned to continuously train African American tank crewmen as replacements for possible battlefield casualties. Once the three tank battalions were activated and fully fielded, there would be no additional African American tank crewmen or support personnel being trained at the Armored Force Replacement Center. The conception of most white officers was that these were experimental units, established to appease Eleanor Roosevelt and convince the African American population that the black soldiers, although serving in a segregated "Jim Crow" army, were given the same opportunities to serve as their white counterparts. But the urgent necessity for well-trained armor support for the infantry divisions caused the army to deploy these token African American tank battalions to overseas theaters of war.

The War Department had a long-standing policy that decreed white Southerners, by virtue of their life experiences, best knew how to handle African American soldiers. Brigadier General R.W. Crawford of the War Department's general staff submitted a memorandum to General Eisenhower. In it, he stated: "Probably the most important consideration that confronts the War Department in the employment of the colored officer is that of leadership qualifications. Although in certain instances, colored officers have been excellent leaders, enlisted men generally function more effectively under white officers. Officers experienced with colored troops lay this to the lack of confidence on the part of the colored enlisted men in the colored officer."[7] This would be a misconception that was carried over from World War I. Many senior officers now on the general staff had served during that war. African American officers were unjustly criticized for having inept leadership skills, for to accept the African American officer as one's peer was to admit that equal status existed between the races.

Attitudes of some of the white officers assigned to the 761st Tank Battalion were not very different from those assigned to the 758th Tank Battalion. When Lieutenant Williams reported into Company C, his new company commander, Captain Charles Wingo, told him: "You gonna learn, lieutenant, you got to have a mean coon ... to keep these boys in line."[8] This, in reference to having inept African American noncommissioned officers in the company that were accustomed to catering to the white officer's whims.

761ST TANK BATTALION

The 761st Tank Battalion (Light) was activated at Camp Claiborne, Louisiana, on 1 April 1942 with Major Edward E. Cruise as its first commanding officer. Enlisted men and some officers of the 758th Tank Battalion made up the cadre for this new unit. It had an initial strength of 27 white officers and 313 African American enlisted men. On 28 May 1942, 216 additional enlisted men, newly trained from the Armored Forces Replacement Training Center at Fort Knox, Kentucky, joined the battalion. On 26 July 1942, the battalion received their first African American officers from the Officer Candidate School (OCS) of the Armored Forces Replacement Center. Second Lieutenants Charles Barbour, Samuel Brown, and Ivan Harrison were first assigned as platoon leaders, but later became staff officers and company commanders. Other African American officers would join the battalion, some coming from the Cavalry Replacement Center at Fort Riley, Kansas.

All warrant officers assigned to the tank battalions would be African American. The commander of the 758th Tank Battalion had requested that it be assigned only white warrant officers due to the fact that he felt African American soldiers lacked the technical expertise to be a warrant officer. This request, in deference to army policy, was turned down by the War Department. This policy provided that in any African American unit which was authorized warrant officer positions would be restricted to utilize only African Americans.

The esprit de corps in these tank battalions, in spite of the racial attitude in a segregated army, remained high regardless of the discriminatory conditions that were prevalent throughout the South. At Camp Clairborne, all the African American units were billeted in the vicinity of the post water sewage treatment plant, far from the white units. All the facilities on the installation, such as the Post Exchange (PX), service clubs, and hospital, were segregated.

The tank battalions, training as part of the 5th Armored Group, though often located at different military installations, had a high sense of mission. Even though their higher headquarters had frequent doubts as to the validity of continuing to train these "experimental" units, the doubts were never communicated to the men of the battalions. Rather, through the leadership of their group and higher headquarters, these tank battalions learned to think of themselves not only as units from which significant results were expected but also as units which could expect to produce these results. Their men, normally volunteers, were not specially selected, nor had they achieved higher aptitude scores on the classification test; but the visible progress of their training and of their potential usefulness, stimulated by their growing familiarity with their weapons, equipment, and tanks, coupled with the gradual appearance of African American officers who advanced up through the ranks to eventually command all of the companies, gave these units a sense of movement toward a visible goal. From maneuvers and field exercises, supporting both white and African American infantry regiments and divisions, they gained a confidence in each other, in their leaders, and in their units. But this was not always the case in many poorly led African American units. More important, higher echelon officers not only visited them, but what they reported to the commanders in the way of commendation was communicated back to the men; what they said in addresses was well enough said to be remembered and acted upon. Accolades to which many white units became accustomed to, struck home to units unaccustomed to being taken as valuable members of a team. The commander of the Tank Destroyer Training Center at Fort Hood, Texas, Brigadier General Ernest J. Dawley, addressed the men the 761st Tank Battalion on three separate occasions. Once, in a farewell speech to the men just prior to their departure for the European Theater, he spoke of the various things that might or might not happen during wartime for which there would be no obvious explanation but which must be laid to the "fog of war." He concluded: "When you get in there, put in an extra round of ammunition, and fire it for General Dawley!" This speech made a lasting impression on the men. When the 761st Tank Battalion entered combat, one of its tanks was named "The Fog of War." To take this point home, several extra rounds of ammunition were put in and fired "for General Dawley" as recorded by the unit's historian, Private Trezzuant Anderson.[9] Anderson, a journalist in civilian life, was a noncommissioned officer in an aviation engineer battalion, and took a reduction in rank to private in order to voluntarily join the 761st Tank Battalion.

On 23 August 1942, the 761st Tank Battalion, with strength of 34 officers and 545 enlisted soldiers, departed Camp Claiborne for the first major training exercise supporting the 78th Infantry Division. The maneuver consisted of a mounted field road march with full combat equipment to Camp Livingston in the Kisatchie National Forest. Armored field operations conducted there pressed into service fire and maneuver tactics against fixed fortifications constructed by the infantrymen. Upon their return to Camp Claiborne on 7 September, the battalion received additional tank crewmen from the Fort Knox Armored Replacement Center, bringing their enlistment strength up to 603 soldiers.

Intensive training continued for the tank battalions at Camp Claiborne. Soldiers had to learn how to operate all the positions within the tank: gunner, loader, and driver. Weapons were disassembled and reassembled while the men were blindfolded. Tanks were cleaned upon returning from field exercises in the Louisiana mud. Live fire exercises were utilized to improve the soldiers' weapon proficiency.

On 25 September, five additional African American second lieutenants joined the 761st Tank Battalion from the Armored Replacement Center. They were Carl Bowman, Spencer Harder, John D. Long, Irvin McHenry, and Warren Taylor. As African American officers reported in to the battalion, white second lieutenants were transferred to white armored units. To lessen the effect of mass transfers of white officers out and African American officers into a unit, commanders of armies, corps, and other field units having assignment jurisdiction over units were authorized, in 1943, to direct attachment rather than relief of white officers for a period of from three to six months. The retained white officers were to train the new African American personnel and help make the transition from one group of officers to the other a smoother and more gradual process.[10] But most commanders did not follow this policy, and white officers, eager to join white units, were quickly transferred out.

On 22 November 1942, newly promoted Lieutenant Colonel Cruise transferred out of the 761st Tank Battalion, and Major John R. Wright assumed command. On 1 April 1943, the third African American battalion, the 784th Tank Battalion (Light), was activated. Personnel from the 761st Tank Battalion provided much of the cadre. On 8 April, the 761st Tank Battalion departed Camp Claiborne for the second phase of the 3rd Army maneuvers. There, they operated with the 85th and 93rd Infantry Divisions, and the 100th Infantry Battalion composed of Japanese-American soldiers. Major General Willis D. Crittenberger, commander of the III Armored Corps, directed the exercise. The senior ranking officers who observed these maneuvers duly noted outstanding performances by the African American tank battalions. Lieutenant General Ben Lear, the commanding general of the Army Ground Force Reinforcement System of the European Theater of Operations, and Lieutenant General Leslie J. McNair, the Chief of the Army Ground Forces, had high praise for the 761st Tank Battalion who distinguished themselves by not losing a single vehicle on an 83-mile mounted road march, unlike the other tank battalions that participated in the maneuvers.

On 4 July 1943, Major Paul L. Bates, the battalion executive officer, assumed command of the 761st Tank Battalion. Commanding an all African American unit was often viewed as a hardship and degrading assignment, and white officers where eligible for reassignment after 18 months. Normally, they were transferred out long before the 18 months had expired. Lieutenant Colonel Bates recalls: "When people heard I'd been assigned to this new all black battalion, they went around saying what bad luck I had. I honestly didn't have any idea what they were talking about. The town I lived in near Los Angeles didn't have a Negro in it, nor did my high school or my college. I had no idea about Negroes one way or another ... I found out that when the first Negroes were to arrive they had a heritage of undeserved attributes that were all on the down side. I never looked at them like that. I never had reason to because I make up my own mind! There is something that exists between men and men and men and women and this is empathy. You can feel towards a person when you first meet them. It has nothing to do with words; you get a feeling between the two of you where you know you are on the same playing field. That happened because of my lack of knowledge and that we made it out together.... My 18 months came up; we were still in the states. And did I want to go? Hell no! I didn't want to go."[11]

In June 1943, Lieutenant Irvin McHenry became the first African American officer to command a company in the 761st Tank Battalion when Captain Wingo relinquished command of Company C to become the battalion executive officer.

CAMP HOOD, TEXAS

On 13 September 1943, the 5th Armored Group was transferred to Camp Hood, Texas, where the armored and tank destroyer training was being consolidated. On 29 October, the 761st Tank Battalion, and later the 784th Tank Battalion were converted from the light tank battalion designation to the standard medium tank battalion. The three line companies and the headquarters company turned in their M5 Stuart light tanks and received the heavier M4 Sherman medium tank with its larger 75-mm main gun. It was also armed with two .30-caliber light machine guns, and a heavy .50-caliber antiaircraft machine gun mounted atop the turret. Tank crew size also increased from four to five crewmen, with the addition of a cannon loader. The M4 Sherman was powered by a 500-horsepower Ford gasoline engine. It had a top speed of 35 miles per hour, and a range of 100 miles. The assault gun platoon turned in their 75-mm self-propelled howitzers for the larger 105-mm armored self-propelled howitzer cannon. Company D was added to the battalion. This company still operated the M5 Stuart light tank for screening and reconnaissance missions. During this reorganization, all the African American officers were transferred from the newly activated 784th Tank Battalion into the 761st Tank Battalion. The battalion also gained the services of Captain Garland

"Doc" Adamson, who would assume the dual duties of the battalion surgeon and commander of the medical detachment. At 50 years old, he was the oldest member of the battalion. Prior to joining the army, he taught obstetrics and gynecology at Meharry Medical School in Tennessee.

On 30 October 1943, First Lieutenant Ivan Harrison assumed command of headquarters company. Lieutenant Harrison remembers sitting in as the commanding officer of headquarters company back at Camp Claiborne during a group photo session in the motor pool: "In the photograph, I was commanding the company because we had a few white officers who didn't want their pictures taken with Negroes. In this case, one was Geist. When he came to the battalion, Lieutenant Colonel Bates briefed him and then asked if he had any questions. Geist told him that he wanted out of this outfit because he didn't want to serve with Negroes. Lieutenant Colonel Bates told him: 'Go down to this company and you are company commander. You will serve here!' Geist in his heart didn't want to but he went ahead and did it. There were men in the company like Thomas Ashly from Washington. He was brilliant with radios and Geist was interested in radios. Geist would stand around and watch him. We also had this thing called a gyrostabilizer, which was new then and classified. It was that thing on the big gun and while you were riding, where you pointed that gun, the gyrostabilizer would keep it on target. It was sealed and only people with top-secret clearances could break one of those seals. But this colored soldier would break that damn seal when something went wrong and fixed it. Geist was amazed that a Negro knew that much, and that son-of-a-gun fell in love with those men and did a complete about face. And during the war when other white officers would not go to the front, he would go forward with those men. He just completely reversed! Russell C. Geist, from Germantown, Pennsylvania. So, in the photo, I was actually a platoon leader but since the two or three white officers refused to have their pictures taken with Negroes, they made me the company commander."[12]

In November 1943, the third African American officer assumed command of a company when First Lieutenant Sam Brown took over Company A. The battalion also received 93 Good Conduct Medals presented to enlisted soldiers who had completed three years of unblemished active duty service. It was during this period of intensified training that the Assault Gun Platoon of headquarters company was singled out for it ability to zero in on a target with one shot and destroy the target with its second round. The commander, Captain Ivan Harrison recalls the efficiency of the platoon: "At Camp Hood, Gates was the commander of the Assault Gun Platoon. There was this white colonel who had been fighting in North Africa who came to Camp Hood. He was an artilleryman and he took a special interest in Gates and that platoon. They would stay for days on a hillside shooting indirect fire, which is an art. There were out there for three, four, or five weeks firing all types of ammunition. They were getting additional ammunition so they were able to fire much more ammunition than any other group firing. That platoon, they were all good men. They were terrific!"[13]

It was also around this time that the 761st Tank Battalion's distinctive insignia and motto were designed with the assistance of newly promoted Captain Ivan Harrison. The insignia had a snarling black panther's head with the motto, "Come Out Fighting." It took several attempts before getting the Department of the Army to approve the design.

On 7 January 1944, the 761st Tank Battalion received 128 additional enlisted men from the Armored Force Replacement Center to fill out Company D. As the war in both the Mediterranean and Pacific Theaters were advancing forward, the buildup of military forces for the invasion of Western Europe was also gaining momentum. The battalion was getting up to their assigned strength in anticipation of hopefully being deployed overseas. Early lessons learned in the war put tank battalions in great demand, and the 5th Armored Group was too valuable a resource to remain stateside. The 761st Tank Battalion had an authorized strength of 39 officers, three warrant officers, and 713 enlisted men. Additional African American officers also joined the battalion. Warrant Officer Clarence I. Godbold from the 92nd Infantry Division became the personnel officer. Second Lieutenant John Roosevelt Robinson from the Cavalry Replacement Center became a platoon leader and the battalion morale officer.

On 6 July 1944, Second Lieutenant Robinson, on a bus from Camp Hood to the local town of Belton, Texas, refused to move to the back of the bus when ordered to do so by a civilian bus driver. Court-martial charges ensued but could not proceed because Lieutenant Colonel Bates would not consent to the charges. The commanding officer of Camp Hood subsequently transferred Second Lieutenant Robinson to the 758th Tank Battalion, where its commander immediately signed the court-martial consent.

Lieutenant Colonel Bates describes the incident: "The worst thing here was the bus situation. The only recreation areas they had was off post here in Killeen, a very small town, and Belton and Temple. The bus drivers took a vicious pleasure on the last bus at night, which was always full of soldiers. They were always in the back area standing. Getting about two or three miles from the post and say the bus was over loaded, some of you have to get out. They would make six or eight of them get out and walk back to post. They clearly enjoyed it! The day came and it actually happened about six weeks before we went overseas when one of our Negro officers came out of the Negro Officer's Club, got on the bus along with a Negress who was so light that she looked like a white woman. She was the wife of an officer friend of his. Instead of going to the back of the bus he sat down in about the middle of the bus. Two more stops and the bus was filled with workers leaving here and somebody pointed out that a Negro officer was not sitting in the back of the bus, he was sitting in the middle of the bus with a white woman. The driver went back and told the man he would have to go to the back of the bus, The man refused to go to the back of the bus. He had a short temper, a short fuse, he refused to go back and told the bus driver he had a choice of either driving the bus himself or he would drive it. The bus driver got on the radio, called the dispatch and said he had an uppity kind of Negro here and I'm going to drive to the MP station, have them wait there for us. They started asking him questions and many of the white people on the bus began yelling that he used bad language; he was disrespectful to the bus driver. The MP was a captain and two enlisted men, the captain and the enlisted men call him nigger. This is a black officer. They sure were talking to the wrong man. That was Jackie Robinson, who later became the star baseball player. Jackie Robinson at that time was the only man from UCLA with four letters in four major sports and that is true still today. He came here from Fort Riley. He had gone to OCS and got an appointment to Fort Riley.... The next day I was called into Group Headquarters and they had heard of the incident in the worst light possible imaginable and said there was probably a court-martial pending. I went back to my headquarters and found Jackie there waiting. He told me his story. I then told him that I think the best thing for you to do is, you have accrued leave, put in a request for a ten-day leave. I will sign it. You go home to Pasadena, California, where the entire atmosphere is different. Think about it. Line up and do whatever you can to help yourself because there is pretty well going to be a court-martial. Copies of telegrams came from the War Department. They said, 'We are being deluged with letters upholding the character and popularity of this man. Proceed in court-martial with great care.' You would think that they would have dropped it."[14]

The court-martial of Second Lieutenant John Robinson opened on 2 August 1944, and

Tankers of Company D, 761st Medium Tank Battalion preparing tanks for combat, European Theater of Operations, August 1944. (National Archives)

lasted for 17 days, in which time the 761st Tank Battalion departed Camp Hood for the European Theater of Operations. Lieutenant Robinson was charged with violation of the 63rd and 64th Articles of War.

Lieutenant Robinson was found not guilty on all charges. After the acquittal, his physical status was amended to permanent limited service. After being assigned to the Tank Destroyers, he ended up in an infantry battalion at Camp Breckinridge. In October 1944, Lieutenant Robinson was given a 30-day leave and assigned to inactive duty.[15]

DEPLOYMENT TO WAR

With the invasion of France on 6 June 1944, hopes diminished that the 761st Tank Battalion would ever be sent overseas to a combat theater. Many members of the battalion had been in training for over three years now, and had seen white tank battalions with less time in service deploy overseas ahead of them. But on 9 June 1944, the 761st Tank Battalion was put on full alert for movement overseas. A request came from the European Theater of Operations to send the best tank battalions that still remained in the United States. The 761st Tank Battalion would have the honor of being the first African American armored battalion to deploy overseas to a theater of war.

On 1 August, an advance party composed of the battalion executive officer, Major Charles Wingo, Warrant Officer Mark Henderson, and Technical Sergeant William Newkirk departed Camp Hood for Camp Kilmer, New Jersey. Eight days later, the remainder of the battalion departed, bound for Camp Shanks, New York, and the port of embarkation. They arrived on 13 August, and departed for Great Britain on 27 August. The battalion sailed on HMS *Esperance Bay*, and arrived at the port of Avonmouth, England, on 8 September. Upon arrival, the battalion had a strength of 36 officers, two warrant officers, and 676 enlisted men. The battalion then proceeded to Wimbourne, England, and began last-minute preparations. They were assigned to the 9th Army and placed on alert to stand by in readiness for movement within a notice of six hours. In England, the battalion acquired new equipment and tanks, most armed with the newer high-velocity 76-mm cannon. On 5 October, the battalion received orders relieving it from the 9th Army and assigning it to General George Patton's 3rd Army. On 9 October, the 761st Tank Battalion departed England and landed on Omaha Beach in Normandy, France. On the eve of entering combat, the companies of the 761st Tank Battalions were now led by: Company A, Captain David J. Williams; Company B, Captain J.R. Lawson; Company C, Captain Irvin McHenry; Company D, Captain Richard English; Headquarters Company, Captain Ivan Harrison; and Service Company, Captain August Bremer.

Upon arrival in France, the battalion was attached to the 26th "Yankee" Infantry Division in XII Corps. Major General Willard S. Paul commanded the 26th Infantry Division. Major General Manton S. Eddy commanded XII Corps. From the Normandy coast, the battalion traveled 400 miles inland without any incident of vehicle losses and arrived at Saint Nicholas-de-Port, east of Nancy, France.

Major General Willard S. Paul, in welcoming the battalion on 31 October, told the tank crewmen and their officers: "I am damned glad to have you with us. We have been expecting you for a long time, and I am sure you are going to give a good account of yourselves. I've got a big hill up there that I want you to take, and I believe that you are going to do a great job of it." Two days later, General Patton visited the battalion and, standing on the same half-track vehicle used by Major General Paul, challenged the unit in characteristic Patton manner: "Men, you're the first Negro tankers to ever fight in the American Army. I would never have asked for you if you weren't good. I have nothing but the best in my Army. I don't care what color you are, so long as you go up there and kill those Kraut sonsabitches. Everyone has their eyes on you and is expecting great things from you. Most of all, your race is looking forward to you. Don't let them down, and damn you, don't let me down!... They say it is patriotic to die for your country. Well, let's see how many patriots we can make out of those German sonsabitches."[16]

At 3rd Army Headquarters, General Patton commented on his inspection of the 761st Tank Battalion: "They gave a very good first impression, but I have no faith in the inherent fighting ability of the race."[17]

Since September, General Patton's 3rd Army had been at a standstill outside of Metz, France. General Eisenhower had diverted badly needed supplies and resources from the United States 3rd Army to British commander Field Marshal Montgomery's 21st Army Group in support of the airborne attack into Holland to seize several key bridges in an attempt to capture the port city of Antwerp. While Operation Market Garden was the focus of the Allied advance, General Patton was able to acquire supplies and personnel for an upcoming major offensive in his sector. Meanwhile, German forces fortified their defensive positions around the vicinity of Metz. Some of the fiercest battles of war would occur in this region as Allied forces were preparing to enter Germany. The United States 5th, 90th and 95th Infantry Divisions were poised to attack Metz from three directions.

BAPTISM BY FIRE

The 761st Tank Battalion took up positions at the Line of Departure (LD) near Athanville, France, for its entry into combat on 8 November. Elements of the battalion, as was normal for separate armored units, were attached to the combat regiments of the 26th Infantry Division or placed in special task forces. Company A of the 761st Tank Battalion was attached to the 104th Infantry Regiment with one platoon of tanks attached to the 101st Infantry Regiment. Company C was attached to the 328th Infantry Regiment. Provisional Task Force A contained Company K of the 3/101st Infantry, combat engineers of the 26th Infantry Division, the 602nd Tank Destroyer Battalion (-), and the remainder of the 761st Tank Battalion (except the mortar, assault gun, and reconnaissance platoons, held in reserve). This task force fell under the command of Lieutenant Colonel Peter J. Kopcsak, commander of the 602nd Tank Destroyer Battalion.[18]

In the predawn hours of 8 November 1944, the 761st Tank Battalion encountered a roadblock at the line of departure. A herd of cattle blocked the intersection, causing a delay in the departure of the task forces. Lieutenant Colonel Bates personally arrested the French cattle herder, possibly a collaborator. Just as the crossroads were cleared, an enemy artillery barrage fell, disabling one tank. As the barrage lifted, the column was attacked by a German patrol, which seriously wounded Lieutenant Colonel Bates. With the battalion commander wounded, the responsibility of command fell to the executive officer, Major Charles Wingo. Prior to the commencement of the main attack, Major Wingo reversed the direction of his tank, and proceeded for the rear area away from the line of debarkation. Lieutenant Colonel Bates describes the situation: "None of our men went psycho that I know of. The only one that went psycho was a white officer, my executive officer. There was this terrible day when the whole 3rd Army was making a big attack and it was delayed, and delayed and delayed for a week. At the last few hours before the attack, a patrol came back and said there is ground out there impassable for tanks. The direction of the tank attack was changed 30 degrees and we got the word out by radio, as they were moving toward the line of departure. I hurried up in a jeep and got up to the line of departure. It was barely breaking daylight and I stood there. I knew they knew me and I was making sure they were going in the right direction. They all went by, waved, buttoned up and kept going. When we got on by, a German patrol nailed me with a burp gun. Unfortunately, that day I went down and my XO (executive officer) cracked up."[19]

Lieutenant John D. Long, who would later command Company B, shows his disgust with the executive officer's action: "The next man in command, Major Wingo, the morning of the attack, turned his tank around and went hell-bent in the opposite direction. He just plain chickened and that SOB was evacuated for combat fatigue. Hell, we hadn't even been in battle yet.... I swore to myself there would never be a headline saying my men and I chickened. A soldier, in time of war, is supposed to accept the idea of dying. That's what he's there for; live with it and forget it. I expected to get killed, but whatever happened I was determined to die an officer and a gentleman."[20]

Elements of the 101st and 104th Infantry Regiments of the 26th Infantry Division with a detachment of combat engineers followed Company A's spearhead through the line of resistance. Captain Williams led two tank platoons in the direction of Vic-sur-Seille, in support of the 104th Infantry Regiment. Lieutenant Joseph Kahoe's tank platoon was in the lead, with Staff Sergeant Ruben Rivers commanding the first tank. First Lieutenant Charles Barbour led the remaining tank platoon of Company A in the direction of the town of Moyenvic, followed by elements of the 101st Infantry Regiment. Traversing minefields, three tanks were disabled due to mines before even reaching their first objective.

Staff Sergeant Rivers encountered a roadblock that impeded the column's advance. With utter disregard for his personal safety, he dismounted his tank in the face of German machine gun and mortar fire, attached a cable to the roadblock, a downed tree, and removed it from the road. Several antipersonnel mines were set off as Staff Sergeant Rivers' tank removed the large tree from the road. His prompt action under heavy enemy fire prevented any further delay and was instrumental to the success of the assault. For his heroic actions on that day, Staff Sergeant Ruben Rivers would be awarded the battalion's first Silver Star Medal.[21]

Shell fragments of exploding artillery struck Private Clifford C. Adams of Waco, Texas, a medic assigned to the 761st Tank Battalion's medical detachment. He was going to the aid of wounded tank crewmen and infantrymen. He died a few hours later, becoming the first member of the 761st Tank Battalion to die in combat.[22]

Company C, commanded by Captain Irvin McHenry, attached to the 328th Infantry Regiment, utilized its twelve tanks in the assault on the town of Bezange-la-Petite and a hill to the southeast. Second Lieutenant Jay E. Johnson, the 761st Tank Battalion's Motor Officer, led Company C's first platoon in the assault. He was seriously wounded and temporarily blinded by a shell burst from a German 88-mm cannon that exploded directly over his exposed position on the opened turret. Company C lost three tanks in that battle, with the complete tank crew of Staff Sergeant Harvey Woodard's tank killed and two additional tank crewmen wounded.

Opposing this American force was the veteran German 11th Panzer Division, which had over 12,000 battle-hardened soldiers, 30 artillery guns, and a large number of Panzer tanks. They had been in action in North Africa and the Russian front. Supporting the Panzer division were the 361st and 559th Volksgrenadier Divisions.

On 9 November, in the season's first snowstorm, the two platoons of Company A supported the 104th Infantry Regiment, which attacked and took the town of Chateau-Salins after four hours of heavy fighting. Company A then turned east toward Morville-les-Vic. The remainder of the battalion in Task Force A, with infantry mounted on its tanks, was then approaching the town of Morville. Two light tank platoons of Company D, with two companies of the 3/101st Infantry, took positions south of Salival, a small town from which enemy machine gun fire enfiladed the western slope of Hill 310 (Cote St. Jean), which was the 26th Infantry Division's main objective for the day. The Stuart tanks of Company D conducted screening operations in an area around Salival. Sergeant Warren G.H. Crecy's tank came out of a wooded area where antitank fire caught him in the open and disabled his tank. He immediately recovered and took over a half-tracked vehicle armed only with a .30-caliber light machine gun. Still under enemy fire, he eliminated the enemy antitank crew that destroyed his tank, and aided in the annihilation of enemy forward artillery observers. Company D shelled the town with its 37-mm cannons and set it afire. Infantry, at dusk, entered Salival, clearing the town of the remaining German soldiers, and passed through it to the woods beyond.

Staff Sergeant Chester Jones from the 961st Tank Ordnance Company recalls: "When you opened the hatches of the wrecked tanks that could be repaired, some of the most ghastly sights you could imagine were exposed: what were once human beings were scrambled all over the interior of these tanks. You didn't stop to figure out which leg or arm went with which remains, if there were a whole torso. You just put it in a plastic container and cleaned the spattered brains and blood from the inside of the vehicle. I was a tank mechanic, but cleaning out those wrecks went with the job...."[23]

As the 761st Tank Battalion approached the village of Morville-les-Vic, they received a barrage of heavy artillery and mortar fire. The units took up defensive positions around the village, with Company A on the east, Company C on the northwest, and Company B in the center, preparing to assault with infantry. Company D conducted screening operations from the direction of Salival. After the tanks of the 761st Tank Battalion and the guns of the 602nd Tank Destroyer Battalion (–) shelled Morville-les-Vic, infantry elements attempted to assault the town by following the tanks of Company B. Tank barricades halted this advance. The infantry suffered heavy casualties as only a few tanks of the company were able to maneuver around the barricades, and were immediately fired upon by well-camouflaged antitank and machine gun fire coming from every direction.

As one of the tanks took a direct hit from a Panzerfaust and caught fire, the tank commander, Sergeant Roy King from Rouge, Michigan, was killed by machine gun fire as he attempted to exit through the right turret hatch. The M4 Sherman tank, with its gasoline engine and loaded with ammunition, was highly volatile when hit with an antitank shell. German tanks were equipped with diesel engines and were not as vulnerable as the Sherman tank, that they nicknamed the *Ronson*, after a famous cigarette lighter. In addition, the German antitank weapons were designed to penetrate five inches of armor, and the Sherman tank was only equipped with three inches of frontal armor plate. The tank crewmen were instructed to evacuate the tank immediately when a round penetrated its armor. Private First Class Nathaniel Ross was severely wounded when he came out of the left turret hatch. Technician Four James Whitby and Private John McNeil exited through the bottom escape hatch, carrying their .45-caliber submachine guns with them. Corporal Herbert Porter, wounded by the shell that hit the tank, exited last. Using their individual weapons, the surviving crewmen sprayed accurate submachine gun fire on enemy infantry and machine gun positions in the upper stories of houses. After sighting the German antitank and machine gun emplacements, Technician Four Whitby reentered the burning tank, and manning the .30-caliber machine gun and 76-mm cannon, was able to kill several enemy soldiers. The Sherman was hit twice more by German antitank fire, but the soldiers remained at their positions, not wanting to leave their fellow wounded crewmen, and maintaining constant suppressing fire on the enemy. This action allowed the soldiers of Company K, 3/101st Infantry to regroup and begin clearing the town of German soldiers.

On the high ground northwest of Morville-les-Vic, Company D assisted the infantry in gaining a foothold. In a furious battle, they broke up an enemy counterattack. Staff Sergeant Jack Gilbert and his tank crew abandoned their M5 tank after it had been hit by antitank fire. The enemy captured and held the tank, firing at the exposed infantry, until Staff Sergeant Gilbert and his crew retook it. In another tank, Private First Class Obie Smith personally accounted for 20 enemy soldiers killed with his bow-mounted .30-caliber light machine gun. Meanwhile, Sergeant Crecy's new tank became bogged down in the mud. Climbing on the rear of his immobile tank, he was able to keep the enemy pinned down, firing the turret-mounted .30-caliber machine gun, while the infantrymen of the 26th Division were able to safely withdraw.

While the enemy concentrated on the tanks of Company B and infantry in the town, Company C attacked with such swiftness that a bridge over the Seille River was crossed before the enemy could destroy it. The Germans quickly recovered and fired antitank rounds at the approaching tanks. Second Lieutenant Kenneth W. Coleman of Washington, D.C., was leading his platoon in the attack when his tank was immobilized by enemy fire. Lieutenant Coleman immediately dismounted his burning tank and courageously led his crew on foot under heavy artillery and machine gun fire. Battling a much larger force, they were able to drive the Germans from their positions with grenades and fire from their .45-caliber submachine guns. This swift action cleared the way and enabled the rest of the tank platoon to proceed. The remaining tanks of Company C then came over a steep hill, and down into an enemy tank trap. Cleverly camouflaged and concealed in buildings were German antitank guns. Unable to maneuver back up over the steep hill, the tanks were immediately fired on by the antitank gun crews and Panzerfaust teams. Seven tanks were immediately hit and disabled.

First Sergeant Samuel J. Turley, a career soldier from Brooklyn, New York, fighting as a tank platoon leader, organized the surviving crewmen into dismounted combat teams. As the company first sergeant, Turley could have remained behind with the rear support detachment, but instead routed a bow gunner from the tank, and went forward with his men. He, like the rest of the battalion, was eager to prove their self-worth in battle. Upon dismounting his burning tank, First Sergeant Turley removed one of the tank's .30-caliber machine guns. He returned fire by shooting the weapon from his hip. Some of the surviving soldiers crawled under their disabled tanks with their individual weapons and placed devastating fire upon enemy gun emplacements. These dismounted teams held off the enemy counterattacks, while crews from other trapped and burning tanks, along with the infantry, escaped along the adjacent tank ditch.[24]

Pinned down by heavy enemy artillery and machine gun fire, many of the beleaguered tankers of Company C were unable to return fire. The Germans were determined to eliminate the surviving tank crewmen. First Sergeant Turley ordered the retreat of his men. Emerging from beneath the protection of a disabled Sherman tank, First Sergeant Turley provided such accurate fire from his machine gun that the enemy gunners had to take cover, and his men were able to retreat along the tank ditch.

The escaping tank crewmen crawled in the freezing, muddy waters of the ditch. Hot shell fragments fell all around, steaming up the water as the ground shook from the explosions. The situation became even more hopeless as German artillery began walking a line toward the ditch. Corporal Dwight Simpson, scrambling for his life, saw Technician 4th Class Horatio Scott of Lynn, Massachusetts, who was seriously wounded and unable to move. With total disregard for his personal safety, Corporal Simpson weaved through artillery fire and moved Scott away from his burning tank. He administered life-saving first aid and remained with his wounded friend until dark. Under the cover of darkness, Simpson evacuated Scott 300 yards to the rear, finally reaching a battalion aid station. For his heroic actions, Corporal Simpson would be awarded the Bronze Star medal.[25]

Company C was nearly annihilated by the time help arrived. The company had nine enlisted men and one officer killed, and seven battle-damaged tanks, four of them recoverable, in the fighting along the tank trap. The relief force, consisting of the headquarters tanks, the 105-mm assault gun platoon, and the 81-mm mortar platoon, opened fire on the enemy positions with devastating effect. An enemy relief column consisting of over 30 vehicles and 200 soldiers was spotted en route to Morville-les-Vic. Despite low visibility caused by the weather, the four howitzers of the battalion's assault gun platoon and the 81-mm mortar crews, aided by the aerial observations of artillery liaison spotter aircraft, completed its indirect firing missions. Their accurate fire scored direct hits on an enemy armored vehicle and four trucks, causing the column to withdraw. Task Force A, finally getting seven tanks through Morville, went on toward the town of Hampont, the tanks assisting the infantry in gaining a foothold in the vicinity of the village of Bois de Geline to the northeast.[26]

On the left flank, Company A completed its mission of capturing the town of Chateau

Officers of the 761st Medium Tank Battalion await action near Nancy, France, on 5 November 1944. Left to right: Captain Ivan H. Harrison, Captain Irvin McHenry and 2nd Lieutenant James C. Lightfoot. (U.S. Army Military History Institute, Carlisle Barracks, Pennsylvania)

Salines with the 104th Infantry Regiment. This was the first major town to be captured by the 26th Infantry Division. As the infantry secured the town and established a forward headquarters for XII Corps, Company A proceeded east toward Morville.

Later on that same day, Lieutenant Colonel Hopis E. Hunt came forward from the 17th Armored Group headquarters to assist the battalion's acting commander, unaware that Major Wingo had already been evacuated. Shortly after his arrival, both Lieutenant Colonel Hunt and Lieutenant Colonel Kopcsak, commander of Task Force A, were wounded by enemy artillery fire. After Lieutenant Colonel Kopcsak was medically evacuated from the battlefield, Lieutenant Colonel Hunt, though slightly wounded, took command of the task force. With the administrative removal of Major Wingo, Lieutenant Colonel Hunt assumed command of the 761st Tank Battalion as well, a position which he retained until the end of November. Major John F. George, also from the 17th Armor Group, became the new battalion's S-3 operations officer.

As night began to fall, the 761st Tank Battalion was ordered to deploy back and regroup. During the initial two days of their baptism by fire, there were men who reentered burning tanks to pull out their trapped comrades, tank commanders who strapped wounded men to their vehicles and successfully evacuated them from the battlefield, and men who, in exposed positions, pulled their machine guns from their disabled tanks and returned German fire on foot. One tank driver, seeing seriously wounded white soldiers of the 26th Infantry Division lying in the open, dismounted from his tank, moved across open terrain under heavy artillery and small arms fire, evacuated the men to the shelter of a disabled tank and administered first aid, and thereby saved the lives of three of the wounded. White infantrymen of Company K similarly attempted to remove the body of the tank crew commander from his burning tank in Morville. A number of men lost their lives or were wounded in the effort. Lieutenant Coleman and First Sergeant Turley would be posthumously awarded Silver Star medals for their heroic deeds in combat.[27] At the close of the second day of combat, the 761st Tank Battalion felt that it had won the right to its motto, "Come Out Fighting."

On 10 November 1944, Company A pushed through Morville-les-Vic with the infantry. They continued to advance forward together as the enemy withdrew slowly in a well-planned and executed retreat, still providing stiff resistance. Technician Horatio Scott died of wounds he received the day before. The fully mechanized 4th Armored Division stood prepared to exploit any signs of a breach in the lines or of a full enemy retreat.

On 11 November, Staff Sergeant Johnnie Stevens led the third platoon of Company A in an assault on Hill 309 near the town of Wuisse, France. German antitank guns opened up on the tanks of the platoon. After his tank had been hit by antitank fire, Staff Sergeant Stevens and the surviving members of his crew were severely wounded. Tankers were trained to immediately evacuate tanks that been hit by enemy gunfire because the Sherman tanks with their gasoline engines were susceptible to explode. After Stevens left his tank, German mortar fire targeted the surviving crew members. As a white sergeant from the 26th Infantry Division was evacuating Stevens from an exposed position, the sergeant was killed by German machine gun fire. Staff Sergeant Stevens would have 11 pieces of shrapnel removed from his legs while he was hospitalized.

During this battle, Technician 5th Class Walter J. Campbell of Hempstead, New York, was killed when the antitank round struck Staff Sergeant Stevens' tank. Sergeant George Shivers of Bainbridge, Georgia, was also killed in action when a German 88-mm round scored a direct hit on the turret of his tank. Captain Adamson, the 761st Tank Battalion's medical officer, proceeded on foot through an enemy artillery barrage to aid the wounded soldiers on the battlefield. There, with his medics, he administered life-saving medical treatment in total disregard for his own personal safety. For his strong devotion to duty, courage, and solicitude for his wounded comrades, he was awarded the Bronze Star medal.[28]

On 12 November two platoons of Company A repulsed an enemy counterattack just outside of Wuisse, destroying two enemy Panzer tanks. The next day, one tank platoon led by First Lieutenant Joseph O. Kahoe, attached to the 2/104th Infantry Battalion, counterattacked on its own initiative, took Wuisse in the afternoon, and defended the town throughout the night. Lieutenant Kahoe had joined the army in 1935 as a $21 per month private in the 10th Cavalry Regiment. He reenlisted in 1942 with the hopes of attending Officers Candidate School. As the only African American officer candidate in his class, he graduated and joined the 761st Tank Battalion.

The 26th Infantry Division's next objective was the town of Benestroff, a vital railroad junction and German communications center. General Patton's 3rd Army had other infantry divisions simultaneously attacking the city of Metz. As the pincer movement closed, the 26th Infantry Division would eliminate any possibility of relief for the enemy. On 16 November 1944, Company A, supporting the 2/101st Infantry Battalion, led an attack on the railroad town of Guebling. As Company A approached the town, it divided its 11 remaining tanks into two platoons. Second Lieutenant Robert Hammond, Jr., of Cleveland, Ohio, led the first platoon with Staff Sergeant Rivers commanding the lead tank. Lieutenant Kahoe led the second platoon of six tanks, including Company A's headquarters tank. As the second platoon reached the summit of a gentle slope, a concentrated barrage of enemy artillery met them. Lieutenant Kahoe had his tank disabled in the artillery barrage and had to be evacuated to the battalion aid station along with another wounded member of his crew. Lieutenant Kahoe's remaining tank crewmen escaped injury, returned to the battalion command post to secure another tank, and rejoined the platoon. The platoon then changed directions and joined Lieutenant Hammond's platoon.

En route to Guebling, Staff Sergeant Rivers' tank struck a double teller antitank mine. The ensuing explosion blew off the right track, the volute springs, and the undercarriage, and tossed the tank on its side. Staff Sergeant Ray Roberson and Corporal Homer Bracey of the medical detachment heard the explosion, rushed forward, and found Rivers behind the tank with a severe leg wound. He had a compound fracture with the bone protruding through the pants leg. He was clearly a case for medical evacuation, but when the medics attempted to administer morphine for the pain, Rivers refused it. After having the wound dressed, Rivers went to the second tank in the column and told Sergeant Conway to get out, as he took over command. Sergeant Conway picked up his submachine gun and took up positions with the infantry. Then as incoming enemy mortar rounds hit their positions, the tanks were ordered to disperse and take up defensive positions around the Guebling railroad complex. Staff Sergeant Rivers' new tank was driven by Technician 5th Class Jonathan Hall, Private First Class Frank Towers was the bow gunner, Private First Class Ivory Hilliard of Houston, Texas, was the loader, and Private Everett Robinson was the cannoneer.

On 17 November, the combat engineers worked at constructing a prefabricated Bailey bridge while the tank crews and infantry exchanged fire with the enemy on the far bank. The bridge was completed that evening and Staff Sergeant Rivers' tank was the first to cross. Despite his wounds, Staff Sergeant Rivers battled two German tanks in Guebling until forcing them to withdraw. Splitting the platoon up into two firing teams, Staff Sergeant Rivers and his companion tank, commanded by Sergeant Walter James, took up firing positions on a gentle slope that offered excellent fields of fire on the town of Bougaltroff. Lieutenant Hammond and his companion tank took up firing positions in an orchard located in the low ground. From these positions, Lieutenant Hammond's platoon would be able to provide cover for the main assault into Bougaltroff, which was scheduled as the next objective. Captain Williams and the remaining tanks of Company A took up positions inside of Guebling. Captain Williams ordered Staff Sergeant Rivers to the rear, as the medical personnel reported infection had set in on his wounded leg. If he did not receive immediate medical attention, there was a possibility of his losing that leg. Staff Sergeant Rivers again refused, stating that he would be needed if the Germans counterattacked. That evening, Germans in captured American uniforms attempted to infiltrate the town. The ensuing battle lasted until daybreak as the Germans withdrew.

On the morning of 19 November, the assault on Bougaltroff began as the tanks of Company A, M10 tank destroyers from the 602nd Tank Destroyer Battalion, and the supporting infantry advanced. Lieutenant Hammond and Staff Sergeant Rivers' tank teams would provide covering fire for the advance. Just outside of Guebling in an open field, enemy antitank and machine gun fortifications fired upon the advancing force. Sergeant Weston's lead tank received a direct hit, which disabled his 76-mm cannon. Captain Williams ordered all armored vehicles on the move to pull back. Staff Sergeant Rivers and Sergeant James spotted the enemy's antitank emplacements from their covered positions behind the slope. They immediately moved forward and placed a concentrated barrage of fire on the advancing enemy Mark IV Panther tanks and the armored Panzerjaegers (tank destroyers). Lieutenant Hammond's tank team also commenced firing on the enemy positions. This allowed the ambushed infantry and armor to escape. Captain Williams then ordered all the armored vehicles to pull back as the 26th Division artillery would begin firing on the German positions. Both tanks in Lieutenant Hammond's team were quickly struck by antitank rounds and disabled. Staff Sergeant Rivers, caught up in the heat of battle, probably did not hear the order to withdraw. Staff Sergeant Rivers' tank continued to battle the German armored vehicles, allowing the remaining forces to safely retreat. The surviving tanks heard Staff Sergeant Rivers over the radio say: "I see them. We'll fight them."[29] Rivers, outnumbered, continued firing on the enemy armored vehicles until antitank rounds were seen going through his turret. "Pull up, driver! Pull back, driver! Oh, Lord," were Staff Sergeant Rivers' last words before his tank exploded. At that moment, the Panzerjaegers began to pursue Sergeant James' tank, which immediately sought cover behind the crest of the hill. The remaining wounded crewmen of Staff Sergeant Rivers' tank were able to evacuate the tank. Private First Class Hilliard, although mortally wounded, was last seen fleeing toward the enemy lines.

The soldiers of the 2/101st Infantry also suffered heavy casualties. When the battalion commander was severely wounded, Captain Williams became the senior officer on the ground. He ordered the infantry to take up defensive positions in the houses in Guebling as the enemy had now outflanked them. The 26th Division artillery was effective in forcing the Germans to retreat. When there was a lull in the battle, Captain Williams had the medics check the disabled tanks for the wounded. Captain Williams recalls: "Then along comes Lieutenant Colonel Hunt, who took Bates' place. He is standing in a half-track looking immaculate and he says, 'Williams, you had quite a battle here.' I said, yes sir! Then the tank destroyer captain said, 'Listen, this company stayed in there.' I didn't have much of a company left and there was infantry all over the place. The infantry takes terrible casualties. I said I want to put Sergeant Rivers in for the Congressional Medal of Honor. He said, 'What did he do? He got the Silver Star already.' I said sir that was for November 8. He's up in that tank there. He said, 'Well, put it in writing.' He didn't show any interest.... It was subtly told to me not to put anything in over the Silver Star. We called it the battalion commander's good conduct medal; I got one. Once they saw 761st with the 'N' behind it: Silver Star. I didn't deserve any more."[30]

At 1300 hours, what remained of Company A and the 2/10th Infantry Battalion were pulled out of Guebling. Company A went to the town of Marimont to reequip, perform emergency maintenance, and reorganize its surviving crewmen. The maintenance section worked diligently repairing the remaining tanks to make them combat-ready for the next mission. On the morning of 21 November, Captain Williams was awakened by Corporal Walter Lewis, who invited him to a memorial service given by the men. The men wanted to say their own personal prayers and just be together. Many had lost friends that they had lived with and served together with for the last few years.

On 20 November, Company C, 761st Tank Battalion, supported the 2/328th Infantry

Battalion for an assault on the town of Kerprich. The assault gun platoon and four medium tanks shelled the town while the infantry initiated their assault. Captain McHenry, the commanding officer of Company C, broke his hand in his cannon's recoil during combat. First Lieutenant Gates, the leader of the assault gun platoon, took over command of that company. The infantry entered and cleared Kerprich that evening of enemy soldiers.

On 22 November, Company C entered the town of Torchville unopposed. From there, they drove northeast through Bois-de-Hessling to the western edge of the city of Munster. One section of the assault gun platoon moved south and shelled the town. The infantry occupied a portion of the town that evening. For the next two days, the battle continued in Munster, with the infantry clearing house by house, and the tanks firing on enemy sniper and mortar positions. After Munster was secured, the remnants of Company C deployed back to Marimont and made preparations for an offensive push against the towns of Benestroff and Dieuze.

The assault gun platoon conducted a fire mission on the Dieuze with such pinpoint accuracy it forced the Germans to withdraw from the town. As the infantry was securing the town, the enemy counterattacked and reoccupied Dieuze. Combat Command A of the 4th Armored Division finally forced the remnants of the German soldiers from Dieuze, and the 761st Tank Battalion advanced 20 miles through the Forest-de-Bride, and launched an attack against the town of Bensetroff, its primary objective. The 26th Reconnaissance Troop, with a platoon of M5 Stuart tanks from Company D, entered the town first, and after a short firefight, the delaying force of German soldiers surrendered.

On 25 November, a platoon of tanks from Company C, led by Lieutenant Bruce, the assault gun platoon, and elements of the 328th Infantry Regiment received orders to assault the town of Honskirch. Due to the muddy fields, the five remaining operational tanks of Company C were ordered to approach the town on the main road in column. On the outskirts of the town, enemy artillery and antitank rounds fired on the column. The last tank in the column was hit first, blocking the egress road to the rear, and trapping the remaining tanks. Unable to retreat due to the road's being blocked, and not capable of advancing due to the devastating enemy fire, the tankers continued to fire back until each tank was finally disabled. As the surviving crewmembers evacuated their tanks, German mortars tried to finish them off. When Sergeant Frank Cochrane's tank was hit, his driver was killed, and the gunner, Private Frank Greenwood, had both of his legs blown off. Sergeant Cochrane evacuated Greenwood from the burning tank and sought the cover of a ditch. Cochrane kept Greenwood's head from becoming submerged in the water of the ditch by resting it on the heel of his foot. It was then that Germans began walking their mortars toward their position. Under heavy fire, Sergeant Cochrane was able to evacuate Private Greenwood to a battalion aid station. Sergeant Emery Thomas saw three wounded crewmen from another tank exposed in the open terrain. After Sergeant Thomas and his crew dismounted their burning tank, he courageously led a few men to the wounded while under heavy mortar and machine gun fire. They dragged the casualties to safety and administered medical aid. Then Thomas personally carried the most seriously wounded man to the battalion aid station and returned to help evacuate the others.

As the enemy continued to fire on the surviving tankers and infantry soldiers along the road, Sergeant Robert A. Johnson of Washington D.C., was on the high ground overlooking the battle with his assault gun platoon. He and his gunner commenced firing on the German positions. When he had exhausted all of their HE rounds, he began to fire white phosphorous shells at the enemy mortar crews. This was all the ammunition that he had left. The phosphorous shells caused the enemy to quit firing because it covered the battlefield with a white cloud, and enabled the surviving tankers and infantrymen to escape to safety.

The Company C commander, Lieutenant Charles Gates, was wounded, and his driver, Technician 5th Class Lane Dunn of Scottsville, Kentucky, was killed. Also killed during this battle were: Corporal Ardis Graham, of Raeford, North Carolina; Private Coleman Simmons, Jr., of Detroit, Michigan; and Private James Welborn, Jr., of Jonesville, North Carolina. Lieutenant Gates recalls: "I became very bitter in the battle of Honskirch. We had been ordered to make an attack. We were able to spot all the major defenses of the Germans. I told this colonel that our approach was very poorly organized and would be pretty tough. I delayed the attack for four hours. Finally, he gave me a direct order to move my tanks straight down a road. It was in defiance to good tactics. Within five minutes, we lost five tanks. Now this colonel had been given command of an infantry regiment. All the combat experience he had was as a finance officer in the United States. He didn't know a thing about combat."[31]

Later, when asked, "Did Patton recognize you?" Lieutenant Gates replied, "Yes he did. He was a person who came to the front frequently. When he'd come around us, he'd talk just as you and I are talking now. He'd start relieving people of the units to which we were attached, starting at the top. At Honskirch, he wanted to know why we lost five tanks in such a short period. Within two weeks, this colonel of whom I had spoken had been shipped back to the United States. I have respect for [Patton]. He might not have liked the Negro any more than anybody else. I know his headquarters didn't, because they never accepted our record."[32]

Casualties in men and tanks were heavy during the month of November. There were 22 men killed in action, two more died of wounds, 81 wounded, 44 non-battle casualties, with 14 tanks lost and 20 damaged.[33] Many of the non-battle casualties were caused by trench foot. The men had no opportunity for personal hygiene and foul conditions existed everywhere. The pace in combat is so intense that when a foot began to lose sensation, there was usually no time to stop for treatment. Finally, when a foot went dead and became useless, the soldier would have to be evacuated to the battalion aid station. In some cases, the limb would have to be removed. But tanks could be recovered and repaired, or even replaced. On the other hand, the 761st Tank Battalion, like the other active African American combat units, had difficulty replacing men. During its first month in combat, no replacements arrived at all and the unit ended November 1944 with a shortage of 113 men.[34]

At the end of November, Lieutenant Colonel Hunt returned to his duties with the 17th Armor Group and Major John George, the battalion S-3 operations officer, moved up and assumed command of the battalion. Also in November, the first of the three African American armored units, the 758th Tank Battalion, deployed overseas to the Mediterranean Theater supporting the 92nd Infantry Division.

On 4 December the first of the replacements arrived at the 761st Tank Battalion. But these were not Armored Force replacements because there were none. The 761st Tank Battalion would have to instruct these soldiers on the job, but presently, the battalion still had a combat mission to perform. Meanwhile, the 26th Infantry Division continued its advance toward the Maginot Line. France built the Maginot Line after World War I in an effort to prevent Germany from reinvading their country. It was a system of well-fortified bunkers and tunnels that stretched from the France/Switzerland border to Belgium. Now, it was the last line of defense for the German army to protect its country from the invasion of General Patton's 3rd Army.

The Maginot Line came under attack by the tanks of Company A in the hard-fought region surrounding the city of Aachen, Company B in the vicinity of Etting, and Company

C around the town of Oermingen. High explosive shells from the 761st's cannons just bounced off the thick pillbox walls. United States Army Air Force bombardment and explosives planted by combat engineers were required to demolish these fortifications. On 9 December 1944, the 761st Tank Battalion pushed through the Maginot Line and assembled at Woelfling for the push into Germany. On 11 December, the 26th Infantry Division was relieved from front line duties, and replaced with the newly arrived 87th Infantry Division. There would be no relief for the soldiers of the 761st Tank Battalion. They were quickly attached to the 87th Infantry Division.

A strong comradeship had developed in combat between the African American tankers and the white infantrymen of the 26th Infantry Division. Each had put their lives on the line to protect their fellow soldiers. In the time frame of only one month, the 761st Tank Battalion gained the reputation of having no fear against the enemy forces that opposed them. The 761st Tank Battalion's work with the 26th Infantry Division in November 1944 elicited special commendation from the corps commander, in addition to commendation that went to all units of the 26th Division and XII Corps[35]:

1. I consider the 761st Tank Battalion to have entered combat with such conspicuous courage and success as to warrant special commendation.
2. The speed with which they adapted themselves to the front line under most adverse weather conditions, the gallantry with which they faced some of Germany's finest troops, and the confident spirit with which they emerged from their recent engagements in the vicinity of Dieuze, Morville les Vic, and Guebling entitle them surely to consider themselves of the veteran 761st.[36]

To this General Paul added: "It is with extreme gratification that the Corps Commander's commendation is forwarded to you. Your battalion has supported this division with great bravery under the most adverse weather and terrain conditions. You have my sincere wish that success may continue to follow your endeavors."[37]

On 14 December 1944, the first of the 761st Tank Battalion's armored vehicles crossed the border into Germany. By 15 December the battalion had lost a majority of its tanks to enemy action and from mechanical failure caused by continuous commitment to combat of all available tanks for extended periods of time. When the battalion returned to Sarre Union for four days of maintenance, only three tanks were fully combat operational. On 16 December, the Germans began their offensive in the Ardennes region of Belgium. Caught totally by surprise, American forces were quickly driven back. Two regiments of the 106th Infantry Division were surrounded and captured, and more than 350 American prisoners of war were massacred at Malmedy. The 82nd and 101st Airborne Divisions, recovering from Operation Market Garden, and the only divisions being held in reserve in France, were rushed to the Ardennes. General Patton's 3rd Army was ordered to change the direction of their attack 90 degrees and proceed to relieve the 101st Airborne Division at Bastogne.

The 761st Tank Battalion, poised to strike the Siegfried Line at Saarbrucken and Zweibrucken, received orders along with the 87th Infantry Division to proceed to what became known as the Battle of the Bulge. Due to the urgency of the battle, one contingent of tanks traveled by train and arrived several days ahead of the rest of the battalion, which negotiated the steep and icy roads to the battlefield of Belgium. Sergeant Robert Johnson, who was responsible for saving so many lives at Honskirch by firing those white phosphorous artillery rounds, was killed in an accident when his assault gun vehicle slid off an icy road. On the march from the Sarre region to Neufchateau, Belgium, southwest of Bastogne, beginning on

24 December and ending on 30 December, ten medium tanks dropped from the column because of maintenance failures.[38]

On the morning of 27 December 1944, elements of the 4th Armored Division reached Bastogne. The 590th Ambulance Company, an African American unit, followed closely behind the advanced elements. They were among the first to reach the badly wounded Americans there.

On 31 December, the 761st Tank Battalion was committed to battle in support of the 347th Infantry Regiment. They captured the towns of Rondu and Nimbermont, Belgium, approximately 15 miles west of Bastogne. With tanks spearheading the attack, the 87th Infantry Division reported: "The 1/347th Infantry was at Remagne, the 3/347th Infantry was at Moircy. Instructions were to close the highway between St. Hubert and Bastogne. Two tanks from the 761st were in front of each infantry company for the attack. On the next day, the 3/347th Infantry reported that three of the tanks were burning and one was damaged beyond use."[39]

On 4 January 1945, in the area around Remagne, Sergeant Walter Woodson, of Company A, had his tank shot out from under him by an 88-mm antitank gun. The delayed-action projectile ricocheted inside the steel walls of the tank and exploded behind the driver, Private Thomas Bragg of Elizabeth, New Jersey, killing him instantly. He had been a popular member of the 761st Orchestra back at Camp Hood. Walter Lewis, the gunner, and his fellow crewmembers, Privates James Jordan and Charles Brooks, received serious wounds. Walter Lewis describes the hit: "We did not move 50 yards before we were hit! It sounded like heavy plate glass bursting into a million ear-splitting pieces. Concussion blew me out of the tank. Had my hatch not been open, all of us would have been killed by the concussion alone. I got up and ran, for I was in a state of hysteria.... My clothing was cut to shreds. [I was] bleeding profusely.... The area was now drawing enemy fire. I ran until I was exhausted. I remember stopping at a monastery. The Germans began shelling this also, so I took off again. In my delirium, I made my way to an aid station about three kilometers from the scene of the battle, running through wooded areas infested with German snipers.... I collapsed. When I came to my senses, I was on a litter. I was evacuated at night in a convoy of ambulances, which slowly moved through minefields and booby-trapped roads. I was operated on the next day in a hospital in Sedan, France."[40] Sergeant James Nelson of Detroit, Michigan, commander of the first Company A tank to cross the German border in December, was killed instantly when an antitank round scored a direct hit on his tank. The towns of Bonnerue, Recongne, Remagne, and Jenneville fell to the advancing 761st Tank Battalion and the 87th Infantry Division. On 5 January, Technician 5th Class Jessie J. Bond of Gates, North Carolina, was killed in action. In this fast-moving battle, the 761st Tank Battalion had to be constantly resupplied with fuel and ammunition. When at times supply trucks could not reach elements of the unit due to icy snow-covered roads, the light M5 tanks of Company D towed ammunition trailers to resupply the medium tanks from forward supply points placed as close to the front battle lines as possible.

On 7 January 1945, the 761st Tank Battalion and elements of the 87th Infantry Division were ordered to attack the enemy fortified positions defended by the 113th Panzer Brigade at Tillet. Company A destroyed an 88-mm antitank gun and a self-propelled 75-mm gun. Company D, relieved of resupply duties, along with the 87th Reconnaissance Troop, diverted enemy attention from the main battle around Tillet with an attack on Gerimont. There, they destroyed an enemy mortar position and an ammunition supply point, killed 50 German soldiers, and captured ten enemy prisoners.

A reconstituted Company C assaulted Tillet with all three tank platoons. Newly promoted Captain Gates, in command of a force of ten tanks with supporting infantry, launched an assault against an organized enemy defensive position following a personal forward reconnaissance. Captain Gates personally directed the attack on foot, keeping his force going forward against heavy opposition. They destroyed eight machine gun emplacements, a Mark IV Panther tank, an ammunition supply point, and three antitank guns. They also killed 106 enemy soldiers. Staff Sergeant Cochrane, leading one of the tank platoons, took three hits on his tank. With his battle-damaged tank, he and his crew fired back and continued to advance. Staff Sergeant Moses Dade, leading another of the platoons, had the turret top fly 50 feet in the air after taking a direct hit from an antitank round. He continued to fire back with his remaining operational weapons. In another action, Staff Sergeant Conway's tank was caught on a hill by several Panzer tanks just outside of Tillet, and had to battle them off alone in spite of having been hit, but the Panzers did not get past his position. At the end of the battle, only two American tanks and a remnant of the infantry remained with the original force. On the evening of 9 January, the enemy could no longer continue its resistance and withdrew in the direction of Fosset and Roumont with the American infantry and tanks in pursuit. The 87th Infantry Division set up barricades on the March/Bastogne Road and blocked the vital supply route to the Germans' offensive operations in the Bulge.

The last of the three African American tank battalions to be activated, the 784th, arrived in France on 25 December 1944, in the midst of the Battle of the Bulge. The 784th Tank Battalion was attached to support the 104th Infantry Division, then located near Eshweiler, Germany. On 26 December, while en route to join the 104th Infantry Division, the battalion came to the aid of a burning Allied ammunition train near Soissons, France. The officer in charge of the ammunition train requested their assistance in saving the undetonated rail cars. Utilizing their tanks as recovery vehicles, the 784th Tank Battalion was able to recover 160 of the original 300 rail cars. The 784th Tank Battalion then joined the 104th Infantry Division on 31 December along the Ruhr River in an area between the towns of Durden and Murken, and helped defend the positions held there. Elements of the 784th Tank Battalion were attached to units of the 104th Infantry Division; a platoon of Company D's light tanks to the 104th Cavalry Reconnaissance Troop; the 81-mm mortar platoon to the 414th Infantry Regiment; Company A (–) and Company B (–) to the 415th Infantry Regiment; Provisional Company "X," made up of one platoon of Company A and one platoon of Company B, to the 413th Infantry Regiment. Company C, which was initially attached to XIX Corps as a part of the reserves, joined the battalion on 25 January. The assault gun platoon was used to reinforce division artillery fire.[41]

On 14 January 1945, the 761st Tank Battalion was attached to the 17th Airborne Division. Newly arrived in the European Theater, the 17th Airborne Division was immediately rushed to the front lines during the Battle of the Bulge. The division relieved the 101st Airborne Division and held a sector of the key point on the road between Liege and Bastogne. Company B took up positions with the 193rd Glider Infantry Regiment near the town of Wicourt with ten M4 Sherman tanks, three assault guns, and three M5 light tanks. The remainder of the battalion pulled back to perform badly needed emergency repairs, to train replacement personnel, and to replace equipment that had been lost throughout two months of continuous combat.

On 20 January, Brigadier General Whitelaw, the assistant division commander of the 17th Airborne Division, visited the 761st Tank Battalion to award the Bronze Star medal to Captain John D. Long, who now commanded Company B. The Bronze Star medal was also awarded to Master Sergeant Ernest D. Hill of the service company, cited for meritorious duty in keeping a maximum number of tanks and service vehicles in operational condition. He accomplished this in spite of extremely hazardous conditions and adverse weather, and without sufficient replacement parts or repair facilities.[42] Staff Sergeants Cochrane and Kitt were also awarded battlefield commissions to second lieutenants for their exemplary combat leadership skills. The battalion, already hard pressed to replace its enlisted ranks, would not receive any armor trained replacement lieutenants.

On 23 January, Company A, supporting the 513th Parachute Infantry Regiment, replaced Company B on the front lines. The assault gun platoon fired on a large wooded area that contained tanks and German forces, forcing a large number of enemy soldiers to surrender. Company D performed screening and reconnaissance missions before joining with elements of the 513th Parachute Infantry Regiment. Together, they captured the town of Watemall. The next day, Company C, in support of the 194th Glider Infantry Regiment, crossed into Luxembourg and engaged an enemy rear-guard unit set up for a delaying action to protect retreating German forces. Company C destroyed an antitank gun and a machine gun emplacement, and killed 35 enemy soldiers. The towns of Gouvy and Hautbillan fell as the combined armored/airborne forces advanced toward Saint Vith, near the German border and the Siegfried Line. The towns of Koppingerberg and Thommen also fell, thus securing the vital road that linked Saint Vith and Bastogne.

Major General William M. Miley, commanding general of the 17th Airborne Division, had not forgotten the 761st Tank Battalion: "What I clearly remember is the very fine support we received from the 761st. The reason I remember it so well is because it was so much better than what we received from units previously providing support. My most vivid recollection of the 761st Tank Battalion was an action in support of the 194th Glider Infantry Regiment. The regiment had been stopped in its attack on a well-fortified hill. When they regrouped to renew the attack, the attack was led by one of the companies of the 761st. They led the way up the hill with so much accurate fire that the hill was seized without the loss of a single airborne soldier.... During the Ardennes operation we had very little armored unit support, but of that we had, the 761st was by far the most effective and helpful."[43]

During the Battle of the Bulge, the 761st Tank Battalion was attached to any unit that required armor support during their advance. By 26 January 1945, the 87th Infantry Division replaced the 17th Airborne Division, and the 761st Tank Battalion returned to duties briefly supporting this division once again. On 28 January, the battalion advanced northeast toward Saint Vith to relieve elements of the 7th Armored Division and the XVIII Airborne Corps. The next day, the remaining five operational tanks of Company C supported a combat team from the 346th Infantry Regiment, a tank destroyer platoon, and a company of tanks from the 7th Armored Division on an advance through the 82nd Airborne Division's sector in an attempt to outflank the enemy. Company B spearheaded an attack on the town of Huem, as the rest of the battalion continued to perform emergency maintenance to keep their vehicles prepared for combat. On 3 February 1945, the 761st Tank Battalion traveled 140 miles to Hermee, Belgium, and was attached to the 95th Infantry Division, commanded by Major General Harry Twaddle. Assigned to XVI Corps of the 9th Army, the 95th Infantry Division was then holding a defensive position along the Maas River. The 761st Tank Battalion set up a command post across the border in Jabeek, Holland.

As January drew to a close, the 761st Tank Battalion suffered five additional men killed in combat, 14 wounded, and 22 non-battle casualties. There were 17 tanks lost to enemy fire, and 16 required maintenance repairs due to continuous combat duties over harsh terrain. The battalion only had 20 tanks that were combat ready. Trained replacement personnel were sorely needed, but none were available. Emergency replacements arrived from a variety of combat service support units then stationed in the European Theater. Completely untrained in armor tactics, these replacements voluntarily took reductions in rank to private as a prerequisite to be afforded the opportunity to serve in the 761st Tank Battalion. An intense two-week training course took place in Holland that covered the basic armor skills. Following this, the replacements received on-the-job training while in combat. Also, men who had been wounded in those early battles during November were slowly returning to the battalion. Christopher Navarre, a 24 year old first sergeant from an ambulance company, took a reduction in rank to private for this opportunity. Navarre was assigned to the badly battered Company C.

On 16 February, Major George received a promotion to Lieutenant Colonel. The following day, Lieutenant Colonel Bates returned and took over command of the battalion. On 20 February, orders reassigned the 761st Tank Battalion to the 79th Infantry Division commanded by Major General Ira T. Wynch. Initially, Company A was attached to the 313th Infantry Regiment, Company B to the 315th Infantry Regiment, Company C to the 314th Infantry Regiment, and Company D to the 79th Reconnaissance Troop. Supporting the 79th Infantry Division in this offensive, which began on 23 February, elements of the 761st Tank Battalion participated in the capture of the town of End, Holland, cut the Roermond-Julich Railway at Milich, and moved on to Erkling, where they crossed the border into Germany on 3 March. The battalion then advanced on to Schwannenberg, where along with supporting the infantry regiments, they cleared bypassed pockets of resistance and captured enemy prisoners left behind by the swift advance of the 2nd Armored Division.

As February 1945 came to a close, the 761st Tank Battalion had an effective strength of 33 officers, three warrant officers, and 680 enlisted men. The battalion lost ten casualties to non-combat mishaps, but none were killed or wounded in action.[44]

The 761st Tank Battalion received orders to proceed to Saverne, France, on 8 March to rejoin the 3rd Army. En route, the battalion received amended orders attaching it to the 103rd Infantry Division of the 7th Army. Major General Anthony McAulliffe, the former artillery commander of the 101st Airborne Division who led that unit during its siege at Bastogne, now commanded the 103rd Infantry Division. The 761st Tank Battalion traveled by train through Luxembourg to Saverne, where they began preparations for a major offensive to again breach the Siegfried Line and move into Germany.

The 784th Tank Battalion was released from attachment to the 104th Infantry Division and attached to the 35th Infantry Division on 3 February 1945 at Geilenkirchen, Germany. On 26 February, Company A assisted elements of the 134th Infantry Regiment in the capture of Hilfarth across the Ruhr River. The following day, a motorized attack force consisting of Company A, 1/137th Infantry Battalion, Company A, 784th Tank Battalion, and a platoon of the 654th Tank Destroyer Battalion attacked and captured the town of Wassenburg. On the same day one platoon of tanks from Company B, attached to the 137th Infantry Regiment, participated in a successful attack on the town of Goldrath.

Task Force Byrne was organized on 28 February with the mission of liberating Venlo, Holland. It contained the 320th Infantry Regiment, motorized; the 784th Tank Battalion (less Company A); the 654th Tank Destroyer Battalion; two field artillery battalions; and attached engineer and medical units, all under the command of Colonel Bernard A. Byrne, the infantry regiment's commander. On 1 March, led by the medium and light tanks of the 784th Tank Battalion carrying a company of infantrymen, the task force attacked from Widenrath, Holland, along the main road to Venlo. Bypassing pockets of resistance, except in towns and villages along the road, the task force moved so swiftly that the enemy, taken totally by surprise, had no time to destroy bridges. With close cooperation between infantry and armor, resistance met was quickly eliminated. The task force advanced twenty-five miles and captured a total of twenty towns and villages. It entered Venlo by 1800 hours.[45]

Following the task force column were the 137th and 134th Regimental Combat Teams. Company A, 784th Tank Battalion, remained supporting the 134th Infantry Regiment. The two regimental combat teams were closing into assembly areas near Venlo, clearing up scattered enemy forces bypassed by Task Force Byrne. The task force set out again at 1000 on 2 March with the mission of seizing, successively, the towns of Straelin, Nieukerk, Sevelen, Linfort, and Rhineberg. Except for scattered resistance and a few destroyed bridges, the task force had little trouble as it forged ahead. One tank was destroyed by Panzerfaust fire in Straelin, but the burning tank was pushed out of the way, and the task force was not delayed. Beyond Nieukerk, a fourteen-foot antitank ditch blown in the road after the tanks had passed, kept the infantry from advancing. Enemy artillery shelled the road, preventing its repair, until Sergeant Walter Hall, exposed to enemy mortar fire, managed to maneuver his bulldozer tank (tank with a bulldozer blade attached to the front to clear obstacles was known as a tankdozer) so as to fill the antitank ditch and enable the task force to continue its mission. He then destroyed an enemy antitank gun that was firing on the column. For his heroic actions, Sergeant Hall was awarded the Bronze Star medal.[46]

A night attack was planned for Sevelen. Here, enemy paratroopers stiffened resistances, and slowed the American advance. Out of the task force, the M5 light tanks of Company D, one medium tank platoon, the assault gun platoon, and a company of infantrymen were chosen to attack the town. This force left Nieukerk at 2200 on 2 March and entered Sevelen at about midnight, meeting little resistance until it reached the center of the town. The enemy then destroyed a bridge over a deep railroad cut at the south entrance to the town, trapping the force in the town and cutting it off from reinforcements and resupply. Nevertheless, at dawn, the soldiers resumed their attack and the town was cleared of resistance by 1100, just as reinforcements entered Sevelen by another route from the north. In addition to seizing huge stores of food and ammunition, the Sevelen force killed 53 and captured 207 of the enemy paratroopers. Wes Gallagher of the *Los Angeles Times* reported: "With a bridge blown behind them, a Negro tank battalion task force staged a miniature 'Bastogne' in Sevelen today, mauling Nazi parachute units in savage street fighting while cut off for 18 hours."[47]

Wes Gallagher went on to report: "The 784th Tank Battalion was fighting its first offensive action beside the 35th Infantry Division. The battalion won a place in the hearts of the men of the battle hardened 35th Division, who fought from St. Lo to Venlo and beyond, by the battle it put up here and the spearhead fighting it did to get here. Sergeant Walter (Pop) Hall, a 47 year old veteran of the last war from Little York, Illinois, who came back in this war as the commander of a tank bulldozer, was called out under fire to fill craters in a road. He went on to knock out a German 88 millimeter anti-tank gun. Sergeant Ambrose Hicks of Mt. Vernon, New York, an artillery mechanic, was sent back to help bring a supply convoy through. He saved three trucks parked near a burning ammunition truck loaded with 2,300 pounds of TNT. There were Negro tank men who climbed out of the shelter of their tanks under mortar and shellfire to refuel.... I had studied the brilliant history of the outfit, and among the ranks of its enlisted men, I had formed some of my most cherished friendships. But I had not seen the battalion under actual combat conditions, the skill and daring of the battalion's colored tank commanders. There were countless stories of how these Negro sergeants carried on alone in the heat of battle, even when their white commanding captains and lieutenants had been wounded or lost in action. Along the lonely German fields and roads that beckoned to the Ruhr, I had a chance to test the truth or falsity of those stories, and I found that the glowing tales of heroism which had been attributed to these brown warriors were only a small part of a much greater truth."[48]

Company A, supporting the 1/134th Infantry, with the tank destroyers, drove against slight enemy resistance to a road junction west of Geldern where they made contact with the 12th Battalion, King's Royal Rifle Corps, of the British 8th Armored Division.[49] Company A was then released from attachment to the 134th Infantry Regiment. Upon its release, the regimental commander wrote to the division commander this letter of commendation for the 784th Tank Battalion:

1. I desire to commend Company A, 784th Tank Battalion, for the splendid performance of that unit while attached to this organization for the period 25 February to 9 March 1945.

2. The Company Commander, Captain Robert L. Groglode, 01017224, and his entire company proved indispensable to the 134th Infantry Regiment in the assaulting of Hilfarth and the Roer River and the dash to Wassenburg, Bergenlen, and Geldern.

3. Their high morale, aggressiveness, and willingness to fight deserve commendation.[50]

Within Task Force Byrne, Company B, 784th Tank Battalion was now attached to the 1/ 320th Infantry Battalion, with Company C supporting the 2/320th Infantry Battalion, and Company A now assigned to the 137th Infantry Regiment. As the soldiers approached the Rhine River, enemy resistance became much stronger. On 4 March 1945, the 1/320th Infantry, supported by the tanks of Company B, attacked Kamperbruch, Germany. The tank platoon leader believed friendly infantry to be in the eastern portion of the town when, in fact, they had been forced to withdraw by a strong German counterattack. The tanks of Company B ran into antitank guns, and had three tanks disabled in the action. One tank commander, Sergeant Douglas F. Kelly, kept his crew in his burning vehicle when his tank was hit and immobilized, and continued to direct fire against the enemy until his ammunition began to explode. He then dismounted, made his way to an artillery command post under mortar and small arms fire and, by using accurate map coordinates, enabled the artillery to destroy four German antitank guns. Technician 5th Class David H. Adams, observing three wounded infantrymen in a burning building, left his tank, which was then pinned down by antitank fire, made his way to the burning building under heavy fire, and evacuated the wounded soldiers. Both men were awarded the Bronze Star medal for their actions. Kamperbruch was secured the following day.[51]

The companies of the 784th Tank Battalion continued to push toward the Rhine with the 35th Infantry Division. Company A, on 5 March, became a part of Task Force Murray, along with the 137th Regimental Combat Team, Combat Command C of the 8th Armored Division, a company of the 654th Tank Destroyer Battalion, and the 692nd Field Artillery Battalion. Under the leadership of Colonel William Murray, commander of the 137th Infantry Regiment, this force had the mission of seizing Wesel and the Rhine River bridge still intact at that point. Task Force Byrne moved ahead, with enemy resistance stiffening toward the late afternoon of 6 March. For the next four days the two task forces fought their way ahead, meeting tenacious resistance in the towns of Ossenberg, Huck, and Milligen. On 10 March, with the 134th Regimental Combat Team relieving it, Task Force Byrne was dissolved. Task Force Murray secured the town of Ossenberg and advanced on to Wallach on the same day, completing its mission. Company A, 784th Tank Battalion, was relieved from attachment to the

137th Infantry Regiment. With the rest of the 784th Tank Battalion, Company A deployed to Tegelen, Holland, where, from 12 to 25 March 1945, the battalion was refitted, performed badly needed maintenance, and trained replacement personnel. Like the 761st Tank Battalion, the 784th only received untrained volunteers from the Combat Service Support Command as replacements.

On 12 March 1945, the 761st Tank Battalion set up their command post in Bosselshausen, where they relieved the 48th Tank Battalion from attachment to the 103rd Infantry Division. Initially, Company A was attached to the 409th Infantry Regiment; Company B to the 411th Infantry Regiment; Company C to the 410th Infantry Regiment; and the Assault Gun Platoon to the 928th Field Artillery Battalion. The tank crewmen made preparation for a division-wide assault called Task Force Cactus, to penetrate the Siegfried Line in the vicinity of Climbach, France. When the 761st Tank Battalion arrived, the 614th Tank Destroyer Battalion (Towed), another African American combat unit, was already attached to the 103rd Infantry Division. The 614th Tank Destroyer Battalion had developed a strong esprit de corps working closely with this division, and one of its platoons from Company C was the first African American unit to be awarded the Presidential Distinguished Unit Citation for valor. The 614th Tank Destroyer Battalion, like the 761st Tank Battalion, was commanded and staffed with five senior white officers; the remainder of its staff and all of its company officers and enlisted personnel were African Americans. Now, each infantry regiment had an African American tank and tank destroyer company attached for fire support.

On 20 March, a platoon of Company C, 761st Tank Battalion, supporting the 411th Infantry Regiment in the assault on Nieder Schlettenbach, destroyed 13 fortified pillboxes, disabled 12 machine gun emplacements, captured one 75-mm antitank gun fully intact with sights and ammunition, and accounted for 35 enemy soldiers killed. This offensive came to a halt due to the Germans' destroying a key bridge as they retreated. Another platoon from Company C spearheaded the 409th Infantry Regiment into Riesdorf, where it destroyed 6 pillboxes, killed 8 Germans, and took 40 prisoners. Riesdorf, well defended with fortified pillboxes and dugouts, was a key point to the division's advance through the Siegfried Line.

On that same day, First Lieutenant Maxwell Huffman, a white officer from Newell, South Dakota, who had recently assumed command of Company A from Captain Williams, was shot by a sniper in the town of Nieder Schlettenbach. Lieutenant Huffman died of his wounds five days later.

Task Force Rhine was formed on 21 March from the 761st Tank Battalion (less Company C); the 2/409th Infantry; a reconnaissance platoon of the 614th Tank Destroyer Battalion; the 103rd Signal Company; and an engineer detachment. They were ordered to the assembly area at the edge of Riesdorf on 22 March and were to be prepared to exploit any breakthrough in the Siegfried Line and to advance on to the Rhine River upon orders. Lieutenant Colonel Bates would command this task force.

Company C, with its tank platoons dispersed, was still spearheading the advances of the 409th and 411th Infantry Regiments. Together, they cleared the approaches to the Siegfried Line and would later join the task force. At Nieder Schlettenbach, in support of the 409th Infantry Regiment, Sergeant Crecy, who had transferred from Company D, destroyed a fortified pillbox high on a hill. The First Sergeant of Company C, William Burroughs, was the gunner in Sergeant Crecy's tank. Through the open hatches of the commander's turret, Sergeant Crecy manned the .50-caliber machine gun and cut down a group of enemy soldiers scurrying from their burning bunker. He then ducked down and closed the hatch just as an 88-mm shell exploded a few feet from his tank.

In support of the 411th Infantry Regiment, a platoon led by newly promoted Second Lieutenant Cochrane fought its way into Nieder Schlettenbach. Using fire and maneuver tactics, they advanced two tanks forward while the remaining tanks provided covering fire. Another pair would follow in the same manner. This battle was fought until the following morning, when the road between Nieder Schlettenbach and Erlenbach had been secured. In its wake, the platoon along with the infantry destroyed seven pillboxes and ten machine gun emplacements, killed 12 enemy soldiers, and captured 64 prisoners of war. Company A sent a platoon of tanks to relieve the battle-weary tankers of Lieutenant Cochrane's platoon. The advance came to a halt at Gundershoffen due to another destroyed bridge. At this point, all the tanks of the battalion were formed into Task Force Rhine.

Task Force Rhine assembled south of Riesdorf on the morning of 22 March. The tanks of the task force fired on the town for over an hour. With Lieutenant Colonel Bates in command, and a reconnaissance platoon of the 614th Tank Destroyer Battalion and the light tanks of Company D, 761st Tank Battalion at its lead, the task force moved through Riesdorf at 1600, attacked pillboxes northeast of the town, and then split into two columns, one going north toward the town of Birkenhordt and the other going southeast toward Bollenborn.

The task force was entirely mechanized with the infantry riding on tanks, trucks, and in half-track armored vehicles, firing at any suspected enemy site. Reaching Birkenhordt, the column advanced against small arms fire and moved through the town until halted by two antitank guns. The force withdrew and called for artillery support, which destroyed most of the town. The force then advanced through the rubble of dead cows, horses and other animals that littered the streets. Four antitank guns were discovered, and the Assault Gun platoon promptly destroyed two, forcing the German crews to abandon the others. At this point, the column came to a halt as soldiers of Company G, 2/409th Infantry, secured the town.

The Bollenborn column encountered obstacles along the road, which impeded their advance. Once the engineer detachment cleared the road, the column proceeded. An antitank gun emplacement, set up to protect the approaches to Bollenborn, quickly disabled two of the lead Sherman tanks. With the road pre-sited by the enemy's artillery observers, the column, forced to withdraw, joined forces with the Birkenhordt column, and were ordered to proceed northwest towards the town of Silz. The tanks of Company B were now leading the column, with First Lieutenant Harold Gary's platoon out front. Sergeant Ervin Latimore, commanding the lead tank, refused to be evacuated after being seriously wounded. He continued to clear a path for the column. For his heroic acts, Sergeant Latimore would be awarded the Silver Star medal. Lieutenant Colonel Bates, while on foot commanding the task force, and prodding the infantrymen riding on the tanks to stay awake after more then 12 hours of continuous fighting, was knocked unconscious by the concussion of an 88-mm artillery blast. Sergeant Crecy dismounted his tank under heavy artillery fire and moved his commander to a place of safety.

At 1800, the 103rd Infantry Division directed the task force to proceed northeast to rendezvous with the 10th Armored Division, reported to be advancing toward Silz. The task force set out into the night. At 1835, a crater in the road beyond Birkenhordt stopped the advance, but repairs were made within an hour by the accompanying engineer detachment and tank dozers. The task force proceeded, using reconnaissance by fire throughout the column to resist several attempts by groups of German soldiers to halt it. On approaching Silz, the swiftly moving column found the enemy rather than the 10th Armored Division in possession. The column was immediately fired on by artillery and mortar rounds. Turning east, the column fought its way through Silz. Firing into one house, the force's guns hit an ammunition supply point. The house exploded, blocking the road. Silz burned brightly, providing illumination as the task force sped through the night over strange and unmarked roads. Shortly after midnight Task Force Rhine reached Munchweiler where its machine gun fire drove enemy crews away from their defending antitank guns.

Just outside Munchweiler, on the way to Klingenmunster, toward which the 36th Infantry Division was to be advancing, a report which, like that of the 10th Armored Division, proved later to be in error, Task Force Rhine overran a retreating German horse-drawn artillery vehicle column. The task force blasted through this column, killing and wounding many of the enemy, and leaving the road blocked with the wreckage of vehicles, dead enemy soldiers and the carcasses of dead horses. The tank-dozer had to be called up to clear the way.

Sergeant William East of the 409th Infantry Regiment describes the situation: "Soon after midnight, the tanks appeared on the outskirts of Silz. The attack was so swift, an enemy antitank gun was knocked out before its crew could man the weapon. The gun was in position and there was plenty of ammunition, but the column had knifed through the darkness so quickly, the enemy was caught unprepared. The town of Silz was burning brightly from the fires started by shells from the tank guns. The experienced Negro soldiers who manned the tanks employed reconnaissance by fire. Every stretch of ground along the line of arch was systematically and mercilessly searched by 75-mm, 76-mm, and 37-mm cannons, and .30 and .50-caliber machine guns. This was power with vengeance. As one of the colored gunners put it: 'Man, we learned this jive from General Patton.' Not to be outdone, the Cactus foot soldiers kept a steady stream of .30-caliber ammunition blazing off into the ditches and hills along the road. M1 rifles and Browning automatics were red hot. The tanks sped unimpeded through Silz. There was an 'end of the world' terror about the place. Hellish fires cast weird shadows, screams of terrified civilians mingled with the agonizing groans of the enemy wounded.... Speeding on toward Munchweiler, the armored column surprised a Wehrmact column of artillery, antitank guns, and supplies that had waited too long before evacuating. This was an opportunity that had never been encountered by the power crazed tank pilots. They sent their steel monsters bulling into the German column, strewing wreckage as they thundered forward. Tanks crushed men and horses. Cannon fire blasted trucks into twisted masses of flaming steel. Erstwhile supermen ran screaming down the road attempting to surrender."[52]

Captain William L. O'Dea, the 761st Tank Battalion Motor Officer, describes how his maintenance section that was trailing the lead vehicles was ambushed: "Company and battalion maintenance sections were combined and consolidated with trains under the protection of the light tanks of Company D. These sections followed the medium tanks closely, until the town of Silz was taken. After which, the trains were ambushed by bypassed enemy infantry. The battalion maintenance platoon half-track caught the brunt of this enemy attack and fought it off with the vehicular .50-caliber machine gun until all the trucks were regrouped with the light tanks. Seven enemy riflemen surrendered to the maintenance section. There were no casualties sustained by maintenance personnel."[53]

Klingenmunster itself was a guarded permanent enemy installation. As Task Force Rhine approached its final objective, it was met by heavy fire, but the combined weapons of the task force were turned on the enemy, many of whom surrendered. This presented another problem. Prisoners taken earlier had been sent to the rear, but the enemy had now closed in behind the task force. Prisoners were loaded on gas and ammunition trucks and every other place where they could possibly ride as the task force moved on into Klingenmunster. One tank platoon with infantry support attempted to enter the town at about 0400 but was driven out by a combination of antitank and small arms fire in the darkness. With the addition of another tank platoon it took up firing positions at the edge of Klingenmunster, shooting all available weapons into the town, and set several buildings on fire. Task Force Rhine, seeing no sign of the expected 36th Infantry Division or of the motorized friendly infantry which was to follow its advance, entered Klingenmunster and consolidated its positions.

It now learned that the 14th Armored Division would pass through the task force's defensive positions and advance on to the Rhine River. By the time the advanced contact party of the 14th Armored Division arrived, Task Force Rhine had penetrated 14 kilometers through well-defended enemy territory. It had destroyed 150 vehicles, 31 fortified pillboxes, 49 machine gun emplacements, 29 antitank guns, and 4 self-propelled guns. At least 170 of the enemy lay dead and hundreds of horses were killed or left to graze by the roadside. It was first estimated that over 1,200 enemy prisoners were taken. The fire strength of the task force was such that the 761st Tank Battalion alone used slightly more than 50 tons of ammunition before it halted.[54]

At the completion of Task Force Rhine, Major General Anthony C. McAuliffe sent a congratulatory message to the participants: "The first stage of our operation has been brilliantly completed. You broke through the famous Siegfried defenses and then boldly exploited your success. You have taken more than 4,700 prisoners. You have fought gallantly and intelligently, and you have led all the way. I congratulate you."[55]

The commander of Task Force Rhine, Lieutenant Colonel Bates pointed out: "On Task Force Rhine, I had about 1,800 men. This was the last of the heavy fighting and I stayed with the leading five tanks where most of the action was. There was extreme bravery, ability, and acceptance of multiple dangerous situations."[56]

After the mission of Task Force Rhine had concluded, the infantry and tankers had to clear bypassed pockets of enemy resistance. The advance to the Siegfried Line had been so rapid, American forces had not secured many of the German defensive positions. On 24 March while escorting jeeps of the 103rd Reconnaissance Troop, Private First Class Crawford O. Pegram and his M5 Stuart tank were fired on by German forces. As the vulnerable jeeps withdrew, Private Pegram moved his tank forward and laid down suppressing fire. His tank destroyed two machine gun emplacements and pinned down one antitank gun crew and two Panzerfaust teams. This allowed the infantrymen to outflank and capture the enemy soldiers. While advancing forward, Pegram's tank was then fired on by a well-concealed antitank gun. Unable to locate the gun, Private Pegram dismounted the tank to reconnoiter on foot. Discovering the antitank gun, Pegram was proceeding back to his tank when he came upon a mortar team from the 103rd Infantry. The mortar team fired five rounds, which disabled the gun and forced the surviving enemy crew to retreat.

Meanwhile, the 761st Tank Battalion received orders from the 103rd Infantry Division that the battalion had been reassigned back to General Patton's 3rd Army for the final offensive thrust through Germany. They were to be attached to the 71st Infantry Division. During the month of March, with the German forces in full retreat, the 761st Tank Battalion only lost five tanks to enemy action. They had fired 300 tons of ammunition and consumed 50,000 gallons of fuel. Only one officer and six enlisted men had been wounded in action. First Lieutenant Max Huffman later died of his wounds.[57]

The 784th Tank Battalion continued its advance to the Rhine River still attached to the 35th Infantry Division. As part of the plan to expand the XVI Corps Rhine River bridgehead into Germany, the 35th Infantry Division was ordered on 25 March 1945 to deploy one regimental combat team across the Rhine River. Company A, 784th Tank Battalion, was again

Privates George Cofield and Howard J. Davis guard a newly constructed bridge site over the Rhine River. Built by U.S. Ninth Army Engineers, 30 March 1945. (National Archives, 111-SC-204770)

attached to the 134th Infantry Regiment as part of Task Force Miltonberger. Under the control of the 78th Infantry Division, the task force crossed the Rhine River at 0800, on 26 March, and assisted in the attack upon a wooded area beyond the town of Dinslaken. The remainder of the 784th Tank Battalion, attached to the 137th Infantry Regiment, crossed the Rhine River and began to attack toward Neukoln. Resistance, consisting mainly of rifle and Panzerfaust fire, was sporadic, but the advance through the wooded area was slow. Infantry/armored teams coordinated their efforts to seek and destroy the enemy's self-propelled antitank guns that were in place to slow the Allied armored advance. In Company A's zone of advance along the German Autobahn north of the Rhine-Herne Canal, the enemy offered only light resistance. In Company B and C's sector south of the Autobahn, resistance was heavier, but the Germans were becoming disorganized and were withdrawing steadily through the Ruhr Valley towns instead of offering their former stiff organized resistance. Both infantry and armor took hundreds of surrendering prisoners. With the Allies advancing from the east and west, defeat was now inevitable.

Staff Sergeant Garrido and Technician 5th Class Dave Adams made their way through mortar and small arms fire and evacuated three wounded men to safety. Lieutenant Peterson then ordered Staff Sergeant Garrido to go and get some infantry support to assist in suppressing the antitank fire. When Staff Sergeant Garrido arrived back with the infantry, he went to the disabled M5 tank and manned the 37-mm cannon. He provided supporting suppressing fire while the infantry attacked the German positions. For their heroic actions under enemy fire, Staff Sergeant Garrido and Technician Adams were awarded the Bronze Star medal. This was Adams' second award of the Bronze Star.[58]

On 30 March 1945, the 761st Tank Battalion received orders attaching it to the 71st Infantry Division of XII Corps, 3rd Army. With the German army in full retreat on all fronts, the battalion crossed the Rhine River and traveled 132 miles to Langenshelbold, Germany, where the 71st Infantry Division was headquartered. Company A was attached to the 5th Infantry Regiment, Company B to the 14th Infantry Regiment, Company C to the 66th Infantry Regiment, and Company D to the 71st Reconnaissance Troop. Together with the 71st Division Artillery, they completely surrounded the elite 6th SS Mountain Division Nord. Attempting to break out from this encirclement on 2 April, three German SS convoys moved southeast, led by captured Sherman tanks, two self-propelled antitank guns, eight American jeeps, and 12 "Deuce-and-a-half" (2½ ton) trucks. The other groups of SS soldiers were also equipped with captured American weapons and vehicles.

Company A split up and led the infantry through the forest and circled Waldenburg. They assisted in the capture of the towns of Buches and Budingen and advanced toward the middle of the enemy lines to force a resupply route through the forest. Company B then advanced north to assist the infantry in clearing bypassed pockets of resistance. The tanks of Company C faced north to take up blocking positions south and east of the enemy's location in order to capture the retreating SS forces. Captain Gates describes what happened when the Germans came out of the wood line: "On one combat mission, we were having difficulty getting the Germans out of the woods. We kept firing low. Finally I told 'em, Gentlemen, raise your fire so it will explode up in the trees. That'll send more shrapnel around, also, some trees down, and get those people out of those woods. They came out waving white flags and calling '*Kameraden*.' I told the men to remain in their tanks with the hatches buttoned up and when the enemy got abreast of 'em, just direct 'em back to the infantry. Well, some guy opened up his hatch a little bit early. The Germans looked and they said, '*Schwarze Soldaten!*' (Black Soldiers!) That word just went through the bunch and they started runnin' back to the damn woods. We figured, we'll be damned if you're gonna get back to those woods. Finally, they figured they'd better go along with these black soldiers."[59]

The German Army could not see how the African American tankers could be in so many places at one time. The two African American tank battalions had built a formidable reputation as ferocious fighters among the German forces. German strategists would plot the known locations of the African American tankers on their field maps. A captured German officer asked Captain Gates, "How many Negro Panzer divisions are there?"[60]

Company D performed screening and reconnaissance missions in coordination with the 71st Reconnaissance Troop. Technician 5 Leonard "Chico" Holland led six M5 Stuart light tanks in the capture of an enemy communications station and two fully stocked armored supply depots near Lake Rotenbach. The tanks of Company D along with the 71st Reconnaissance Troop killed an estimated 200 enemy soldiers in intense fighting on this mission.

The assault gun platoon divided into two sections. Platoon leader Lieutenant James R. Burgess took the first section and covered the forward movement of the 608th Field Artillery Battalion. Staff Sergeant Richard L. Sparks led the other section, and fired 105-mm howitzer rounds on the enemy positions in the heavily wooded areas around the towns of Spielberg, Streitburg, and Leisenwald. Staff Sergeant Sparks also had the mission of supporting the 66th Infantry Regiment on their attack into Leisenwald. Coordinating his fire through a forward artillery observer, his guns neutralized fortified pillboxes at the edge of town, allowing the infantry to proceed unimpeded. When the infantry captured the town, they discovered that the assault guns left most of Leisenwald's stone houses destroyed with the stench of decomposing bodies everywhere. The houses left standing were filled with wounded German soldiers being attended to by their medical personnel, who paid little attention to their captors as they went about their work. The infantrymen captured a German payroll and dutifully forwarded it to regimental headquarters. They also repatriated ten American "Deuce-and-a-half" trucks, which they utilized throughout the rest of the war on their rapid advance through Germany.

By 4 April, the entire 6th SS Mountain Division Nord was rendered useless as a combat force, with its soldiers either killed, captured, or in a state of hasty, disorganized retreat. The 71st Infantry Division headed east toward Fulda in pursuit of the enemy. In Company B, First Lieutenant Harold B. Gary's tank platoon, while in pursuit of a retreating German general, destroyed ten machine gun emplacements set up for delaying action outside of the city of Fulda.

On 7 April, the 761st Tank Battalion reached Meiningen, Germany. In a nearby salt mine outside of Merkers, combat engineers from XII Corps discover a hidden Nazi gold cache. Directly inside the underground vault stood canvas bags filled with priceless metals, Reichsmarks, American dollars, British pounds, French francs, and Norwegian crowns. Along with the money were heirlooms taken from Jewish families arriving at Nazi concentration camps. Packed in crates were priceless paintings by Rembrandt, Raphael, and Renoir.

The 761st Tank Battalion, along with the 71st Infantry Division, continued to pursue the retreating German Army. On 12 April, the infantry entered the city of Coburg and along with the light tanks of Company D, eliminated all enemy resistance. The tanks' 37-mm cannon destroyed several upper story rooms where enemy snipers had been seen. On 14 April, Kulmback came under attack from the American forces. The tanks of Company B, along with the infantry, destroyed one armored car and 15 machine gun emplacements, killed more than 100 German soldiers, and captured 200 enemy prisoners. Company C accounted for 19 enemy vehicles destroyed, killed 125 enemy soldiers, and forced the surrender of two full German battalions, along with an unattached enemy company. Company C also freed two American officers and an enlisted man that were being held captive by the Germans.[61] During the battle for Kulmback, Corporal Fred Brown, of the Bronx, New York, the gunner in tank number 6 of Company B, was mortally wounded by an 88-mm shell that exploded directly overhead as he was attempting to reenter his tank.[62]

The 71st Infantry Division continuing their assault through Germany then proceeded to the city of Bayreuth. Company B, spearheading for the 14th Infantry Regiment, destroyed one Panzer tank and killed 75 enemy soldiers before the remaining 200 Germans surrendered. Company C, while supporting the 66th Infantry Regiment, destroyed nine machine gun emplacements as they attacked the Bindlach Aerodrome, north of Bayreuth. First Sergeant William Burroughs, who dismounted his tank to personally locate a machine gun emplacement that had pinned down the infantry, was shot over the left eye. He had to be medically evacuated, and later lost that eye.[63] The 66th Infantry Regiment S-2 noted that 520 enemy soldiers had been taken prisoner in this battle, as the will to put up resistance to the American onslaught was now crumbling. But the town of Bayreuth continued to hold out against the Americans. After two days of continuous shelling by the 11th Armored Division, the 65th Infantry Division, the 71st Infantry Division and the 761st Tank Battalion, the commander of the city's defenders surrendered to the commander of the 14th Infantry Regiment.

On 18 April, near the town of Neuhaus, Staff Sergeant Johnnie Stevens would be awarded the Bronze Star Medal for singlehandedly destroying an M42 machine gun emplacement that had an American infantry platoon pinned down. After dismounting the safety of his tank, Staff Sergeant Stevens deployed forward to scout the forward positions. Sighting the German position, he crawled to within 15 yards of the position and started throwing grenades and spraying the machine gun emplacement with his M2 submachine gun. By the time the infantrymen from the 71st Infantry Division moved forward, Stevens had killed nine soldiers, and 36 more were captured.[64]

On 19 April, two tank platoons from Company C, led by Second Lieutenants Frank Cochrane and Moses Dade, spearheaded for elements of the 66th Infantry Regiment in their assaults on Neuhaus and Velden. Elite SS soldiers were fortified behind the walls of Luftwaffe chief Hermann Goring's Veldenstein Castle. The tanks covered the infantry's advance up the hill, but their shells bounced off the 500 year old walls. As the infantry infiltrated the castle, the SS forces retreated toward Velden. As the tanks pursued, they became engaged in a fierce battle with enemy armored forces. When the fighting ceased, destroyed were a Mark IV Panzer tank, an antitank gun and six enemy machine gun emplacements.[65]

That evening, Major Reynolds, Captain Long, Sergeant Fields and Technician 4th Class Stanford were reported missing and presumed captured while on a reconnaissance mission in the Lindenhardt area.

On 22 April, Company B and elements of the 14th Infantry Regiment cleared the city of Amberg. On the following day, they found Captain Long, Sergeant Fields, and Technician Stanford. Several days later, the 14th Calvary Group liberated Major Reynolds and returned him to duty. The next day, Company B engaged the enemy at Auerbach, where the combined armor/infantry force captured 75 Germany prisoners. Company C and the 66th Infantry Regiment made contact with the enemy at Perkam, where they destroyed three machine gun emplacements and took 140 prisoners. They also liberated two captured American soldiers from the 80th Infantry Division. The advance continued southeast toward Austria to rendezvous with the Soviet forces advancing from the northeast. The towns of Schwandorf, Burglengenfeld, Regenstauf, Durn, Pirkensee, and Zeitlern fell as the tanks advanced toward the Danube River and Regensburg. There, the 71st Infantry Division was to establish a forward command post for General Patton's 3rd Army Headquarters. Initially, the enemy rejected a surrender ultimatum, and the American artillery and tankers bombarded the city. On 26 April, Regensburg capitulated, and it was just a matter of clearing out stubborn pockets of resistance.

Company A with the 5th Infantry Regiment captured Straubing and helped liberate surviving slave laborers at a nearby camp on 28 April. Company B took up positions in the town of Sarching with the 14th Infantry Regiment, and Company C took up positions in Perkan with the 66th Infantry Regiment. On 30 April, Adolf Hitler committed suicide in his underground command bunker as the Soviet Army was attacking Berlin above.

As April drew to a close, the 761st Tank Battalion had an effective strength of 38 officers, three warrant officers, and 642 enlisted men. Corporal Fred Brown died of his wounds on 14 April. One officer and seven enlisted men were wounded in action. The battalion suffered 33 non-battle casualties and lost one assault gun vehicle, two Sherman medium tanks, and two Stuart light tanks in battle.[66]

The 784th Tank Battalion continued the offensive in the north, supporting various infantry divisions of the 9th Army. On 10 April 1945, Companies B and C were attached to the 17th Airborne Division for an attack on the towns of Oberhausen and Mulheim, providing armored support. On 13 April, the rest of the battalion was assigned to support the 35th Infantry Division, where they patrolled the wooded region around the town of Blatz on the west bank of the Elbe River. There, they cleared bypassed pockets of resistance and captured enemy soldiers.

As the war in Europe was coming to a halt, Russian soldiers advancing from the east, and American, British, Canadian, and French forces closing in on the west, forced the Germans to try to eliminate all witnesses to the atrocities that had occurred. SS soldiers evacuating French, Polish, Russian, and Jewish inmates from concentration camps in the east soon discovered American forces closing in on them. The prisoners were put in a hangar at the edge of the town of Gardelegen. The Germans locked the doors to the hangar and then set it on fire. Those prisoners able to escape the inferno were machine-gunned. As defeat was inevitable, SS Chief Heinrich Himmler ordered the liquidation of all the inmates of the concentration camps in keeping with Hitler's goal of a *Judenfrei* (Jew Free) world.

The American advance was ordered to halt. It had been agreed that the Russian forces would have the honor of capturing Berlin. For the American forces, which had endured many months of combat, this was a welcome relief because the Russians suffered many casualties in this last major battle of the war in Europe. When the Americans met the Russian Army at the Elbe River, two companies of the 784th Tank Battalion would be there. On 26 April, the battalion deployed to Immensen, where it performed occupation duties and control over that town and its surrounding communities. As the war in Europe drew to a close, the 784th Tank Battalion assumed occupation duties as it reequipped and prepared for movement to the Pacific Theater. On 26 May 1945, the battalion relocated to Kelberg to perform military governing duties. When the war in the Pacific suddenly ended, the 784th Tank Battalion was slated to be deactivated. Throughout their combat career, the 784th Tank Battalion performed its duties supporting the white infantry divisions in a highly extraordinary manner. They suffered over 140 casualties with 24 men killed in action. On 29 April 1946, just three years after their activation, the last of the three "experimental" African American tank battalions returned to the United States and was deactivated at Camp Kilmer, New Jersey. Many of its soldiers volunteered to remain on active duty in Germany, some transferring to the 761st Tank Battalion.

As the 761st Tank Battalion advanced through Bavaria in late April, they also liberated smaller satellite camps of the infamous Dachau Concentration Camp. Samuel Pisar, who had been imprisoned originally in Poland at Auschwitz, and then in Germany at Buchenwald, was transferred to one of the satellite camps of Dachau in 1944. As an inmate of one of those liberated concentration camps, he recalls his initial meeting with Sergeant Bill Ellington of the 761st Tank Battalion: "I ran down the ladder and looked out through the slats and I saw a tank. I tried to find the hated swastika, and I couldn't find it. Instead, all I could see was a white star. What is a white star? Why a white star? And suddenly it blew my mind; I realized that after four years of slavery, torture, hunger, I was actually looking at the insignia of the U.S. Army. And like a madman, I ran out toward the tank. It was a stupid thing to do, because I was in the middle of a battlefield. Machine guns were barking, bullets were flying on all sides. But by then, I thought nothing could destroy me; I had taken so many risks and been so close to death, and freedom was coming at me and I couldn't just stand there. I couldn't stop; I was just running and running, closer to the tank. Suddenly its cannon let out a belch. And all the firing ceased. And as I approached, the hatch opened and a tall, helmeted black man climbed out. I had never seen a black man before. I thought, maybe he has soot on his face. I didn't know how to signal him ... how to explain that I was a prisoner, that I needed help. He must have seen that I was weak, maybe sick looking, with a shaven head. But it was a dangerous situation, so the only thing I could think of was to kneel, to put my arms around his legs and begin to yell, in the few words of English my mother had sighed when she prayed for our deliverance. 'God Bless America!' And that he understood. He picked me up in his arms, he led me to the tank and took me with him through the hatch and into the womb of freedom."[67]

When it became apparent that the war would end in a few days, orders were issued restricting the issuance of fuel. It was decided that the 761st Tank Battalion would not be issued any more fuel from the 71st Infantry Division, thus halting the unit's advance to share in the final victory. Second Lieutenant Horace Jones of the battalion S-4 logistics section, using his own initiative, went outside of the division and located an African American quartermaster company. From them, he was able to acquire 30,000 gallons of fuel. Company A was the first to reach the Austrian border, arriving at 0430 hours on 2 May near the town of Ering. The tanks destroyed two machine gun emplacements that were located on the far bank of the Inn River. This allowed the infantry and smaller vehicles to cross a dam into Austria. Unable to negotiate a safe crossing at this location, the 761st Tank Battalion advanced up the river to a larger dam at Egelfing. There, with the tank tracks wider than the road space on the dam, no guardrails, and no margin for error, the tankers made their way across the river. On 4 May, the last of the 761st Tank Battalion's Sherman tanks crossed into Austria. This would be the sixth European country that the 761st Tank Battalion had fought in.

The 761st Tank Battalion proceeded down the Salzburg-Vienna Highway capturing towns infested with the enemy soldiers before encountering stiff resistance in the town of Wels. After a brief battle, the enemy soldiers also surrendered there. A major airstrip on the town's eastern outskirts was also secured, with the tankers destroying the remaining enemy aircraft, along with their hangars. Aircraft attempting to take off were quickly shot down. The battalion was then ordered to advance toward the city of Steyr, located along the Enns River. Outside of the town of Lambach, Company A ran into a formidable force of enemy soldiers. After a hard-fought battle, the enemy had lost two Mark IV Panzer tanks, two machine gun emplacements, and several Panzerfaust teams. The accompanying infantry captured over 300 enemy soldiers.

Finally, on 6 May 1945, after 183 continuous days in combat, the fighting ceased for the 761st Tank Battalion. Since its baptism by fire, the 761st Tank Battalion had aided in the capture or liberation of more than 30 major towns, four airfields, three ammunition supply depots, several branch concentration camps, and one communications station. They destroyed 461 wheeled vehicles, 34 Panzer tanks, 87 antitank guns, 27 large artillery pieces, 58 fortified pillboxes, 49 machine gun emplacements, and an untold number of small arms and crew-served weapons. In combined efforts with the infantry, the tankers inflicted a reported 129,640 enemy casualties, and captured 15,818 prisoners. But the Panthers paid a high price for this victory. They suffered 304 combat casualties, almost fifty percent of the battalion, in which 34 men were killed in action. They also had 201 non-combat casualties. Losses in equipment were 33 tanks to antitank fire, 19 to land mines, eight to Panzerfaust fire, seven to artillery, and four tanks lost in battle with German Panzers.[68]

The 761st Tank Battalion had fought in France, Belgium, Luxembourg, Holland, Germany, and Austria, serving under the commands of the Third, Seventh, and Ninth Armies. The had lived, fought, and died among the white soldiers of the 17th Airborne, 26th, 71st, 79th, 87th, 95th, and 103rd Infantry Divisions, and had proven themselves in battle. Although being a separate battalion, and often not being recognized for their heroic feats while attached to the various infantry divisions, the 761st received Campaign Streamers for battles in Northern France, Rhineland, Ardennes-Alsace, and Central Europe. Individual awards include 10 Silver Star and 38 Bronze Star medals. Staff Sergeants Moses Dade, Leonard Holland, Horace Jones, William Kitt, Joseph Tates, Theodore Weston, Frank Cochrane, and Warren Crecy all received battlefield commissions to second lieutenant for their leadership in combat. Warrant Officer Clarence I. Godbold also received a commission to second lieutenant for performing the duties of both the personnel officer and the battalion adjutant throughout the entire period that the 761st Tank Battalion was engaged in combat.[69]

On 25 July 1945, Captain Ivan Harrison, while acting as temporary commander of the 761st Tank Battalion, submitted a recommendation that the unit be awarded the Distinguished Unit Citation. This is the highest honor that can be bestowed upon a military unit. The recommendation consisted of a four-page narrative, four exhibits, a report of damage inflicted on the enemy, remarks by Undersecretary of War Robert L. Patterson, and a Chart of Path of Origin. The exhibits are letters of commendation from the commanding general of XII Corps along with the commendations from the commanding generals of the 26th, 103rd, and 71st Infantry Divisions. The recommendation stated: "This unit has distinguished itself by extraordinary heroism in battle and has exhibited great gallantry, determination, and esprit de corps in operations against the enemy, overcoming such hazardous conditions as adverse weather, mountainous terrain, and heavily fortified enemy positions."[70]

General Eisenhower's staff forwarded the recommendation to the 3rd Army Headquarters for an evaluation. The reply, dated 18 August 1945, stated:

1. Not favorably considered.
2. After a careful study of the 761st Tank Battalion described in the basic communication, it is considered that the action, while commendable, was not sufficiently outstanding to meet the requirements for a unit citation as set forth in Section IV, Circular 333, War Department, dated 22 December 1943.

The letter was signed: "For the Commanding General: R.W. Hartman, Lt. Col., Assistant Adjutant General."[71]

On 12 February 1946, the final decision from General Eisenhower's headquarters regarding the Distinguished Unit Citation came down to the commander of the 761st Tank Battalion.

1. Disapproved.
2. While the operations of the 761st Tank Battalion were commendable, it is not felt that they meet the requirements for a Distinguished Unit Citation.

That letter was signed: "By Command of General McNarney L.S. Ostrander, Brigadier General, USA, Adjutant General."[72]

During 1947 and 1948, a formal board took into consideration the compiled facts of this case and concluded with disapproval. Since that time, numerous requests for reconsideration have been denied as no new evidence was uncovered that could substantially affect the initial denial of the citation. During World War II, there were only two Distinguished Unit Citations awarded to African American units. The 103rd Infantry Division Headquarters submitted the recommendation for one of these awards for the 3rd Platoon, Company C, 614th Tank Destroyer Battalion for leading the assault on Climbach, France. The other recommendation, for the 969th Field Artillery Battalion, was submitted for all the units that were involved with the defense of Bastogne during the Battle of the Bulge. But racism and prejudices associated with the approving authority for granting military awards and decorations would deny many soldiers of color the honor of receiving the recognition that this country should have rightly bestowed upon them. Of the 440 Medals of Honor awarded during World War II, none were awarded to African Americans, and only one was presented posthumously to an Asian American.

After the cessation of hostilities in Europe, the 761st Tank Battalion assumed the duties of an occupation force. On 30 July 1945, after being detached from the 71st Infantry Division and assigned to the 6th Armored Group, the battalion relocated their command post to the Bavarian town of Teisendorf, Germany. They conducted occupation duty there and performed armor training near the town of Chiemsee. The training emphasized cannon fire, and familiarization with the new M26 Pershing Tank with its larger 90-mm cannon, which was replacing the battle-worn M4 Shermans, and the M24 Chaffee with its 75-mm gun, which replaced the M5 Stuart light tank. Headquarters Company, the Service Company, and the Medical Detachment set up operations in the town of Teisendorf; Company A in Neukirchen, Company B in Siegsdorf; Company C in Petting; and Company D in Anger. When the war in the Pacific Theater ended in September, some of the men in the battalion were rotated back to the United States, but many decided to remain in Europe with the unit.

The first of the African American armored units, the 758th Tank Battalion, after supporting the 92nd Infantry Division and the 442nd Regimental Combat Team during the final allied offensive in Italy, was deactivated on 25 September 1945. On 14 June 1946, the battalion was reactivated at Fort Knox, Kentucky, and became part of the Armored Force School until 1948 when the battalion, although still segregated, was specifically requested by Major General John Gavin to be transferred to Fort Bragg, North Carolina, and become part of his 82nd Airborne Division.

On 5 November 1945, Lieutenant Colonel Bates left the 761st Tank Battalion, transferring to the 90th Infantry Division, which was departing for the United States. Captain Ivan Harrison temporarily assumed command until the new white commander, Lieutenant Colonel Frank K. Britton, arrived. In an After Action Report for the last quarter of 1945, Lieutenant Colonel Britton wrote: "During the period 1 October 1945 to 31 December 1945, the 761st Tank Battalion redeployed 432 enlisted men and seven officers. Enlisted replacements received were negligible as they were just below the critical score and in turn were redeployed. Therefore the battalion has exerted every effort toward maintaining the integrity of the unit. One hundred eleven men reenlisted in the Regular Army, all for the battalion. The majority of these reenlistees are tank trained and many are specialists. Thirty officers volunteered to remain on active duty until 30 June 1947.... During the period the men of the 761st Tank Battalion wrote the battalion history [*Come Out Fighting*] and publication was commenced in Salzburg, Austria. The book was paid for by popular subscription and will be mailed to all former members of the battalion. Cost of publication was $1,040 for 2000 copies."[73]

The 761st Tank Battalion remained in Germany until 1 June 1947 when it was deactivated. The 761st was reactivated on 24 November 1947 at Fort Knox, Kentucky, initially as a training battalion until its final deactivation on 15 March 1955.

When the tankers of the 761st Tank Battalion returned to the United States in 1947, after nearly three years in Europe, they encountered the same racism that had prevailed when they departed in 1944.

AFTERMATH

Lieutenant John Roosevelt Robinson, after being discharged, played professional football in Hawaii with the Honolulu Polar Bears until his old ankle injury began to give him problems. He then joined the Kansas City Monarchs of the Negro National Baseball League. While playing as their starting shortstop, he was selected by Mr. Branch Rickey of the Brooklyn Dodgers to be the first African American to integrate the major leagues. In 1947, his first year, he led the National League in stolen bases and was voted Rookie of the Year, and in 1949 was voted the league's Most Valuable Player. He retired from baseball in 1957, and was elected to the Baseball Hall of Fame in 1962.

In November 1949, the 758th Tank Battalion was redesignated the 64th Heavy Tank Battalion and then reassigned to the 2nd Armored Division at Fort Hood, Texas, after serving under Major General Gavin and successfully supporting the 82nd Airborne Division. Although President Truman had issued his Executive Order #9981, integrating the military forces the previous year, the army was slow at implementing the change. World War II had proved that a segregated military was not a viable solution for successful operations in combat or in peacetime. But the 64th Heavy Tank Battalion remained segregated as some military commanders held onto their old ways for as long as possible. In July 1950, the battalion received orders for deployment to Korea and was assigned to support the 3rd Infantry Division. The battalion commander and the senior officers on his staff were white, while the remainder to the battalion was African American. Upon arrival in Japan, the battalion quickly familiarized and trained with the new M48 Patton heavy tanks.

Deploying to combat in November 1950, the 64th Heavy Tank Battalion supported the 3rd Infantry Division in the assault landing at Wonson, North Korea, where it relieved elements of the 1st Marine Division who were withdrawing under the massive Chinese assault. The battalion assisted in the evacuation of United States Marines and Korean civilians by containing the final line of resistance in which 105,000 marines and soldiers, over 100,000 civilians, and 17,500 vehicles were withdrawn in the largest beachhead evacuation in U.S. military history. In early 1951, the battalion formed part of Task Force Bartlett to clear a path for the advance of the 25th Infantry Division. The tankers inflicted heavy enemy casualties in one of the early major United Nations victories of the war. In March, the 64th Heavy Tank Battalion participated in Operation Tomahawk. While supporting the 3rd Infantry Division, they had the mission of rendezvousing with the airborne assault of the 187th Airborne Regimental Combat Team, the 4th Ranger Company, and the African American 2nd Ranger Company, which had parachuted behind enemy lines on 23 March 1951. Many former soldiers of the 555th Parachute Infantry Battalion would finally meet the test of combat, as they were now members of the airborne units that jumped into battle that day. The mission was to encircle and trap retreating communist forces. By 29 March, the 64th Heavy Tank Battalion was one of the first units to cross the 38th Parallel in 8th Army's advance north.

From May 1951 through July 1953, the battalion held and defended positions around the 38th Parallel while supporting the 3rd Infantry Division. It was also during this period that the battalion was finally fully integrated. As trained armored soldiers were required to replace casualties and troops that rotated back to the United States, the army could ill afford to repeat the mistakes that hampered their forces during World War II. In its final battle of the Korean War, the battalion repelled a communist attack into the United Nations' lines. Company A, while supporting an infantry advance, drove into an enemy regimental assembly area. There, overwhelmed by a numerically superior force, the company's tanks fired at point blank range, having to finally call in artillery on their positions in order to halt the attack. When the battle finally ended, over 300 dead enemy soldiers where found surrounding their perimeter. For their gallant action, Company A, 64th Heavy Tank Battalion received the Distinguished Unit Citation. By November 1954, when the battalion departed Korea, in addition to the Distinguished Unit Citation, it had also been awarded two Korean Presidential Unit Citations.

Presidential Unit Citation (Later renamed the Distinguished Unit Citation)

Criteria: The Presidential Unit Citation is awarded to units of the Armed Forces of the United States and co-belligerent nations for extraordinary heroism in action against an armed enemy occurring on or after 7 December 1941. The unit must display such gallantry, determination, and esprit de corps in accomplishing its mission under extremely difficult and hazardous conditions as to set it apart from and above other units participating in the same campaign. The degree of heroism required is the same as that which would warrant award of a Distinguished Service Cross to an individual. Extended periods of combat duty or participation in a large number of operational missions, either ground or air, is not sufficient. Units that have participated in single or successive actions covering relatively brief time spans will normally earn this award. It is not reasonable to presume that entire units can sustain Distinguished Service Cross performance for extended time periods except under the most unusual circumstances. Only on rare occasions will a unit larger than battalion qualify for award of this decoration.[74]

The surviving members of the 761st Tank Battalion continued in their efforts to have the Distinguished Unit Citation presented to them for their service during World War II. In 1967, Congressman Frank Annunzio from Illinois unsuccessfully introduced a bill before Congress that would enable the president to award the citation to the battalion. In 1977, Congressman John Conyers of Michigan sent a letter to the Secretary of the Army, Clifford Alexander, which resulted in the reopening of this case. The summary of consider partially stated: "After seven months of intensive research covering the National Archives, the Library of Congress, Office of the Chief of Military History, and the Eisenhower Library in Abilene, Kansas, extensive documentary materials were compiled which taken together, are credible evidence and have not been viewed in total context with the previous evidence; that there are clear indications that racial discrimination and inadvertent neglect on the part of those in authority, at the time the recommendations were originally considered, may have been a factor in the disapprovals; that the climate created by the Army commanders could only have made it difficult to provide proper recognition for a 'Negro' unit during the period 1944–1947; that the accomplishments of the unit are quite impressive and the high enemy casualties and equipment losses were achieved despite documented adverse weather conditions and problems in resupply peculiar only to a dispersed 'Negro' unit attached to several other units in a segregated Army; that under the configuration the 761st operated in, with no controlling headquarters element, it would have been very difficult for the unit to compile timely statistical information necessary to prepare well documented and timely recommendations; thus resulting in submission of recommendations after the close of hostilities."[75]

Captain Charles Gates, upon the conclusion of World War II, volunteered to command a unit of the Missouri National Guard in 1949. He retired as a Lieutenant Colonel in 1964. As the president of the 761st Tank Battalion and the Allied Veterans Association in 1977, in a letter written to President Jimmy Carter, dated 16 March 1977, he stated: "Sir, would the President consider aiding a small group of World War II Veterans in the quest to secure two citations which, we feel, should be included to the outstanding combat record of the 761st Tank Battalion? The citations we are interested in being granted and added to our record are the Presidential Unit Citation and the French Croix de Guerre.... Enclosed is a novel written by Mr. David J. Williams, one of our unit commanders during World War II, which truthfully, brutally, and dramatically describes some of our ordeals and achievements during the combat phase of World War II in a fictitious manner. The novel is entitled *Eleanor Roosevelt's*

Niggers and this title is explained in the preface of the book.... Members of our Washington, D.C. Chapter, Mr. David Williams, or I would be most honored to meet with you or your appropriate staff representatives for a few minutes to discuss the worthiness of the battalion to receive these citations. This quest has been a 32-year effort and will be continued. Thank you, Mr. President. For your consideration."[76]

General Orders
No. 5

HEADQUARTERS
DEPARTMENT OF THE ARMY
WASHINGTON, DC
10 APRIL 1978

THE PRESIDENTIAL UNIT CITATION (ARMY). Award of the Presidential Unit Citation (Army) by the President of the United States of America to the following unit of the Armed Forces of the United States is confirmed in accordance with paragraph 9-2, AR 672-5-1. The text of the citation, signed by President Jimmy Carter on 24 January 1978, reads as follows: By virtue of the authority vested in me as President of the United States and as Commander in Chief of the Armed Forces of the United States, I have today awarded

THE PRESIDENTIAL UNIT CITATION (ARMY)
FOR EXTRAORDINARY HEROISM
TO THE
761st TANK BATTALION, UNITED STATES ARMY

The 761st Tank Battalion distinguished itself by extraordinary gallantry, courage, professionalism and high esprit de corps displayed in the accomplishment of unusually difficult and hazardous operations in the European Theater of Operations from 31 October 1944 to 6 May 1945. During 183 days in combat, elements of the 761st — the first United States Army tank battalion committed to battle comprised of black soldiers — were responsible for inflicting thousands of enemy casualties and for capturing, destroying, or aiding in the liberation of more than 30 major towns, 4 airfields, 3 ammunition supply dumps, 461 wheeled vehicles, 34 tanks, 113 large guns, 1 radio station, and numerous individual and crew-served weapons. This was accomplished while enduring an overall casualty rate approaching 50 percent, the loss of 71 tanks, and in spite of extremely adverse weather conditions, very difficult terrain not suited to armor operations, heavily fortified enemy positions and units, and extreme shortages of replacement personnel and equipment. The accomplishments are outstanding examples of the indomitable spirit and heroism displayed by the tank crews of the 761st. In one of the first major combat actions of the 761st, in the vicinity of Vic-sur-Seille and Morville-les-Vic, France, the battalion faced a reinforced enemy division. Despite the overwhelming superiority of enemy forces, elements of the battalion initiated a furious and persistent attack, which caused defending enemy elements to withdraw. While pursuing the enemy, tanks of the 761st were immobilized before an anti-tank ditch. Savage fire from enemy bazooka and rocket launcher teams, positioned 50 yards beyond the ditch, disabled many of the vehicles. Crewmen dismounted the disabled tanks, crawled under them with their 50 caliber weapons, and placed withering fire upon the enemy positions. This resulted in the elimination of many of the positions and virtually destroyed two enemy companies while permitting the escape of other tanks and crews and eventual completion of the mission. From 5 January 1945 to 9 January 1945, the 761st engaged the 15th SS Panzer Division in the vicinity of Tillet, Belgium. Suffering severe casualties and damage to their tanks, the 761st attacked and counterattacked throughout the five-day period against a numerically superior force in both personnel and equipment, and on 9 January 1945 the men of the 761st routed the enemy from Tillet and captured the town. This action was significant in that the men of the 761st prevented the enemy from further supply of its forces encircling Bastogne, and the United States troops there, because of the closing of the Brussels-Bastogne highway. One of the most significant accomplishments of the 761st began 20 March 1945 when, acting as the armor spearhead, the unit broke through the Siegfried Line into the Rhine plain, allowing units of the 4th Armored Division to move through to the Rhine River. During the period 20 March 1945 to 23

March 1945 the battalion, after operating far in advance of friendly artillery, encountered the fiercest of enemy resistance in the most heavily defended area of the war theater. Throughout the 72-hour period of the attack, elements of the 761st assaulted and destroyed enemy fortifications with a speed and intensity that enabled the capture or destruction of 7 Siegfried towns, 31 pillboxes, 49 machine gun emplacements, 61 antitank guns, 451 vehicles, 11 ammunition trucks, 4 self-propelled guns, one 170mm artillery piece, 200 horses, and one ammunition dump. Enemy casualties totaled over 4,100 and of those captured it was determined that the 761st in its Siegfried Line attack had faced elements of 14 different German divisions. The accomplishments of the 761st in the Siegfried area were truly magnificent as the successful crossing of the Rhine River into Germany was totally dependent upon the accomplishment of their mission. The men of the 761st Tank Battalion, while serving as a separate battalion with the 26th, 71st, 79th, 87th, 95th, and 103rd Infantry Divisions, the 17th Airborne Division, and 3rd, 7th, and 9th Armies in 183 continuous days in battle, fought major engagements in six European countries, participated in four major Allied campaigns and on 6 May 1945, as the easternmost American soldiers in Austria, ended their combat missions by joining with the First Ukrainian Army (Russian) at the Enn River, Steyr, Austria. Throughout this period of combat, the courageous and professional actions of the members of the "Black Panther" battalion, coupled with their indomitable fighting spirit and devotion to duty, reflect great credit on the 761st Tank Battalion, the United States Army, and this Nation.

There are several lasting monuments to the soldiers of the 761st Tank Battalion. In Mannheim, Germany, a *Kaserne* (military post) has been posthumously renamed in honor of First Sergeant Samuel J. Turley. In Gelnhausen, a *Kaserne* has been posthumously renamed for Lieutenant Kenneth W. Coleman, and in Giessen, Germany, there is one for Staff Sergeant Ruben Rivers. Fallen comrades are buried in three of the World War II cemeteries erected on foreign soil. At the Saint Avold-Lorraine American Cemetery in France, 22 members of the battalion are interred. At Margraten American Cemetery in Holland there is one, and there is also one at the Luxembourg American Cemetery. The others were sent back to the United States for interment.

In October 1993, an obelisk was dedicated at the Fort Knox, Kentucky (Home of the Armored Forces), Memorial Park to the 761st Tank Battalion for their valiant actions during World War II. On 15 September 1993, at Fort Hood, Texas, where the 761st was stationed at in 1943–1944, a monument was dedicated to the battalion, located near the main gate of the post. On 16 October 1994, Fort Hood's Headquarters Avenue was renamed the 761st Tank Battalion Avenue. The ceremony was addressed by the III Corps and Fort Hood commander, Lieutenant General Paul E. Funk, who stated, "It is about time those brave soldiers were justly honored. As you know, they were embroiled on two fronts, in the battle at home against segregation and racism, and abroad against the Germans. The history of this elite unit is not well known, but it is becoming more well known. Everyone knows that our services in those days were rigidly segregated, and most of the books have neglected or ignored the services of black servicemen. And more importantly, their sacrifices. Courage is colorblind. The acts of courage of the 761st were frequent, and certainly possessed uncommon valor."[77]

761st Tank Battalion Members Killed in Action During World War II

Name	Rank	Date	Hometown
ADAMS, CLIFFORD C.	PVT	11/8/44	Waco, TX
ANDERSON, ALEXANDER S.	PVT	11/9/44	Washington, PA
ARMSTRONG, EMILE I.	PVT	11/9/44	Cincinnati, OH
BOND, JESSE J.	TECH-5	1/5/45	Gates, NC

(761st Tank Battalion Members Killed in Action — *continued*)

Name	Rank	Date	Hometown
BRAGG, THOMAS S.	PVT	1/4/45	Elizabeth, NJ
BRISCOE, ROBERT W.	PVT	11/9/44	Baltimore, MD
BROWN, FRED L.	CPL	4/14/45	The Bronx, NYC
BYRD, L.C.	PVT	11/8/44	Tuscaloosa, AL
CAMPBELL, WALTER J.	TECH-4	11/11/44	Hempstead, NY
CHAPMAN, CARLTON	CPL	11/8/44	Pembroke, VA
COLEMAN, KENNETH W.	2LT	11/9/44	Washington, DC
COOPER, THEODORE R.	PVT	11/9/44	Camden, SC
DEVORE, WILLIE J.	TECH-5	1/9/45	Greenwood, SC
DUNN, LANE	TECH-5	11/25/44	Scottsville, KY
EWING RODERICK	TECH-5	11/19/44	Oklahoma City, OK
GRAHAM, ARDIS E.	CPL	11/25/44	Raeford, NC
HAMMOND, ROBERT C.	2LT	11/19/44	Cleveland, OH
HARRISON, JAMES W.	SGT	11/9/44	Brooklyn, NY
HILLIARD, IVORY V.	PFC	11/19/44	Houston, TX
HUFFMAN, MAXWELL	1LT	3/20/44	Newell, SD
JOHNSON, HORACE G.	TECH-5	12/19/44	Tabor City, NC
JOHNSON, ROBERT A.	SGT	1/3/45	Washington, DC
KING, ROY	SGT	11/9/44	River Rouge, MI
LOFTON, WILLIE C.	PVT	11/9/44	Corsicana, TX
MANN, CLAUDE	TECH-4	11/8/44	Chicago, IL
NELSON, JAMES W.	SSG	1/4/45	Detroit, MI
RIVERS, RUBEN	SSG	11/19/44	Holtuka, OK
SCOTT, HORATIO	TECH-4	11/10/44	Lynn, MA
SHIVERS, GEORGE	SGT	11/11/44	Bainbridge, GA
SIMMONS, COLEMAN JR.	PVT	11/25/44	Detroit, MI
SIMMONS, NATHANIEL	PVT	11/8/44	Beaufort, SC
TURLEY, SAMUEL J.	1SG	11/9/44	The Bronx, NYC
WELBORN, JAMES JR.	PVT	11/25/44	Jonesville, NC
WOODARD, HARVEY	SSG	11/8/44	Howard, GA

Chapter XIV

Conclusion

THE UNITED STATES CAME OUT OF WORLD WAR II completely changed as a nation. Now the predominant world power, America would be thrust into the leadership role in ensuring world peace. As for the soldiers who had served their country, the end of hostilities meant a return of normalcy to one's life. The African American soldiers, many of whom had fought to preserve democracy for the world, would not yet enjoy the fruits of freedom in their own country. Many decided to remain with the army, stationed in foreign countries as members of the occupation forces. Growing up during the depression years, the military offered many a sense of security and better opportunities than they would have if they returned to civilian life. But the majority chose to resume their lives in the civilian world.

To ease the transition back into civilian life, legislation was passed to support the returning soldiers. On 22 June 1944, President Franklin D. Roosevelt signed the Servicemen's Readjustment Act of 1944, popularly known as the "GI Bill of Rights." Many African American soldiers took advantage of the benefits provided in this bill to become more productive citizens. The first GI Bill provided six benefits:

- education and training
- loan guaranty for a home, farm, or business
- unemployment pay of $20 a week for up to 52 weeks
- job-finding assistance
- top priority for building materials for VA hospitals
- military review of dishonorable discharges

To be eligible for GI Bill education benefits, a World War II veteran had to serve 90 days or more after 16 September 1940, and have other than a dishonorable discharge. Veterans of the war were entitled to one year of full-time training plus a period equal to their time in service, up to a maximum of 48 months.

The Veterans Administration paid the educational institution up to a maximum of $500 a year for tuition, books, fees, and other training costs. The Veterans Administration also paid the single veteran a subsistence allowance of up to $50 a month. This was increased to $65 a month in 1946 and to $75 a month in 1948. Allowances for veterans with dependents were higher. This program ended on 25 July 1956. In the peak year of 1947, veterans accounted for 49 percent of all college enrollments. Out of a veteran population of 15,440,000, some 7.8 million took advantage of these benefits, including:

- 2,230,000 in college
- 3,480,000 in other technical schools
- 1,400,000 in on-the-job training
- 690,000 in farm training

Total cost of the World War II education program was $14.5 billion. Millions who would have flooded the labor market, instead opted for education, which reduced joblessness during the demobilization period. When they did enter the labor market, most were better prepared to contribute to the support of their families and society.[1]

First Lieutenant Bradley Briggs of the 555th Parachute Infantry Battalion decided to remain in the army after the war. Over 100,000 wartime reserve officers applied for the 9,800 regular officer positions that would be available in the peacetime army. Lieutenant Briggs would be one of only 31 African American officers that were granted regular army commissions.[2] First Lieutenant Vernon Baker, who had won the Distinguished Service Cross with the 92nd Infantry Division, remained in Italy, assigned to ordnance and maintenance companies until February 1947. He then graduated from the United States Army Airborne School and volunteered to join the 555th Parachute Infantry Battalion. Returned to his prewar enlisted rank, Baker now became the first sergeant of one of the airborne companies. On 9 December 1947, the 555th Parachute Infantry Battalion was deactivated and reflagged as the 3/505th Infantry Battalion, officially becoming part of the 82nd Airborne Division. Major General Gavin felt the army should be in the forefront of changing racial attitudes, instead of waiting for society to change. Many of the African American soldiers of the 555th Parachute Infantry Battalion now found themselves working side by side with the white paratroopers of the division, as they were transferred to other units and were assigned different duties within the 82nd Airborne Division. This would be the first effort in fully desegregating a division within the army.

But this would not change the racist ideology adhered to by many of the white officers remaining in the army in the late 1940s. First Sergeant Baker recalls an encounter with a colonel in Fayetteville, North Carolina, that ordered him to remove the Distinguished Service Cross ribbon from his dress uniform. "Sergeant, git that DSC ribbon off a yer uniform. Ah you a hearing me, nigger? Get that goddamn ribbon off a yer uniform. Ain't no nigger I ever saw deserved no Distinguished Service Cross." First Sergeant Baker refused to remove the ribbon and told the colonel to check his service record if he did not believe he earned the award.[3]

On 26 July 1948, President Truman issued Executive Order 9981, which banned segregation, and established equality of treatment and opportunity in the Armed Services.

EXECUTIVE ORDER 9981

Establishing the President's Committee on Equality of Treatment and Opportunity In the Armed Forces.

WHEREAS it is essential that there be maintained in the armed services of the United States the highest standards of democracy, with equality of treatment and opportunity for all those who serve in our country's defense:

NOW THEREFORE, by virtue of the authority vested in me as President of the United States, by the Constitution and the statutes of the United States, and as Commander in Chief of the armed services, it is hereby ordered as follows:

1. It is hereby declared to be the policy of the President that there shall be equality of treat-

ment and opportunity for all persons in the armed services without regard to race, color, religion or national origin. This policy shall be put into effect as rapidly as possible, having due regard to the time required to effectuate any necessary changes without impairing efficiency or morale.

2. There shall be created in the National Military Establishment an advisory committee to be known as the President's Committee on Equality of Treatment and Opportunity in the Armed Services, which shall be composed of seven members to be designated by the President.

3. The Committee is authorized on behalf of the President to examine into the rules, procedures and practices of the Armed Services in order to determine in what respect such rules, procedures and practices may be altered or improved with a view to carrying out the policy of this order. The Committee shall confer and advise the Secretary of Defense, the Secretary of the Army, the Secretary of the Navy, and the Secretary of the Air Force, and shall make such recommendations to the President and to said Secretaries as in the judgment of the Committee will effectuate the policy hereof.

4. All executive departments and agencies of the Federal Government are authorized and directed to cooperate with the Committee in its work, and to furnish the Committee such information or the services of such persons as the Committee may require in the performance of its duties.

5. When requested by the Committee to do so, persons in the armed services or in any of the executive departments and agencies of the Federal Government shall testify before the Committee and shall make available for use of the Committee such documents and other information as the Committee may require.

6. The Committee shall continue to exist until such time as the President shall terminate its existence by Executive order.

Harry Truman
The White House
July 26, 1948[4]

For many, the executive order meant that little would change. The segregationists associated with the military set out to try to ensure that integration of the armed forces would not be the end result of this presidential decree. The Chief of Staff, General Omar Bradley, argued that the army was no place for social experiments. With resistance bordering on insubordination, President Truman forced a written apology from General Bradley.[5] Of all branches of the military services, the army provided the strongest opposition to the executive order. Many commanders interpreted integration to mean having a segregated battalion or regiment assigned to their division or corps, thus preserving racial separation. Secretary of the Army Kenneth C. Royall, while addressing the Fahy Senatorial Committee in March 1949, stated that the army "was not an instrument for social evolution and that integration would undermine the army's efficiency." He reported that during the past two world wars the Negroes had failed to prove themselves in combat, and believed them only qualified for laborer duties. A few weeks after the report to the committee, Secretary Royall was forced to resign.[6] Gordon Gray, a lawyer from North Carolina, became the new Secretary of the Army. In his efforts to enforce Presidential policy, he met strong resistance from the army's senior command staff, and there would be only minimal integration conducted.

It would be the Korean War that would finally end segregation in the army. On 25 June 1950, more than 100,000 North Korean soldiers, supported by 1,400 artillery pieces and 125 Soviet-built T-34 tanks, crossed the 38th Parallel and invaded South Korea. The 24th Infantry Regiment, still segregated and on occupation duty in Japan since the end of World War II, became part of the 25th Infantry Division and were immediately rushed into the conflict. Ill-prepared, led by officers who were marginally qualified and rejected by white units, and with little or no combat training, the 24th Infantry Regiment was immediately deployed into battle to stop the flow of onrushing enemy forces. They were met by a numerically superior force, and the results were disastrous. One battalion of the regiment withdrew from their defensive positions without orders, leaving the flanks exposed to enemy attacks.

While the unit overall was rated poor in its combat performance, there were several individual acts of heroism. On 2 August 1950, Private First Class William Thompson from New York City, assigned to Company M, 3/24th Infantry Battalion, would win the first Congressional Medal of Honor awarded to an African American soldier since the Spanish American War. Near Haman, South Korea, while his weapons platoon was reorganizing under cover of darkness, fanatical enemy forces in overwhelming strength launched a surprise attack on the unit. Private First Class Thompson set up his machine gun in the path of the onslaught and swept the enemy with withering fire, pinning them down momentarily, thus permitting the remainder of his platoon to withdraw to a more tenable position. Although hit repeatedly by grenade fragments and small arms fire, he resisted all efforts of his comrades to induce him to withdraw, steadfastly remained at his machine gun and continued to deliver deadly, accurate fire until mortally wounded by an enemy grenade. Private First Class Thompson, in Korea only five weeks, refused to evacuate his post and fired his machine gun until enemy soldiers overran his position.[7]

Sergeant Cornelius H. Charlton, from East Gulf, West Virginia, assigned to Company C, 1/24th Infantry Battalion, would posthumously be awarded the regiment's second Medal of Honor while engaged in an assault on Hill 542, near Chipo-ri, Korea, on 2 June 1951. Leading the platoon after his lieutenant was wounded, Sergeant Charlton personally eliminated two machine gun emplacements while killing six of the enemy with his rifle fire and grenades. He continued to lead his platoon up the slope until the unit suffered heavy casualties and became pinned down. Regrouping the men, he led them forward only to be again hurled back by a shower of grenades and machine gun fire. Despite a severe chest wound, Sergeant Charlton refused medical attention and led a third daring charge, which carried to the crest of the ridge. Observing that the remaining machine gun emplacement, which had slowed the advance, was situated on the reverse slope, he charged it alone, was again hit by grenade fragments, but raked the position with a devastating fire, which eliminated it and routed the defenders. Though severely wounded, he refused medical evacuation, regrouped his men and continued to lead the assault on the hill. He would later succumb to his wounds.[8] However, individual acts of bravery were not enough to change the perception of the 24th Infantry Regiment as a unit that "melted away" under fire.

In late September 1950, two months after the beginning of the Korean War, the commander of the 25th Infantry Division, Major General William B. Kean, requested that the 8th Army disband the 24th Infantry Regiment because it had demonstrated that it was "untrustworthy and incapable of carrying out missions expected of an infantry regiment."[9]

When the 9th Infantry Regiment of the 2nd Infantry Division arrived in Korea in July 1950, it had two under-strength white battalions and one over-strength African American battalion assigned. The regimental commander, Colonel John G. Hill, transferred the excess African American soldiers to the white battalions. Colonel Hill later noted that "the mixed units worked well and that he never had any doubt that they would do so because at a time like that, misery loves company."[10]

While the 9th Infantry Regiment and other early-arriving front-line units of the 8th Army in Korea integrated their units to meet the demands of combat, the overall commander of the United States and United Nations forces did not support this practice. Not a single African American enlisted man or officer ever served on General MacArthur's headquarters staff. His chief of staff, Lieutenant General Almond, former commander of the 92nd Infantry Division, obviously shared his views. When given command of 10th Corps for the invasion of Inchon, General Almond immediately began to reverse the policies of integration. General Almond ordered that no additional African American soldiers be assigned to any white combat units, and that those already assigned, not be replaced when rotated out. Under General Almond's command, African American soldiers were relegated to rear-area service and support units. Even when casualties outnumbered replacements, and units were fighting far below their authorized strength, Generals MacArthur and Almond refused to integrate their front-line forces.

When President Truman relieved General MacArthur on 11 April 1951, General Matthew B. Ridgeway, who had commanded the 82nd Airborne Division and 18th Airborne Corps during World War II, replaced him. General Ridgeway, who opposed segregation on the moral grounds that it was both un–American and un–Christian, paused only long enough to request that the Department of the Army formally approve his desegregation efforts. After gaining approval from Washington, General Ridgeway started disbanding all segregated African American and Puerto Rican units, transferring their personnel to white units. Replacement personnel arriving from Japan were no longer restricted to the type of unit they could be assigned to, based solely on the color of their skin. These moves vastly improved the efficiency of combat readiness in Korea and eventually led to the integration of all training facilities throughout the army.

The needs of war had finally made the integration policy a reality in the army. By 1953, more than 90 percent of the African American soldiers served in integrated units, and by the end of 1954, the remaining all-black units were either integrated or disbanded. The four original African American regiments founded at the end of the Civil War were either converted or deactivated. The 9th Cavalry Regiment was converted to the 509th Tank Battalion on 20 October 1950, and fully integrated on 7 March 1953. The 10th Cavalry Regiment was converted to the 510th Tank Battalion on 20 October 1950, and was integrated on 31 December 1953. Two of the battalions of the 25th Infantry Regiment became the 94th and 95th Infantry Battalions before being deactivated on 20 and 22 December 1952. The regiment's third battalion became the 25th Armored Infantry Battalion of the 1st Armored Division on 20 November 1952. The 24th Infantry Regiment never survived the poor reputation and criticism it received in the opening months of the Korean War. It was officially deactivated on 1 October 1951, and replaced in the 25th Infantry Division by the 37th Infantry Regiment. Soldiers of the 24th Infantry integrated into the 37th Infantry Regiment, and other units within the division that badly needed replacements. While the soldiers continued to serve proudly in their integrated units, the 24th Infantry Regiment's reputation would forever remain tarnished.[11]

Integration of the military forces would continue to proceed in the military throughout the 1950s and 1960s. The Vietnam conflict would mark the first time that the United States entered a war with a totally integrated military force. While the military had made strides to improve race relations, they were well ahead of society's will to integrate. A soldier may have experienced totally integrated facilities while being on the military installation, but on many bases, especially in the South, as soon as they stepped through the front gates, it was back to the Jim Crow laws and segregation. Also, integration did not change the racist attitudes of many soldiers. Racial tensions that were prevalent in society during the late 1960s were also reflected in the military.

By the 1970s, the armed forces had implemented a program of race relations and equal opportunities. Some commands implemented mandatory seminars where the soldiers of different races and ethnicities were taught to interact with each other and to dispel racial stereotypes. Officers and noncommissioned officers received specialized training in order to conduct this training.

Racial segregation in the military, as well as in society, proved to be a dismal failure. During World War II, a valuable resource of manpower was denied the opportunity to fully defend their country due to accepted discrimination policies. Many casualties could have been prevented had the higher command put aside their racist views and fully utilized the manpower resources that were available. "Separate but equal" was a method of justifying discrimination based on race. The experiment of assigning segregated African American units in combat for the most part would be judged a failure by the white general staffs, based solely on the perceived performances of the 92nd and 93rd Infantry Divisions. Inept leadership by their white commanders and discrimination were never considered a cause of these failures. The combat performances of the 92nd Infantry Division in Italy would not have been any worse than a comparable white infantry division had they been adequately led. Little was known of the stellar combat records of the African American armor and artillery units that were assigned to the European Theater of Operations supporting white units. The 761st Tank Battalion, the 614th Tank Destroyer Battalion, and the 969th Field Artillery Battalion would all go on to receive the Distinguished Unit Citation, the most prestigious award presented to a unit in combat. Nor have our history books dedicated anything more than a footnote to the combat support personnel who kept the units supplied; built the roads, airfield and bridges; and provided the critical logistical support, which was vital to the victory of Allied armies in this global conflict. All this was accomplished while having to tolerate discrimination at home and overseas, and being treated as second-class citizens.

During World War II, no African American soldier was awarded the Medal of Honor. Many felt that racism during the time was a major factor in this decision. In 1993, after pressure from various veterans groups to reexamine the issue, the army contracted Shaw University in Raleigh, North Carolina, to research and prepare a study "to determine if there was a racial disparity in the way Medal of Honor recipients were selected." Shaw University's team, headed by Dr. Daniel K. Gilbran, researched the matter for over three years, and, finding that there was indeed disparity, recommended the army consider a group of 10 soldiers for the Medal of Honor. Of those 10, seven were recommended to receive the award. In October of 1996 Congress passed the necessary legislation, which waived the 1952 approval deadline date for all World War II Medal of Honor recipients, and allowed the president to award these Medals of Honor.[12]

President William Clinton presented the Medals of Honor in a ceremony on 13 January 1997 at the White House. Vernon Baker, at age 76, was the only surviving recipient present to receive his long-awaited award. He stated that he wished the other six could have been honored in their lifetimes: "It's been late, but it's never too late to say it was a job well done. I'm so very, very sorry that they're not here."[13] The other six soldiers received their awards posthumously, with their medals being presented to surviving family members. George Watson, of Birmingham, Alabama, the first African American soldier to receive the Distinguished Service Cross during World War II, had no surviving family members, and his Medal of Honor is located on display at the Quartermaster Museum at Fort Lee, Virginia.

Appendix: The Medal of Honor

BAKER, VERNON

Citation: For extraordinary heroism in action on 5 and 6 April 1945, near Viareggio, Italy. Then Second Lieutenant Baker demonstrated outstanding courage and leadership in destroying enemy installations, personnel and equipment during his company's attack against a strongly entrenched enemy in mountainous terrain. When his company was stopped by the concentration of fire from several machine gun emplacements, he crawled to one position and destroyed it, killing three Germans. Continuing forward, he attacked an enemy observation post and killed two occupants. With the aid of one of his men, Lieutenant Baker attacked two more machine gun nests, killing or wounding the four enemy soldiers occupying these positions. He then covered the evacuation of the wounded personnel of his company by occupying an exposed position and drawing the enemy's fire. On the following night Lieutenant Baker voluntarily led a battalion advance through enemy mine fields and heavy fire toward the division objective. Second Lieutenant Baker's fighting spirit and daring leadership were an inspiration to his men and exemplify the highest traditions of the Armed Forces.

CARTER, EDWARD A., JR.

Citation: For extraordinary heroism in action on 23 March 1945, near Speyer, Germany. When the tank on which he was riding received heavy bazooka and small arms fire, Sergeant Carter voluntarily attempted to lead a three-man group across an open field. Within a short time, two of his men were killed and the third seriously wounded. Continuing on alone, he was wounded five times and finally forced to take cover. As eight enemy riflemen attempted to capture him, Sergeant Carter killed six of them and captured the remaining two. He then crossed the field using as a shield his two prisoners from which he obtained valuable information concerning the disposition of enemy troops. Staff Sergeant Carter's extraordinary heroism was an inspiration to the officers and men of the 7th Army Infantry Company Number 1 (Provisional) and exemplifies the highest traditions of the Armed Forces.

FOX, JOHN R.

Citation: For extraordinary heroism against an armed enemy in the vicinity of Sommocolonia,

Italy on 26 December 1944, while serving as a member of Cannon Company, 366th Infantry Regiment, 92nd Infantry Division. During the preceding few weeks, Lieutenant Fox served with the 598th Field Artillery Battalion as a forward observer. On Christmas night, enemy soldiers gradually infiltrated the town of Sommocolonia in civilian clothes, and by early morning the town was largely in hostile hands. Commencing with a heavy barrage of enemy artillery at 0400 hours on 26 December 1944, an organized attack by uniformed German units began. Being greatly outnumbered, most of the United States Infantry forces were forced to withdraw from the town, but Lieutenant Fox and some other members of his observer party voluntarily remained on the second floor of a house to direct defensive artillery fire. At 0800 hours, Lieutenant Fox reported that the Germans were in the streets and attacking in strength. He then called for defensive artillery fire to slow the enemy advance. As the Germans continued to press the attack towards the area that Lieutenant Fox occupied, he adjusted the artillery fire closer to his position. Finally he was warned that the next adjustment would bring the deadly artillery right on top of his position. After acknowledging the danger, Lieutenant Fox insisted that the last adjustment be fired, as this was the only way to defeat the attacking soldiers. Later, when a counterattack retook the position from the Germans, Lieutenant Fox's body was found with the bodies of approximately 100 German soldiers. Lieutenant Fox's gallant and courageous actions, at the supreme sacrifice of his own life, contributed greatly to delaying the enemy advance until other infantry and artillery units could reorganize to repel the attack. His extraordinary valorous actions were in keeping with the most cherished traditions of military service, and reflect the utmost credit on him, his unit, and the United States Army.

JAMES, WILLY F., JR.

Citation: For extraordinary heroism in action on 7 April 1945 near Lippoldsberg, Germany. As lead scout during a maneuver to secure and expand a vital bridgehead, Private First Class James was the first to draw enemy fire. He was pinned down for over an hour, during which time he observed enemy positions in detail. Returning to his platoon, he assisted in working out a new plan of maneuver. He then led a squad in the assault, accurately designating targets as he advanced, until he was killed by enemy machine gun fire while going to the aid of his fatally wounded platoon leader. Private First Class James' fearless, self-assigned actions, coupled with his diligent devotion to duty exemplified the finest traditions of the Armed Forces.

RIVERS, RUBEN

Citation: For extraordinary heroism in action during the 15–19 November 1944, toward Guebling, France. Though severely wounded in the leg, Staff Sergeant Rivers refused medical treatment and evacuation, took command of another tank, and advanced with his company in Guebling the next day. Repeatedly refusing evacuation, Sergeant Rivers continued to direct his tank's fire at enemy positions through the morning of 19 November 1944. At dawn, Company A's tanks began to advance towards Bougaktroff, but were stopped by enemy fire. Sergeant Rivers, joined by another tank, opened fire on the enemy tanks, covering Company A as they withdrew. While doing so, Sergeant Rivers' tank was hit, killing him and wounding the crew. Staff Sergeant Rivers' fighting spirit and daring leadership were an inspiration to his unit and exemplify the highest traditions of military service.

THOMAS, CHARLES L.

Citation: For extraordinary heroism in action on 14 December 1944, near Climbach, France. While riding in the lead vehicle of a task force organized to storm and capture the village of Climbach, France, then First Lieutenant Thomas' armored scout car was subjected to intense enemy artillery, self-propelled gun, and small arms fire. Although wounded by the initial burst of hostile fire, Lieutenant Thomas signaled the remainder of the column to halt and, despite the severity of his wounds, assisted the crew of the wrecked car in dismounting. Upon leaving the scant protection which the vehicle afforded, Lieutenant Thomas was again subjected to a hail of enemy fire, which inflicted multiple gunshot wounds in his chest, legs, and left arm. Despite the intense pain caused by these wounds, Lieutenant Thomas ordered and directed the dispersion and emplacement of two antitank guns, which in a few moments were promptly and effectively returning the enemy fire. Realizing that he could no longer remain in command of the platoon, he signaled to the platoon commander to join him. Lieutenant Thomas then thoroughly oriented him on enemy gun dispositions and the general situation. Only after he was certain that his junior officer was in full control of the situation did he permit himself to be evacuated. First Lieutenant Thomas' outstanding heroism was an inspiration to his men and exemplifies the highest traditions of the Armed Forces.

WATSON, GEORGE

Citation: For extraordinary heroism in action on 8 March 1943. Private Watson was on board a ship, which was attacked and hit by enemy bombers. When the ship was abandoned, Private Watson, instead of seeking to save himself, remained in the water assisting several soldiers who could not swim to reach the safety of the raft. This heroic action, which subsequently cost him his life, resulted in the saving of several of his comrades. Weakened by his exertions, he was dragged down by the suction of the sinking ship and was drowned. Private Watson's extraordinarily valorous actions, daring leadership, and self-sacrificing devotion to his fellow man exemplify the finest traditions of military service.[1]

Chapter Notes

Introduction

1. Lorenzo J. Green, "Some Observations on the Black Regiment of Rhode Island in the American Revolution," *Journal of Negro History* 37 (1952): pp. 142–143, 152.
2. Bruce Catton, *This Hallowed Ground: The Story of the Union Side of the Civil War* (New York, 1956), p. 222.
3. Luis F. Emilio, *A Brave Black Regiment: The History of the 54th Massachusetts, 1863–1865* (Boston, 1894), pp. 1–2.
4. Major John Bigelow, Jr., Historical Sketch, 10th United States Cavalry, 1866–1892, United States Army Commands, Records Group 98, National Archives.
5. Henry O. Flipper, *Black Frontiersman: The Memoirs of Henry O. Flipper, First Black Graduate of West Point*, compiled and edited by Theodore Harris (Fort Worth, Texas: Texas Christian University Press, 1997), pp. 15–20; Organizational Returns, 10th Cavalry, August 1881 and July 1882, National Archives; William Leckie, *The Buffalo Soldiers: A Narrative of the Negro Cavalry in the West* (University of Oklahoma Press, 1967), pp. 237–238.
6. U.S. Army War College, *Colored Soldiers in the U.S. Army* (Washington, D.C., 1942), p. 15.
7. U.S. Supreme Court, *Plessy v. Ferguson* (163 U.S. 537, 16S.Ct. 1138), 18 May 1896.
8. Vincent C. Jones, *American Military History: Transition and Change, 1902–1917* (Center of Military History, Washington, D.C., 1969), p. 351.
9. Michael L. Lanning, *The African-American Soldier: From Crispus Attucks to Colin Powell* (Trenton, NJ, 1999), p. 104.
10. Ibid., p. 106.
11. Ann Lane, *The Brownsville Affair: National Crisis and Black Reaction* (New York, 1971), p. 103.
12. John D. Weaver, *The Brownsville Raid* (New York, 1970), p. 172.

I. World War I

1. Robert Haynes, *A Night of Violence: The Houston Riot of 1917* (Louisiana, 1976), pp. 54–60.
2. Lanning, *The African-American Soldier*, p. 125.
3. Ibid., p. 126.
4. W.E.B. Dubois, *The Crisis* (18 January 1918): p. 114.
5. James W. Johnson, *Along This Way* (New York, 1933), pp. 322–323.
6. Arthur E. Barbeau and Florette Henri, *The Unknown Soldiers: African-American Troops in World War I* (New York, 1996), p. 17; Letter, *Literary Digest* 55 (June 1917): pp. 342–343; W.E.B. Dubois Papers, Amistad Research Center, Fisk University, Nashville, Tennessee, Chapter 4, "Black France," pp. 12–13.
7. Ibid., W.E.B. Dubois Papers, Chapter 4, "Black France," pp. 13–22.
8. Letter, Henry Jervey to the Adjutant General, 29 Dec 1917, Records Group 165, Item 8142-62; Letter, General Frank McIntyre to the Adjutant General, 1 Aug 1918, Records Group 165, Item 8142-181; National Archives.
9. John L. Thompson, *History and Views of the Colored Officers Training Camp* (Des Moines, Iowa), 1917, pp. 6–7; Barbeau and Henri, *The Unknown Soldiers*, p. 217.
10. Barbeau and Henri, *The Unknown Soldiers*, p. 61; Allison W. Sweeney, *History of the American Negro in the Great World War* (Chicago, 1919), p. 79.
11. U.S. Army War College, *Colored Soldiers in the U.S. Army*, p. 127.
12. Barbeau and Henri, *The Unknown Soldiers*, pp. 62–63.
13. James P. Finley, "Colonel Charles Young—Black Cavalryman, Huachuca Commander, and Early Intelligence Officer," *Huachuca Illustrated: A Magazine of the Fort Huachuca Museum*; Volume 1, *The Buffalo Soldiers at Fort Huachuca* (1993).
14. George B. Rodney, *As a Cavalryman Remembers* (Caldwell, Idaho, 1944), pp. 262–263.
15. Letter, Command General Punitive Expedition, U.S. Army, Colonia Dublan, Mexico, to the Adjutant General, 21 Aug 1916, Subject: Recommendation of Officers to Command Militia in the Federal Service, National Archives; quoted in *The Crisis* 15 (March 1918): p. 218.
16. Addie W. Hunton and Katherine M. Johnson, *Two Colored Women with the American Expeditionary Forces* (Brooklyn, 1920), pp. 43–44; Ulysses Lee, *The Employment of Negro Troops: Special Study, The United States Army in World War II* (Washington, D.C., 1966), p. 10; Barbeau and Henri, *The Unknown Soldiers*, pp. 66–67.
17. Newton D. Baker Papers, Library of Congress, Man-

uscript Division, Washington, D.C., item 216 (Wilson to Baker, 25 Jun 1917).

18. Ibid., item 219 (Baker to Wilson, 26 Jun 1917, unsigned carbon copy).

19. Ibid., item 7-2 (Letter Wilson to John Sharp Williams, 29 Jun 1917).

20. Finley, "Colonel Charles Young — Black Cavalryman, Huachuca Commander, and Early Intelligence Officer," *Huachuca Illustrated.*

21. Lee, *The Employment of Negro Troops*, p. 4.

22. Emmett J. Scott, *Scott's Official History of the American Negro in the World War* (New York, 1969), pp. 32–34; Barbeau and Henri, *The Unknown Soldiers*, pp. 70–71.

23. Arthur Little, *From Harlem to the Rhine* (New York, 1936), pp. 50–51; Barbeau and Henri, *The Unknown Soldiers*, p. 74.

24. Scott, *Official History of the American Negro in the World War*, pp. 80–81.

25. Barbeau and Henri, *The Unknown Soldiers*, pp. 76–77; William L. Judy, *A Soldier's Diary* (Chicago, 1930), pp. 36–37.

26. Chester D. Heywood, *Negro Combat Troops in the World War* (Worcester, Massachusetts, 1928), p. 1; Scott, *Official History of the American Negro in the World War*, p. 231; Barbeau and Henri, *The Unknown Soldiers*, p. 79.

27. Thomas Shipley, *The History of the AEF* (New York, 1920), p. 110; Scott, *Official History of the American Negro in the World War*, pp. 130–131; Barbeau and Henri, *The Unknown Soldiers*, p. 82; *New York Times*, 10 Oct 1917, p. 4.

28. Letter, Chief of Staff of the Army to the Adjutant General, R.G 165, Item 8142-29, 7 Oct 1917, National Archives.

29. List of Officers Assigned to the 92nd Infantry Division, Records Group 120, File 28-12.6, National Archives; Scott, *Official History of the American Negro in the World War*, pp. 131–134.

30. Scott, *Official History of the American Negro in the World War*, pp. 131–132; Barbeau and Henri, *The Unknown Soldiers*, p. 84.

31. Sweeney, *History of the American Negro in the Great World War*, pp. 206–207; Osceola McKaine, "The Buffaloes," *Outlook* 119 (22 May 1918).

32. Report of First Lieutenant Oscar C. Brown, 351st Machine Gun Battalion, Records Group 130, File 16-11.4, National Archives; William N. Colson and A.B. Nutt, "The Failure of the 92nd Division," *Messenger* (September 1919): pp. 22–24.

33. Barbeau and Henri, *The Unknown Soldiers*, p. 85.

34. Letter, Colonel E.D. Anderson to the Chief of Staff, Records Group 165, Item 8142-150, 16 May 1918, p.1, National Archives.

35. Letter, General Bliss to the Adjutant General, Records Group 165, Item 8689-26, 7 Aug 1917; General Orders 107, 14 Aug 1917; Service of Supply records from Base Section 5, typescript History of the Stevedores, Records Group 120, File 121-12.0; National Archives.

36. Letter, General H.L. Scott, Chief of Staff, to the Adjutant General, Records Group 165, Item 8689-42, 19 Sep 1917; Authorized in General Order 125, 22 Sep 1917, National Archives; Barbeau and Henri, *The Unknown Soldiers*, p. 92.

37. Report of from Camp Taylor, Records Group 120, File 168-11.4, 1 Dec 1918, National Archives.

38. Historical Narrative of the Port of Embarkation, Hoboken, NJ, Records Group 120, File 11.4, National Archives; Walter Delsarte, *The Negro, Democracy, and the War* (Detroit, 1919), p. 15; Barbeau and Henri, *The Unknown Soldiers*, p. 102.

39. Report, "Cable History of Colored Soldiers," Records Group 120, File 7-12.5; General Pershing's cable number 454, Jan-Feb 1918; National Archives.

40. John J. Pershing, *My Experiences in the World War* (New York, 1931); Barbeau and Henri, *The Unknown Soldiers*, p. 112.

41. Carter G. Woodson, *The Negro in Our History* (Washington, D.C., 1921), p. 524; Herbert Aptheker, *Toward Negro Freedom* (New York, 1956), p. 119; Barbeau and Henri, *The Unknown Soldiers*, pp. 114–115; France, Asemblee Nationales, n.s., 1919, Session Ordinaire, Chambre, *Debats*, 25 Jul 1919, p. 3365.

42. Barbeau and Henri, *The Unknown Soldiers*, pp. 114–115.

43. Ibid., pp. 192–201; *New York Times*, 21 May 1918, p. 6.

44. *The Army Times*, 3 March 2003, pp. 4–5.

45. Report, Colonel Hayward to l'Esperance, Records Group 120, File 16-11.4, pp. 3–4, 9–10, National Archives; Barbeau and Henri, *The Unknown Soldiers*, pp. 120–121.

46. U.S. Army War College, *Colored Soldiers in the U.S. Army*, pp. 83–84; *The Crisis* (January 1919): p. 113.

47. Ibid., pp. 60–61.

48. Barbeau and Henri, *The Unknown Soldiers*, pp. 122–123.

49. Colonel Roberts After Action Report, Records Group 120, File 293-11.4, 2 Jan 1919, National Archives; Sweeney, *History of the American Negro in the Great World War*, p. 157.

50. Dubois, W.E.B., "An Essay Toward a History of the Black Man in the Great War," *The Crisis* (June 1919): pp. 75–76.

51. Warren H. Miller, *The Boys of 1917* (Boston, 1939), pp. 366–367; Heywood, *Negro Combat Troops in the World War*, p. 181; Records Group 120, File 16-11.4, National Archives.

52. Barbeau and Henri, *The Unknown Soldiers*, p. 131; General Headquarters, French Armies of the East, Orders Number 12,291 D, 15 Jan 1919.

53. Citation Medal of Honor, Center of Military History; Robert F. Dorr, *The Army Times*, "America 70 Years Late in Honoring World War I Soldier," 19 May 2003.

54. Monroe Mason and Arthur Furr, *The American Negro with the Red Hand of France* (Boston, 1920), pp. 43–44; Barbeau and Henri, *The Unknown Soldiers*, p. 136.

55. Robert L. Bullard, *Personalities and Reminiscences of the War* (New York, 1925), pp. 291–295.

56. Jerome Dowd, *The Negro in American Life* (New York, 1926), p. 102; Letter General Charles C. Ballou, Commander 92nd Division, to Assistant Commandant, General Staff College, 14 Mar 1920, National Archives.

57. Emmett J. Scott, Papers of Emmett J. Scott, Morgan State University, Baltimore, Maryland, box 114, file 2 (Charles Williams' report on the 92nd Infantry Division).

58. Hunton and Johnson, *Two Colored Women with the American Expeditionary Forces*, pp. 60–61; Barbeau and Henri, *The Unknown Soldiers*, p. 143.

59. Barbeau and Henri, *The Unknown Soldiers*, p. 138.

60. Letter, Colonel Lochridge to the Chief of Staff, Records Group 94, File 48-46.1, 20 Oct 1918; List of Officers of the 92nd Infantry Division, Records Group 120, File 292-65.1, 1 Nov 1918, National Archives.

61. Edward M. Coffman, *War to End All Wars* (New York, 1968), p. 319.

62. Hunton and Johnson, *Two Colored Women with the American Expeditionary Forces*, pp. 53–54.

63. After Action Report, Colonel Brown and Appendix D, Major Elser, Records Group 120, File 292-33.6, National Archives.

64. Ibid.; Dubois, "An Essay Toward a History of the

Black Man in the Great War," *The Crisis* (June 1919): pp. 81–82.

65. Shipley, *The History of the AEF*, pp. 257–258; Barbeau and Henri, *The Unknown Soldiers*, p. 152.

66. Dubois, "An Essay Toward a History of the Black Man in the Great War," *The Crisis* (June 1919): pp. 82.

67. After Action Report, "Inefficiency of Negro Officers" (no signature), Colonel Brown, Commander 368th Infantry Regiment, Records Group 120, File 16-11.4, National Archives; Barbeau and Henri, *The Unknown Soldiers*, pp. 153–154.

68. After Action Report on the Argonne Offensive, Colonel Brown, Commander 368th Infantry Regiment, 15 Nov 1918, Records Group 120, File 292-33.6, National Archives.

69. Scott, Papers of Emmett J. Scott 113-5, Letter, Ralph Tyler to Scott.

70. Barbeau and Henri, *The Unknown Soldiers*, pp. 154–155; *New York Times*, 8 Nov 1918, p. 8.

71. Scott, Papers of Emmett J. Scott 112-6, Letter Major Dean to Scott; After Action Report, "Inefficiency of Negro Officers" (no signature), Colonel Brown, Commander 368th Infantry Regiment, Records Group 120, File 16-11.4, National Archives.

72. After Action Report on the Argonne Offensive, Colonel Brown, Commander 368th Infantry Regiment, 15 Nov 1918, Records Group 120, File 292-33.6, National Archives.

73. Dubois, "An Essay Toward a History of the Black Man in the Great War," pp. 81–82; After Action Report on the Argonne Offensive, Colonel Brown, 15 Nov 1918, Appendix Z, Records Group 120, File 292-33.6, National Archives; W.E.B. Dubois, Dubois Papers, Amistad Research Center, Fisk University, Nashville, Tennessee, chapters 14–18 (Wright's report on medical services within the 92nd Infantry Division).

74. Herbert Seligmann, *The Negro Faces America* (New York, 1920), p. 39.

75. Barbeau and Henri, *The Unknown Soldiers*, p 166.

76. Records of the 5th Infantry Division, Endorsement by Brigadier General D.E. Nolan, G-2, American Expeditionary Force Headquarters, Records Group 120, File 205-27.7, National Archives.

77. Scott, Papers of Emmett J. Scott, 115-3; *The Crisis* (July 1919): pp. 128–129; Memorandum of Captain Louis Mehllinger, 368th Infantry Regiment, 24 Nov 1918, Records Group 120, File 292-36, National Archives.

78. United States Congress, Senate, *Alleged Executions Without Trial in France* (Washington, D.C., Government Printing Office, 1923), pp. 55–59.

79. Ibid., pp. 494–505, 568.

80. Carter G. Woodson, *Negro Makers of History* (Washington, D.C., 1928), pp. 330–331; *Chicago Defender*, 9 Apr 1919, p. 16; *New York Times*, 19 Dec 1919, p. 3; Barbeau and Henri, *The Unknown Soldiers*, p. 171.

81. National Association for the Advancement of Colored People, *Annual Reports For 1919* (New York, NAACP, 1917–1920): pp. 39–40; *New York Times*, 1 Nov 1919, p. 3.

82. Scott, Papers of Emmett J. Scott, 110-3, Press release from Scott's office, 7 May 1919.

83. Ibid., 113-5; Letter, Colonel Greer to Senator McKellar, 6 Dec 1918; Woodson, *Negro in Our History*, pp. 521–522.

84. Ibid., 113-5, Letter Ralph Tyler, from Marbache, France, to Scott, 8 Dec 1918.

85. Sweeney, *History of the American Negro in the Great World War*, p. 237; Barbeau and Henri, *The Unknown Soldiers*, p. 244.

86. Lanning, *The African-American Soldier*, pp. 147–148.

II. Between the Wars

1. Walter F. White, *Rope and Faggot* (New York, 1929), p. 112; *Chicago Defender*, 10 May 1919, p. 10; NAACP, *Report For 1919*, p. 19; Barbeau and Henri, *The Unknown Soldiers*, pp. 177–178.

2. Woodson, *The Negro in Our History*, p. 528.

3. Lee, *The Employment of Negro Troops in World War II*, 1966, pp. 15–16.

4. Ibid.

5. Ibid., p. 20.

6. Personal letter, Major General Douglas MacArthur, Chief of Staff, to Major General Edwin B. Winas, Commanding General, 8th Corps Area; Letter, Frederick H. Payne, Acting Secretary of War to Walter White, Secretary NAACP, 11 Aug 1931; both in File AG320.2 (6-17-31)(1) Section, National Archive.

7. Letter, Adjutant General to all the Commanding Generals, File AG320.2 (17 Jun 1931), Enlisted; Letter, Adjutant General to all the Commanding Generals Corps Area, File AG320-2 (25 Jun 1934) Enlisted, National Archives.

8. Letter, Walter White, NAACP to President Hoover, 29 Jul 1931, File AG320.2 (6-17-31) (1) sec, National Archive.

9. Letter, Robert Moton to President Hoover, 18 Sep 1931, Forwarded to War Department, 22 Sep 1931, File AG620 (4-23-31) (1) sec, National Archives.

10. Letter, Adjutant General to Senator Elmer Thomas, Oklahoma, 13 Apr 1939, File AG291.21 (4-10-39), National Archives.

11. Letter, Walter D. McClure, Jr. (Roxbury, MA) to Secretary of War, 13 Apr 1941, and answer Adjutant General to McClure, 18 Apr 1941, File AG291.21 (4-13-41) (1); Report, Lieutenant Colonel Willis J. Tack, University of Akron, re: Allegations of Samuel R. Shepard, Concerning Racial Discrimination in ROTC, 3 Dec 1941, File AG291.21 (11-14-41) (3), National Archives.

12. Memorandum, Tab C, G-1 to the Army Chief of Staff, 28 Sep 1940, File AG210.31 ORC, National Archives.

13. Mobilization Regulations 1–2, 1 Sep 1938, Modified in May 1939, National Archives; Lee, *The Employment of Negro Troops in World War II*, pp. 40–41.

14. Appendix D, Percentages of Negro Manpower, Letter Adjutant General to the Chiefs of Arms, Services, Bureaus, Corps Area Commanders, Commanding General Headquarters Air Force, Superintendent United States Military Academy, Commandants General Service Schools, 3 May 1939, File AG381 (3-3-39), National Archives.

15. Memorandum, G-3 for the Army Chief of Staff, 5 Jun 1940, File G-3/6541-Gen-527; Annex 2, War Department Protective Mobilization Plan, 1940, National Archives.

16. Lanning, *The African-American Soldier*, p. 164; Memorandum, G-3 for the Army Chief of Staff, 12 Jun 1940, File AG011, Records Group 612-40 (1), National Archives.

17. Letter, Secretary of War to Senator Morris Sheppard, Chairman Senate Military Affairs Committee, 13 Jun 1940, File AG011, Records Group 612-40 (1), National Archives.

18. Public Law 703, 76th Congress, Approved 2 Jul 1940, Published to the Army in War Department Bill 17, 2 Aug 1940, National Archive.

19. Memorandum, Office of the Chief of Staff (initialed G.C.M. for General George C. Marshall) for Major Person, 20 Jul 1940, File OCS 20 Records Group 602-2, and penciled note thereon, AG of 1 (6-20-40); Memorandum Office of the Chief of Staff for the G-1, G-2, G-3, G-4, and the War Department, 19 Jun 1940, File OCS 20, Records

Group 602-61; Lee, *The Employment of Negro Troops in World War II*, p. 69.

20. *The Crisis* (November 1940); Lee, *The Employment of Negro Troops in World War II*, pp. 74–75; Lanning, *The African-American Soldier*, p. 164.

21. Lanning, *The African-American Soldier*, p. 164; Stimson, Henry, Diary Entries, Henry Simpson Papers, Yale University, New Haven Connecticut.

22. Memorandum, Assistant Secretary of War for the President, 8 Oct 1940; Letter, Secretary to the President (Stephan Early) for the Assistant Secretary of War, 9 Oct 1940, File AG291.21 (10-9-40) (1), National Archives.

23. Enclosure to Memorandum, Assistant Secretary of War for the President, 8 Oct 1940, distributed to the Army on 16 Oct 1940, by Letter, File AG291.21 (10-9-40) (1), National Archives.

24. *Pittsburgh Courier*, 19 Oct 1940; *Time Magazine*, 28 Oct 1940; Lee, *The Employment of Negro Troops in World War II*, p. 76.

25. *The Crisis* (December 1940): p. 375.

26. Congressional Record 86, 13610, 13827, United States Congress, 7 Nov 1940.

27. Lanning, *The African-American Soldier*, p. 165; Lee, *The Employment of Negro Troops in World War II*, p. 80.

28. Letter, Secretary of War to Dean William H. Hastie, 25 Oct 1940, File — Office Assistant Secretary of War, Personnel #601, and Memorandum, Assistant Secretary of War to Major General James H. Burns, 25 Oct 1940, same file, National Archives.

29. Jerry N. Ness, "Oral History Interview with Judge William Hastie," in *The Truman Papers*, 5 Jan 1972 (Harry S. Truman Library, Independence, Missouri).

30. Hearings, Senate, military Establishment Appropriations Bill for 1941, File H.R. 9209, United States Congress, 14 May 1940, p. 365.

31. Lanning, *The African-American Soldier*, p. 168.

32. Memorandum, Secretary of the General Staff for G-1, G-3, and Chief of Staff Air Services, 25 Nov 1941, File AG322.97 (11-25-41) (1), National Archives.

33. Memorandum, War Department for the Chief of Staff, 26 Sep 1940, File AG324.71 (9-26-40) (1), National Archives.

34. Memorandum, G-3 to the War Department, 5 Oct 1940, File AG324.71 (9-26-40)(1), National Archives.

35. Executive Order 8802, Fair Employment Practice Order, 25 Jun 1941, http://www.eeoc.gov/35th/thelaw/eo-8802.html.

36. Ness, "Oral History Interview with Judge William Hastie."

37. Memorandum in response to Judge Hastie's Memorandum dated 22 Sep 1941, By the G-1/G-3 for the Chief of Staff's submission to the Secretary of War, 1 Dec 1941, File OCS/20602-219, National Archives; Lee, *The Employment of Negro Troops in World War II*, pp. 138–140.

38. Ibid.; Lanning, *The African-American Soldier*, pp. 169–170.

III. The African American Press

1. *Pittsburgh Courier*, 19 Feb 1938–28 Sep 1940; Letters to the Adjutant General's Office, 3 AG 322.99, 23 Feb 1938, National Archives.

2. Lee H. Finkle, *Forum for Protest: The Black Press During World War II* (East Rutherford, New Jersey), 1975, pp. 130–132.

3. Hayward Farrar, *The Baltimore Afro-American: 1892–1950* (Westport, Connecticut), 1998, p. 167.

4. Editorial, *Baltimore Afro-American*, 13 Dec 1941.

5. Minutes of the General Council, 22 Feb 1943, p.5, 1 Mar 1943, p. 2; Letter Walter White to the Secretary of War, Office of the Secretary of War File 291.2, National Archives; Editorial, *The Crisis* (Mar 1943): p. 72.

6. Editorial, Baltimore *Afro-American*, 26 Jun 1943.

7. Letter, The Adjutant General to Commanding Generals All Corps Areas, File AG320-2, 11 Aug 1943, National Archives.

8. War Department Circulars 271, 355, 365 and 392, 1943, National Archives.

9. Lee, *The Employment of Negro Troops*, p. 383.

10. Ibid., p. 384.

11. Ibid.

12. Patrick Washburn, *A Question of Sedition: The Federal Government's Investigation of the Black Press During World War II* (New York, 1986), p. 98; Farrar, *The Baltimore Afro-American*, p. 169.

13. Finkle, *Forum for Protest*, p. 9.

14. Virginius Dabney, "Nearer and Nearer the Precipice," *Atlantic Monthly* (January 1943), pp. 94–100.

15. Farrar, *The Baltimore Afro-American*, pp. 170–171.

16. Phillip McGuire, ed., *Taps for a Jim Crow Army: Letters Black Soldiers in World War II* (Lexington: University Press of Kentucky, 1983), p. 239.

IV. Combat Service Support Units

1. Letter, Office of the Chief of Engineers to the Adjutant General, 24 Jan 1941, File AG324.71 (1-24-41) (1) sec 12, National Archives.

2. Memorandum, G1 for the Adjutant General, 1 Feb 41, and first endorsement, 5 Feb 41, both in File AG324.71 (1-24-41) (1) sec 12, National Archives.

3. Memorandum, G3 for the Adjutant General, and attached Memorandum for Record, File AG-3/46578, 7 Aug 1941; Letter, the Adjutant General to the Chief of the Army Air Forces, 25 Aug 1941, File AG324.71 (8-7-41) E-C, National Archives.

4. Memorandum, Operations Division War Department for the Commanding General, Army Ground Forces and Service of Supply (SOS), 6 May 1942, File AGF 320.2/14 (Chemical Warfare Service), National Archives; Letter War Department to Commanding Generals Central and Western Defense Commands and Edgewood Arsenal, Maryland., 16 May 1942, File AG320.2 (5-15-42), National Archives.

5. Memorandum, G3 for the G1, 5 Nov 1940, File AG-3/42108, National Archives; Memorandum, G1 for the Adjutant General, 13 Nov 1940, National Archives.

6. Memorandum for Record, attached to Memorandum, G-3 for the Adjutant General, 27 Feb 1941, File AG320.2 (2-27-41), National Archives.

7. Consolidated files, Minutes of the Chief of Staff General Council, Feb 1943, National Archives.

8. Historical Files, Army Nurses Corps, 1941–1945, National Archives.

9. Letter, Adjutant General to the Provost Marshal General *et al.*, 26 Sep 1941, File AG320.2 (9-26-41) MR-M-A, National Archives.

10. Memorandum, Office of the Chief Signal Officer for the Assistant Chief of Staff for Training and Operations, dated 28 May 1940, File OCSIGO-320.2, National Archives.

11. Historical Files, Army Signal Corps, 1941–1945, National Archives.

12. Letter, Field Artillery School to Commanding General Replacement and School Command, 2 Oct 1942, File AGF 352/402 (Field Artillery School), National Archives.

13. McGuire, *Taps for a Jim Crow Army*, pp. 67–69.

14. Letter, Parachute School to Commanding General, Army Ground Forces, 27 July 1942, File AGF 322.999/2 (Colored Troops) (7-27-42).

15. History 810th Engineer Aviation Battalion, Air Force Archives, National Archives.

16. History United States Army Forces Far East, 1943–1945, appendix 10, Office of the Chief of Military History Files, National Archives.

17. Letter, Headquarters 376th Engineer Battalion (Separate), to Engineer Office Base Section (Italy), 23 Mar 1945, National Archives.

18. History, 811th Aviation Engineer Battalion (Lieutenant Saul Cohen), 23 Sep–18 Dec 1944, Air Force Archives.

19. Historical Files and Diary 96th Engineer Battalion (Separate), National Archives.

20. Historical Files, Army Corps of Engineers, 1941–1945, National Archives.

21. Summary of the History of the 96th Engineer General Service Regiment (Lieutenant Nils R. Holmes), 21 Apr 1944, National Archives.

22. Ibid.

23. Historical Summary 91st Engineers (Captain Paul Miller), 4 May 1944, National Archives.

24. Designations in parentheses indicate the numerical designation assigned after port companies became separate in 1943.

25. Historical Summary, 394th Port Battalion (Transportation Corps), 1 May 1944, National Archives.

26. Citations, Distinguished Service Cross, Center for Military History, Washington, D.C.; Quartermaster Museum, Fort Lee, Virginia.

27. Memorandum, War Plans Division for the Chief of Staff, 18 Jan 1942, and Letter, Secretary of War to the Secretary of State, 21 Jan 1942, both in File WPD 4376-10, National Archives.

28. Memorandum, War Plans Division for the Commanding Generals Army Ground Forces, Army Air Forces, Supply of Services, 16 Mar 1942, File WPD 381/DO (3-16-42) National Archives; Letter, Headquarters Army Ground Forces to Commanding General Second Army, 20 Mar 1942, File AGF 320.2/76 OPN; Memorandum, Operations Division War Department for Colonel Wood, 25 May 1942, File OPD 381 Liberia (5-25-42), National Archives.

29. History 367th Infantry Battalion (Separate), 1 Mar 1942–18 May 1944, National Archives.

30. General Order 23, Headquarters, United States Army Forces in Liberia, 22 Dec 1943, National Archives.

31. The Alaska Highway, A Report Compiled for the Commanding General, Army Service Forces (May 1945), II, Office of the Chief of Military History, National Archives.

32. Planning Division, Office of the Director of Plans and Operations, Army Service Forces (11 vols.), I, v–7, Office of the Chief of Military History, National Archives.

33. History 83rd Engineer Aviation Battalion, 1943, National Archives.

34. Historical Report, 45th Engineer General Service Regiment, 15 Jun 1941–30 Jun 1944, National Archives.

35. History, 76th Engineer Light Pontoon Company, 1944, National Archives.

36. Ibid.; History, 76th Engineer Light Pontoon Company, 1944, National Archives.

37. History, Service of Supply, India-Burma Theater, app. 12, Construction Service, 23 Apr–24 Oct 1944, Office of the Chief of Military History, National Archives.

38. History, Service of Supply, India-Burma Theater, app. 4, Advance Section Three, 25 Oct 44–20 May 45, pp. 223–224.

39. Ibid.; Unit History 3841st Quartermaster Truck Company, 25 Oct 42–23 Dec 1944; History 518th Quartermaster Battalion Mobile, 1 Jan 1944–31 Dec 1944, National Archives.

40. History 352nd Engineer General Service Regiment; Technical Intelligence Report 1943, Problems Encountered in 352nd Engineer Regiment, 28 May 1945, National Archives.

41. Charles F. Romanus and Riley Sunderland, *Time Runs Out in CBI* (Washington, D.C, 1959), p. 348.

42. Ledo Road, I, VI-8, Memorandum in Office of the Chief of Military History; History of Service of Supply, India-Burma Theater, Administrative Section, 25 Oct 1944–20 May 1945, Memorandum in Office of the Chief of Military History, National Archives.

43. History 858th Engineer Aviation Battalion, 8 Jan 1944–15 Sep 1945, National Archives.

44. General Order 32, Headquarters Service of Supply, India-Burma Theater, 6 Dec 1944, National Archives.

45. History Service of Supply, India-Burma Theater, app. 4, Advance Section Three, p. 116, Washington, D.C.

46. Ibid., p. 88.

47. Ibid., p. 89.

48. Strength of the Army, File STM-30, 1 Dec 1945, National Archives.

49. Ibid., 1 Jan 1945, National Archives.

50. Letter, Staff Sergeant H.A.W., *Stars and Stripes* (October 12, 1944); Benjamin C. Bowker, *Out of Uniform* (New York: Norton, 1946), pp. 193–212.

51. Strength of the Army, File STM-30, 1 Sep 1944, National Archives.

52. Letter, Headquarters, European Theater of Operations, United States Army to Commanding Generals and Commanding Officers, 16 Jul 1942, File ETOUSA AG-Misc 291.2-A, National Archives.

53. Letter, Headquarters, Service of Supply, European Theater of Operations, United States Army, to Base Section Commanders and All Commanding Officers, 7 Aug 1942, File AG291.2, National Archives.

54. Motor Transport Service, chapter V, volume V, part 2 of the Historic Report Transportation Corps in the European Theater of Operations, p. 7, Washington, D. C., 1945.

55. Ibid., pp. 11–23. See also Joseph Bykofsky and Harold Larson, *The Transportation Corps: Operations Overseas: United States Army in World War II* (Washington, D.C., 1957), chapter 8.

56. "Gasoline," *The Quartermaster Review* 24 (May-June 1945): p. 23.

57. History 22nd Quartermaster Truck Regiment (Group), National Archive; Letter, Headquarters Peninsular Base Section (Colonel Roger W. Whitman) to Brigadier General H.S. Clarkson, Headquarters Mediterranean Theater of Operations, 19 Jul 1945, File WDSSP 291.2, National Archives.

58. History 609th Port Company (Transportation Corps), Oct–Dec 1944 (2nd Lieutenant Weaver A. Turner), National Archives.

59. United States Army Forces Pacific Operations Area, Report of Part in the Iwo Jima Campaign, File 98-USF4-0.3 (23284), National Archives.

60. History 24th Chemical Decontamination Company, National Archives; Paul W. Pritchard, *Smoke Generator Operations in the Mediterranean and European Theaters of Operation*, Chemical Corps Historical Studies 1 (Washington, D.C., 1946), pp. 53–54.

61. After Action Report, S-1, 387th Engineer Battalion (Separate), Jan–Mar 1944, National Archives.

62. Charles Broadwell, "The Long Run," interview with Vernon Castle Stephens for *The Fayetteville Observer*, 5 Dec 1999.

63. Historical Records, 320th Antiaircraft Balloon Battalion (VLA), Center for Military History, Washington, D.C.
64. Address, Brigadier General Charles Lanham (formerly commanding officer of the 22nd Infantry Regiment, 4th Infantry Division) before American Council on Race Relations, transcribed from a broadcast over radio station WMCA, New York, 12 Jul 1946.
65. The Transportation Corps in the Battle of France (Historic Report, Transportation Corps in the European Theater of Operations, V), Motor Transport Brigade, pp. 9–10.
66. After Actions Report 261st Ordnance Battalion, 1944, National Archives.
67. After Action Report, 666th Quartermaster Truck Company, 16 Dec 1943–15 Dec 1944; 16 Dec 1944–31 Mar 1945, National Archives.
68. General George S. Patton Jr., *War as I Knew It* (Boston, 1947), p. 194; Franl E.G. Weil, "The Negro in the Armored Forces," *Social Forces* 26 (1947–1948), p. 97.

V. Women's Army Corps

1. Judith A. Bellafaire, *The Women's Army Corps: A Commemoration of World War II Service* (CMH Publication 72-15, Office of Military History, Washington, D.C., 1947).
2. Ibid.
3. Charity Adams Earley, *One Woman's Army: A Black Officer Remembers the WAC* (College Station, Texas: Texas A&M University Press, 1989), pp. 3–14.
4. Ibid., p. 22.
5. Memorandum, Colonel Tasker for Colonel Hobby, 14 May 1942, G-1 File AG291.21 Women's Army Corps; Disposition Form, G-1 for Military Personnel Department, Services of Supply, 24 Aug 1942, File WDGAP 322.99; Memorandum, Military Personnel Department, Services of Supply for the G-1, 12 Sep 1942, File SPGAM 322.5 Women Army Auxiliary Corps, in G-1 File 291.21 Women's Army Corps; all in the National Archives.
6. File of action is WA 291.21 (5-27-42), 1942, National Archives.
7. Letter, Walter White, Secretary of the NAACP to the Director of the Women Army Auxiliary Corps, 8 Jun 1942 and reply, File SPWA 291.2; Letter, Major Harriet West to Frances L. Munson, 1 Sep 1943, File SPWA 291.2, National Archives.
8. *New York Times*, July 1942, p. 6.
9. Memorandum, Military Personnel Division, Service of Supply for G1, 12 Sep 1942, File SPGAM/3225 (Women Army Auxiliary Corps) (8-24-42), National Archives.
10. Planning Project 5, May 1943, Sample of 1400 of each race. Women's Army Auxiliary Corps Planning Service Files, National Archives.
11. Bellafaire, *The Women's Army Corps*.
12. Letter, Commandant Fort Des Moines to Executive Women's Army Auxiliary Corps, File SPWA 319.1, 13 May 1943; Letter, Detroit NAACP to the Secretary of War, with endorsements, File SPWA 291.2, 29 Sep 1943, National Archives.
13. Disposition Form, Operations Service, Surgeon General's Office, for the Military Training Division, Army Services Forces, in Surgeon General's Office Historical Division, File SPMCM 322.5-1, 17 Aug 1944, National Archives.
14. Western Flying Training Command News Release, undated Folder Negroes—Army Air Forces, War Department Bureau of Public Relations Files; Women's Army Corps, Army Air Forces History, pp. 14, 40, National Archives.
15. Study conducted by the Surgeon General's Office (incidental to determining factors in health records) of 22,000 accepted applicants, Surgeon General' Office Medical Statistics Division, Oct 1943–Mar 1944, National Archives.
16. History, 6888th Central Postal Directory Battalion, Office of Military History, National Archives.
17. Report on Postal System in the European Theater of Operations, 10 Jan 1945—15 Feb 1945, Report 30 Headquarters European Theater of Operations, General Inspectorate Section. Copy in War Department Women's Army Corps File 333.5, National Archives.
18. Earley, Charity Adams. *One Woman's Army*, p. 215.
19. Treadwell, *The Women's Army Corps*, pp. 408, 460.
20. Ibid., Appendix A, Table 8, p. 774; Adjutant General's Office, Women's Army Corps Awards and Decorations, 30 Jan 1947–Distributed by War Department Bureau of Public Relations, Office Department of the Women's Army Corps Reference File, Awards and Decorations, Chief Military History, National Archives.
21. Memorandum, Assistant Chief of Staff, G-1, to The Under Secretary of War, through the Chief of Staff, 15 Jan 1946, subject: Future Utilization of Female Personnel in the Postwar Military Establishment, File 326.5; Organized Reserve Corps, Records Group 165, National Archives.

VI. Artillery

1. The howitzer has an arched trajectory, while the artillery gun has a straight trajectory.
2. Narrative, Westervelt Board Results, Artillery Corps, United States Army, 1921, National Archives.
3. Artillery Corps Statistics for 1944, National Archives.
4. Memorandum, Army Service Forces Manpower Personnel Division for the Commanding General Army Service Forces, 31 Aug 1943, File APGAM 320.2 (30 Aug 1943), National Archives.
5. Report of Artillery with the VIII Corps in the Reduction of Brest, 22 Aug–19 Sep 1944, National Archives.
6. After Action Report, 969th Field Artillery Battalion, Jul–Dec 1944, National Archives.
7. After Action Report 333rd Field Artillery Battalion, Dec 1944, National Archives.
8. Historical Reports, 106th Infantry Division, Center of Military History, Washington, DC, http://www.ibiblio.org/hyperwar/USA/OOB/106-Division.html.
9. World War II Prisoner of War Database, National Archives.
10. After Action Report, "Discovery of American Bodies," Major James L. Baldwin, S-2, 395th Infantry Regiment, Feb 1945, National Archives.
11. After Action Report 578th Field Artillery Battalion, Dec 1944, National Archives.
12. Ibid.; Personal Report and Journal, 101st Division Artillery, Dec 1944, National Archives.
13. After Action Report, 771st Field Artillery Battalion, Dec 1944; After Action Report and Journal, 333rd Field Artillery Group, Dec 1944, National Archives.
14. After Action Report, S-1 969th Field Artillery Battalion, Dec 1944, National Archives.
15. Letter, Headquarters 101st Airborne Division to Commanding Officer 969th Field Artillery Battalion, through Commanding General VIII Corps, 3 Jan 1945, copy in 969th Field Artillery Battalion After Action Report, Jan 1945; National Archives.
16. First Endorsement to the letter cited in note 16.
17. 3rd Army General Order 31, dated 7 Feb 1945, National Archives.

18. After Action Report 578th Field Artillery Battalion, Dec 1944, National Archives.
19. After Action Report 578th Field Artillery Battalion, Jan–May 1945, National Archives.
20. After Action Reports 999th Field Artillery Battalion, Feb–May 1945; 969th Field Artillery Battalion, Feb–May 1945; 686th Field Artillery Battalion, Feb–May 1945.
21. After Action Report 969th Field Artillery Battalion, Feb–May 1945, National Archives.
22. History of the 777th Field Artillery Battalion, 15 Aug 1943–31 Dec 1944; After Action Report and Journal 777th Field Artillery Battalion, Feb–May 1945; After Action Report and Journal 349th Field Artillery Group, Feb–Mar 1945; National Archives.
23. Antiaircraft Artillery Branch Statistics for 1944, National Archives.
24. After Action Report, 191st Field Artillery Battalion, 31 Aug 1944, National Archives.
25. Citation, Silver Star Medal, Headquarters XII Corps, General Order 3, 9 Jan 1945; Headquarters XII Corps, General Order 4, 13 Jan 1945; National Archives.
26. After Action Reports and Operations Reports, 452nd Antiaircraft Artillery Automatic Weapons Battalion, Aug 1944-May 1945.

VII. Tank Destroyers

1. After Action Report, United States Tank Destroyer Command to the Assistant Chief of Staff, G-1, Jan. 1945, National Archives.
2. Steven J. Zaloga, *M10 and M36 Tank Destroyers: 1942–1943* (Osprey Publishing Co., 2002), p. 14.
3. Lee, *The Employment of Negro Troops in World War II*, p. 121.
4. Journal 614th Tank Destroyer Battalion, Dec 1944; Narrative Report 614th Tank Destroyer Battalion, Dec 1944, National Archives.
5. Field Order 3, 103rd Infantry Division, 7 Dec 1944, National Archives.
6. William F. Barclay, ed., *103rd Infantry Division Signal Company Remembrances: 1918–1945* (1995), http://www.pierce-evans.org/remembrancesa.htm.
7. Citation, Distinguished Service Cross, Headquarters 7th Army, General Order 58, 20 Feb 1945, Center for Military History and the National Archives.
8. Barclay, *103rd Infantry Division Signal Company Remembrances*.
9. Narrative Report, 614th Tank Destroyer Battalion, Dec 1944; S3 Report, Company C, 614th Tank Destroyer Battalion, 13–14 Dec 1944, Battalion S3 Journal; Operations Report (Narrative, annex 1), 103rd Infantry Division, Dec 1944–Apr 1945, National Archives; Personal Narrative, Sergeant Dillard Booker, 3rd Platoon, Company C, 614th Tank Destroyer Battalion, File AGF 314.7, National Archives; Ralph Mueller and Jerry Turk, *Report After Action: The Story of the 103rd Infantry Division* (Headquarters, 103rd Infantry Division, Innsbruck, Austria, 1945), pp. 48–50; Citations Distinguished Service Cross, Silver Star Medal, and Bronze Star Medal, Headquarters 103rd Infantry Division, General Order 88, 27 Dec 1944, and General Order 89, 28 Dec 1944; National Archives.
10. Narrative Report, 614th Tank Destroyer Battalion, Dec 1944, National Archives.
11. Joseph Galloway, "Military Injustice," *U.S. News and World Report*, 6 May 1996.
12. Narrative Report 614th Tank Destroyer Battalion, Jan 1945, XV Corps Daily Tank Destroyer Reports, Dec 1944–Jan 1945, National Archives.
13. Narrative Report 614th Tank Destroyer Battalion, Apr–May 1945; Operations Report, 103rd Infantry Division, Apr–May 1945, National Archives.
14. Barclay, *103rd Infantry Division Signal Company Remembrances*.
15. Report of Investigation, 827th Tank Destroyer Battalion, After Action Review 827th Tank Destroyer Battalion, National Archives; Lee, *The Employment of Negro Troops*, p. 681.
16. Letter, Headquarters 7th Army, 6 Jan 1945 (copy in the History, 827th Tank Destroyer Battalion), National Archives.
17. Report of Investigation, 827th Tank Destroyer Battalion, 15–19 Jan 1945, Chief of Military History, National Archives.
18. Report of Investigation, 827th Tank Destroyer Battalion; After Action Report 813th Tank Destroyer Battalion, Jan 1945, National Archives.
19. After Action Report 813th Tank Destroyer Battalion, Jan 1945; Unit Journal 3/313th Infantry, Jan 1945, National Archives.
20. First Endorsement to the Report of Investigation, Headquarters VI Corps to Commanding General 7th Army, 26 Jan 1945, National Archives.
21. Letter, Headquarters 7th Army to Commanding General 6th Army Group, 31 Jan 1945, Adjutant General File AG333.5-C, 6th Army Group File AG322-3 (Jan 1945), National Archives.
22. 12th Armored Division G1 Operations Reports, Feb 1945; 12th Armored Division Inspector General Reports, Feb 1945, National Archives.
23. Lee, *The Employment of Negro Troops*, p. 686; 5th through 8th Endorsements, 27 Mar 1945–19 Apr 1945, to Letter, Headquarters 7th Army to Commanding General 6th Army Group, 31 Jan 1945, National Archives.

VIII. Separate Infantry Regiments

1. Memorandum, Adjutant General, 13 Jan 1941, sub: Constitution and Activation of Units, Files AG320.2, Record Group 407, National Archives.
2. After Action Report, 24th Infantry Regiment, Apr 1942–Jun 1943; 23 Feb–30 Jun 1943; Dated 1 Oct 1943, National Archives.
3. Historical Record and History, 24th Infantry Regiment, 1 Oct 1943, National Archives.
4. Historical Record and History, 24th Infantry Regiment, 1 Jan–31 Mar 1944, National Archives.
5. General Order 453, Headquarters U.S. Army Forces in the South Pacific Area, 30 Mar 1944, subject: Reorganized and Redesignated 2nd Battalion, 54th Coast Artillery, National Archives.
6. Historic Reports, 49th Coast Artillery Battalion (155-mm), 15 Feb 1941–Jun 1944; G-3 Section XIV Corps, Report of Operations on Bougainville; Commanding General XIV Corps, Report of Lessons Learned in the Bougainville Operation, National Archives.
7. Memorandum, The Inspector General for Deputy Chief of Staff, 14 May 1945, File WDSIG 330.13-24th Infantry Regiment; National Archives.
8. Ibid.; Memorandum, Deputy Chief Pacific Theater, for General Hull, 16 May 1945, File OPD 330.13 (14 May 1945); National Archives.
9. Letter, Headquarters Army Ground Forces to Commanding General 3rd Army, 9 Jun 1942, File AGF320.2/8 Infantry, National Archives.
10. Unpublished manuscript, Captain Robert Thomson, "Reminiscence of a Black Infantry Regiment," 30 May 1994. In Archives Branch, U.S. Army Military History Institute, Carlisle Barracks, Pennsylvania.

11. Inspector General (IG) Report of Investigation, 31 Oct 1942, subject: Investigation of Matters Reported to the Chief of Chaplains Relating to the 364th Infantry, and, in Particular, to Lieutenant Colonel Hugh D. Adair, 0-7452 (RA), Executive Officer, 364th Infantry Regiment. Inter-Office of the Inspector General, General Correspondence 1939, File 333.9, Records Group 159, National Archives.

12. Report of Investigation, Headquarters, Southern Land Frontier Sector, Western Defense Command (by Major Earl F. Bradfield), 30 Oct 1942, subject: Report of Investigation, 364th Infantry. In Office of the Inspector General, General Correspondence 1939-1947, Files 333.9, Records Group 159, National Archives.

13. Memorandum, G-3 for the Commanding General Army Ground Forces, 16 Apr 1943, File WDGCT291.21, National Archives.

14. Minutes of the General Council, 22 Feb 1943, p. 5, and 1 Mar 1943, p. 2; Letter Walter White to the Secretary of War, Office of the Secretary of War, File WD291.2, National Archives; Editorial, *The Crisis* (March 1943): p. 72.

15. Report of Investigation (undated), Colonel C.C. Park, Inspector General, 3rd U.S. Army, subject: Report of Investigation of Disorder in 364th Infantry Regiment, 27 May 1943. In Records of Headquarters 3rd U.S. Army, Adjutant General, General Correspondence File AG291.1 thru AG300.3, Records Group 338, National Archives. (See Encl 2.)

16. Ibid.

17. Military Personnel Records of Technician 4 Booket Watkins, National Personnel Records Center, St. Louis, Missouri.

18. Thomson, *Reminiscence of a Black Infantry Regiment*; telephone interview, Thomson with Lieutenant Colonel Charles T. Graul, 16 Jun 1999.

19. Ibid.

20. Memorandum, Major General Virgil L. Peterson for Deputy Chief of Staff, 8 Jun 1943, subject: 364th Infantry, Camp Van Dorn, Mississippi. In Headquarters Army Ground Forces, General Correspondence, 1942-1948, File AG291.2, Records Group 335, National Archives; Memorandum, Acting Civilian Aide to the Secretary of War for the Deputy Chief of Staff, 15 June 1943, subject: Inspector General's Memorandum Regarding the 364th Infantry Regiment, Records Group 107, National Archives.

21. Memorandum (Agent Report), Agent George F. Kennedy, Counter Intelligence Corps (CIC), 12 Jun 1943, subject: Negro Conditions, Camp Van Dorn, Mississippi. In Records of Headquarters 4th Service Command, File 291.2, Records Group 338, National Archives. (See Encl 3.)

22. Memorandum, Agent Homer B. Scretchings, CIC, for Director, Intelligence Division, 4th Service Command, 10 Nov 1943, subject: Survey Relative to Existing Conditions at Camp Van Dorn, Mississippi. In Records of Headquarters 4th Service Command, File 291.2, Records Group 338, National Archives. (See Encl 4.)

23. Memorandum, Chief of Staff, for Commanding Generals, Army Air Forces, Army Ground Forces, and Army Service Forces, 14 Jul 1943, subject: Negro Troops, File AGC 291.2 (9-1-43) to (4-30-44), Records Group 407, National Archives.

24. Letter, Office of the Inspector General for the Inspector General, 21 Sep 1943, Headquarters Army Ground Forces, General Correspondence, 1942-1948, File AG291.2/25, Records Group 337, National Archives.

25. Memorandum, Office of the War Department, G3 (Major General Ray E. Porter), for Chief, Organization-Mobilization Branch, 6 Nov 1943, (G3) Files AG291.2 to AG291.22, Records Group 165, National Archives.

26. Report of Test Alert at Shemya 19–21 April 1945. Alaska Department, Adjutant General Section, Classified Historical Reports of Military Installations 1941-1947, Entry Alaska Defense Command, Records Group 338, National Archives.

27. Report of Test Alert Amchitka 8 March 1945. Alaska Department, Adjutant General Section, Classified Historical Reports of Military Installations 1941-1947, Entry Alaska Defense Command, Records Group 338, National Archives.

28. Memorandum, Army Ground Forces for the Operations Division, Department of War, 14 Oct 1943, File AGF291.2/25, National Archives; Disposition Form, Operations Division, Department of War to Commanding General, Army Ground Forces, 19 Oct 1943, File AGF 291.2/11, National Archives.

29. Letter, The Adjutant General to the Commanding General Second Corps Area, 13 Dec 1941, File AG370.5 (12-11-41), National Archives; Letter, The Adjutant General to the Commanding General Second Corps Area, 26 Apr 1942, File AG370.5 (4-22-42), National Archives; Memorandum, Operations Division War Department for the Chief of Staff, 20 Apr 1943, File OPD 322.97, National Archives.

30. Memorandum, Operations Division War Department for the Deputy Chief of Staff, 26 Nov 1943, National Archives; Reply Form, Assistant Secretary of the General Staff for the Operations Division War Department, 2 Dec 1943; Disposition Form, Operations Division War Department for the G-3, 3 Dec 43; all included in File OPD 320.2 (20 Nov 43), National Archives.

31. United States Army, *Participation of Puerto Ricans in the Armed Services with Emphasis on World War I, World War II, and the Korean War* (Headquarters Antilles Command, U.S. Army Center of Military History, Fort McNair, Washington, D.C. July 1965), Section II, p. 1.

32. *Participation of Puerto Ricans in the Armed Services*, Section II, pp. 2–3.

33. U.S. Army Forces Antilles and MDPR, "60th Anniversary United States Army in Puerto Rico," *The Sentinel* (12 December 1958): p. 4-B, Puerto Rican National Guard Museum, San Juan, Puerto Rico.

34. Jose Norat Martinez, *Historia del Regimento 65 de Infanteria* (San Juan, Puerto Rico, 1992), p. 55.

IX. Paratroopers

1. General Orders 40, Paragraph 1, Headquarter, Airborne Corps, Army Ground Forces, Camp Mackall, North Carolina, 23 Dec 1943.

2. Historical Records, 555th Parachute Infantry Battalion, National Archives.

3. Bradley Biggs, *The Triple Nickles: America's First All-Black Parachute Unit* (North Haven, Connecticut, 1986), pp. 29–30.

4. Letter, Headquarters Parachute School, subject: Transfer of 555th Parachute Infantry Company, 13 July 1944, File AG325, Records Group 445, National Archives.

5. War Department General Orders 13, Headquarters Airborne Corps, Army Ground Forces, subject: Activation of the 555th Parachute Infantry Battalion, 21 Nov 1944, Historical Files, 555th Parachute Infantry Battalion, National Archives.

6. Historical Files, 555th Parachute Infantry Battalion, Attachment Orders to the 9th Service Command, May 1945, National Archives.

7. Ronald. H. Bailey, ed., *The Home Front: USA* (Alexandria, Virginia: Time-Life Books, 1978), p. 107.

8. Al Greenwood, "Tribute Honors Black Paratroopers," *The Fayetteville Observer*, 9 Feb 2003.

9. After Action Report, Operation Firefly, 555th Parachute Infantry Regiment, Jul–Oct 1945, National Archives.
10. Attachment Orders, 82nd Airborne Division, Feb 1946, National Archives; Biggs, *The Triple Nickles*, p. 73.

X. 2nd Cavalry and 93rd Infantry Divisions

1. Vernon Baker, *Lasting Valor* (New York, 1997), p 123.
2. Action Memorandum, Chief of Cavalry for the Chief of Staff, United States Army, 20 Sep 1940, File AG320.2 Cavalry (9-20-40), National Archives.
3. Memorandum, Headquarters Army Ground Forces for G-3, 12 May 1942: Memorandum, G-3 for Commanding General, Army Ground Forces, 14 May 1942. Both in File AGF 320.2/165 GNGPS (5-11-42), National Archives.
4. McGuire, *Taps for a Jim Crow Army*, p. 115.
5. Memorandum — Detailed Plans for Implementation of 1944 Troop Basis, Tab A, G-3 for the Chief of Staff, 20 Jan 1944, File AG320.2 (17 Aug 1943) (2) section 1. Approved 21 Jan 1944. National Archives.
6. Memorandum, G-3 for the Chief of Staff, 7 Dec 1943, War Department File GCT 320 TB (7 Dec 1943); Approved 15 Jan 1944 as amended File AG320.2 (17 Aug 1943) section 1; National Archives.
7. Arnold M. Rose, "1947 Army Policies Toward Negro Soldiers — A Report on a Success and a Failure," *Journal of Social Issues* (Fall 1947): pp. 26–31.
8. L.D. Reddick, "The Negro Policy of the United States Army, 1775–1945," *Journal of Negro History* (1949): p. 29.
9. Henry Stimson, 1944 Diary entry, January 27. Henry Simpson Papers, Yale University, New Haven Connecticut.
10. Ibid.
11. *Chicago Defender*, 4 March 1944a and b; *Cleveland Call & Post*, 4 March 1944; *Norfolk Journal and Guide*, 18 March 1944; Johnson 1944.
12. Advisory Committee in MacGregor and Nalty 1977: Volume 5, pp. 326–331.
13. Richard Dalfiume, *Desegregation of the U.S. Armed Forces: Fighting on Two Fronts, 1939–1954* (Columbia: University of Missouri Press, 1969).
14. Lee, Ulysses, *The Employment of Negro Troops in World War II*, pp. 492–494.
15. Lieutenant General M.F. Harmon, The Army in the South Pacific, Operations Division War Department File 314.7 PTO, Case 14; Operations Report, 37th Infantry Division, National Archives.
16. Letter, Commanding General, United States Army Forces in South Pacific Area to Commanding General XIV Corps, 23 Mar 1944, National Archives.
17. Operations Memorandum 9, Headquarters Americal Division, 30 Mar 1944; National Archives.
18. After Action Report, 25th Regimental Combat Team, 31 Mar 1944; National Archives.
19. General Order 20, Citation for the Bronze Star Medal, 4 Aug 1944; National Archives.
20. After Action and Monthly Casualty Reports, G-1/G-3, 93rd Infantry Division, 30 Apr 1944; National Archives.
21. Letter, Headquarters Americal Division Artillery to the Officers and Enlisted Men, 593rd Field Artillery Battalion, 4 Apr 1944, 93rd Infantry Division; National Archives.
22. Letter, Captain Curran, Commanding Officer Company K to Commanding General, United States Army Forces in the Central Pacific Area, 9 May 1944, subject: Posthumous Award of Bronze Star, 93rd Division Files; National Archives.
23. Lee, *The Employment of Negro Troops in World War II*, p. 508.
24. Investigation of Company K, 25th Infantry Patrol of 6 April 1944, conducted by Lieutenant Colonel Frank Lucas, Inspector General, Americal Division, APO 716, 14 Apr–2 May 1944, 93rd Infantry Division File 333; National Archives.
25. General Order 131, Citation for the Silver Star Medal, 93rd Infantry Division, 31 Oct 1944; National Archives.
26. Interview with General Marshall by Dr. Sidney T. Mathews, Dr. Howard M. Smyth, Major Roy Lamson, and Major James Hamilton, 25 Jul 1940, Office of the Chief of Military History files.
27. Major General Griswold Report, 10 May 1944, Operations Division War Department 322.97; National Archives.
28. Memorandum, Secretary of War (initialed H.L.S.) to Assistant Secretary of War McCloy, forwarded to Colonel Pasco, General Marshall, noted Deputy Chief of Staff, 5 Jun 1944, File WDCSA 370.2 (27 May 1944); National Archives.
29. Appendix to the Congressional Record, Volume 92- Part 9, 14 Jan 1946, to 8 Mar 1946; National Archives.
30. 1st Headquarters XIV Corps to Commanding General Provisional Brigade, 93rd Infantry Division, on Report of Investigation, 15 May 1944, 93rd Infantry Division Files 333; National Archives.
31. Headquarters 25th Infantry Regiment (Colonel Yon) to the Commanding General 93rd Infantry Division, 27 Jun 1944, on Letter, Headquarters Americal Division to Commanding General XIV Corps, 10 May 1944; National Archives.
32. Headquarters, U.S. Army Forces in the South Pacific Area, General Order 1097, 29 Jul 1944; Citation, Silver Star Medal; National Archives.
33. After Action Report, 49th Coastal Artillery Battalion, 31 Mar 1944; Citation for the Bronze Star Medal, Headquarters, XIV Corps Artillery; National Archives.
34. Memorandum, Walter White (Hollandia) for the President, 12 Feb 1945, Assistant Secretary of War's copy in File WDCSA 291.2 Negroes; National Archives.
35. Ibid.
36. Radio Message, General MacArthur to General Marshall, 5 Mar 1945, National Archives.
37. Letter, Walter White (Hollandia) to General Douglas MacArthur, 5 Mar 1945, Assistant Secretary of War's copy in File WDCSA 291.2 Negroes; National Archives.
38. Memorandum, Walter White for the President, 8 Mar 1945; Enclosure Letter Walter White for General MacArthur, 8 Mar 1945; Both enclosed to a memorandum address to the Assistant Secretary of War for Brigadier General Henry I. Hodes, Operations Division; National Archives.
39. McGuire, *Taps for a Jim Crow Army*, pp. 56–57.
40. Historical Records, 369th Infantry Regiment, 1944–1945, 93rd Infantry Division, National Archives.
41. Field Order 5, Headquarters 93rd Infantry Division, 8 Apr 1945; Field Order 7, Headquarters 93rd Infantry Division, 5 May 1945; Field Order 8, Headquarters 93rd Infantry Division, 18 May 1945; National Archives.
42. G-3 After Action Report, Capture of Colonel Ouchi; Citation Silver Star and Bronze Star Medals, 93rd Infantry Division Files, Aug 1945; National Archives.
43. Commanding Officer, USS *Charette* (DD581) to Commander in Chief U.S. Fleet, 17 Aug 1945; Letter, Commander Seventh Fleet to Commanding General 93rd Infantry Division, 24 Oct 1945; both in the 93rd Division Files; National Archives.
44. G-3 After Action Report, 93rd Infantry Division Files, Sep 1945; National Archives.

45. Field Order 4, Armed Forces Western Pacific Command, 1 Nov 1945; National Archives.
46. United States Army, *The Army Almanac: A Book of Facts Concerning the Army of the United States* (U.S. Government Printing Office, Washington, D.C., 1950), pp. 510–592; Center for Military History.

XI. 92nd Infantry Division

1. Thomas St. John Arnold., *Buffalo Soldiers: The 92nd Infantry Division and Reinforcements in World War II, 1942–1945* (Manhattan, Kansas, 1999), p. 7.
2. McGuire, *Taps for a Jim Crow Army*, pp. 45–46.
3. Letter, Headquarters 4th Army to Commanding General, Army Ground Forces, 9 May 1944, File AGF322/6 (92nd Infantry Division), National Archives.
4. Notes, Chief of Staff, 92nd Infantry Division, 15 Oct 1944, Enclosure (History) Combat Efficiency Analysis, 92nd Infantry Division Files; National Archives.
5. Headquarters, 92nd Infantry Division, General Order 14, 92nd Infantry Division Files, National Archives.
6. Baker, *Lasting Valor*, p 76.
7. Message, Lieutenant General Devers to General Marshall, 8 Jun 1944, File CM-IN 6151, National Archives.
8. Captain John Bowditch III, *Fifth Army History*, vol. 7, *The Gothic Line* (Florence, Italy: L'Impronta Press, 1945), pp. 13–19.
9. Foreword, History of Task Force 45, 29 Jul 1944 to 28 Jan 1945, Operation Reports File 105-81.1 (15093), National Archives.
10. 1st Armored Division Field Orders 21, 23 Aug 1944; 1st Armored Division G-3 Journal, 24 Aug 1944, National Archives.
11. General Mark W. Clark, *Calculated Risk* (New York: Harper's, 1950), p. 392.
12. Arnold, *Buffalo Soldiers*, p. 221.
13. Hondon B. Hargrove, *Buffalo Soldiers in Italy: Black Americans in World War II* (Jefferson, North Carolina, 1985), p. 18.
14. Citation, Silver Star, Center for Military History, Washington, D.C.; Historical Files, 370th Infantry Regiment, National Archives.
15. Paul Goodman, *A Fragment of Victory: A Special Study of the 92nd Infantry Division* (Army War College, Carlisle Barracks, Pennsylvania, 1952), p. 1.
16. Arnold, *Buffalo Soldiers*, p 34.
17. Baker, *Lasting Valor*, pp. 72–73.
18. After Action Report, 370th Infantry Regiment, Oct–Nov 1944, National Archives.
19. Memorandum, Headquarters Army Service Force for Colonel Roamer (copies to Army Service Force Branches, War Department General Staff Secretaries, Civilian Aide), 6 Dec 1944, File OPD 322.97 (6-12-44), National Archives.
20. Letter, Commanding General 5th Army (General Clark) to Commanding General Mediterranean Theater of Operation, United States Army (General McNarney), 14 Dec 1944; Cover Letter General McNarney to General Handy, and first endorsement, 19 Dec 1944, File OPD 322.97, National Archives.
21. Lee, *The Employment of Negro Troops*, p. 562.
22. Memorandum, Civilian Aide for the Assistant Secretary of War, 20 Dec 1944, Subject: Negro Troops-Alpha, File ASW 291.2, National Archives.
23. Citation Silver Star Medal, Center for Military History; Historical Files, 371st Infantry Regiment, National Archives; Hargrove, *Buffalo Soldiers in Italy*, pp. 43–44.
24. Ibid.
25. Ibid.
26. Operations Report, 370th Combat Team, Aug–Dec 1944, November 1944, National Archives.
27. Hargrove, *Buffalo Soldiers in Italy*, p. 46.
28. Arnold, *Buffalo Soldiers*, p. 63.
29. Hargrove, *Buffalo Soldiers in Italy*, p. 47; Second Lieutenant Sidney Thompson, questionnaire, 25 June 1981.
30. Ibid.; First Lieutenant John T. Letts, questionnaire, 26 June 1980.
31. Letter, Commanding Officer 366th Infantry Regiment to the Commanding General 5th Army, 11 Dec 1944, 92nd Infantry Division Files, National Archives.
32. Arnold, *Buffalo Soldiers*, pp. 221–222.
33. After Action Report, 366th Infantry Regiment, Dec 1944, National Archives; Citation Silver Star Medal, Center for Military History.
34. Citation Silver Star Medal, Center for Military History.
35. Arnold, *Buffalo Soldiers*, p. 71.
36. Ibid, p. 74.
37. Intelligence Journal, G-2, Headquarters 92nd Infantry Division, 20–31 Dec 1944, National Archives.
38. "Critique after Battle," interview conducted by Lieutenant Colonel Thomas Arnold with Brigadier General Fretter Pico, commander 148th Grenadier Division, Munich, Germany, Nov 1948–Feb 1949, 92nd Infantry Division Files, National Archives.
39. Journal, S-2 and S-3, 2/366th Infantry, Dec 1944; After Action Report, 366th Infantry Regiment, Jan 1945; 92nd Infantry Division Files, National Archives.
40. After Action Report, 370th Infantry Regiment S-3, 92nd Infantry Division Historical Files, Dec 1944, National Archives.
41. Citation of the Silver Star Medal, 366th Infantry Regiment Historical Files, National Archives; Hargrove, *Buffalo Soldiers in Italy*, pp. 63–64.
42. Major E.A. Raymond, "Black Buffalo," *Field Artillery Journal* (January 1946): p. 15.
43. Citation for the Distinguished Service Cross, 366th Infantry Regiment Historical Files, National Archives; Hargrove, *Buffalo Soldiers in Italy*, p. 65.
44. Hargrove, *Buffalo Soldiers in Italy*, p. 65; First Lieutenant Lewis Flagg III, interview, 9 Sep 1980.
45. Citation, Silver Star Medal, Historical Files, 366th Infantry Regiment, National Archives; Hargrove, *Buffalo Soldiers in Italy*, p 66.
46. *Transmittal of Resume of Events, 26–27 December 1944, Serchio Valley Sector*, 92nd Infantry Division Historical Files, National Archives; Letter to Commanding General, 92nd Infantry Division from Captain John J. Kelly, S-1/Adjutant, 370th Infantry Regiment, 4 Mar 1945, National Archives.
47. Captain Samuel Tucker, S-2, 2/366th Infantry, Letter to Hondo Hargrove, 14 Jul 1980.
48. Goodman, *A Fragment of Victory*, p. 80.
49. Clark, *Calculated Risk*, p. 413.
50. Lieutenant General L.K. Truscott, Jr., *Command Missions: A Personal Story* (New York, 1954), p. 455.
51. Kelly, *Transmittal of Resume of Events, 26–27 December 1944*.
52. Citation Silver Star Medal, Center for Military History; Hargrove, *Buffalo Soldiers in Italy*, p. 81.
53. Fifth Army Operations Instructions #2, 9 Jan 1945, 5th Army Historical Files, National Archives.
54. *Plan Fourth Term: The Enemy Situation*, Headquarters, 92nd Infantry Division, 15 Jan 1945, National Archives.
55. Goodman, *A Fragment of Victory*, p. 94.
56. *Plan Fourth Term*, Headquarters, 92nd Infantry Division Operations Orders, 15 Jan 1945, National Archives.
57. Operations Reports, 365th Infantry Regiment, Jan.–

Jul. 1945, National Archives; Operation Highlights, 365th Infantry Regiment, Oct 1944–Aug 1945, 5 Sep 1945, National Archives.
58. Hargrove, *Buffalo Soldiers in Italy*, pp. 84–87.
59. Intelligence Annex No. 2 to Field Orders No. 4, 23 Dec 1944, Major General Almond, National Archives.
60. Narrative of Action, Headquarters, 2/370th Infantry, 8–11 Feb 1945, National Archives.
61. Citation, Silver Star Medal, Historical Files 370th Infantry Regiment, 92nd Infantry Division, National Archives.
62. Citation Silver Star Medal, Center for Military History; After Action Reports, S-1, 371st Infantry Regiment, Feb 1945, National Archives.
63. Citation, Silver Star Medal, 371st Infantry Regiment, 92nd Infantry Division, National Archives; Hargrove, *Buffalo Soldiers in Italy*, p. 97.
64. First Lieutenant Dennette Harrod, questionnaire, 6 May 1980; Hargrove, *Buffalo Soldiers in Italy*, p. 99.
65. Colonel W.F. Millice, Field Artillery, *Report to Army Ground Forces: Reduction of Concrete Emplaced Coast Defense Guns*, 1945.
66. Goodman, *A Fragment of Victory*, p. 106.
67. Ibid.
68. First Lieutenant Dennette Harrod, interview, 18 May 1980; Hargrove, *Buffalo Soldiers in Italy*, p. 103.
69. Citation, Silver Star Medal, Historical Files, 366th Infantry Regiment, National Archives; Hargrove, *Buffalo Soldiers in Italy*, p. 104.
70. Arnold, *Buffalo Soldiers*, pp. 105–107.
71. Ibid.
72. Major Alvin D. Wilder, Jr., After Actions Report, *Operations of the 317th Engineer Combat Battalion, during 4th Term Operation, 8–11 Feb., inclusive*, 21 Feb 1945, National Archives.
73. Arnold, *Buffalo Soldiers*, p. 106.
74. Citation Silver Star Medal, Historical Files, 317th Engineer Battalion, National Archives; Hargrove, *Buffalo Soldiers in Italy*, p. 106.
75. Regimental History, 370th Infantry Regiment, Jan.–Aug. 1945, National Archives.
76. Narrative of Operations, 3/370th Infantry, 8–12 Feb 1945, National Archives.
77. Lieutenant General Truscott, Commanding General 5th Army, Operations Report, 8–11 Feb 1945, National Archives.
78. Major Sanford P. Russell, S-3, 371st Infantry Regiment, Operations Report, 8–11 Feb 1945 (21 Feb 45), National Archives; Hargrove, *Buffalo Soldiers in Italy*, p. 111.
79. Arnold, *Buffalo Soldiers*, p. 109.
80. Lieutenant Colonel E.J. Rowney, Combat Engineers, Operations of Task Force One, Annex #2, 11 Feb 1945, National Archives.
81. Jefferson Hightower, interview, 25 Aug 1996.
82. After Action Report, Task Force One, 1/370th Infantry Battalion Historical Records, 11 Feb 1945, National Archives.
83. Narrative of the Attack Phase, 8–11 Feb 1945, Headquarters 3/371st Infantry, 19 Feb 1945, National Archives.
84. *History, The Legionnaires*, 371st Infantry Regiment Historical Files, Feb 1945; National Archives.
85. 371st Infantry Regiment, Operations Report, 8–11 Feb 1945 (21 Feb 45); National Archives.
86. Operations in Italy, Headquarters 760th Tank Battalion, Feb 1945, National Archives.
87. Operations Report, 8–11 Feb 1945, Headquarters 1/370th Infantry (19 Feb 45), National Archives.
88. *History, The Legionnaires*, 371st Infantry Regiment Historical Files, Feb 1945; National Archives.
89. Citation, Silver Star Medal, 370th Infantry Regiment Historical Files, National Archives.
90. Citation, Silver Star Medal, 370th Infantry Regiment Historical Files, National Archives; Hargrove, *Buffalo Soldiers in Italy*, p. 144.
91. Consolidated Casualty Report for Period, 8–11 Feb 1945 (Totals do not include casualties in Serchio Valley, 5–8 Feb 1945), Adjutant, 92nd Infantry Division, Feb 1945; National Archives.
92. Arnold, *Buffalo Soldiers*, p. 111.
93. Truscott, Operations 8–11 Feb 1945, National Archives.
94. Truscott, *Command Missions*, p. 455.
95. Headquarters, 5th Army, Plans, P/114 Future Operations, 27 Feb 1945, National Archives; 5th Army Plans, 23 Jan–27 Feb 1945, National Archives.
96. Arnold, *Buffalo Soldiers*, p. 117.
97. Hargrove, *Buffalo Soldiers in Italy*, p. 147.
98. Milton Bracker, "Americans Lose Ground in Italy," *New York Times*, 14 Feb 1945. See also "The Luckless 92nd," *Newsweek* 25 (26 February 1945): pp. 34–35.
99. Report, Civilian Aide to General Nelson, 12 Mar 1945, Assistant Secretary of War files, National Archives.
100. Memorandum, Civilian Aide to Secretary of War for the Assistant Secretary of War, 23 Apr 1945, "Operations of Colored Troops," National Archives.
101. Milton Bracker, "Negro Courage Upheld in Inquiry," *New York Times*, 15 Mar 1945.
102. Editorial, "Somebody's Gotta Go!" *Chicago Defender*, 24 Mar 1945.
103. *Michigan Chronicle*, 24 Mar 1945; Adam Clayton Powell Jr., "The Gibson Folly," *New York People's Voice*, 24 Mar 1945.
104. George S. Schuyler in "Views and Reviews," *Pittsburgh Courier*, 31 Mar 1945. (Schuyler's views were not necessarily those of the paper in which the column appeared.)
105. Editorial, "Too Much Ado About the 92nd Division Episode," *Norfolk Journal and Guide*, 14 Apr 1945.
106. *Baltimore African American*, Editorial, "Remove General Almond," 24 Mar 1945. For a similar opinion, see also Harry McAlpin, "Uncovering Washington," *Philadelphia Tribune*, 31 Mar 1945.
107. "Collins George Cables From Rome: Reporters Term Criticism of Truman Gibson Unfair," *Pittsburgh Courier*, 7 April 1945.
108. *Washington African American*, 15 Apr 1945. See also "The Social Front: Armed Forces," *A Monthly Summary of Trends in Race Relations* 11 (April 1945): p. 253.
109. Arnold, *Buffalo Soldiers*, p. 226.
110. The 100th Infantry Battalion was the first Japanese-American infantry unit to deploy to a combat theater. When they became part of the 442nd, they retained their unit designation. The 1/442nd Infantry remained in the United States to train Japanese-American and native Hawaiian infantry replacements.
111. Headquarters IV corps, Annex #1, *G-2 Estimate of the Enemy Situation to Accompany Plan "Second Wind,"* 25 Feb 1945, National Archives.
112. 5th Army History, vol. IX. The 442nd was formally attached to the 92nd Infantry Division on 3 Apr 1945 by radio message from IV Corps. Operations Report, 442nd Regimental Combat Team, Apr 1945, National Archives.
113. Historical Files, 679th Tank Destroyer Battalion, National Archives.
114. Arnold, *Buffalo Soldiers*, p. 129.
115. Lieutenant Colonel Ernest V. Murphy, *Narrative of Action*, 1/370th Infantry, 5 Apr 1945, National Archives.

116. Interview Vernon Baker, *Honor Deferred*, Documentary, Cat. No. AAE-75400, A&E Television Networks, 2006.

117. Captain Runyon Report, 12 Apr 45, War Department SSP Records Group 113 (Mediterranean Theater of Operations) (App. II), National Archives; Lee, *The Employment of Negro Troops*, p. 583.

118. Narrative of the Attack by 370th Infantry Regiment, 5–8 Apr 1945, Colonel Sherman, Commander 370th Infantry Regiment, War Department SSP Records Group 113 (Mediterranean Theater of Operations), National Archives; Lee, *The Employment of Negro Troops*, p. 582.

119. Headquarters, 92nd Infantry Division, *Citation of Unit (442nd Infantry Regiment)*, 7 Oct 1945, National Archives.

120. Citation Medal of Honor, Center for Military History.

121. Lieutenant Colonel C.H. Daughette, Commanding Officer, 3/370th Infantry, *Summary of the Third Battalion During period 1210, 3 April 1945 to 2400*, dated 11 Apr 1945, National Archives.

122. Citation, Distinguished Service Cross, 442nd Infantry Regiment Historical Files, 92nd Infantry Division Historical Records, National Archives, and the Center for Military History.

123. Headquarters, 92nd Infantry Division, *Distinguished Unit Citation (442nd Infantry Regiment)*, 7 Oct 1945, National Archives.

124. Lee, *The Employment of Negro Troops*, p. 585.

125. After Action Report, 679th Tank Destroyer Battalion, 30 April 1945, National Archives.

126. Ibid., p. 586.

127. Citation, Distinguished Service Cross, Center for Military History; Historical Files, 442nd Infantry Regiment, Apr 1945; After Action Report, G-3 92nd Infantry Division, Apr 1945, National Archives.

128. Command Historian, Defense Language Institute, Study to determine if Americans of Asian/Pacific Region Distinguished Service Cross awardees were to be upgraded to Medal of Honor status, 1996; Rudy Williams, *Armed Forces Information Service*, "21 Asian American World War II Vets to Get Medal of Honor," 19 May 2000.

129. Arnold, *Buffalo Soldiers*, Foreword.

130. Citation, Distinguished Service Cross, Center for Military History.

131. Field Order Number 11, Headquarters, 92nd Infantry Division, 24 Apr 1945, National Archives.

132. Arnold, *Buffalo Soldiers*, p. 181.

133. Letter, Private Robert R. Thompson, Infantry, in "Mail Call," *Stars and Stripes Newspaper* (Italy), 8 Jun 1945.

134. Personal letter, Lieutenant Colonel Ray, Commander 600th Field Artillery Battalion, to Truman Gibson, 14 May 1945, File WDGAP/291.2, National Archives.

135. General Order 70, Headquarters 5th Army, 10 Jun 1945, National Archives.

136. Official Program, 92nd Infantry Division Armistice Day Program, 11 Nov 1945, in Italy.

XII. Combat Infantry Replacements

1. After Action Report on Manpower Strength, G-1, 3rd United States Army, Jul 1944, National Archives.

2. History Ground Forces Reinforcement Command, V, pt. II (6 Jun 1944–8 May 1945), National Archives.

3. Papers in European Theater of Operations File AG 322 (Replacement Units), Dec 1944, National Archives.

4. History of Special Section of the Office of the Inspector General (29 Jun 1941–16 Nov 1945), National Archives.

5. Letter, Headquarters Communications Zone, European Theater of Operations, to Commanders of Colored Troops Communications Zone, 26 Dec 1944, European Theater of Operations Adjutant General (322 X 353 XSGS), National Archives.

6. Ibid.

7. History of the Special Section of the Office of the Inspector General (29 Jul 1941–16 Nov 1945), Office of the Chief of Military History; National Archives.

8. Address, Brigadier General Charles Lanham (Assistant Division Commander, 104th Infantry Division) before American Council on Race Relations, New York City, 12 July 1946, Radio Station WMCA transcripts, National Archives.

9. Personnel Action, After Action Review, 104th Infantry Division, Mar 1945, National Archives.

10. Baker, *Lasting Valor*, p. 296; Citation, Medal of Honor, Office of Military History.

11. Letter, General Davis to Inspector General Section, 25 Apr 45, Report 60, European Theater of Operations, File AG331.1, National Archives.

12. Headquarters, 3rd Army General Order 255, 18 Sep 1945, National Archives; Captain Joseph B. Mittelman, *Eight Stars to Victory* (Washington: 9th Infantry Division Association, 1948), p. 366; Office of Military History, Citation Distinguished Service Cross — World War II.

13. Letter, 26th Infantry Regiment to Commanding General, 1st Infantry Division, 20 Jun 1945; Enclosure to Letter, Headquarters XII Corps to Commanding General Third Army, 21 Jun 1945, European Theater of Operations, File AG353, National Archives.

14. Letter, 18th Infantry Regiment to Commanding General, 1st Infantry Division, 20 Jun 1945, Enclosure 2 to the above, National Archives.

15. Letter, Headquarters 99th Infantry Division to Commanding General XII Corps, 21 Jun 1945, European Theater of Operations, File AG319.1, National Archives.

16. Lieutenant Robert Lewis, "Negroes Under Fire" *The Progressive and LaFollette's Magazine* 9 (September 3, 1945).

17. Headquarters 7th Army General Order 580, 4 Oct 1945, Citation, Distinguished Service Cross, National Archives; Office of Military History, Citation Medal of Honor.

18. Letter, Headquarters 7th Army to Commanding General 12th Army Group, 23 Apr 1945, European Theater of Operations, File AG322-C, National Archives.

19. Joseph Carter, *The History of the 14th Armored Division* (Atlanta, Georgia: Albert Love Enterprises, 1945), chapter 13. (This unofficial history contains a detailed account of the employment of the 7th Army Provisional Company No. 4 along with a detailed account of all the units in the 14th Armored Division.)

XIII. Armed Forces

1. Memorandum, Headquarters Armored Force to Liaison Officer Armored Force, 5 Dec 1940, File AG320.2 (6-5-40) (3) Sec. 3-D, National Archives.

2. Ibid.

3. Memorandum, G3 for the Chief of Staff, 15 Feb 1941, Approved 25 Feb 1941, G3/6541-Gen-527; Letter, Adjutant General to Chief Armored Force, 4 Mar 1941, File AG320.2 (2-25-41) M (ret) M-C, National Archives.

4. Letter, Headquarters Armored Force to Adjutant General, 6 Mar 1941, and 1st Endorsement, Adjutant General to Chief Armored Force, 31 Mar 1941, File AG320.2 (3-6-41), National Archives.

5. Memorandum, Chief of Staff for the War Depart-

ment, 14 Apr 1941, File USW 291.2 Race, Negro, National Archives.

6. David Williams, speech given at the Medal of Honor Conference in Los Angeles, CA, 27 Feb 1994.

7. Lou Potter, Bill Miles, and Nina Rosenblum, *Liberators Fighting on Two Fronts* (Orlando, Florida, 1992).

8. David Williams, speech given at the Medal of Honor Conference in Los Angeles, CA, 27 Feb 1994.

9. Private Trezzvant W. Anderson, 761st Historian, *Come Out Fighting: The Epic Tale of the 761st Tank Battalion, 1942–45* (Austria: Salzburger Druckerei and Verlag, 1946), p. 15.

10. Letter, Commanding General, 2nd Army to Commanding General, Army Ground Forces, 19 Feb 1943, File AG 210.31/464, National Archives; http://www.army.mil/CMH-PG/books/wwii/11-4/chapter8.htm#b6.

11. Paul L. Bates, speech, Fort Hood 761st Tank Battalion Monument Banquet, 11 Feb 1994.

12. Ivan Harrison, interview, 23 Aug 1996.

13. Wilson, *The 761st "Black Panther" Tank Battalion in World War II*, pp. 35–37.

14. Paul L. Bates, speech, Fort Hood 761st Tank Battalion Monument Banquet, 11 Feb 1994.

15. Bob Stone, "Interview with Jackie Robinson," *Yank Magazine*, 23 Nov 1945.

16. Battalion Notes, 761st Tank Battalion, Office of the Adjutant General, National Archives; Anderson, *Come Out Fighting*, pp. 15, 21; Lee, *The Employment of Negro Troops in World War II*, p. 661.

17. Martin Blumensen, *The Patton Papers,* vol. 2 (U.S. Army Military History Institute, Carlisle Barracks, Pennsylvania, 1945), p. 567.

18. Journal 602nd Tank Destroyer Battalion, European Theater of Operations I, in L-292 with the 26th Infantry Division, National Archives; Lee, *The Employment of Negro Troops in World War II*, p. 661.

19. Paul L. Bates, speech, Fort Hood 761st Tank Battalion Monument Banquet, 11 Feb 1994.

20. Mary Motley, *The Invisible Soldier* (Detroit: Wayne State University Press, 1975).

21. SSG Ruben Rivers, Silver Star Medal, Headquarters, 26th Infantry Division, General Orders, 2 Dec 1944, National Archives.

22. Special After Action Report, 761st Tank Battalion, Nov 1944, File L-292, 26th Infantry Division, National Archives.

23. David J. Williams, *Hit Hard* (New York: Bantam Books, 1983).

24. After Action Report, 761st Tank Battalion S-2/S-3, Nov 1944, National Archives; Anderson, *Come Out Fighting*, pp. 20–33.

25. Citation Bronze Star Medal, After Action Report, 761st Tank Battalion, Nov 1944, National Archives.

26. After Action Report, 761st Tank Battalion S-2/S-3, Nov 1944, National Archives; Anderson, *Come Out Fighting*, pp. 20–33.

27. Commendations Binder, 761st Tank Battalion Files, National Archives; Anderson, *Come Out Fighting*, pp. 35, 102–112.

28. Commendations Binder, 761st Tank Battalion Files, National Archives; After Action Report, 26th Infantry Division, Nov 1944, National Archives.

29. David Williams, speech given at the Medal of Honor Conference in Los Angeles, CA, 27 Feb 1994.

30. David Williams, speech given at the Medal of Honor Conference in Los Angeles, CA, 27 Feb 1994.

31. Terkel, *The Good War*, pp. 361–364.

32. Ibid.

33. After Action Report, 761st Tank Battalion Medical Detachment, 29 Nov 1944; After Action Report, 761st Tank Battalion S-1, 2 Dec 1944; After Action Report, 761st Tank Battalion Motor Maintenance Office, 2 Dec 1944, National Archives; Lee, *The Employment of Negro Troops in World War II*, p. 664.

34. 26th Infantry Division G-1 Reports, Nov 1944, National Archives.

35. Letter, Headquarters 3rd Army to Commanding General XII Corps, 24 Nov 1944, File AG200-6, National Archives; Letter Headquarters 26th Infantry Division to all members of the 26th Infantry Division, 26 Nov 1944, National Archives.

36. Letter, Headquarters XII Corps to Commanding Officer 761st Tank Battalion, 9 Dec 1944, File AG380.19 (G-1), 761st Tank Battalion Files, National Archives.

37. 1st Endorsement, Letter, Headquarters 26th Infantry Division to Commanding Officer 761st Tank Battalion, File AG201.22, 761st Tank Battalion Files, National Archives.

38. After Action Review, 761st Tank Battalion Motor Maintenance Office, Dec 1944, National Archives.

39. United States Army 87th Infantry Association, *Stalwart and Strong: The Story of the 87th Infantry Division* (Flourtown, Pennsylvania, 1993).

40. Potter, Miles, and Rosenblum, *Liberators Fighting on Two Fronts.*

41. After Action Report 104th Infantry Division, Jan–Apr 1945, National Archives.

42. Bronze Star Medal, Headquarters, 17th Airborne Division, General Order, 20 Jan 1945, National Archives.

43. Letter, General W.M. Miley to Philip W. Latimer, 7 Jun 1981.

44. After Action Report, 761st Tank Battalion S-1, Feb 1945, National Archives.

45. Operational Unit Status Report, 784th Tank Battalion, Feb–Mar 1945, 784th Tank Battalion Files, National Archive; After Action Report 35th Infantry Division, Feb–Mar 1945, National Archives.

46. Headquarters 35th Infantry Division, Citation Bronze Star Medal, General Order 26, 12 Apr 1945, National Archives.

47. Wes Gallagher, *Los Angeles Times*, 10 Apr 1945; Gallagher, "Negro Tank Outfit Repeats Bastogne," *New York Times*, 5 Mar 1945.

48. Ibid.

49. After Actions Report, 35th Infantry Division, Mar 1945 National Archives; Operations Report, 784th Tank Battalion, Mar 1945, National Archives; Lee, *The Employment of Negro Troops in World War II*, p 676.

50. Letter, Headquarters 134th Infantry Regiment to the Commanding General 35th Infantry Division, 5 Mar 1945, National Archives; First Endorsement, Letter, Headquarters 35th Infantry Division to Commanding Officer, 784th Tank Battalion, 784th Tank Battalion Files, National Archives.

51. Citation, Bronze Star Medal, Headquarters 35th Infantry Division, General Orders 26, 12 Apr 1945, National Archives; After Actions Report, 35th Infantry Division, Mar 1945; Operations Report, 784th Tank Battalion (Intelligence Analysis), Mar 1945, 784th Tank Battalion Files, National Archives.

52. Donald East and William Gleason, *The 409th Infantry in World War II* (Nashville, Tennessee, 1986).

53. After Action Report, 761st Tank Battalion Motor-Maintenance Office, Mar 1945, 761st Tank Battalion Files, National Archives.

54. Journal and After Action Report, 761st Tank Battalion, Mar 1945, National Archives; After Action Report, 409th Infantry Regiment, Mar 1945, 103rd Infantry Division Files, National Archives; Letter Headquarters, 761st Tank Battalion to Chief of Staff 103rd Infantry Division,

May 1945, 761st Tank Battalion Files; Historical Data File, 103rd Infantry Division, National Archives; Anderson, *Come Out Fighting*, pp. 67–76.

55. Letter, Commanding General, 103rd Infantry Division to Commanding Officer, 761st Tank Battalion, Mar 1945, 761st Tank Battalion Files, National Archives; Anderson, *Come Out Fighting*, p. 77.

56. Letter, Paul Bates to Joe Wilson Jr., 4 Mar 1994; Wilson, *The 761st "Black Panther" Tank Battalion in World War II*, p. 161.

57. After Action Report, 761st Tank Battalion Medical Detachment, Mar 1945; After Action Report, 761st Tank Battalion S-1, Mar 1945; After Action Report, 761st Tank Battalion Motor Maintenance Office, Mar 1945, 761st Tank Battalion Files, National Archives.

58. After Action Report, 784th Tank Battalion, Apr 1945, 784th Tank Battalion Files, National Archives; Citation for the Bronze Star Medal, 784th Tank Battalion Files, National Archives.

59. Terkel, *The Good War*, p. 364.

60. Ibid.

61. After Action Report, 71st Infantry Division, Mar-Apr 1945, 71st Infantry Division Files, National Archives; After Action Report, 761st Tank Battalion S-3 Operations, Apr 1945, National Archives.

62. Casualty Report, Medical Detachment, 761st Tank Battalion, Apr 1945, National Archives.

63. Ibid.

64. 71st Infantry Division General Orders, Bronze Star Medal, 4 Jun 1945, National Archives.

65. After Action Report, 66th Infantry Regiment, 71st Infantry Division Files, Apr 1945, National Archives.

66. After Action Report, 761st Tank Battalion Medical Detachment, Apr 1945; After Action Report, 761st Tank Battalion S-1, Apr 1945; After Action Report, 761st Tank Battalion Motor Maintenance Office, Apr 1945, National Archives.

67. Potter, Miles, and Rosenblum, *Liberators Fighting on Two Fronts*, New York, 1992.

68. 761st Tank Battalion Historical Files; After Action Report, 761st Tank Battalion Medical Detachment, May 1945; After Action Report, 761st Tank Battalion S-1, May 1945; After Action Report, 761st Tank Battalion Motor Maintenance Office, May–Jun 1945, National Archives.

69. Ibid.

70. White House Central File, Jimmy Carter Presidential Library.

71. Ibid.

72. Ibid.

73. Operations Report, 761st Tank Battalion, Oct–Dec 1945, dated 1 Feb 1946, National Archives.

74. Army Regulation 670-1; Army Regulation 600-8-22; Army Regulation 840-10.

75. White House Central File, Jimmy Carter Presidential Library; Wilson, *The 761st "Black Panther" Tank Battalion in World War II*, p. 241.

76. Ibid.

77. John Clark, *Temple Daily Telegram*, 15 Oct 94.

XIV. Conclusion

1. *History of the GI Bill*, Veterans Administration Pamphlet for Education Assistance.

2. Biggs, *The Triple Nickles*, p. 77.

3. Baker, *Lasting Valor*, p. 240.

4. Executive Order 9981, Truman Papers, Harry S. Truman Presidential Museum and Library, Independence, Missouri.

5. Letter, General Bradley to President Truman, 30 Jul 1948; Letter President Truman to General Bradley, 4 Aug 1948, both in File CS 2912, Records Group 319, National Archives.

6. Lanning, *The African-American Soldier*, pp. 223–224.

7. Citation, Congressional Medal of Honor, Center for Military History, Washington, D.C.; Historical Files, 24th Infantry Regiment, Korean War, National Archives.

8. Ibid.

9. After Action Report, 25th Infantry Division, 30 Sep 1950; Letter Commanding General 25th Infantry Division to Commanding General 8th Army, 30 Sep 1950, Historical Files 25th Infantry Division, Korean War, National Archives.

10. Lanning, *The African-American Soldier*, p. 230.

11. Ibid., pp. 233–234.

12. Title 10 of the United States Code stipulates that Medal of Honor recommendations had to be submitted through military channels no later than May 1951, and approved by the President no later than May 1952.

13. Associated Press, "Seven Black World War II Heroes in Line to Get The Medal of Honor," *The Los Angeles Times*, 28 Apr 1996.

Appendix

1. Citation, Medals of Honor, Center for Military History, Washington, D.C. 1997.

Bibliography

Books

Anderson, Trezzvant W. *Come Out Fighting: The Epic Tale of the 761st Tank Battalion, 1942–45.* Austria: Salzburger Druckerei and Verlag, 1946.
Aptheker, Herbert. *Toward Negro Freedom.* New York, 1956.
Arnold, Thomas St. John. *Buffalo Soldiers: The 92nd Infantry Division and Reinforcements in World War II, 1942–1945.* Manhattan, Kansas, 1993.
Bailey, Ronald, H., ed. *The Home Front: USA.* Alexandria, Virginia: Time-Life Books, 1978.
Baker, Vernon. *Lasting Valor.* New York, 1997.
Barbeau, Arthur E., and Florette Henri. *The Unknown Soldiers: African-American Troops in World War I.* New York, 1996.
Barclay, William F., ed. *103rd Infantry Division Signal Company Remembrances: 1918–1945* (1995), http://www.pierce-evans.org/remembrancesa.htm.
Biggs, Bradley. *The Triple Nickles: America's First All-Black Parachute Unit.* North Haven, Connecticut, 1986.
Bowker, Benjamin C. *Out of Uniform.* New York, 1946.
Carter, Joseph. *The History of the 14th Armored Division.* Atlanta, Georgia: Albert Love Enterprises, 1945.
Catton, Bruce. *This Hallowed Ground: The Story of the Union Side of the Civil War.* New York, 1956.
Coffman, Edward M. *War to End All Wars.* New York, 1968.
Dalfiume, Richard. *Desegregation of the U.S. Armed Forces: Fighting on Two Fronts, 1939–1954.* Columbia: University of Missouri Press, 1969.
Delsarte, Walter. *The Negro, Democracy, and the War.* Detroit, 1919.
Dowd, Jerome. *The Negro in American Life.* New York, 1926.
Earley, Charity Adams. *One Woman's Army: A Black Officer Remembers the WAC.* College Station, Texas: Texas A&M University Press, 1989.
East, Donald, and William Gleason. *The 409th Infantry in World War II.* Nashville, Tennessee, 1986.
Emilio, Luis F. *A Brave Black Regiment: The History of the 54th Massachusetts, 1863–1865.* Boston, 1894.
Farrar, Hayward. *The Baltimore Afro-American: 1892–1950.* Westport, Connecticut, 1998.
Finkle, Lee H. *Forum for Protest: The Black Press During World War II.* East Rutherford, New Jersey, 1975.
Flipper, Henry O. *Black Frontiersman: The Memoirs of Henry O. Flipper, First Black Graduate of West Point.* Compiled and edited by Theodore Harris. Fort Worth, Texas: Texas Christian University Press, 1997.
Hargrove, Hondon B. *Buffalo Soldiers in Italy: Black Americans in World War II.* Jefferson, North Carolina: McFarland, 1985.
Haynes, Robert. *A Night of Violence: The Houston Riot of 1917.* Louisiana, 1976.
Heywood, Chester D. *Negro Combat Troops in the World War.* Worcester, Massachusetts, 1928.
Hunton, Addie W., and Katherine M. Johnson. *Two Colored Women with the American Expeditionary Forces.* New York, 1920.
Johnson, James W. *Along This Way.* New York, 1933.
Lane, Ann. *The Brownsville Affair: National Crisis and Black Reaction.* New York, 1971.
Lanning, Michael L. *The African-American Soldier: From Crispus Attucks to Colin Powell.* Trenton, New Jersey, 1999.
Leckie, William. *The Buffalo Soldiers: A Narrative of the Negro Cavalry in the West.* University of Oklahoma Press, 1967.
Little, Arthur. *From Harlem to the Rhine.* New York, 1936.
Martinez, Jose Norat. *Historia del Regimento 65 de Infanteria.* San Juan, Puerto Rico, 1992.
Mason, Monroe, and Arthur Furr. *The American Negro with the Red Hand of France.* Boston, 1920.
McGuire, Phillip, ed. *Taps for a Jim Crow Army: Letters from Black Soldiers in World War II.* Lexington: University Press of Kentucky, 1983.
Miller, Warren H. *The Boys of 1917.* Boston, 1939.
Motley, Mary. *The Invisible Soldier.* Detroit, Wayne State University Press, 1975.

Norat, Jose Angel. *The Puerto Rican National Guard.* San Juan, Puerto Rico, 1987.

Potter, Lou, Bill Miles, and Nina Rosenblum. *Liberators Fighting on Two Fronts.* Orlando, Florida, 1992.

Rodney, George B. *As a Cavalryman Remembers.* Caldwell, Idaho: Caxton Printers, 1944.

Scott, Emmett J. *Scott's Official History of the American Negro in the World War.* New York, 1969.

Seligmann, Herbert. *The Negro Faces America.* 1920. Reprint, New York: Harper & Row, 1969.

Shipley, Thomas. *The History of the AEF.* New York, 1920.

Sweeney, Allison W. *History of the American Negro in the Great World War.* Chicago, 1919.

Terkel, Studs. *The Good War: An Oral History of World War II.* New York, 1984.

Thompson, John L. *History and Views of the Colored Officers Training Camp.* Des Moines, Iowa, 1917.

Washburn, Patrick. *A Question of Sedition: The Federal Government's Investigation of the Black Press During World War II.* New York, 1986.

Weaver, John D. *The Brownsville Raid.* New York, 1970.

White, Walter F. *Rope and Faggot.* New York, 1929.

Williams, David J., II. *Hit Hard.* New York, Bantam Books, 1983.

Wilson, Joe, Jr. *The 761st Black Panther Tank Battalion in World War II.* Jefferson, North Carolina: McFarland, 1999.

Woodson, Carter G. *The Negro in Our History.* Washington, D.C., 1921.

―――. *Negro Makers of History.* Washington, D.C., 1928.

Zaloga, Steven J. *M10 and M36 Tank Destroyers: 1942–1943.* Osprey Publishing, 2002.

Government Publications

Bellafaire, Judith A. *The Women's Army Corps: A Commemoration of World War II Service.* Chief of Military History Publication 72–15, Center of Military History, Washington, D.C., 1947.

Bigelow, Major John Jr. *Historical Sketch, 10th United States Cavalry, 1866–1892.* United States Army Commands, Records Group 98, National Archives, Washington, D.C.

Blumensen, Martin. *The Patton Papers,* Vol. 2. United States Army Military History Institute, Carlisle Barracks, Pennsylvania, 1945.

Bowditch, Captain John. *Fifth Army History.* Vol. 7: *The Gothic Line.* Florence, Italy: L'Impronta Press, 1945.

Bykofsky, Joseph, and Harold Larson. *The Transportation Corps: Operations Overseas: United States Army in World War II.* Washington, D.C., 1957.

Conn, Stetson, et. al. *United States in World War II, The Western Hemisphere: Guarding the United States and Its Outposts.* Center of Military History, Washington, D.C, 1989.

Dyer, Lieutenant Colonel George. *United States Army XII Corps, Spearhead of Patton's 3rd Army.* Headquarters XII United States Army Corps, 1947.

Goodman, Paul. *A Fragment of Victory: A Special Study of the 92nd Infantry Division.* Carlisle Barracks, Pennsylvania: Army War College, 1952.

Jones, Vincent C. *American Military History: Transition and Change, 1902–1917.* Center of Military History, Washington, D.C., 1969.

Lee, Ulysses. *The Employment of Negro Troops in World War II.* Washington, D.C., 1966.

Mittelman, Captain Joseph B. *Eight Stars to Victory.* 9th Infantry Division Association, Center of Military History, Washington, D.C., 1948.

Mueller, Ralph, and Jerry Turk. *Report After Action: The Story of the 103rd Infantry Division.* Headquarters, 103rd Infantry Division, Innsbruck, Austria, 1945.

Ness, Jerry N. "Oral History Interview with Judge William Hastie." In *The Truman Papers,* 5 Jan 1972. Harry S. Truman Library, Independence, Missouri.

Pritchard, Paul W. *Smoke Generator Operations in the Mediterranean and European Theaters of Operation.* Chemical Corps Historical Studies 1, United States Center of Military History, Washington, D.C., 1946.

Romanus, Charles F., and Riley Sunderland. *Time Runs Out in CBI.* Office of the Chief of Military History, Washington, D.C, 1959.

Thomson, Captain Robert. *Reminiscence of a Black Infantry Regiment.* Unpublished manuscript, Archives Branch, United States. Army Military History Institute, Carlisle Barracks, Pennsylvania, 1994.

Treadwell, Mattie E. *United States Army in World War II, Special Studies, The Women's Army Corps.* Washington, D.C., 1954.

United States Army. *The Army Almanac: A Book of Facts Concerning the Army of the United States.* Washington, D.C.: U.S. Government Printing Office, 1950.

United States Army. *Historic Report Transportation Corps in the European Theater of Operations.* Washington, D.C., 1945.

United States Army. *History, Service of Supply, India-Burma Theater,* app. 12. Construction Service, Office of the Chief of Military History, Fort McNair, Washington, D.C., 1944.

United States Army. *Participation of Puerto Ricans in the Armed Services with Emphasis on World War I, World War II, and the Korean War.* Headquarters Antilles Command, United States Army Center of Military History, Fort McNair, Washington, D.C., 1966.

United States Army. *The Transportation Corps in the Battle of France: Historic Report, Transportation Corps in the European Theater of Operations.* Office of the Chief of Military History, Washington, D.C., 1947.

United States Army 87th Infantry Association. *Stalwart and Strong: The Story of the 87th Infantry Division.* Flourtown, Pennsylvania, 1993.

United States Army War College. *Colored Soldiers in the U.S. Army.* Washington, D.C.: U.S. Government Printing Office, 1942.

United States Congress, Senate. *Alleged Executions Without Trial in France.* Washington, D.C.: Government Printing Office, 1923.

White House Central File. *Presidential Unit Citation for the 761st Tank Battalion.* Jimmy Carter Presidential Library, Atlanta, Georgia.

Personal Narratives

Bullard, Robert L. *Personalities and Reminiscences of the War.* New York, 1925.
Clark, General Mark W. *Calculated Risk.* New York: Harper's Publications, 1950.
Dubois, W.E.B. Dubois Papers, Amistad Research Center, Fisk University, Nashville, Tennessee.
Judy, William L. *A Soldier's Diary.* Chicago, 1930.
Patton, General George S., Jr. *War as I Knew It.* Boston, 1947.
Pershing, General John J. *My Experiences in the World War.* New York, 1931.
Robinson, Jackie. "Jackie Tells Own Story." *Washington Post,* 23 Aug 1949.
Scott, Emmett J. Papers of Emmett J. Scott, Morgan State University, Baltimore, Maryland, File 2.
Stimson, Henry. Diary Entries, Henry Simpson Papers, Yale University, New Haven, Connecticut, 1946.
Truscott, Lieutenant General L.K. *Command Missions: A Personal Story.* New York, 1954.

Newspapers and Periodicals

Associated Press. "Seven Black World War II Heroes in Line to Get The Medal of Honor." *The Los Angeles Times,* 28 Apr 1996.
Bracker, Milton. "Americans Lose Ground in Italy." *New York Times,* 14 Feb 1945.
—————. "Negro Courage Upheld in Inquiry." *New York Times,* 15 Mar 1945.
Broadwell, Charles. "The Long Run," interview with Vernon Castle Stephens for *The Fayetteville Observer,* 5 Dec 1999.
Colson, William N., and A.B. Nutt. "The Failure of the 92nd Division." *Messenger* (September 1919): pp. 22–24.
Dabney, Virginius. "Nearer and Nearer the Precipice." *Atlantic Monthly* (January 1943): pp. 94–100.
Dodge, Lieutenant Colonel (Quartermaster Corps) Abbott. "The Bundles for Burma Boys." *The Quartermaster Review* 24 (November-December 1944): pp. 47–48.
Dorr, Robert F. "America 70 Years Late in Honoring World War I Soldier." *The Army Times,* 19 May 2003.
Dubois, W.E.B. "An Essay Toward a History of the Black Man in the Great War." *The Crisis* (June 1919): pp. 63–85.
Finley, James P. "Colonel Charles Young — Black Cavalryman, Huachuca Commander, and Early Intelligence Officer." *Huachuca Illustrated: A Magazine of the Fort Huachuca Museum;* Volume 1: *The Buffalo Soldiers at Fort Huachuca* (1993).
Gallagher, Wes. *Los Angeles Times,* 10 Apr 1945.
—————. "Negro Tank Outfit Repeats Bastogne." *New York Times,* 5 Mar 1945.
Galloway, Joseph. "Military Injustice." *U.S. News and World Report,* 6 May 1996.
"Gasoline." *The Quartermaster Review* 24 (May-June 1945): p. 23.
George, Collins. "Collins George Cables From Rome: Reporters Term Criticism of Truman Gibson Unfair." *Pittsburgh Courier,* 7 April 1945.
Green, Lorenzo J. "Some Observations on the Black Regiment of Rhode Island in the American Revolution." *Journal of Negro History* 37 (1952).
Greenwood, Al. "Tribute Honors Black Paratroopers." *The Fayetteville Observer,* 9 Feb 2003.
Lewis, Lieutenant Robert. "Negroes Under Fire." *The Progressive and LaFollette's Magazine* 9 (3 September 1945).
"The Luckless 92nd." *Newsweek* 25 (26 February 1945): pp. 34–35.
McAlpin, Harry. "Uncovering Washington." *Philadelphia Tribune,* 31 Mar 1945.
McKaine, Osceola. "The Buffaloes." *Outlook* 119 (22 May 1918).
National Association for the Advancement of Colored People. *Annual Reports For 1919.*
New York: NAACP, 1917–1920.
Powell, Adam Clayton, Jr. "The Gibson Folly." *New York People's Voice,* 24 Mar 1945.
Raymond, Major E.A. "Black Buffalo." *Field Artillery Journal* (January 1946).
Reddick, L.D. "The Negro Policy of the United States Army, 1775–1945." *Journal of Negro History* (1949): p. 29.
Rose, Arnold M. "1947 Army Policies Toward Negro Soldiers — A Report on a Success and a Failure." *Journal of Social Issues* (Fall 1947): pp. 26–31.
Schuyler, George S. "Views and Reviews." *Pittsburgh Courier,* 31 Mar 1945.
Stone, Bob. "Interview with Jackie Robinson." *Yank Magazine,* 23 Nov 1945.
Thompson, Private Robert R., 92nd Infantry Division, in "Mail Call Letters," *Stars and Stripes* (Italy), 8 Jun 1945.
United States Army Forces Antilles and the Military Department of Puerto Rico. "60th Anniversary United States Army in Puerto Rico." *The Sentinel,* 12 December 1958, p. 4-B, Puerto Rican National Guard Museum, San Juan, Puerto Rico.
Weil, Franl E.G. "The Negro in the Armored Forces." *Social Forces* 26 (1947–1948): p. 97.

Newspapers

Army Times
Baltimore Afro-American
Chicago Defender
Cleveland Call & Post
Fayetteville Observer
Los Angeles Times
Michigan Chronicle
New York Times
Norfolk Journal and Guide
Philadelphia Tribune
Pittsburgh Courier
Stars and Stripes
Washington Post

Index

2nd Armored Division 309, 324
2nd Cavalry Division 49, 60, 114, 167–172, 184, 206
2nd French Armored Division 123–124
2nd Infantry Division 115–116
3rd Infantry Division 123–124, 324
4th Armored Division 115, 119, 129, 140, 278, 300, 303, 306, 326
9th Cavalry Regiment 8, 11, 14, 40, 44, 169, 333
10th Cavalry Regiment 2–3, 6–7, 11, 14–16, 19–20, 33–35, 40, 168–169, 300, 333
14th Armored Division 140, 198, 202, 278, 282, 315
17th Airborne Division 164, 275, 307, 309, 316, 319, 321, 327
24th Infantry Regiment 7–14, 20, 35, 39, 57, 145–150, 157, 174–175, 180–181, 331–333
25th Infantry Regiment 2, 6–9, 11, 35, 39, 53, 73, 145, 150, 168, 173, 175–177, 179–183, 188, 324, 331–333
25th Station Hospital 75–76
26th Infantry Division 294–301, 304–305
27th Cavalry Regiment 169
28th Cavalry Regiment 169
35th Infantry Division 309–311, 315, 319
41st Engineer Regiment 68, 73, 75–76
64th Heavy Tank Battalion 324
65th Infantry Regiment 160–161
78th Light Tank Battalion 285–286
79th Infantry Division 140–141, 309, 321, 327
82nd Airborne Division 87, 93, 162, 165–166, 308, 323–324, 330, 333

83rd Engineer Aviation Battalion 77–78
92nd Cavalry Reconnaissance Squadron 140, 193, 207, 211, 215–219, 263
92nd Engineer General Service Regiment 91
92nd Infantry Division 3, 14, 16, 18–19, 22, 24–27, 29, 31, 33–34, 58, 66, 114, 138, 159–160, 163, 169, 171–173, 192–199, 202–212, 214–220, 222–224, 227–229, 232, 235, 237–238, 242, 246–254, 257, 259–264, 267–273, 292, 304, 323, 330, 333–334, 336
93rd Infantry Division 3, 16–18, 21, 24, 29, 33–34, 57–58, 66, 113–114, 153, 159–160, 167, 169, 171–177, 180–185, 187–190, 193–194, 204, 206, 290, 334
95th Engineer Regiment 77
95th Infantry Division 294, 308, 333
96th Engineer Regiment 71–72, 74–75
97th Engineer Regiment 77
101st Airborne Division 24, 93, 117–121, 124–125, 162, 305, 307, 309
103rd Infantry Division 133, 135–138, 309, 312–313, 315, 321–322
104th Infantry Division 278–279, 307–308, 309
106th Infantry Division 115–116, 305
187th Airborne Regimental Combat Team 324
333rd Artillery Battalion 115–120, 123, 126, 134
333rd Artillery Group 114–120, 122–123
364th Infantry Regiment 150–160, 194

365th Infantry Regiment 18–19, 22, 29, 34, 163, 193, 207, 210, 220, 224–225, 236, 248–249, 251, 253–254, 264, 270
366th Infantry Regiment 19, 26, 145, 159–160, 168, 192, 210–213, 215–221, 224–227, 232–234, 236, 239–241, 244, 246–249, 251, 270, 336
367th Infantry Regiment 18–19, 30, 34, 75–76, 145, 150–151, 153, 168
368th Infantry Regiment 18–19, 27–30, 34, 145–146, 160, 168, 172–173, 187–189
369th Infantry Regiment 17, 20, 22, 30–31, 34, 37, 39, 44, 114, 160, 172, 187–188
370th Infantry Regiment 17, 22–23, 163, 193, 196, 198–204, 207–211, 213–224, 226–229, 234–249, 251–263, 265, 268–271
371st Infantry Regiment 18, 23–24, 34, 160, 162–163, 193, 204, 207–208, 211–212, 227, 230–236, 238–239, 242–246, 253–254, 260–261, 264, 270
372nd Infantry Regiment 18, 23, 34, 37, 145, 159, 194, 210, 216
442nd Infantry Regiment 160–161, 196, 200, 247–248, 251–254, 257–270, 323
452nd Antiaircraft Artillery Battalion 126, 128–130
578th Artillery Battalion 115–117, 120–123
614th Tank Destroyer Battalion 133–138, 140, 142–143, 277, 312–313, 322, 334
679th Tank Destroyer Battalion 138–139, 144, 252, 264, 268–269
758th Tank Battalion 49, 222, 224, 226, 240, 252–252, 259,

357

261–262, 267–268, 286–288, 292, 304, 323–324
760th Tank Battalion 214, 218–219, 222, 224, 226–227, 234, 238–239, 241, 243, 252–253, 259, 261–262, 268
761st Tank Battalion 137–138, 277, 285, 287–297, 299–300, 302–309, 312–315, 317–323, 325–328, 334
777th Artillery Battalion 123, 126–127
784th Tank Battalion 277, 285, 289–290, 307, 309–312, 315–316, 319–320
827th Tank Destroyer Battalion 137–144, 281
969th Artillery Battalion 115, 117–121, 123–126, 322, 334
999th Artillery Battalion 123–125
6888th Postal Battalion 105–108

Almond, Maj. Gen. Edward M. 192–193, 195, 202, 204–206, 210–211, 220–221, 223, 227, 231, 244, 248–249, 251–252, 258, 261, 271, 333
Anderson, Trezzvant 289
Arnold, Lt. Col. Thomas 214, 234–235, 239–240, 268
Atlanta Daily World 52, 169, 192

Baker, Secretary of War Edward 163–164
Baker, Newton 14, 16–19, 22, 28
Baker, Vernon J. 168, 203, 222–223, 252, 255, 258, 271, 330, 334
Baltimore Afro-American 53–54, 250–251
Barbour, Lt. Charles 288, 295
Barnes, Lt. Col. Hubert D. 115, 118, 120
Bastogne, Belgium 115, 117–121, 305–309, 322, 326
Bates, Lt. Col. Paul L. 290–292, 295, 302, 309, 312–313, 315, 323
Battle of the Bulge 93–94, 116, 120, 136, 140, 169, 278, 305, 307–308, 322
Briggs, Lt. Bradley 330
Brown, Lt. Samuel 288
Burma Road 77

Camp Carson, Colorado 133
Camp Clairborne, Louisiana 288
Camp Funston, Kansas 18, 169
Camp Hood, Texas 138–139, 142, 290–293, 306
Camp Jackson, South Carolina 18
Camp Kilmer, New Jersey 133, 272, 293, 320
Camp Lee, Virginia 47, 103
Camp Meade, Maryland 18

Camp Shelby, Mississippi 73, 266
Camp Van Dorn, Mississippi 54, 153–158
Carter, Edward 282
Carter, Jimmy 325–326
Chicago Defender 52–53, 250
Clark, Gen. Mark W. 199–200, 205, 220, 248–249, 268–269
Cochrane, Lt. Frank 303, 307–308, 313, 319, 321
Congressional Medal of Honor 7, 9, 24, 257, 266, 302, 332, 334
Crecy, Lt. Warren 296–287, 312–313, 321

D-Day 84, 86, 89–92, 114, 253, 274
Dade, Lt. Moses 307, 319, 321
Davis, Benjamin, O., Jr. 36, 51
Davis, Gen. Benjamin O., Sr. 3, 35, 44, 152, 171, 198

Earley, Charity A. 98–99, 108
Eisenhower, Gen. Dwight D. 84, 108, 275–276, 287, 294, 322, 325

Flipper, Henry O. 6–7
Fort Benning, Georgia 10, 35, 50, 68, 145–146, 162, 164, 172, 193
Fort Clark, Texas 169
Fort Des Moines, Iowa 98, 101–104
Fort Huachuca, Arizona 11, 15, 53–54, 64, 100, 103, 145, 153, 168, 173, 192–194
Fort Knox, Kentucky 286–289, 323, 327
Fort Riley, Kansas 102, 168–169, 288, 292
Fox, Lt. John R. 216–217, 335–336

Gates, Capt. Charles 291, 303–304, 306–307, 317, 325
Gibson, Truman 102, 156–157, 171, 205–207, 249–251, 270–271

Hammond, Lt. Robert 301–302, 328
Harrison, Capt. Ivan 288, 291, 294, 299, 322–323
Harrison, Sgt. James W. 328
Harrison, Sgt. William H. 202
Hastie, William H. 3, 44–45, 48–49, 250
Hitler, Adolf 126, 287, 319–320
Holland, Lt. Leonard 317, 321
Huffman, Lt. Maxwell 328

Johnson, Maj. Gen. Harry J. 169, 184–186, 189
Johnson, Sgt. Henry 22
Johnson, Sgt. Robert 305, 328, 464
Johnson, Samuel 129

Liberian Task Force 75

MacArthur, Douglas 72, 108, 174, 185, 332–333; USS *Mason* 50
Miller, Dorie 8, 49
Mountford Point Marines 50
Mussolini, Benito 223, 269

NAACP 13, 30, 35, 41, 44, 47, 52, 56, 58, 67, 102, 184

Operations Market Garden 93, 294, 305

Patton, Gen. George 119–120, 274, 282, 294, 301, 304–305, 314–315, 319
Pittsburgh Courier 52–53, 287

Red Ball Express 85–86, 127
Rivers, Ruben 295–296, 301–302, 327–328, 336
Roberts, Needham 22
Robinson, John "Jackie" 292–293, 323
Robinson, Samuel 163
Roosevelt, Eleanor 46, 277, 285, 287, 325
Roosevelt, Franklin D. 1–3, 5, 40, 42–45, 46–47, 52–53, 56, 65, 97, 153, 159, 162; Executive Order 8044 44; Executive Order 8802 47, 65
Roosevelt, Theodore 7, 9

Sherman, Col. Raymond 195, 217, 221, 255–256, 271–272
Stowers, Freddie 24

Thomas, Charles L. 134, 136, 336–337
Thompson, William 332
Truman, Harry S. 109, 324, 330, 331, 333; Executive Order 9981 324, 330
Truscott, Gen. Lucian K. 213, 220, 246–249, 262
Turley, Samuel 287, 298, 300, 327–328
Tuskegee Airmen 22, 50, 75; 99th Pursuit Squadron 49–51, 75
Tuskegee, Alabama 64

Watson, George 75, 334, 337
Watson, Tom 30
White, Walter 41, 56, 184
Williams, Capt. David J. 287–288, 294–295, 301–302
Williams, Col. James 6
Williams, Sen. John 16
Women's Army Corps 59, 96–99, 101–110, 274

Young, Charles 15–16, 36, 44

www.ingramcontent.com/pod-product-compliance
Lightning Source LLC
Chambersburg PA
CBHW081536300426
44116CB00015B/2651